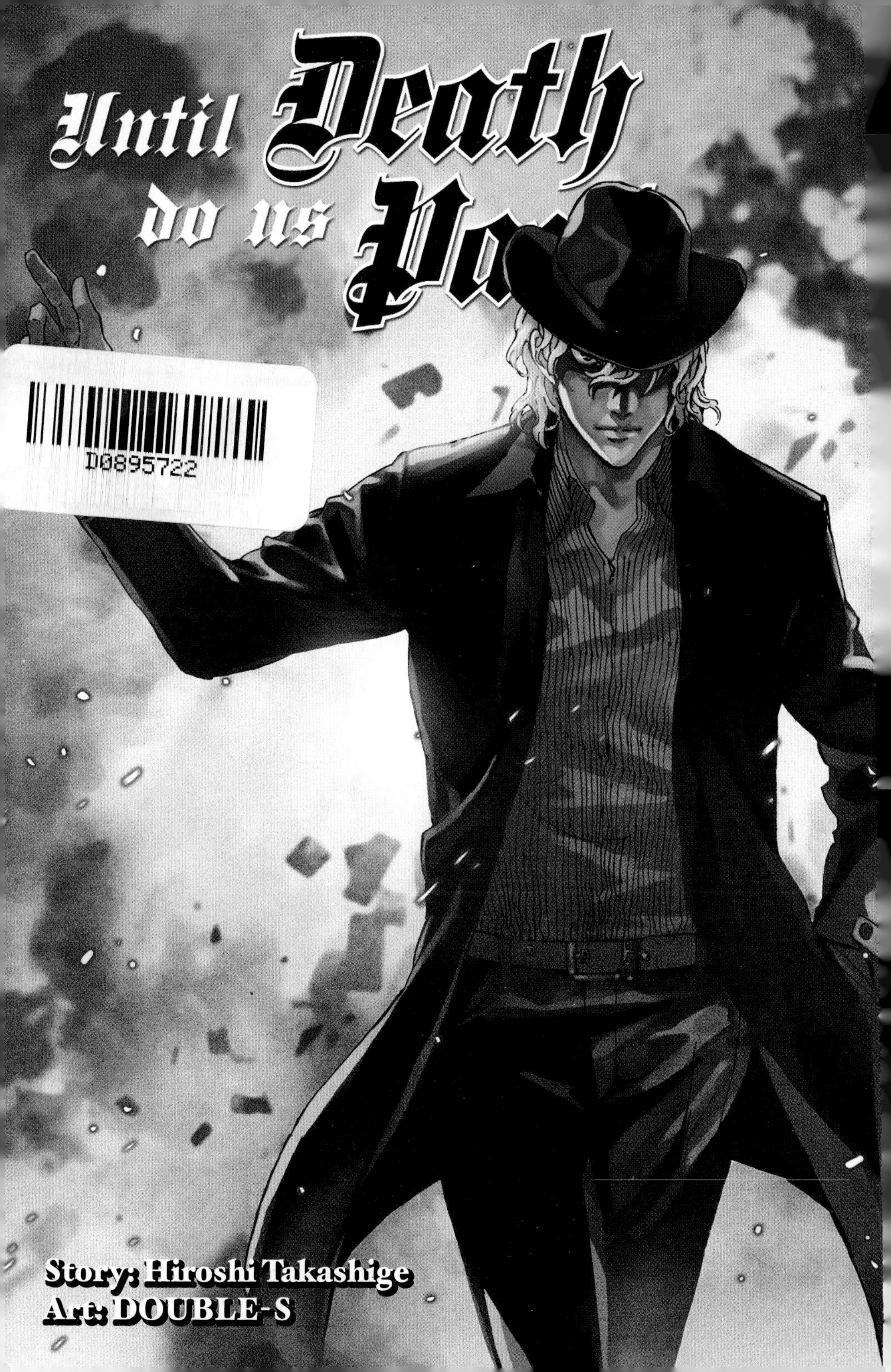
Until Death
do us Pa

Story: Hiroshi Takashige
Art: DOUBLE-S

Until Death do us Part

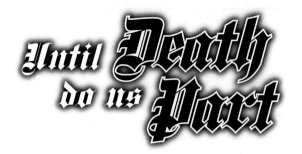

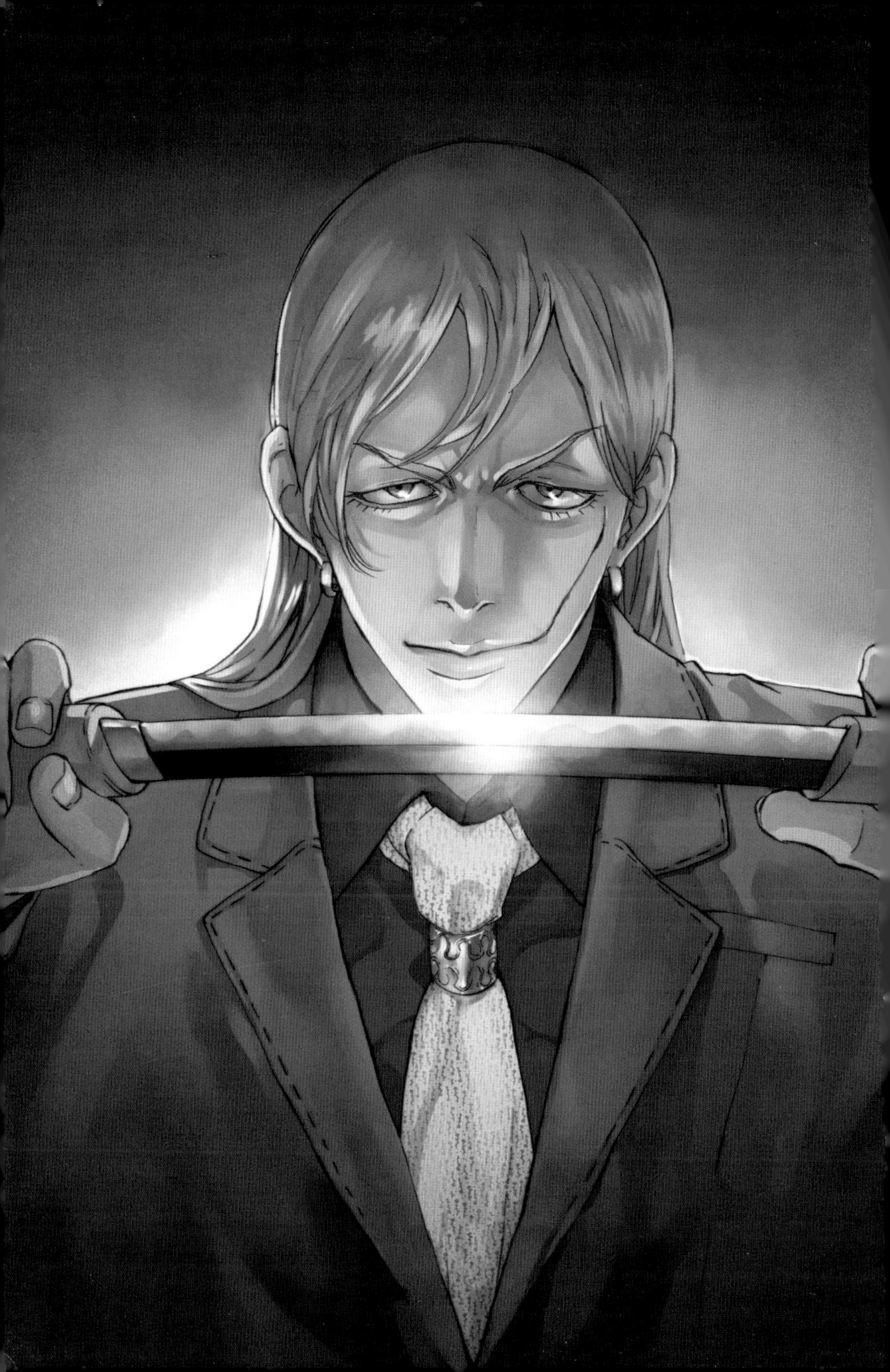

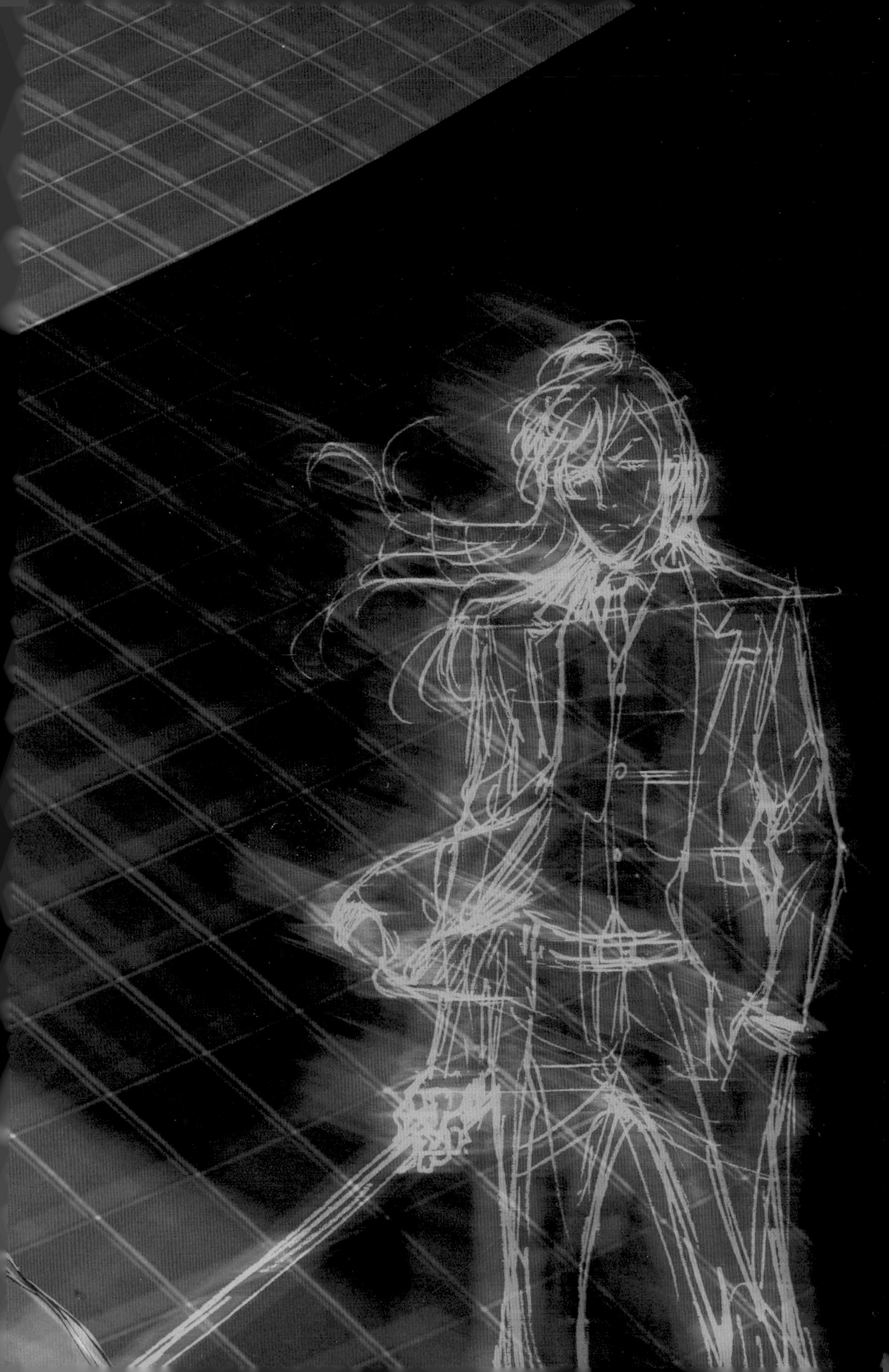

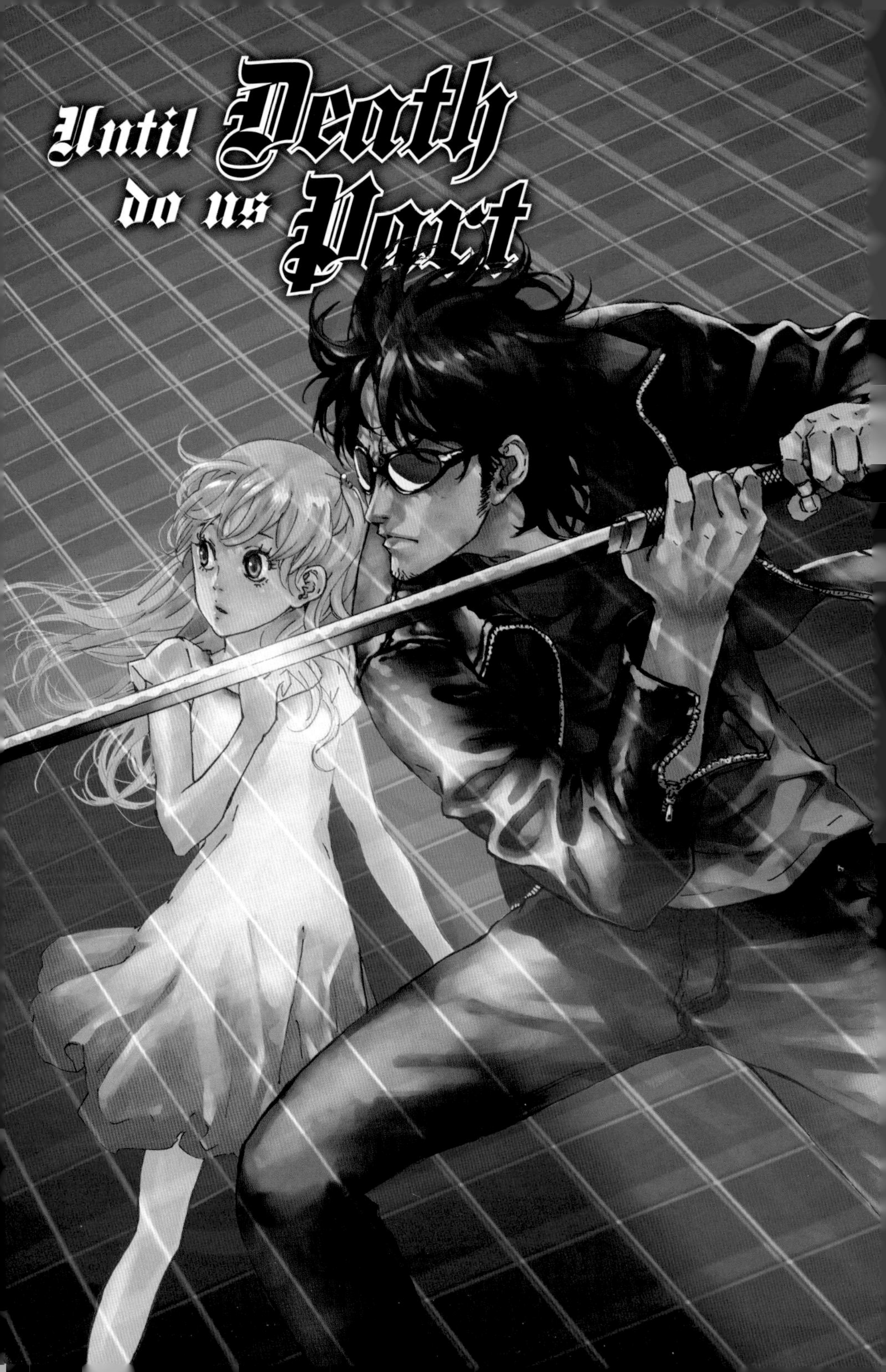
Until Death
do us Part

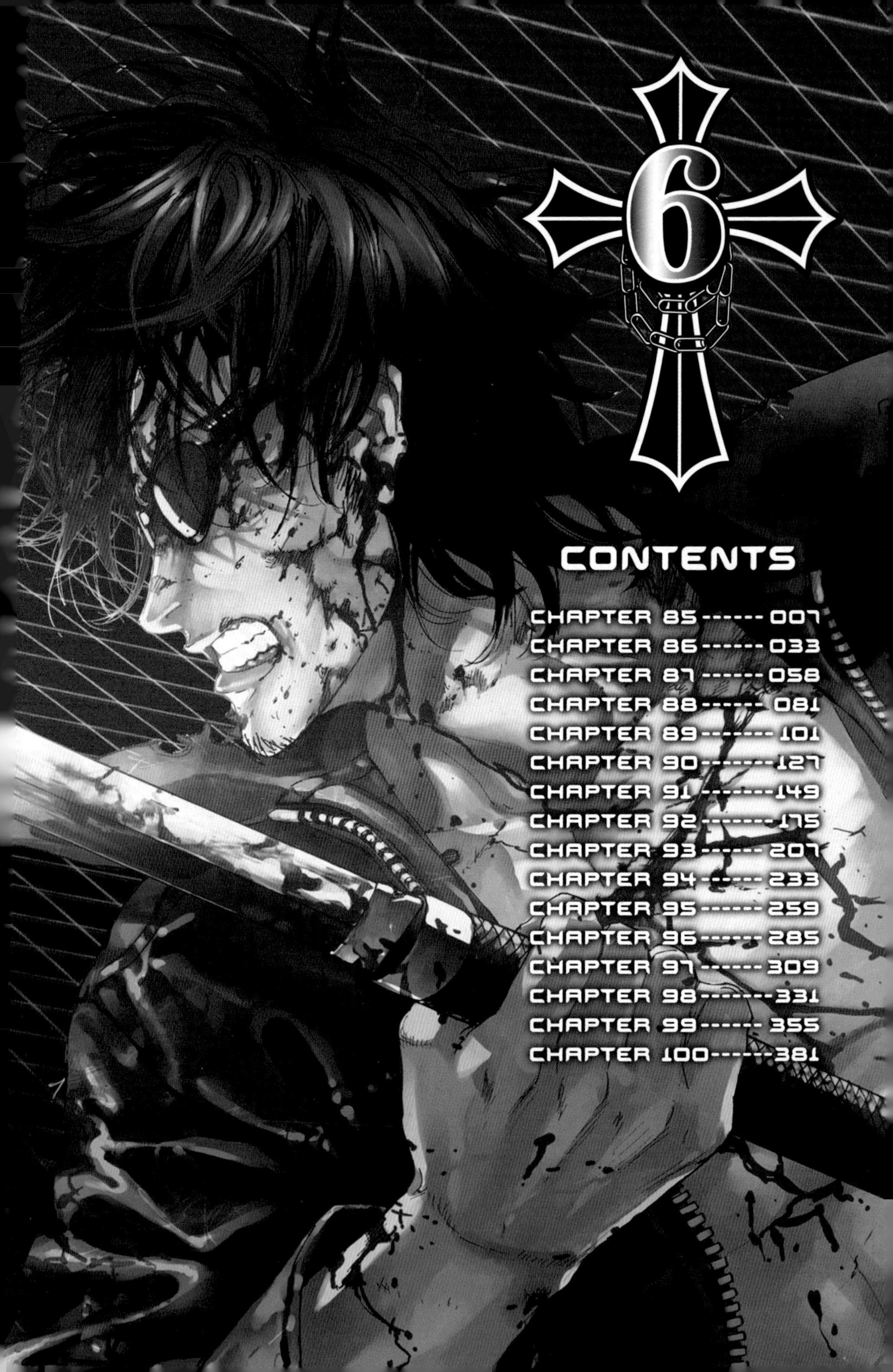

CONTENTS

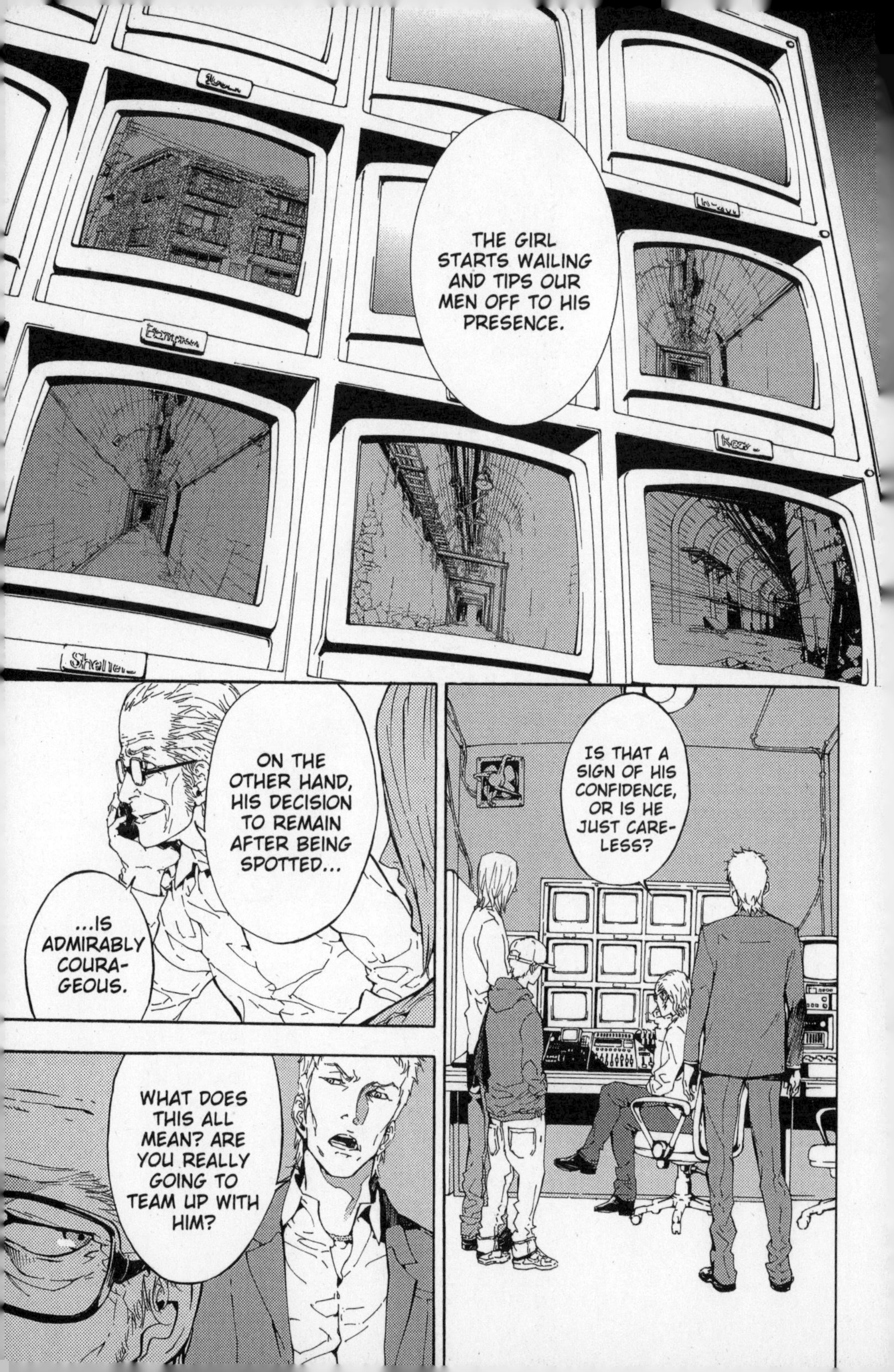
THE GIRL STARTS WAILING AND TIPS OUR MEN OFF TO HIS PRESENCE.
IS THAT A SIGN OF HIS CONFIDENCE, OR IS HE JUST CARE-LESS?
ON THE OTHER HAND, HIS DECISION TO REMAIN AFTER BEING SPOTTED...
...IS ADMIRABLY COURA-GEOUS.
WHAT DOES THIS ALL MEAN? ARE YOU REALLY GOING TO TEAM UP WITH HIM?

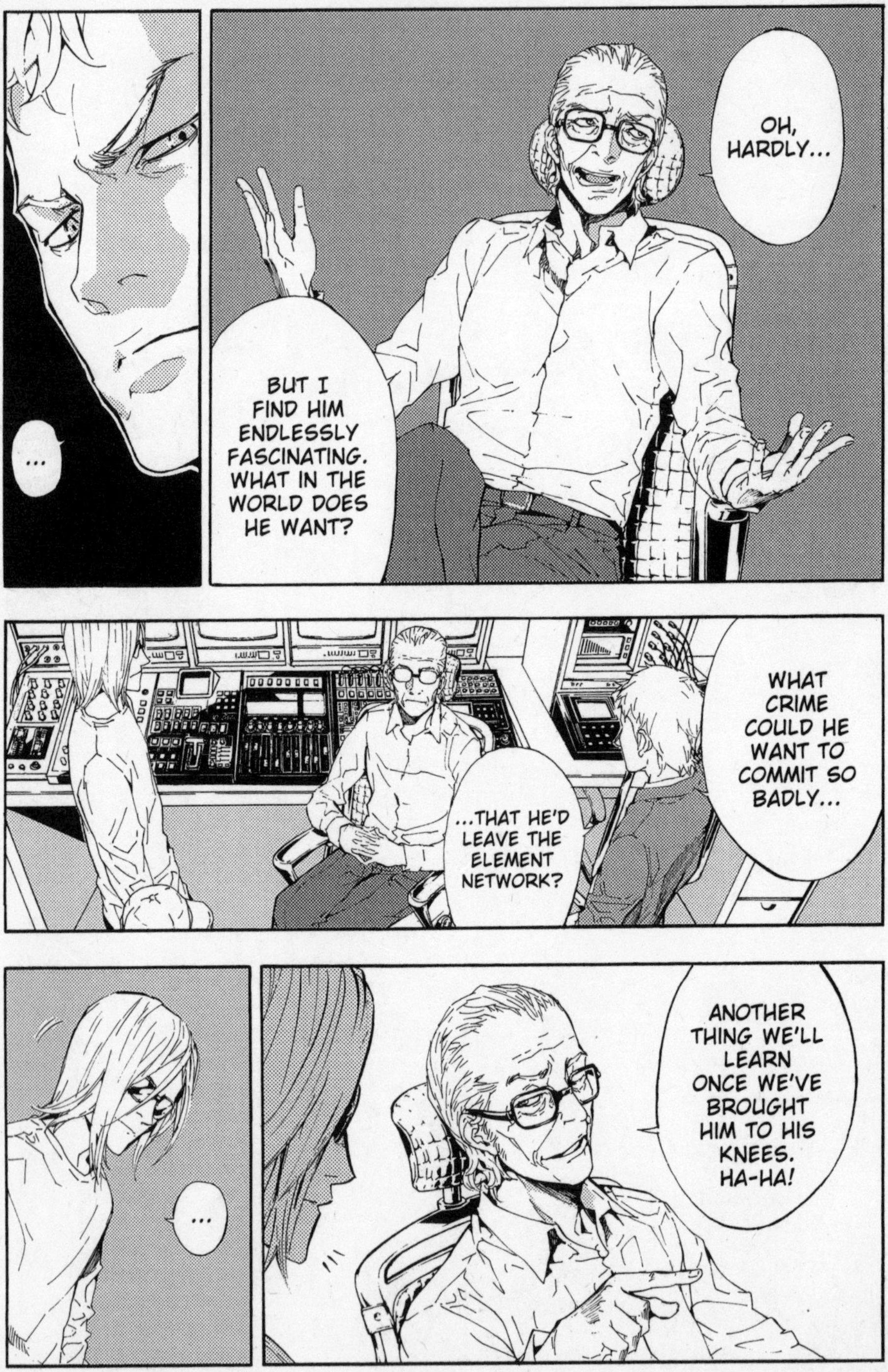
OH, HARDLY...
BUT I FIND HIM ENDLESSLY FASCINATING. WHAT IN THE WORLD DOES HE WANT?
...
WHAT CRIME COULD HE WANT TO COMMIT SO BADLY...
...THAT HE'D LEAVE THE ELEMENT NETWORK?
ANOTHER THING WE'LL LEARN ONCE WE'VE BROUGHT HIM TO HIS KNEES. HA-HA!
...

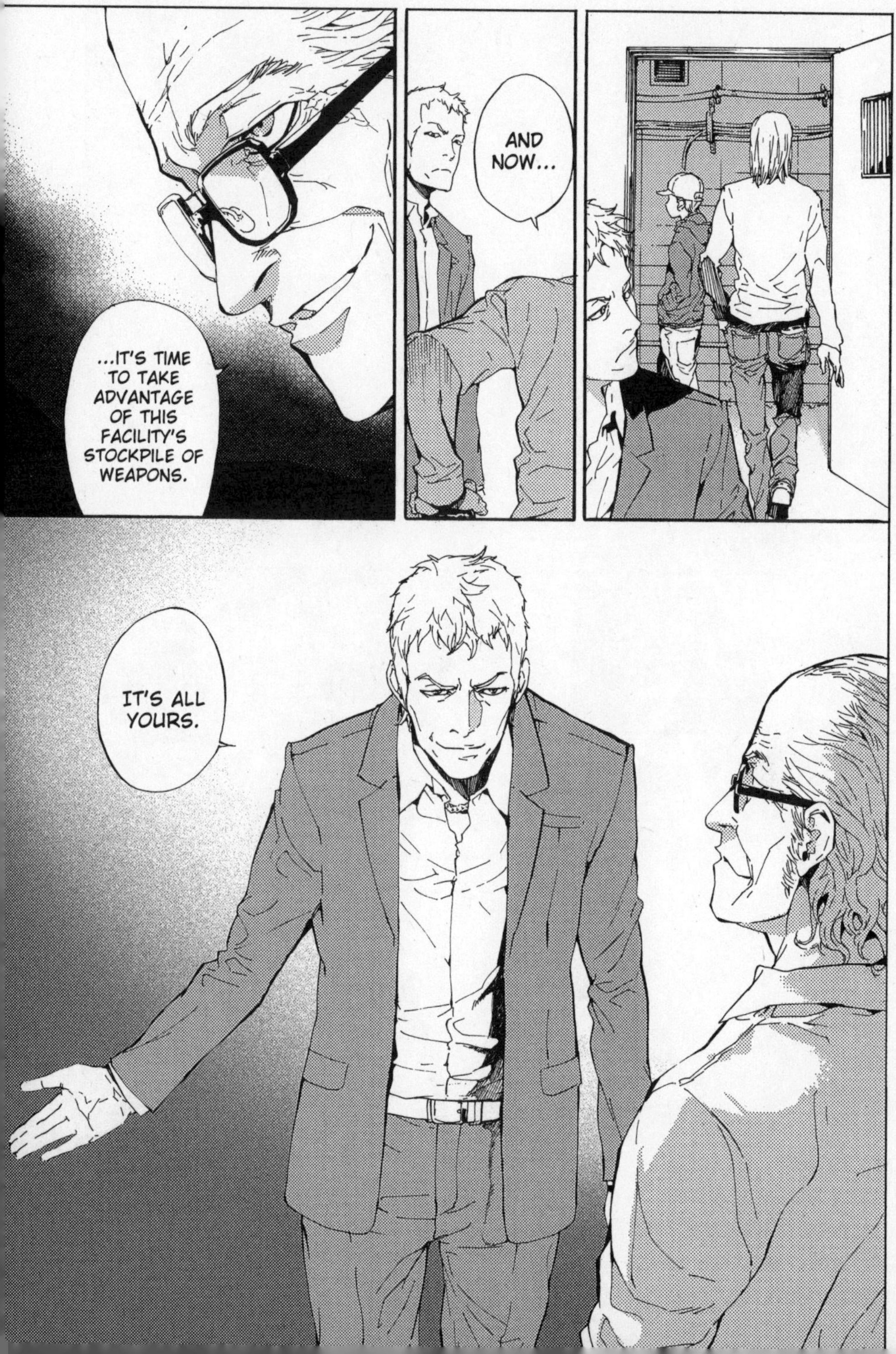
AND NOW...
...IT'S TIME TO TAKE ADVANTAGE OF THIS FACILITY'S STOCKPILE OF WEAPONS.
IT'S ALL YOURS.

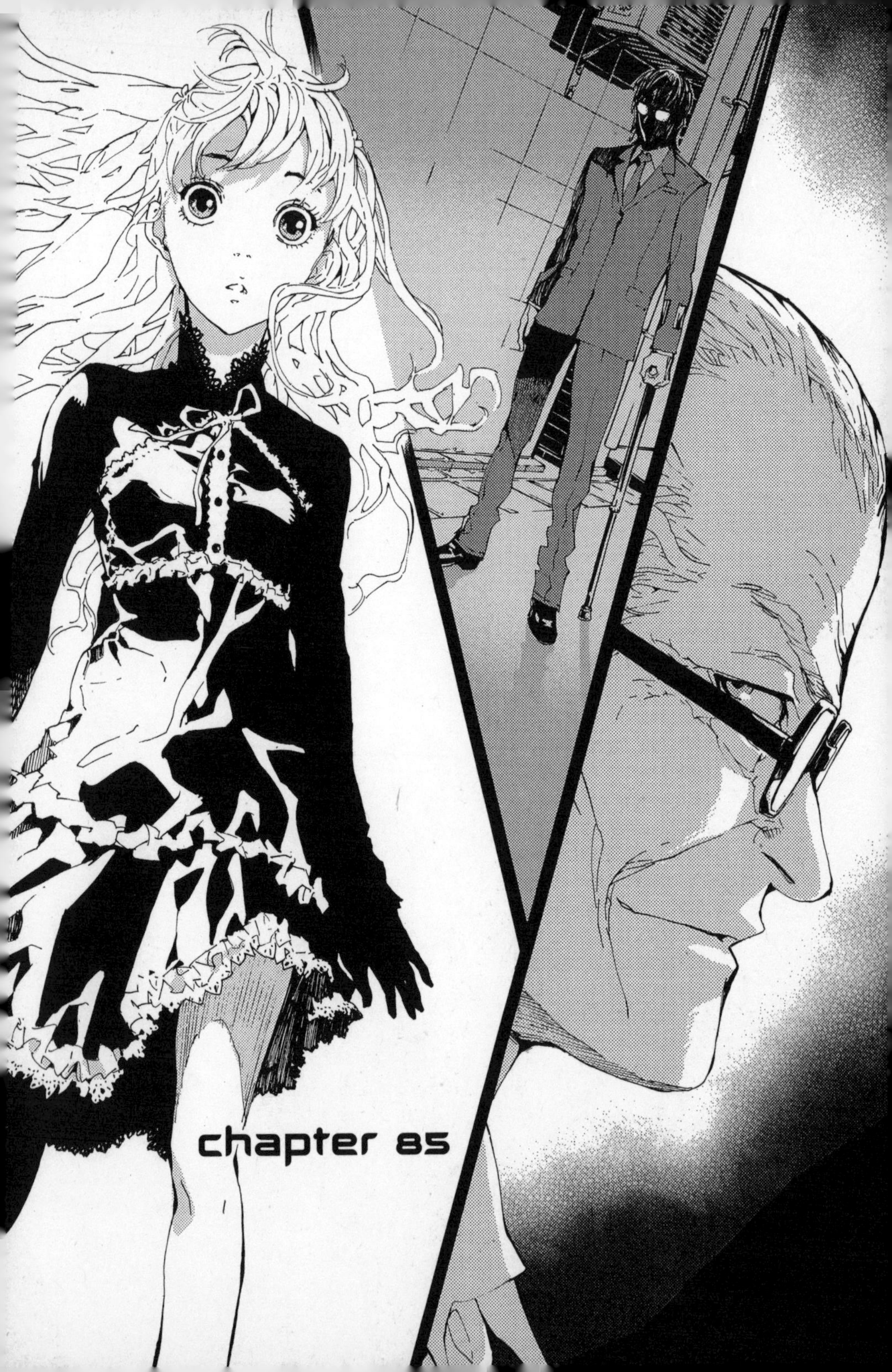
chapter 85

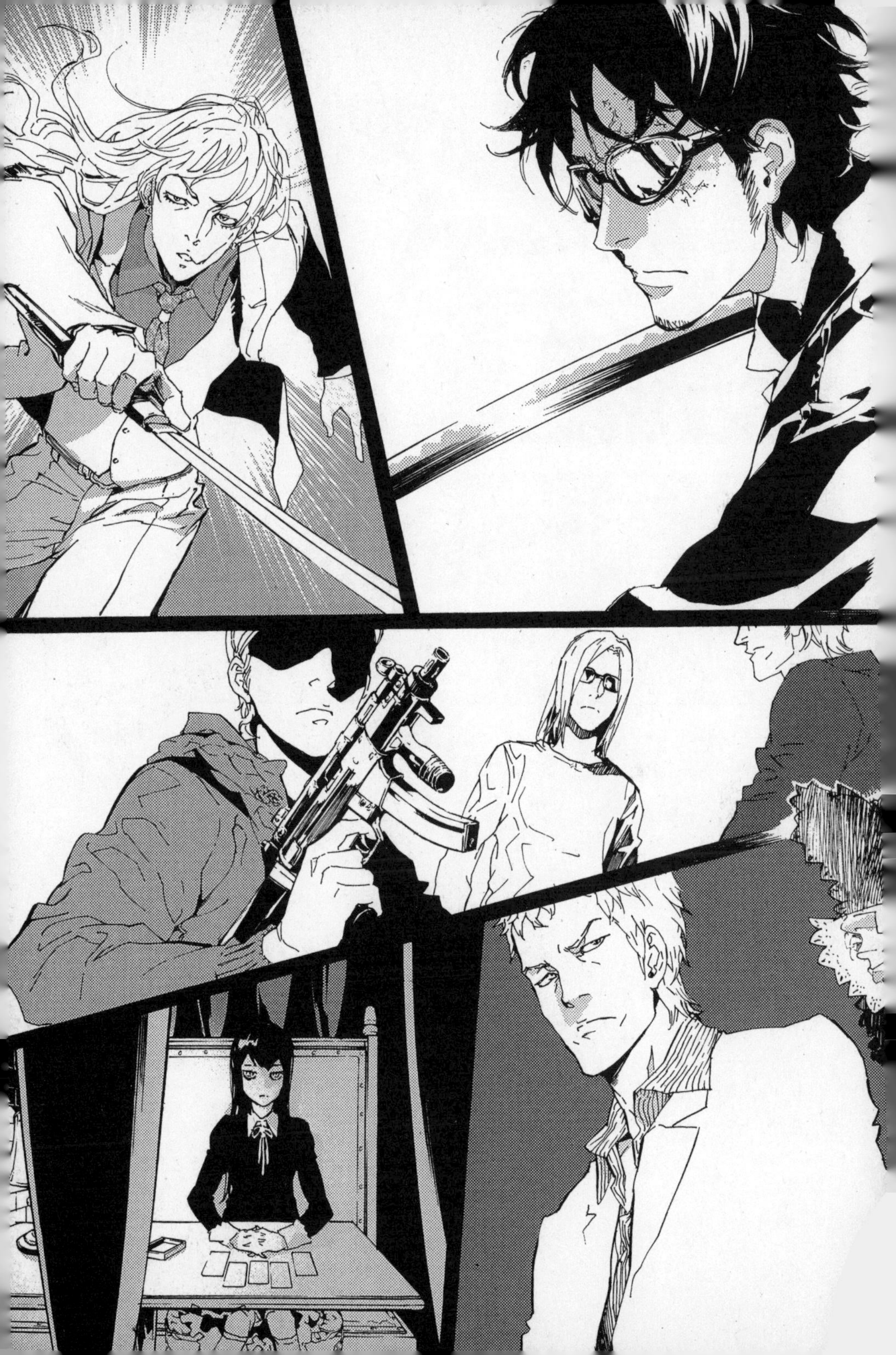

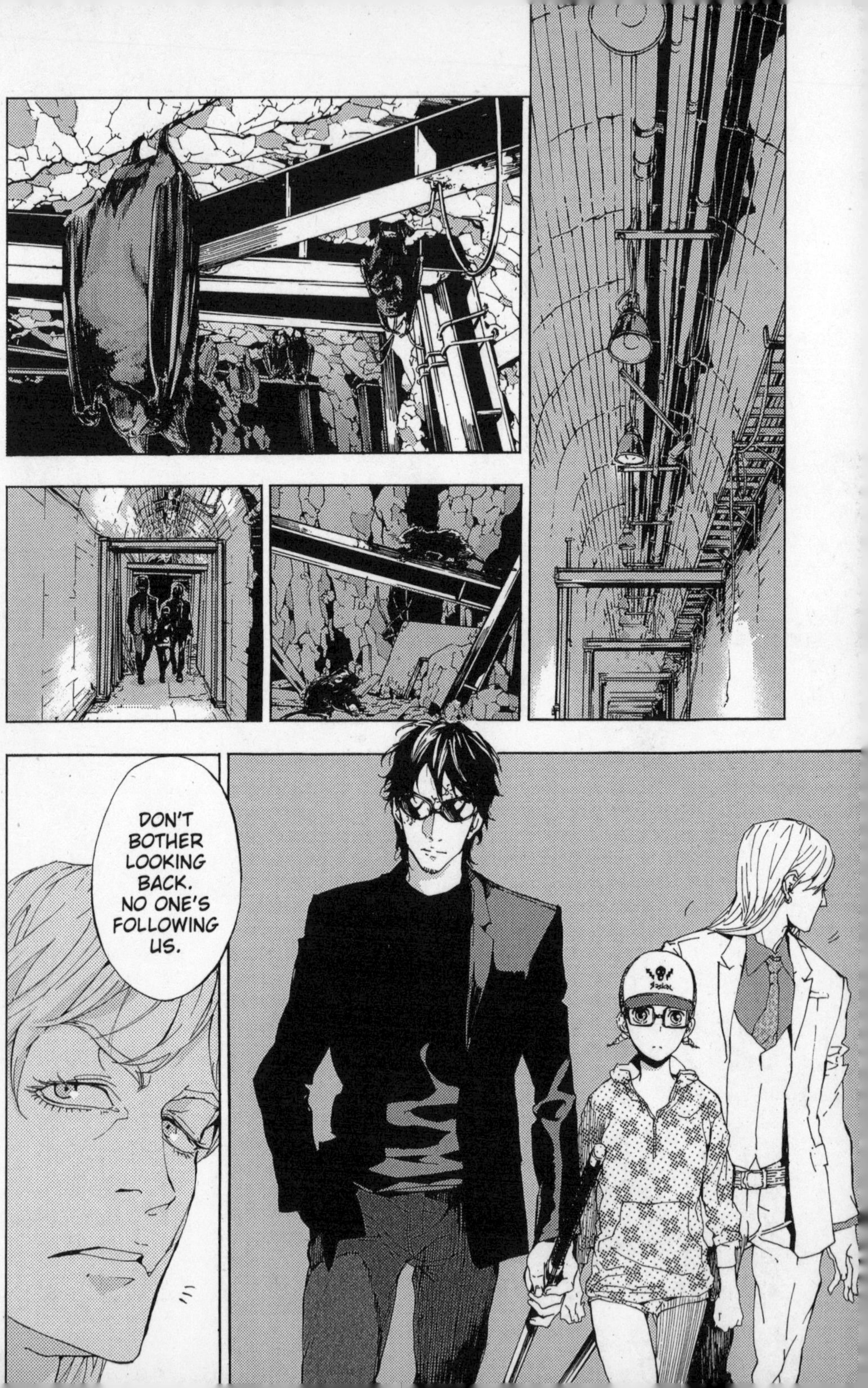
DON'T BOTHER LOOKING BACK. NO ONE'S FOLLOWING US.

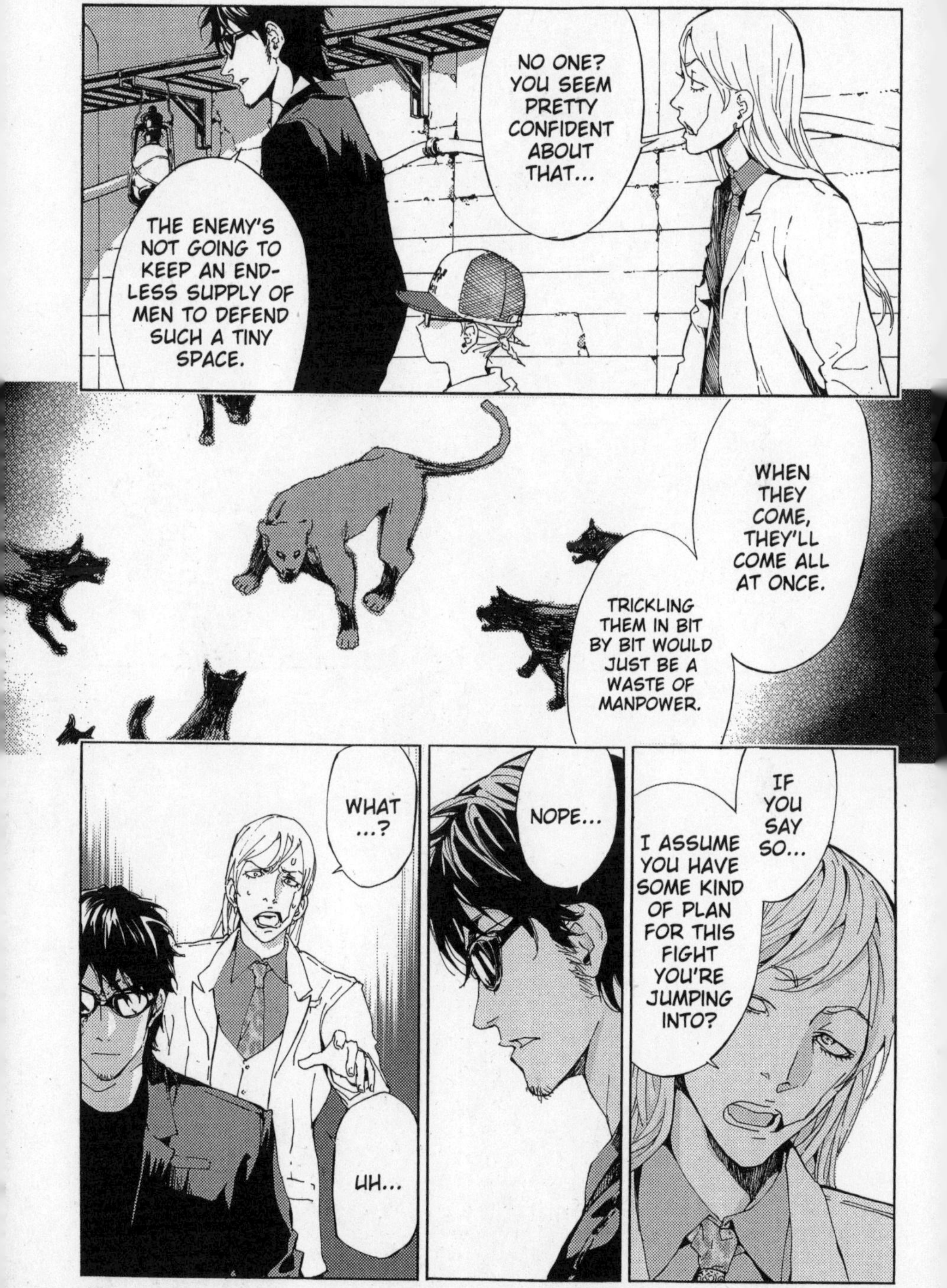
NO ONE? YOU SEEM PRETTY CONFIDENT ABOUT THAT...
THE ENEMY'S NOT GOING TO KEEP AN END-LESS SUPPLY OF MEN TO DEFEND SUCH A TINY SPACE.
WHEN THEY COME, THEY'LL COME ALL AT ONCE.
TRICKLING THEM IN BIT BY BIT WOULD JUST BE A WASTE OF MANPOWER.
IF YOU SAY SO...
I ASSUME YOU HAVE SOME KIND OF PLAN FOR THIS FIGHT YOU'RE JUMPING INTO?
NOPE...
WHAT ...?
UH...

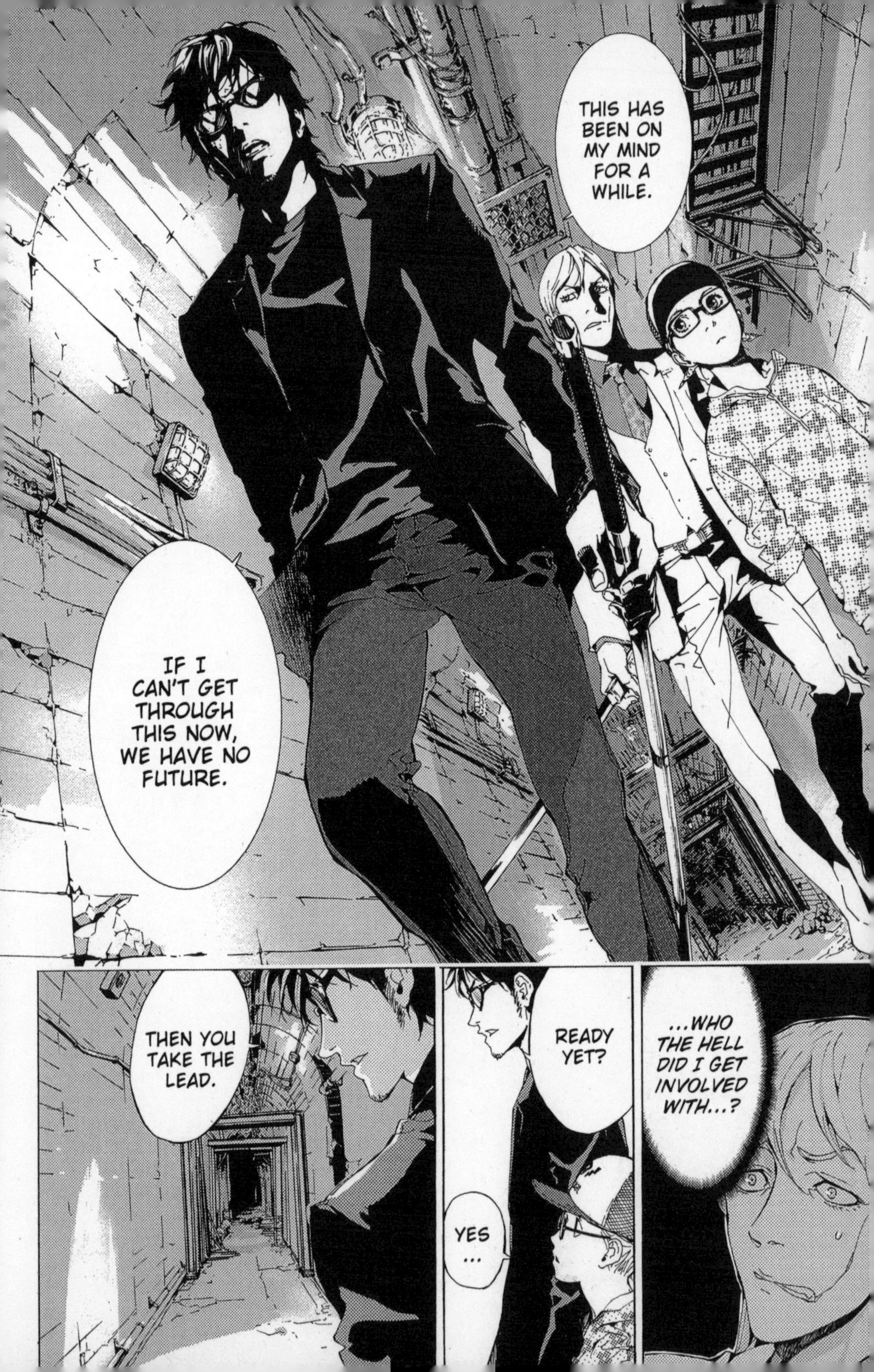
THIS HAS BEEN ON MY MIND FOR A WHILE.
IF I CAN'T GET THROUGH THIS NOW, WE HAVE NO FUTURE.
...WHO THE HELL DID I GET INVOLVED WITH...?
READY YET?
YES ...
THEN YOU TAKE THE LEAD.

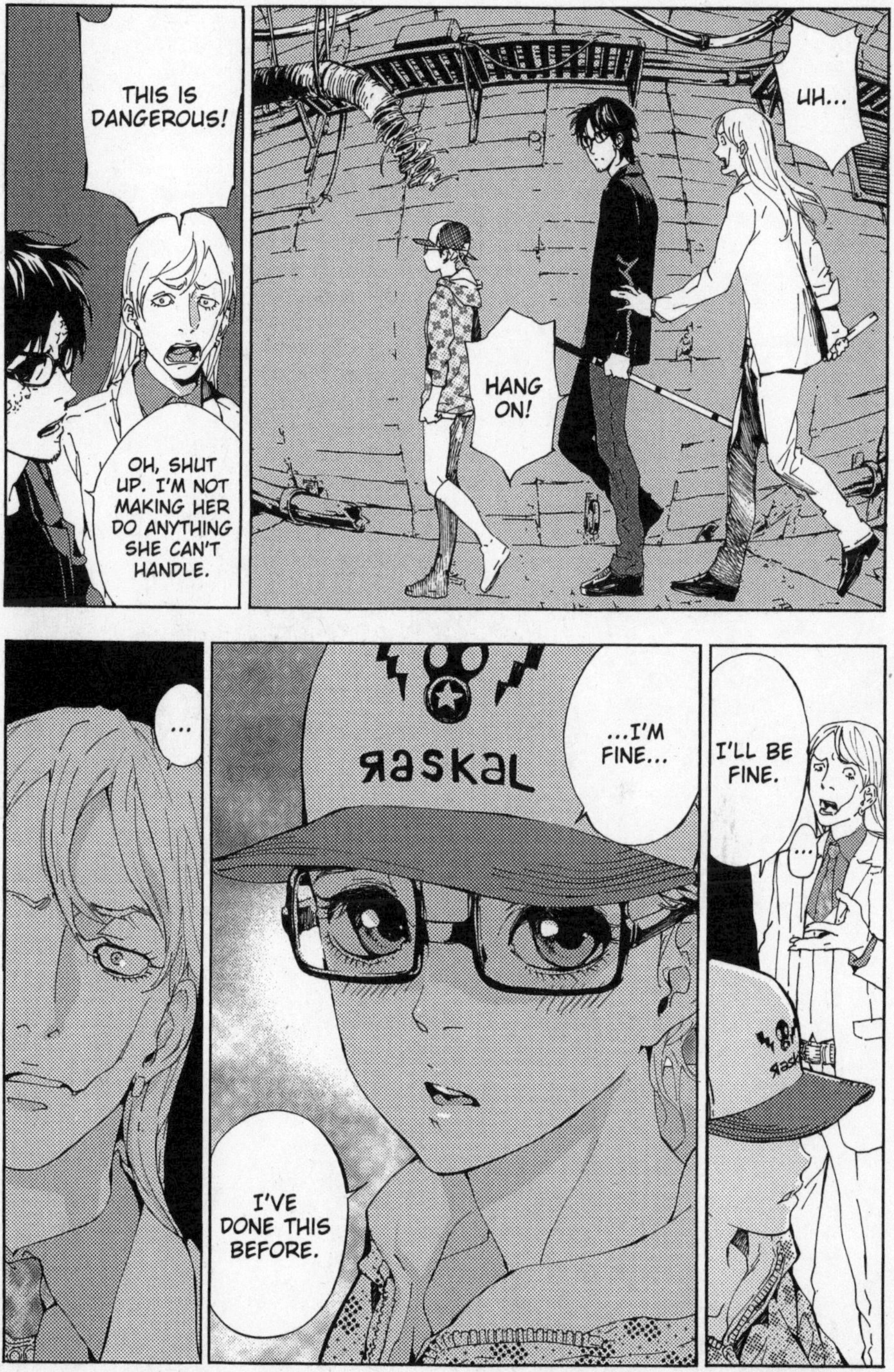
UH...
HANG ON!
THIS IS DANGEROUS!
OH, SHUT UP. I'M NOT MAKING HER DO ANYTHING SHE CAN'T HANDLE.
I'LL BE FINE.
...
...I'M FINE...
raskal
I'VE DONE THIS BEFORE.
...

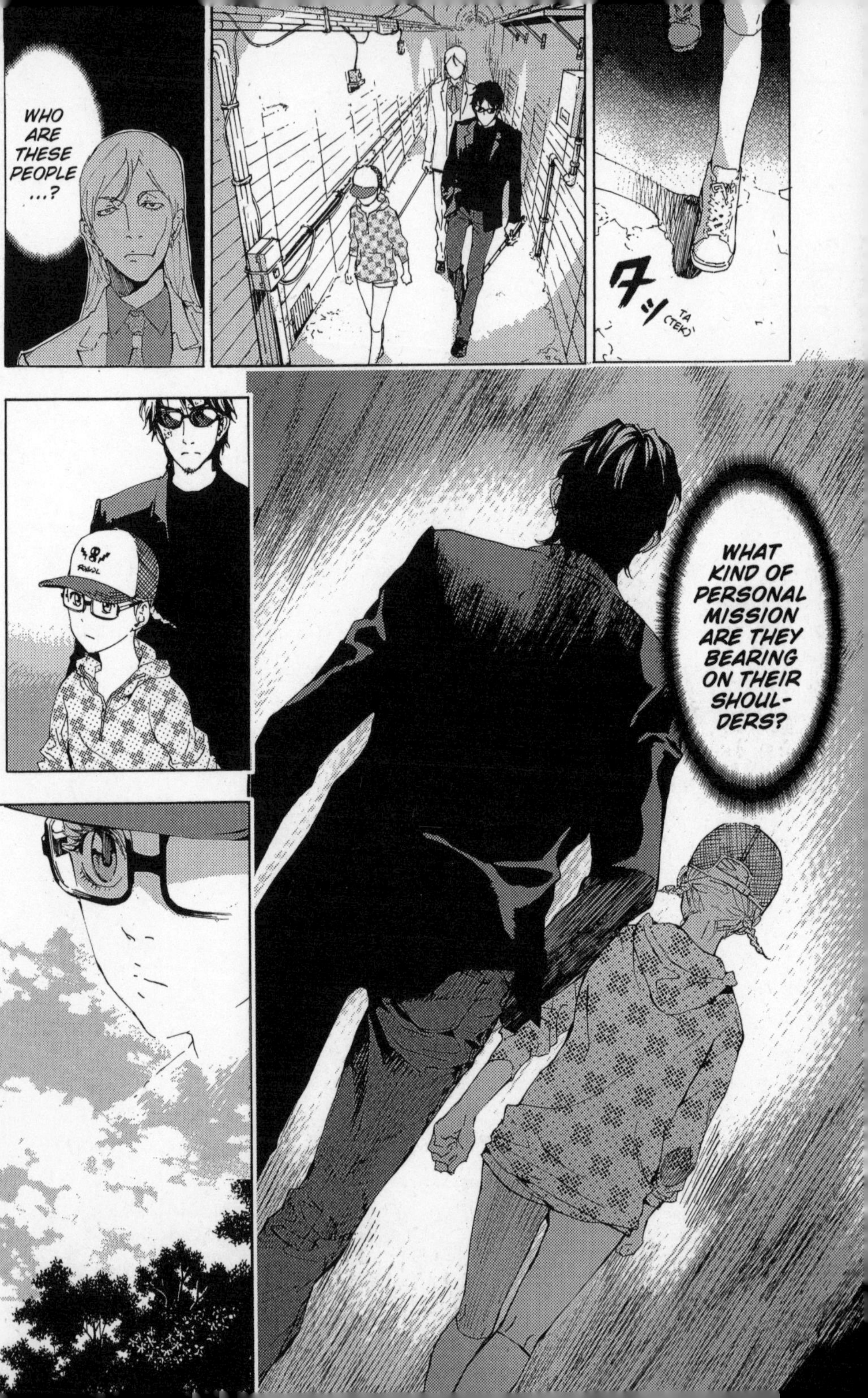

タッ
TA (TEK)
WHO ARE THESE PEOPLE ...?
WHAT KIND OF PERSONAL MISSION ARE THEY BEARING ON THEIR SHOUL-DERS?

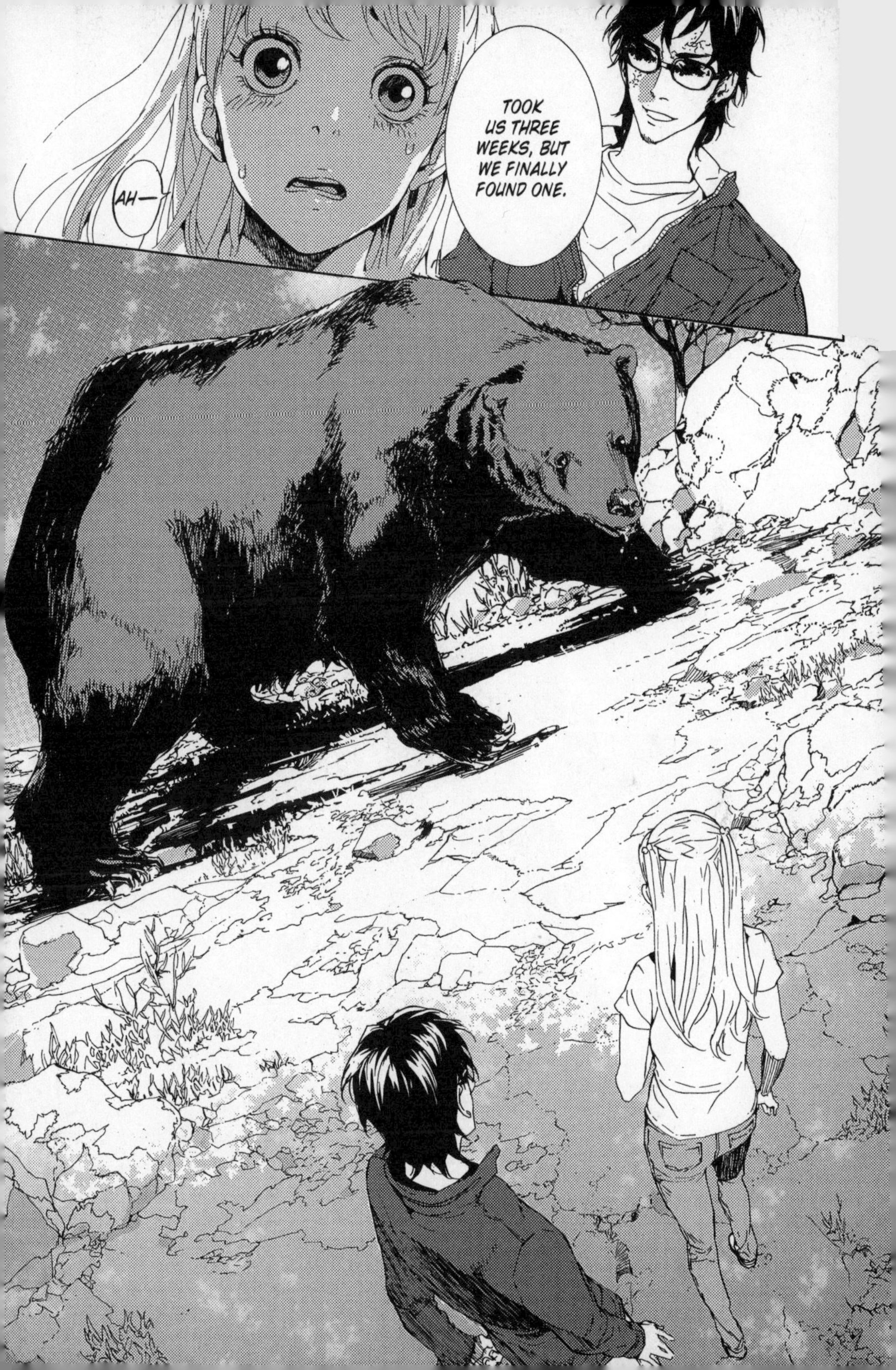
TOOK US THREE WEEKS, BUT WE FINALLY FOUND ONE.
AH—

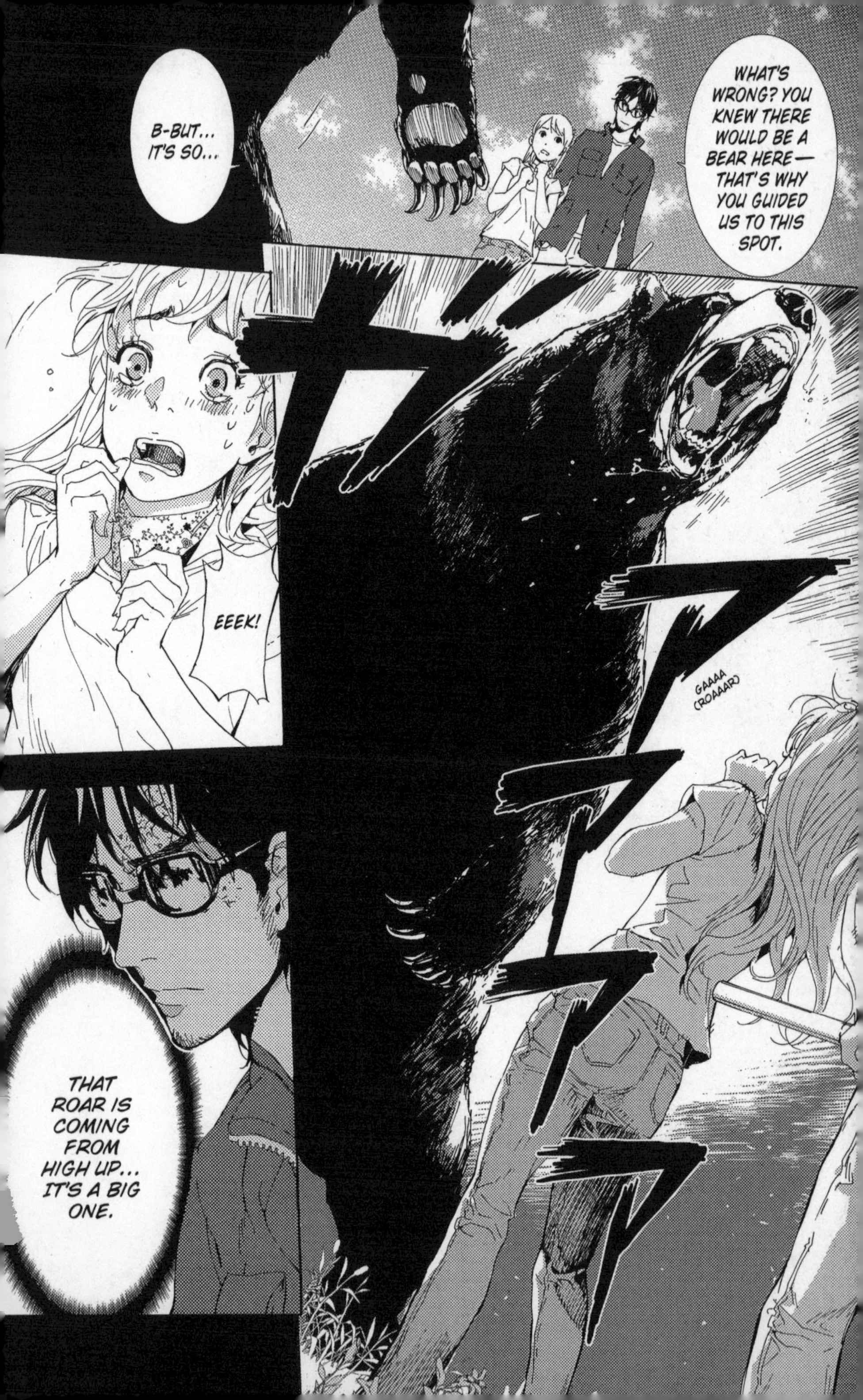
WHAT'S WRONG? YOU KNEW THERE WOULD BE A BEAR HERE—THAT'S WHY YOU GUIDED US TO THIS SPOT.
B-BUT... IT'S SO...
GAAAA (ROAAAR)
EEEK!
THAT ROAR IS COMING FROM HIGH UP... IT'S A BIG ONE.

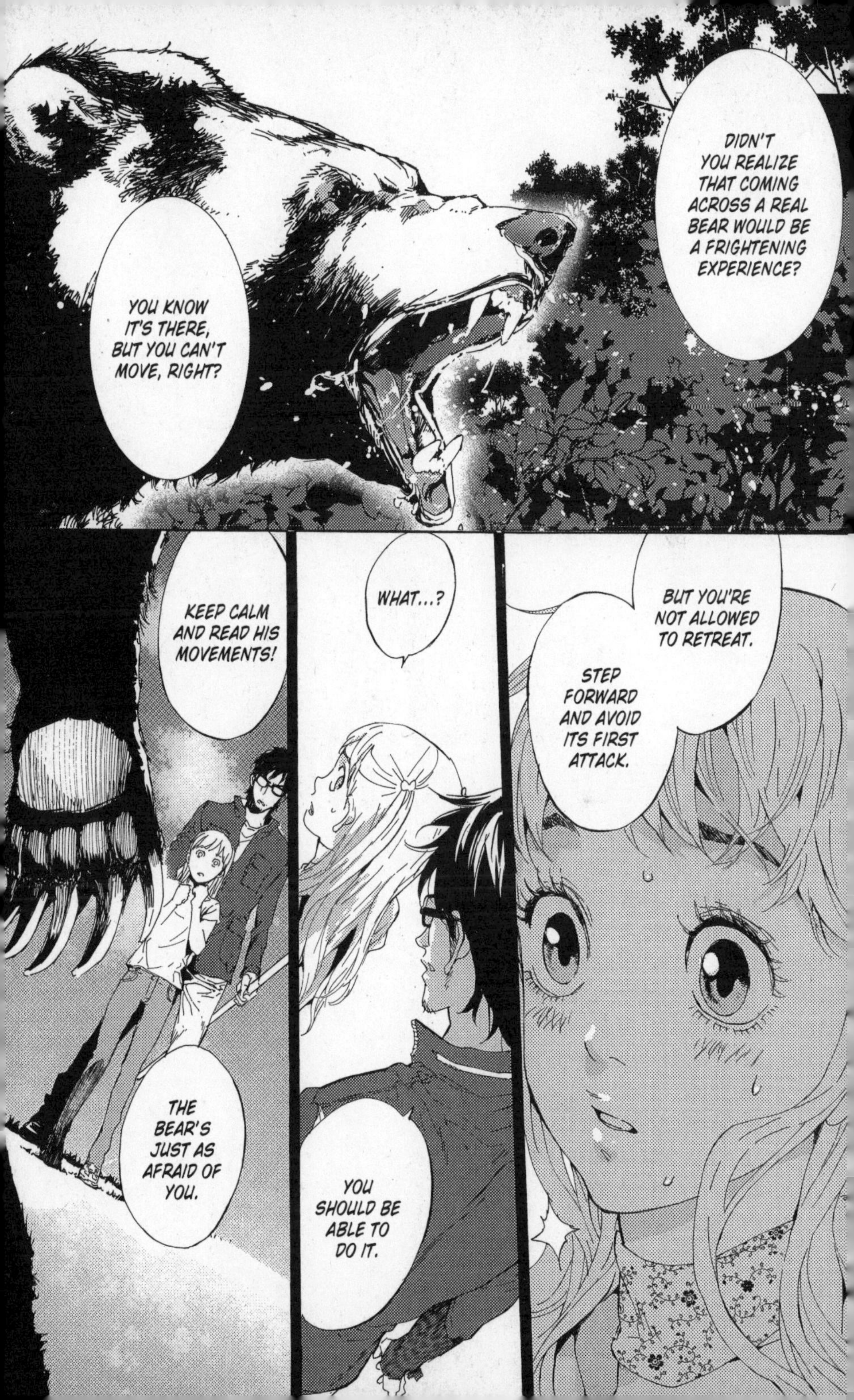
DIDN'T YOU REALIZE THAT COMING ACROSS A REAL BEAR WOULD BE A FRIGHTENING EXPERIENCE?
YOU KNOW IT'S THERE, BUT YOU CAN'T MOVE, RIGHT?
BUT YOU'RE NOT ALLOWED TO RETREAT.
STEP FORWARD AND AVOID ITS FIRST ATTACK.
WHAT...?
YOU SHOULD BE ABLE TO DO IT.
KEEP CALM AND READ HIS MOVEMENTS!
THE BEAR'S JUST AS AFRAID OF YOU.

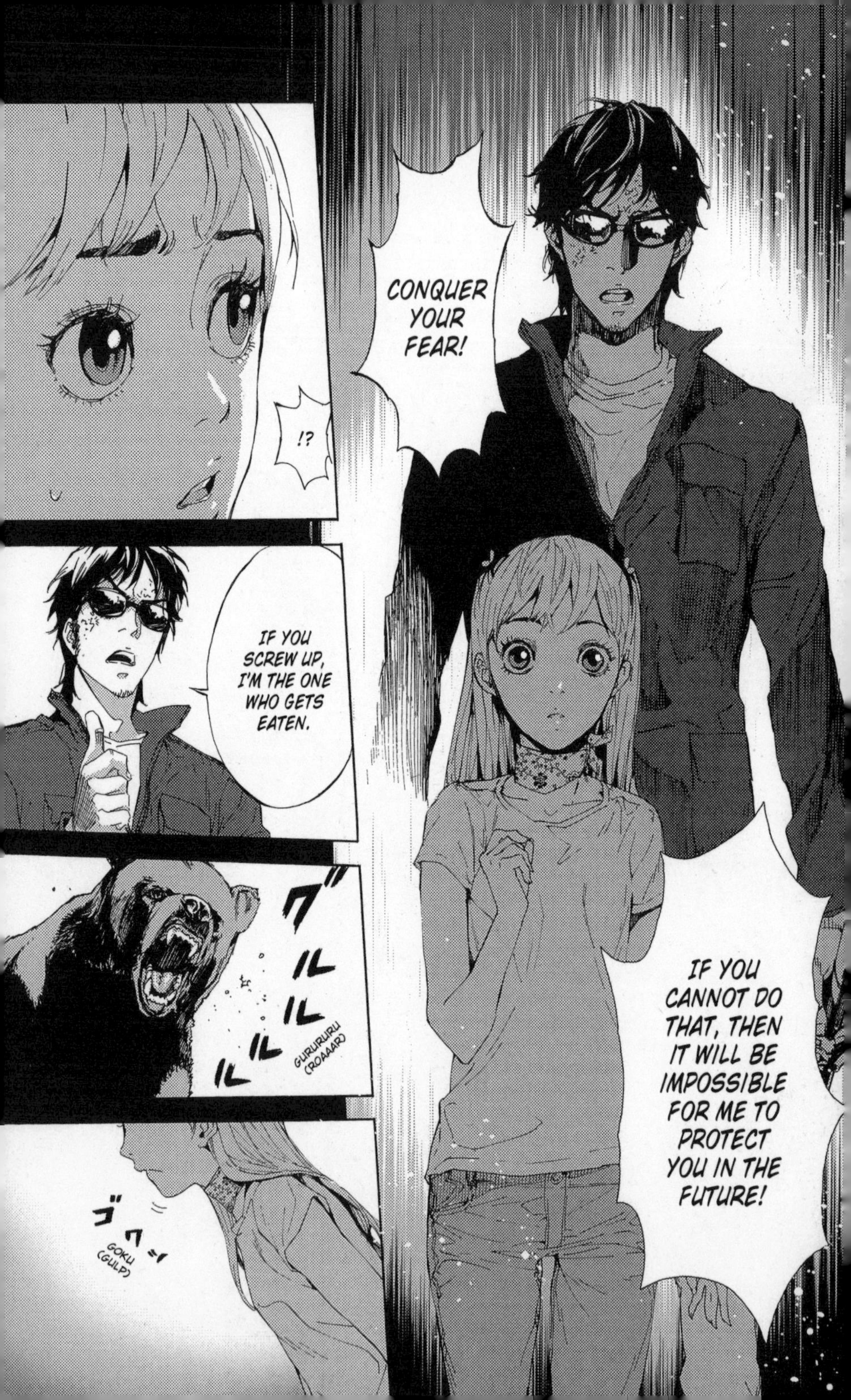

CONQUER YOUR FEAR!
IF YOU CANNOT DO THAT, THEN IT WILL BE IMPOSSIBLE FOR ME TO PROTECT YOU IN THE FUTURE!
!?
IF YOU SCREW UP, I'M THE ONE WHO GETS EATEN.
GURURURU (ROAAAR)
GOKU (GULP)

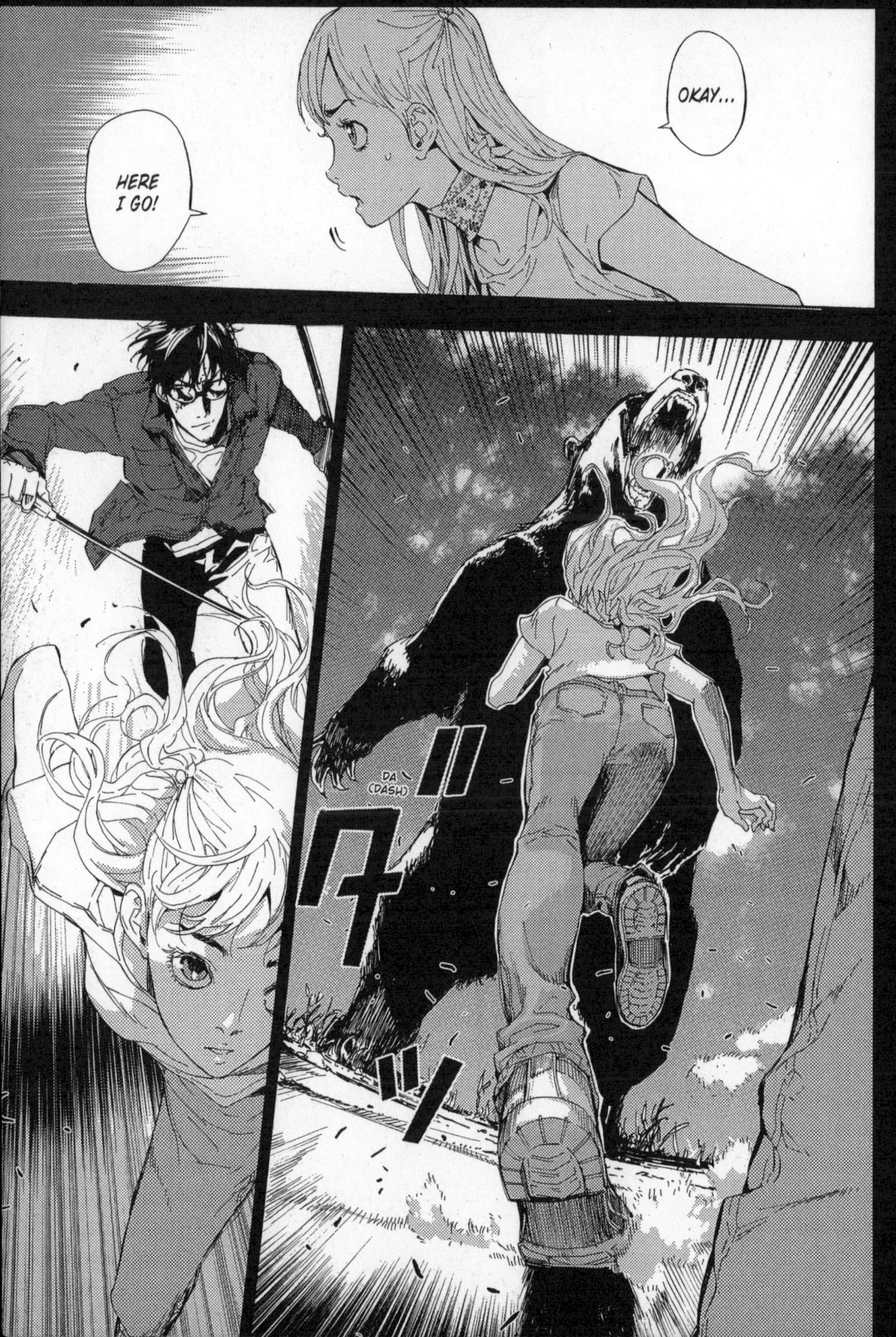
OKAY...
HERE I GO!
DA (DASH)

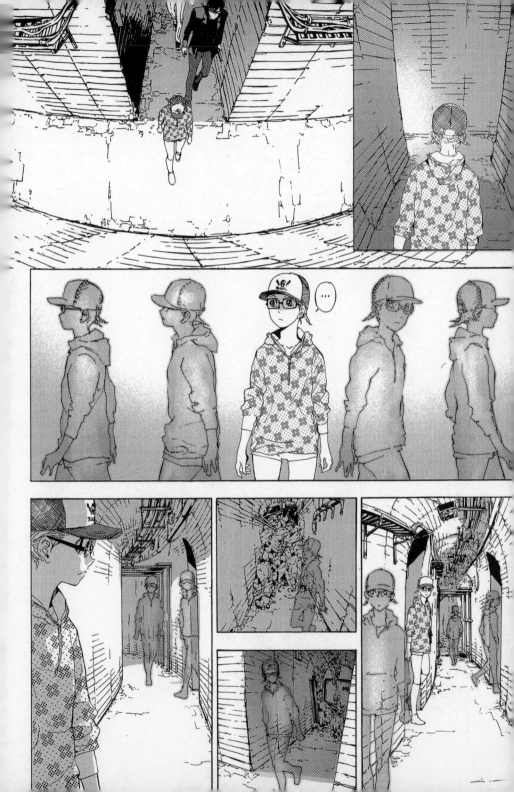

TO
(TMP)
トッ

FU
(FFT)
フッ

フッ
FU

クル
KURU
(SPIN)

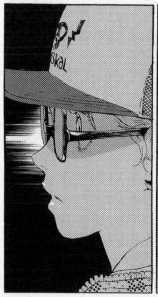

?

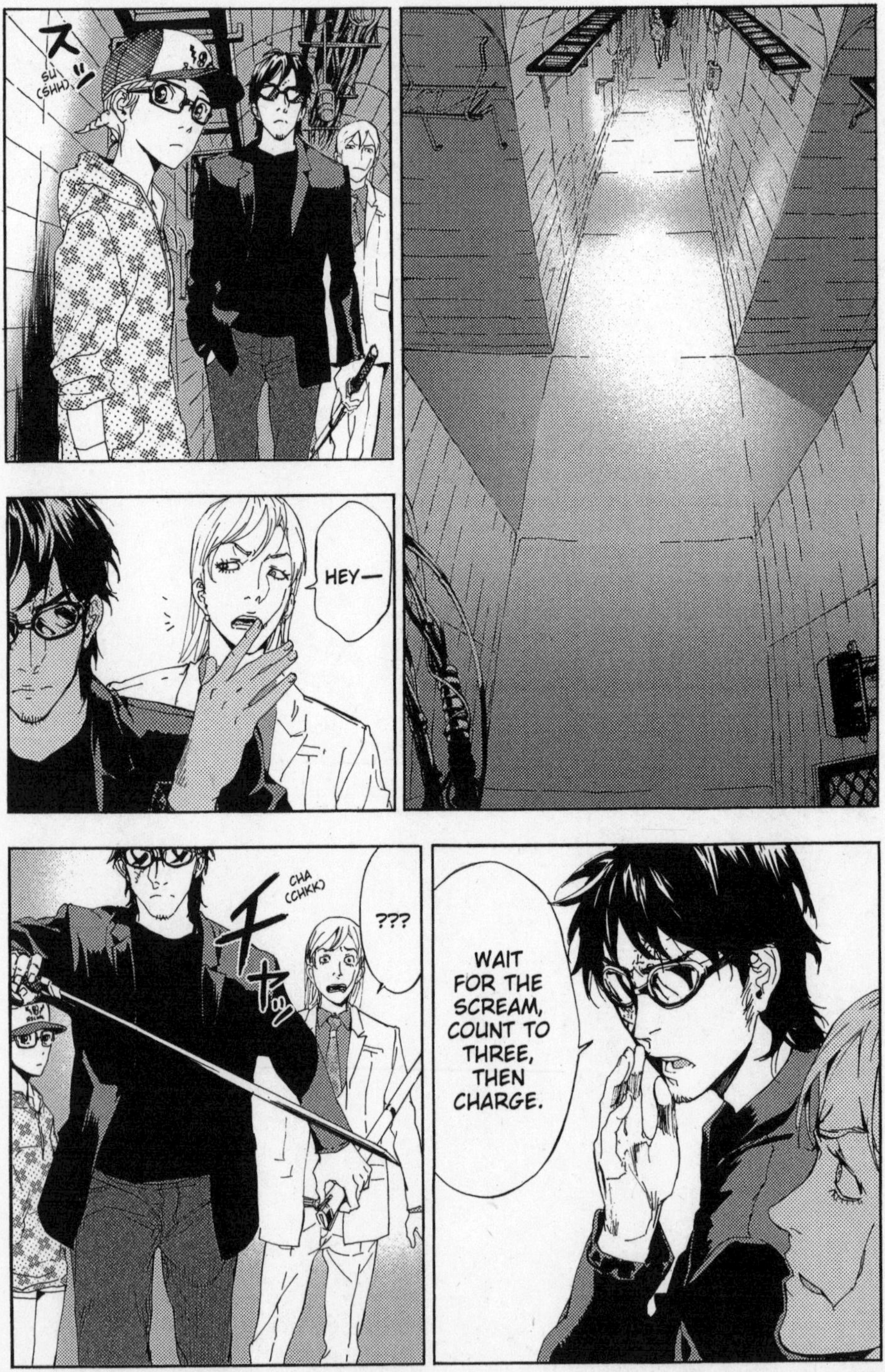

スッ
SU (SHH)
HEY—
WAIT FOR THE SCREAM, COUNT TO THREE, THEN CHARGE.
チャッ
CHA (CHKK)
???

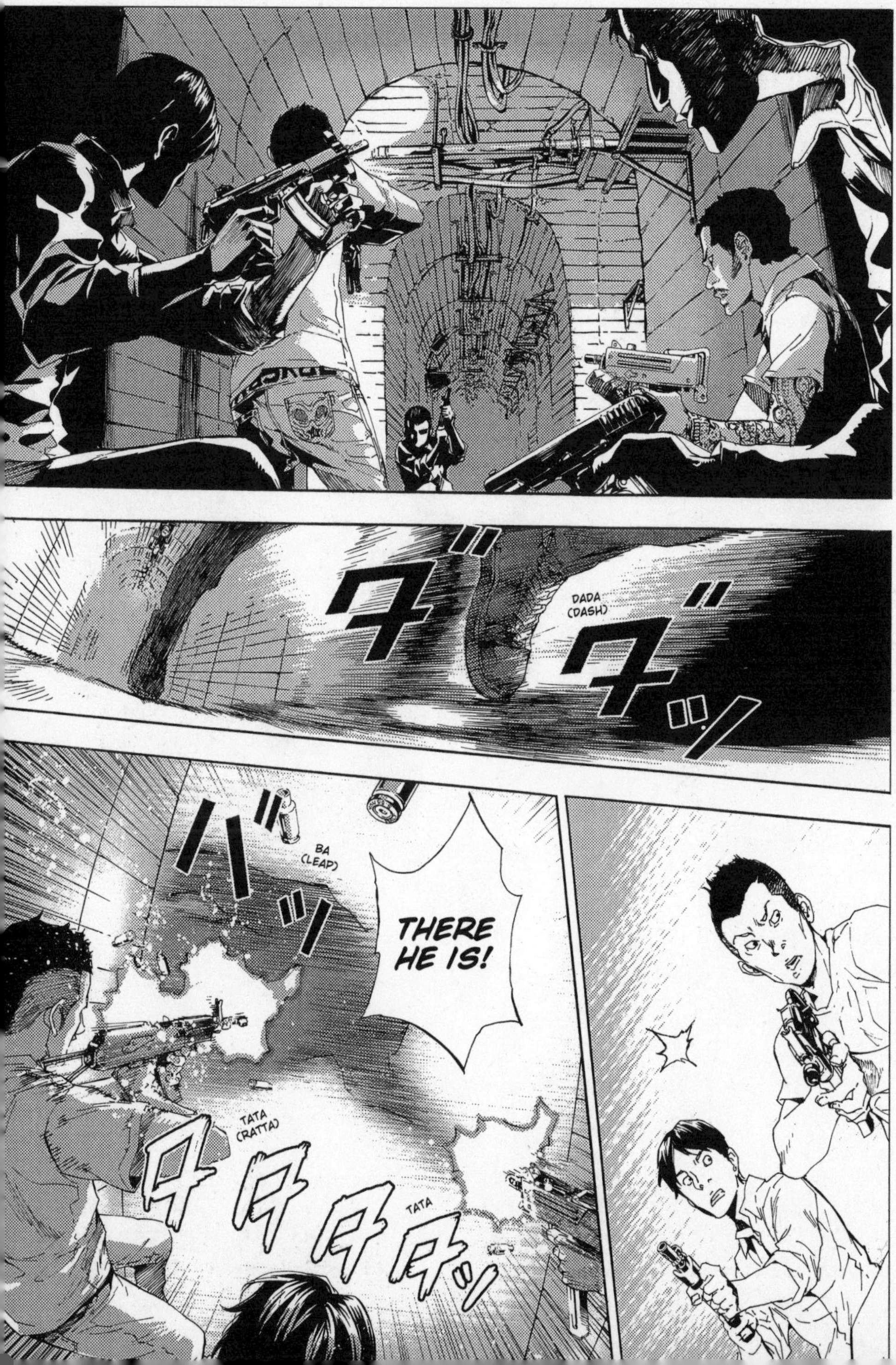
DADA
(DASH)
BA
(LEAP)
THERE HE IS!
TATA
(RATTA)
TATA

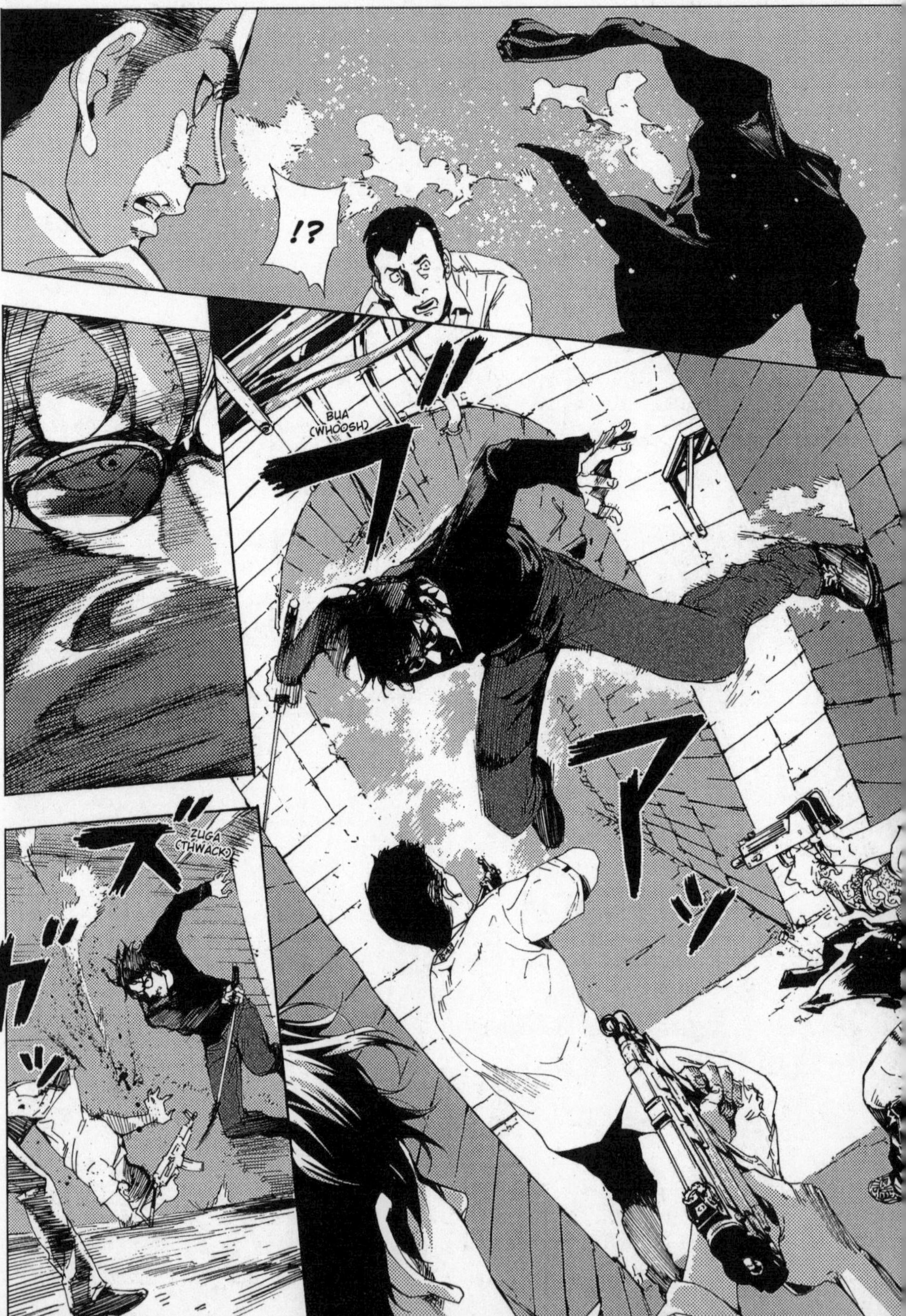
!?
BUA
(WHOOSH)
ZUGA
(THWACK)

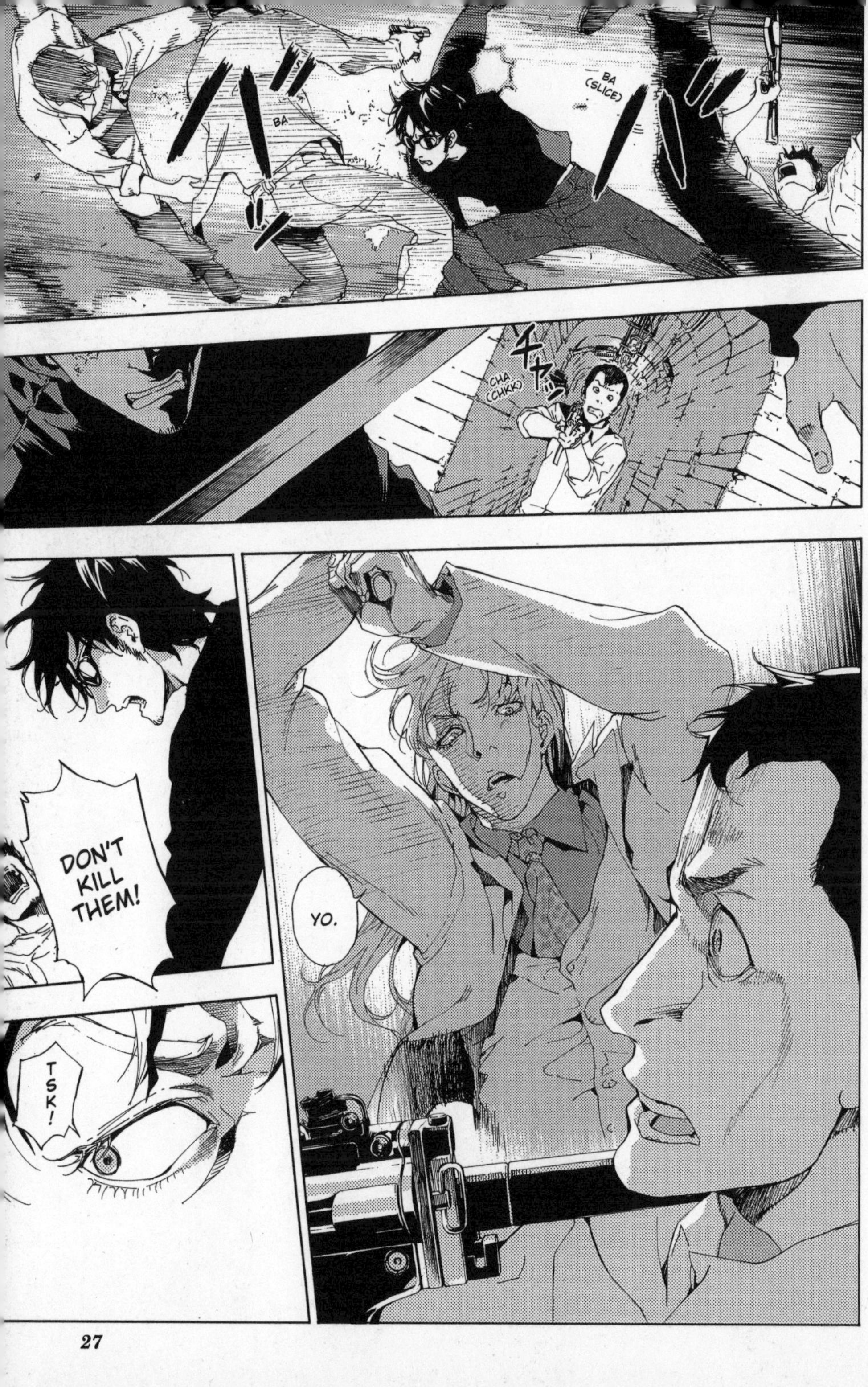
BA
(SLICE)
BA
チャッ
CHA
(CHKK)
YO.
DON'T KILL THEM!
TSK!

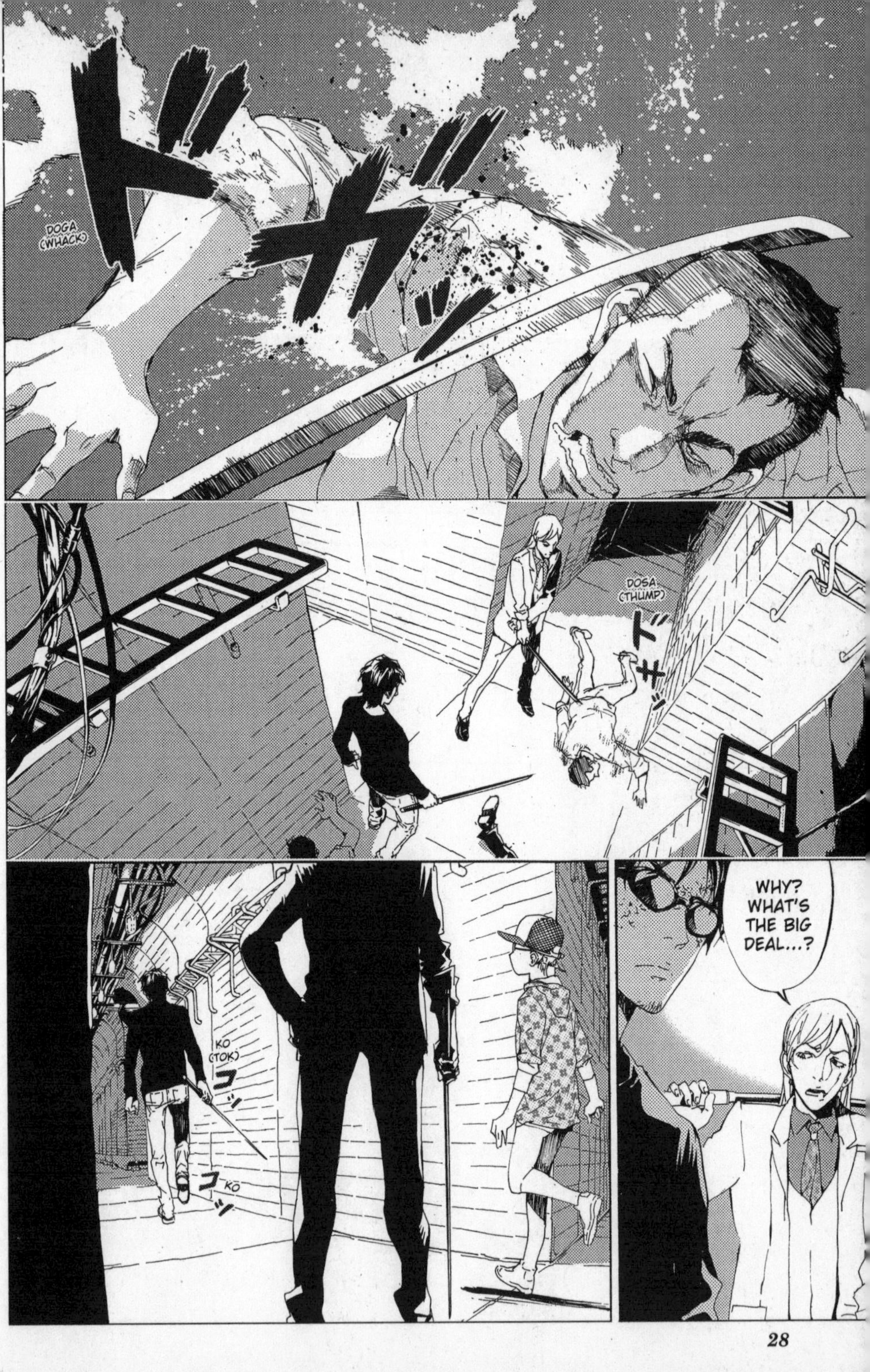
ドガッ
DOGA (WHACK)
DOSA (THUMP)
ドサッ
WHY? WHAT'S THE BIG DEAL...?
KO (TOK)
コッ
コッ
KO

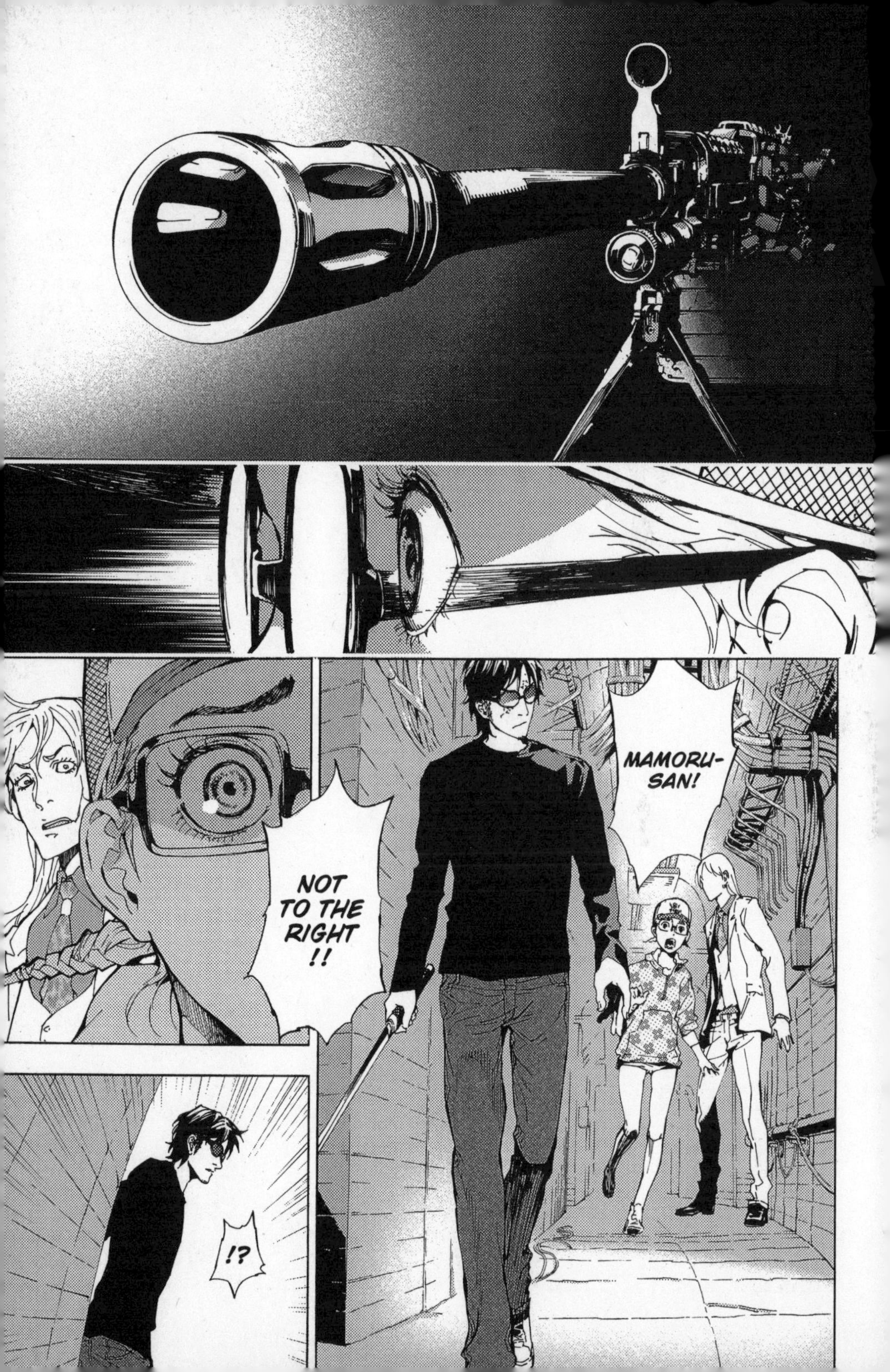
MAMORU-SAN!
NOT TO THE RIGHT !!
!?

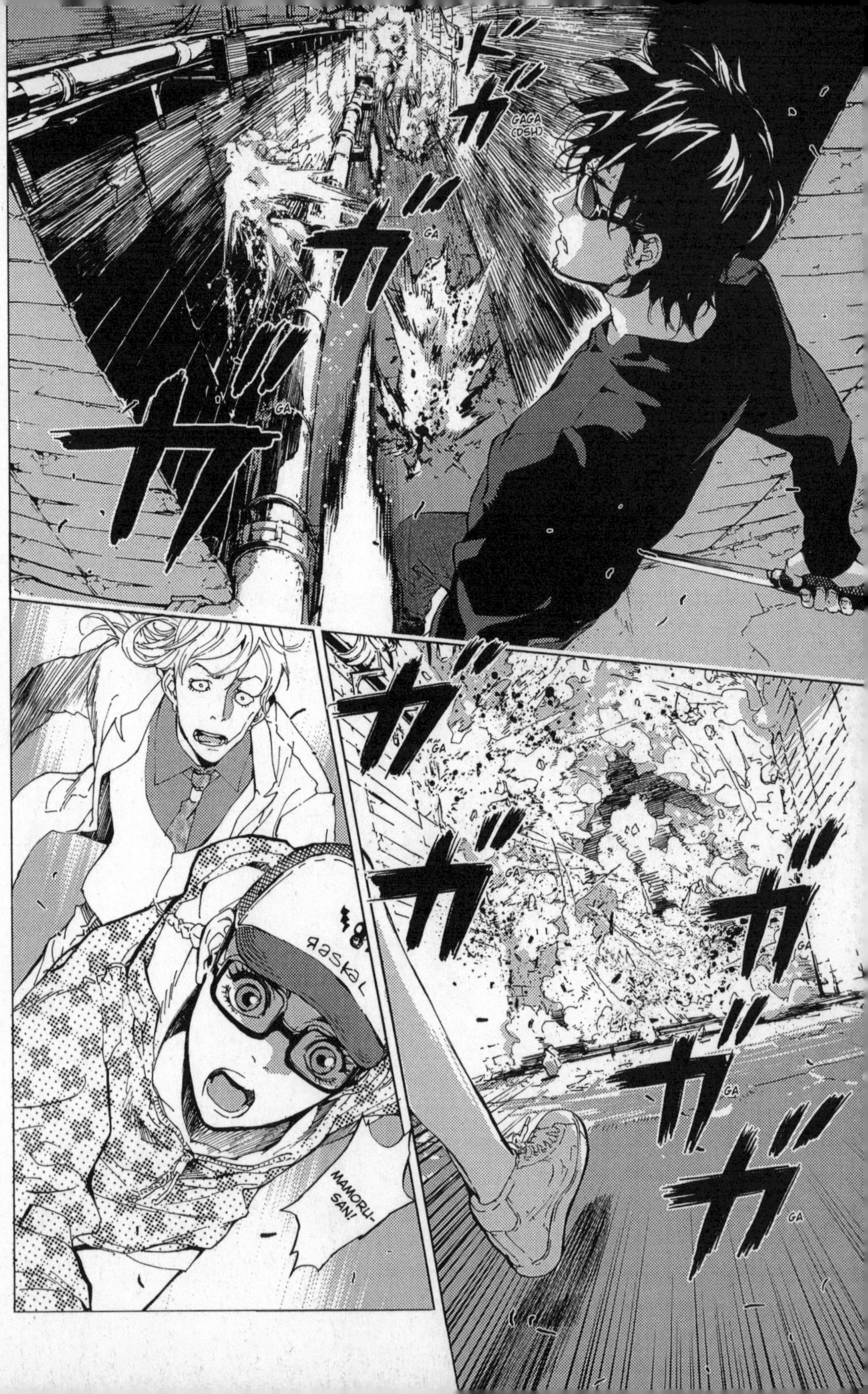
GAGA (DSH)
GA
GA
GA
GA
GA
GA
GA
MAMORU-SAN!

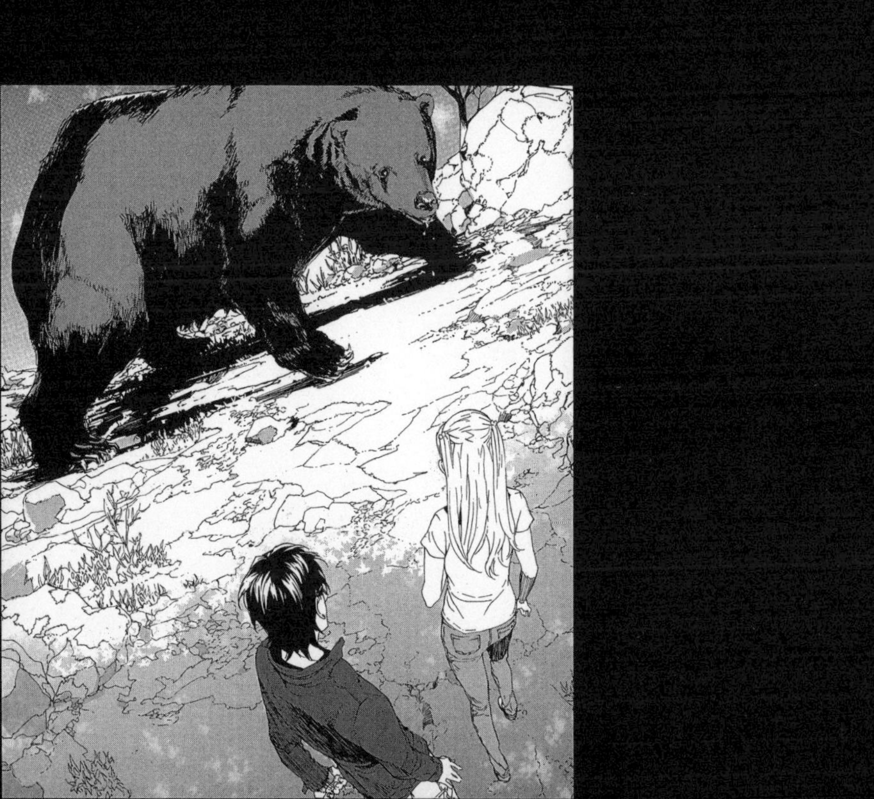

Until Death do us Part

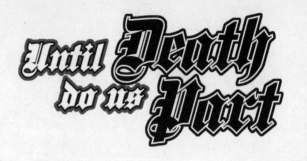

chapter 86

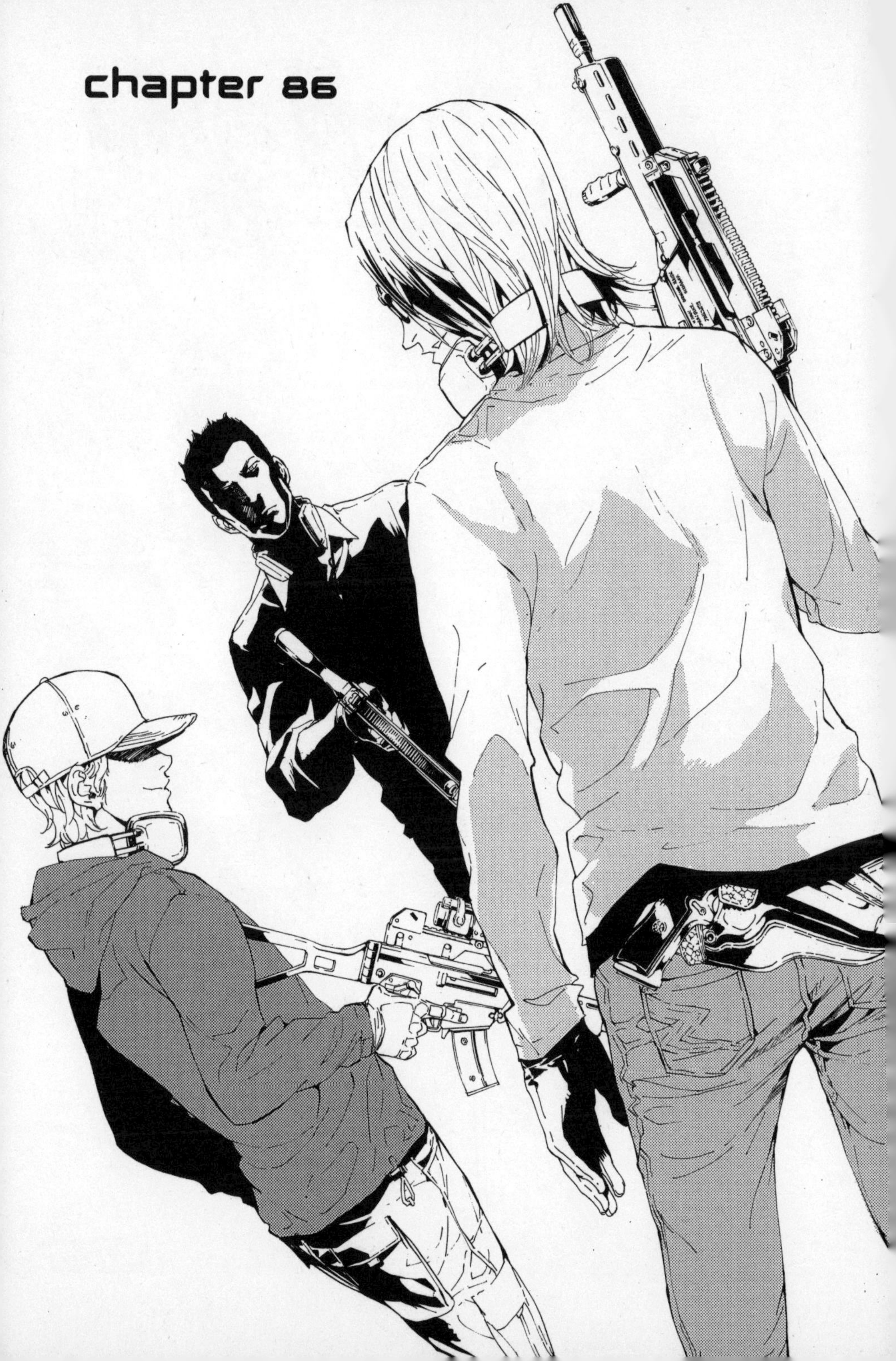

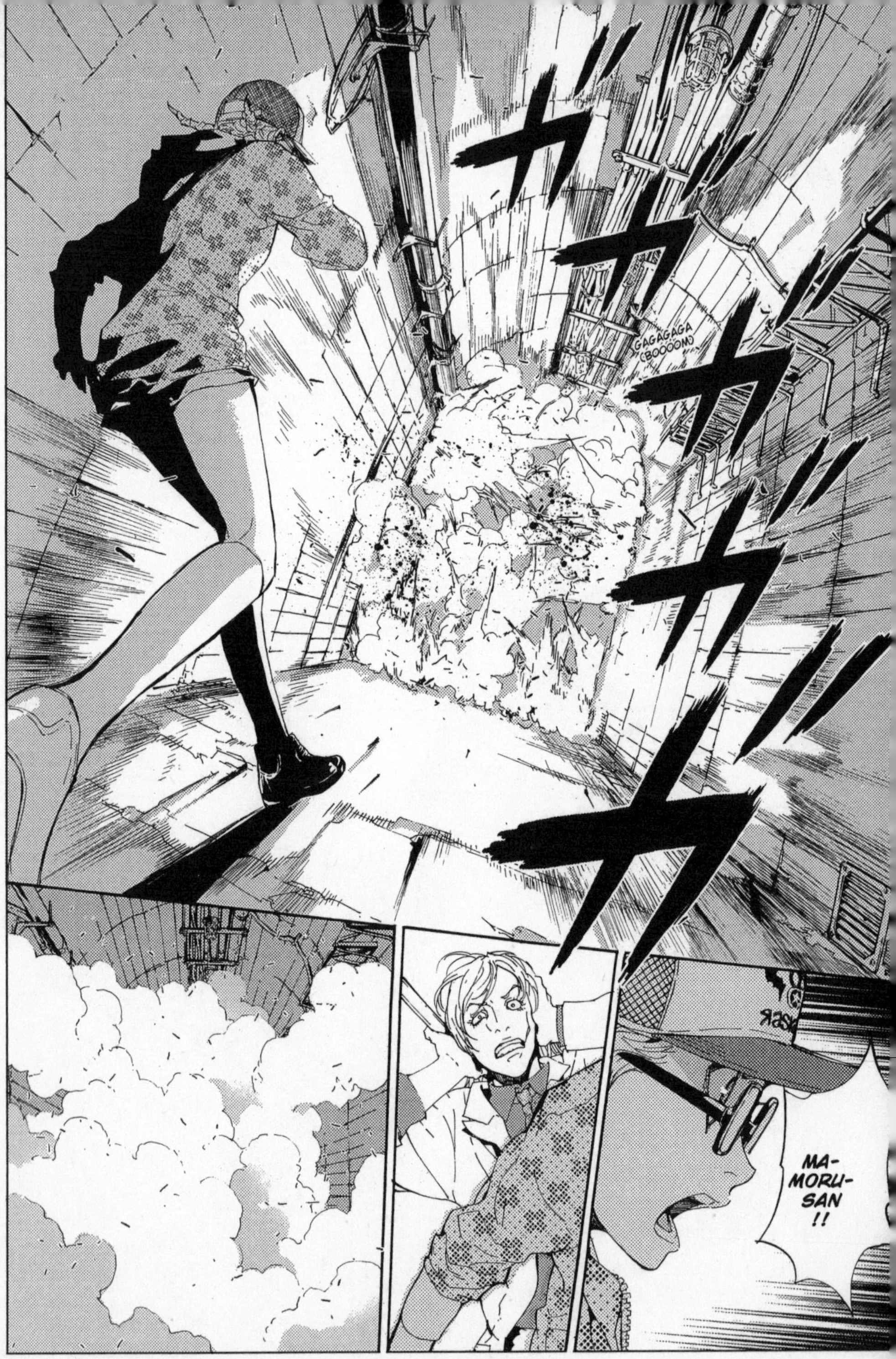
GAGAGAGA (BOOOOM)
MA-MORU-SAN!!

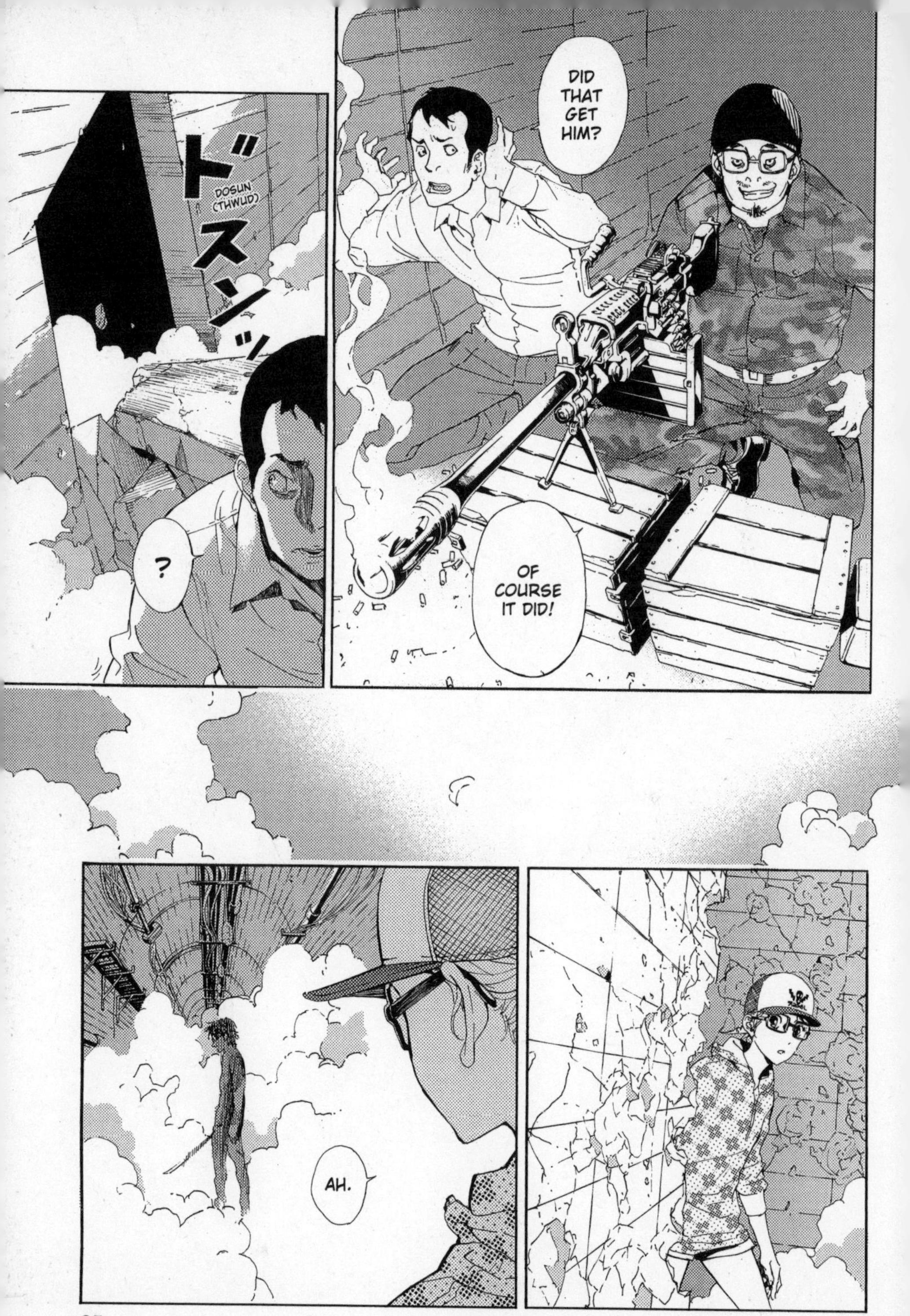
DID THAT GET HIM?
OF COURSE IT DID!
ドスン
DOSUN (THWUD)
?
AH.

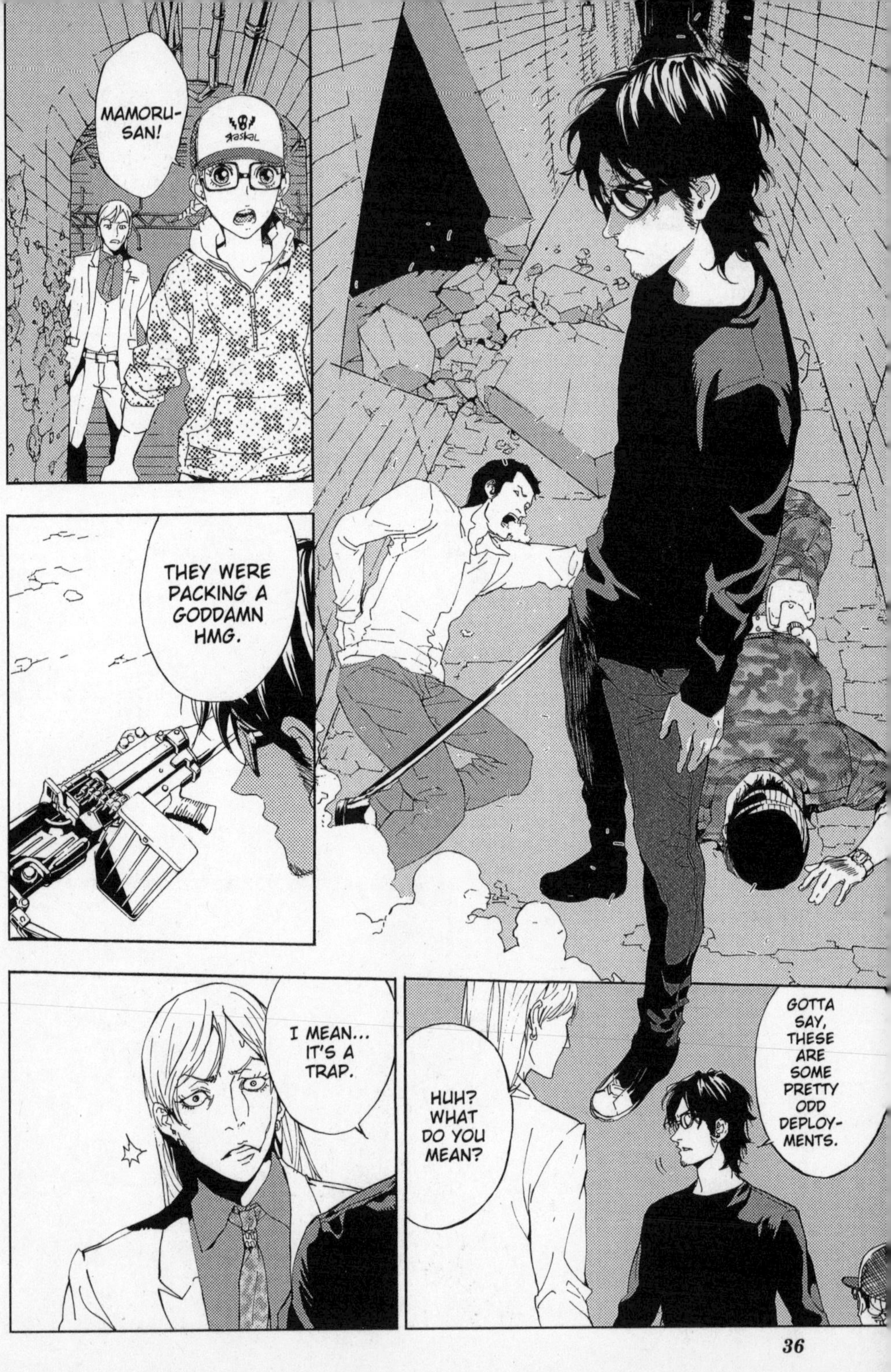
MAMORU-SAN!
THEY WERE PACKING A GODDAMN HMG.
GOTTA SAY, THESE ARE SOME PRETTY ODD DEPLOY-MENTS.
HUH? WHAT DO YOU MEAN?
I MEAN... IT'S A TRAP.

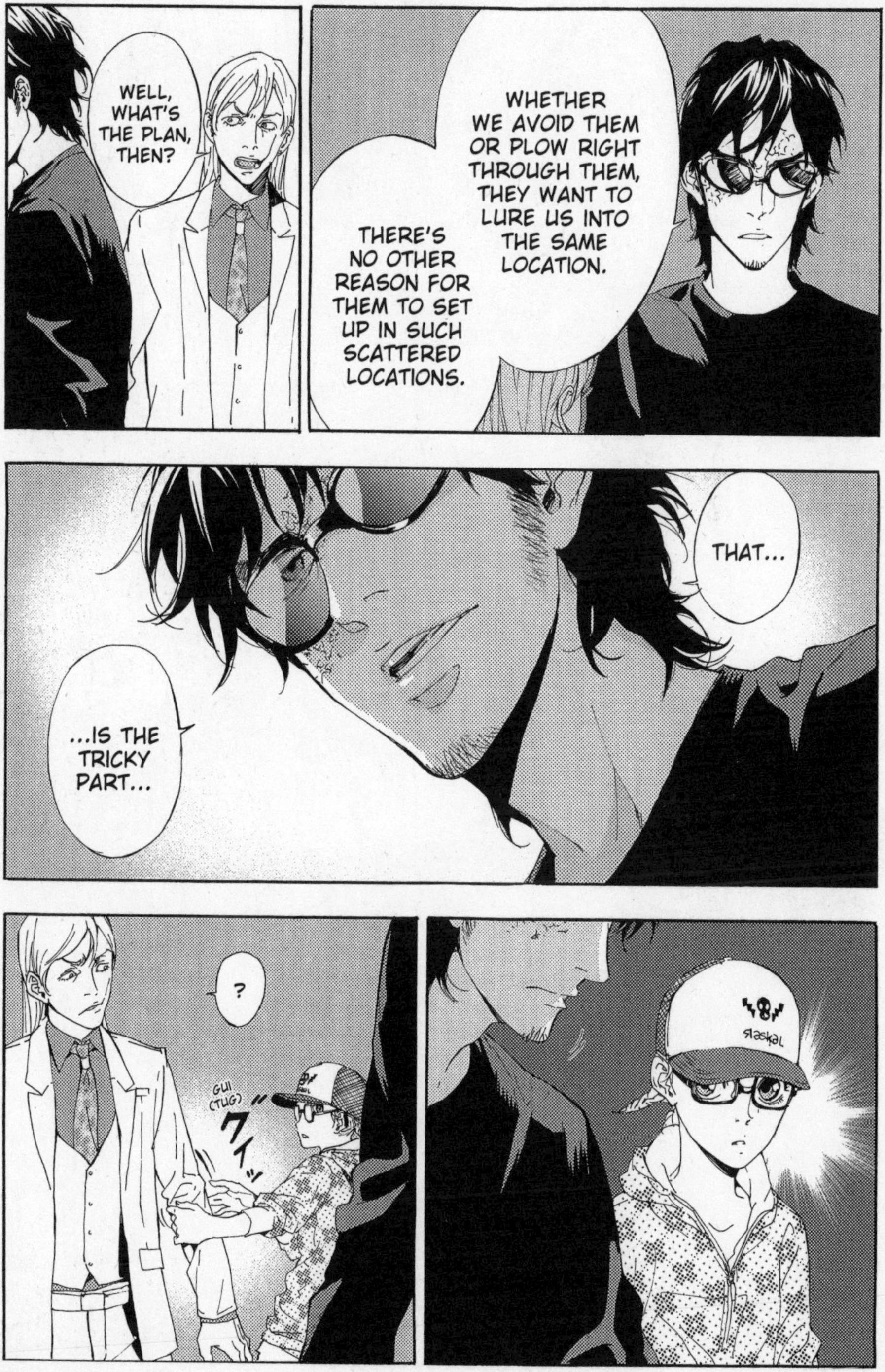
WHETHER WE AVOID THEM OR PLOW RIGHT THROUGH THEM, THEY WANT TO LURE US INTO THE SAME LOCATION.
THERE'S NO OTHER REASON FOR THEM TO SET UP IN SUCH SCATTERED LOCATIONS.
WELL, WHAT'S THE PLAN, THEN?
THAT...
...IS THE TRICKY PART...
?
GUI (TUG)
グイッ

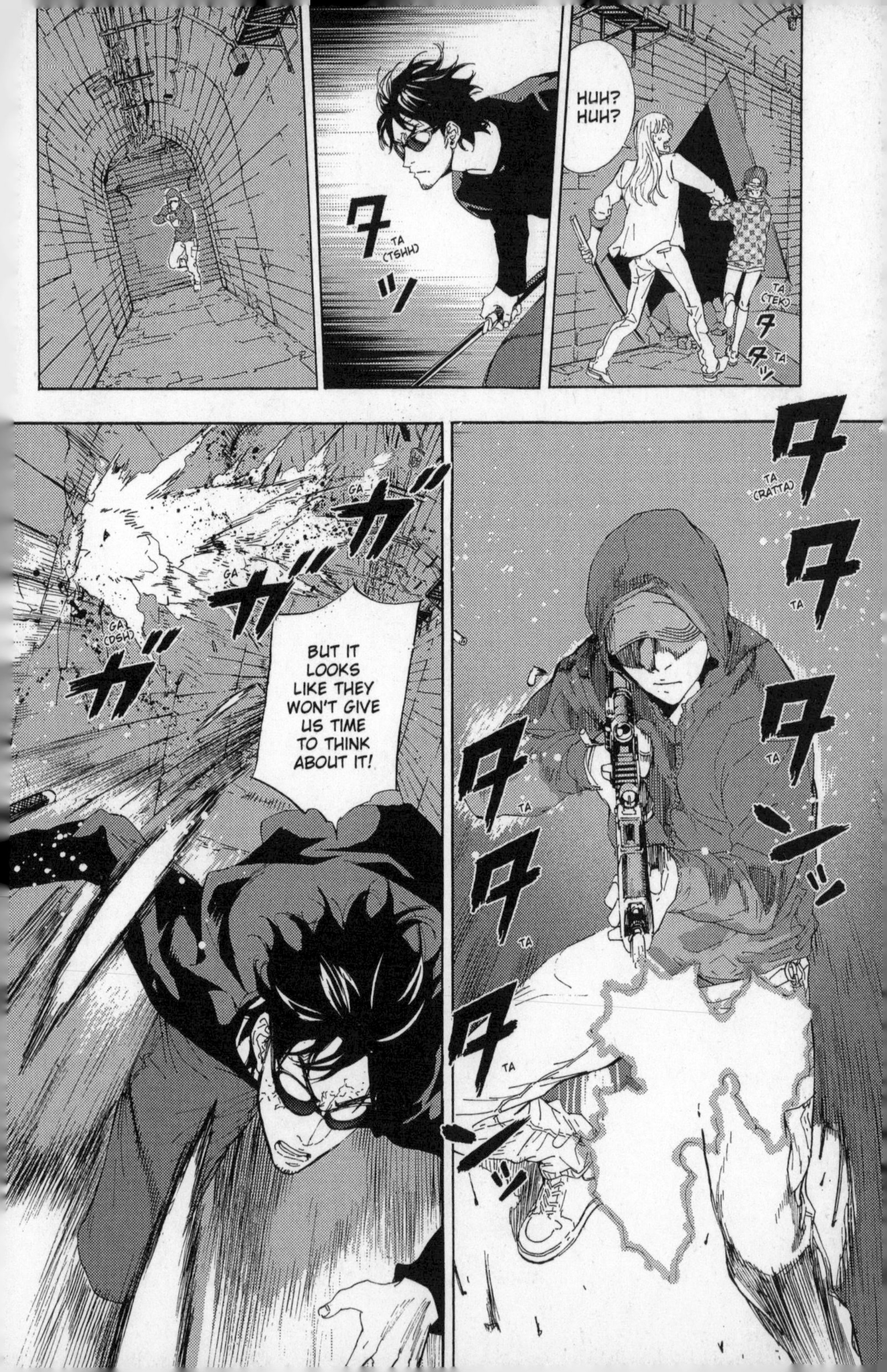
HUH? HUH?
TA (TEK)
TA
TA (TSHH)
TA (RATTA)
TA
TA
TA
TA
TA
GA
GA
GA (DSH)
BUT IT LOOKS LIKE THEY WON'T GIVE US TIME TO THINK ABOUT IT!

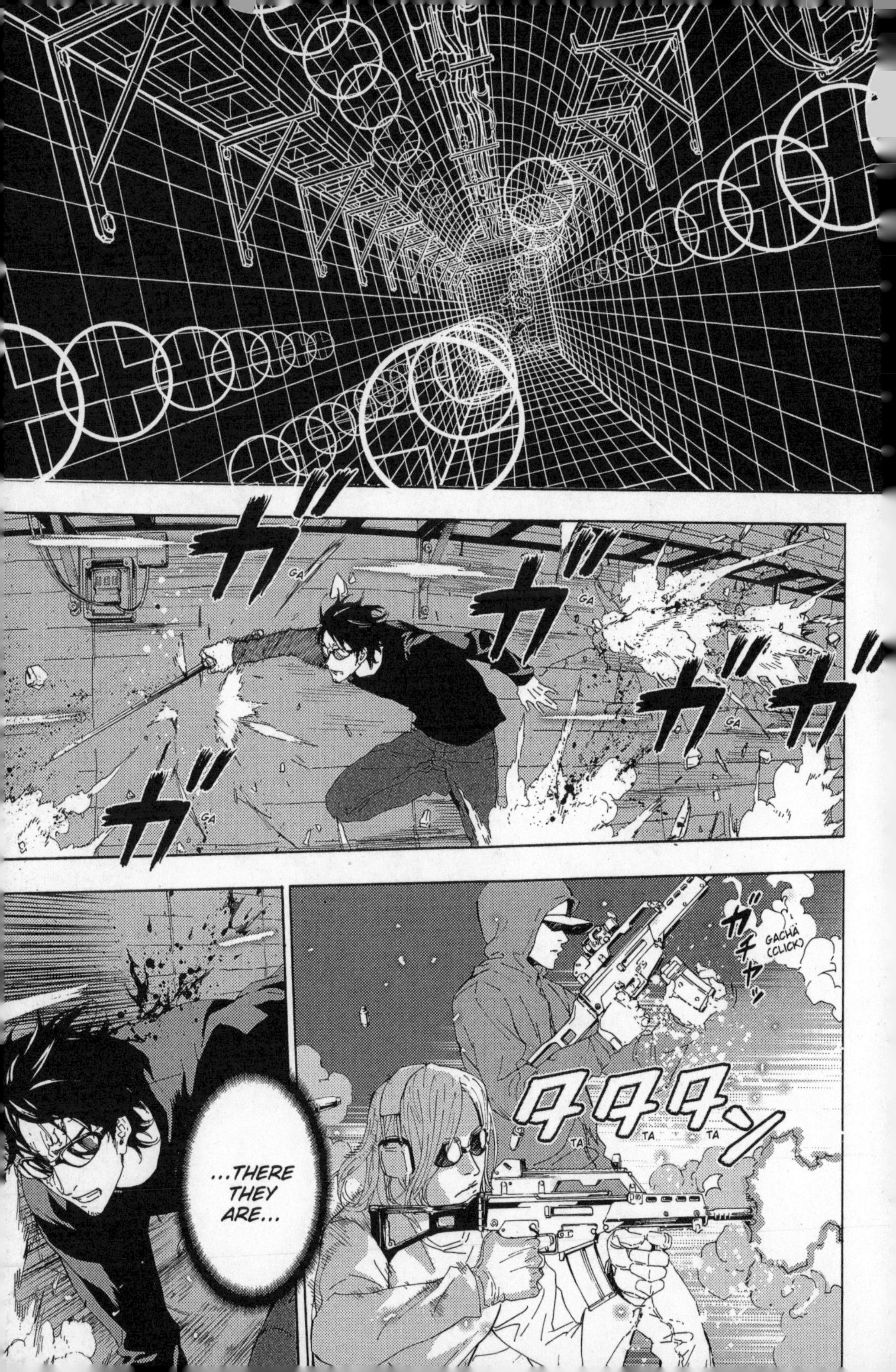
ガ
GA
ガ
GA
ガ
GA
ガ
GA
ガ
GA
ガチャッ
GACHÄ (CLICK)
タタタン
TA TA TA
...THERE THEY ARE...

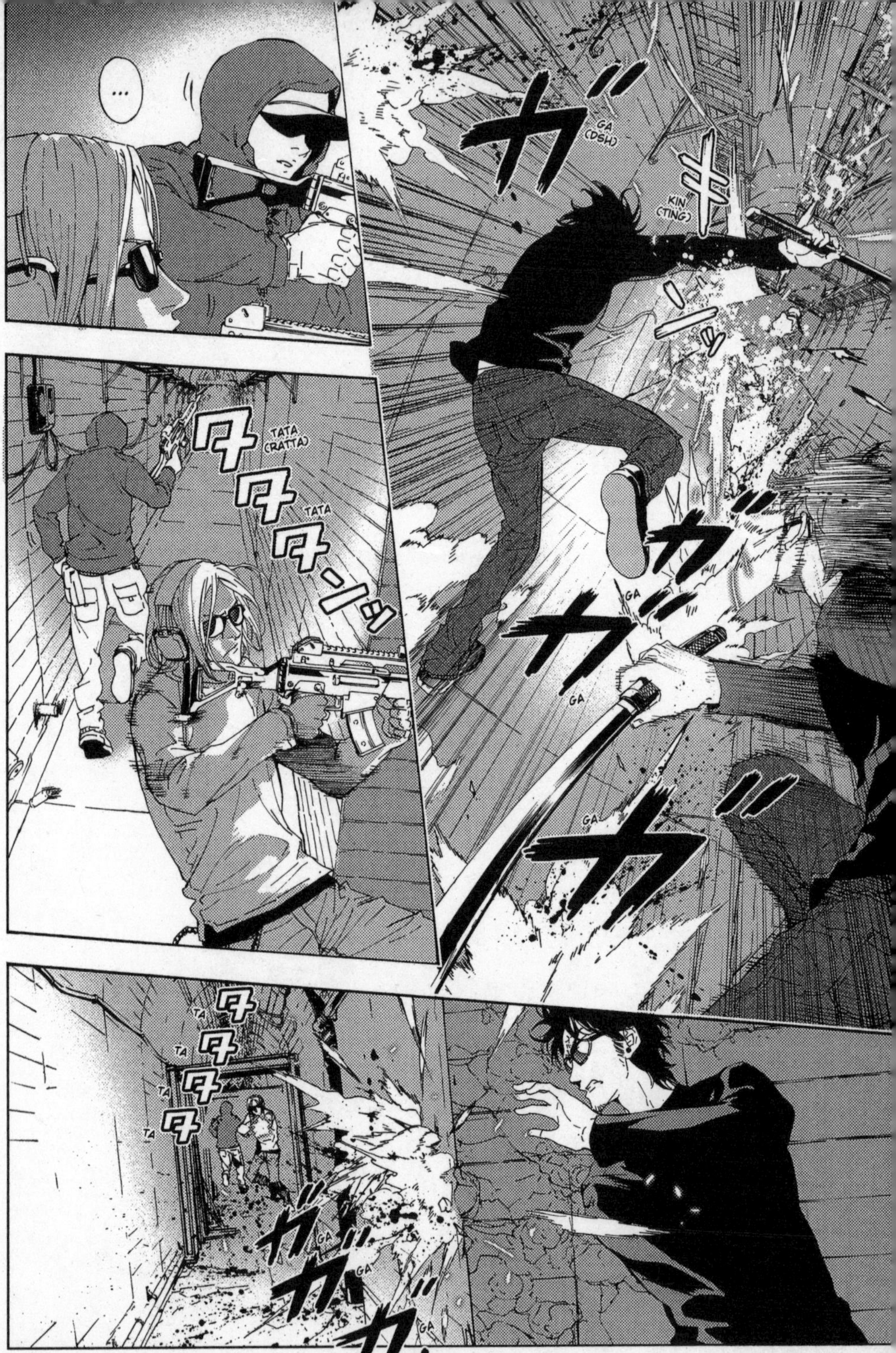

GA (DSH)
KIN (TING)
GA
GA
GA
...
TATA (RATTA)
TATA
TA
TA
TA
TA
GA
GA
GA

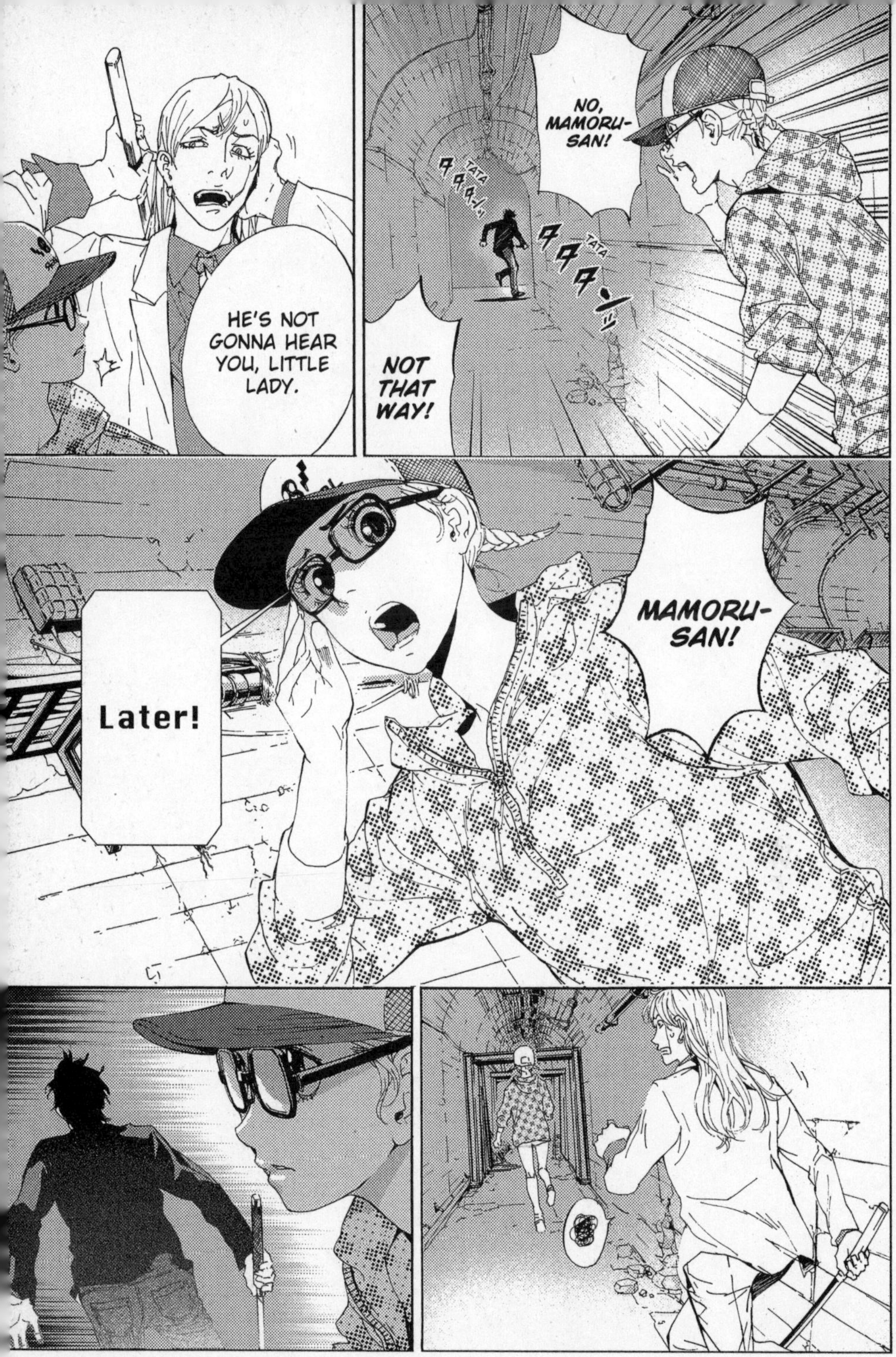
NO, MAMORU-SAN!
TATA
TATA
NOT THAT WAY!
HE'S NOT GONNA HEAR YOU, LITTLE LADY.
MAMORU-SAN!
Later!

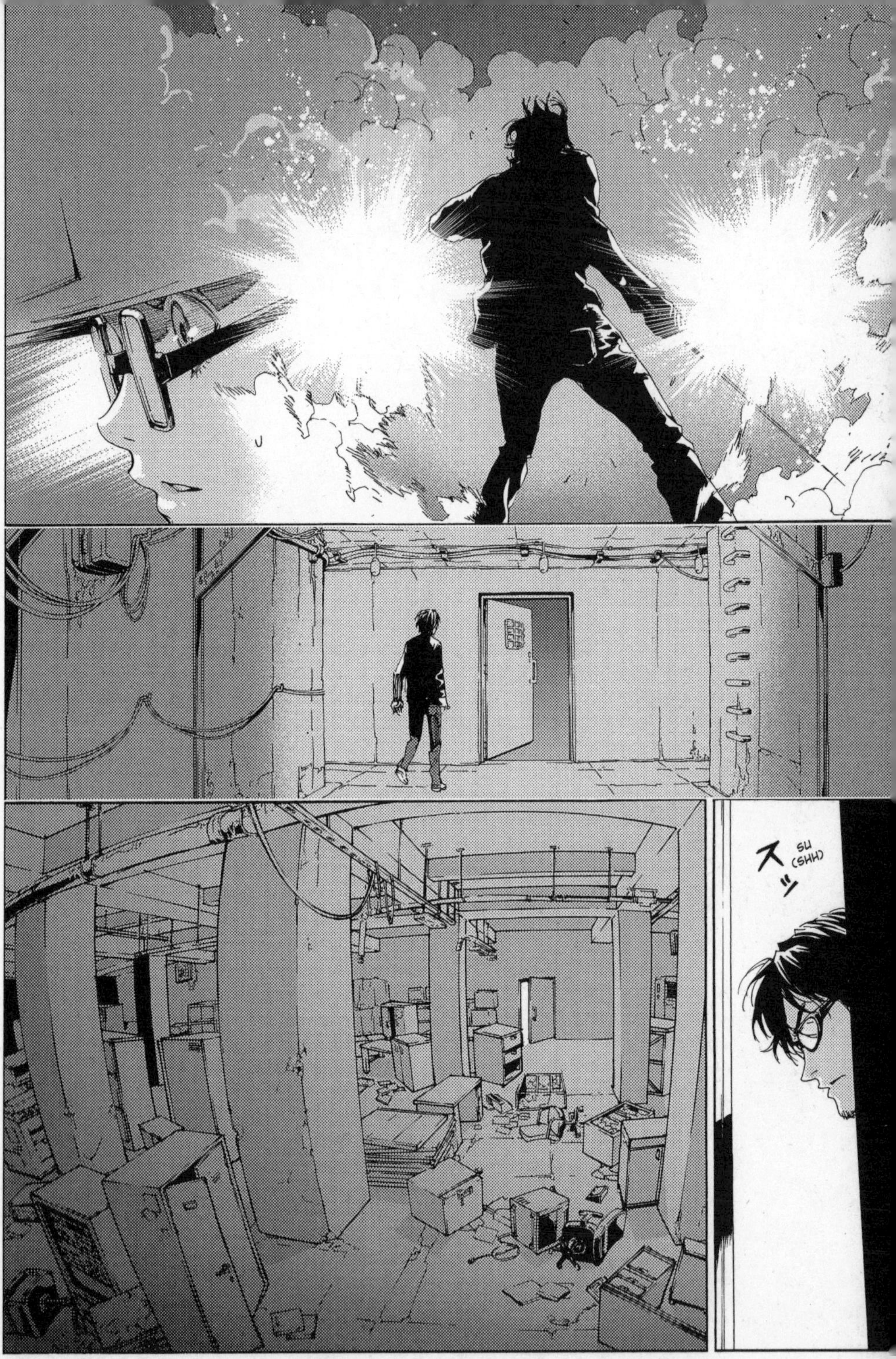
スッ
SU
(SHH)

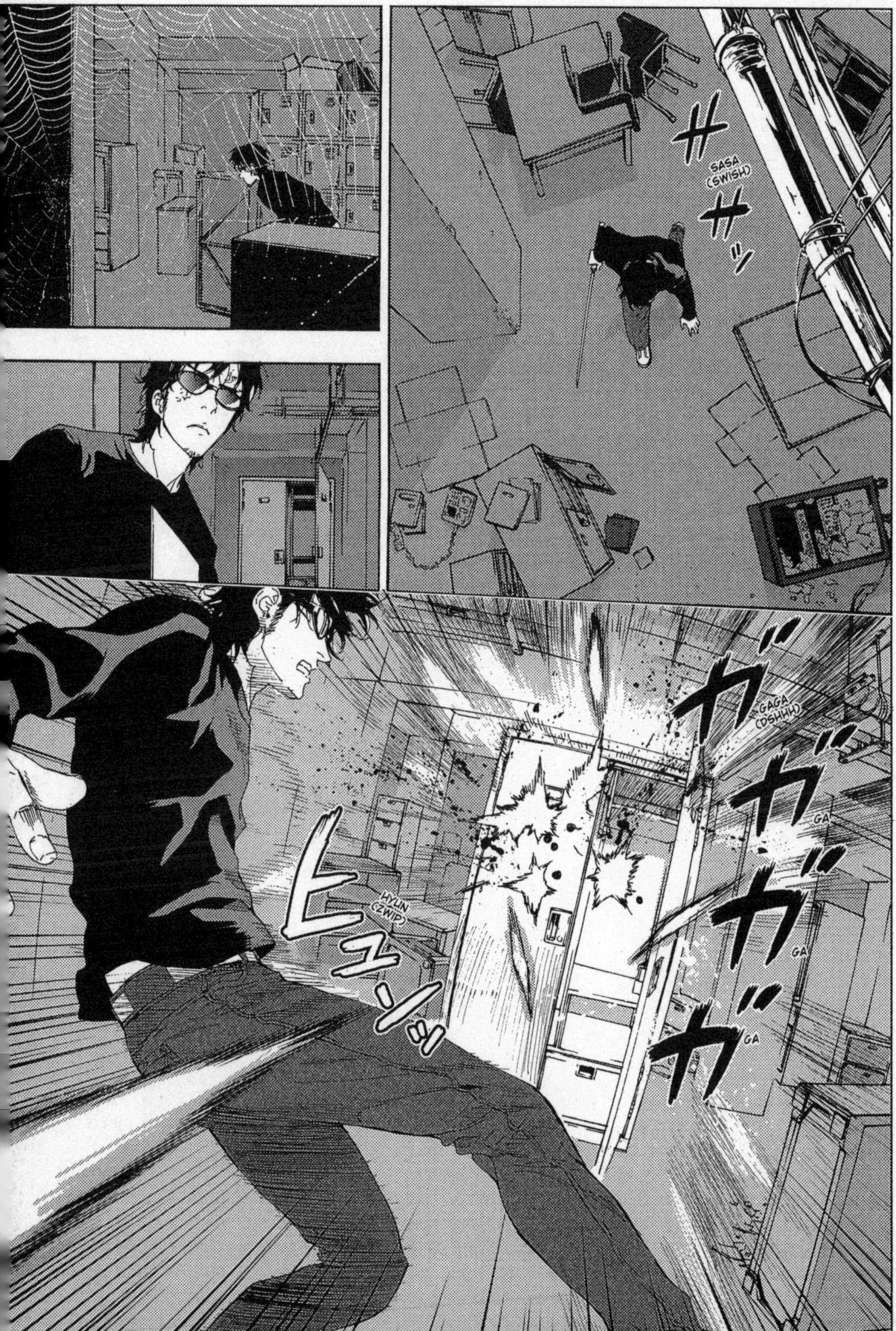
SASA (SWISH)
GAGA (DSHHH)
GA
GA
GA
HYUN (ZWIP)

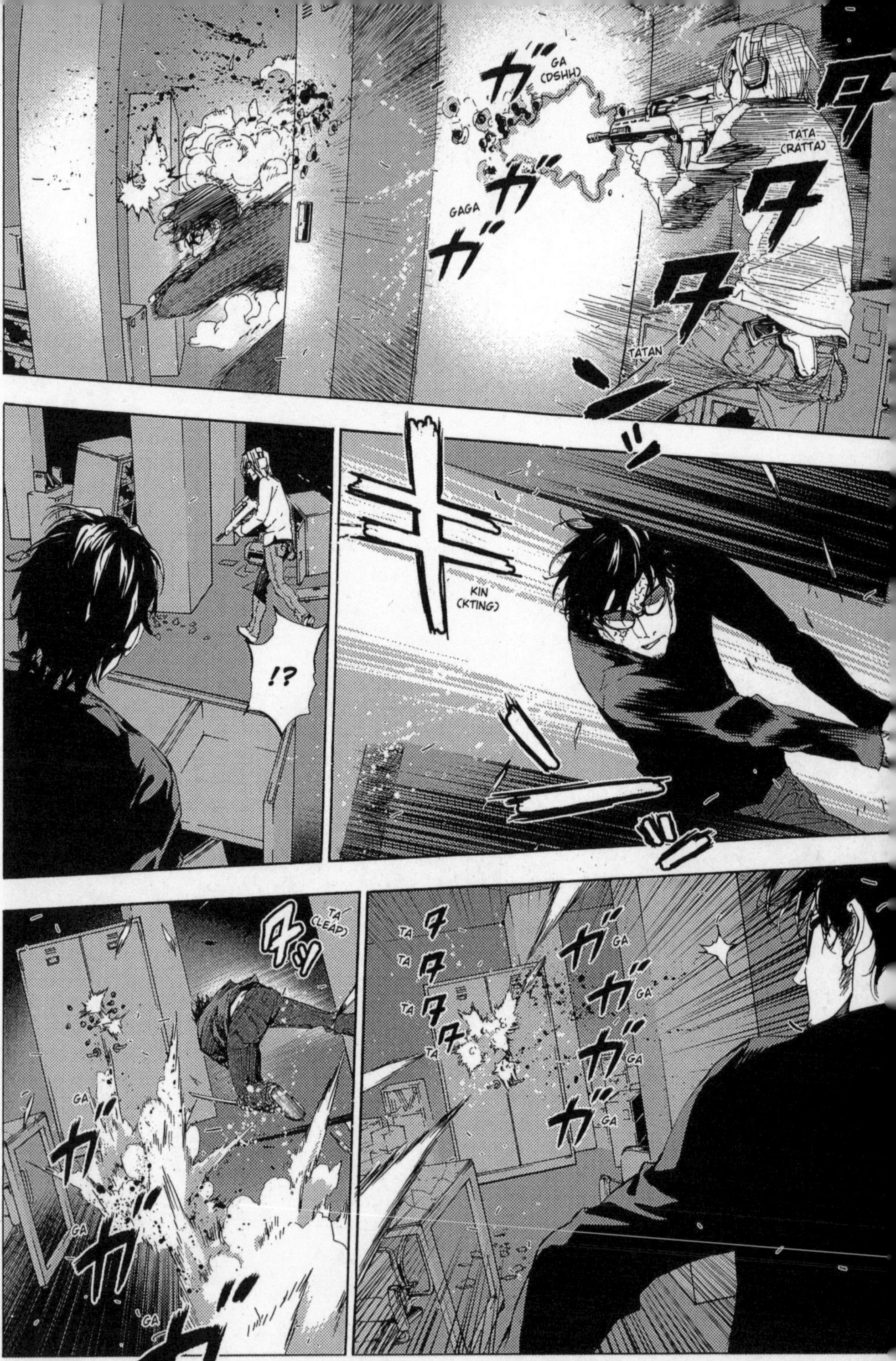
TATA (RATTA)
GA (DSHH)
GAGA
TATAN
KIN (KTING)
!?
TA
TA
TA
TA
GA
GA
GA
GA
TA (LEAP)
GA
GA
GA

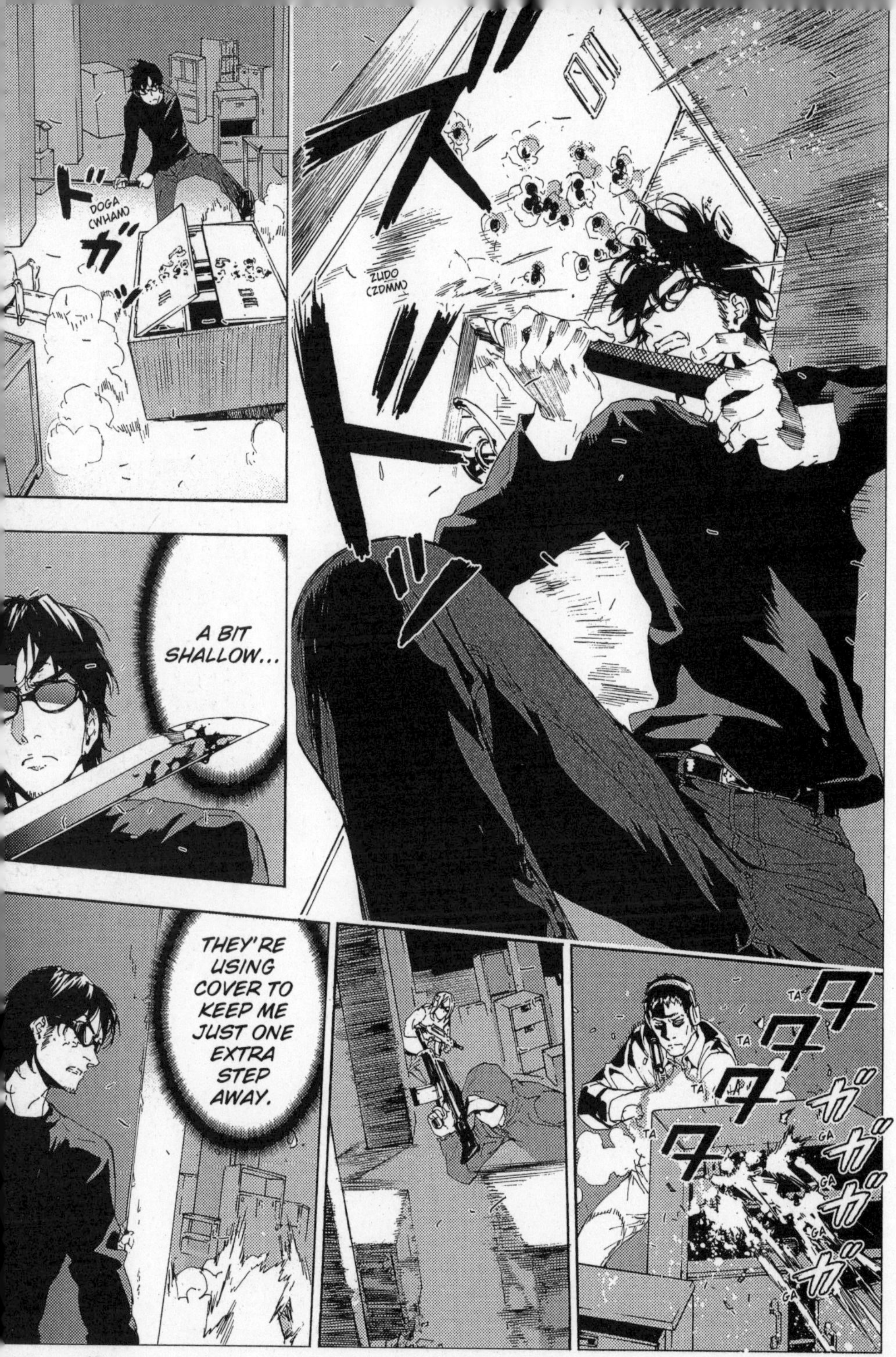

ZUDO (ZDMM)
DOGA (WHAM)
A BIT SHALLOW...
TA
TA
TA
TA
GA
GA
GA
GA
THEY'RE USING COVER TO KEEP ME JUST ONE EXTRA STEP AWAY.

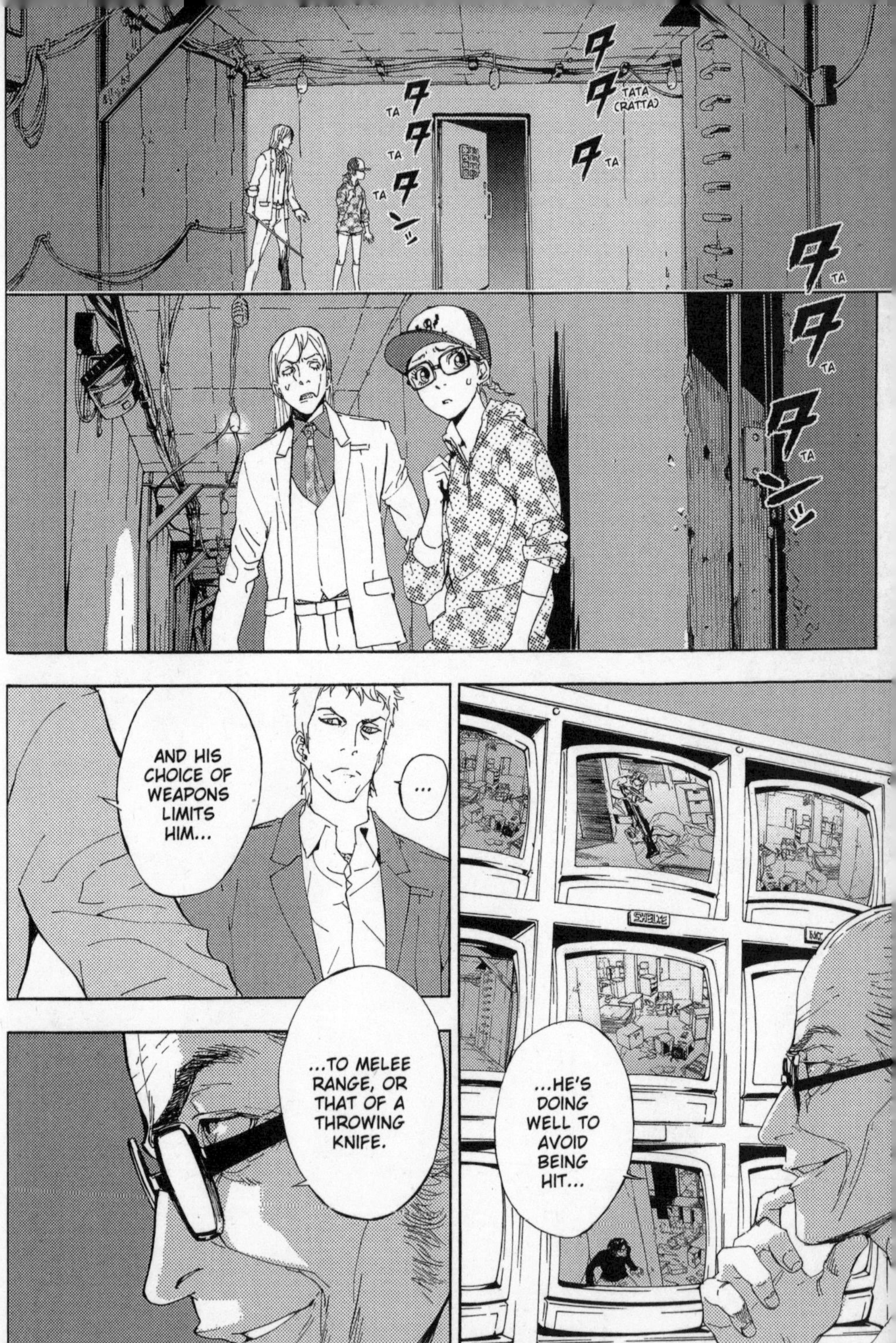
TATA (RATTA)
TA
TA
TA
TA
TA
TA
TA
TA
...HE'S DOING WELL TO AVOID BEING HIT...
AND HIS CHOICE OF WEAPONS LIMITS HIM...
...
...TO MELEE RANGE, OR THAT OF A THROWING KNIFE.

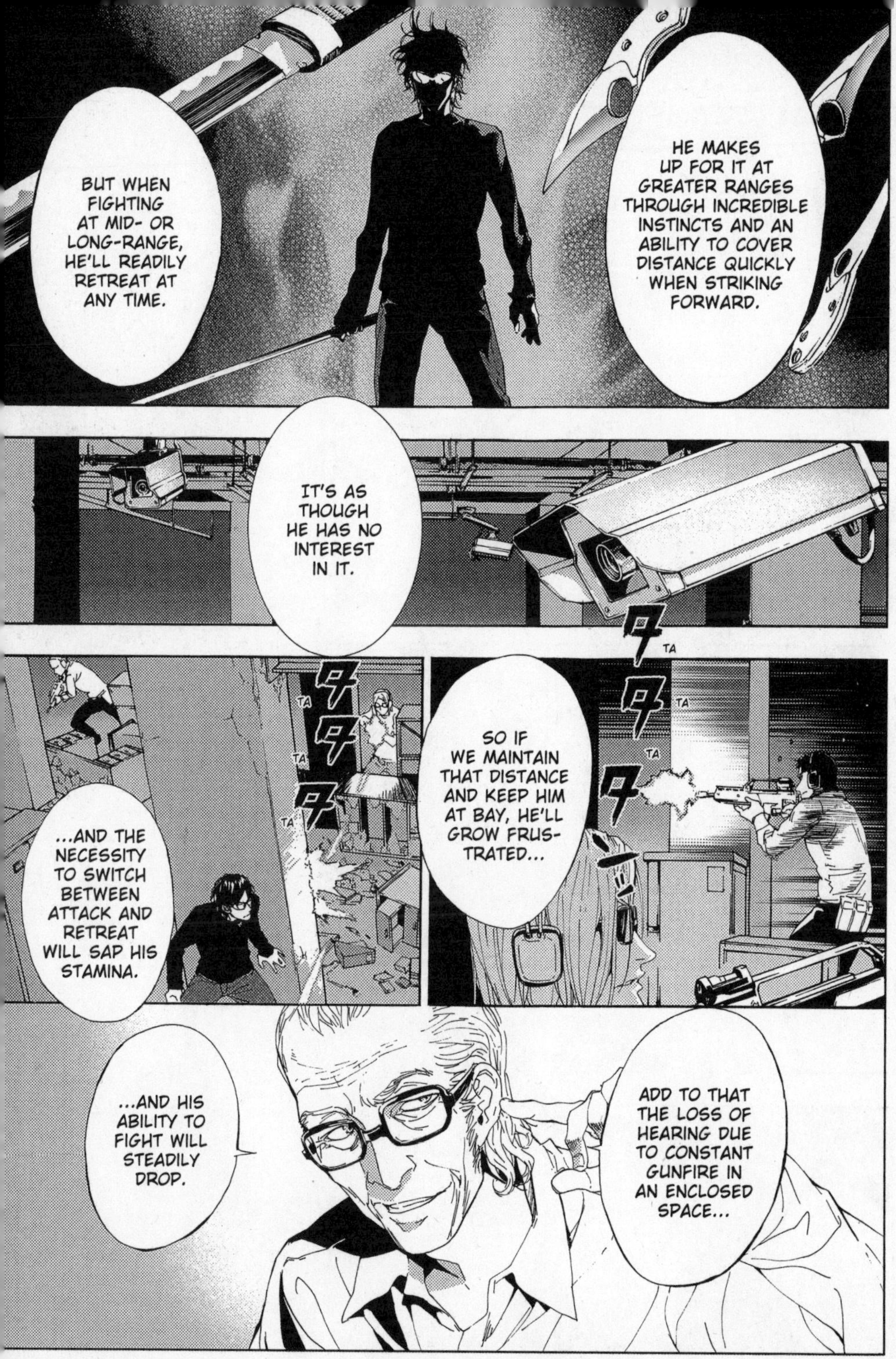
HE MAKES UP FOR IT AT GREATER RANGES THROUGH INCREDIBLE INSTINCTS AND AN ABILITY TO COVER DISTANCE QUICKLY WHEN STRIKING FORWARD.
BUT WHEN FIGHTING AT MID- OR LONG-RANGE, HE'LL READILY RETREAT AT ANY TIME.
IT'S AS THOUGH HE HAS NO INTEREST IN IT.
TA
TA
TA
TA
SO IF WE MAINTAIN THAT DISTANCE AND KEEP HIM AT BAY, HE'LL GROW FRUS-TRATED...
TA
TA
TA
...AND THE NECESSITY TO SWITCH BETWEEN ATTACK AND RETREAT WILL SAP HIS STAMINA.
ADD TO THAT THE LOSS OF HEARING DUE TO CONSTANT GUNFIRE IN AN ENCLOSED SPACE...
...AND HIS ABILITY TO FIGHT WILL STEADILY DROP.

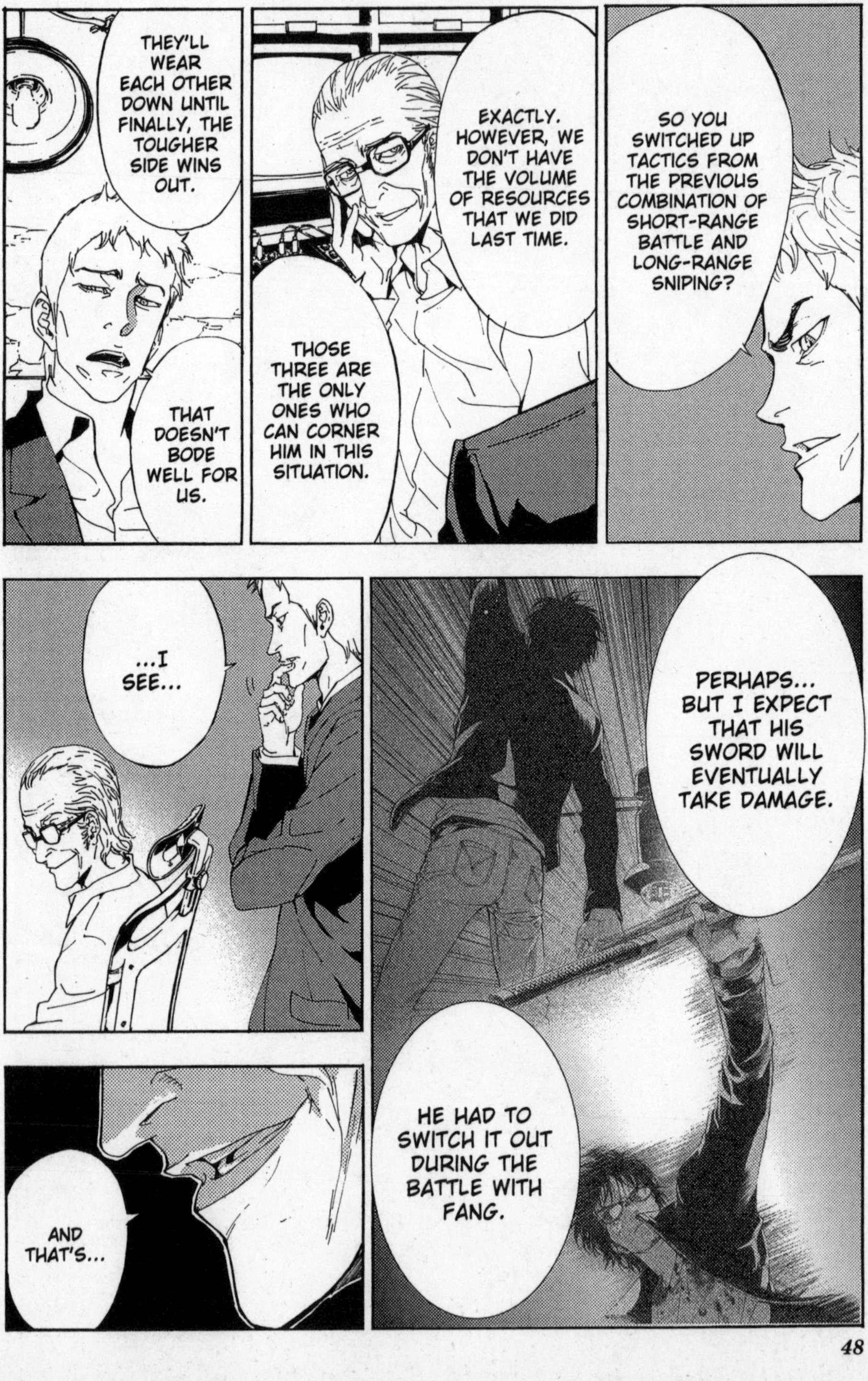
SO YOU SWITCHED UP TACTICS FROM THE PREVIOUS COMBINATION OF SHORT-RANGE BATTLE AND LONG-RANGE SNIPING?
EXACTLY. HOWEVER, WE DON'T HAVE THE VOLUME OF RESOURCES THAT WE DID LAST TIME.
THOSE THREE ARE THE ONLY ONES WHO CAN CORNER HIM IN THIS SITUATION.
THEY'LL WEAR EACH OTHER DOWN UNTIL FINALLY, THE TOUGHER SIDE WINS OUT.
THAT DOESN'T BODE WELL FOR US.
PERHAPS... BUT I EXPECT THAT HIS SWORD WILL EVENTUALLY TAKE DAMAGE.
HE HAD TO SWITCH IT OUT DURING THE BATTLE WITH FANG.
...I SEE...
AND THAT'S...

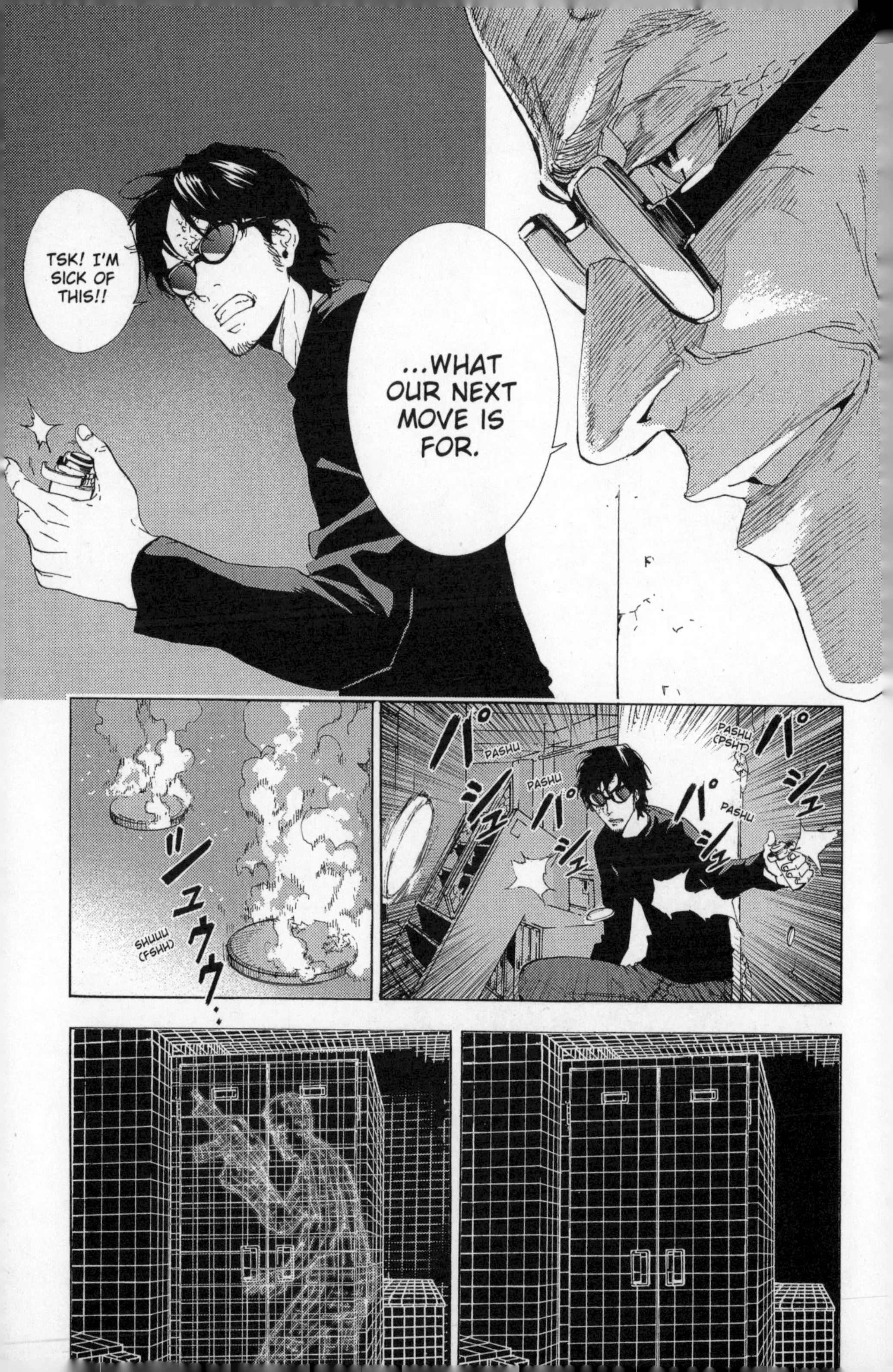
...WHAT OUR NEXT MOVE IS FOR.
TSK! I'M SICK OF THIS!!
パシュ
PASHU (PSHT)
パシュ
PASHU
PASHU
パシュ
PASHU
パシュ
シュウウ..
SHUUU (FSHH)

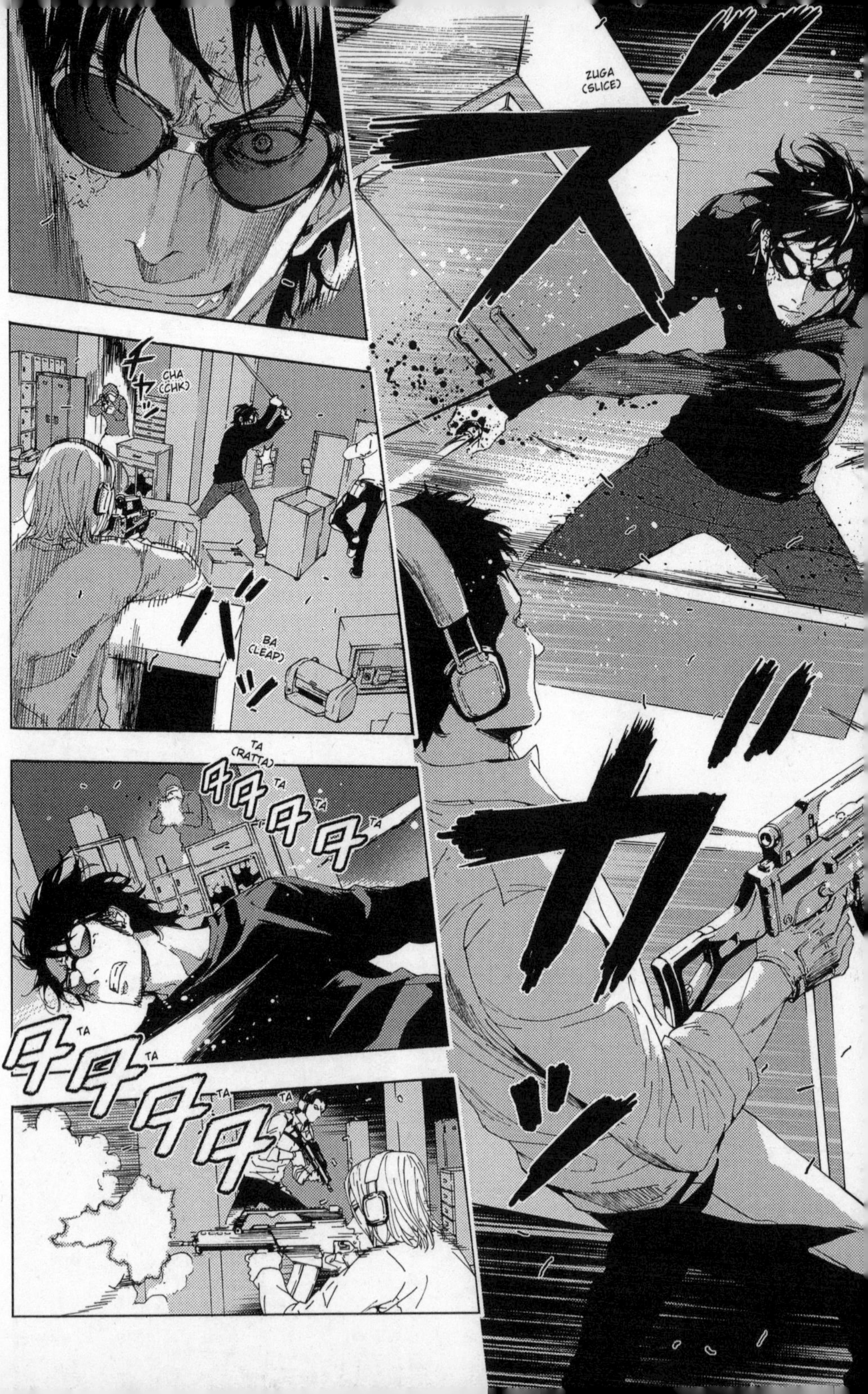
ZUGA (SLICE)
CHA (CHK)
BA (LEAP)
TA (RATTA)
TA
TA
TA
TA
TA
TA
TA

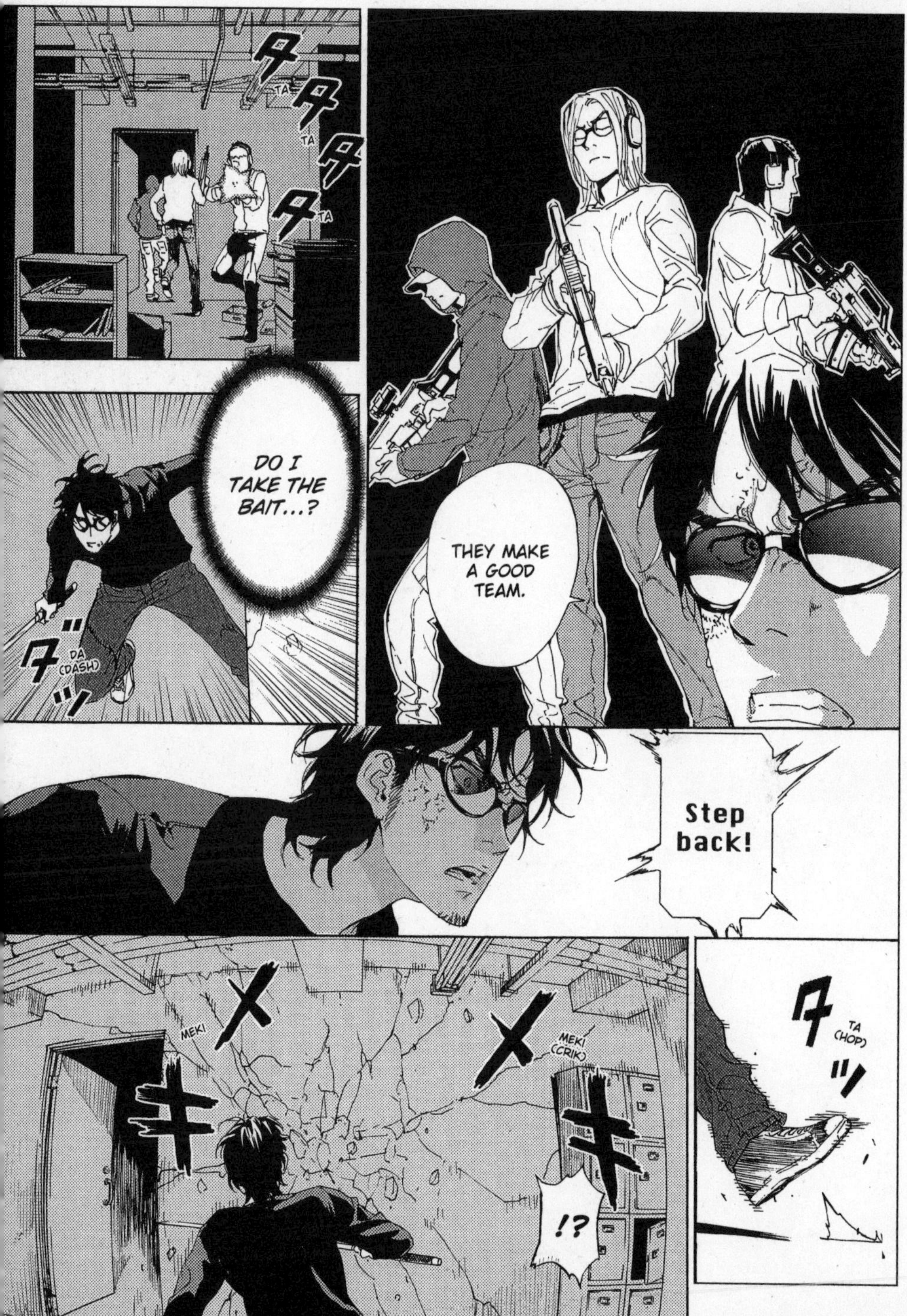
THEY MAKE A GOOD TEAM.
TA
TA
TA
DO I TAKE THE BAIT...?
DA (DASH)
Step back!
TA (HOP)
MEKI (CRIK)
MEKI
!?

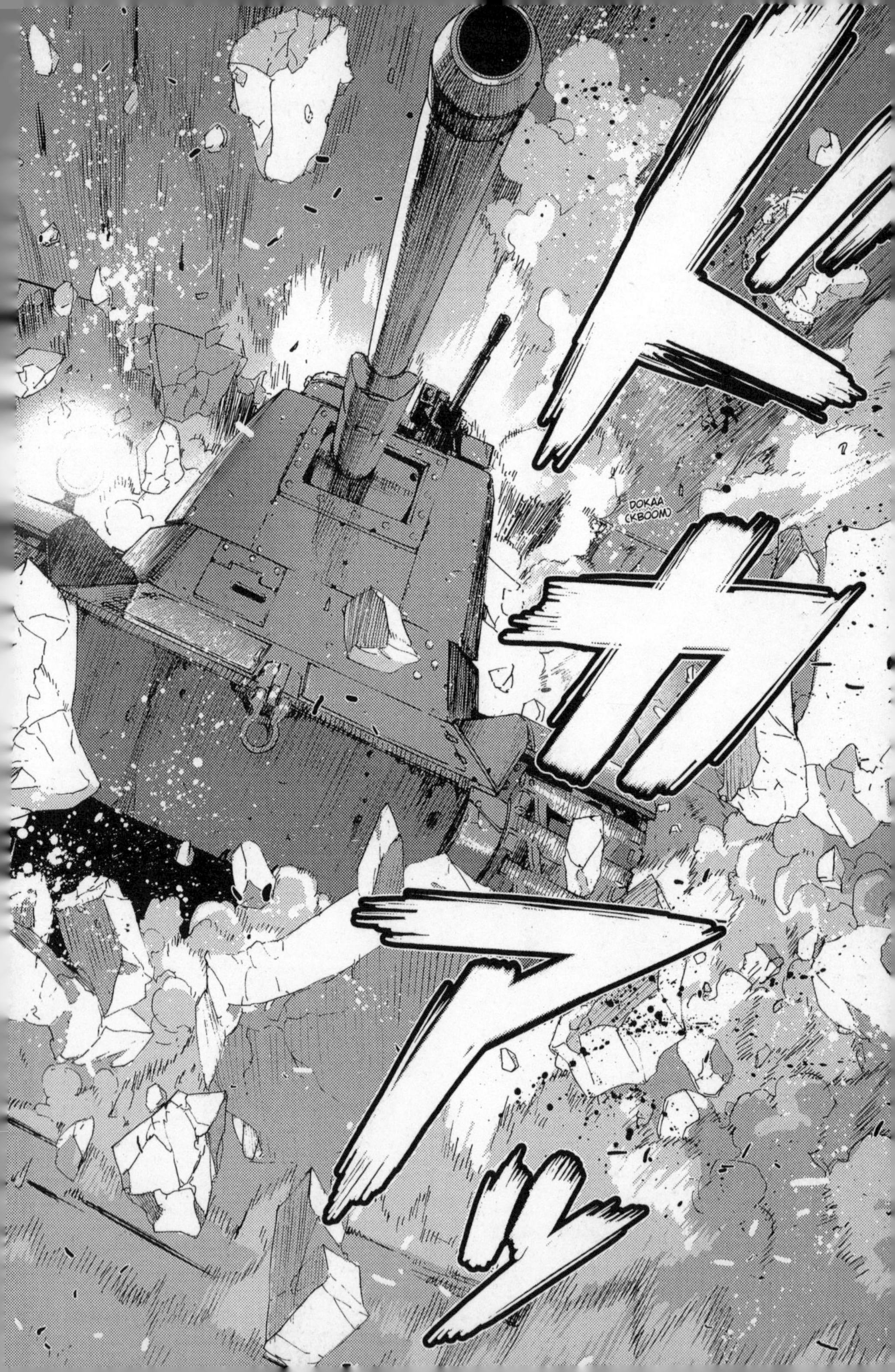
DOKAA
(KBOOM)

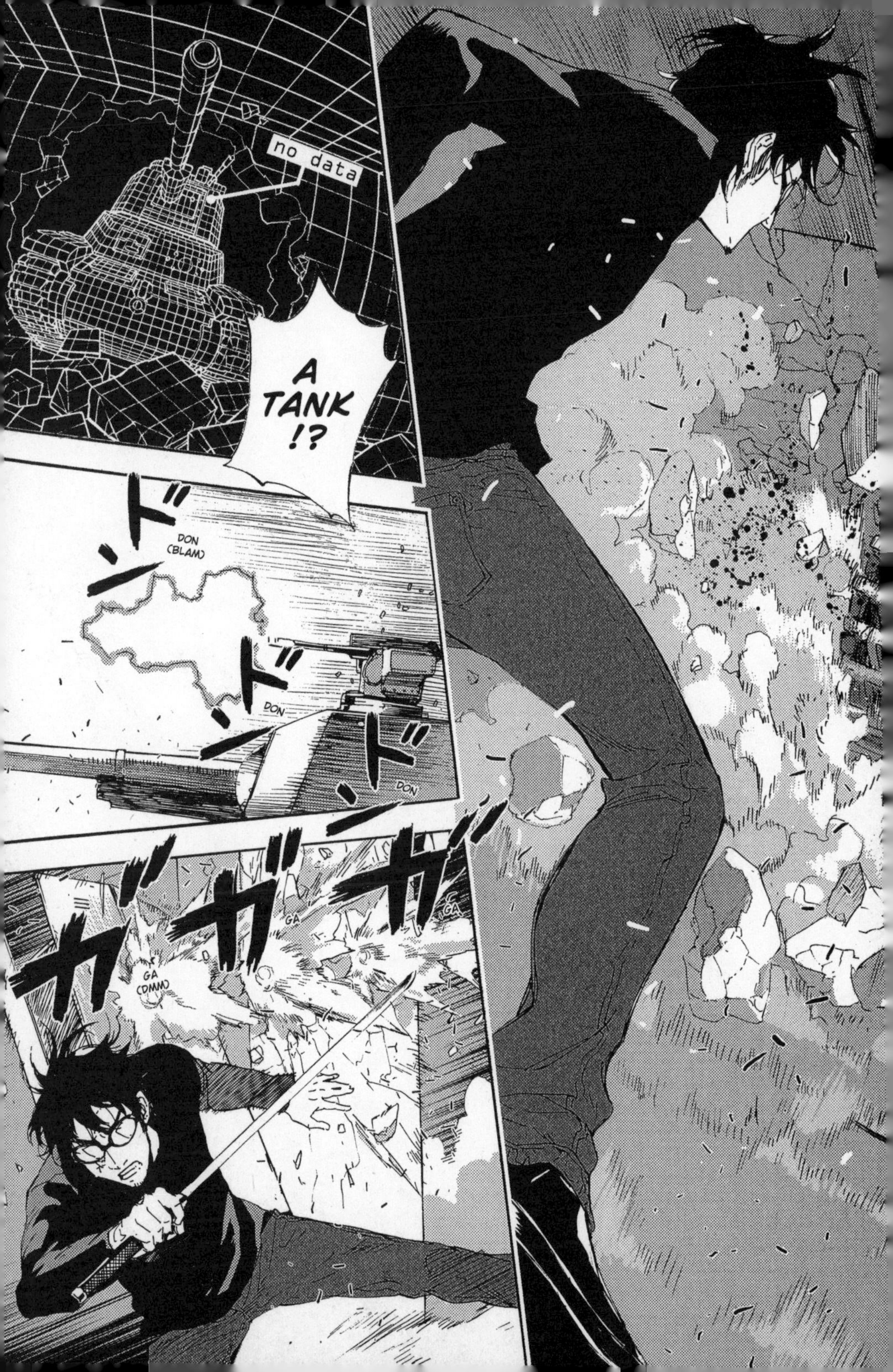
no data
A TANK !?
DON (BLAM)
DON
DON
GA
GA
GA (DMM)

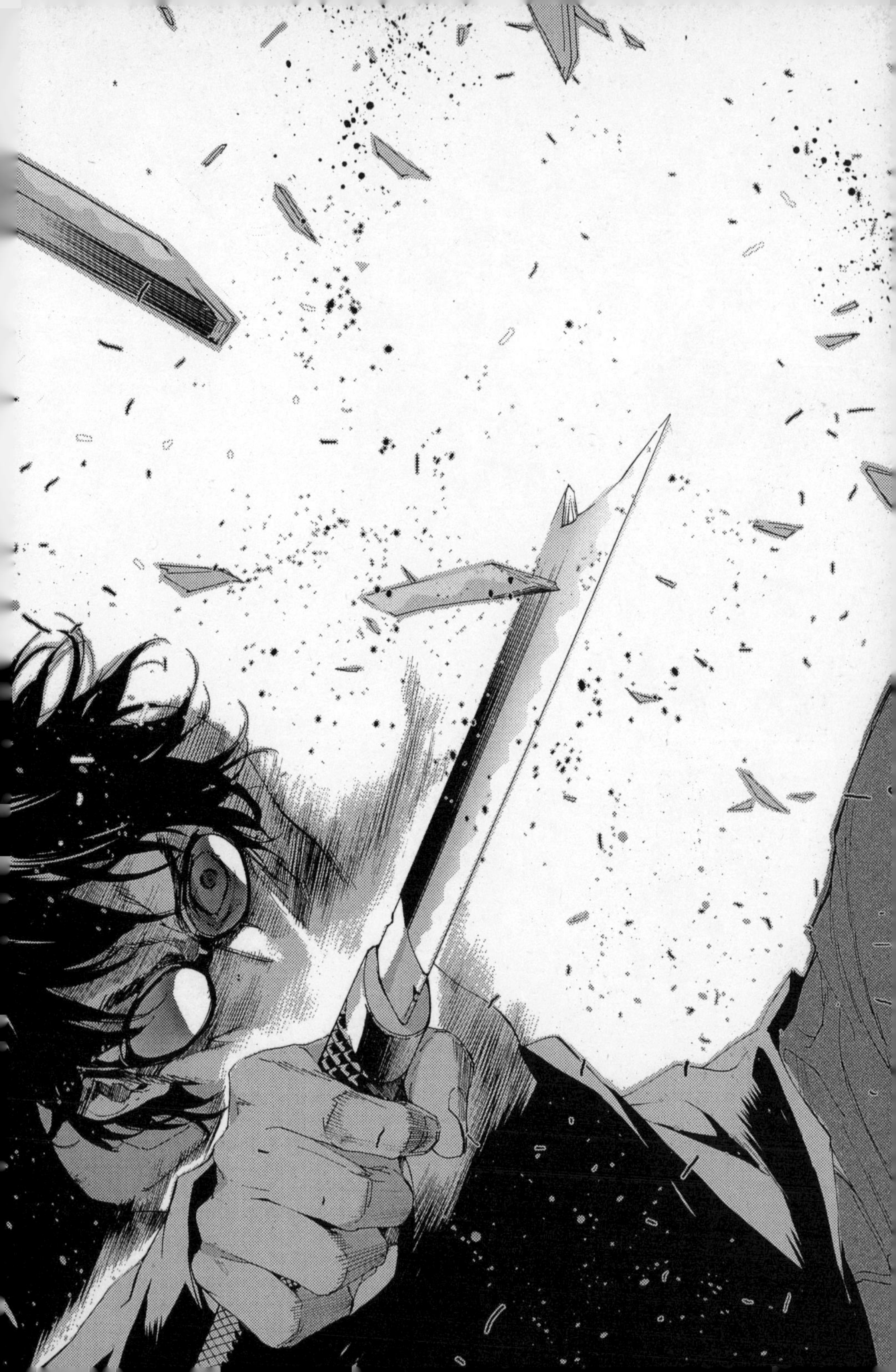

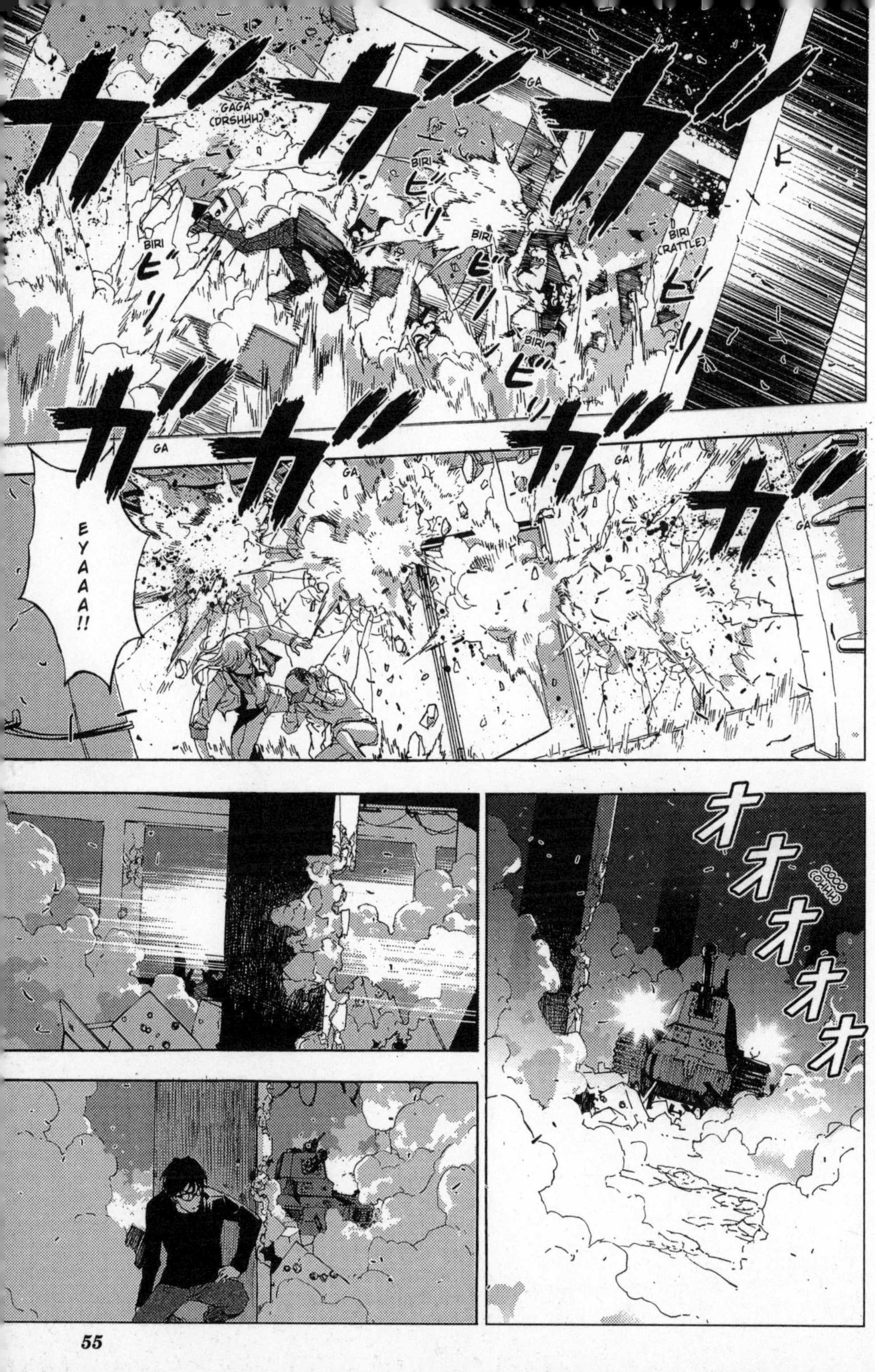

BIRI (RATTLE)
BIRI
BIRI
BIRI
BIRI
GA
GAGA (DRSHHH)
GA
GA
GA
GA
EYAAAA!!
OOOO (OHHH)

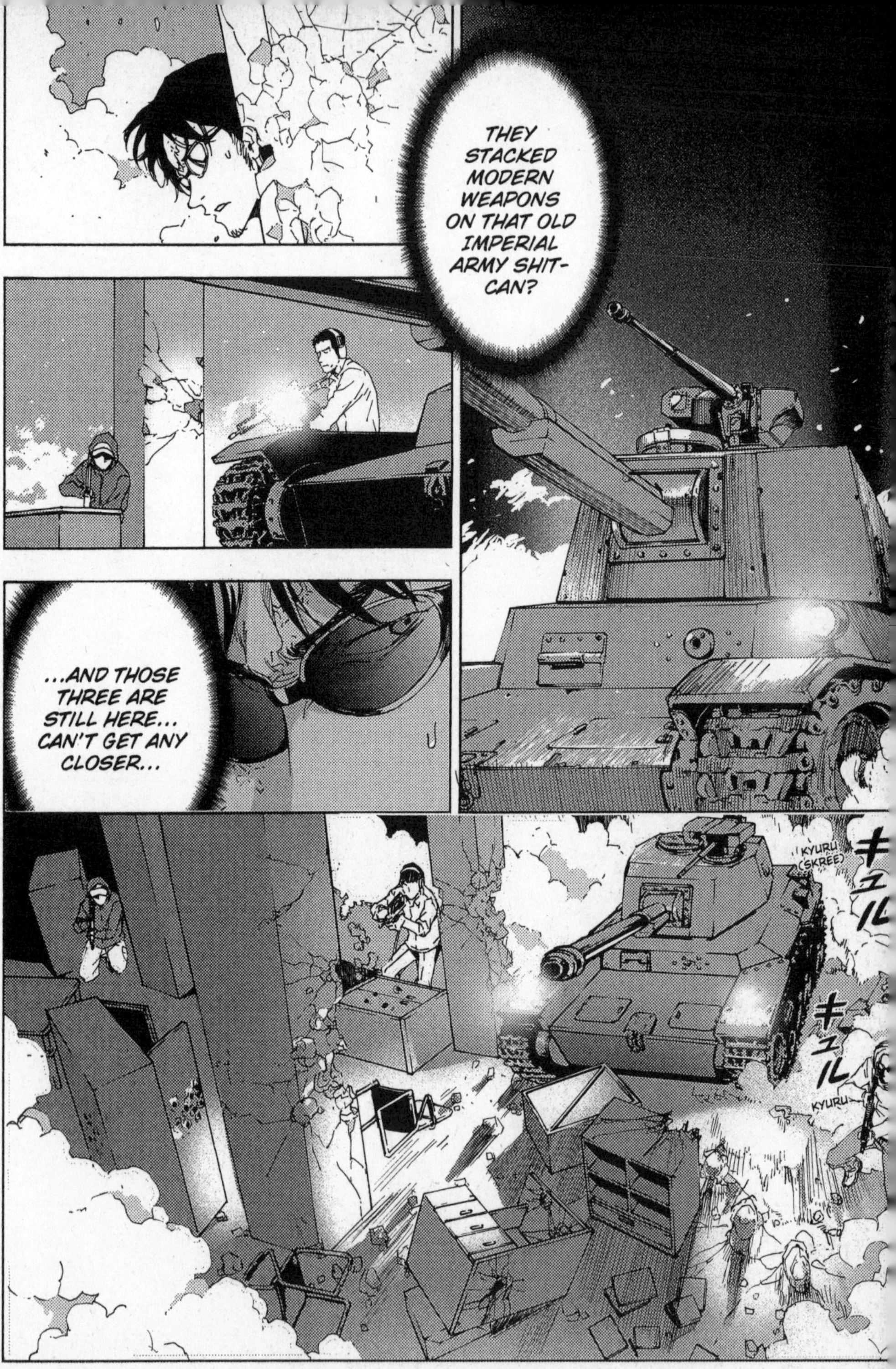
THEY STACKED MODERN WEAPONS ON THAT OLD IMPERIAL ARMY SHIT-CAN?
...AND THOSE THREE ARE STILL HERE... CAN'T GET ANY CLOSER...
キュル
KYURU (SKREE)
キュル
KYURU

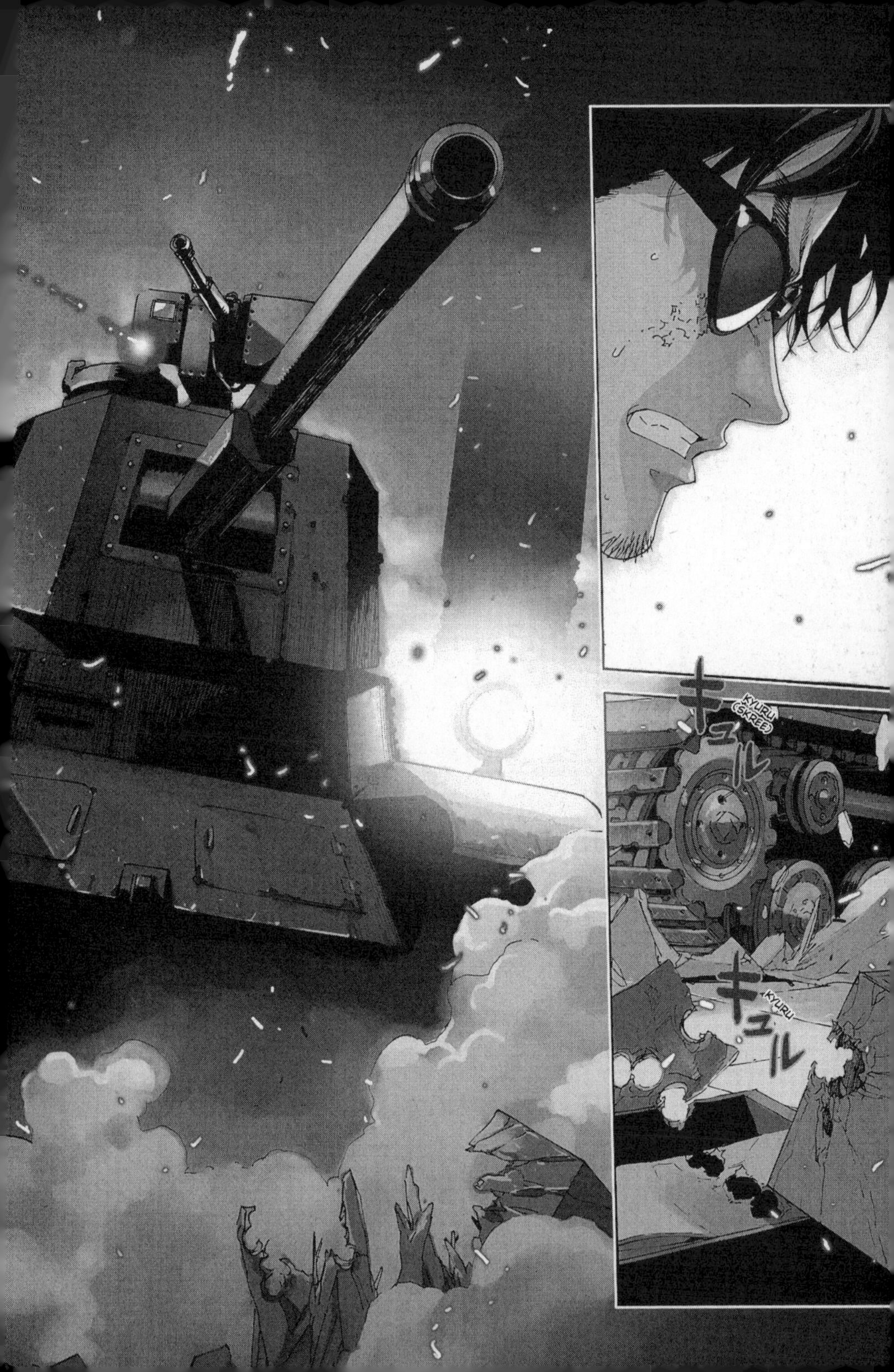
キュル
KYURU (SKREE)
キュル
KYURU

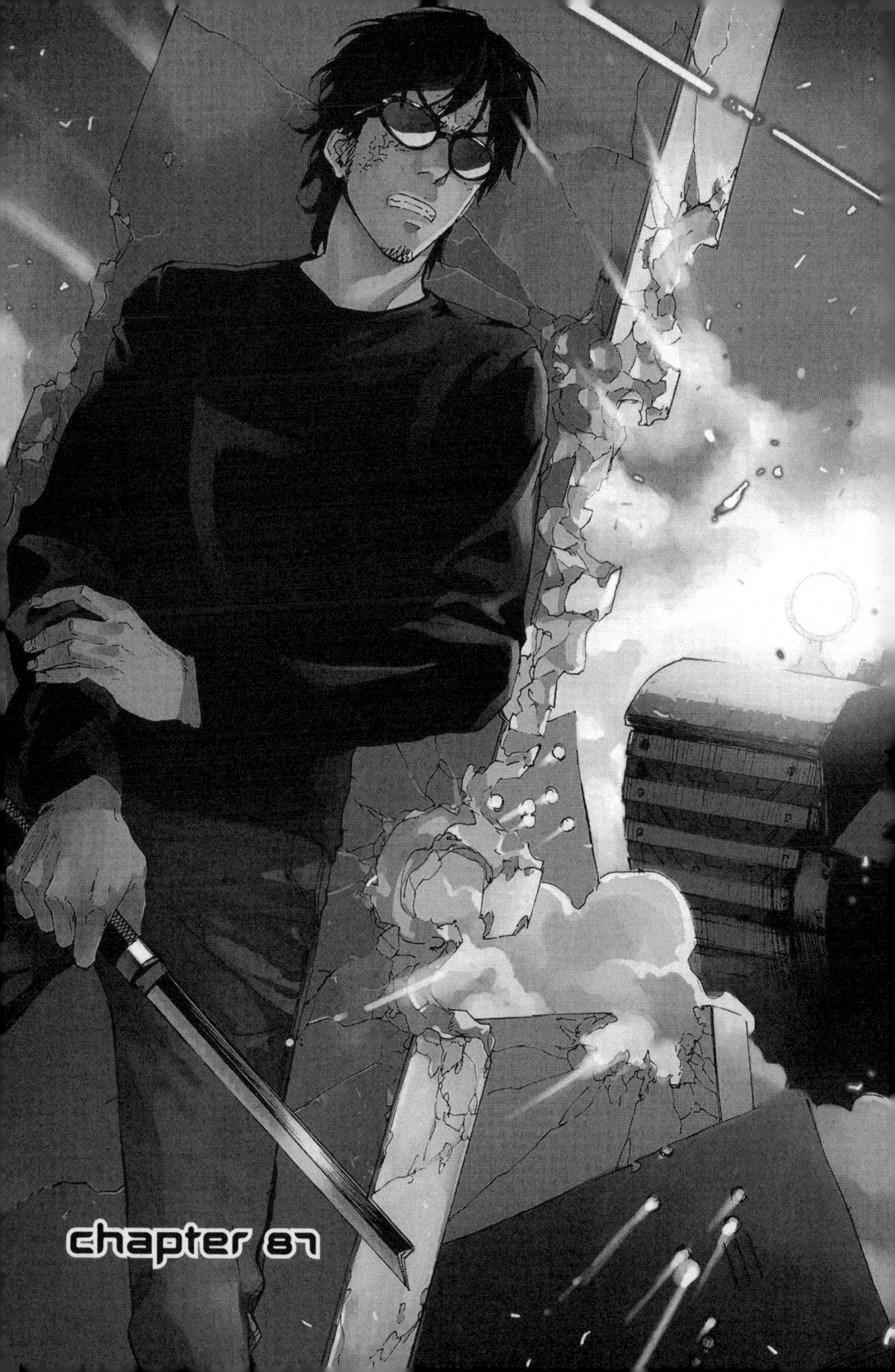
chapter 87

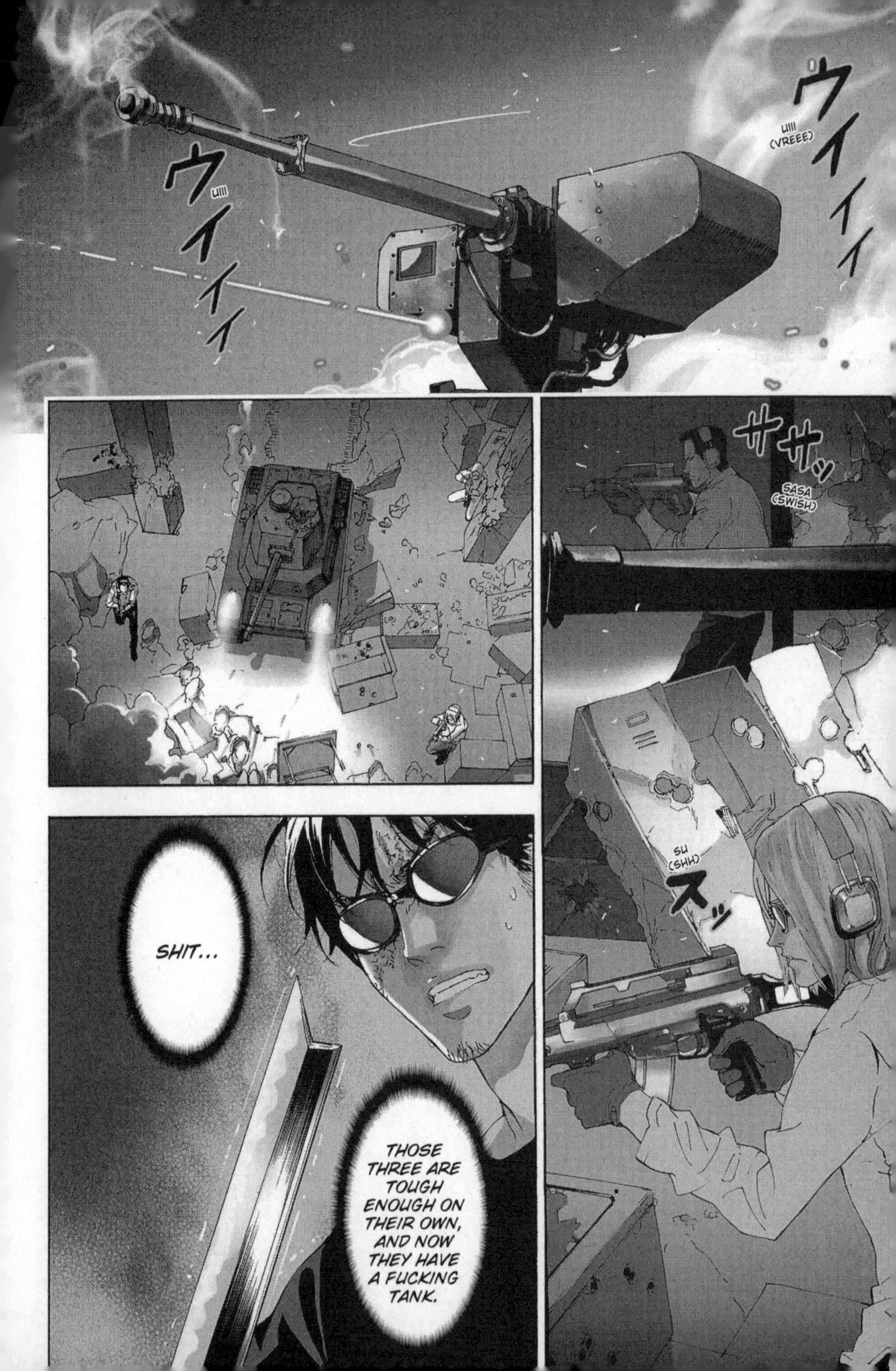
ウィィィ
UIII (VREEE)
ウィィィ
UIII
ササッ
SASA (SWISH)
スッ
SU (SHH)
SHIT...
THOSE THREE ARE TOUGH ENOUGH ON THEIR OWN, AND NOW THEY HAVE A FUCKING TANK.

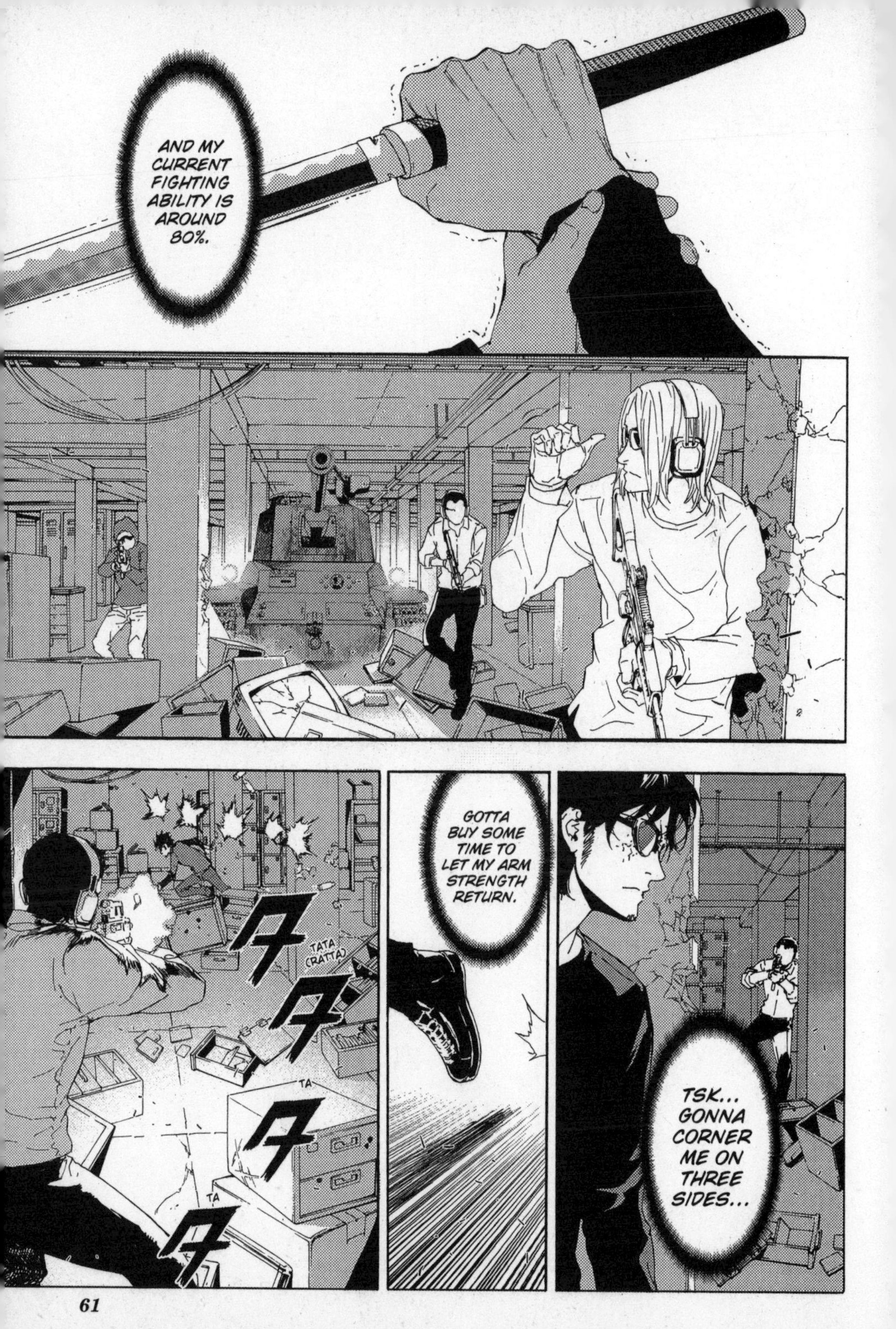
AND MY CURRENT FIGHTING ABILITY IS AROUND 80%.
TSK... GONNA CORNER ME ON THREE SIDES...
GOTTA BUY SOME TIME TO LET MY ARM STRENGTH RETURN.
TATA (RATTA)
TA
TA

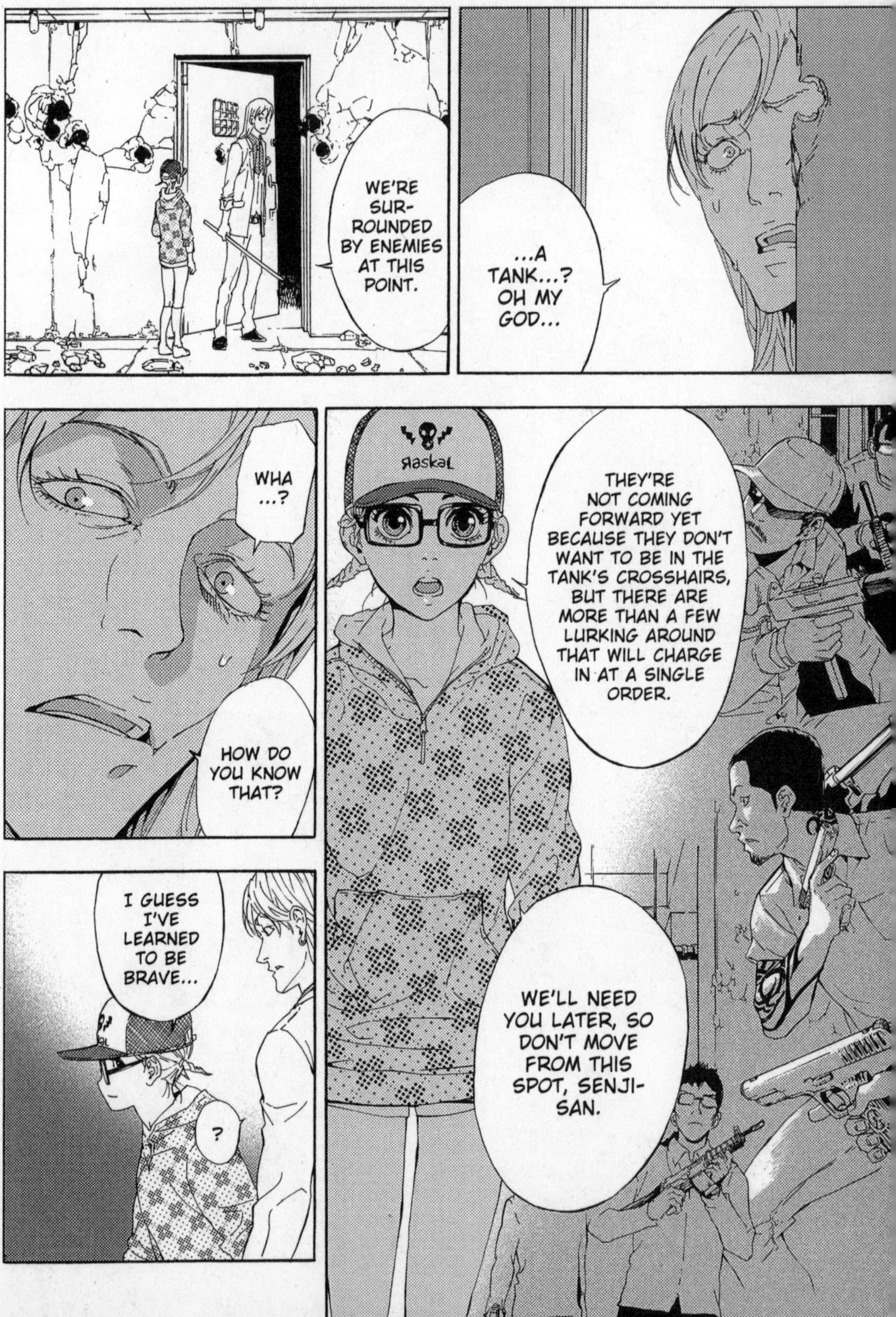
...A TANK...? OH MY GOD...
WE'RE SURROUNDED BY ENEMIES AT THIS POINT.
THEY'RE NOT COMING FORWARD YET BECAUSE THEY DON'T WANT TO BE IN THE TANK'S CROSSHAIRS, BUT THERE ARE MORE THAN A FEW LURKING AROUND THAT WILL CHARGE IN AT A SINGLE ORDER.
WE'LL NEED YOU LATER, SO DON'T MOVE FROM THIS SPOT, SENJI-SAN.
WHA...?
HOW DO YOU KNOW THAT?
I GUESS I'VE LEARNED TO BE BRAVE...
?

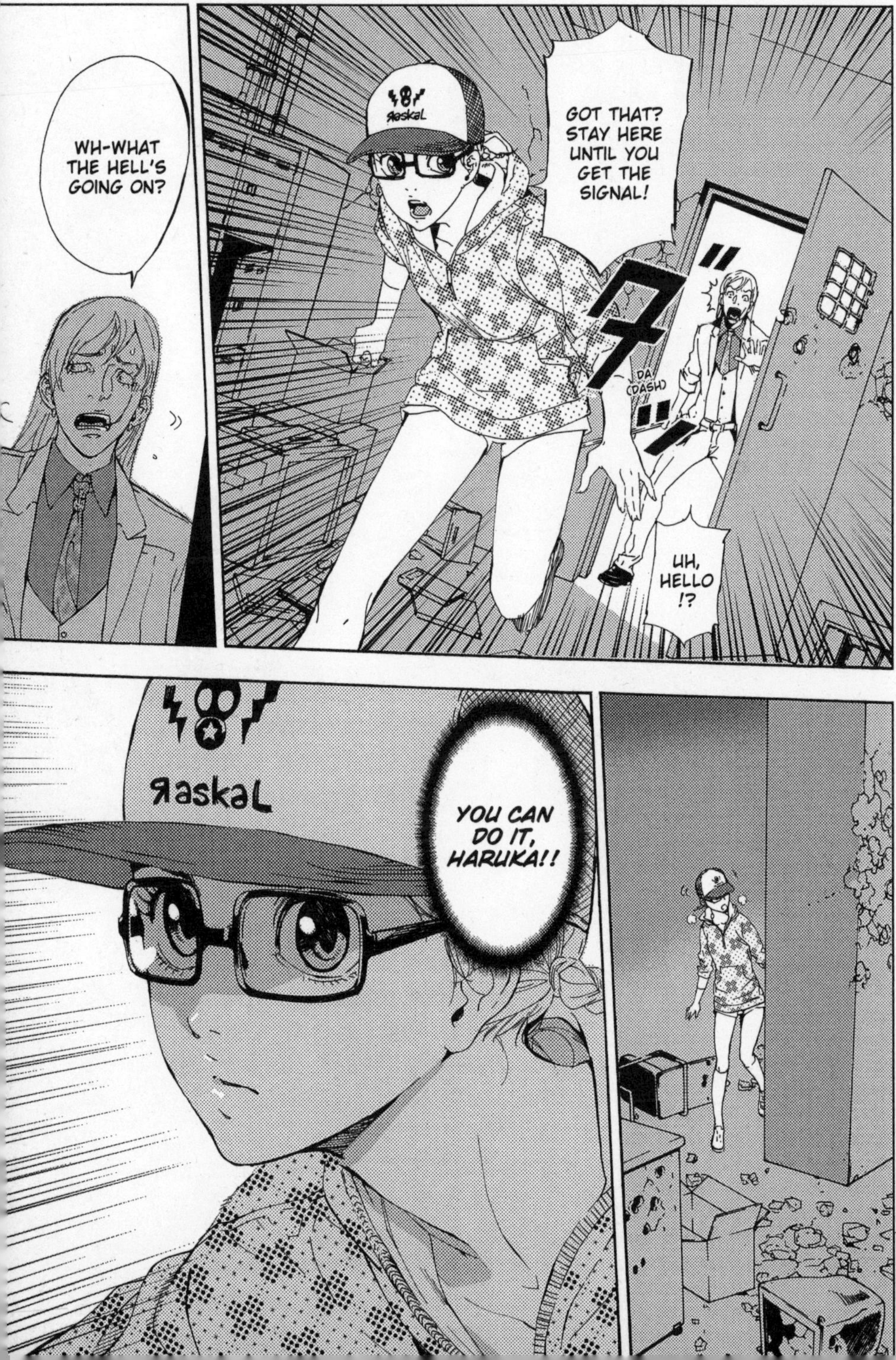
GOT THAT? STAY HERE UNTIL YOU GET THE SIGNAL!
DA (DASH)
UH, HELLO !?
WH-WHAT THE HELL'S GOING ON?
YOU CAN DO IT, HARUKA!!

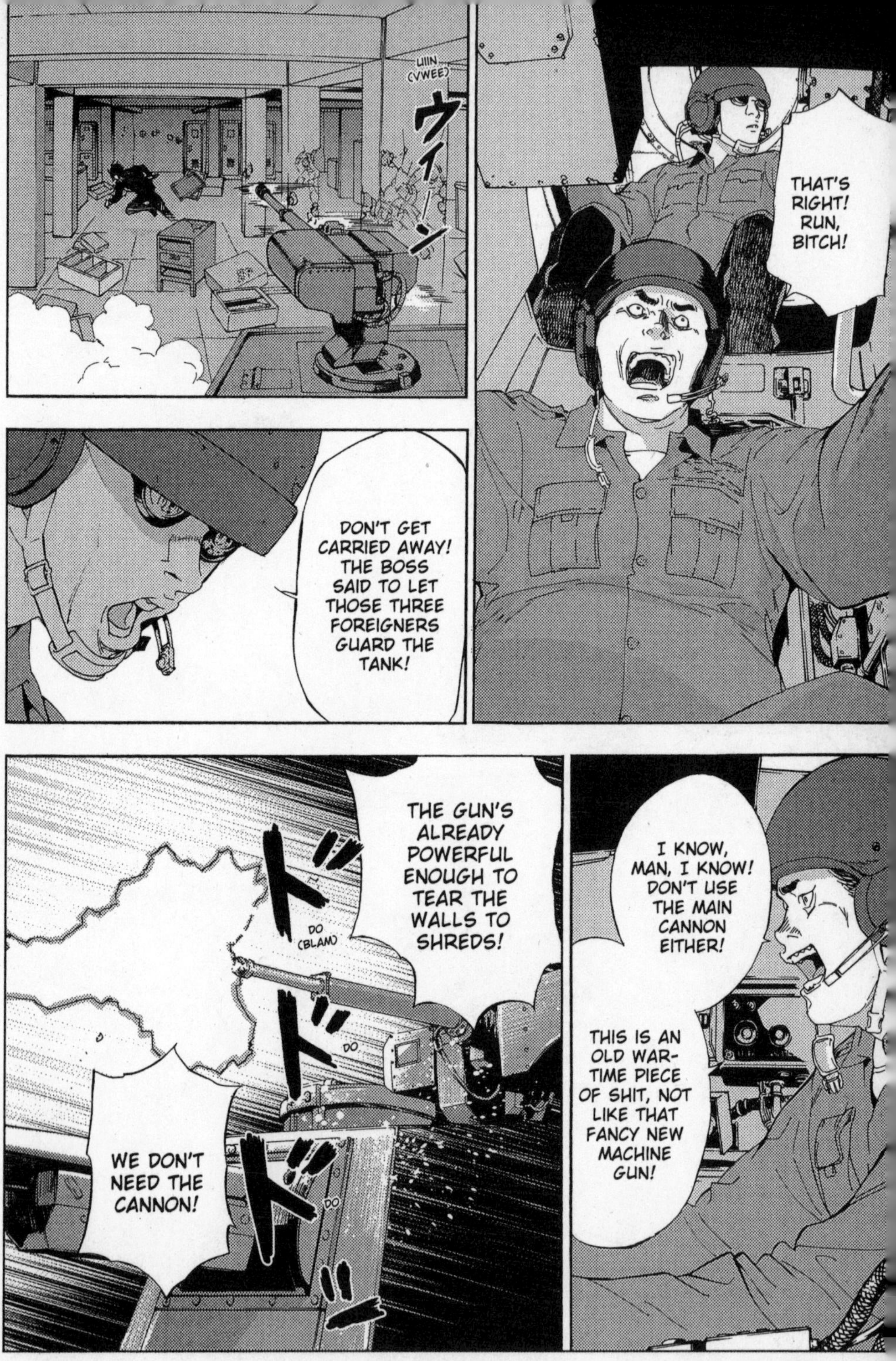
THAT'S RIGHT! RUN, BITCH!
UIIN (VWEE)
DON'T GET CARRIED AWAY! THE BOSS SAID TO LET THOSE THREE FOREIGNERS GUARD THE TANK!
I KNOW, MAN, I KNOW! DON'T USE THE MAIN CANNON EITHER!
THIS IS AN OLD WAR-TIME PIECE OF SHIT, NOT LIKE THAT FANCY NEW MACHINE GUN!
THE GUN'S ALREADY POWERFUL ENOUGH TO TEAR THE WALLS TO SHREDS!
DO (BLAM)
DO
DO
WE DON'T NEED THE CANNON!

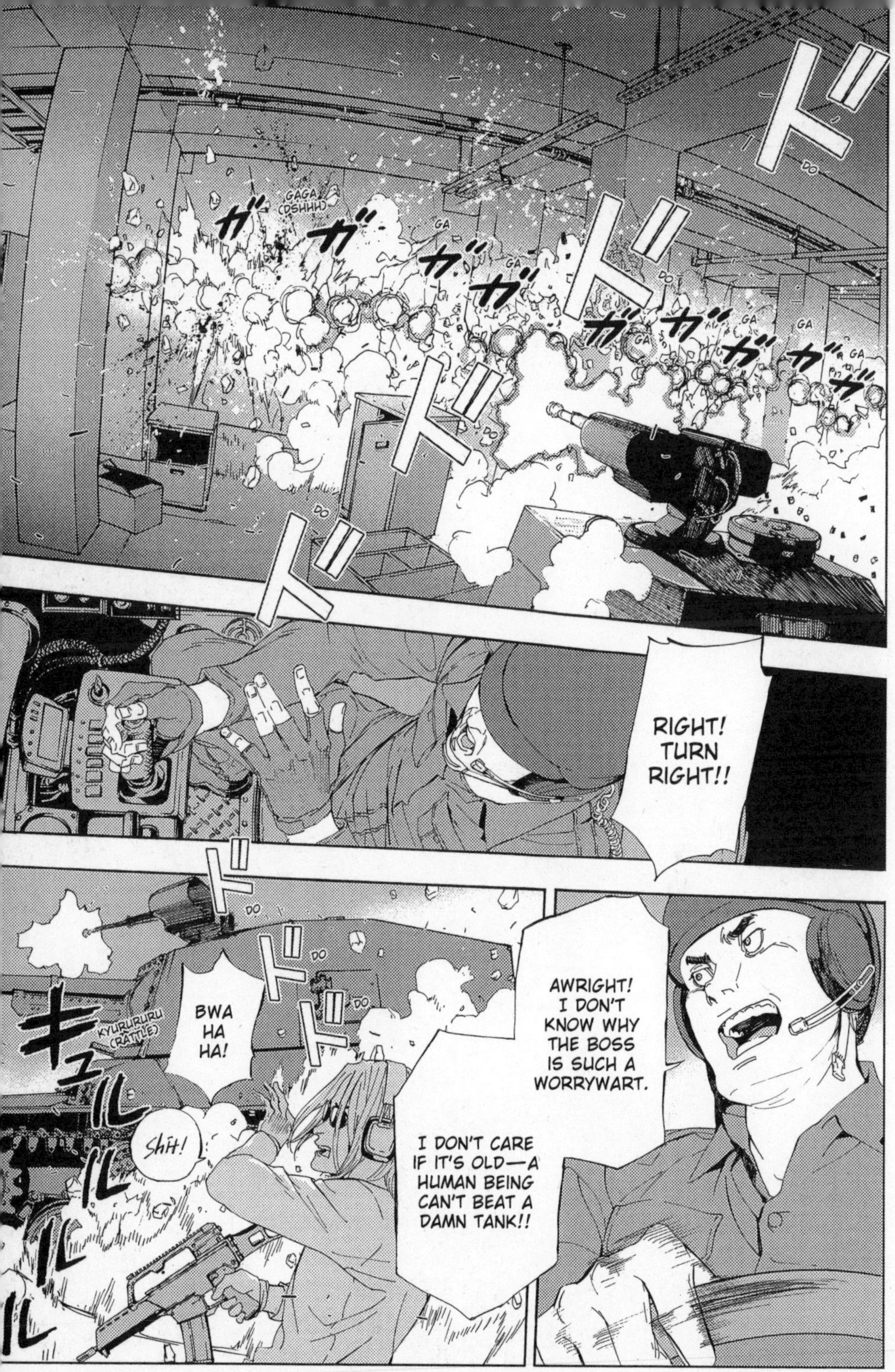
DO
GAGA (DSHHH)
GA
GA
DO
GA
GA
GA
DO
DO
RIGHT! TURN RIGHT!!
AWRIGHT! I DON'T KNOW WHY THE BOSS IS SUCH A WORRYWART.
I DON'T CARE IF IT'S OLD—A HUMAN BEING CAN'T BEAT A DAMN TANK!!
DO
DO
DO
BWA HA HA!
KYURURURU (RATTLE)
Shit!

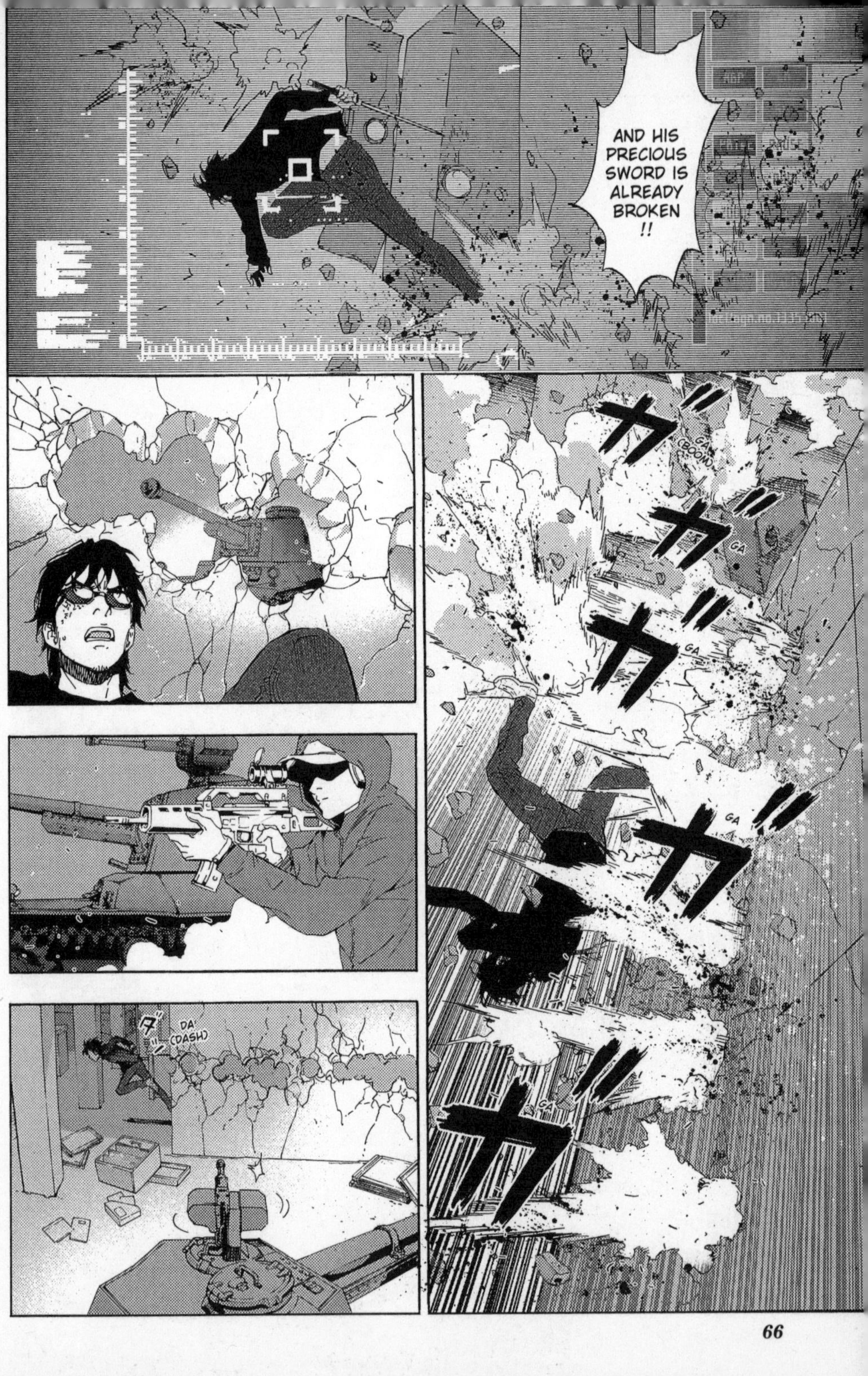
AND HIS PRECIOUS SWORD IS ALREADY BROKEN !!
ガ
GA (BOOM)
ガ
GA
ガ
GA
ガ
GA
ガ
GA
ダッ
DA (DASH)

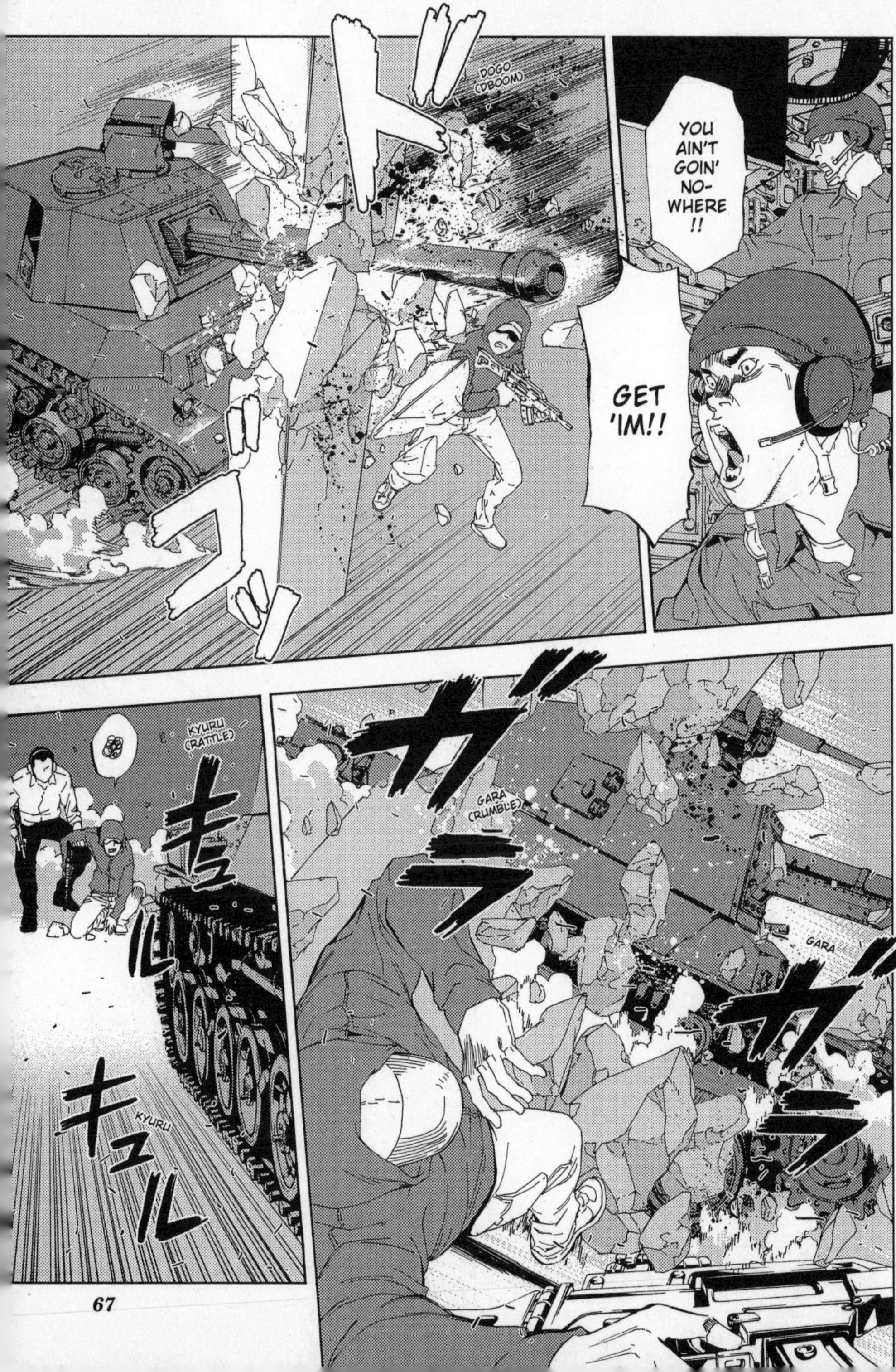
YOU AIN'T GOIN' NO-WHERE!!
GET 'IM!!
DOGO (DBOOM)
GARA (RUMBLE)
GARA
KYURU (RATTLE)
KYURU

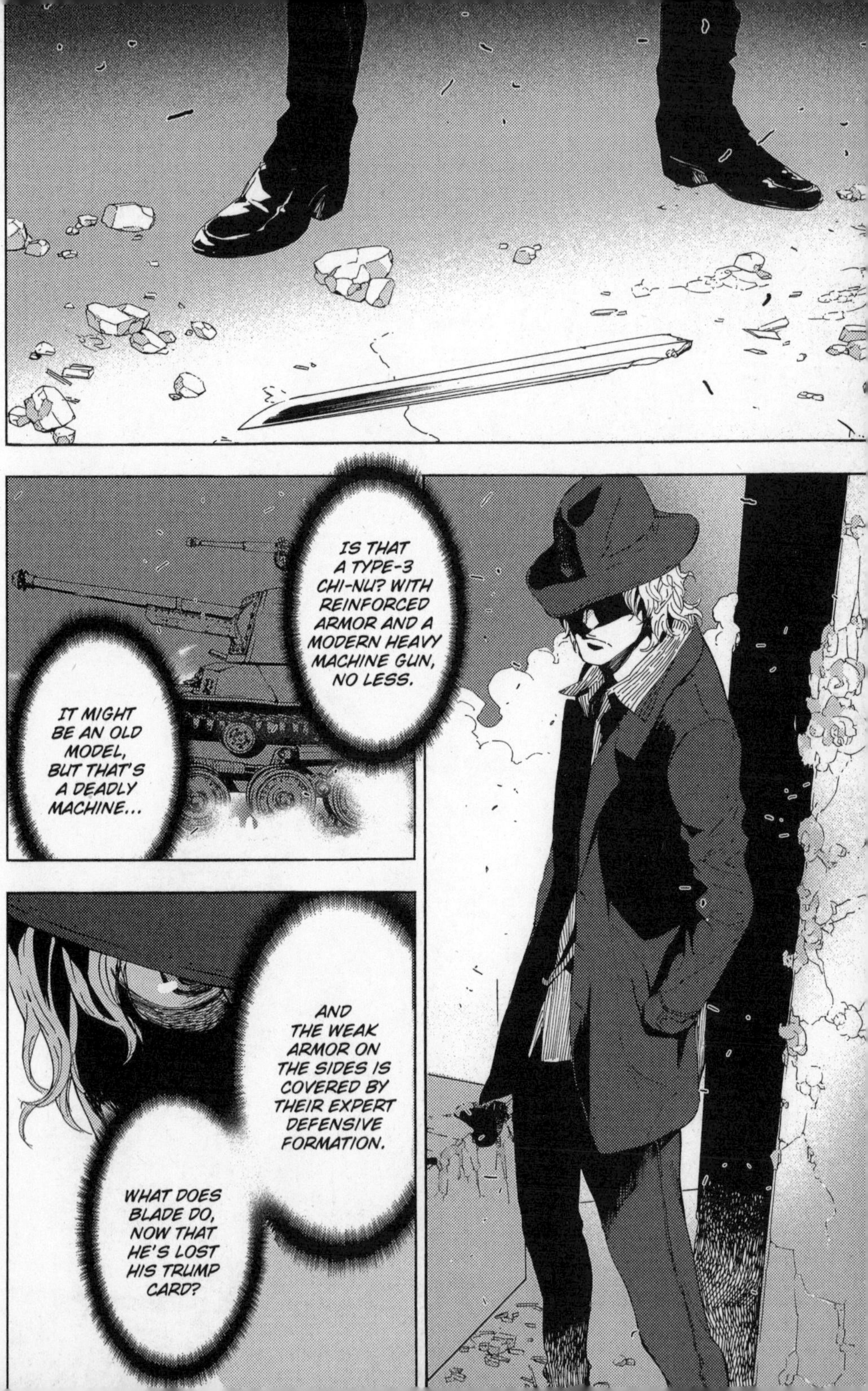
IS THAT A TYPE-3 CHI-NU? WITH REINFORCED ARMOR AND A MODERN HEAVY MACHINE GUN, NO LESS.
IT MIGHT BE AN OLD MODEL, BUT THAT'S A DEADLY MACHINE...
AND THE WEAK ARMOR ON THE SIDES IS COVERED BY THEIR EXPERT DEFENSIVE FORMATION.
WHAT DOES BLADE DO, NOW THAT HE'S LOST HIS TRUMP CARD?

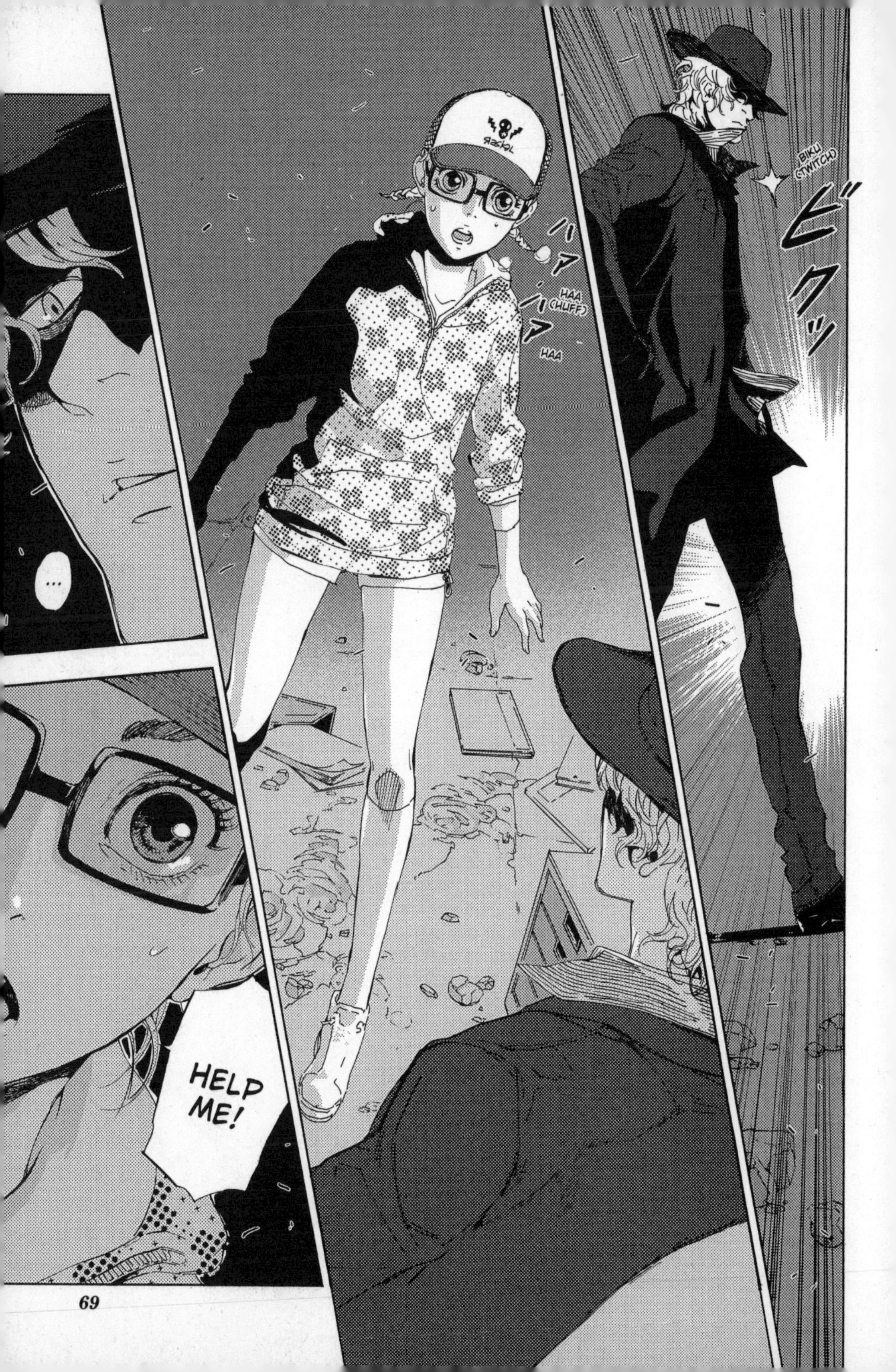
BIKU (TWITCH)
ビクッ
ハァ
HAA (HUFF)
ハァ
HAA
...
HELP ME!

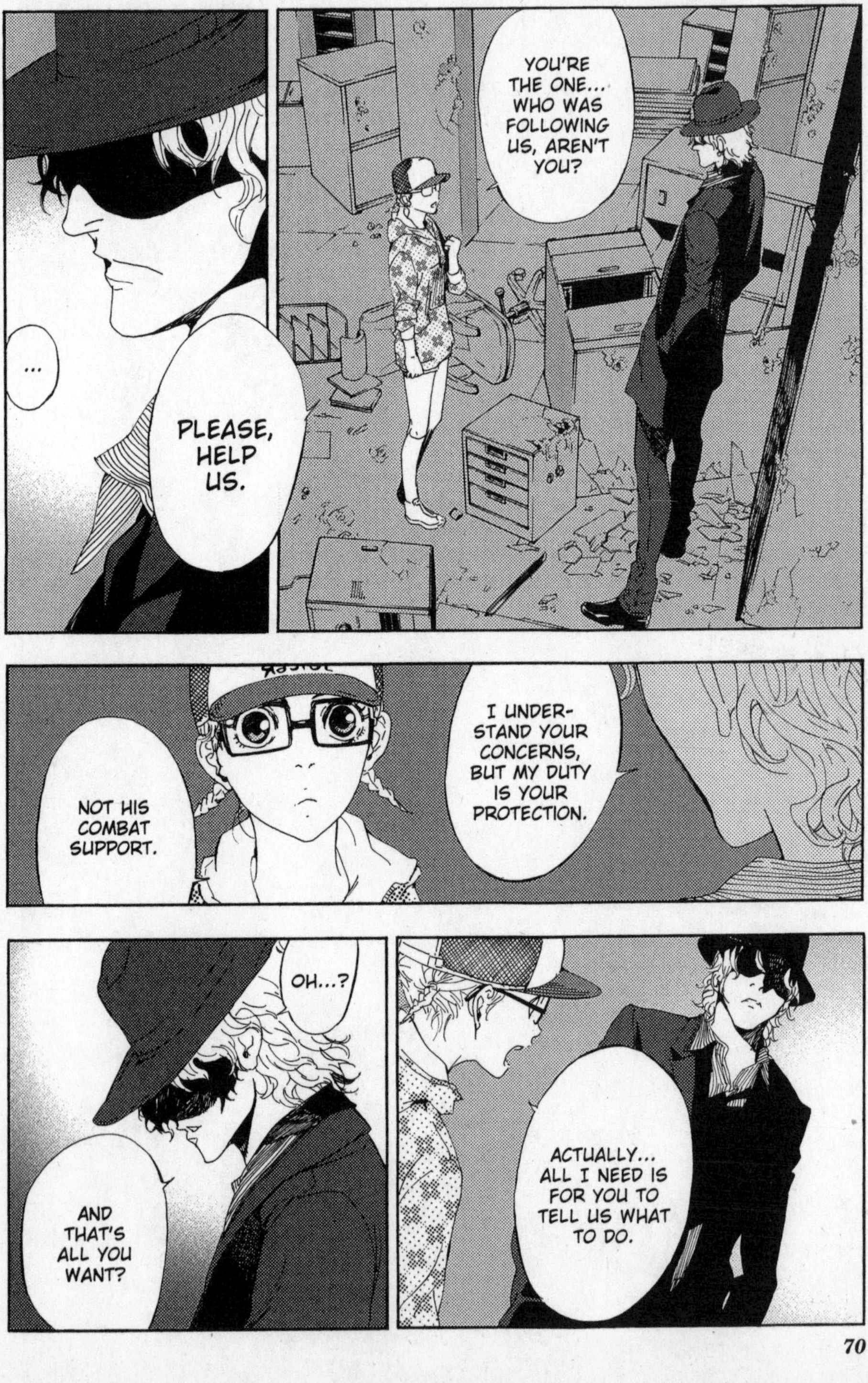
YOU'RE THE ONE... WHO WAS FOLLOWING US, AREN'T YOU?
PLEASE, HELP US.
...
I UNDER-STAND YOUR CONCERNS, BUT MY DUTY IS YOUR PROTECTION.
NOT HIS COMBAT SUPPORT.
ACTUALLY... ALL I NEED IS FOR YOU TO TELL US WHAT TO DO.
OH...?
AND THAT'S ALL YOU WANT?

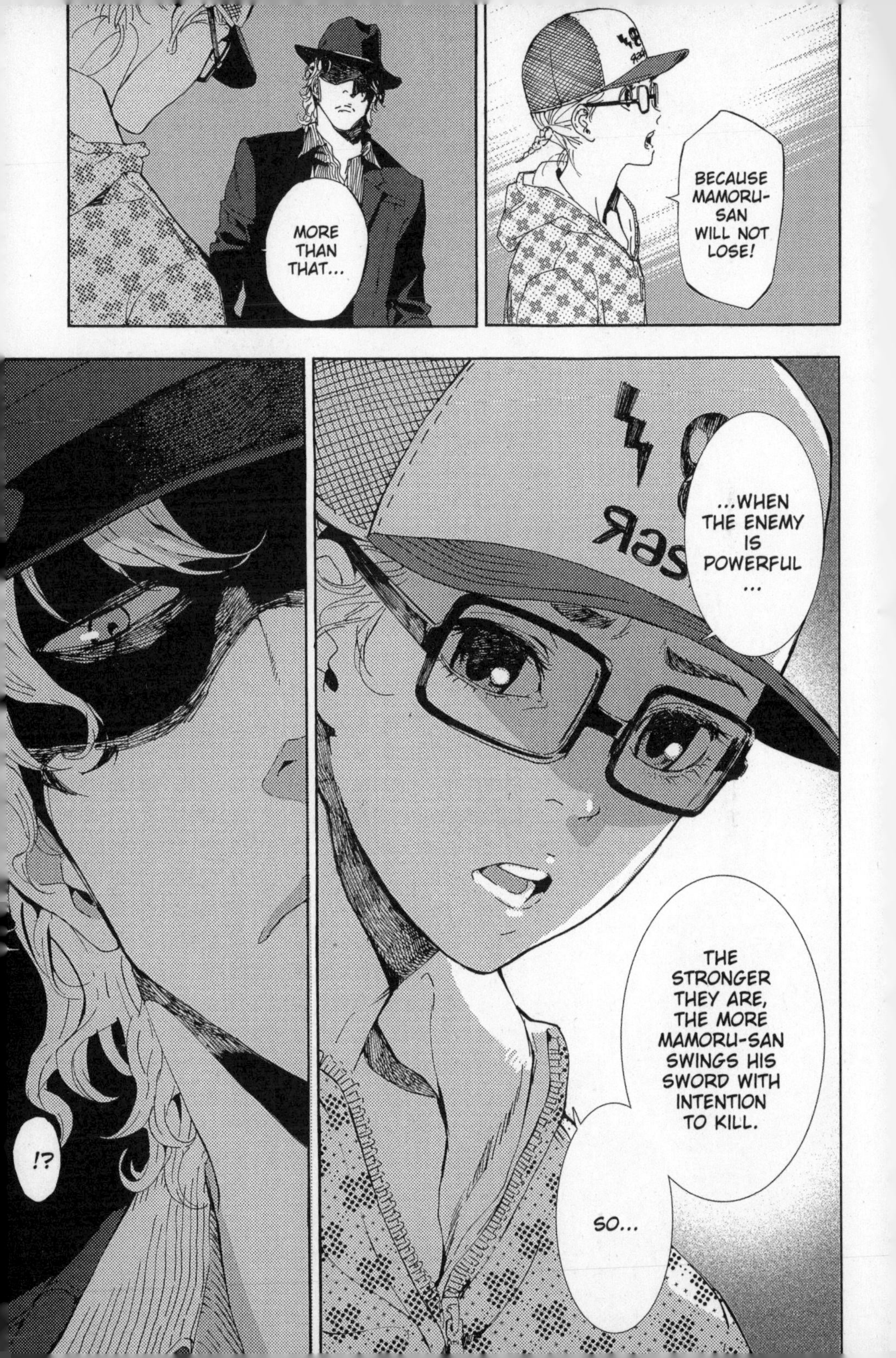
BECAUSE MAMORU-SAN WILL NOT LOSE!
MORE THAN THAT...
...WHEN THE ENEMY IS POWERFUL ...
THE STRONGER THEY ARE, THE MORE MAMORU-SAN SWINGS HIS SWORD WITH INTENTION TO KILL.
SO...
!?

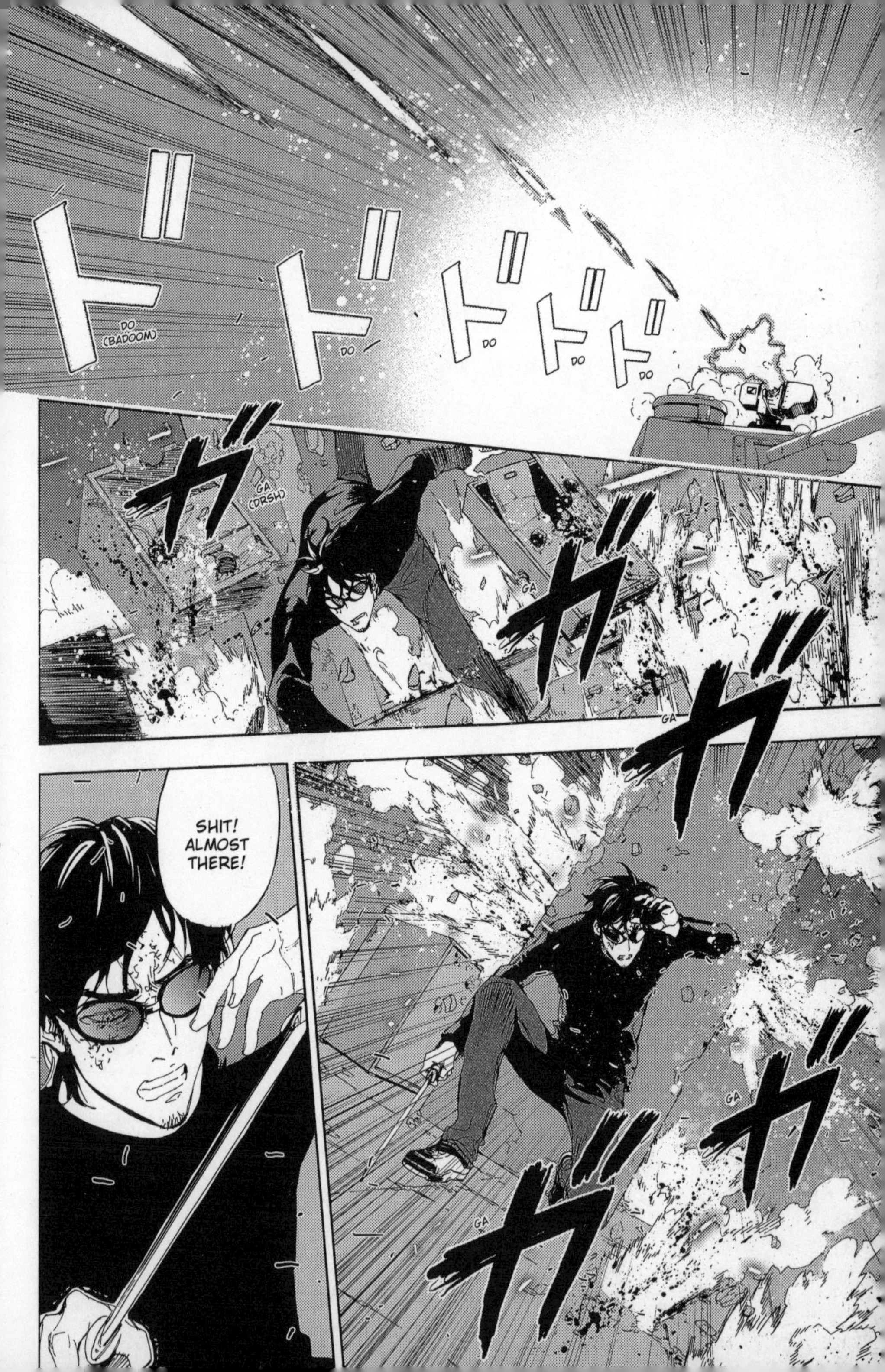
DO
(BADOOM)
DO
DO
DO
DO
GA
(DRSH)
GA
GA
GA
GA
GA
SHIT! ALMOST THERE!

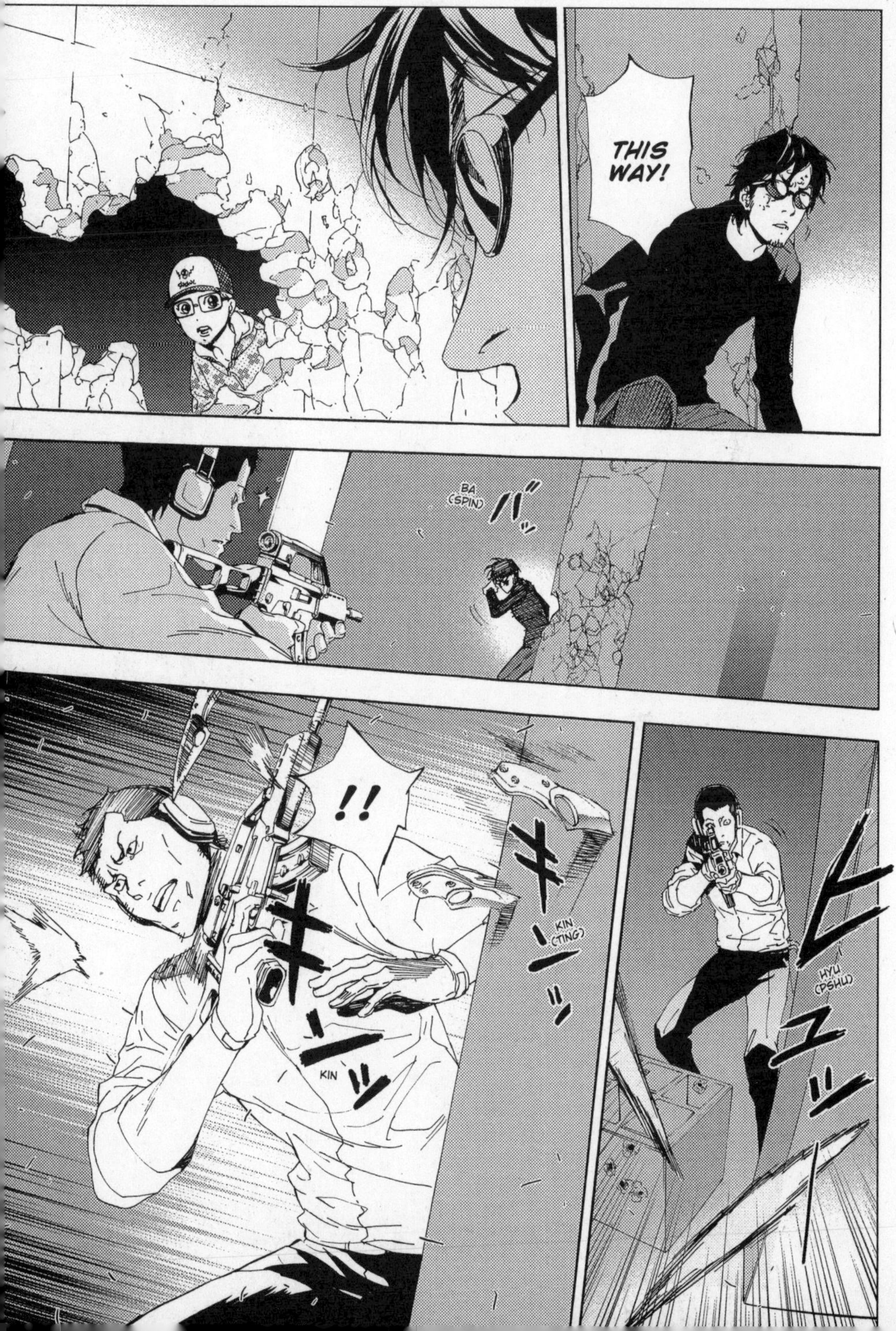
THIS WAY!
BA (SPIN)
HYU (PSHU)
!!
KIN (TING)
KIN

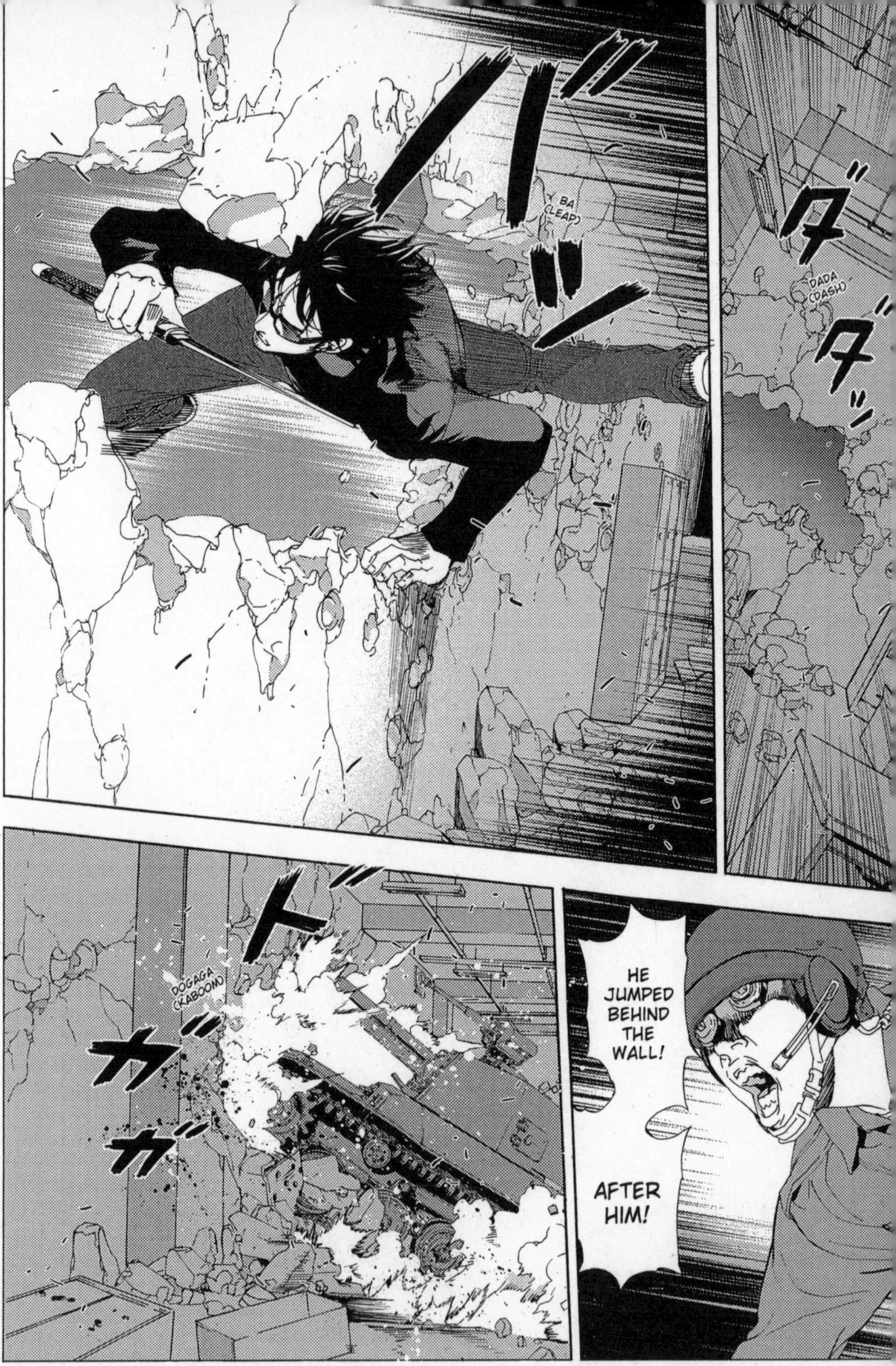
DADA (DASH)
BA (LEAP)
HE JUMPED BEHIND THE WALL!
AFTER HIM!
DOGAGA (KABOOM)

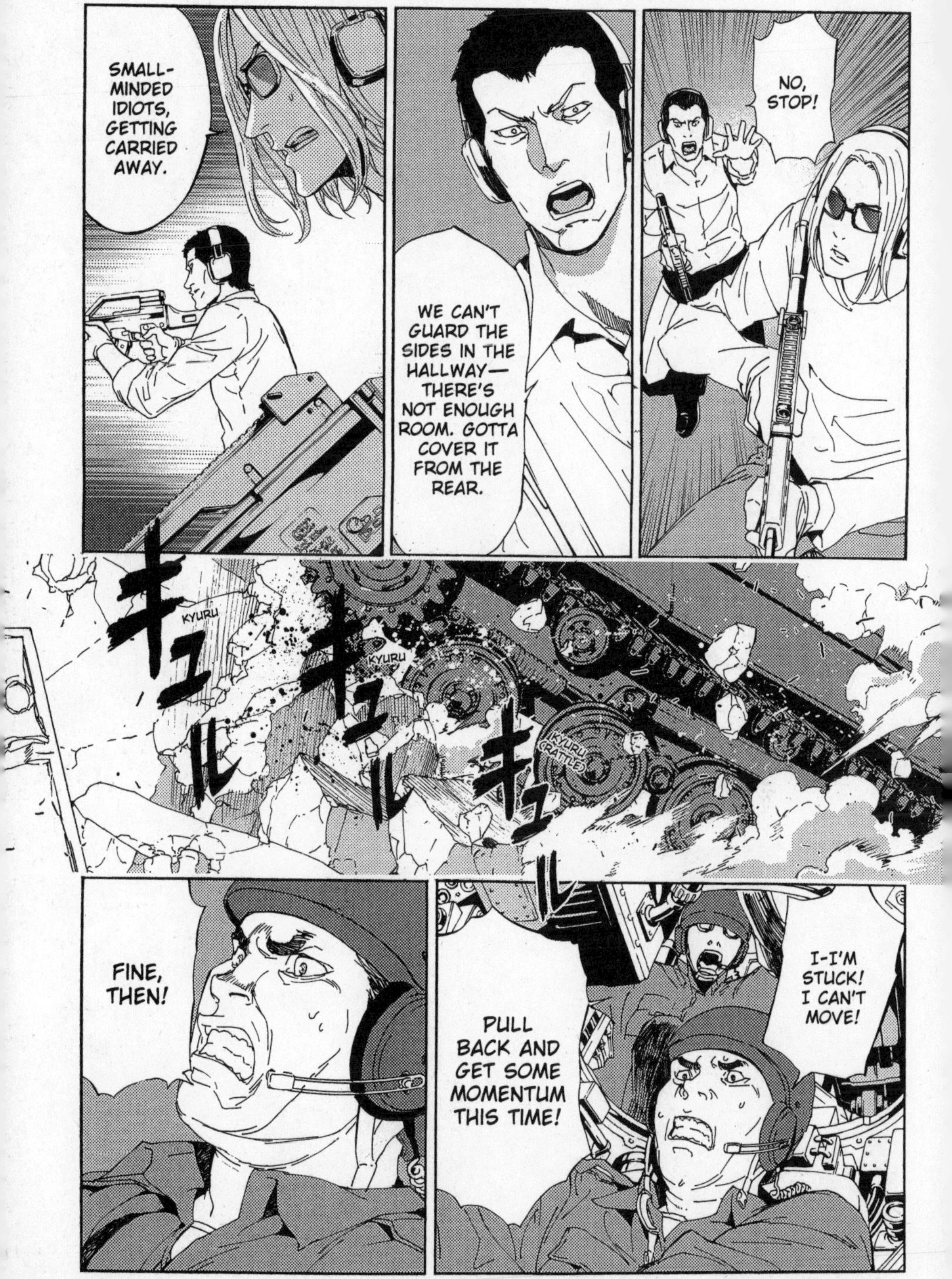
NO, STOP!
WE CAN'T GUARD THE SIDES IN THE HALLWAY— THERE'S NOT ENOUGH ROOM. GOTTA COVER IT FROM THE REAR.
SMALL-MINDED IDIOTS, GETTING CARRIED AWAY.
KYURU
KYURU
KYURU (RATTLE)
I-I'M STUCK! I CAN'T MOVE!
PULL BACK AND GET SOME MOMENTUM THIS TIME!
FINE, THEN!

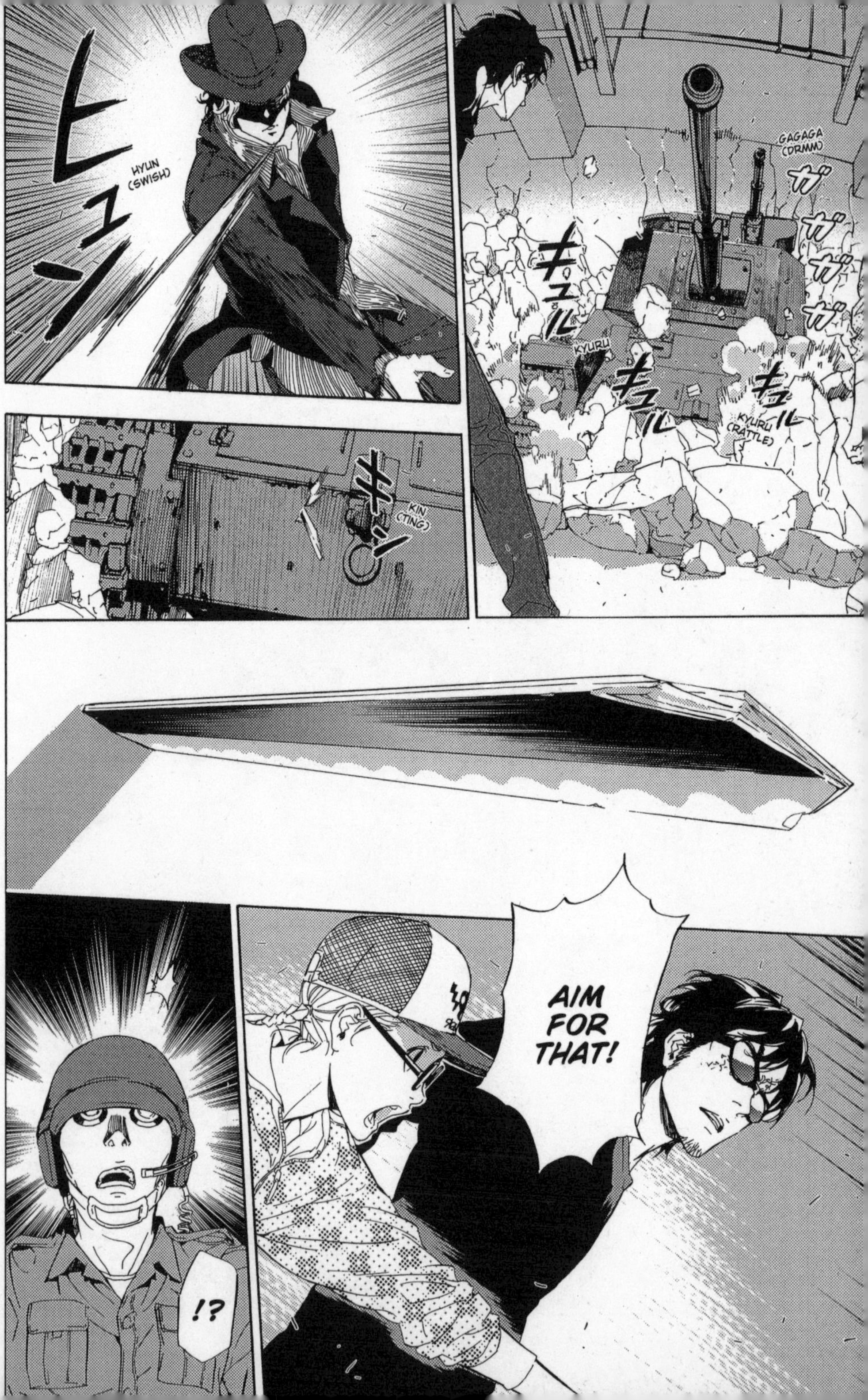
GAGAGA (DRMM)
ガガガガ
キュル
KYURU
キュル
キュル
KYURU (RATTLE)
ヒュン
HYUN (SWISH)
キン
KIN (TING)
AIM FOR THAT!
!?

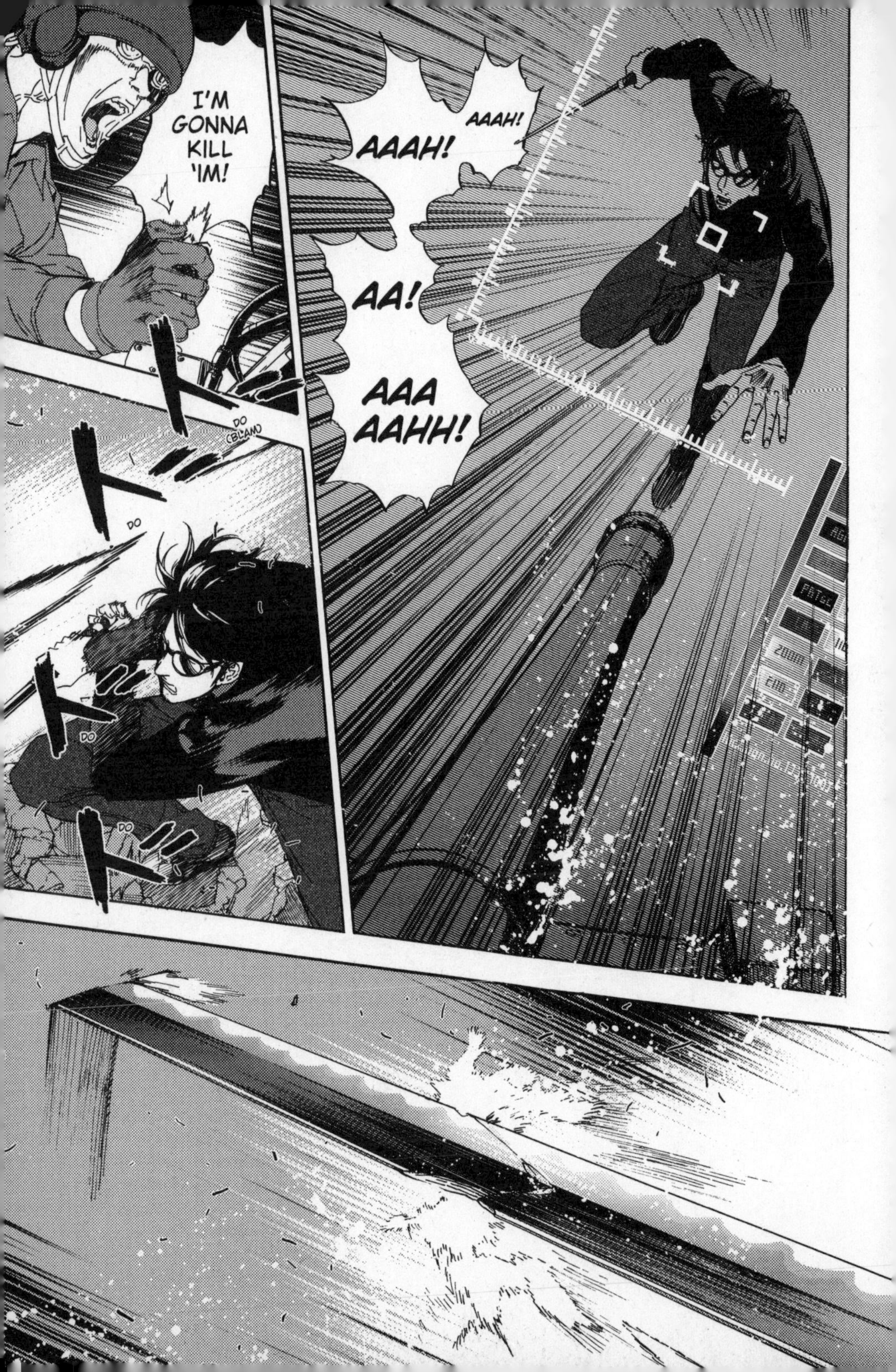
AAAH!
AAAH!
AA!
AAA AAHH!
I'M GONNA KILL 'IM!
DO (BLAM)
DO
DO
DO

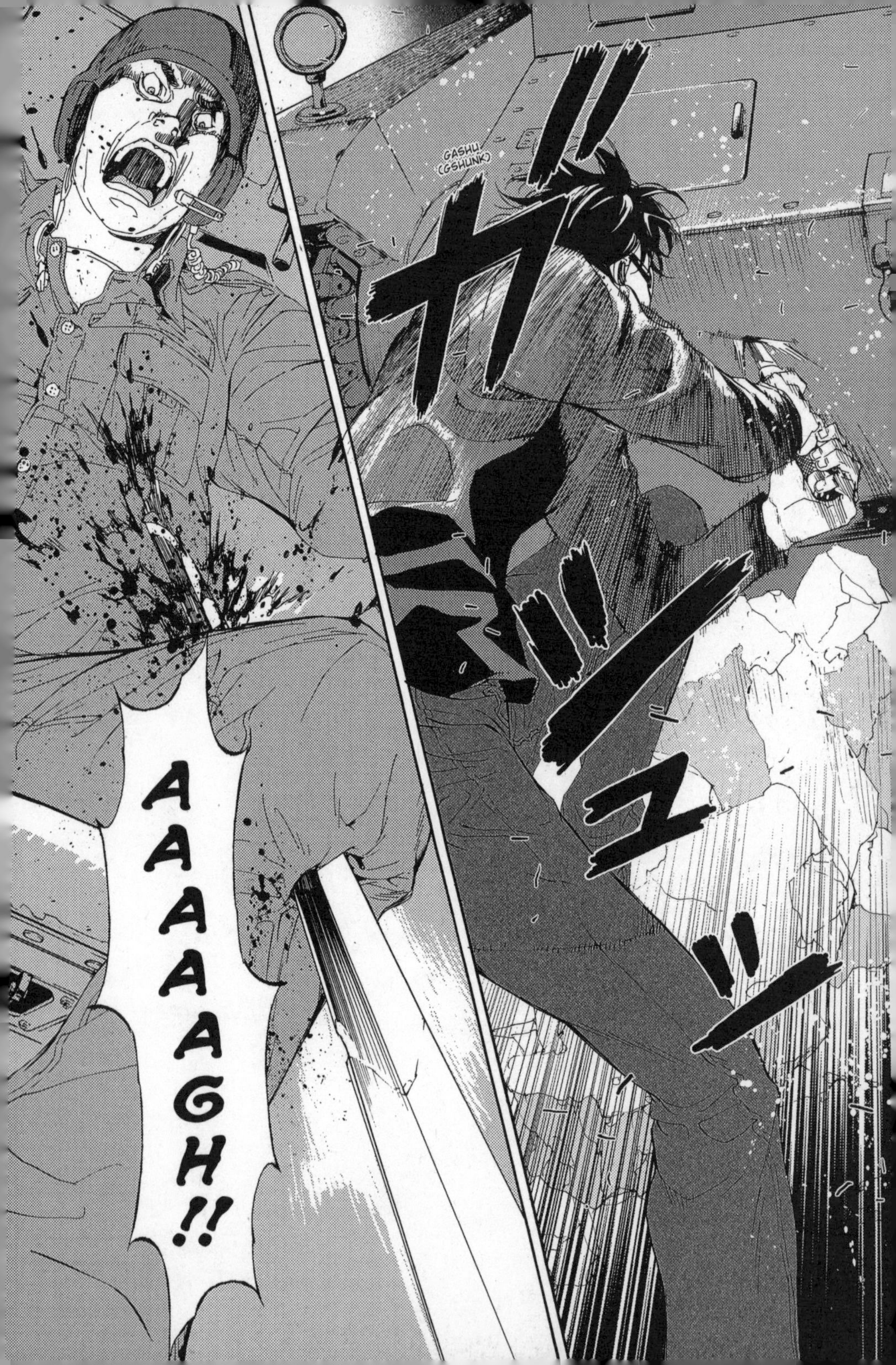
GASHU
(GSHUNK)
AAAAAGH!!

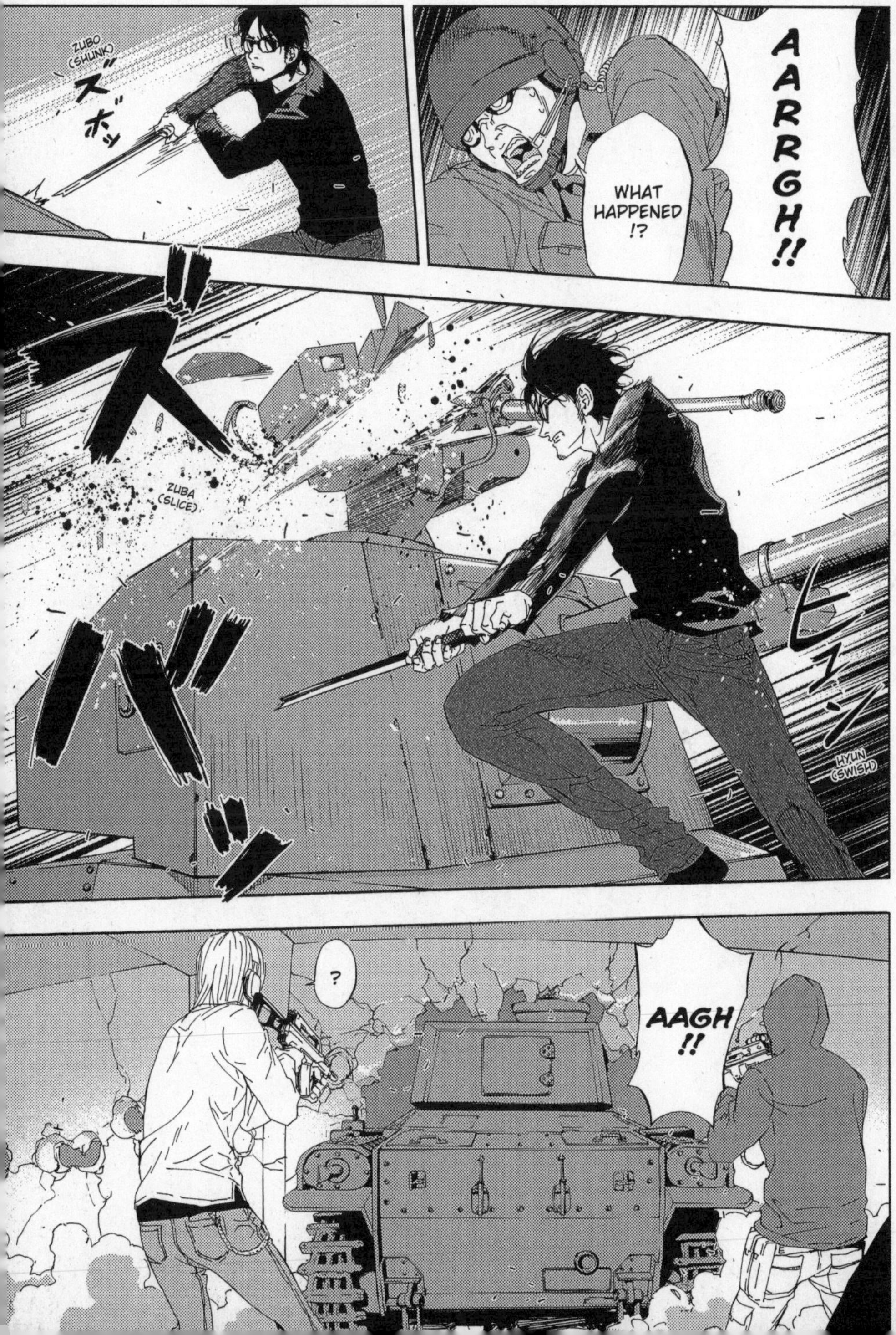
AARRGH!!
WHAT HAPPENED!?
ZUBO (SHUNK)
ズボッ
ヒュン
HYUN (SWISH)
ズバッ
ZUBA (SLICE)
AAGH!!
?

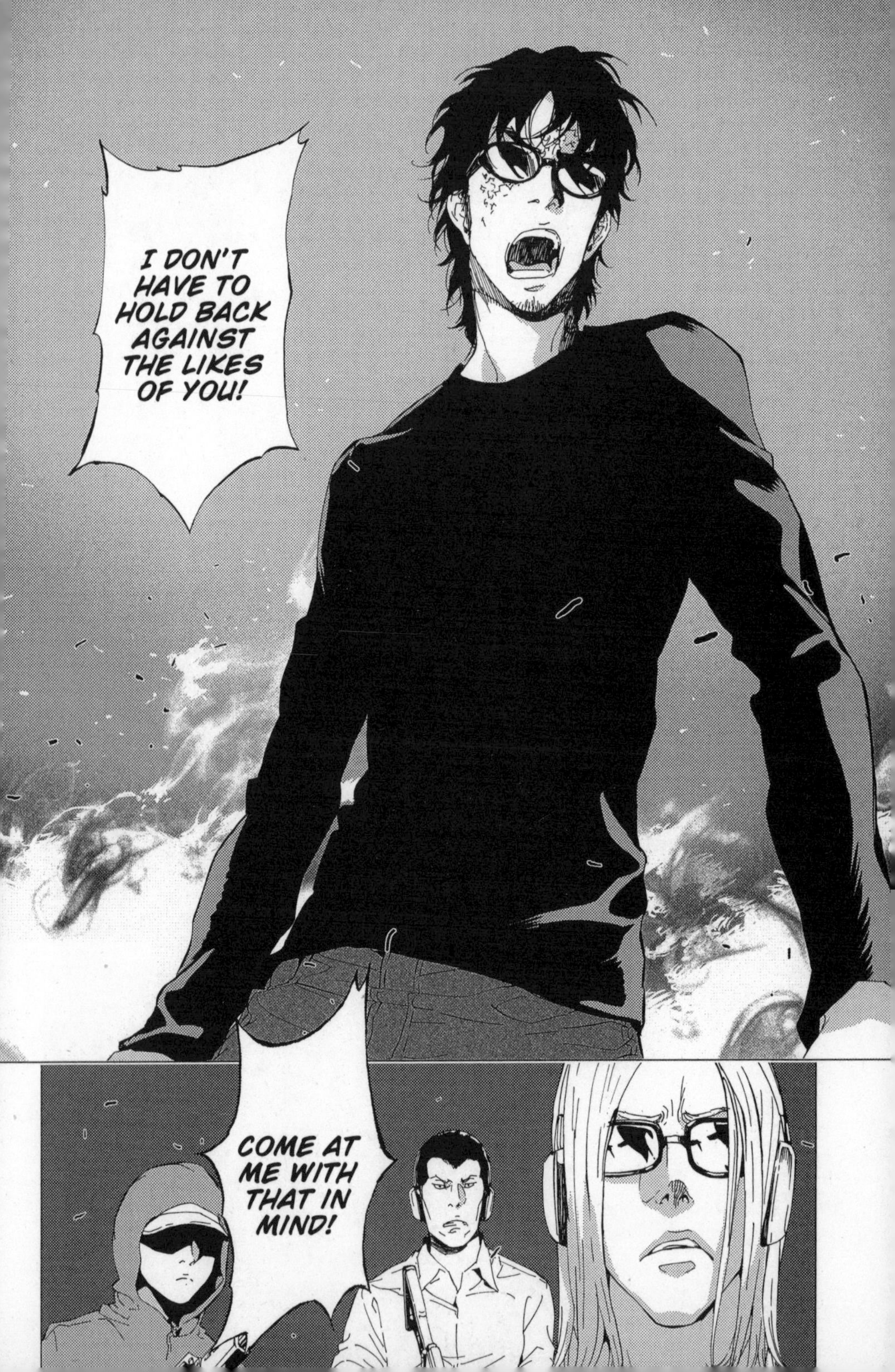
I DON'T HAVE TO HOLD BACK AGAINST THE LIKES OF YOU!
COME AT ME WITH THAT IN MIND!

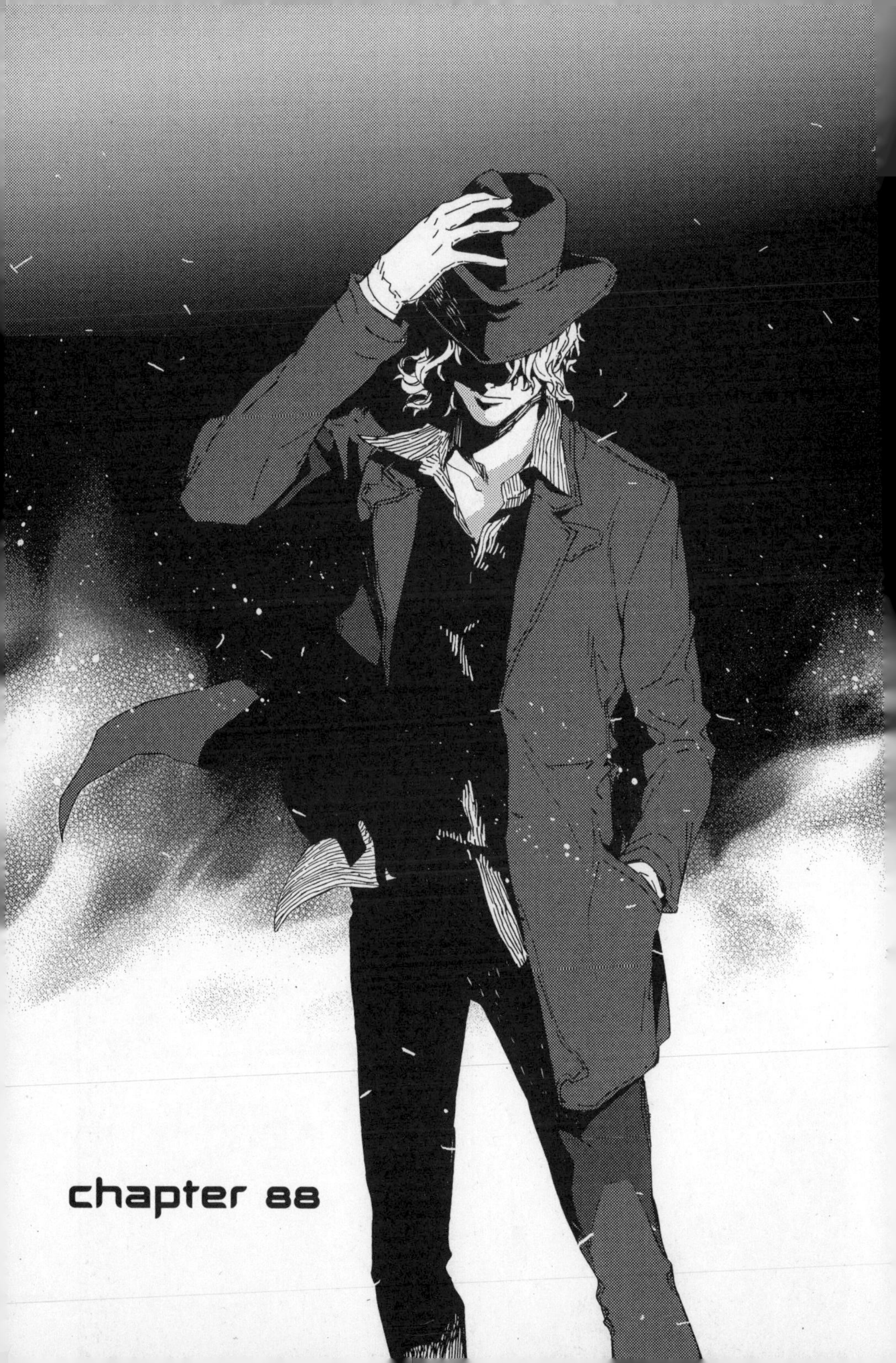
chapter 88

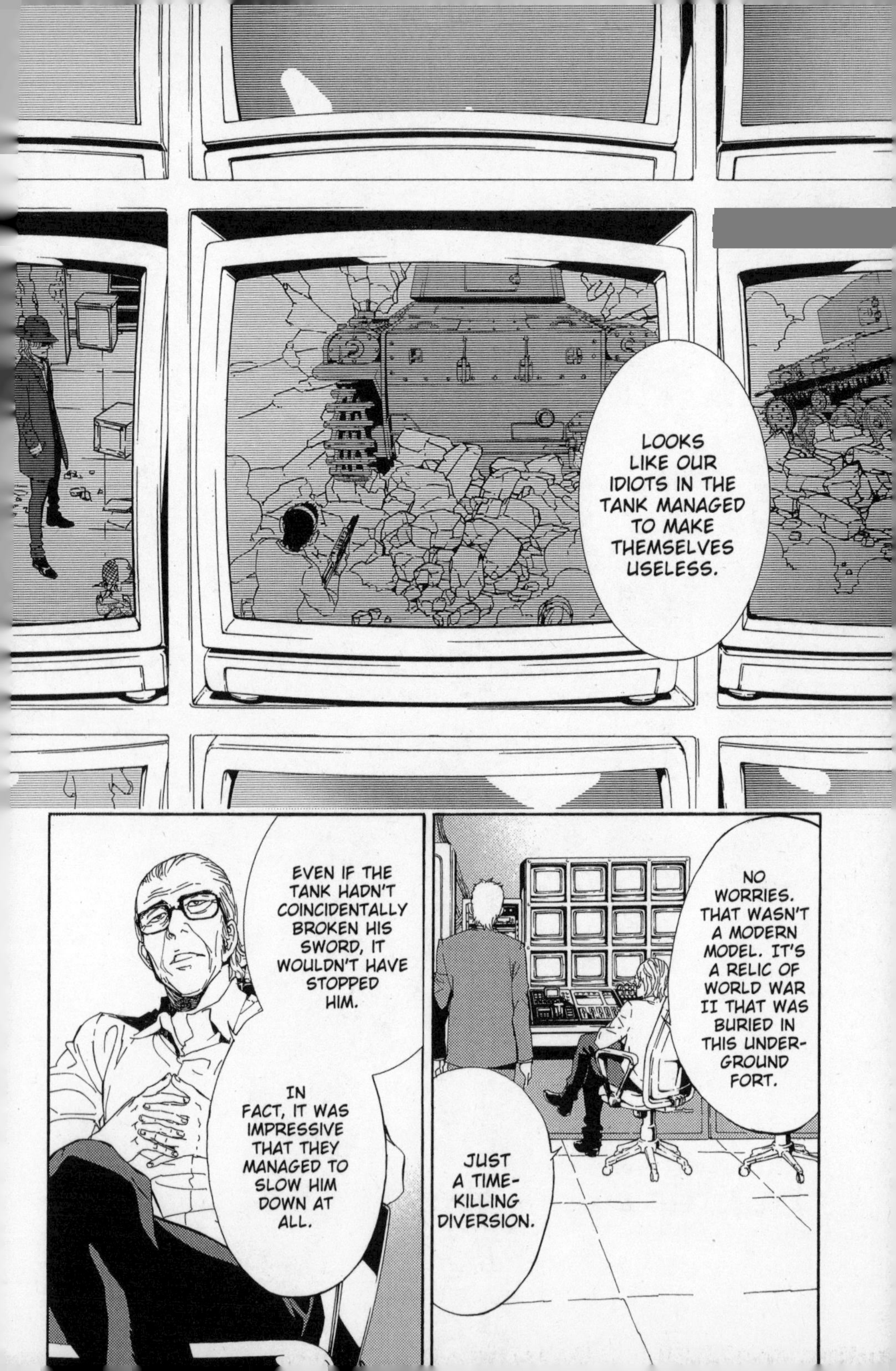
LOOKS LIKE OUR IDIOTS IN THE TANK MANAGED TO MAKE THEMSELVES USELESS.
NO WORRIES. THAT WASN'T A MODERN MODEL. IT'S A RELIC OF WORLD WAR II THAT WAS BURIED IN THIS UNDER-GROUND FORT.
JUST A TIME-KILLING DIVERSION.
EVEN IF THE TANK HADN'T COINCIDENTALLY BROKEN HIS SWORD, IT WOULDN'T HAVE STOPPED HIM.
IN FACT, IT WAS IMPRESSIVE THAT THEY MANAGED TO SLOW HIM DOWN AT ALL.

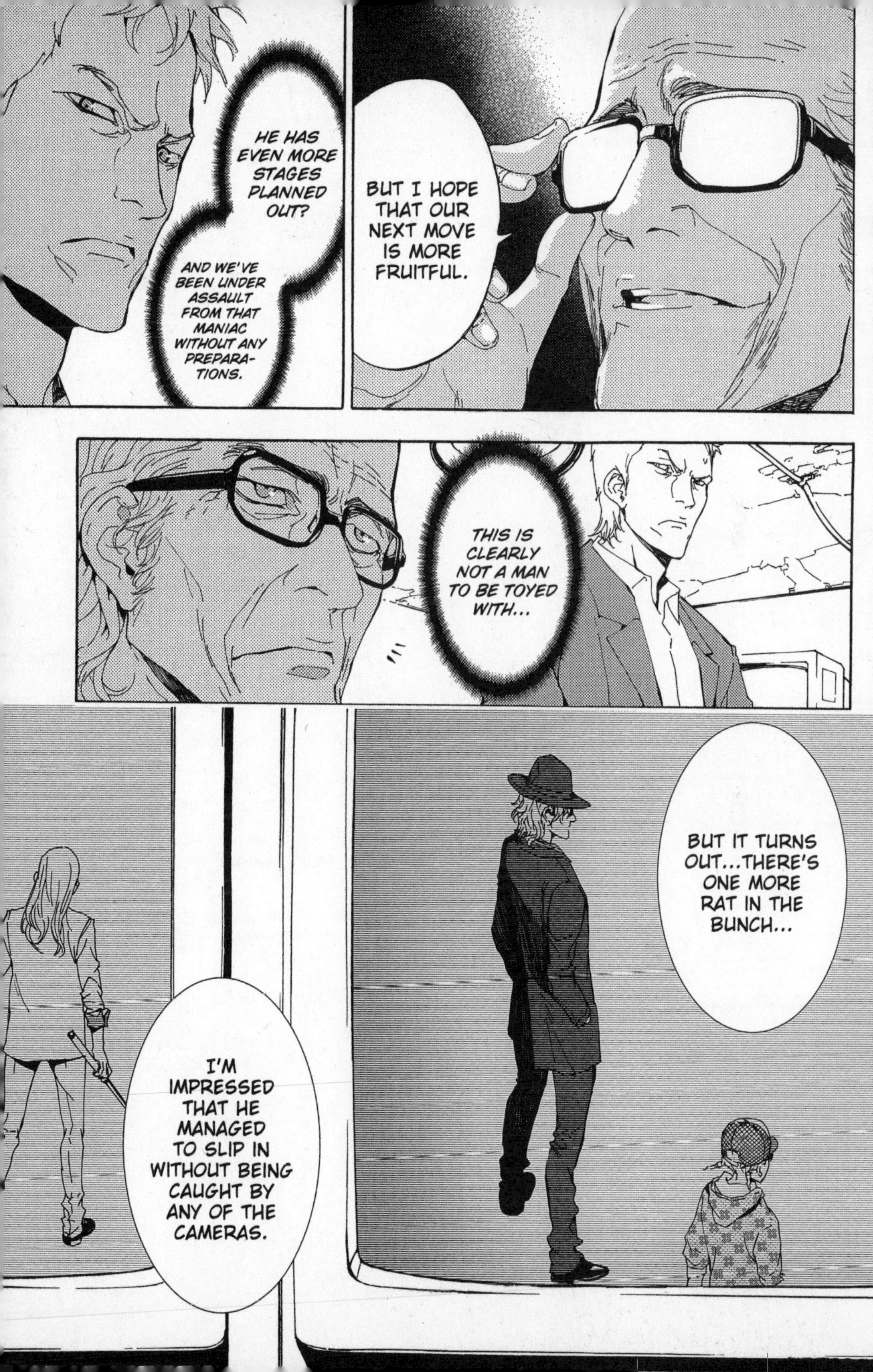
BUT I HOPE THAT OUR NEXT MOVE IS MORE FRUITFUL.
HE HAS EVEN MORE STAGES PLANNED OUT?
AND WE'VE BEEN UNDER ASSAULT FROM THAT MANIAC WITHOUT ANY PREPARATIONS.
THIS IS CLEARLY NOT A MAN TO BE TOYED WITH...
BUT IT TURNS OUT...THERE'S ONE MORE RAT IN THE BUNCH...
I'M IMPRESSED THAT HE MANAGED TO SLIP IN WITHOUT BEING CAUGHT BY ANY OF THE CAMERAS.

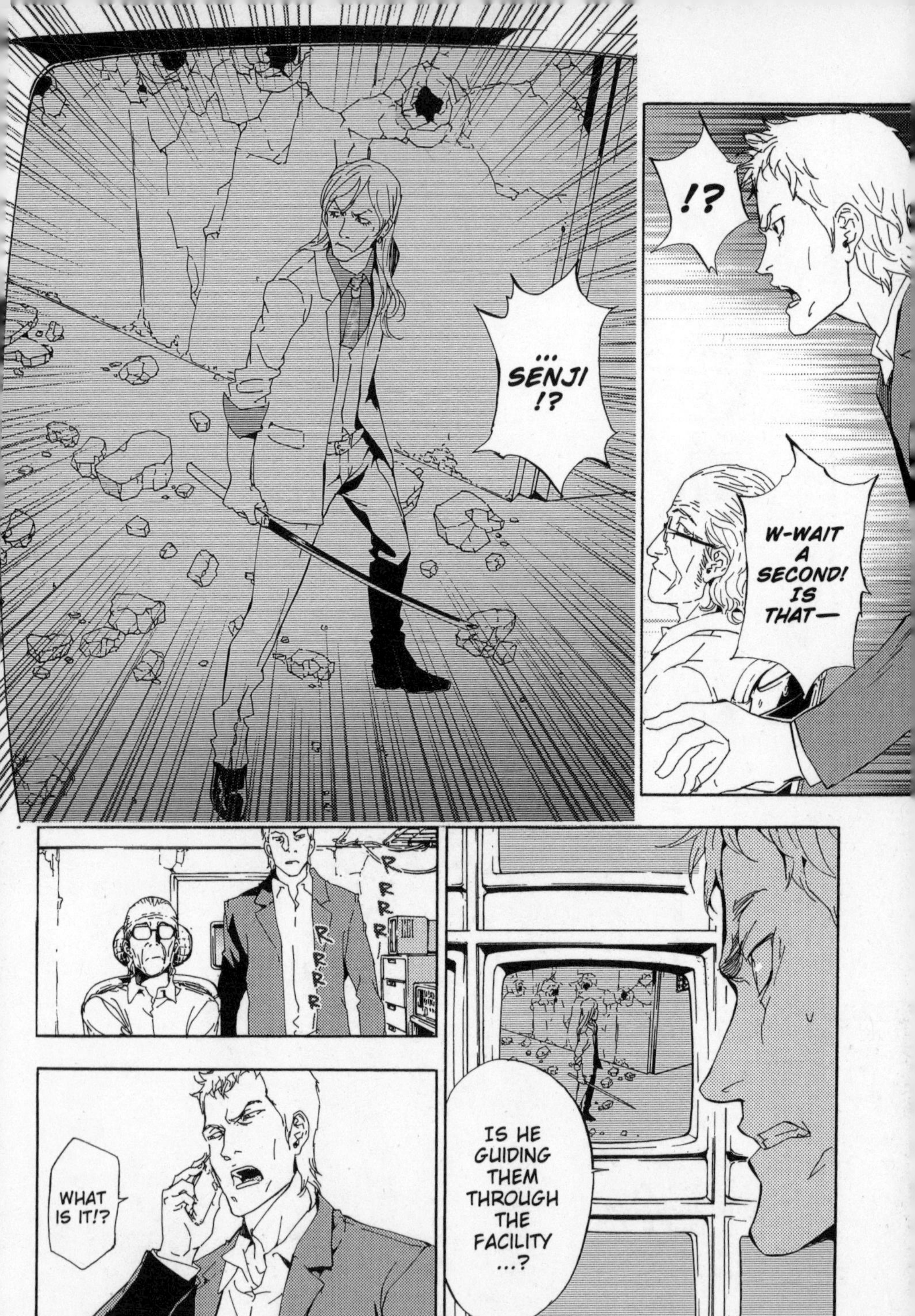
!?
W-WAIT A SECOND! IS THAT—
...SENJI!?
IS HE GUIDING THEM THROUGH THE FACILITY ...?
RRRRRRRR
WHAT IS IT!?

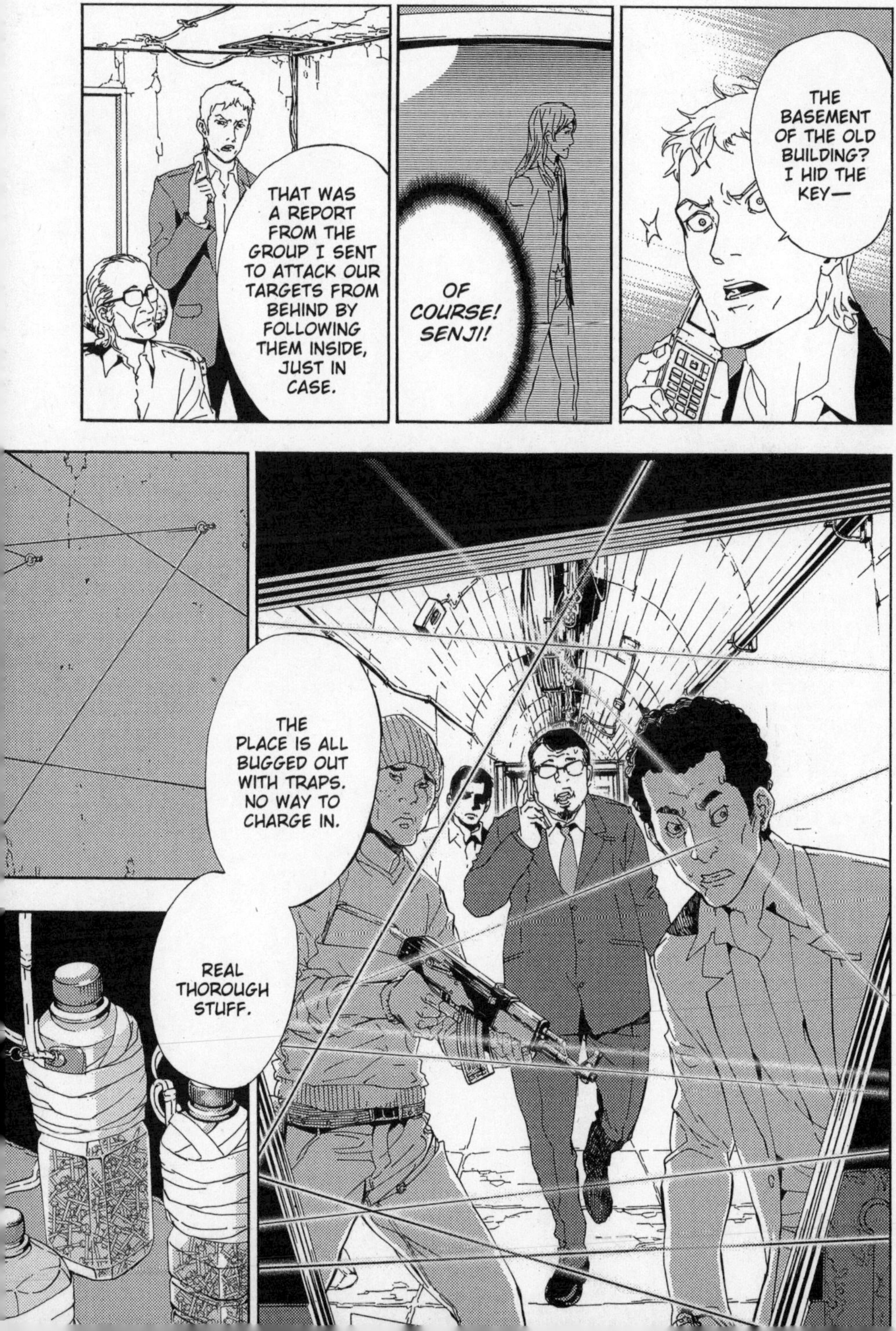
THE BASEMENT OF THE OLD BUILDING? I HID THE KEY—
OF COURSE! SENJI!
THAT WAS A REPORT FROM THE GROUP I SENT TO ATTACK OUR TARGETS FROM BEHIND BY FOLLOWING THEM INSIDE, JUST IN CASE.
THE PLACE IS ALL BUGGED OUT WITH TRAPS. NO WAY TO CHARGE IN.
REAL THOROUGH STUFF.

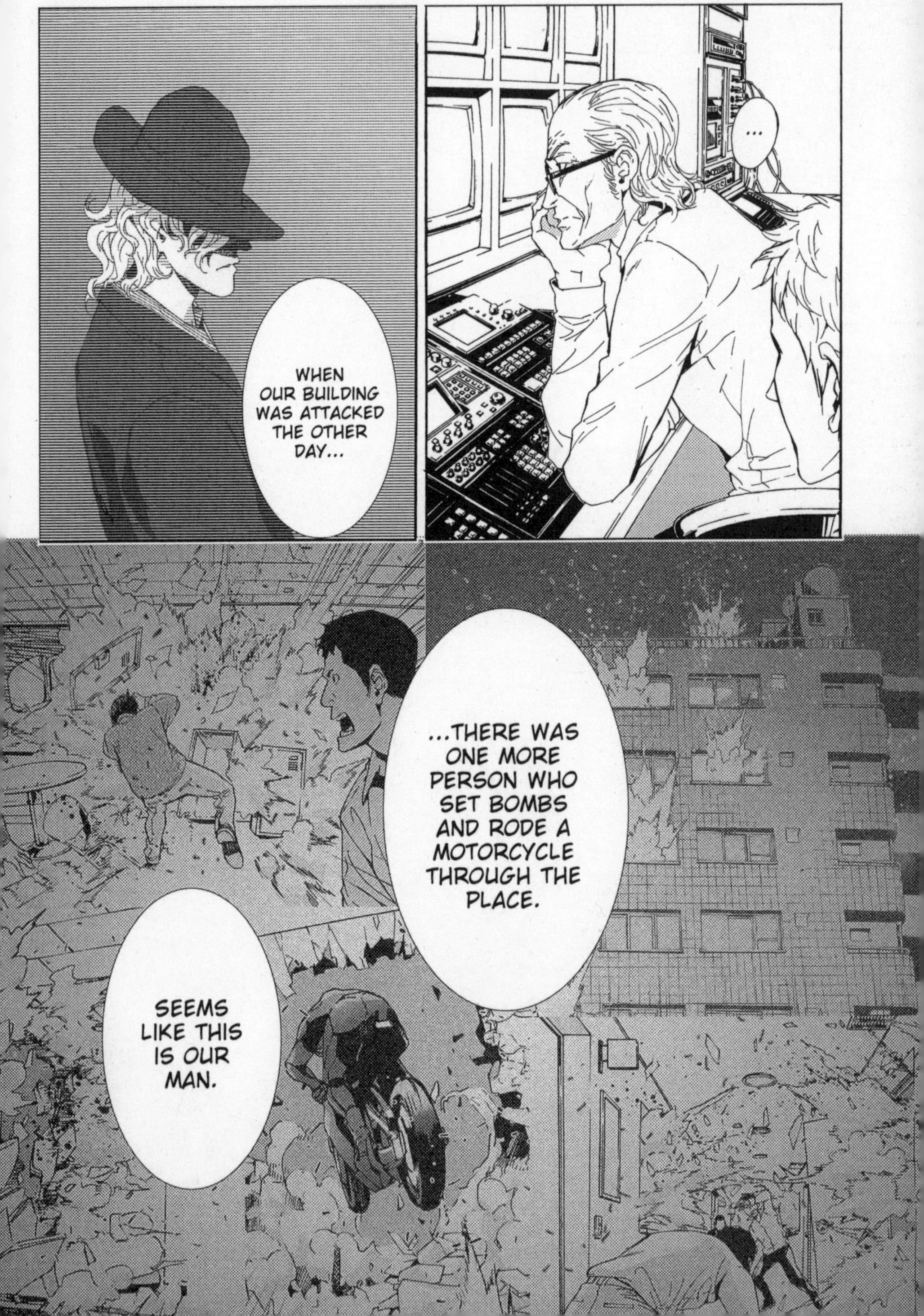
...
WHEN OUR BUILDING WAS ATTACKED THE OTHER DAY...
...THERE WAS ONE MORE PERSON WHO SET BOMBS AND RODE A MOTORCYCLE THROUGH THE PLACE.
SEEMS LIKE THIS IS OUR MAN.

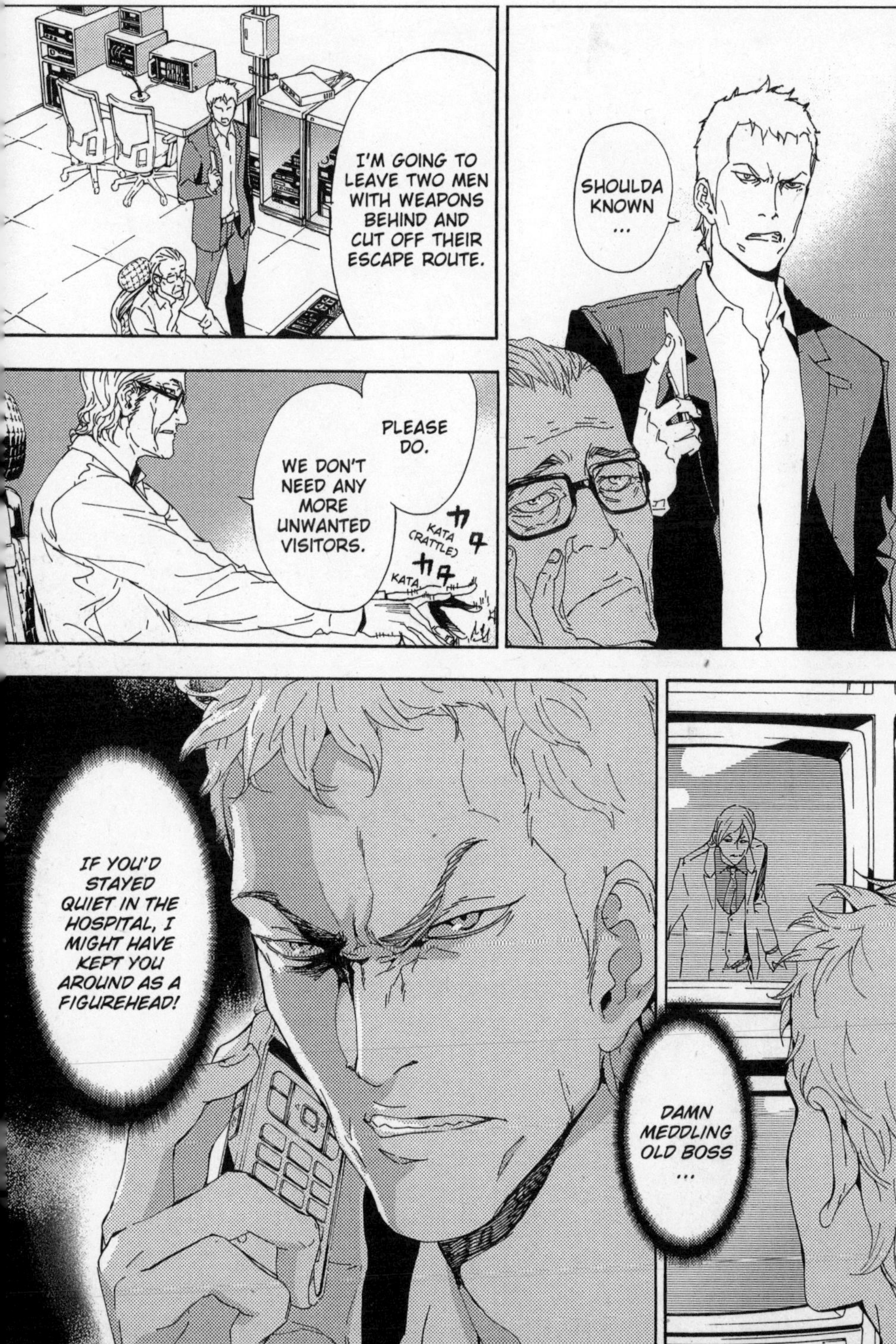
SHOULDA KNOWN ...
I'M GOING TO LEAVE TWO MEN WITH WEAPONS BEHIND AND CUT OFF THEIR ESCAPE ROUTE.
PLEASE DO.
WE DON'T NEED ANY MORE UNWANTED VISITORS.
カタ
KATA (RATTLE)
カタ
KATA
DAMN MEDDLING OLD BOSS ...
IF YOU'D STAYED QUIET IN THE HOSPITAL, I MIGHT HAVE KEPT YOU AROUND AS A FIGUREHEAD!

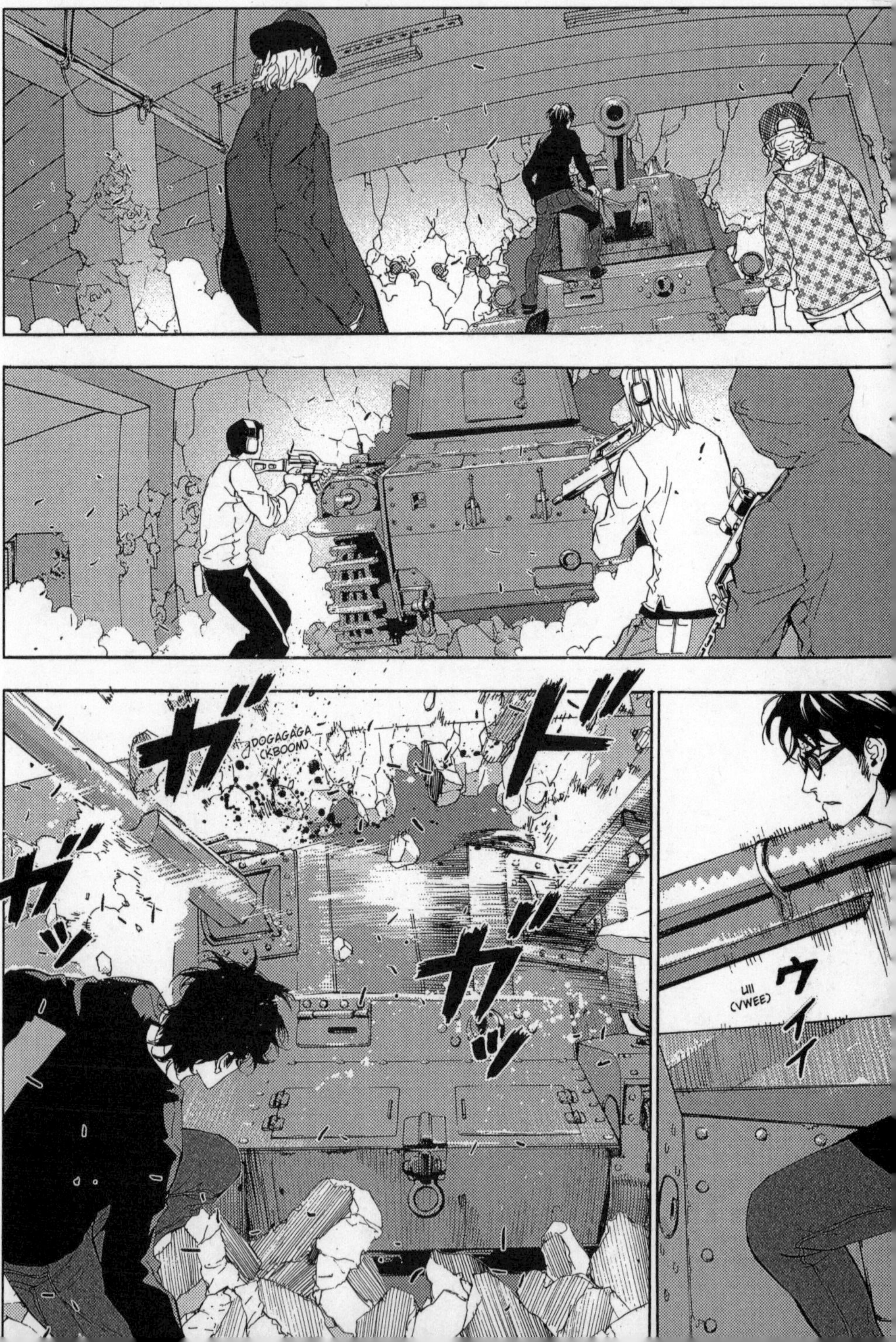
UII
(VWEE)
ウイイ
DOGAGAGA
(KBOOM)
ドガガガ

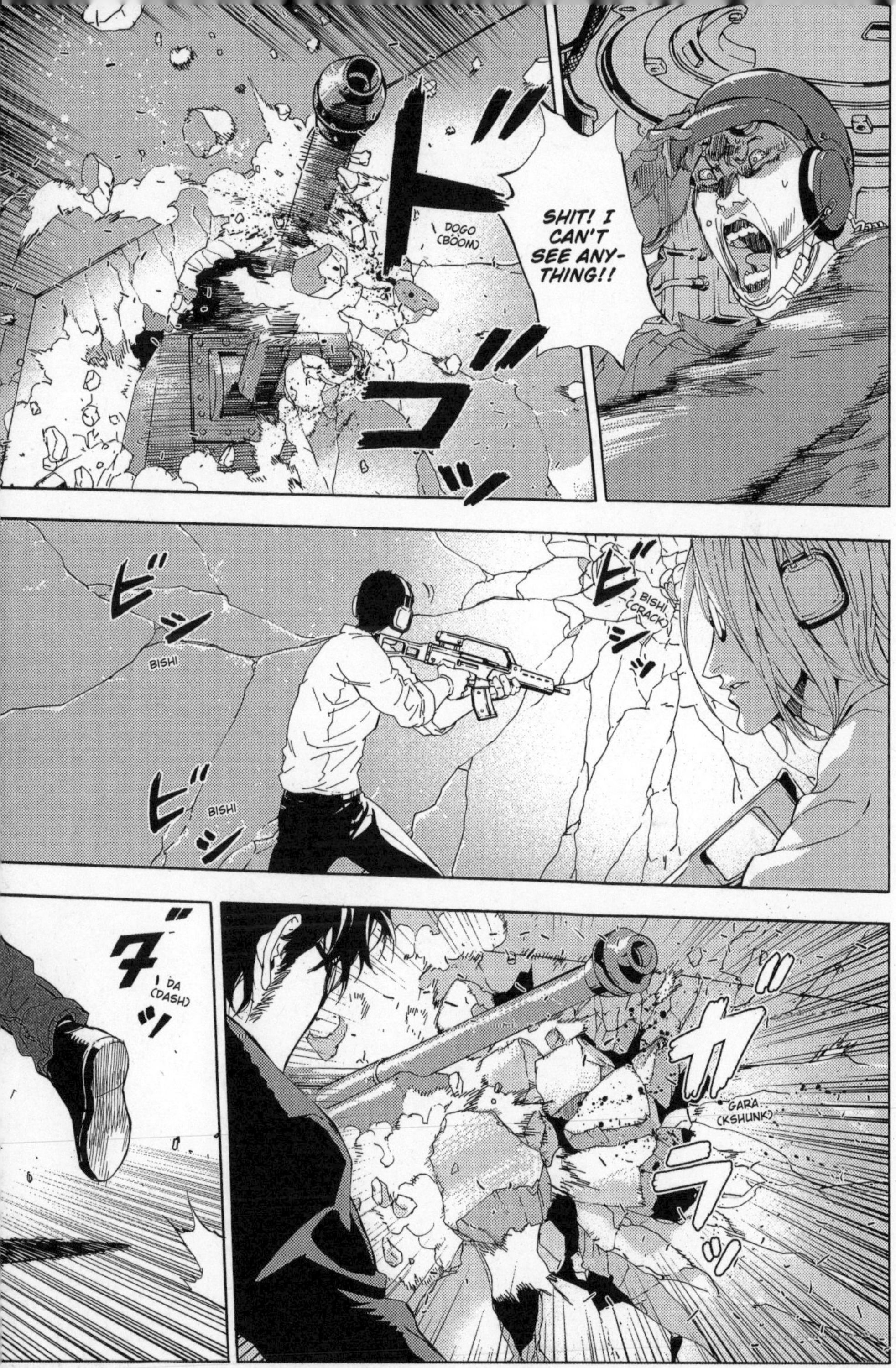
SHIT! I CAN'T SEE ANY-THING!!
DOGO (BOOM)
BISHI (CRACK)
BISHI
BISHI
GARA (KSHUNK)
DA (DASH)

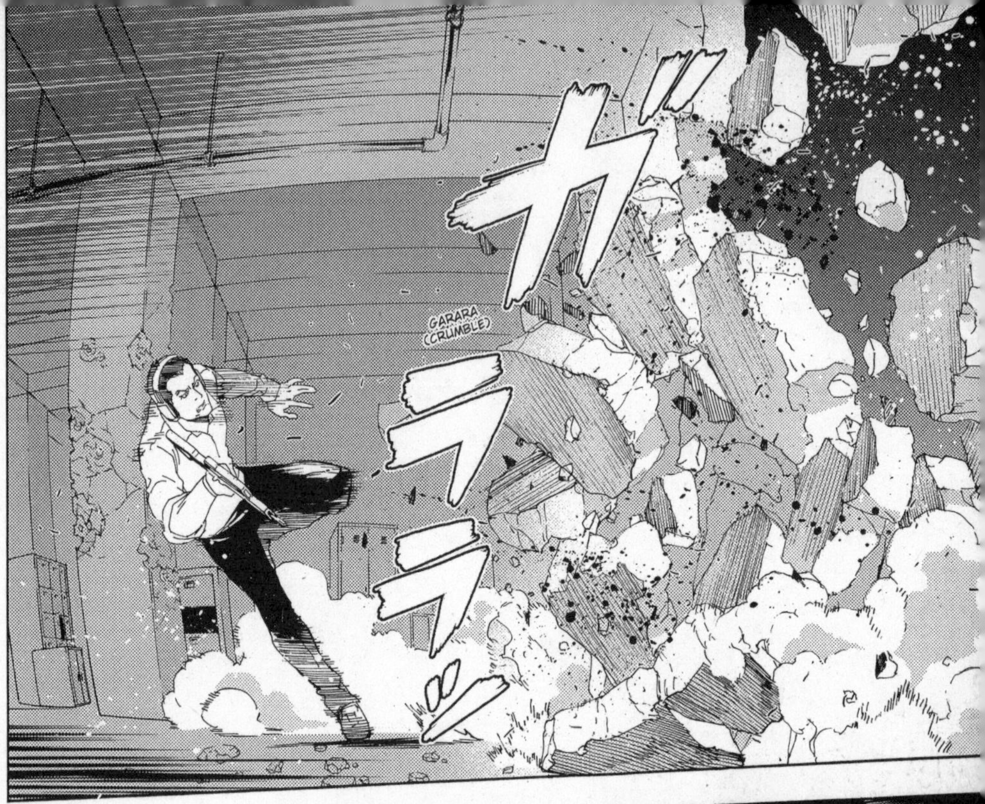
GARARA
(CRUMBLE)
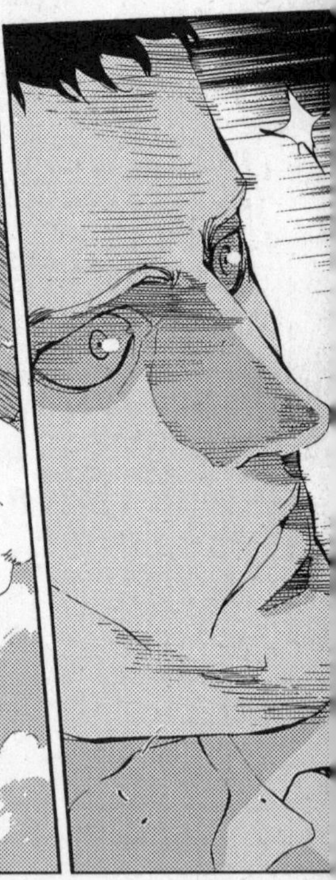
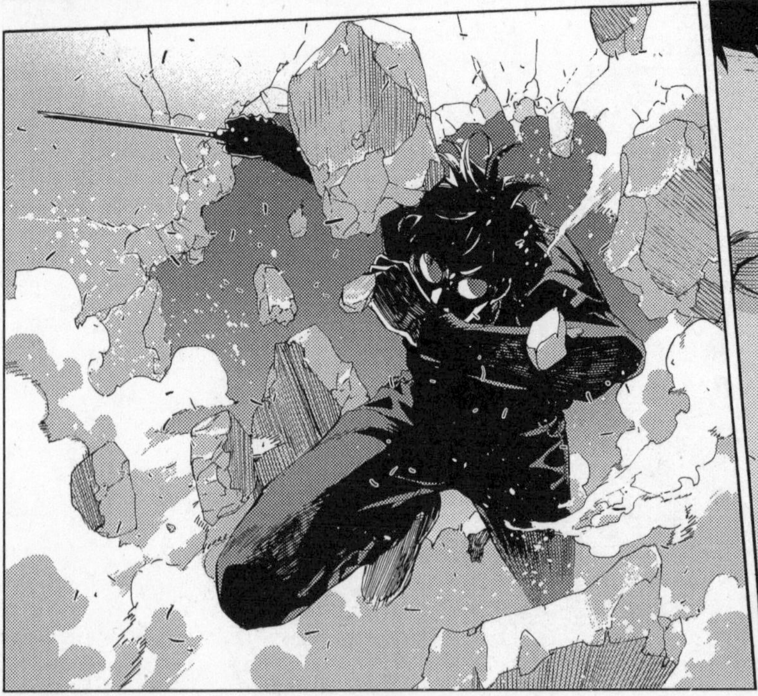

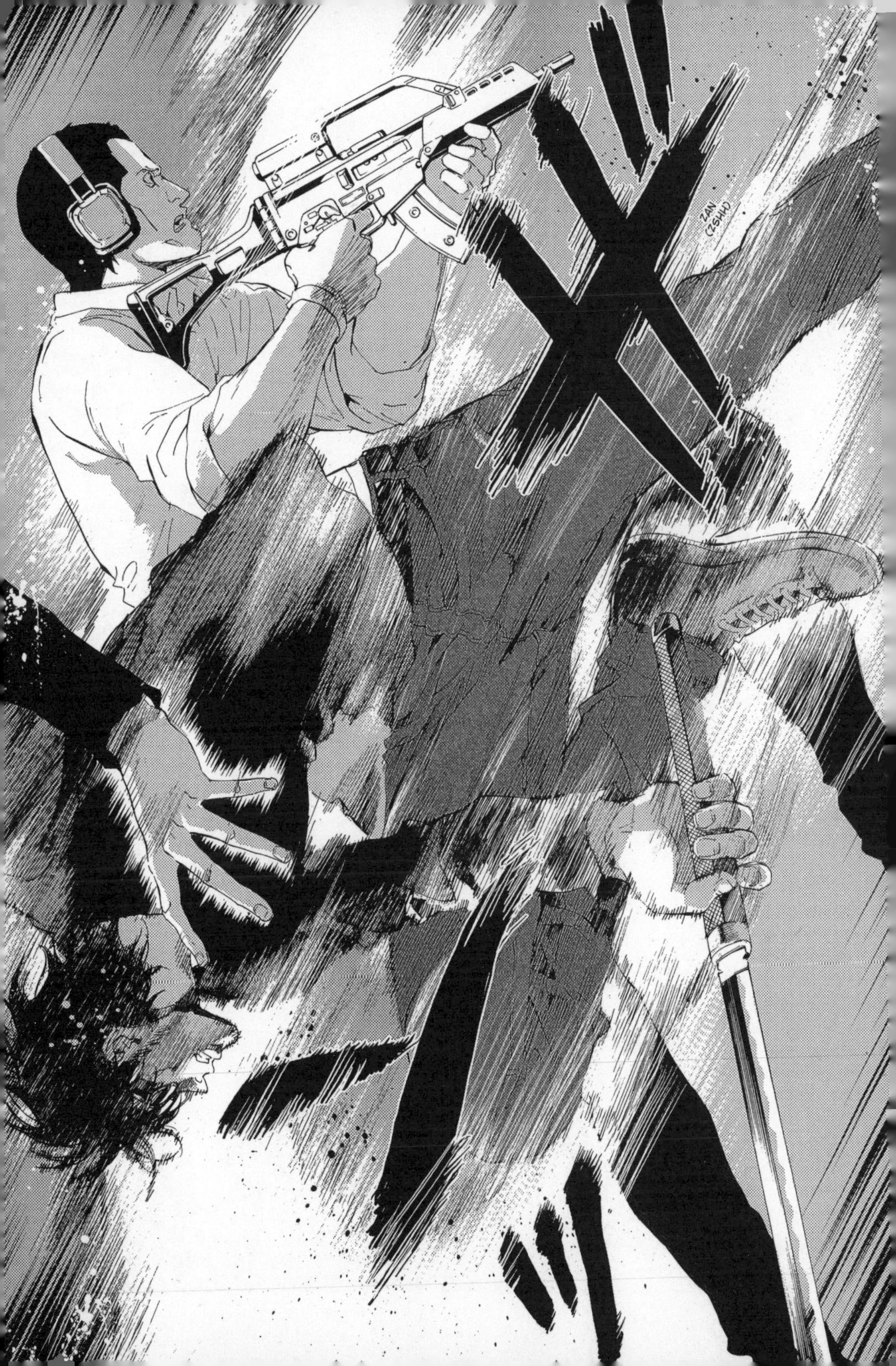
ZAN (ZSHH)

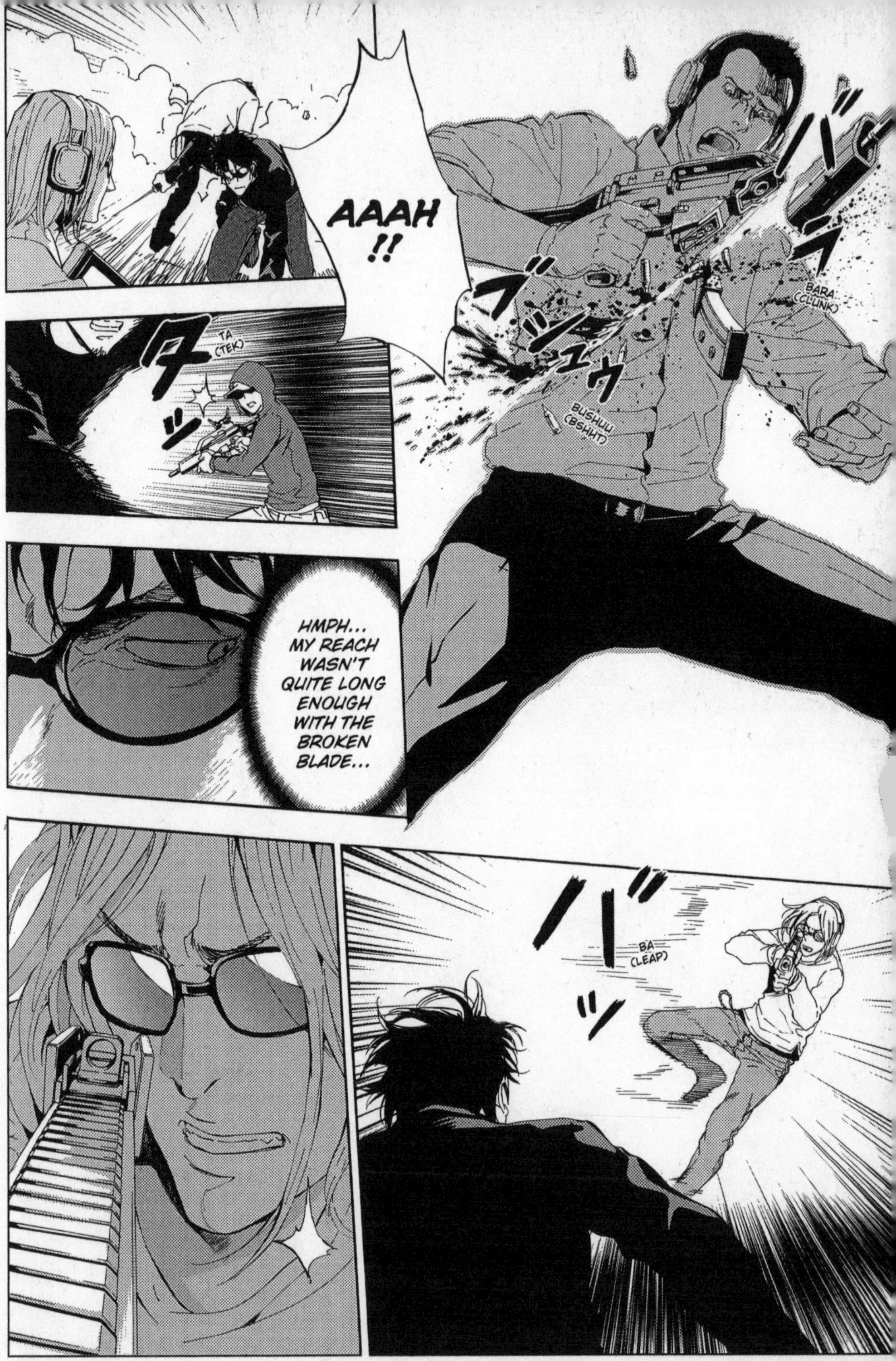
AAAH !!
BARA (CLUNK)
BUSHUU (BSHHT)
TA (TEK)
HMPH... MY REACH WASN'T QUITE LONG ENOUGH WITH THE BROKEN BLADE...
BA (LEAP)

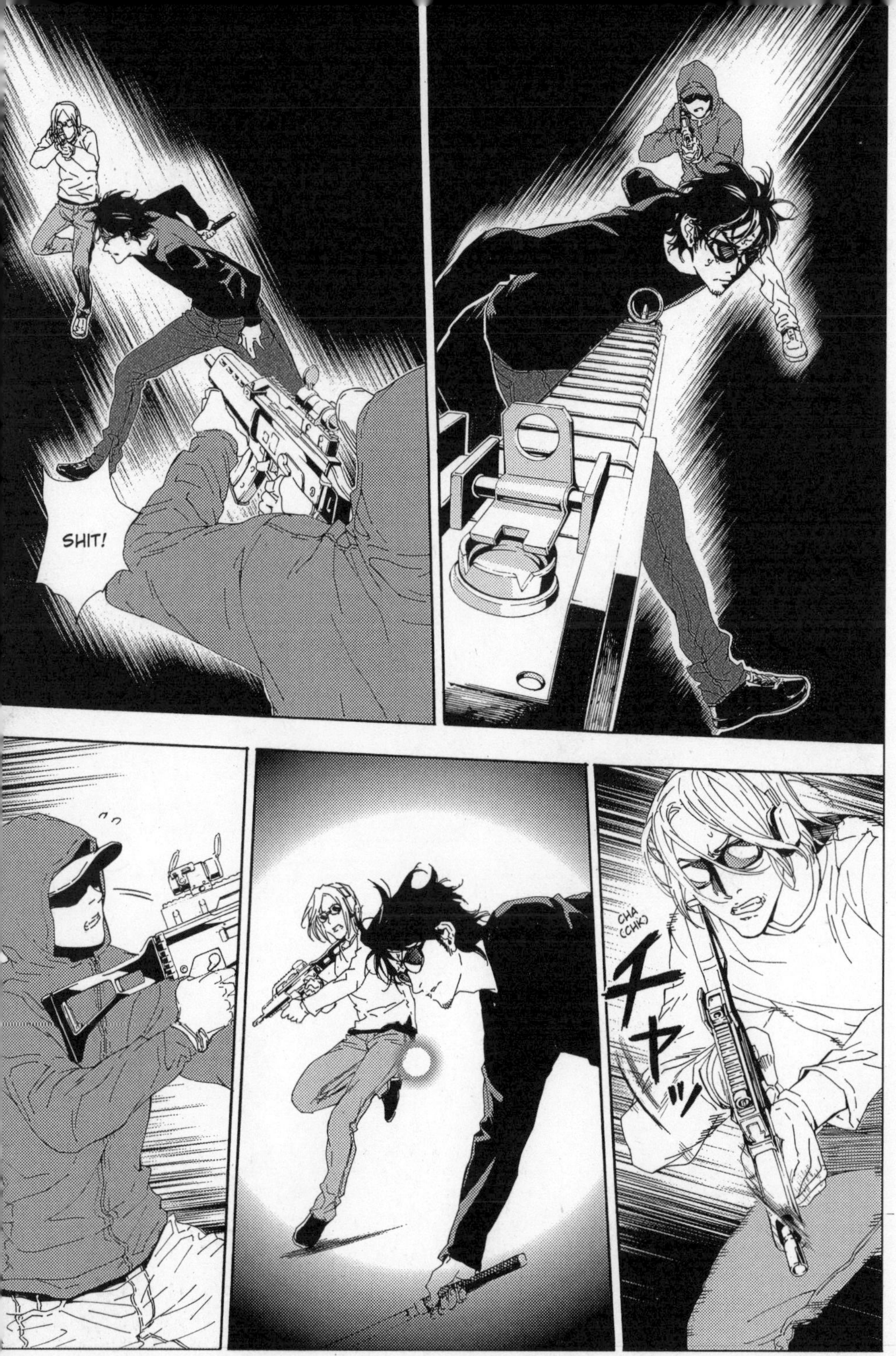
SHIT!
CHA (CHK)
チャッ

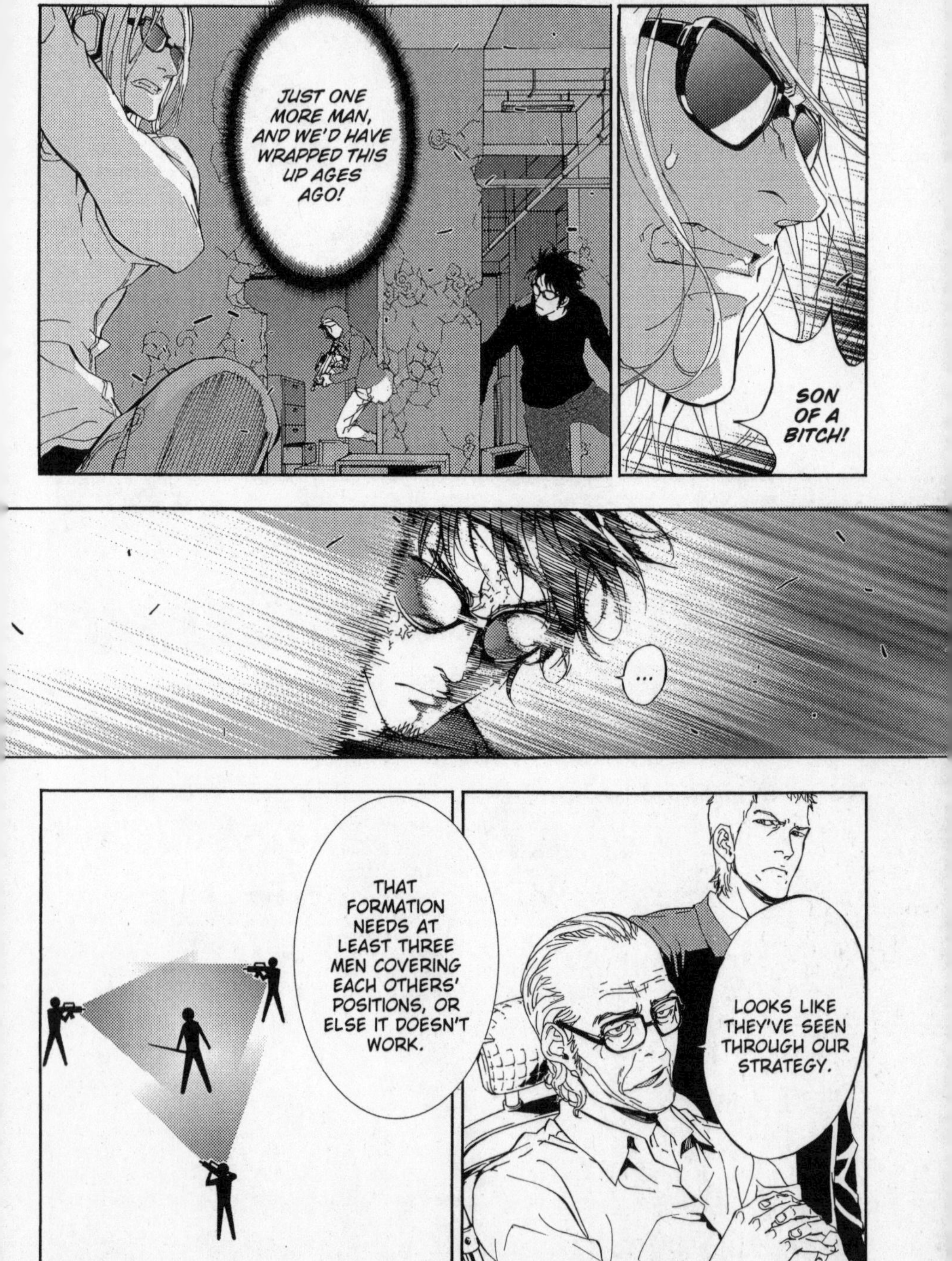
SON OF A BITCH!
JUST ONE MORE MAN, AND WE'D HAVE WRAPPED THIS UP AGES AGO!
...
LOOKS LIKE THEY'VE SEEN THROUGH OUR STRATEGY.
THAT FORMATION NEEDS AT LEAST THREE MEN COVERING EACH OTHERS' POSITIONS, OR ELSE IT DOESN'T WORK.

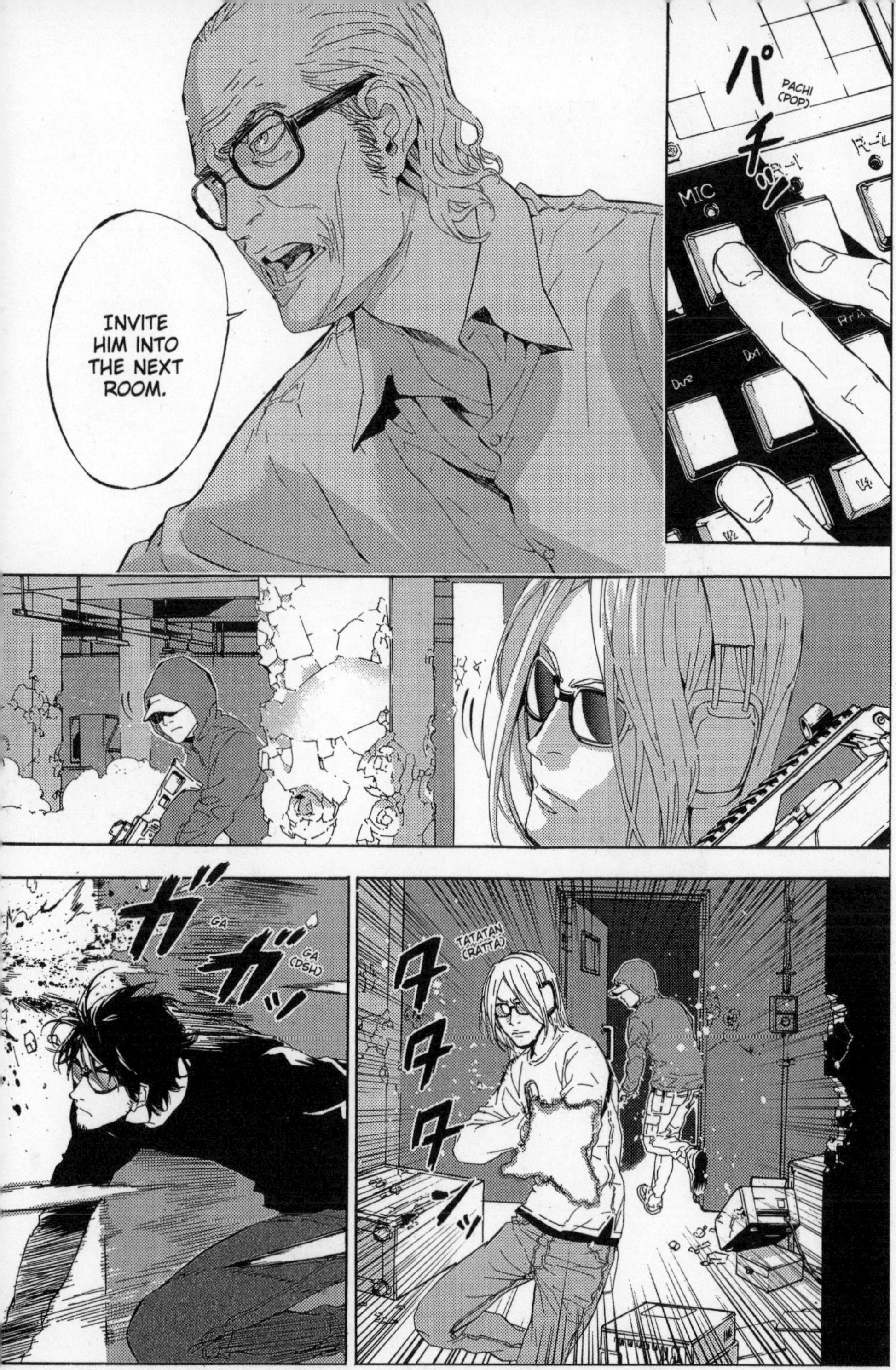

パチッ
PACHI (POP)
MIC
INVITE HIM INTO THE NEXT ROOM.
タタタンッ
TATATAN (RATTA)
ガガッ
GA
GA (DSH)

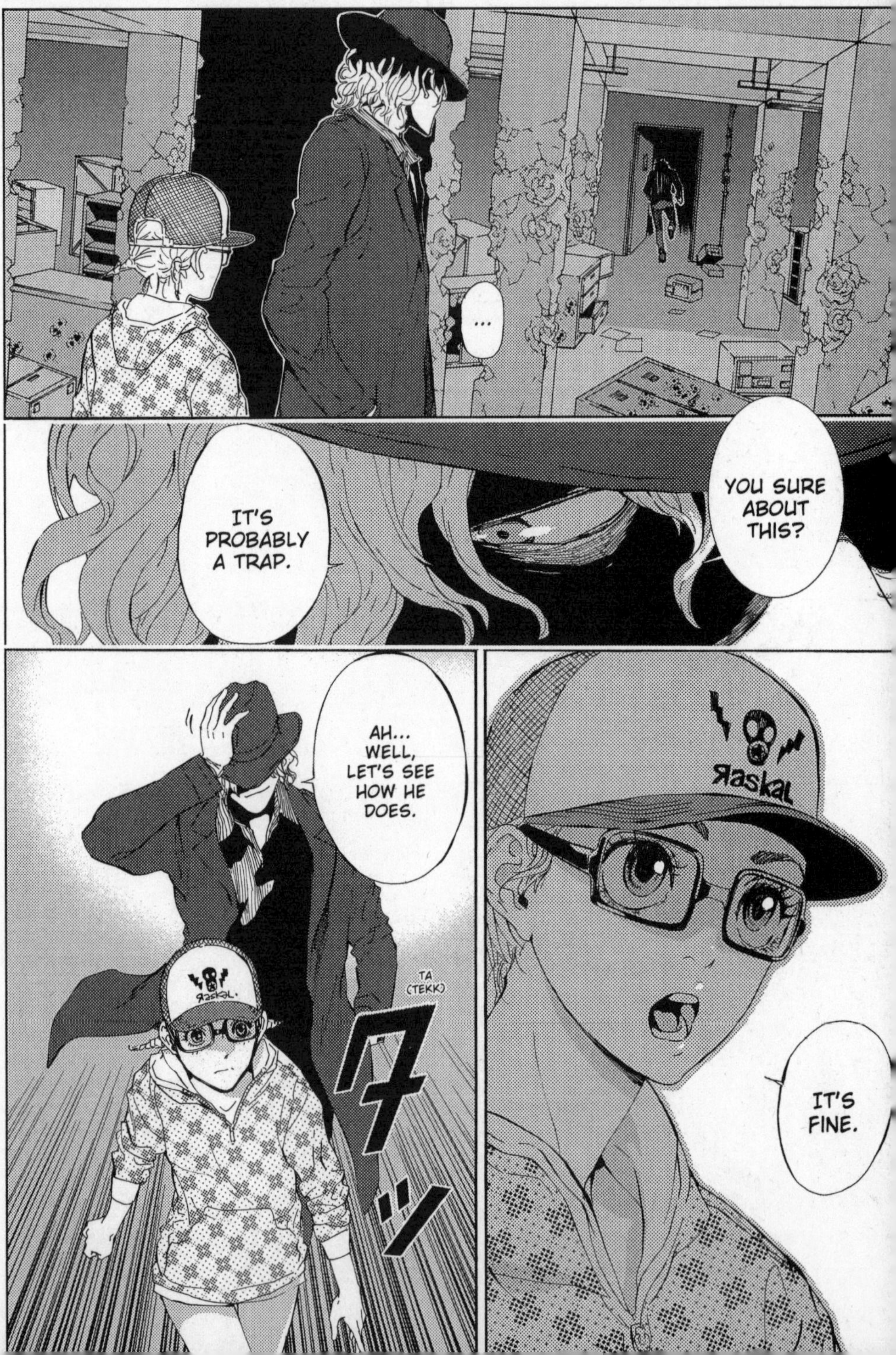
...
YOU SURE ABOUT THIS?
IT'S PROBABLY A TRAP.
IT'S FINE.
AH... WELL, LET'S SEE HOW HE DOES.
TA (TEKK)

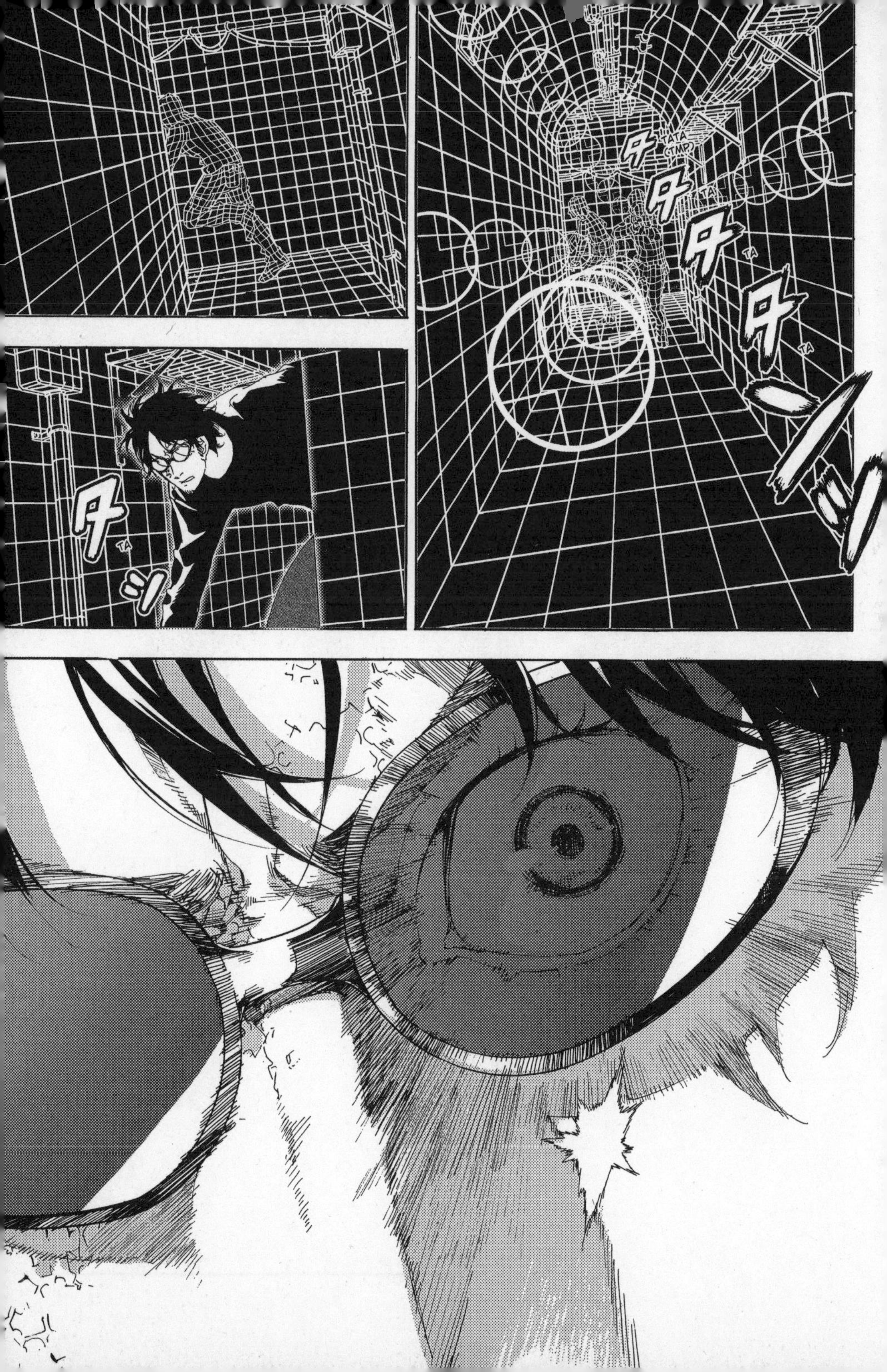
タタタタッ
TATA (TMP)
TA
TA
TA
タッ
TA

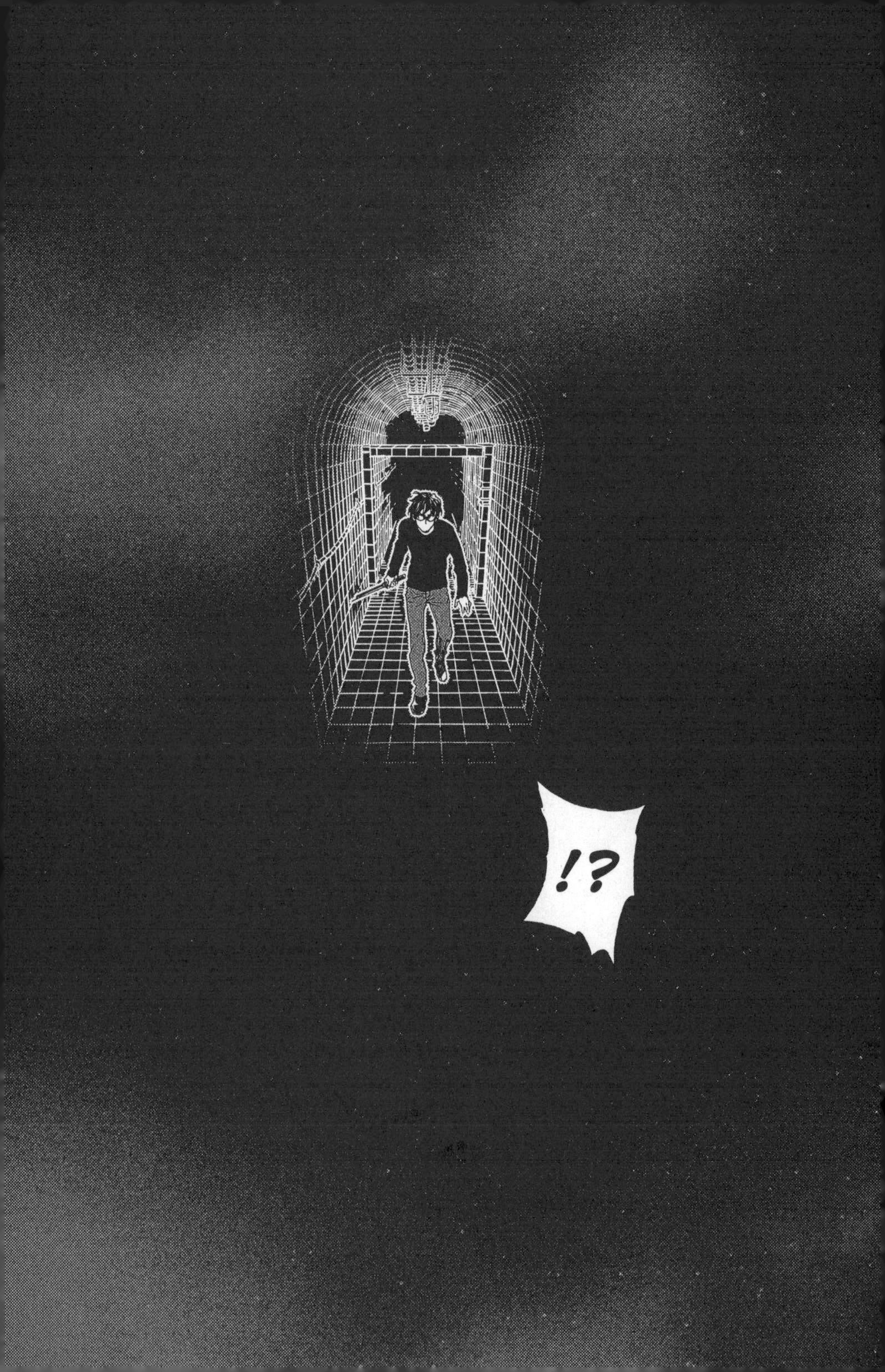
!?

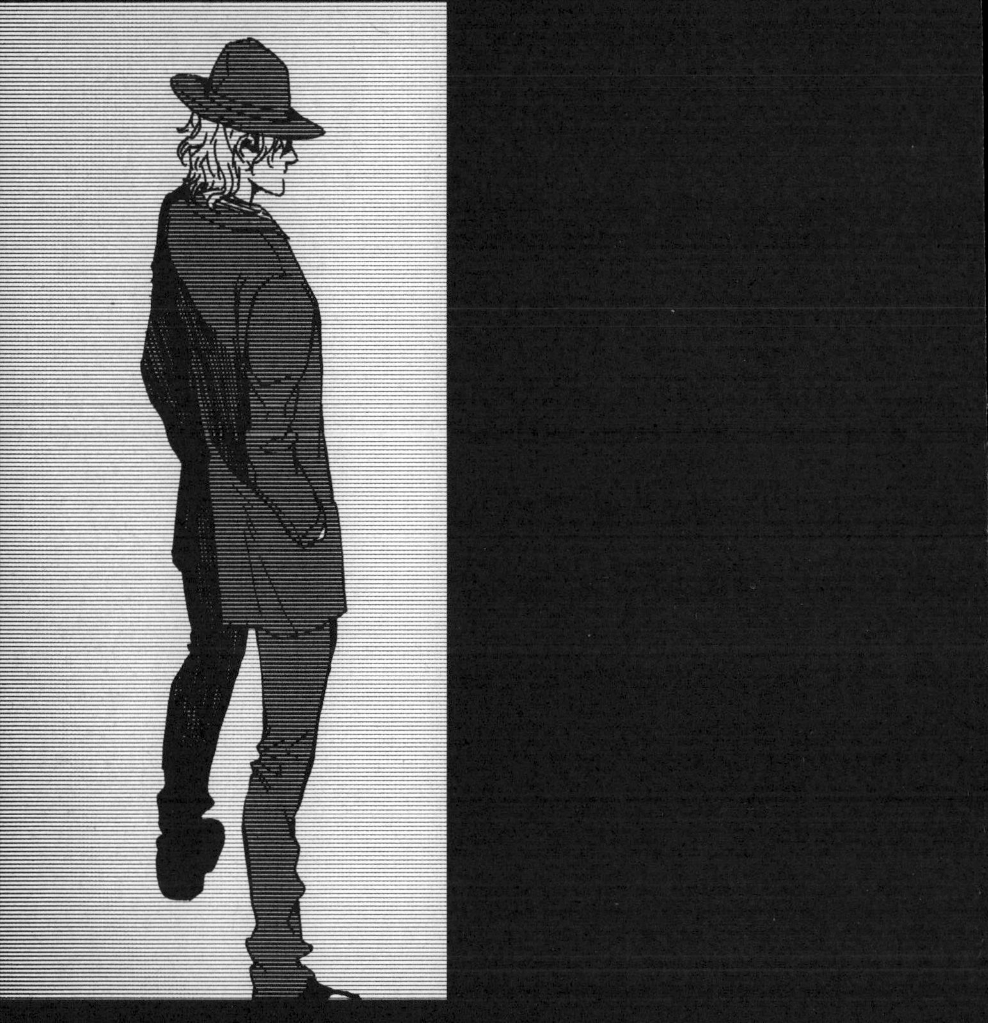

Until Death do us Part

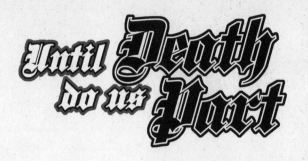

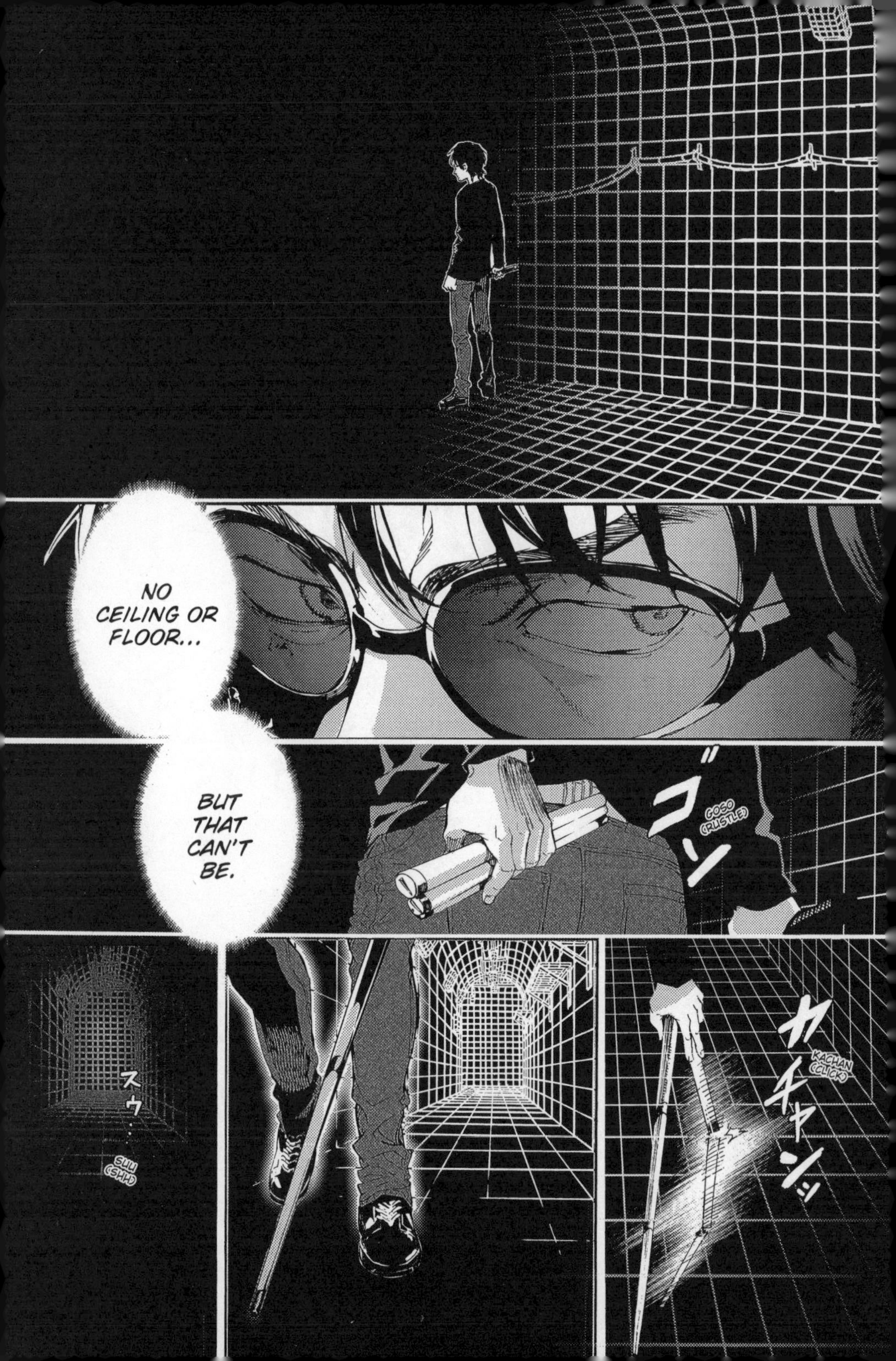

NO CEILING OR FLOOR...
ゴソ
GOSO (RUSTLE)
BUT THAT CAN'T BE.
カチャン
KACHAN (CLICK)
スウ…
SUU (SHH)

chapter 89

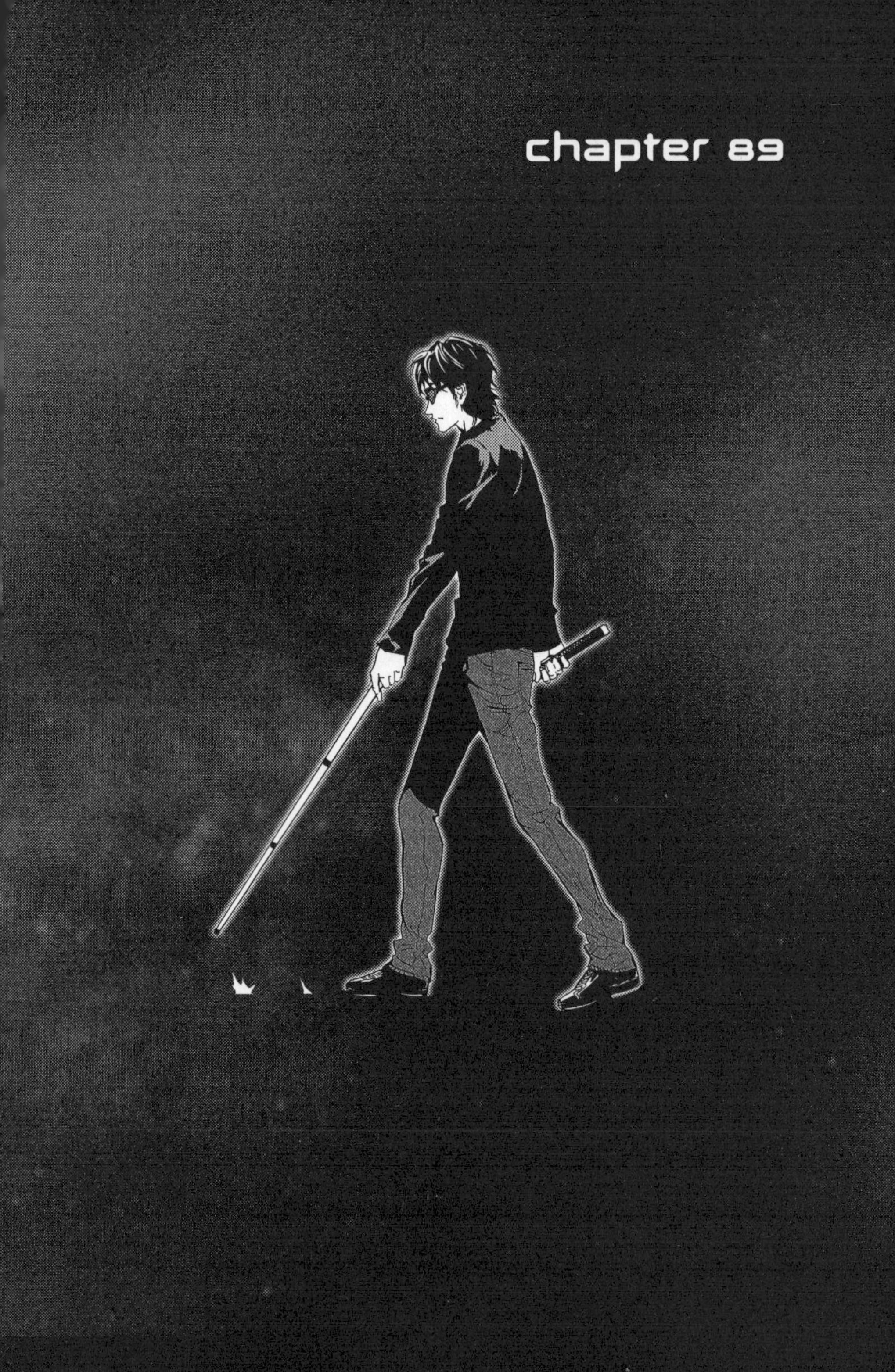

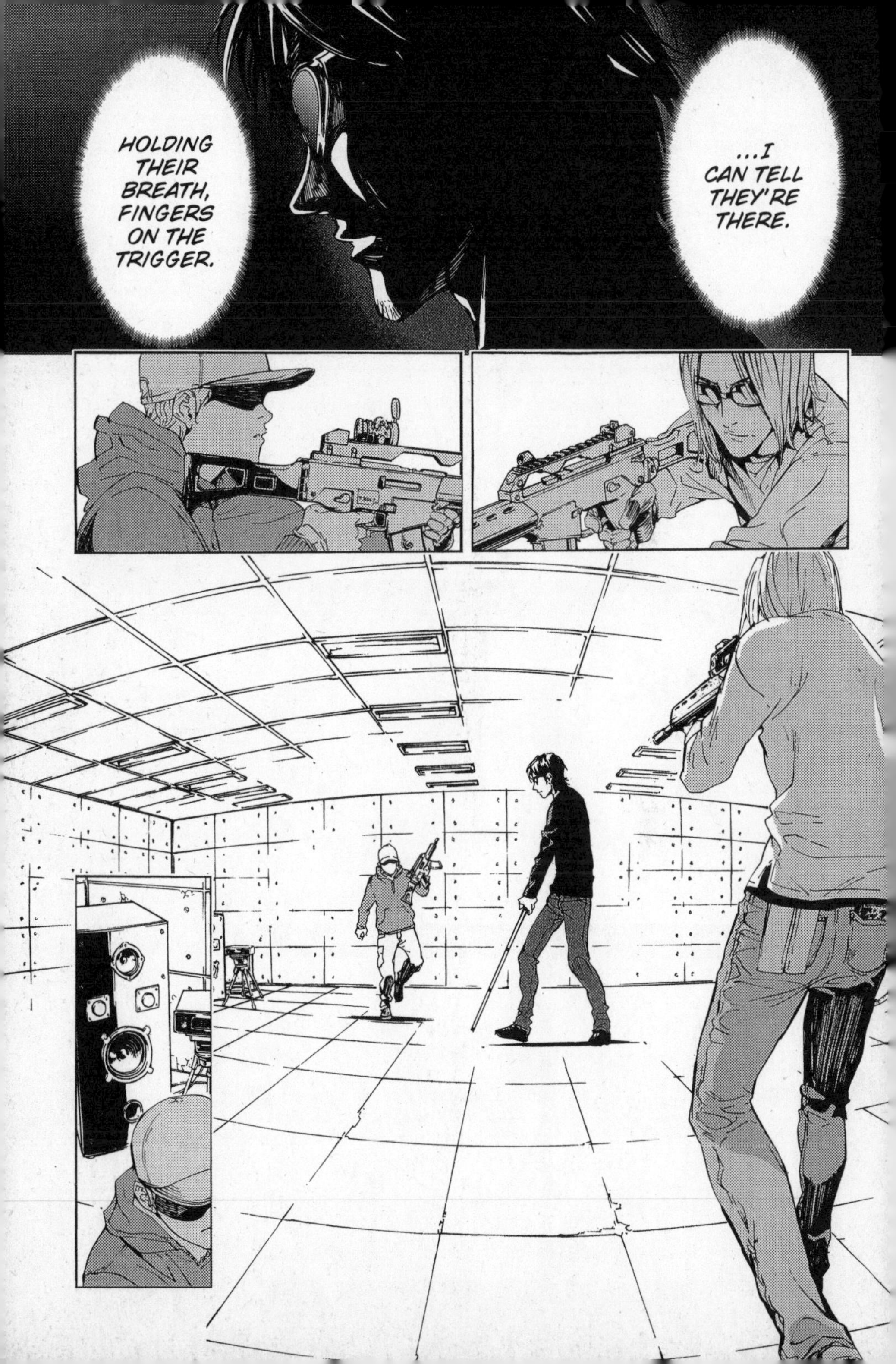
...I CAN TELL THEY'RE THERE.
HOLDING THEIR BREATH, FINGERS ON THE TRIGGER.

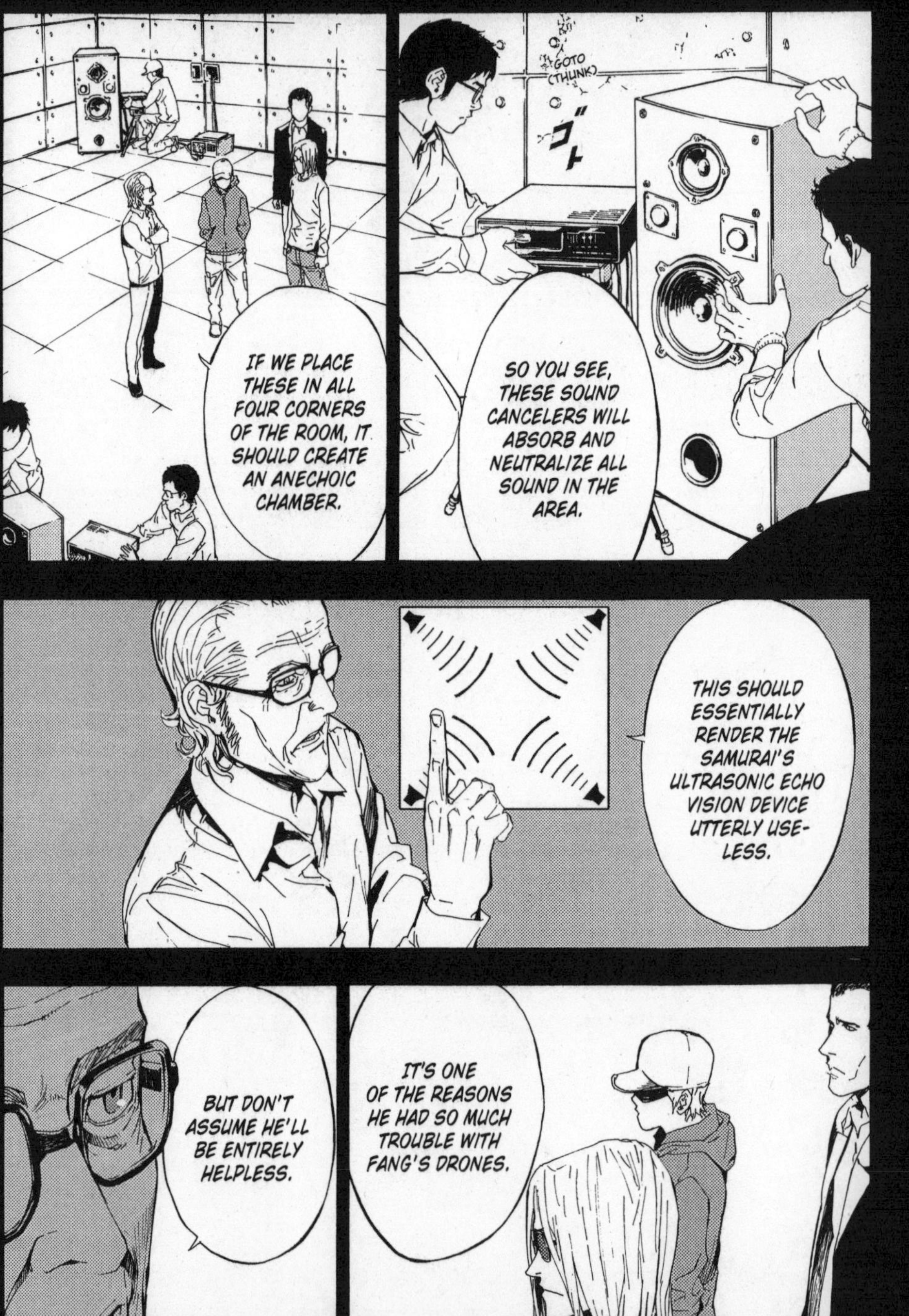
GOTO
(THUNK)
SO YOU SEE, THESE SOUND CANCELERS WILL ABSORB AND NEUTRALIZE ALL SOUND IN THE AREA.
IF WE PLACE THESE IN ALL FOUR CORNERS OF THE ROOM, IT SHOULD CREATE AN ANECHOIC CHAMBER.
THIS SHOULD ESSENTIALLY RENDER THE SAMURAI'S ULTRASONIC ECHO VISION DEVICE UTTERLY USE-LESS.
IT'S ONE OF THE REASONS HE HAD SO MUCH TROUBLE WITH FANG'S DRONES.
BUT DON'T ASSUME HE'LL BE ENTIRELY HELPLESS.

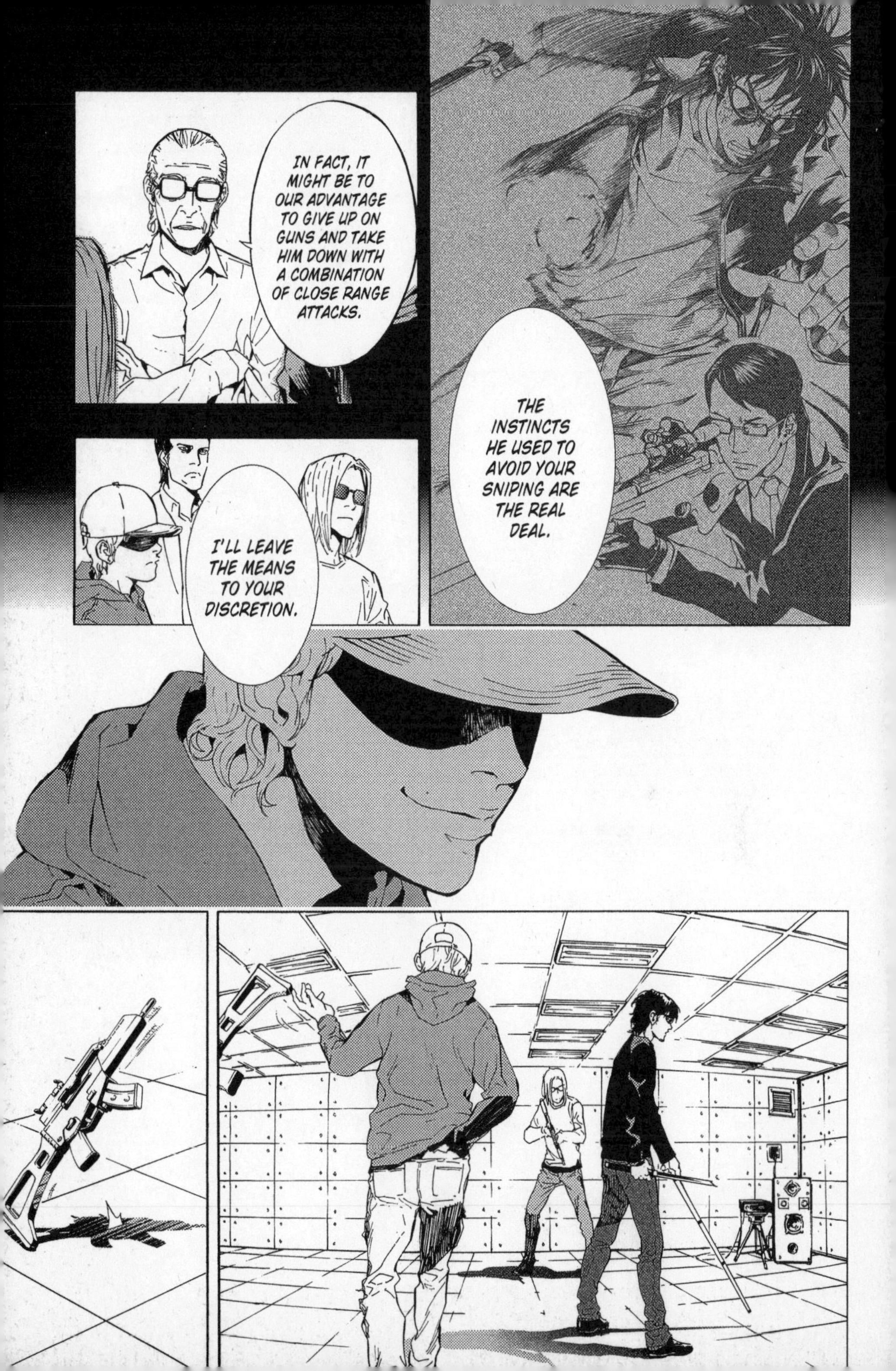
THE INSTINCTS HE USED TO AVOID YOUR SNIPING ARE THE REAL DEAL.
IN FACT, IT MIGHT BE TO OUR ADVANTAGE TO GIVE UP ON GUNS AND TAKE HIM DOWN WITH A COMBINATION OF CLOSE RANGE ATTACKS.
I'LL LEAVE THE MEANS TO YOUR DISCRETION.

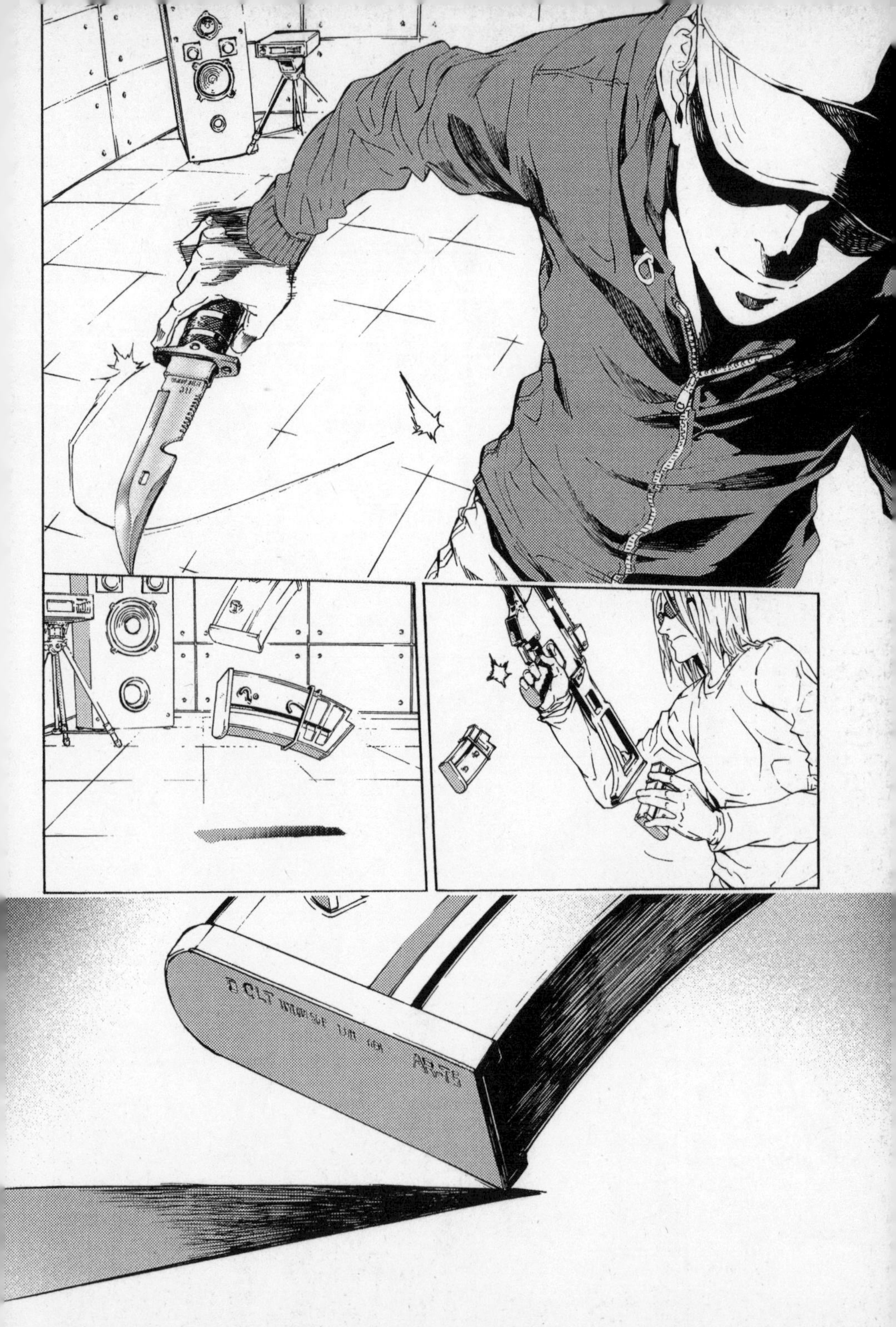
CLT
AR-15

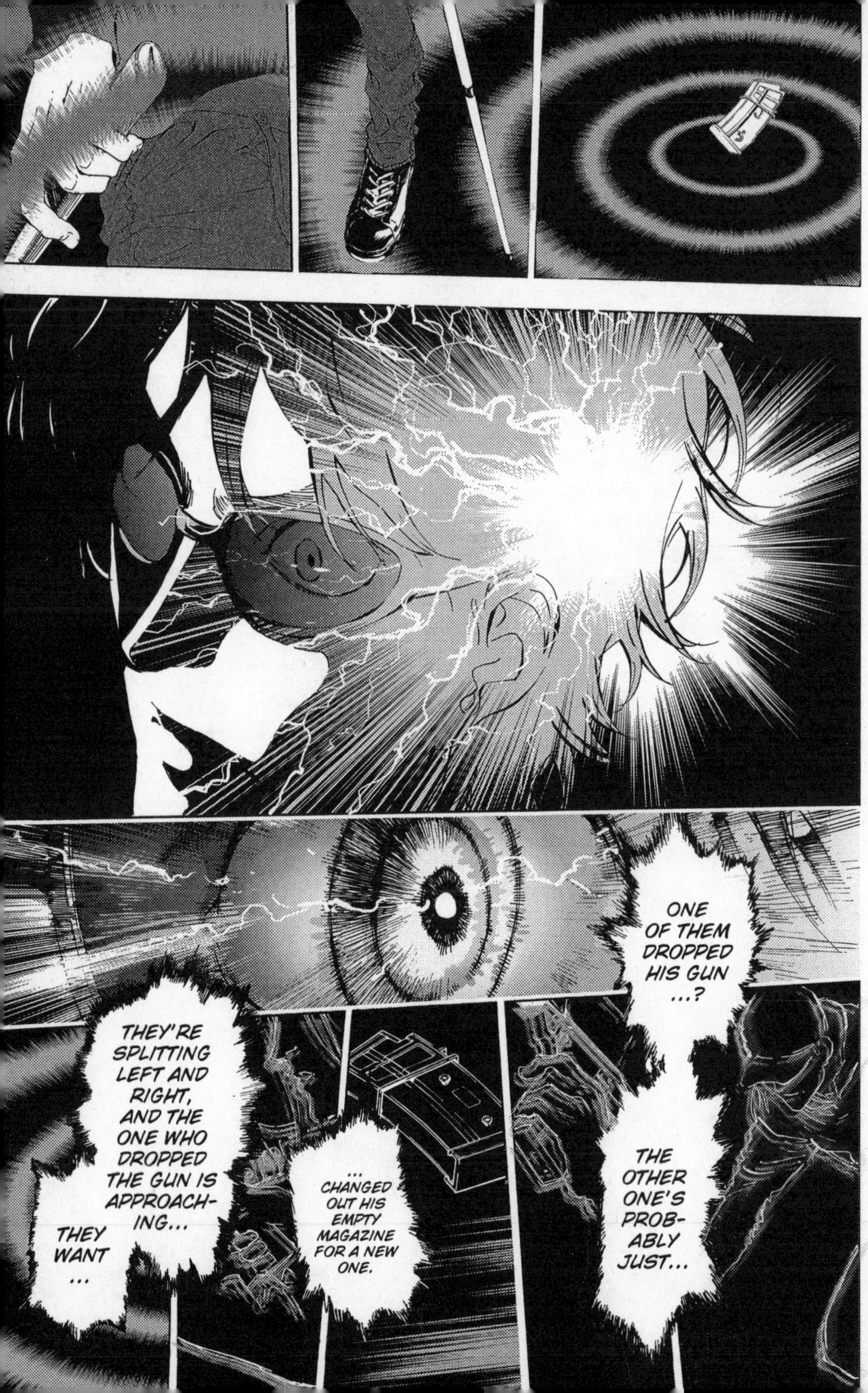
ONE OF THEM DROPPED HIS GUN ...?
THE OTHER ONE'S PROBABLY JUST...
...CHANGED OUT HIS EMPTY MAGAZINE FOR A NEW ONE.
THEY'RE SPLITTING LEFT AND RIGHT, AND THE ONE WHO DROPPED THE GUN IS APPROACHING...
THEY WANT ...

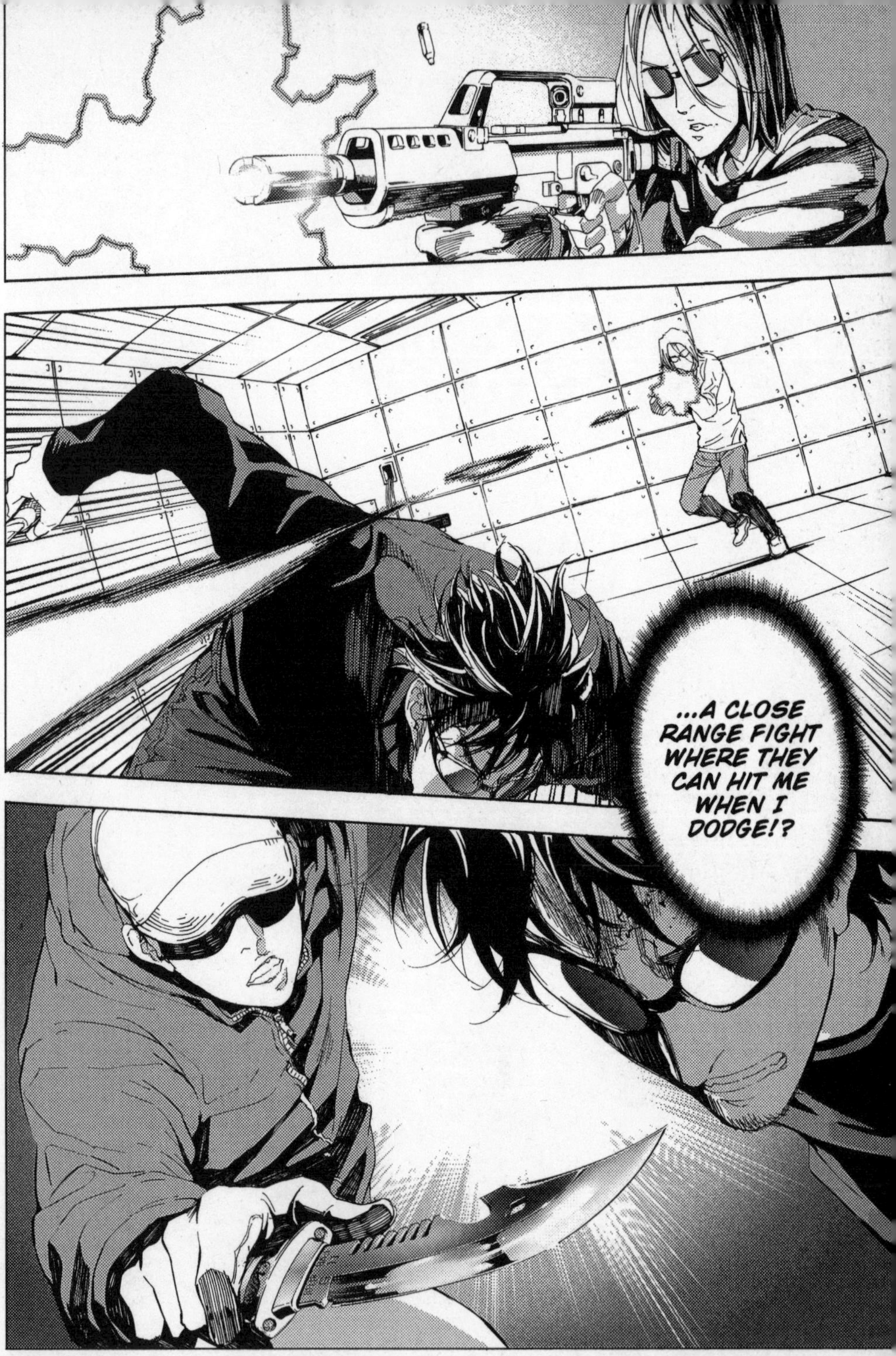
...A CLOSE RANGE FIGHT WHERE THEY CAN HIT ME WHEN I DODGE!?

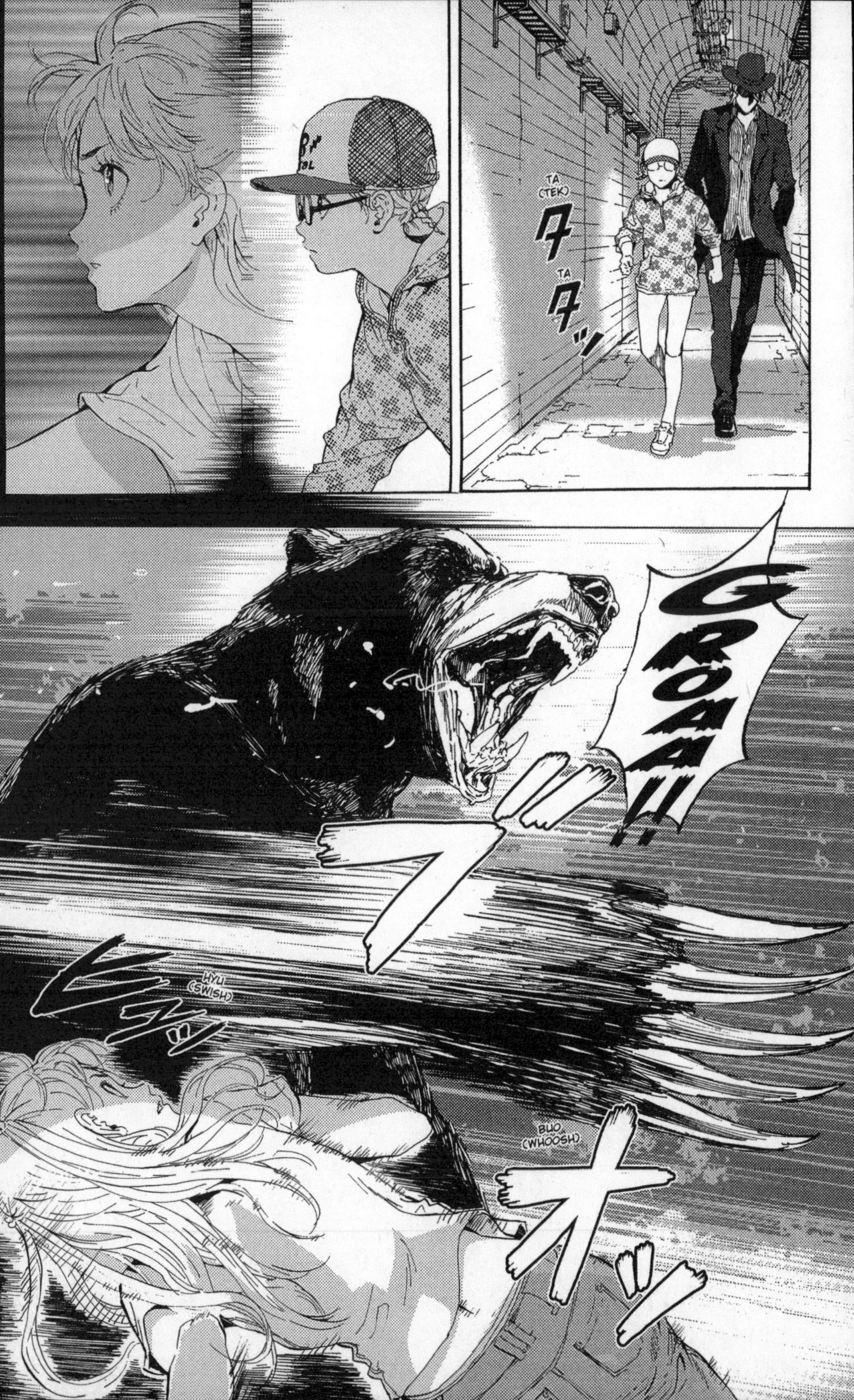
TA (TEK)
TA
GROAAH!!
BUO (WHOOSH)
HYU (SWISH)

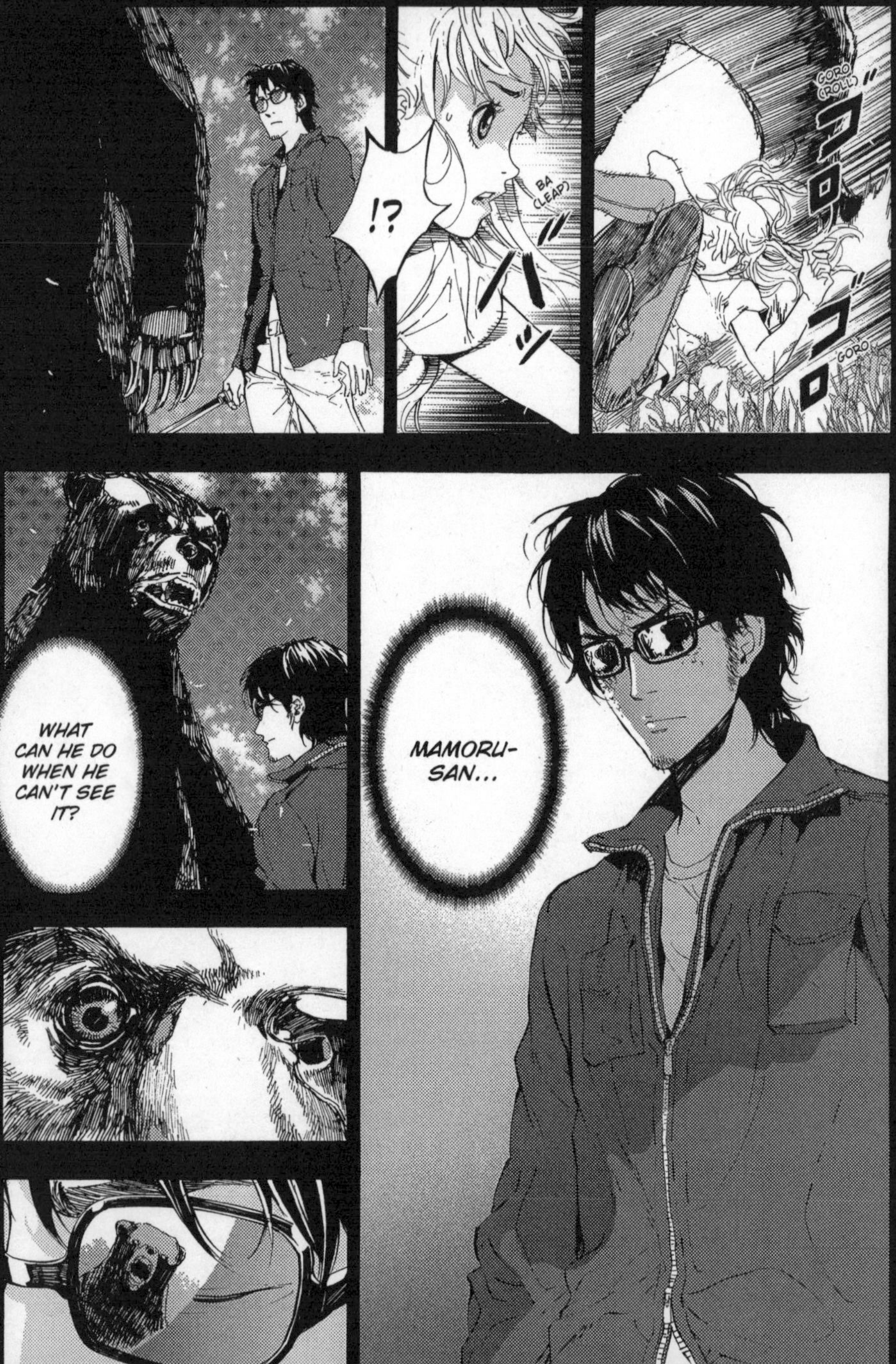
GORO (ROLL)
ゴロ
ゴロ
GORO
!?
BA (LEAP)
バッ
MAMORU-SAN...
WHAT CAN HE DO WHEN HE CAN'T SEE IT?

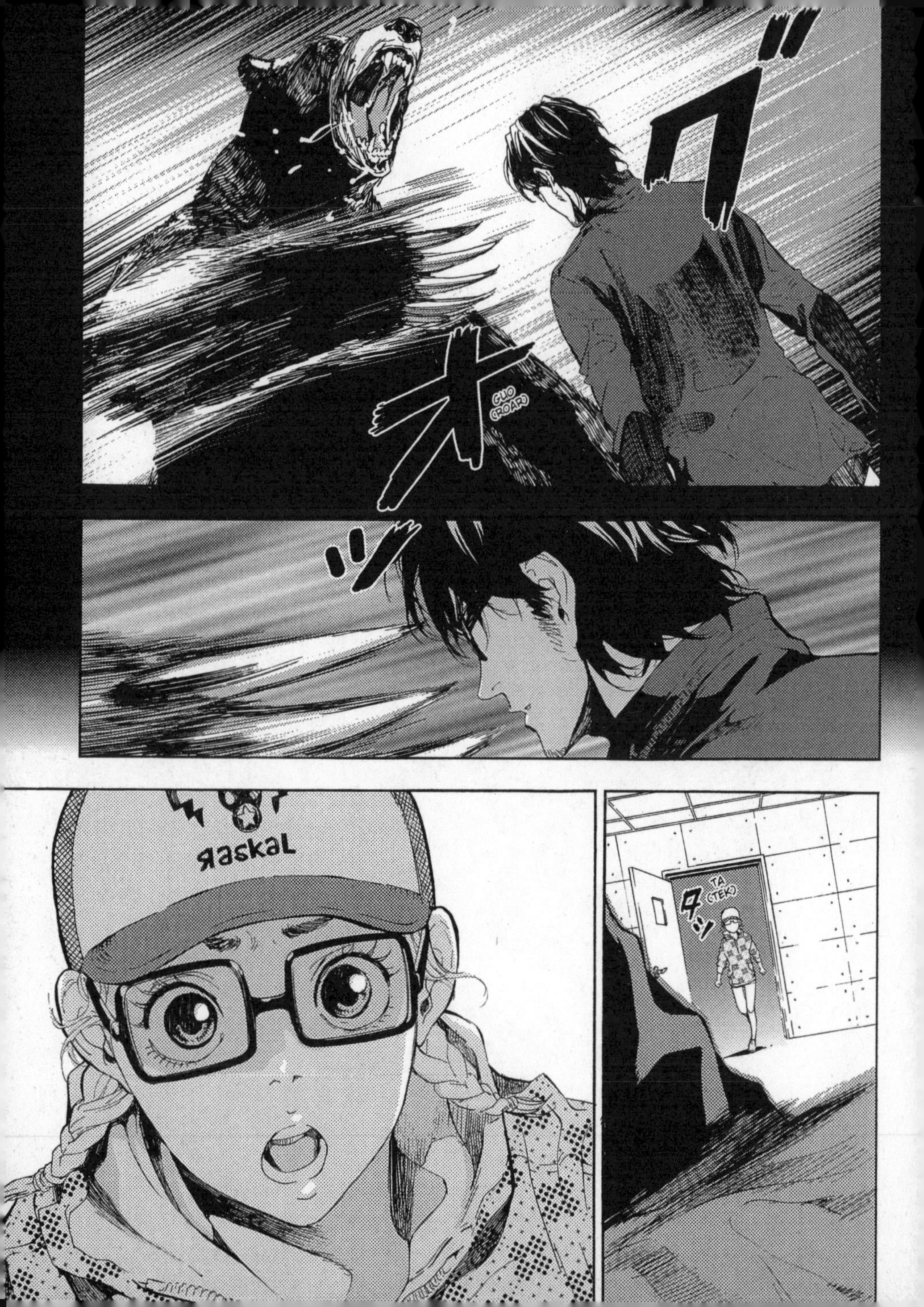
GUO (ROAR)
TA (TEK)
Raskal

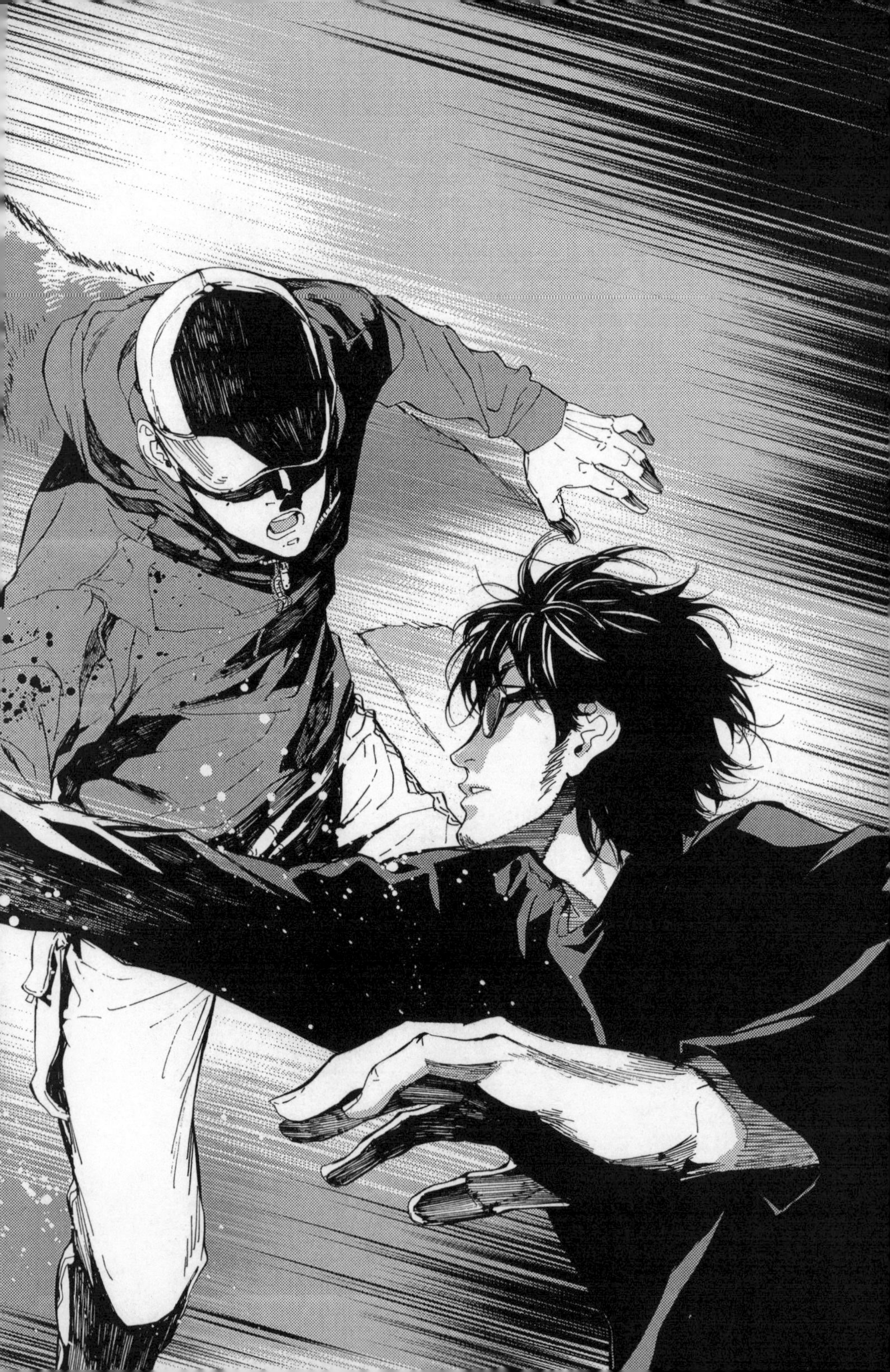

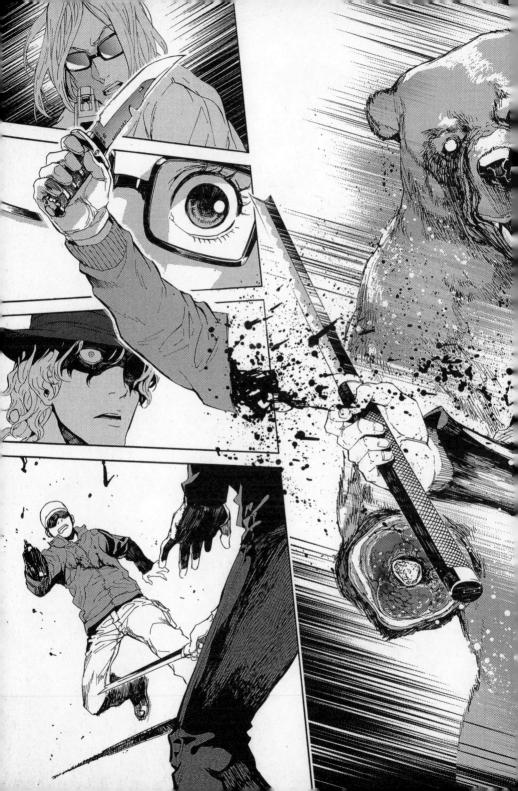

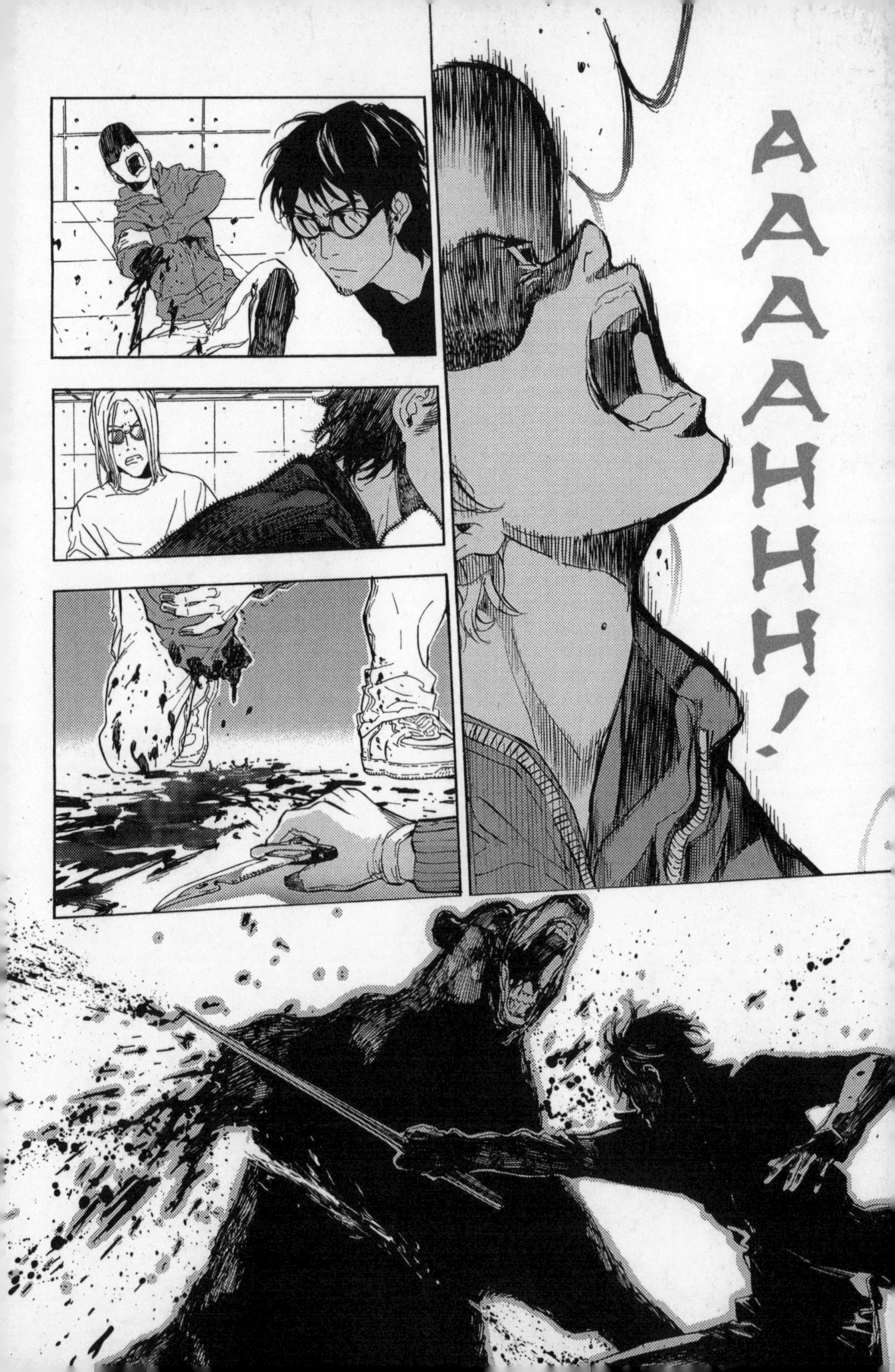
AAAAHHH!

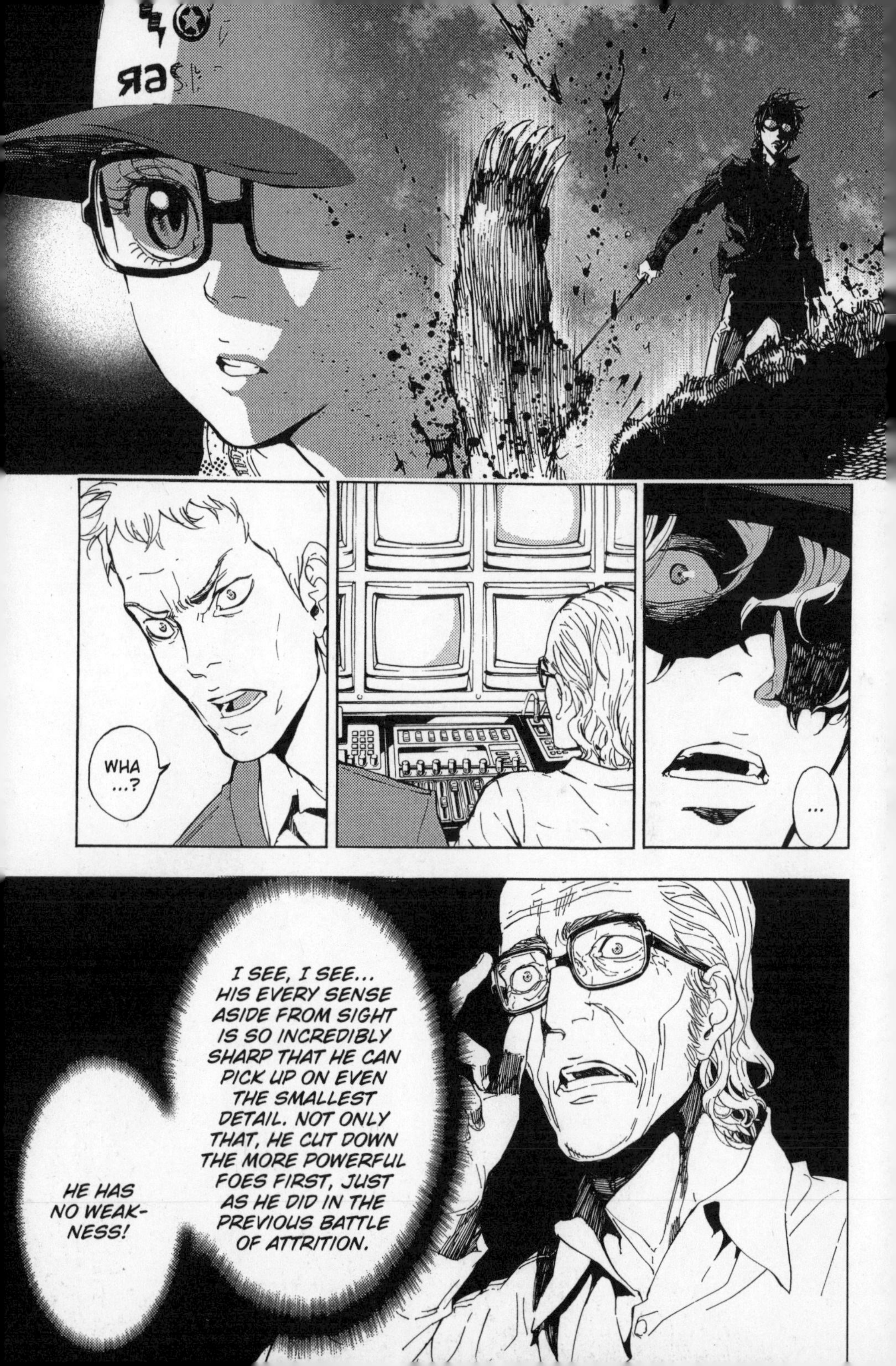
...
WHA ...?
I SEE, I SEE... HIS EVERY SENSE ASIDE FROM SIGHT IS SO INCREDIBLY SHARP THAT HE CAN PICK UP ON EVEN THE SMALLEST DETAIL. NOT ONLY THAT, HE CUT DOWN THE MORE POWERFUL FOES FIRST, JUST AS HE DID IN THE PREVIOUS BATTLE OF ATTRITION.
HE HAS NO WEAK-NESS!

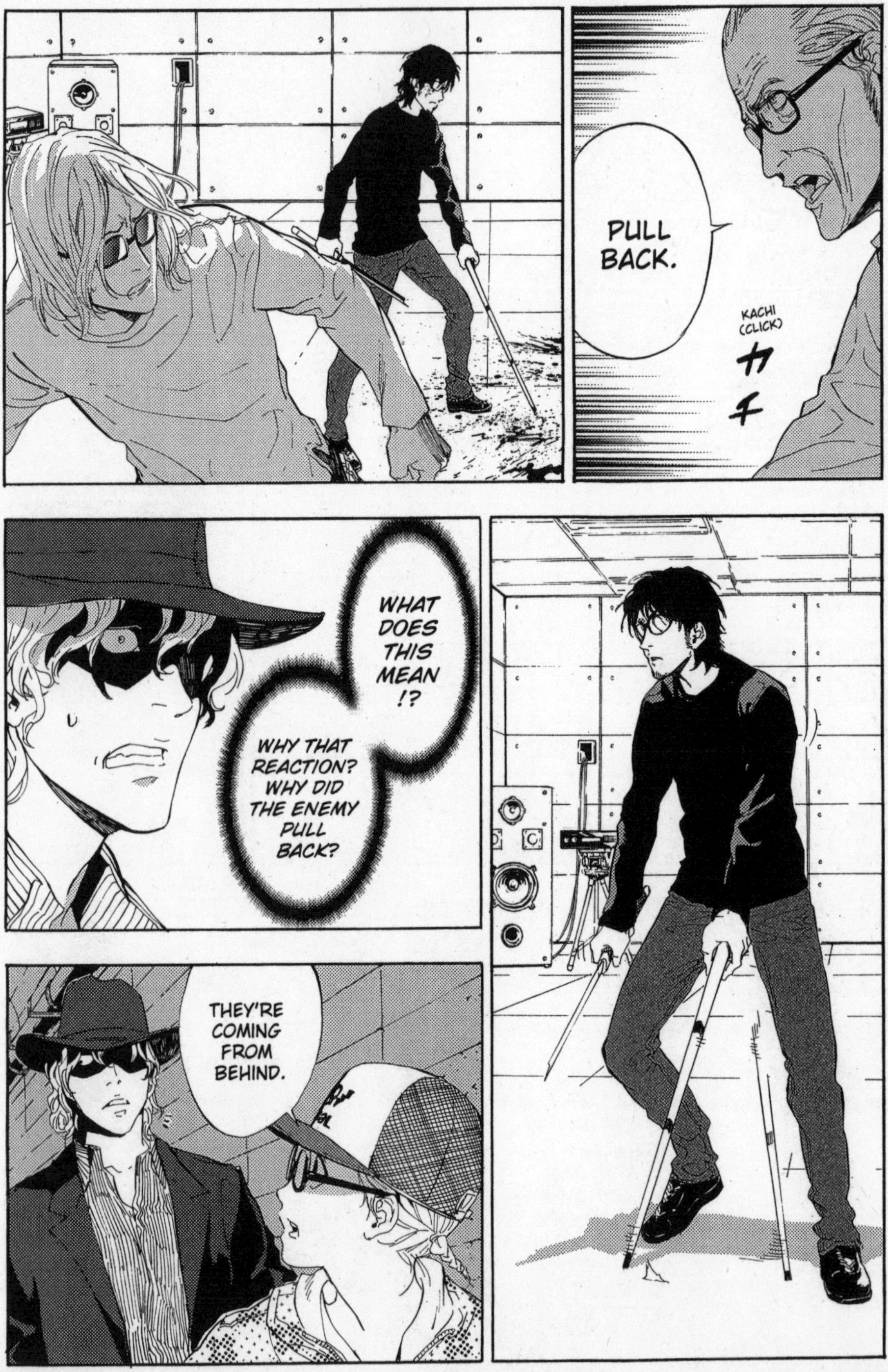
PULL BACK.
KACHI (CLICK)
カチ
WHAT DOES THIS MEAN !?
WHY THAT REACTION? WHY DID THE ENEMY PULL BACK?
THEY'RE COMING FROM BEHIND.

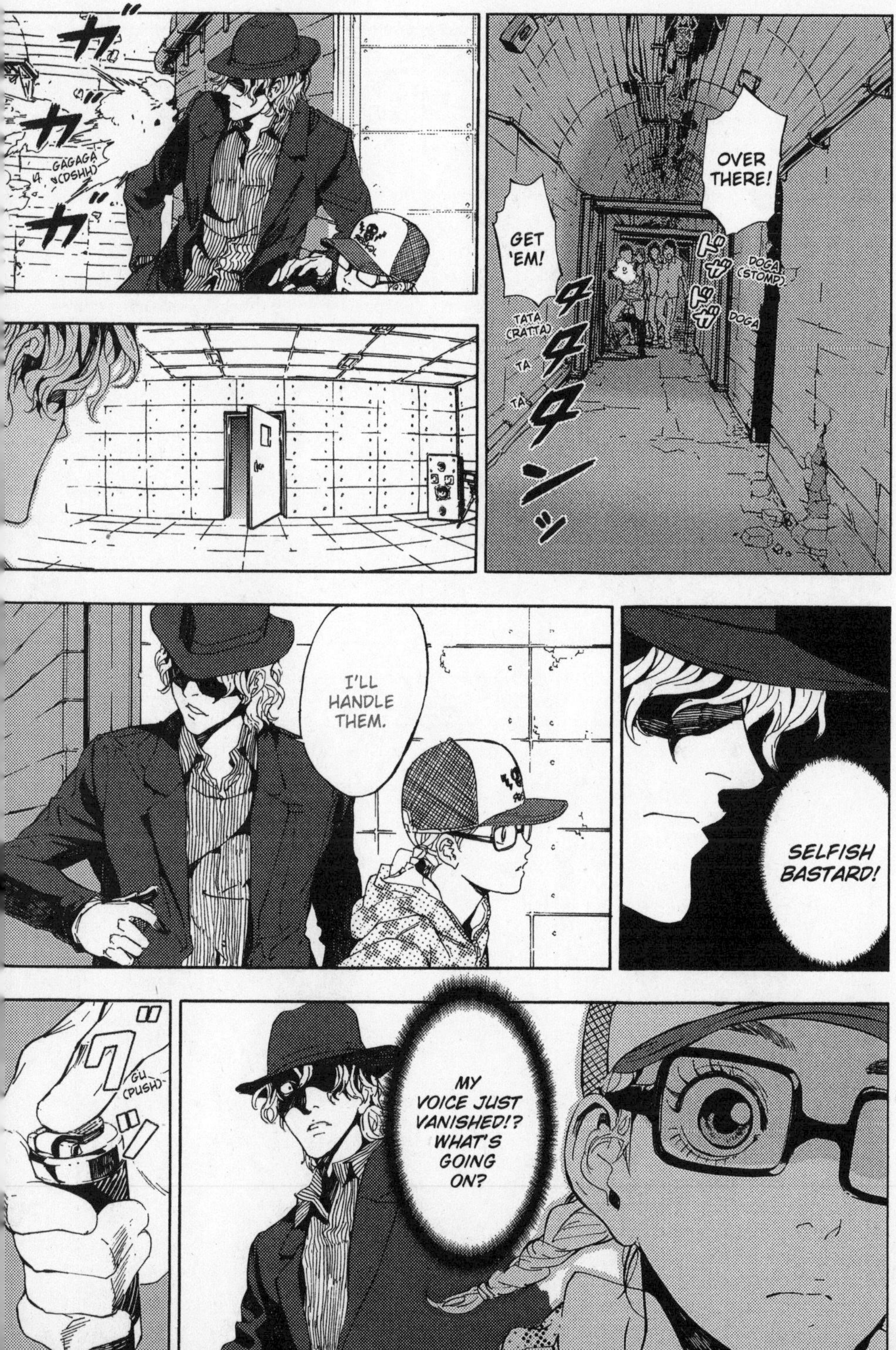
OVER THERE!
GET 'EM!
DOGA (STOMP)
DOGA
TATA (RATTA)
TA
TA
GAGAGA (DSHH)
SELFISH BASTARD!
I'LL HANDLE THEM.
MY VOICE JUST VANISHED!? WHAT'S GOING ON?
GU (PUSH)

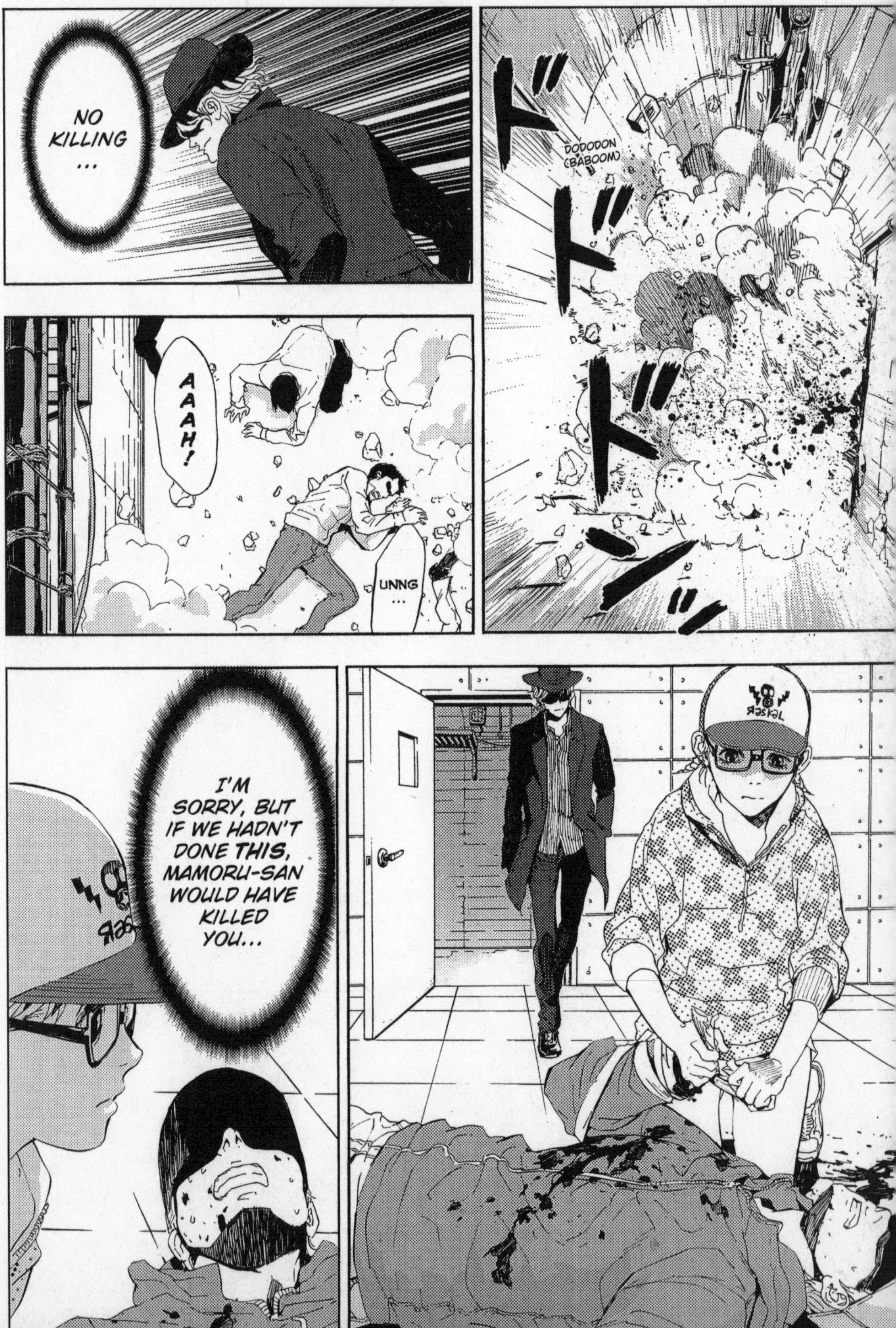
DODODON (BABOOM)
NO KILLING ...
AAAH!
UNNG ...
I'M SORRY, BUT IF WE HADN'T DONE THIS, MAMORU-SAN WOULD HAVE KILLED YOU...

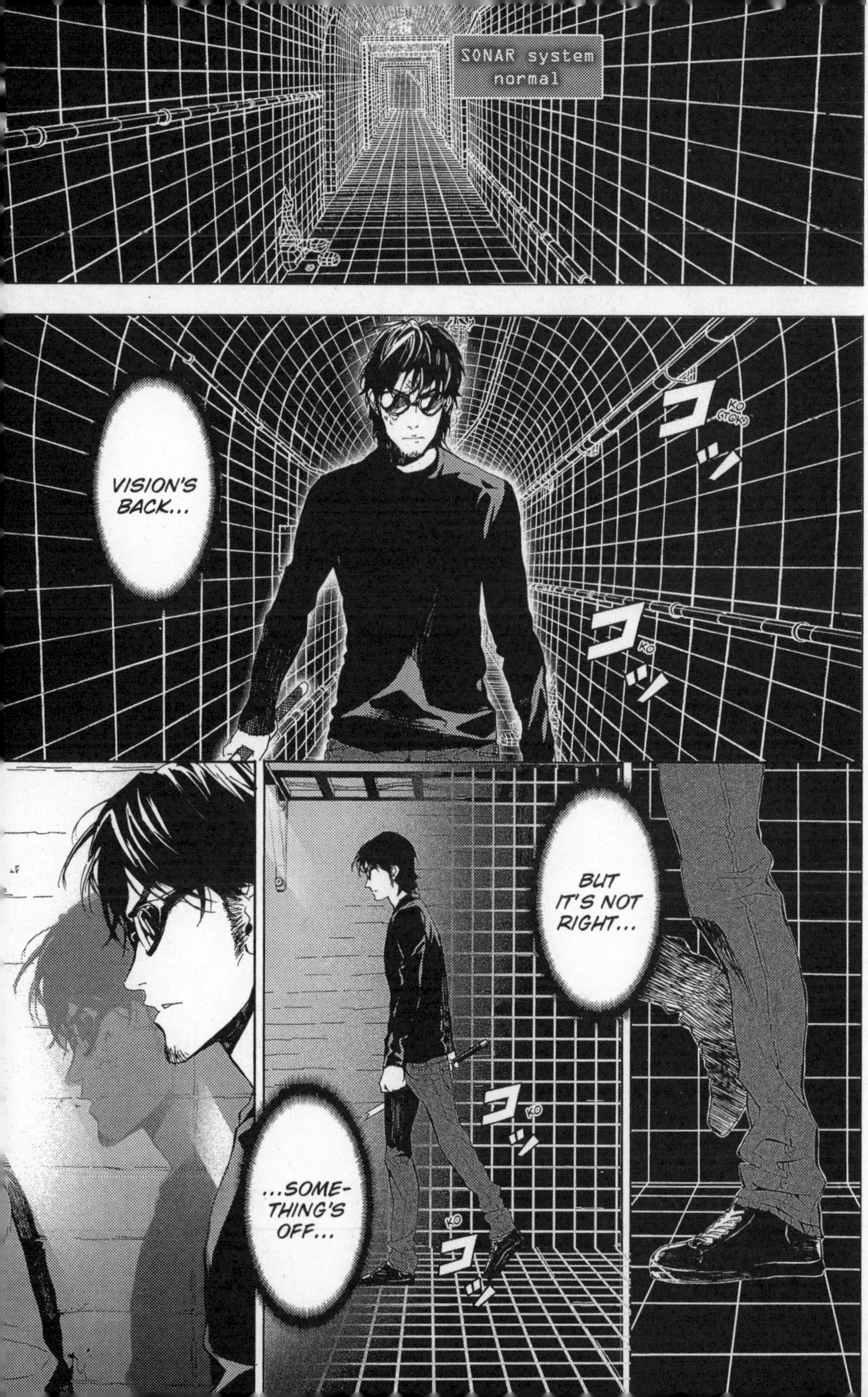
SONAR system normal
KO (STOK)
VISION'S BACK...
KO
BUT IT'S NOT RIGHT...
KO
...SOME-THING'S OFF...
KO

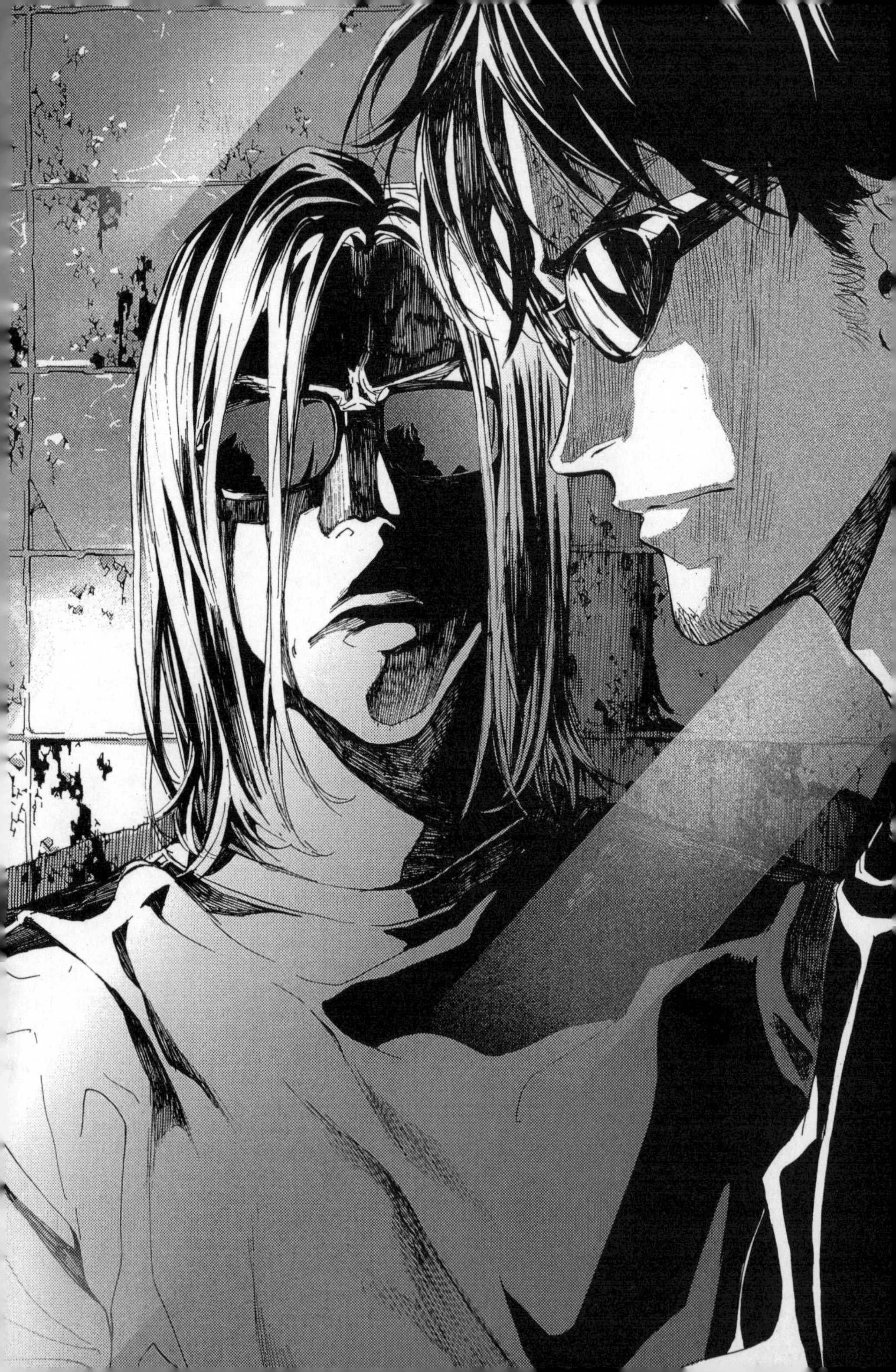

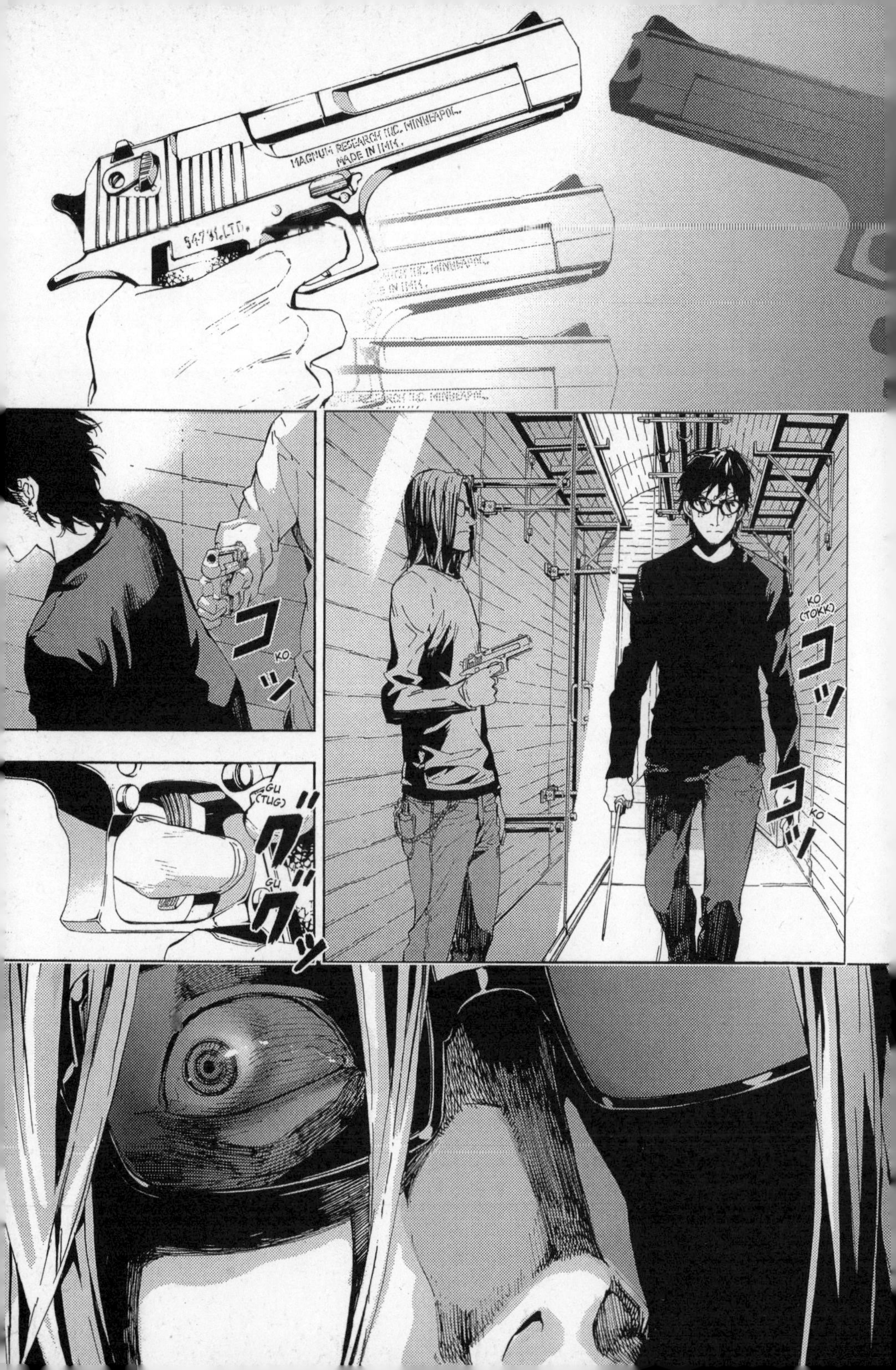

KO (TOKK)
コッ
コッ
KO
KO.
コッ
GU (TUG)
グ
GU.
グッ

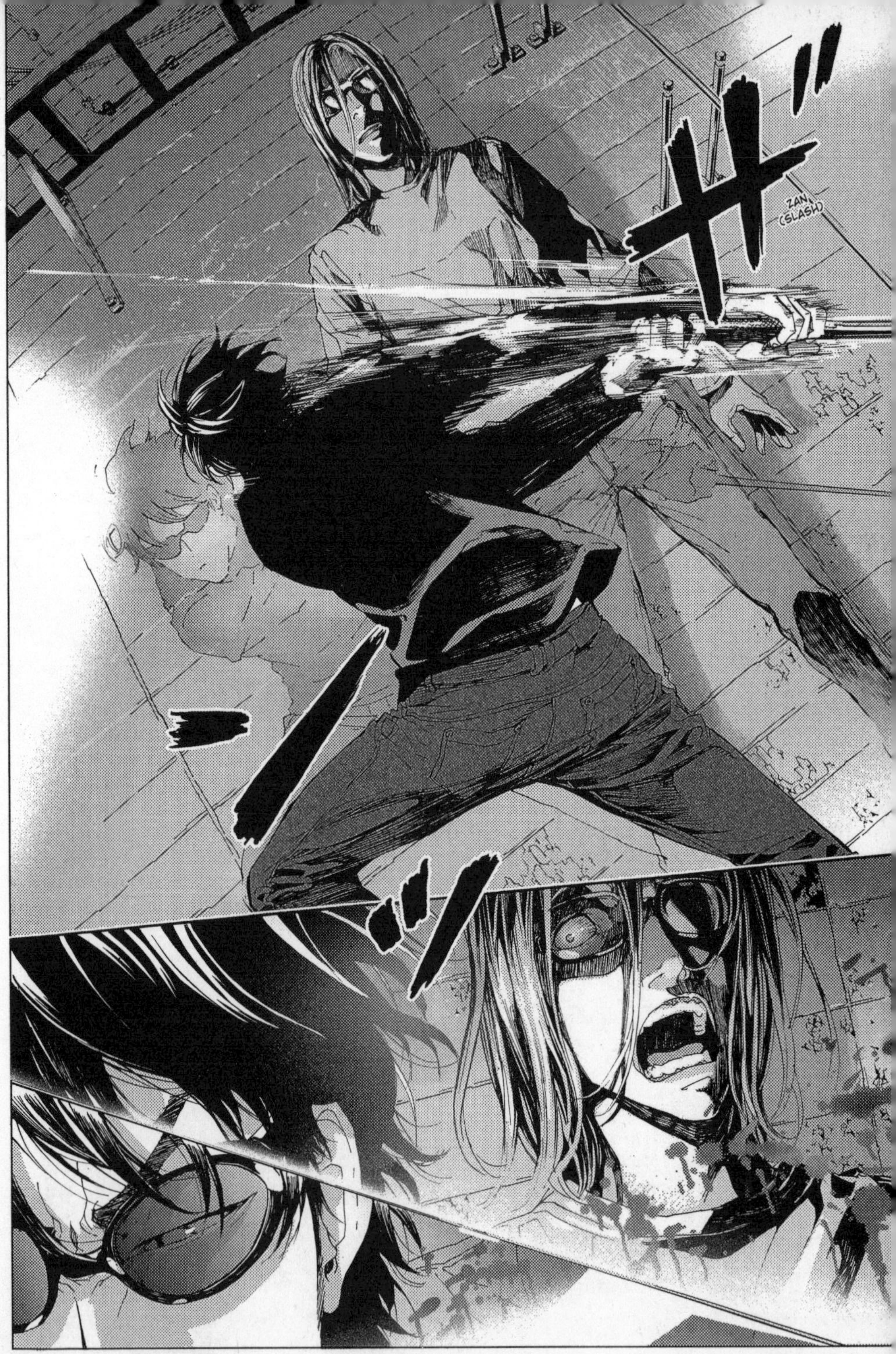
ZAN
(SLASH)

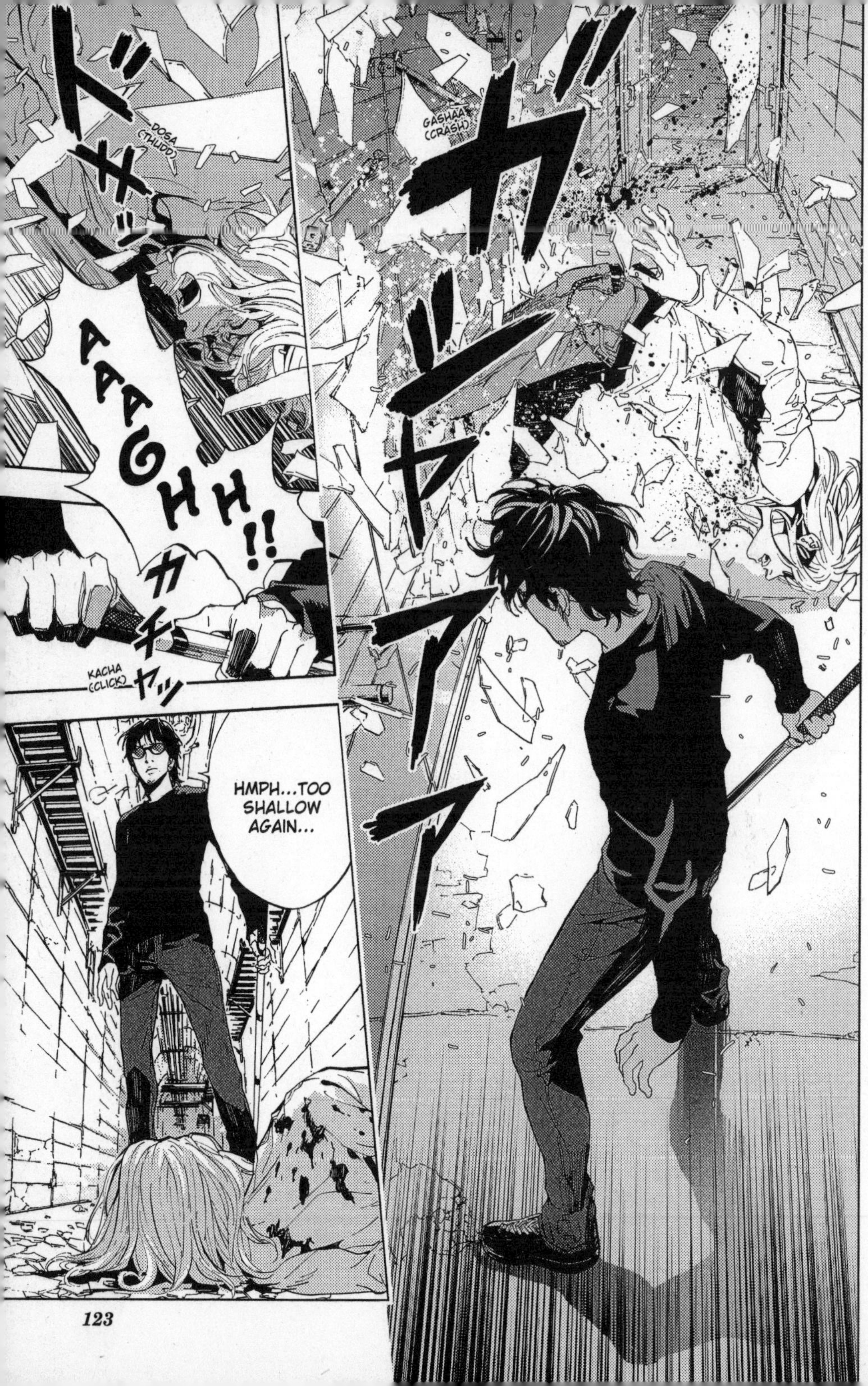

GASHAA (CRASH)
DOSA (THUDD)
AAAGHH!!
KACHA (CLICK)
HMPH...TOO SHALLOW AGAIN...

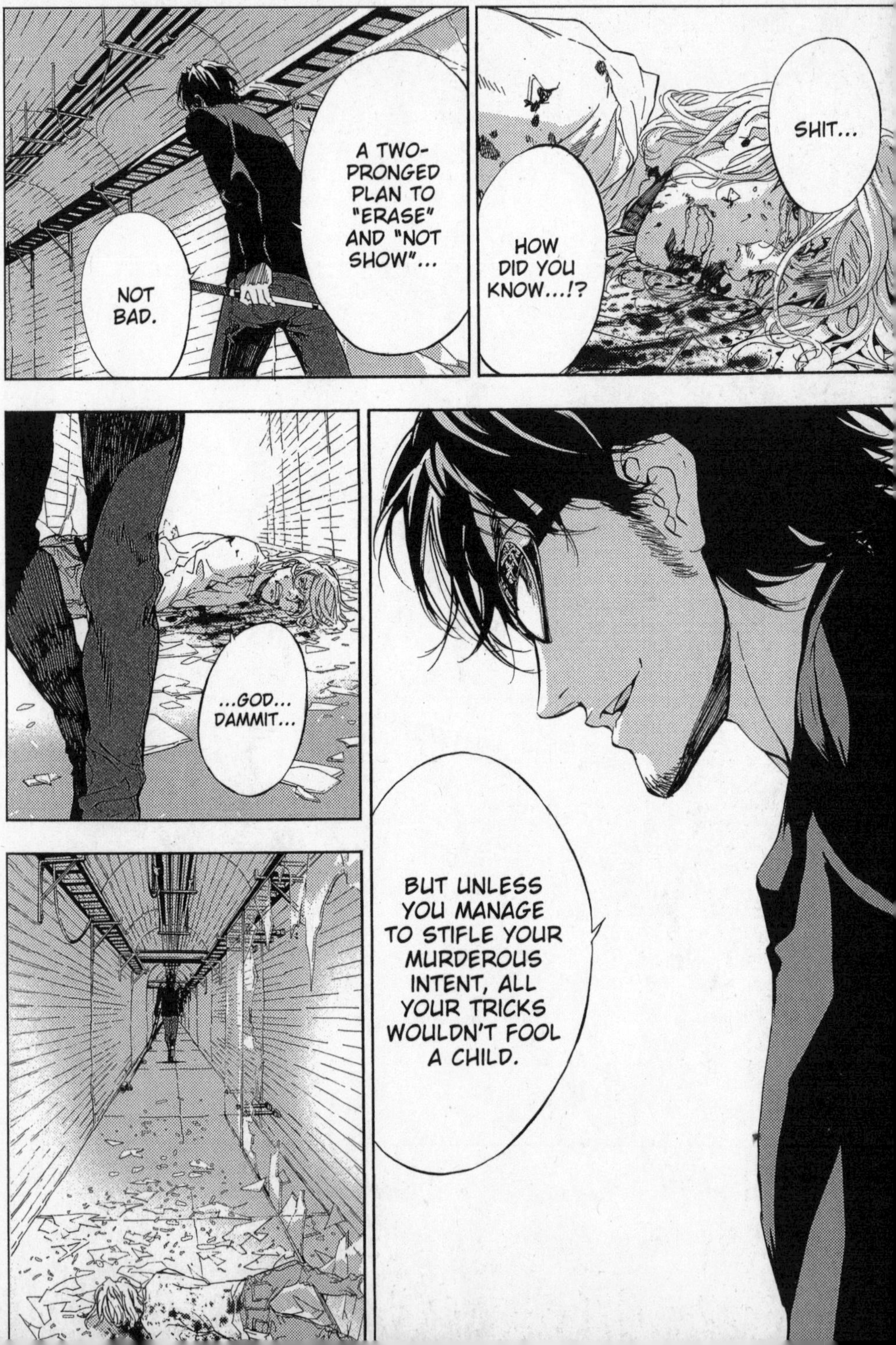
SHIT...
HOW DID YOU KNOW...!?
A TWO-PRONGED PLAN TO "ERASE" AND "NOT SHOW"...
NOT BAD.
BUT UNLESS YOU MANAGE TO STIFLE YOUR MURDEROUS INTENT, ALL YOUR TRICKS WOULDN'T FOOL A CHILD.
...GOD... DAMMIT...

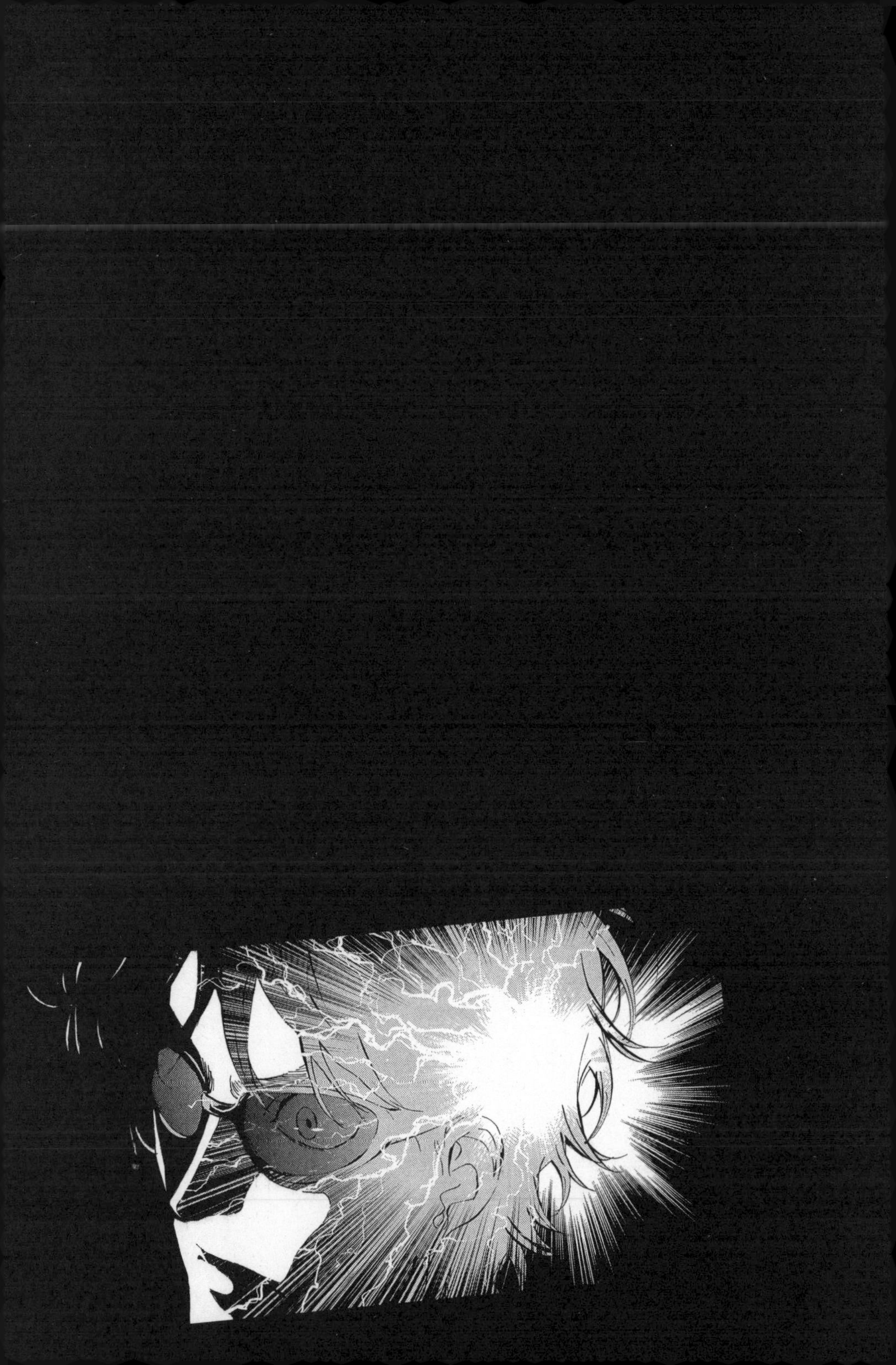

Until Death do us Part

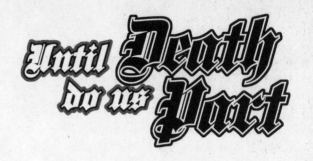

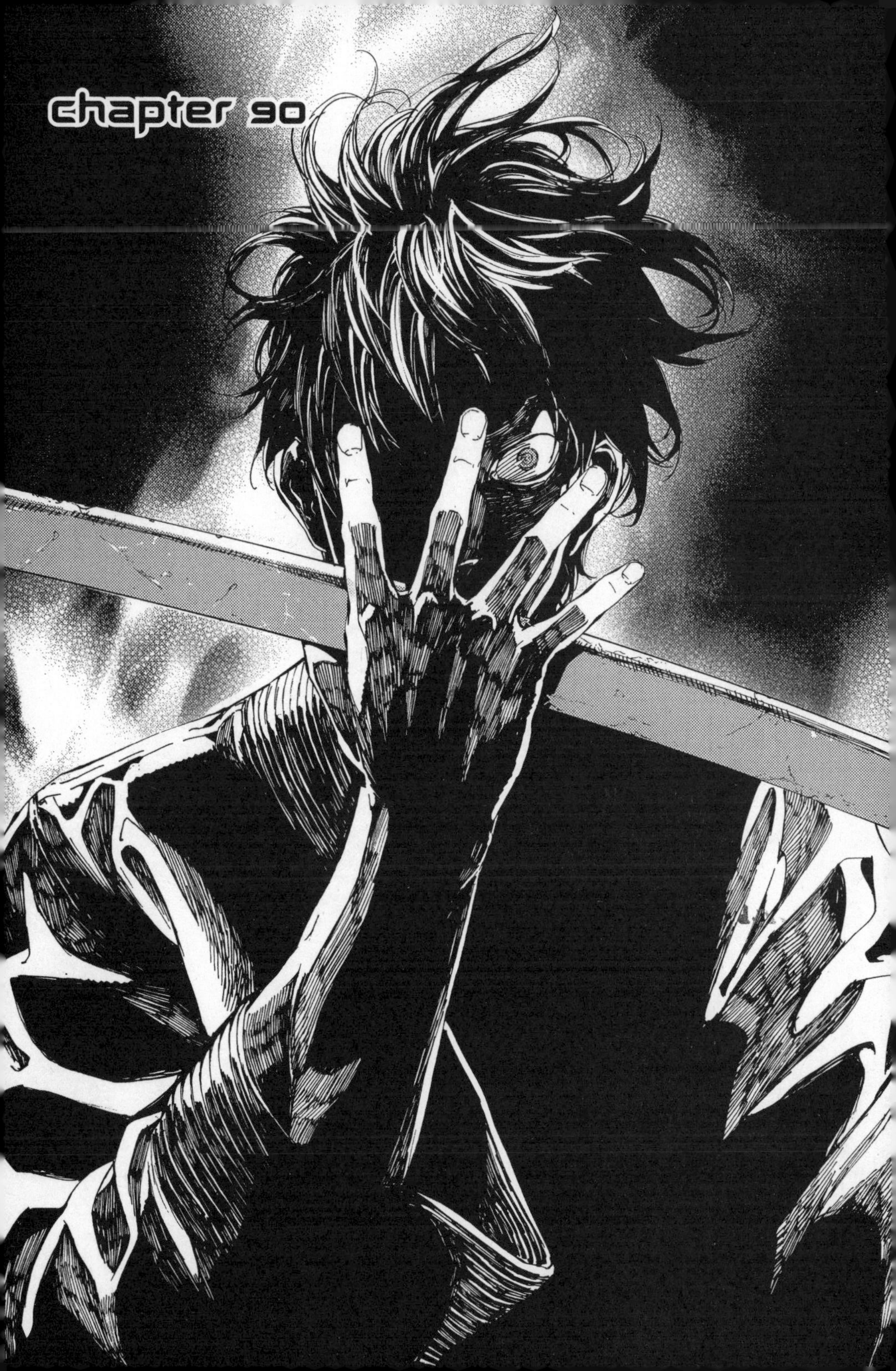
chapter 90

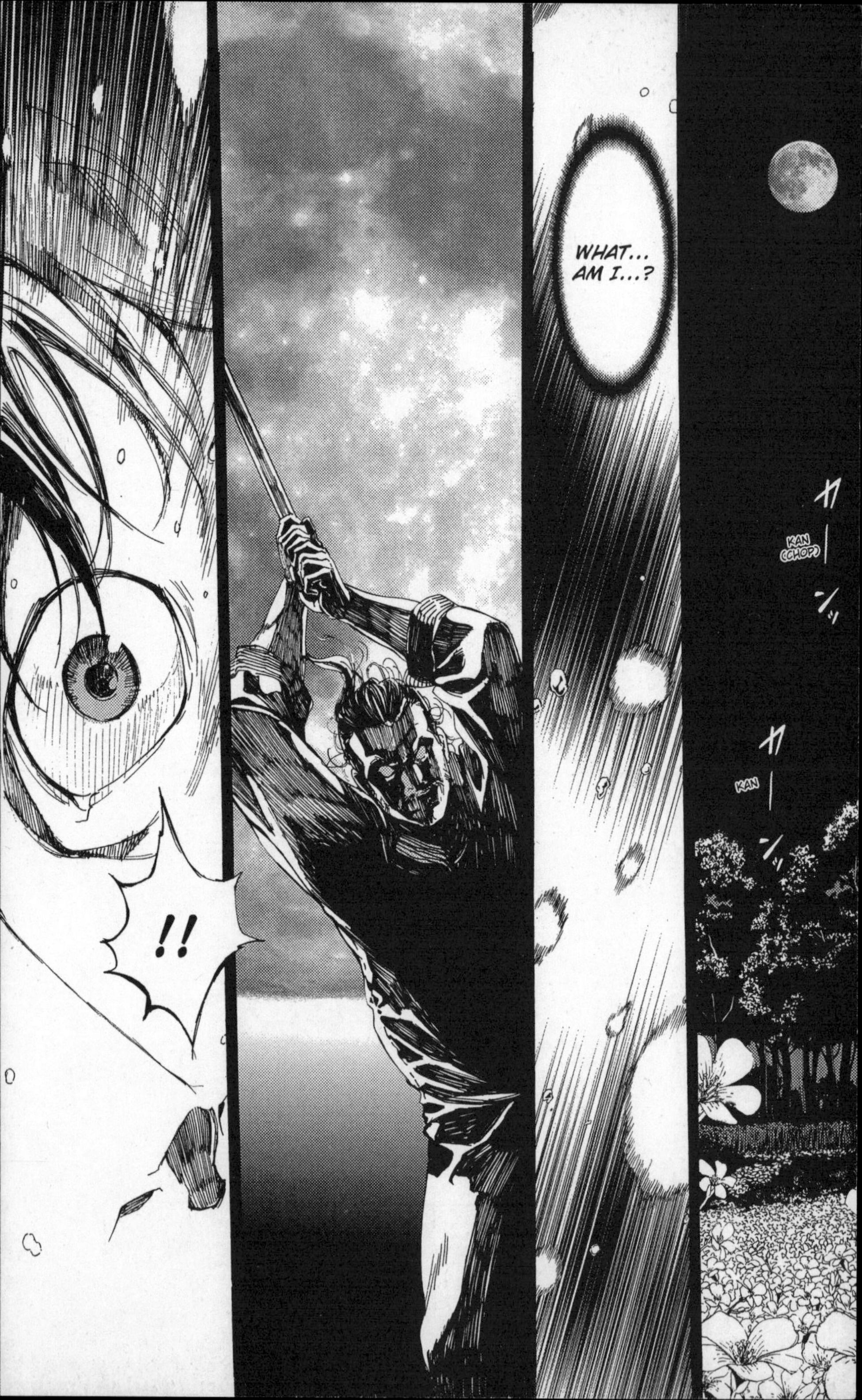
KAN (CHOP)
KAN
WHAT... AM I...?
!!

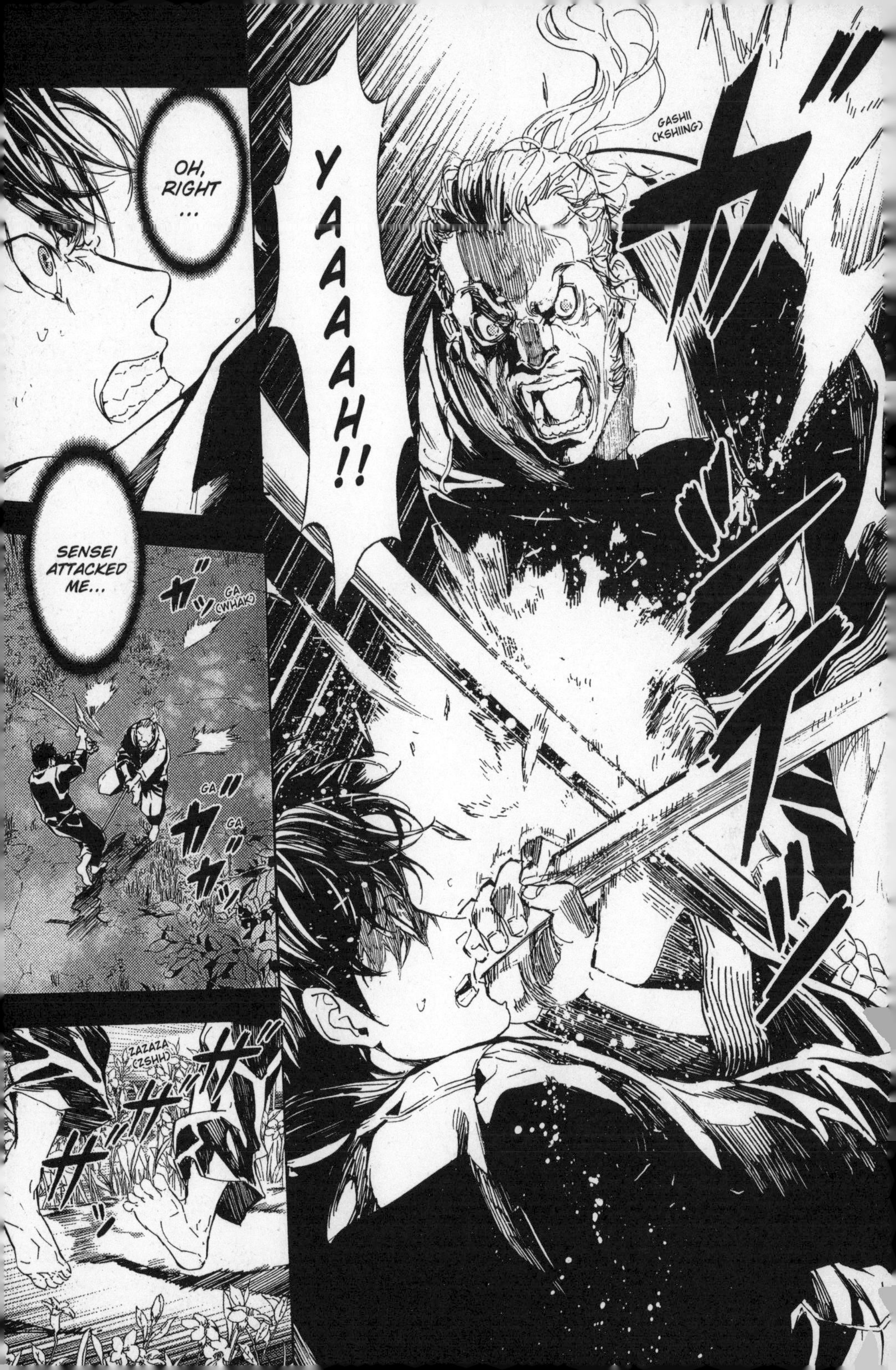
GASHII (KSHIING)
YAAAAAH!!
OH, RIGHT ...
SENSEI ATTACKED ME...
GA (WHAK)
GA
GA
ZAZAZA (ZSHH)

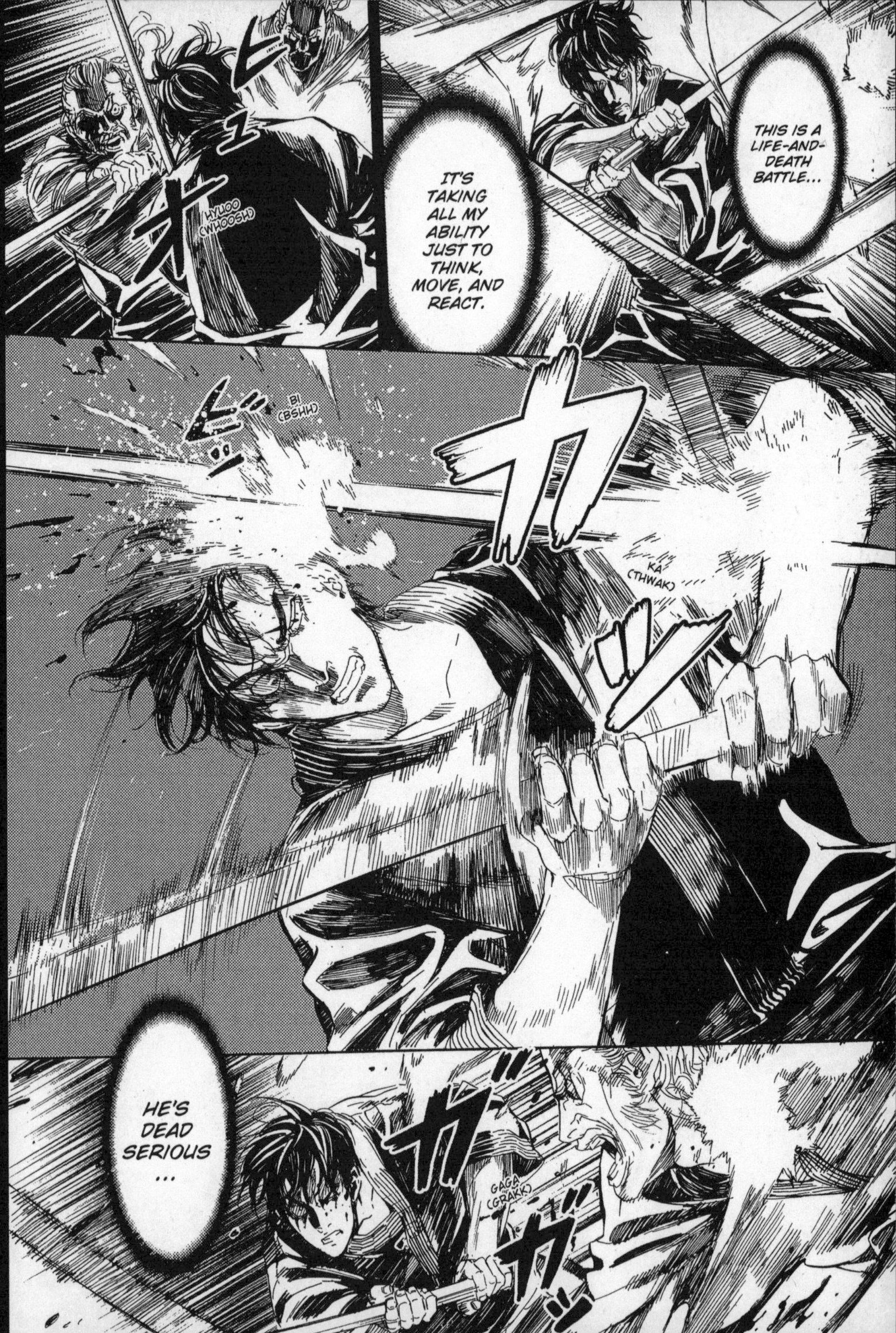
THIS IS A LIFE-AND-DEATH BATTLE...
IT'S TAKING ALL MY ABILITY JUST TO THINK, MOVE, AND REACT.
HYUOO (WHOOSH)
KA (THWAK)
BI (BSHH)
GAGA (GRAKK)
HE'S DEAD SERIOUS ...

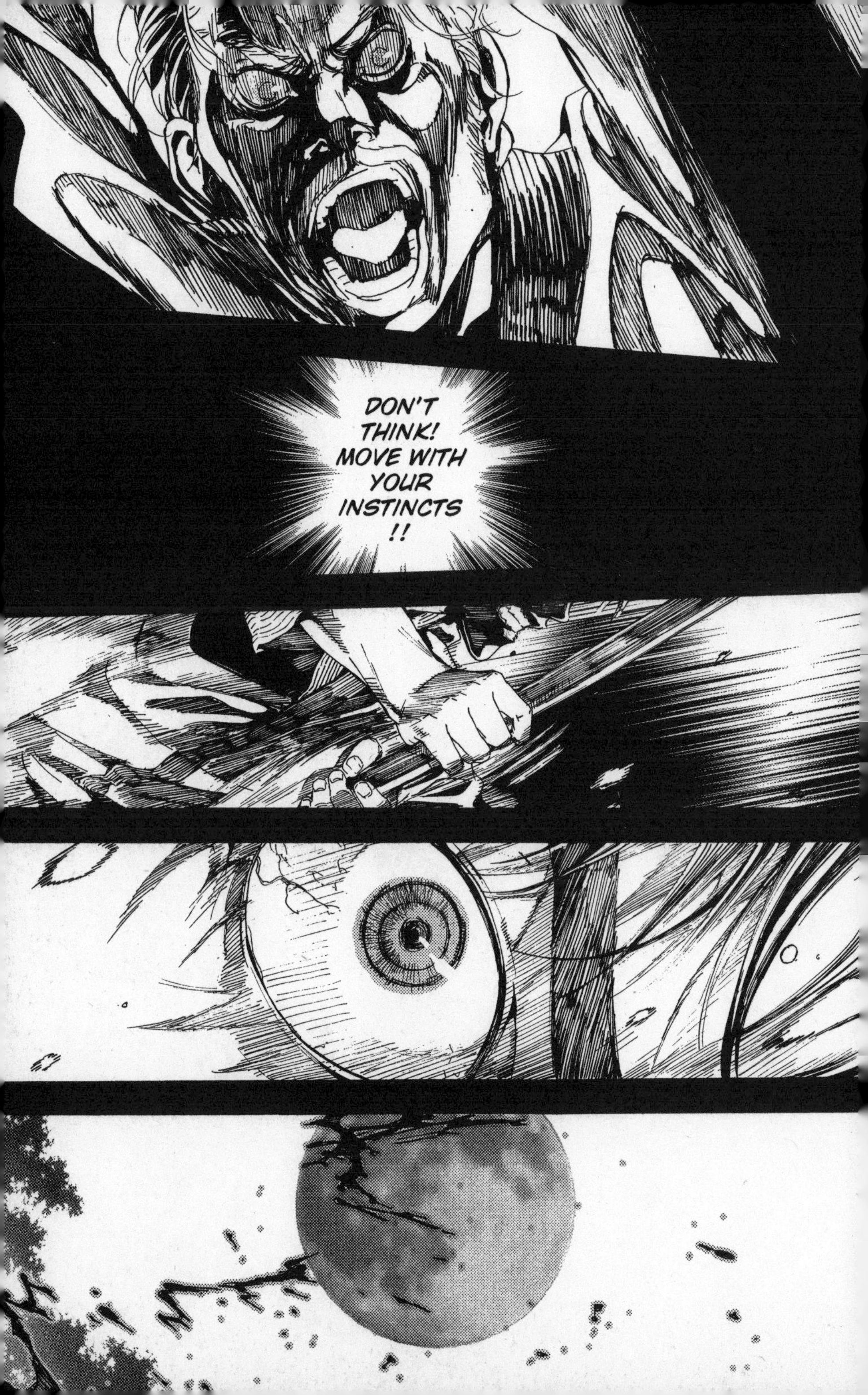
DON'T THINK! MOVE WITH YOUR INSTINCTS !!

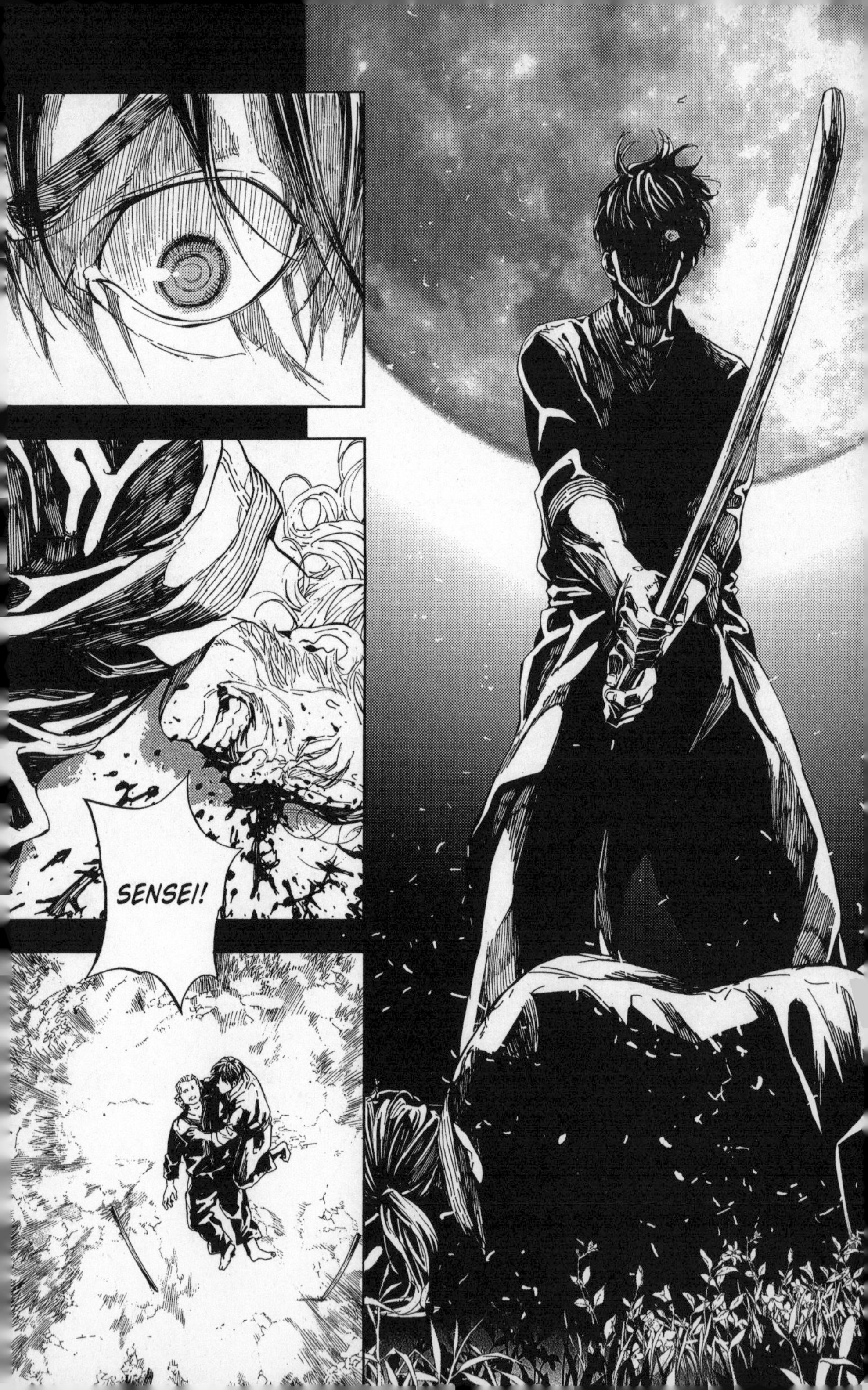
SENSEI!

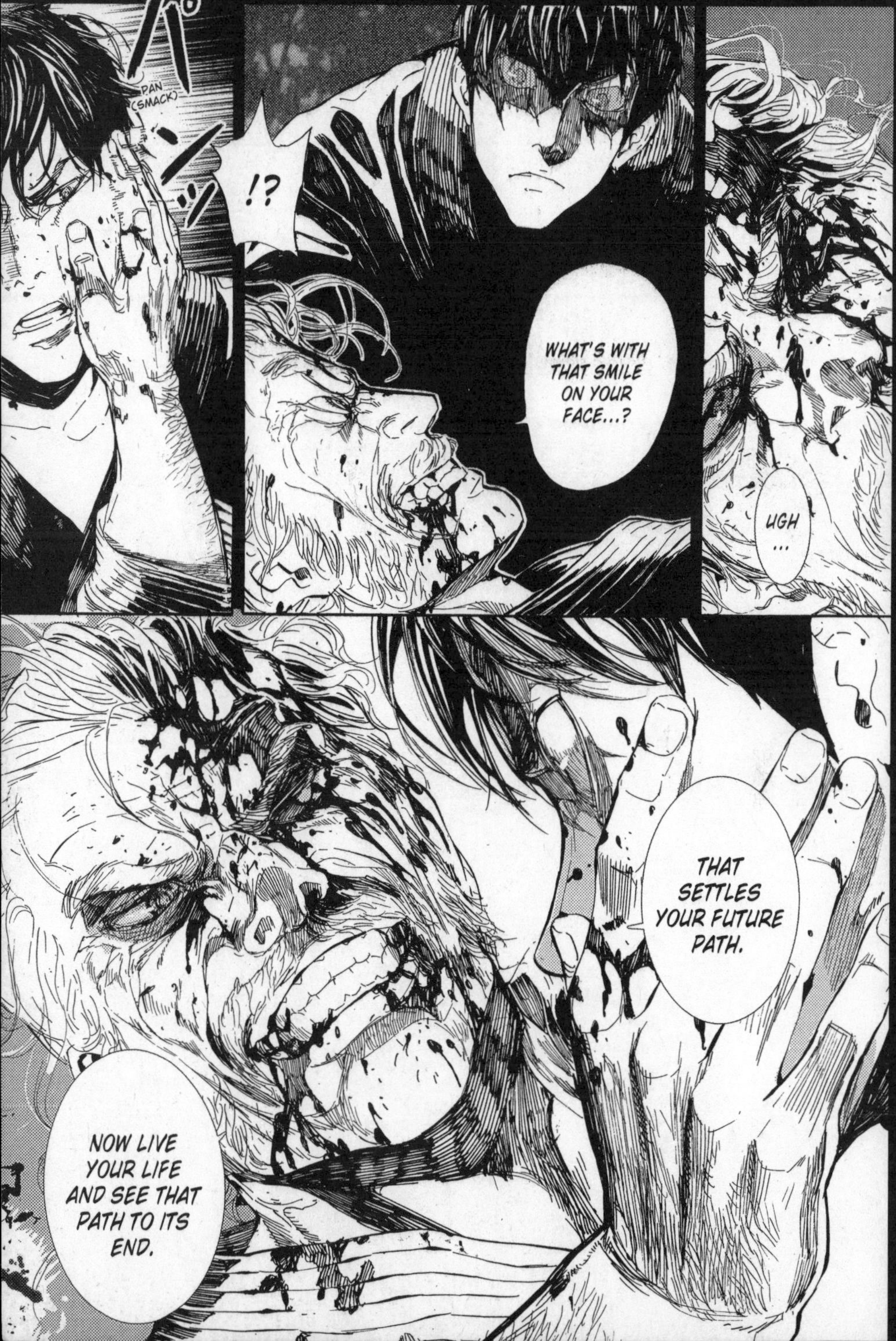
UGH ...
!?
WHAT'S WITH THAT SMILE ON YOUR FACE...?
PAN (SMACK)
THAT SETTLES YOUR FUTURE PATH.
NOW LIVE YOUR LIFE AND SEE THAT PATH TO ITS END.

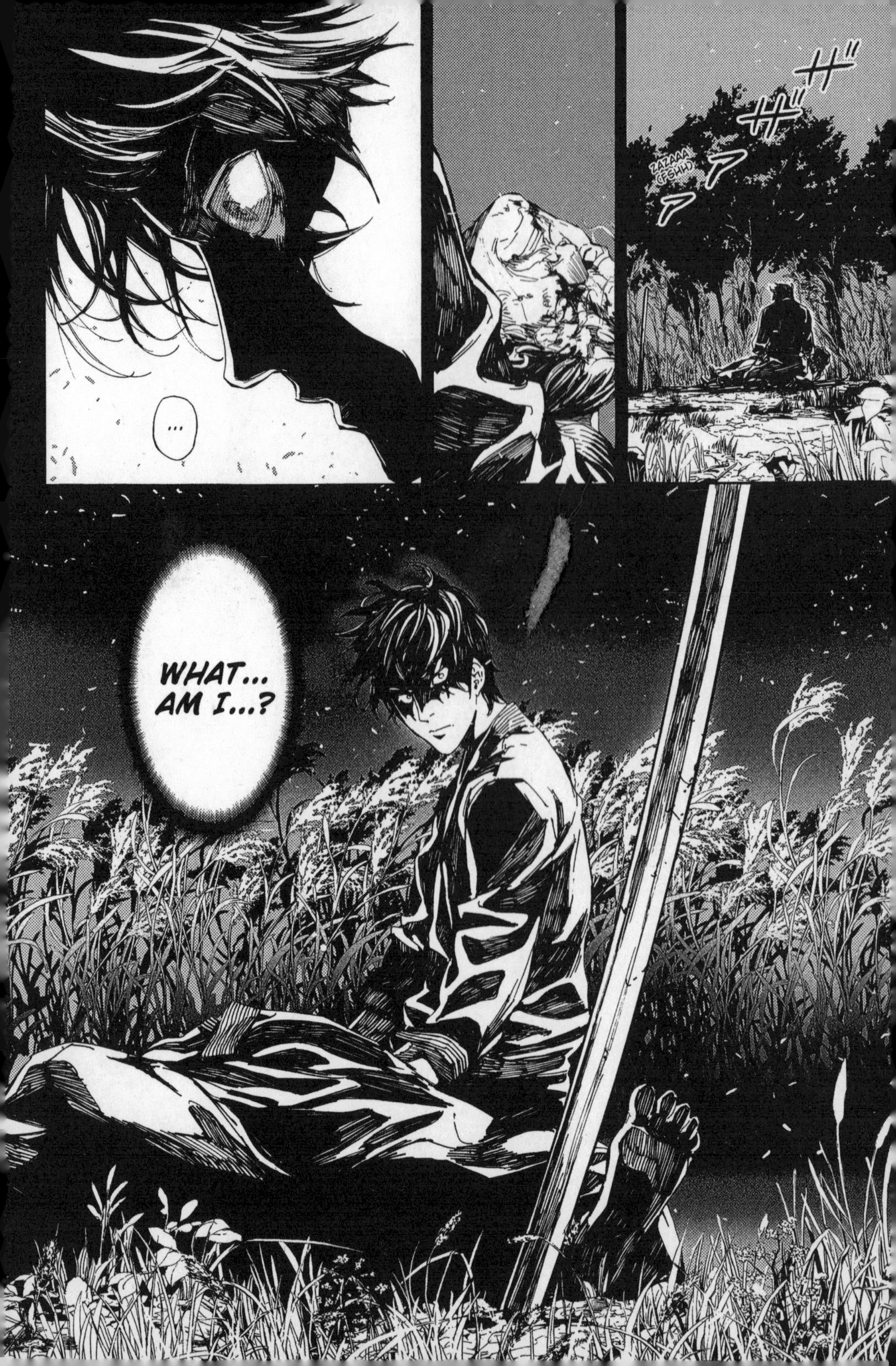

ZAZAAA (FSHH)
...
WHAT... AM I...?

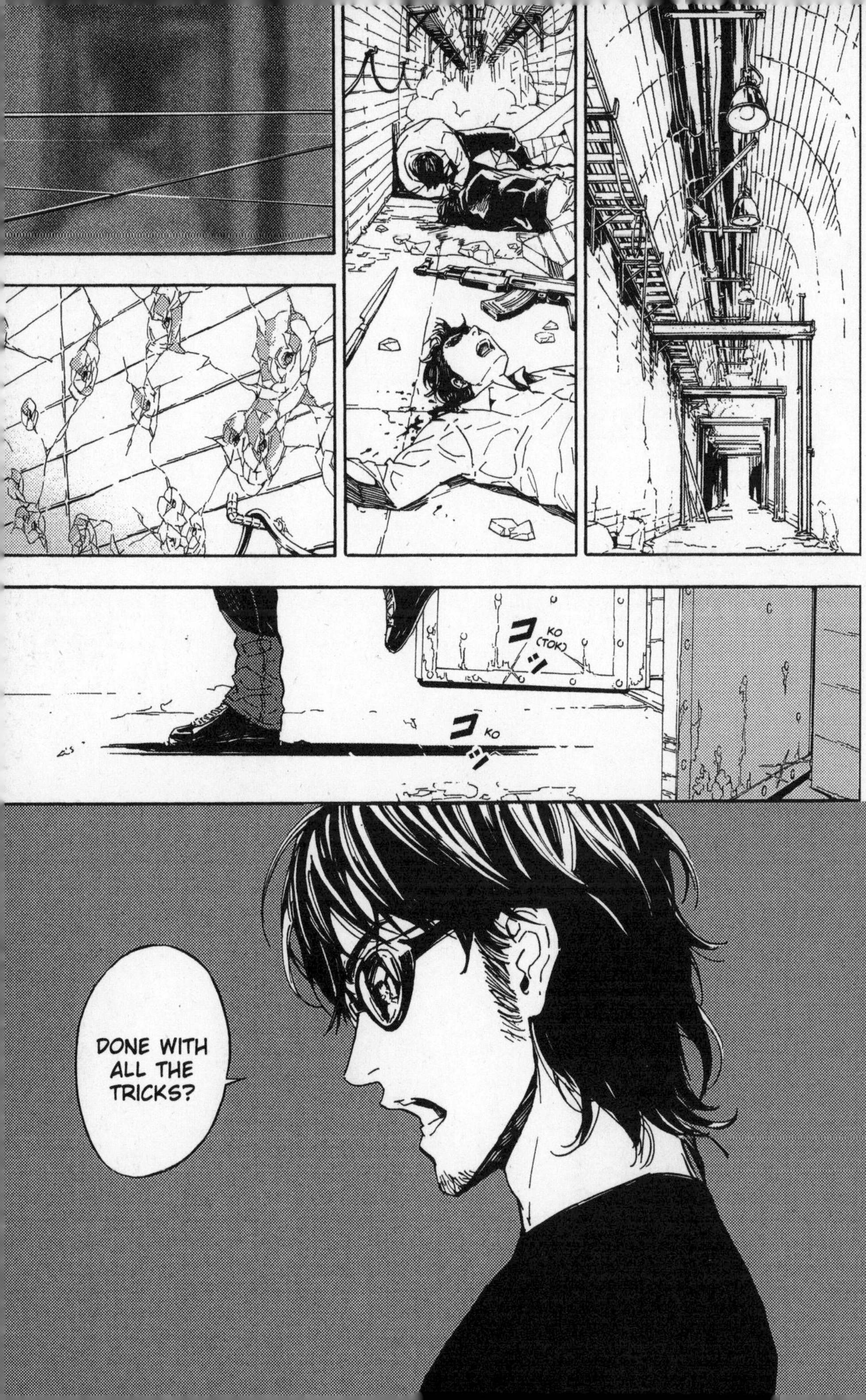
KO (TOK)
KO
DONE WITH ALL THE TRICKS?

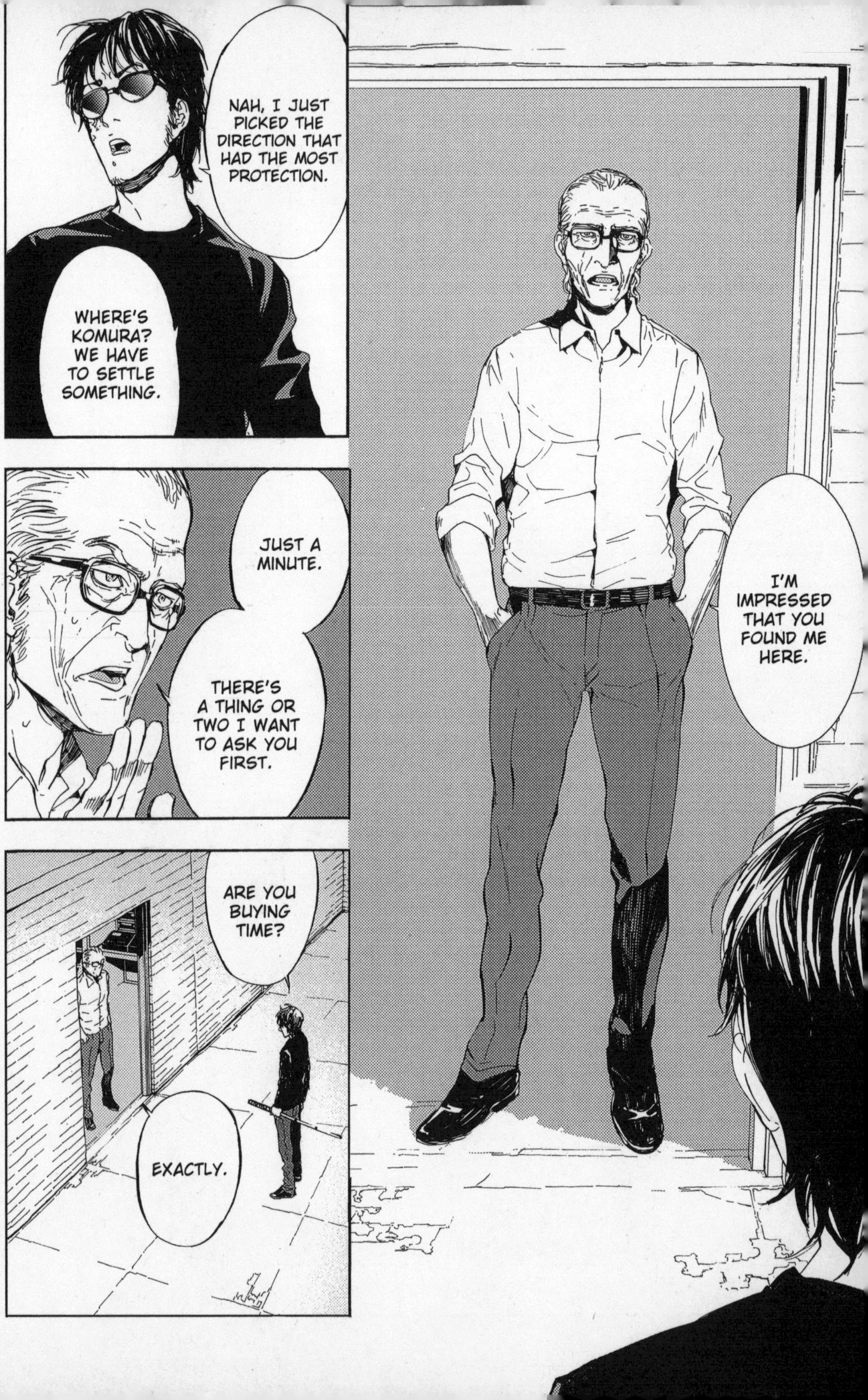
I'M IMPRESSED THAT YOU FOUND ME HERE.
NAH, I JUST PICKED THE DIRECTION THAT HAD THE MOST PROTECTION.
WHERE'S KOMURA? WE HAVE TO SETTLE SOMETHING.
JUST A MINUTE.
THERE'S A THING OR TWO I WANT TO ASK YOU FIRST.
ARE YOU BUYING TIME?
EXACTLY.

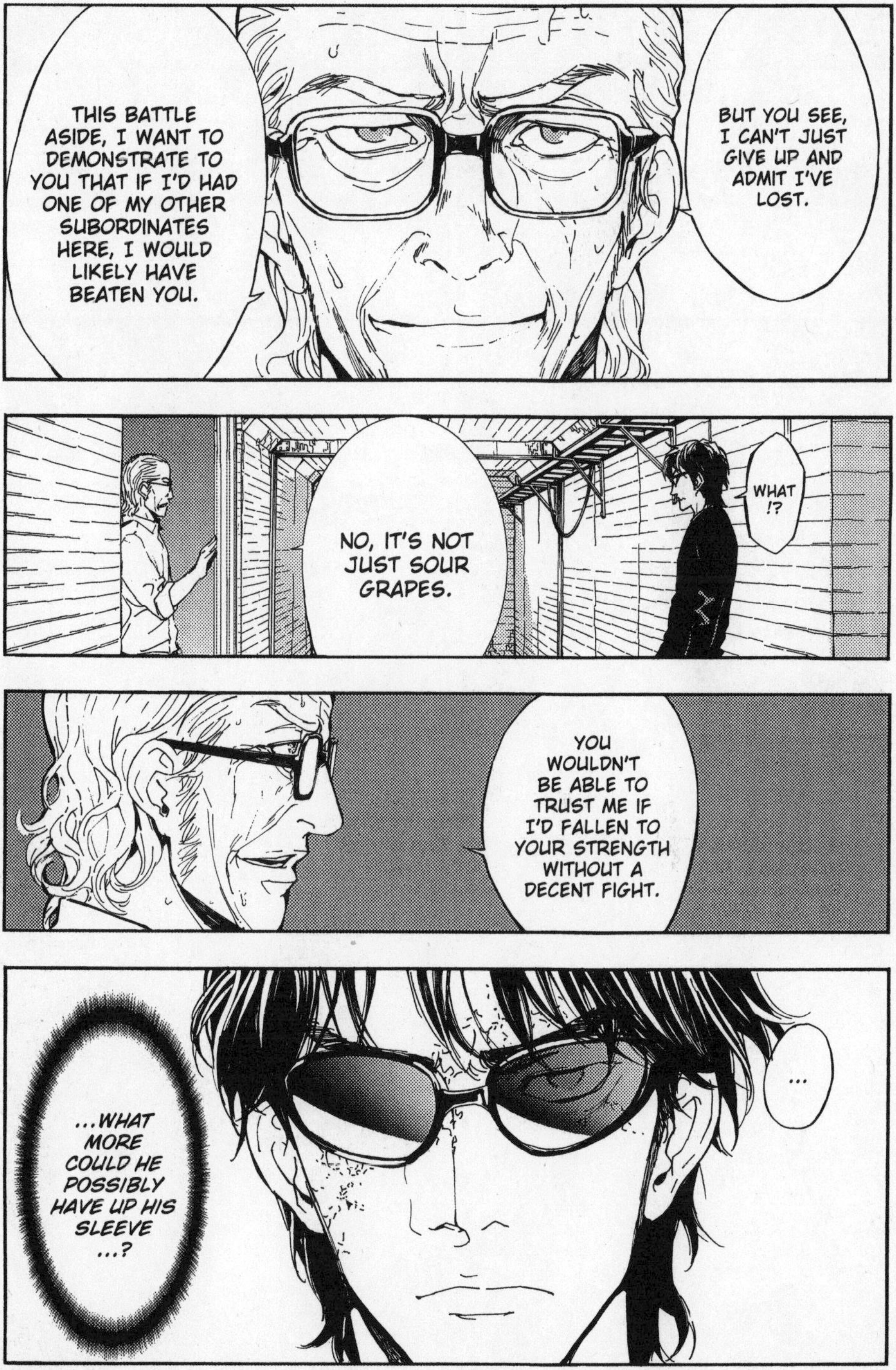
BUT YOU SEE, I CAN'T JUST GIVE UP AND ADMIT I'VE LOST.
THIS BATTLE ASIDE, I WANT TO DEMONSTRATE TO YOU THAT IF I'D HAD ONE OF MY OTHER SUBORDINATES HERE, I WOULD LIKELY HAVE BEATEN YOU.
WHAT !?
NO, IT'S NOT JUST SOUR GRAPES.
YOU WOULDN'T BE ABLE TO TRUST ME IF I'D FALLEN TO YOUR STRENGTH WITHOUT A DECENT FIGHT.
...
...WHAT MORE COULD HE POSSIBLY HAVE UP HIS SLEEVE ...?

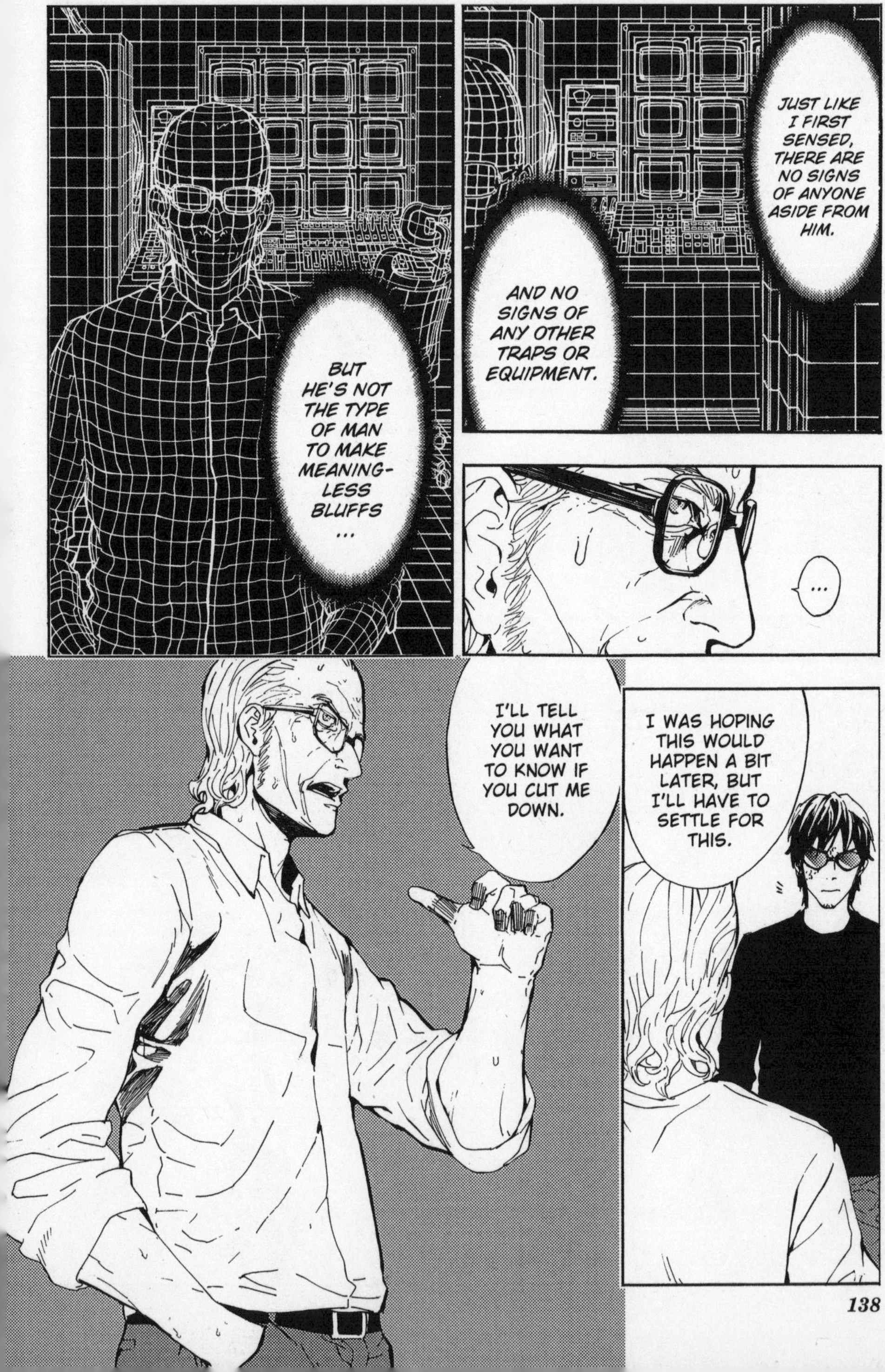
JUST LIKE I FIRST SENSED, THERE ARE NO SIGNS OF ANYONE ASIDE FROM HIM.
AND NO SIGNS OF ANY OTHER TRAPS OR EQUIPMENT.
...
BUT HE'S NOT THE TYPE OF MAN TO MAKE MEANING-LESS BLUFFS ...
I WAS HOPING THIS WOULD HAPPEN A BIT LATER, BUT I'LL HAVE TO SETTLE FOR THIS.
I'LL TELL YOU WHAT YOU WANT TO KNOW IF YOU CUT ME DOWN.

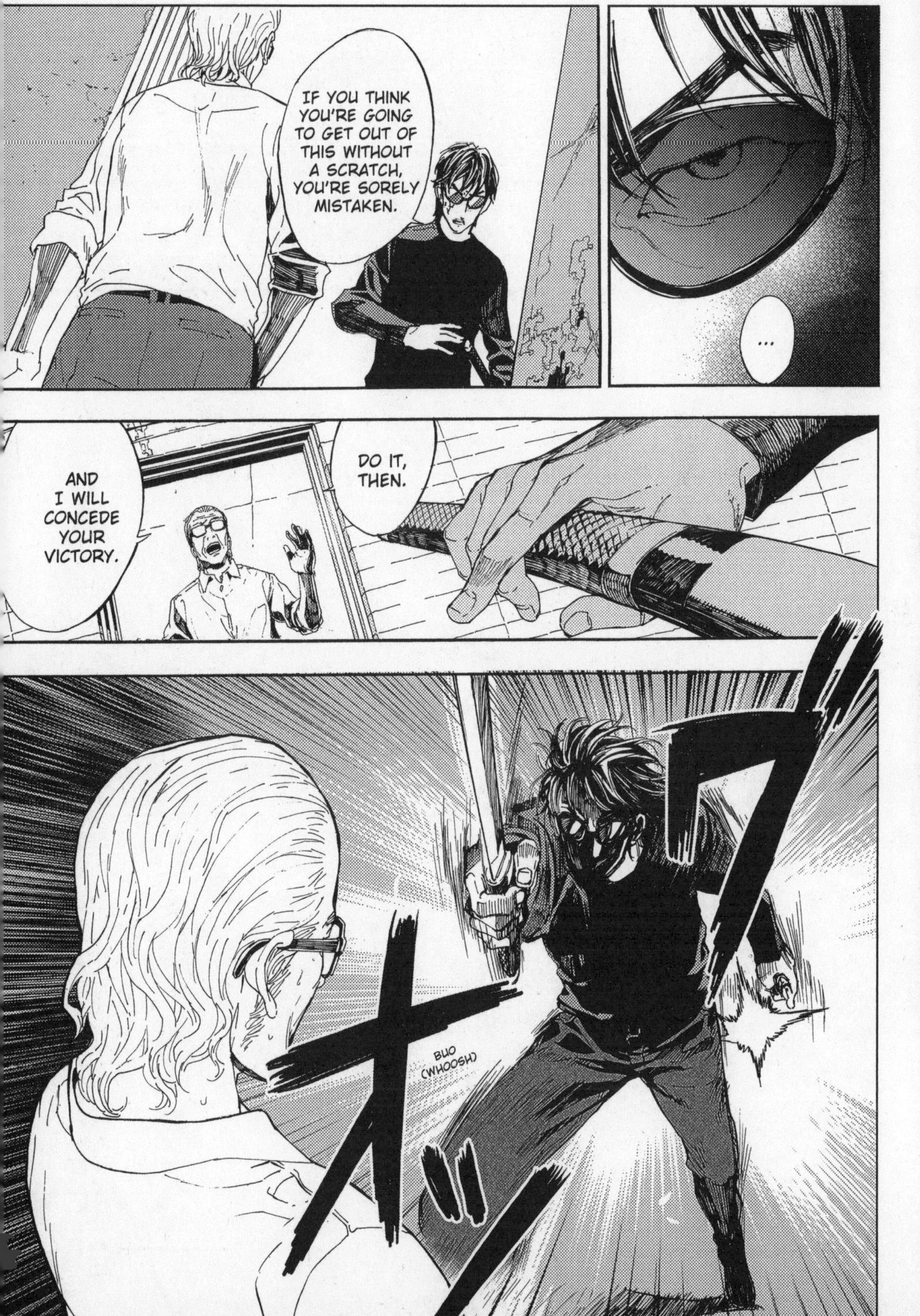
...
IF YOU THINK YOU'RE GOING TO GET OUT OF THIS WITHOUT A SCRATCH, YOU'RE SORELY MISTAKEN.
DO IT, THEN.
AND I WILL CONCEDE YOUR VICTORY.
BUO (WHOOSH)

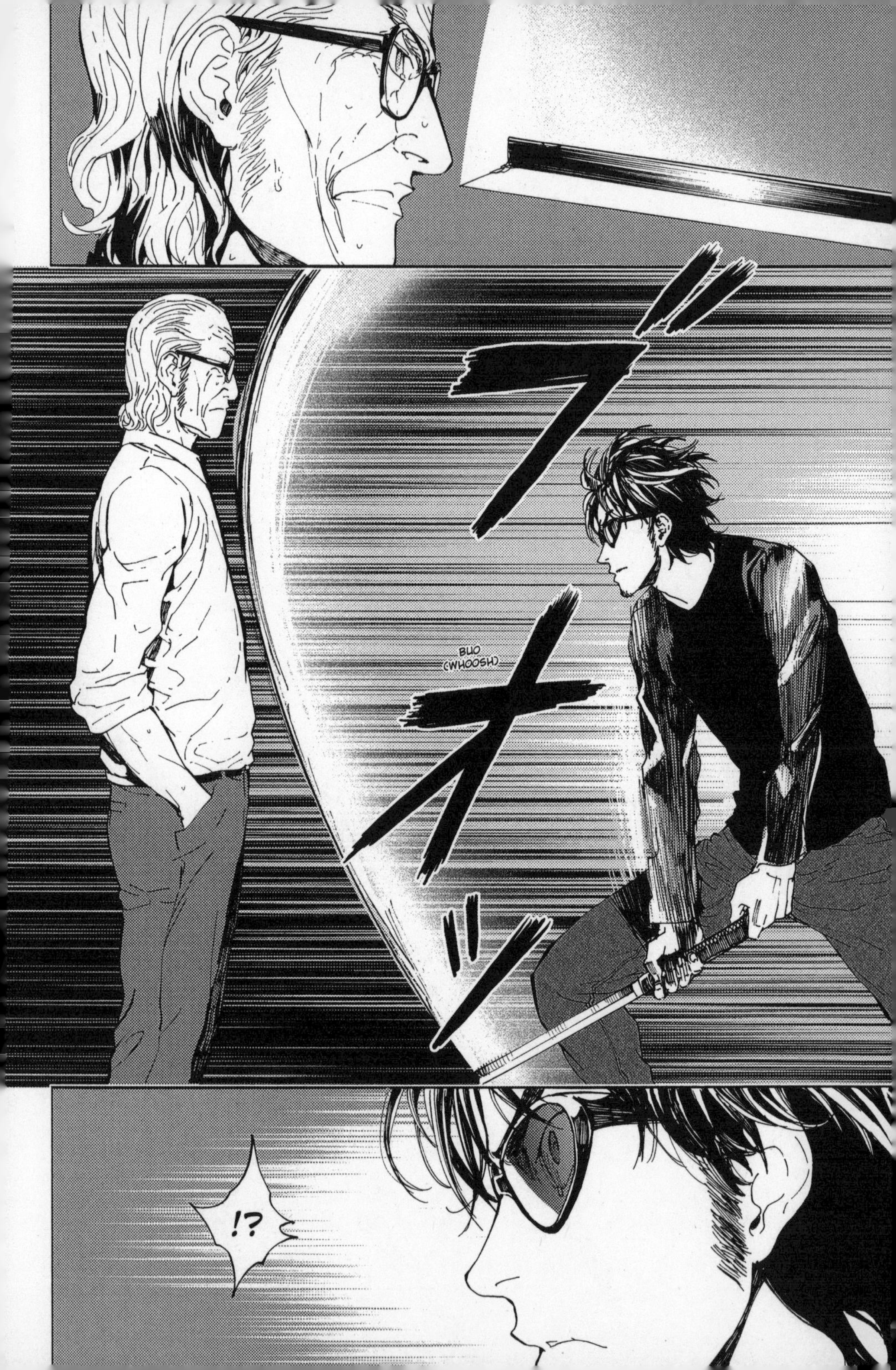
ブオン
BUO
(WHOOSH)
!?

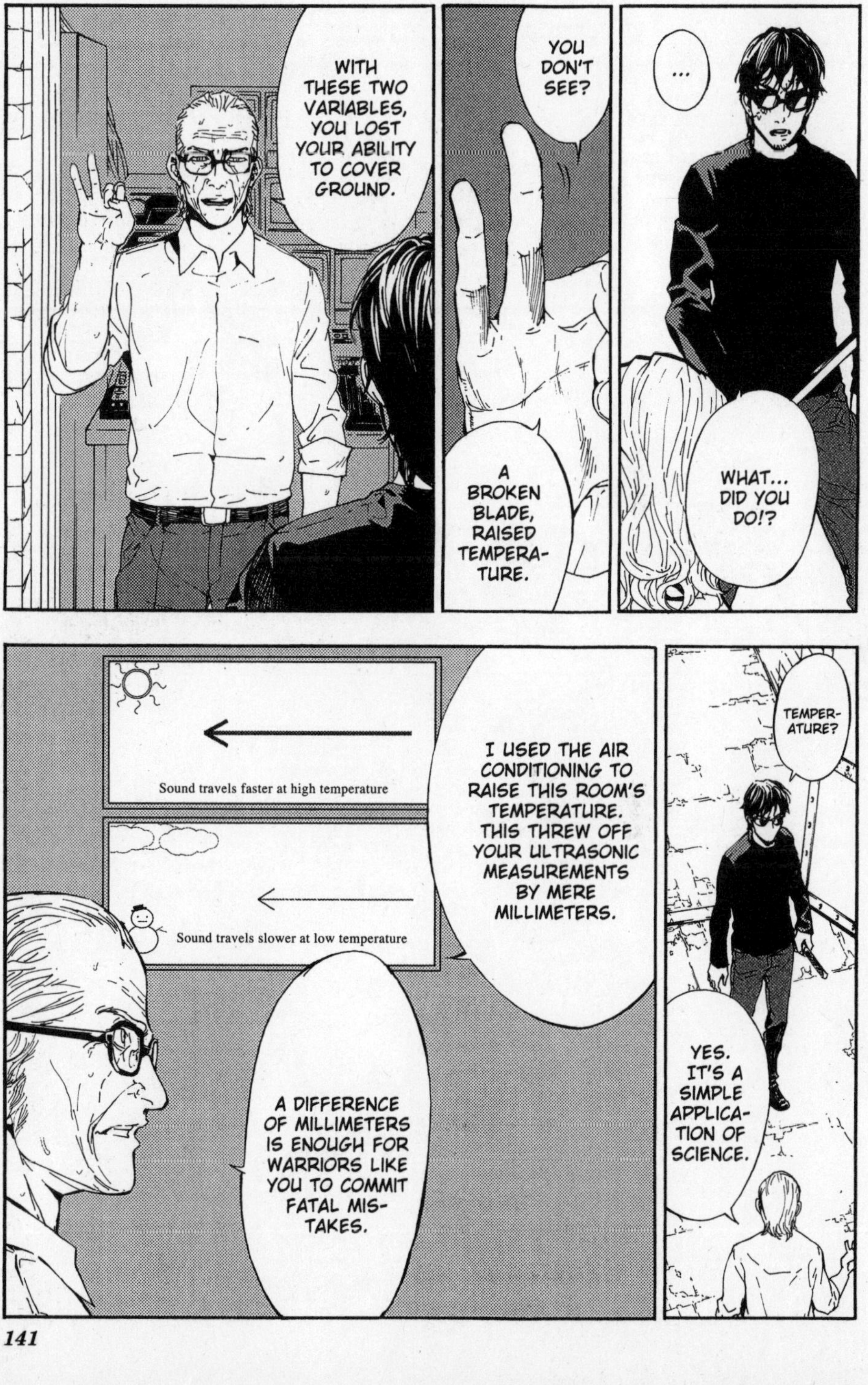
...
WHAT... DID YOU DO!?
YOU DON'T SEE?
A BROKEN BLADE, RAISED TEMPERATURE.
WITH THESE TWO VARIABLES, YOU LOST YOUR ABILITY TO COVER GROUND.
TEMPERATURE?
YES. IT'S A SIMPLE APPLICATION OF SCIENCE.
I USED THE AIR CONDITIONING TO RAISE THIS ROOM'S TEMPERATURE. THIS THREW OFF YOUR ULTRASONIC MEASUREMENTS BY MERE MILLIMETERS.
Sound travels faster at high temperature
Sound travels slower at low temperature
A DIFFERENCE OF MILLIMETERS IS ENOUGH FOR WARRIORS LIKE YOU TO COMMIT FATAL MISTAKES.

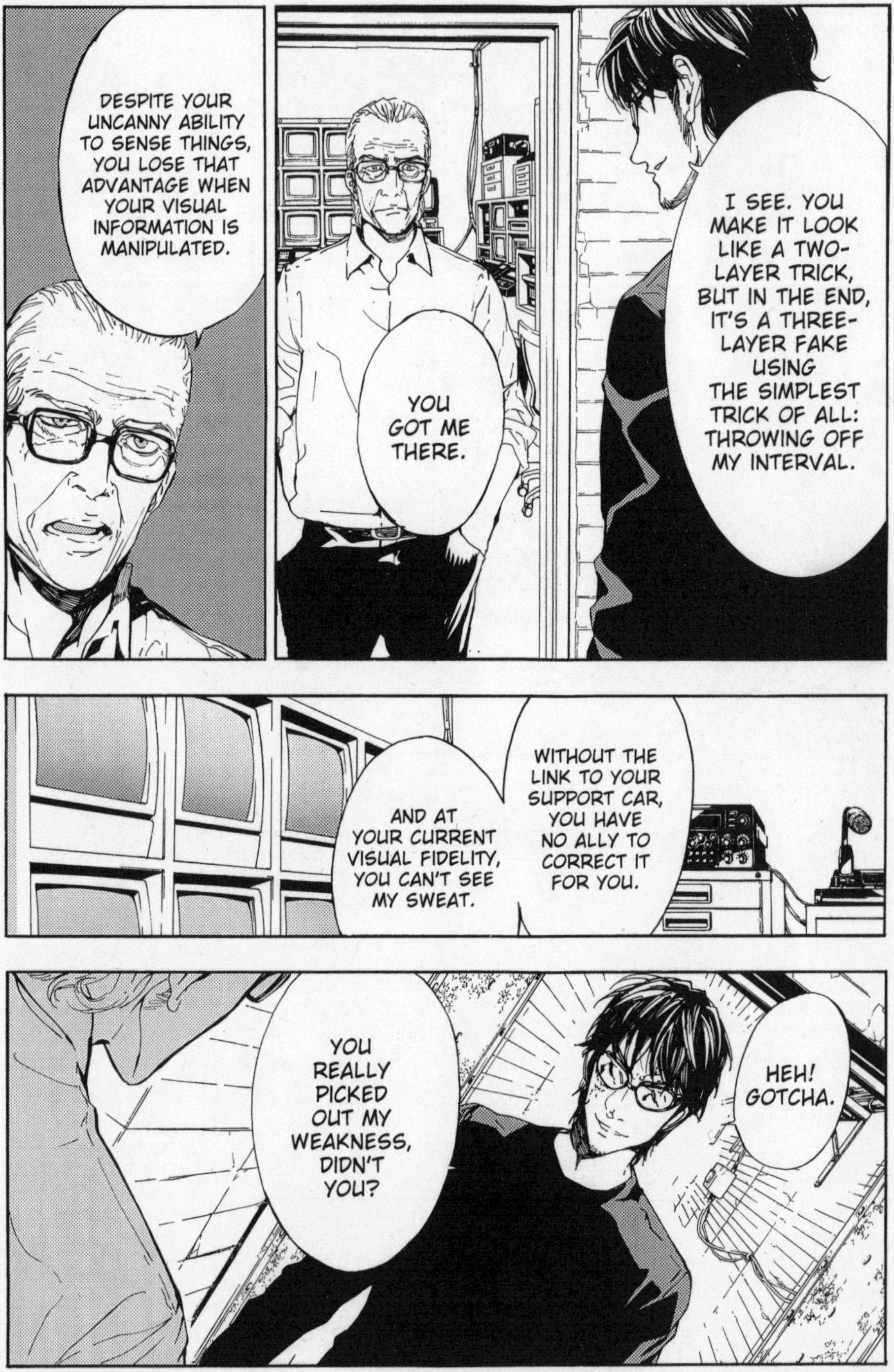
I SEE. YOU MAKE IT LOOK LIKE A TWO-LAYER TRICK, BUT IN THE END, IT'S A THREE-LAYER FAKE USING THE SIMPLEST TRICK OF ALL: THROWING OFF MY INTERVAL.
YOU GOT ME THERE.
DESPITE YOUR UNCANNY ABILITY TO SENSE THINGS, YOU LOSE THAT ADVANTAGE WHEN YOUR VISUAL INFORMATION IS MANIPULATED.
WITHOUT THE LINK TO YOUR SUPPORT CAR, YOU HAVE NO ALLY TO CORRECT IT FOR YOU.
AND AT YOUR CURRENT VISUAL FIDELITY, YOU CAN'T SEE MY SWEAT.
HEH! GOTCHA.
YOU REALLY PICKED OUT MY WEAKNESS, DIDN'T YOU?

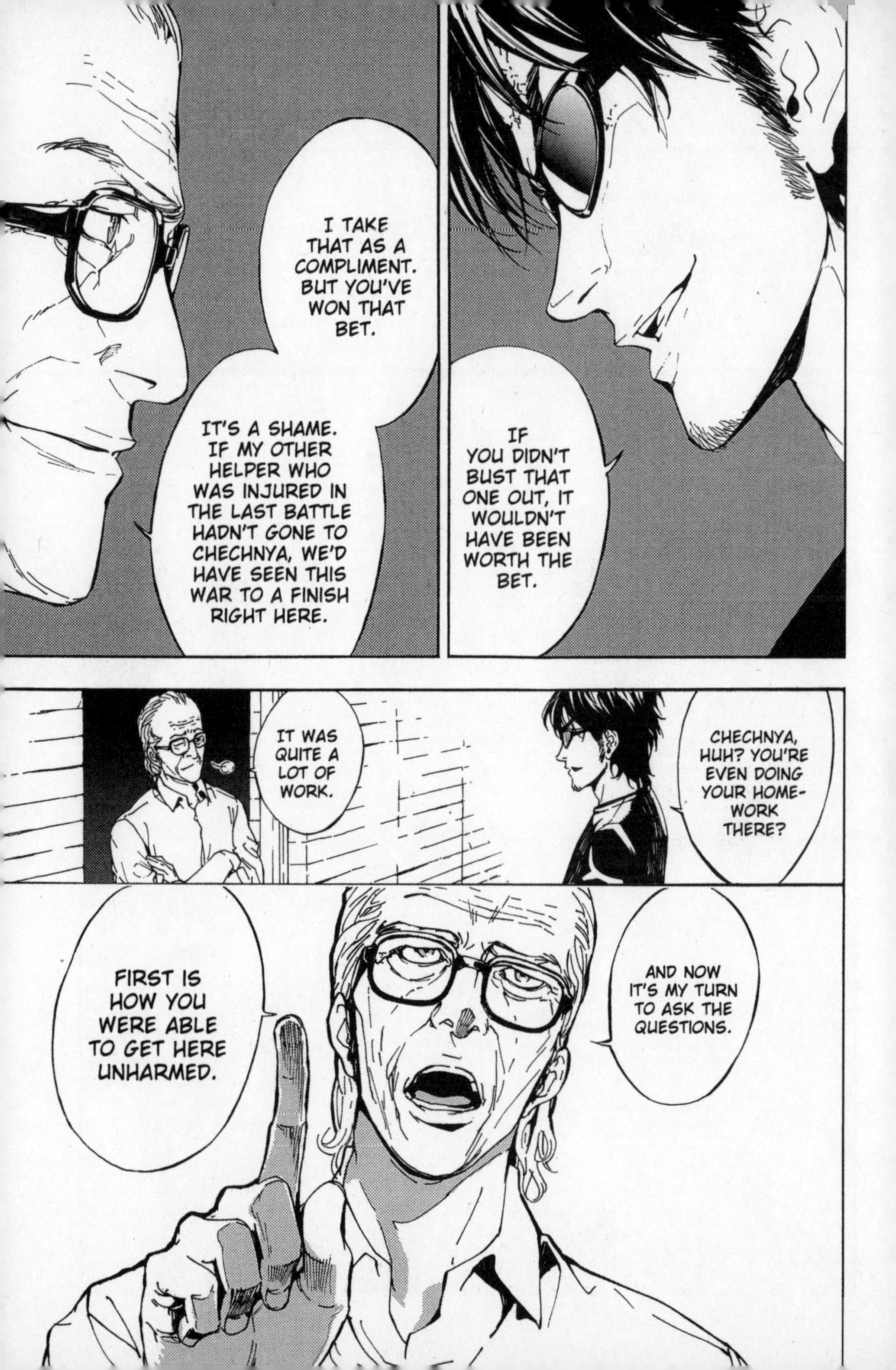
IF YOU DIDN'T BUST THAT ONE OUT, IT WOULDN'T HAVE BEEN WORTH THE BET.
I TAKE THAT AS A COMPLIMENT. BUT YOU'VE WON THAT BET.
IT'S A SHAME. IF MY OTHER HELPER WHO WAS INJURED IN THE LAST BATTLE HADN'T GONE TO CHECHNYA, WE'D HAVE SEEN THIS WAR TO A FINISH RIGHT HERE.
CHECHNYA, HUH? YOU'RE EVEN DOING YOUR HOME-WORK THERE?
IT WAS QUITE A LOT OF WORK.
AND NOW IT'S MY TURN TO ASK THE QUESTIONS.
FIRST IS HOW YOU WERE ABLE TO GET HERE UNHARMED.

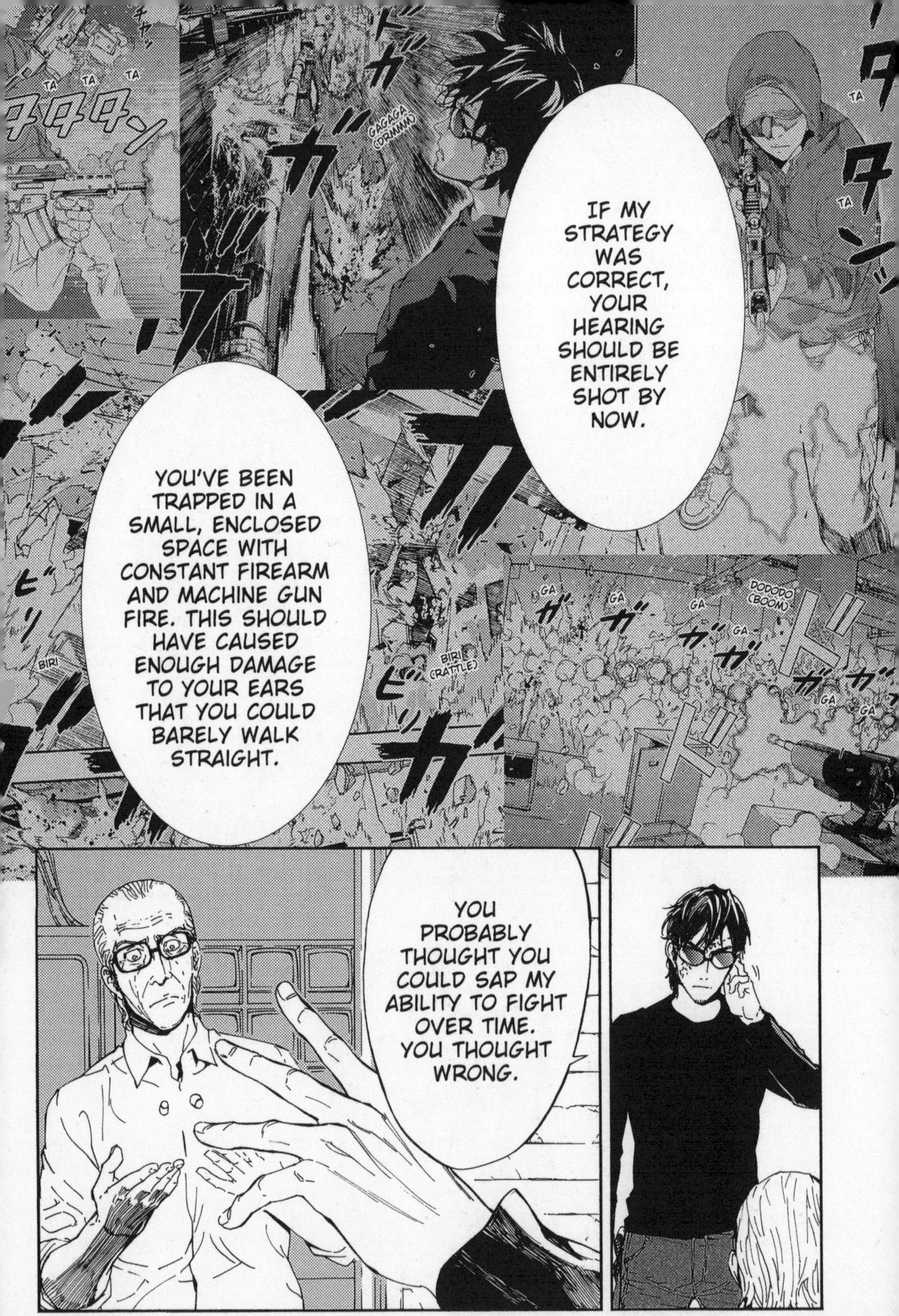
TA
TA
GAGAGA (DRMMM)
TA TA TA
IF MY STRATEGY WAS CORRECT, YOUR HEARING SHOULD BE ENTIRELY SHOT BY NOW.
YOU'VE BEEN TRAPPED IN A SMALL, ENCLOSED SPACE WITH CONSTANT FIREARM AND MACHINE GUN FIRE. THIS SHOULD HAVE CAUSED ENOUGH DAMAGE TO YOUR EARS THAT YOU COULD BARELY WALK STRAIGHT.
DODODO (BOOM)
GA GA GA GA GA GA GA
BIRI (RATTLE)
BIRI
YOU PROBABLY THOUGHT YOU COULD SAP MY ABILITY TO FIGHT OVER TIME. YOU THOUGHT WRONG.

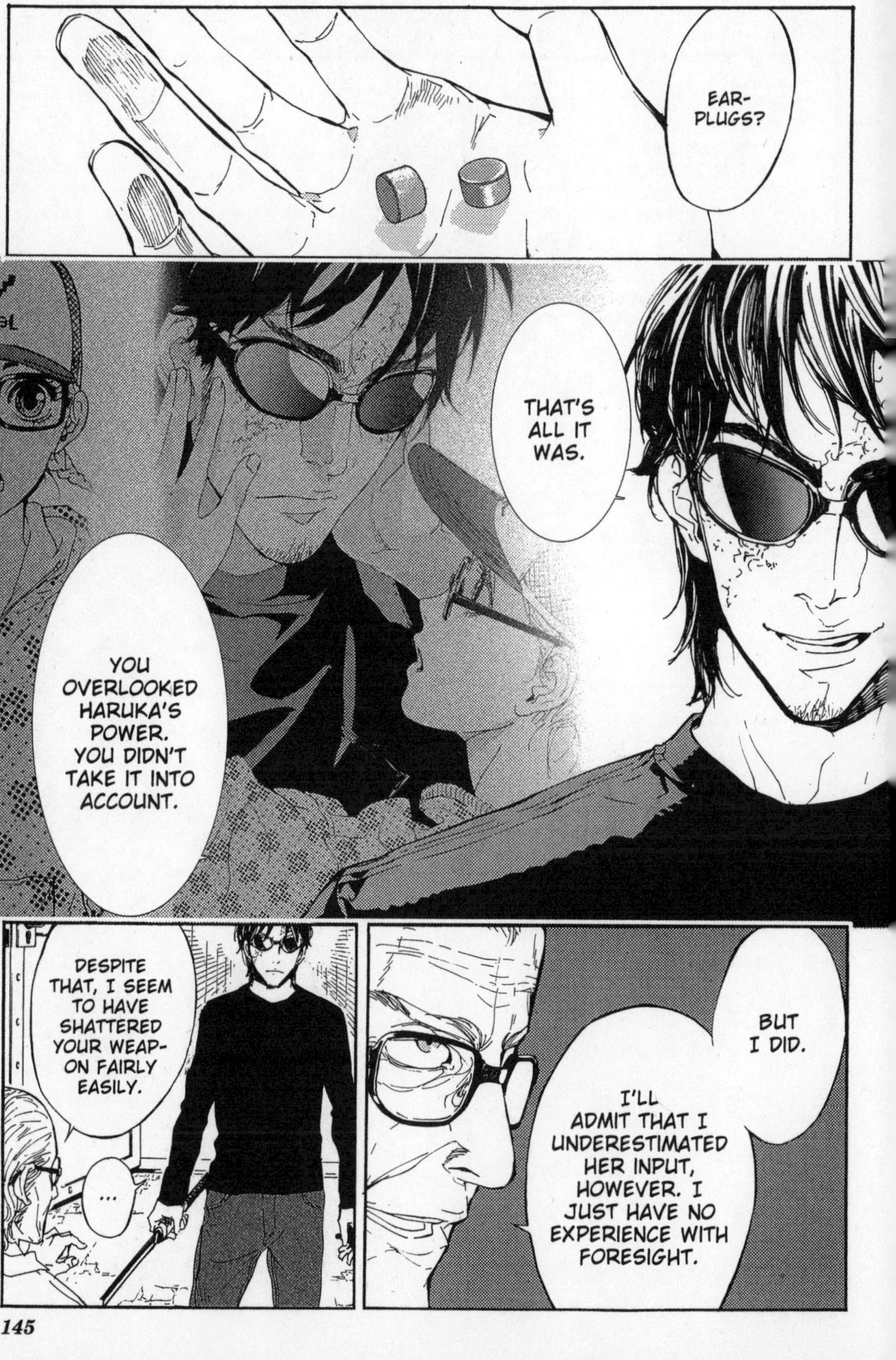
EAR-PLUGS?
THAT'S ALL IT WAS.
YOU OVERLOOKED HARUKA'S POWER. YOU DIDN'T TAKE IT INTO ACCOUNT.
BUT I DID.
I'LL ADMIT THAT I UNDERESTIMATED HER INPUT, HOWEVER. I JUST HAVE NO EXPERIENCE WITH FORESIGHT.
DESPITE THAT, I SEEM TO HAVE SHATTERED YOUR WEAP-ON FAIRLY EASILY.
...

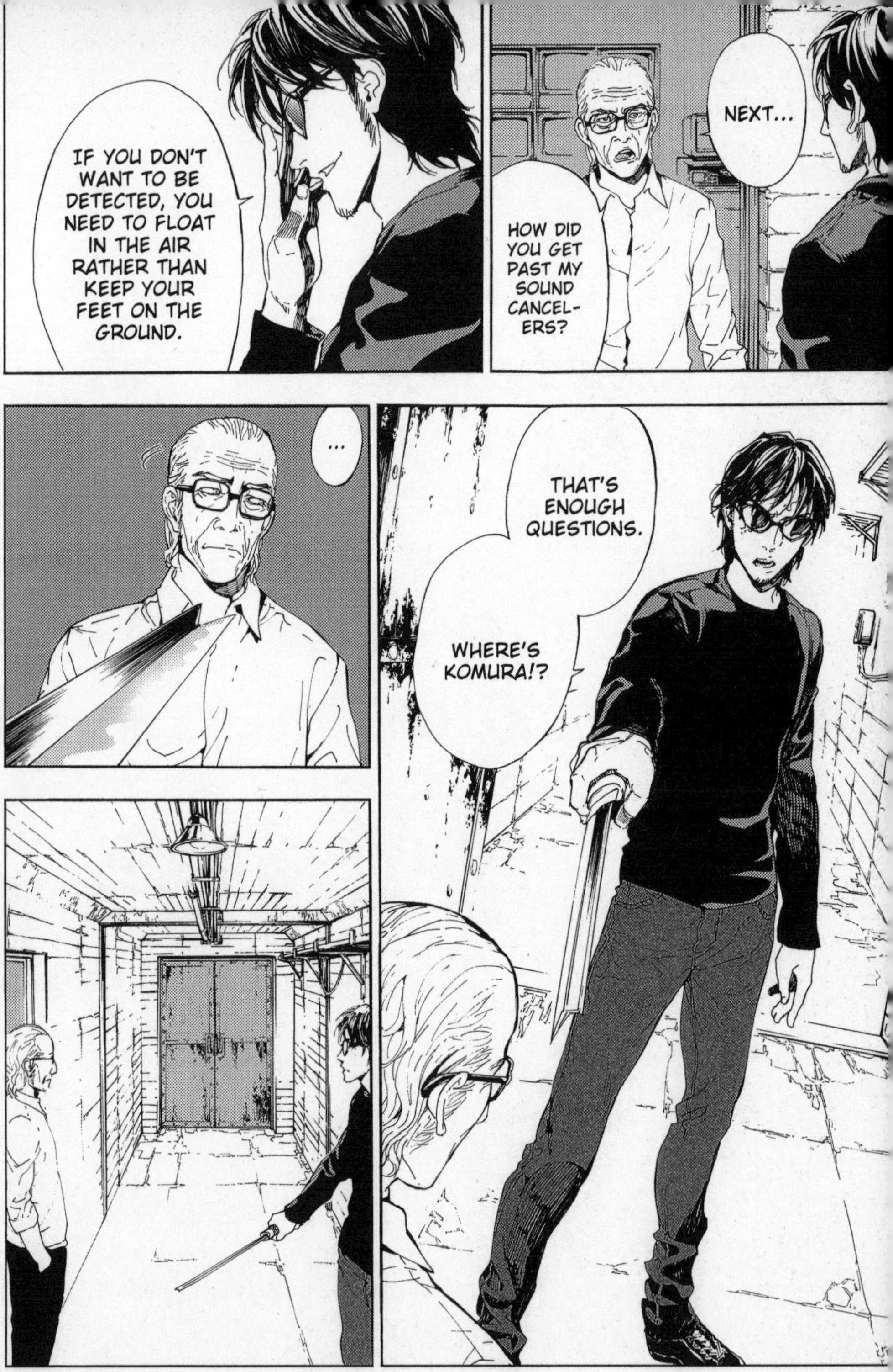
NEXT...
HOW DID YOU GET PAST MY SOUND CANCEL-ERS?
IF YOU DON'T WANT TO BE DETECTED, YOU NEED TO FLOAT IN THE AIR RATHER THAN KEEP YOUR FEET ON THE GROUND.
THAT'S ENOUGH QUESTIONS.
WHERE'S KOMURA!?
...

Until Death do us Part

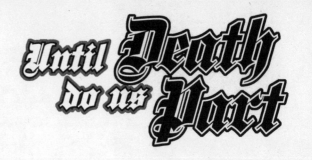

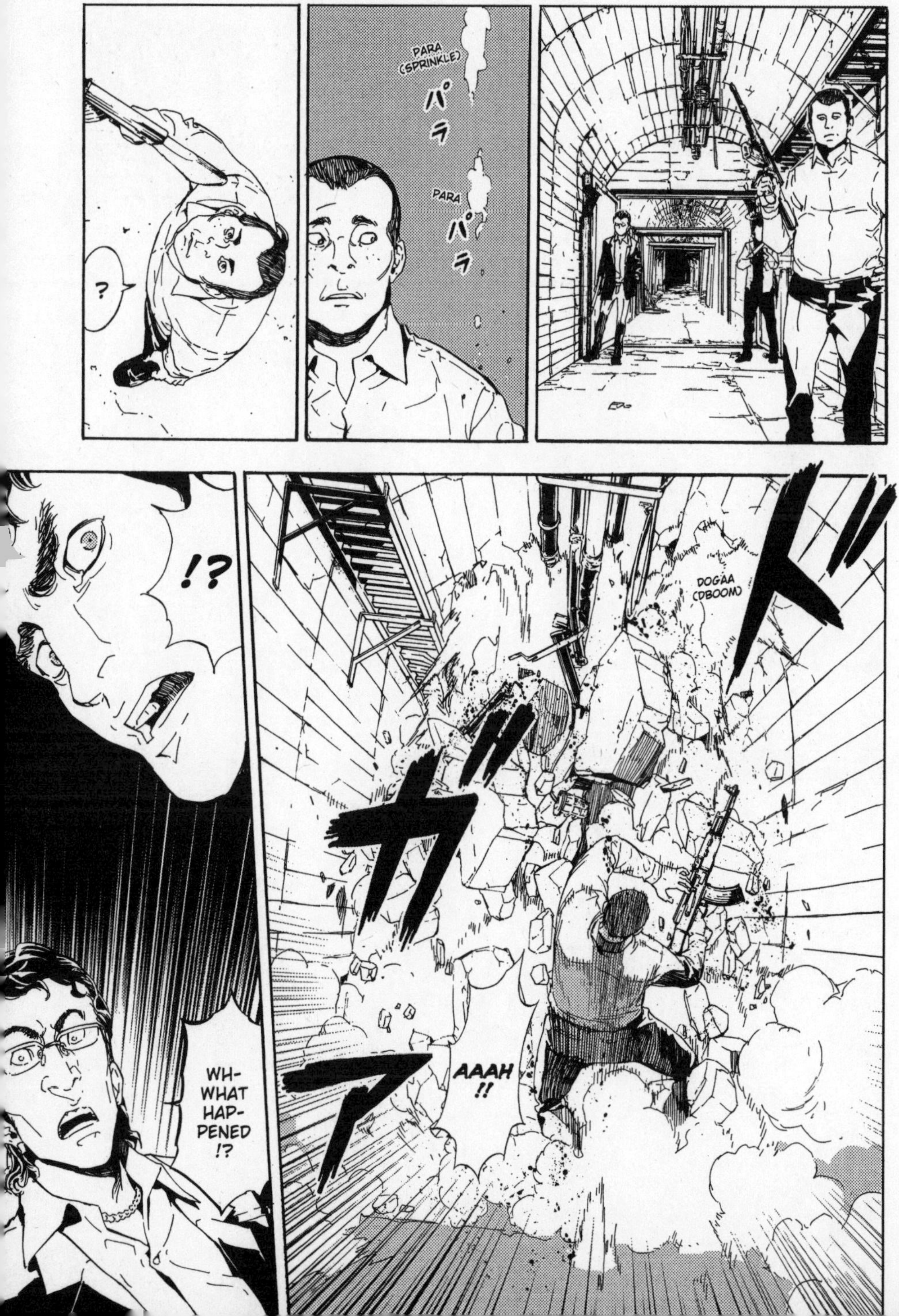

PARA (SPRINKLE)
パラ
PARA
パラ
?
DOGAA (DBOOM)
ドガァ
AAAH!!
!?
WH-WHAT HAPPENED!?

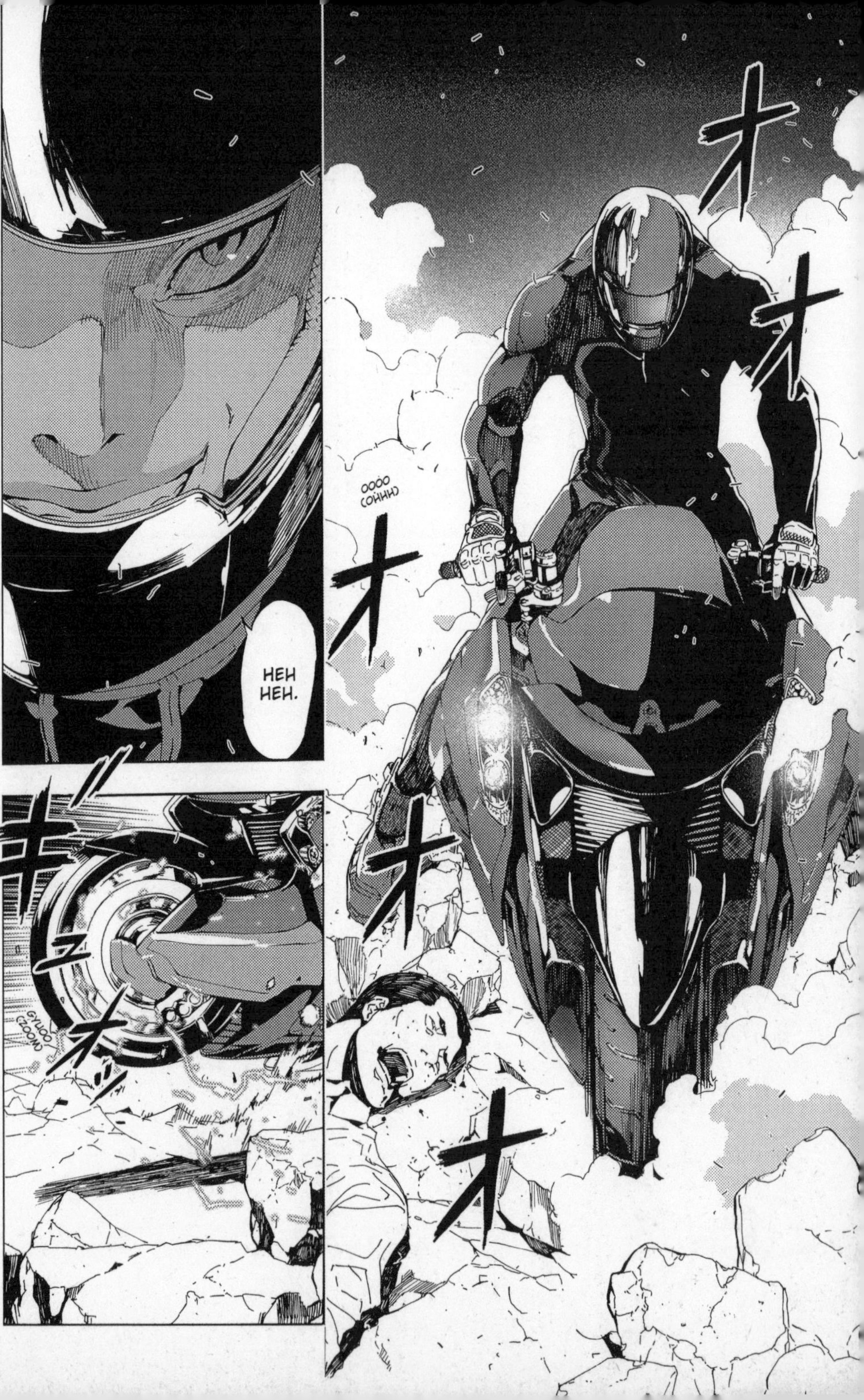
OOOO (OOHH)
HEH HEH.
GYUOO (ZOOM)

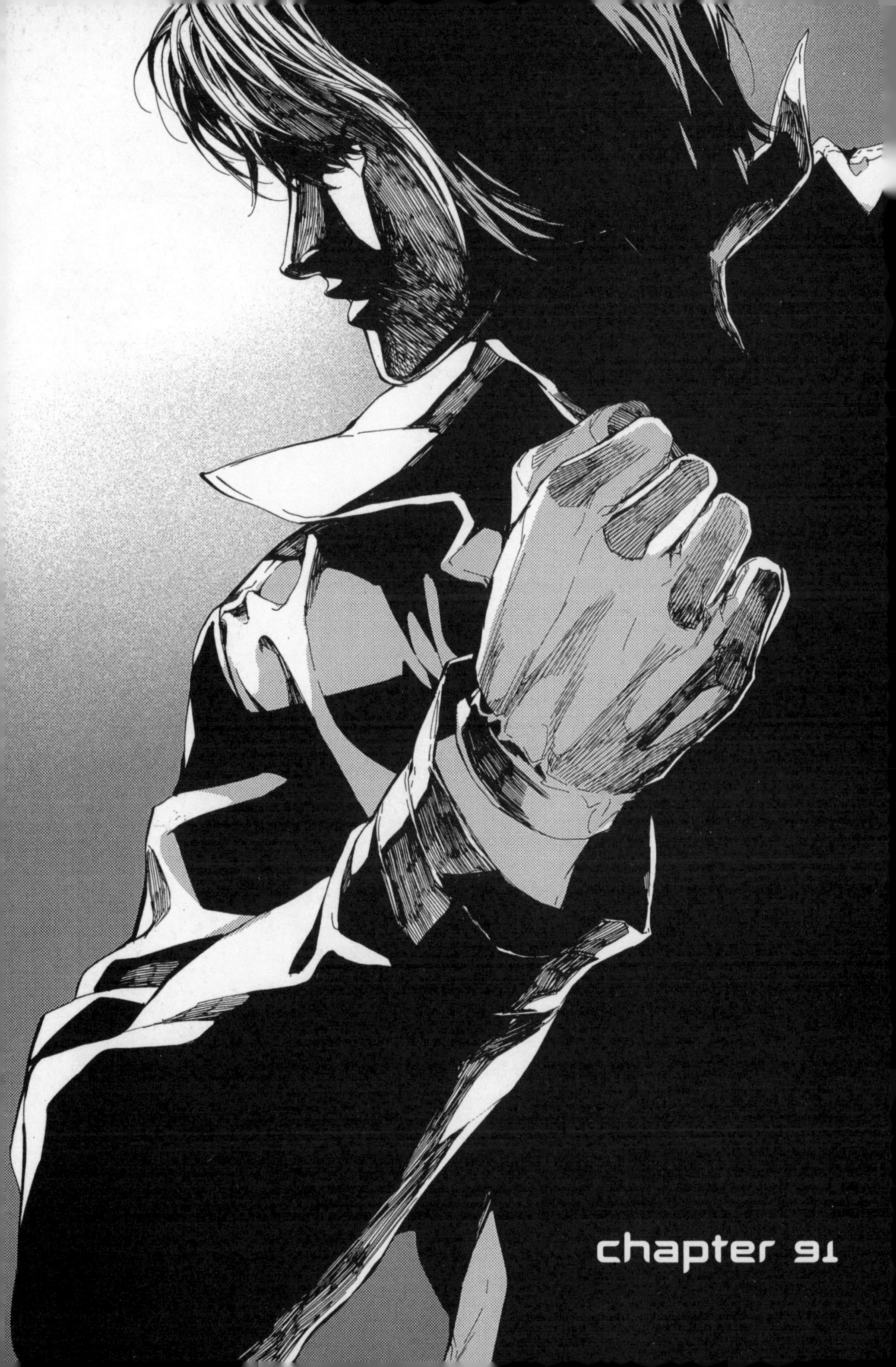
chapter 91

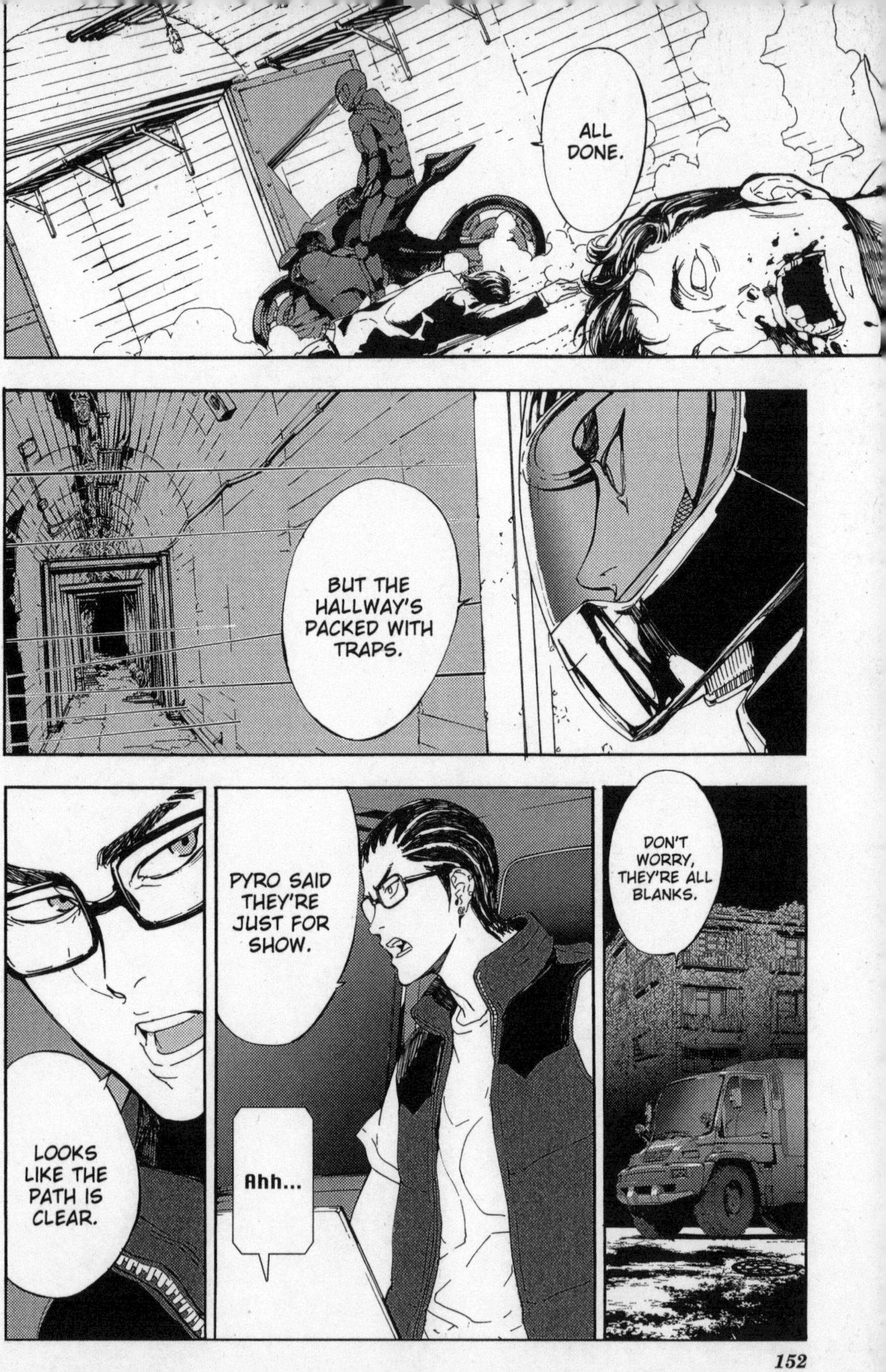
ALL DONE.
BUT THE HALLWAY'S PACKED WITH TRAPS.
DON'T WORRY, THEY'RE ALL BLANKS.
PYRO SAID THEY'RE JUST FOR SHOW.
Ahh...
LOOKS LIKE THE PATH IS CLEAR.

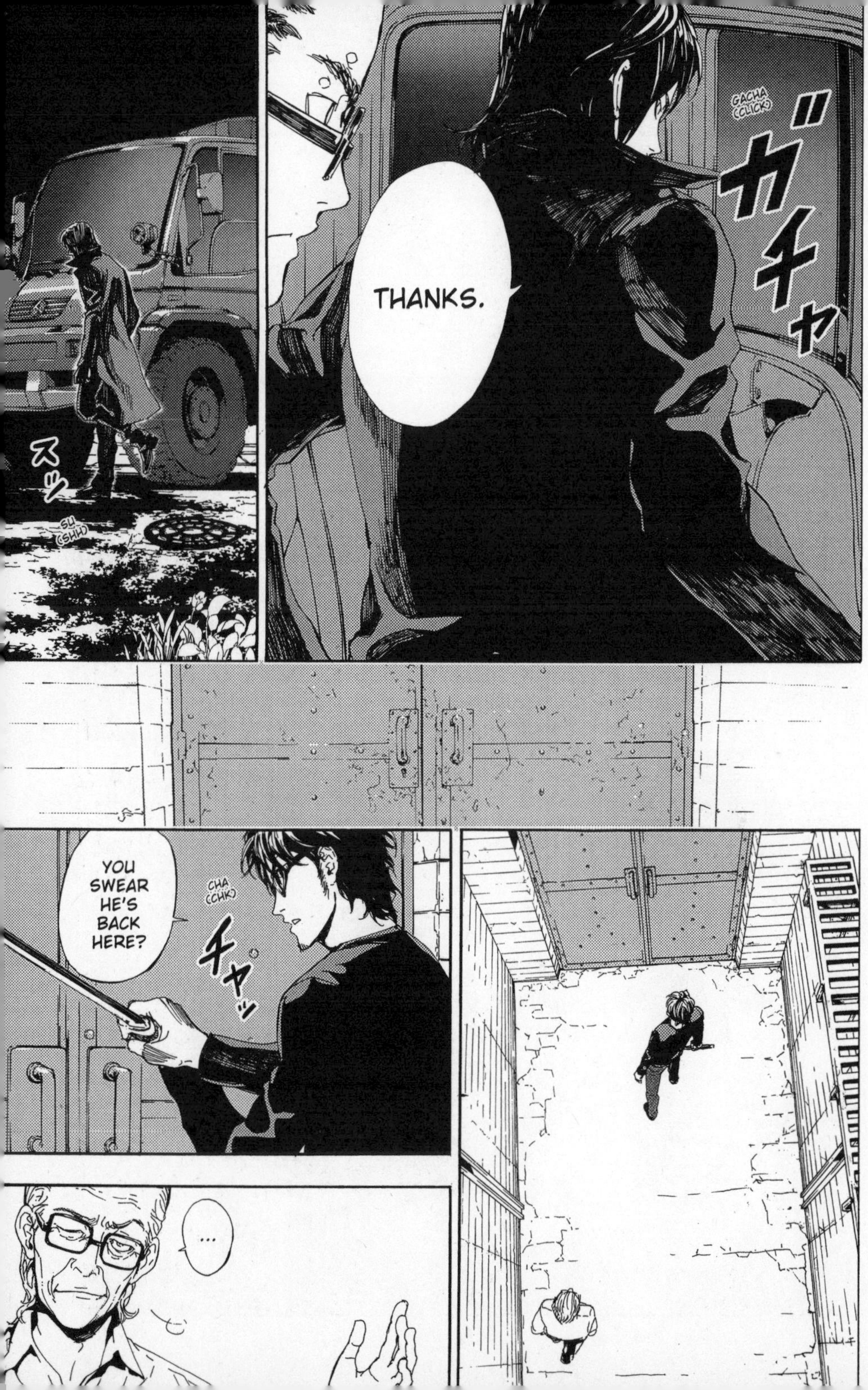

THANKS.
GACHA (CLICK)
ガチャ
スッ
SU (SHH)
YOU SWEAR HE'S BACK HERE?
CHA (CHK)
チャッ
...

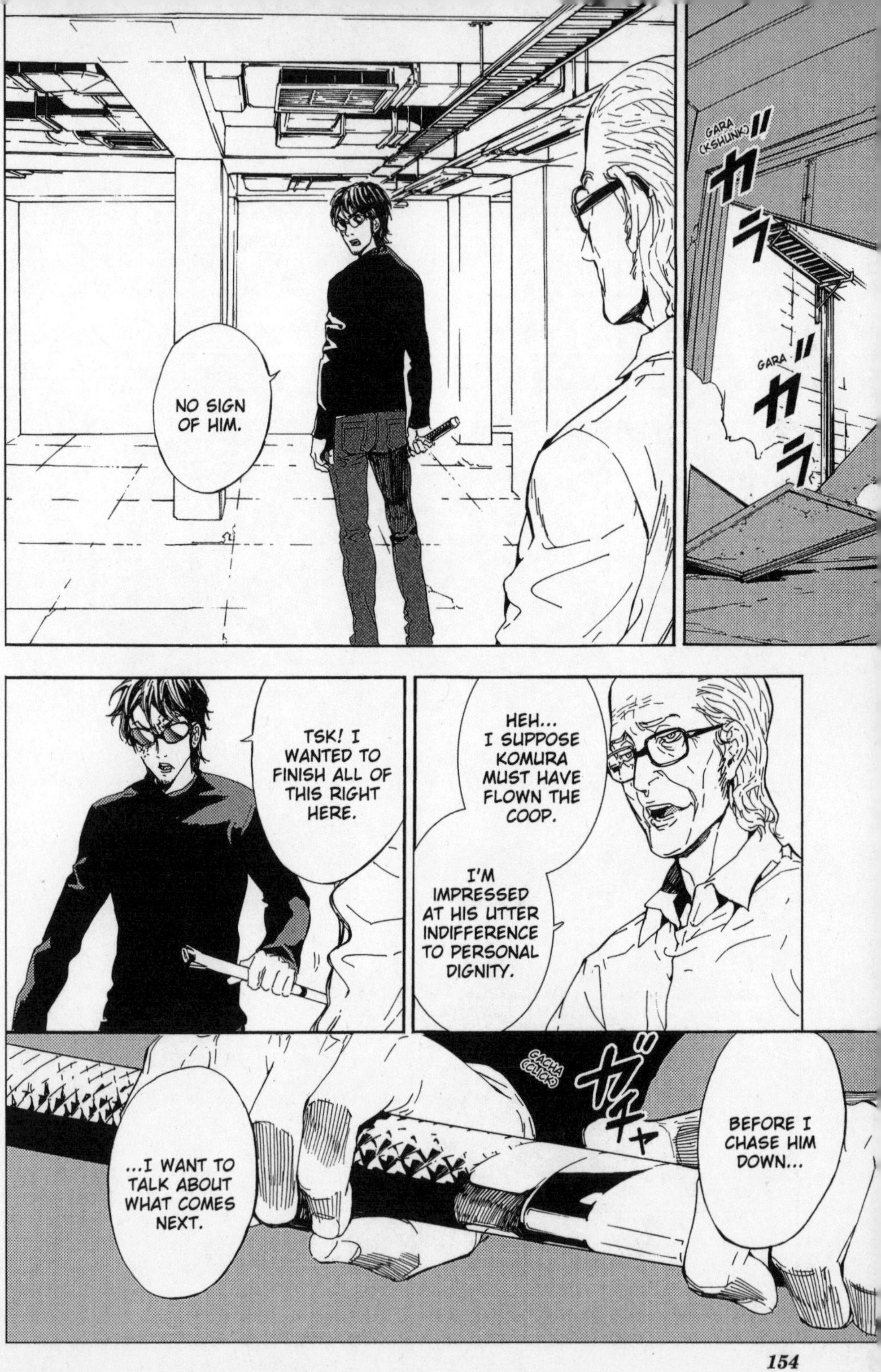
GARA (KSHUNK)
ガラ
GARA
ガラ
NO SIGN OF HIM.
HEH... I SUPPOSE KOMURA MUST HAVE FLOWN THE COOP.
I'M IMPRESSED AT HIS UTTER INDIFFERENCE TO PERSONAL DIGNITY.
TSK! I WANTED TO FINISH ALL OF THIS RIGHT HERE.
BEFORE I CHASE HIM DOWN...
GACHA (CLICK)
ガチャ
...I WANT TO TALK ABOUT WHAT COMES NEXT.

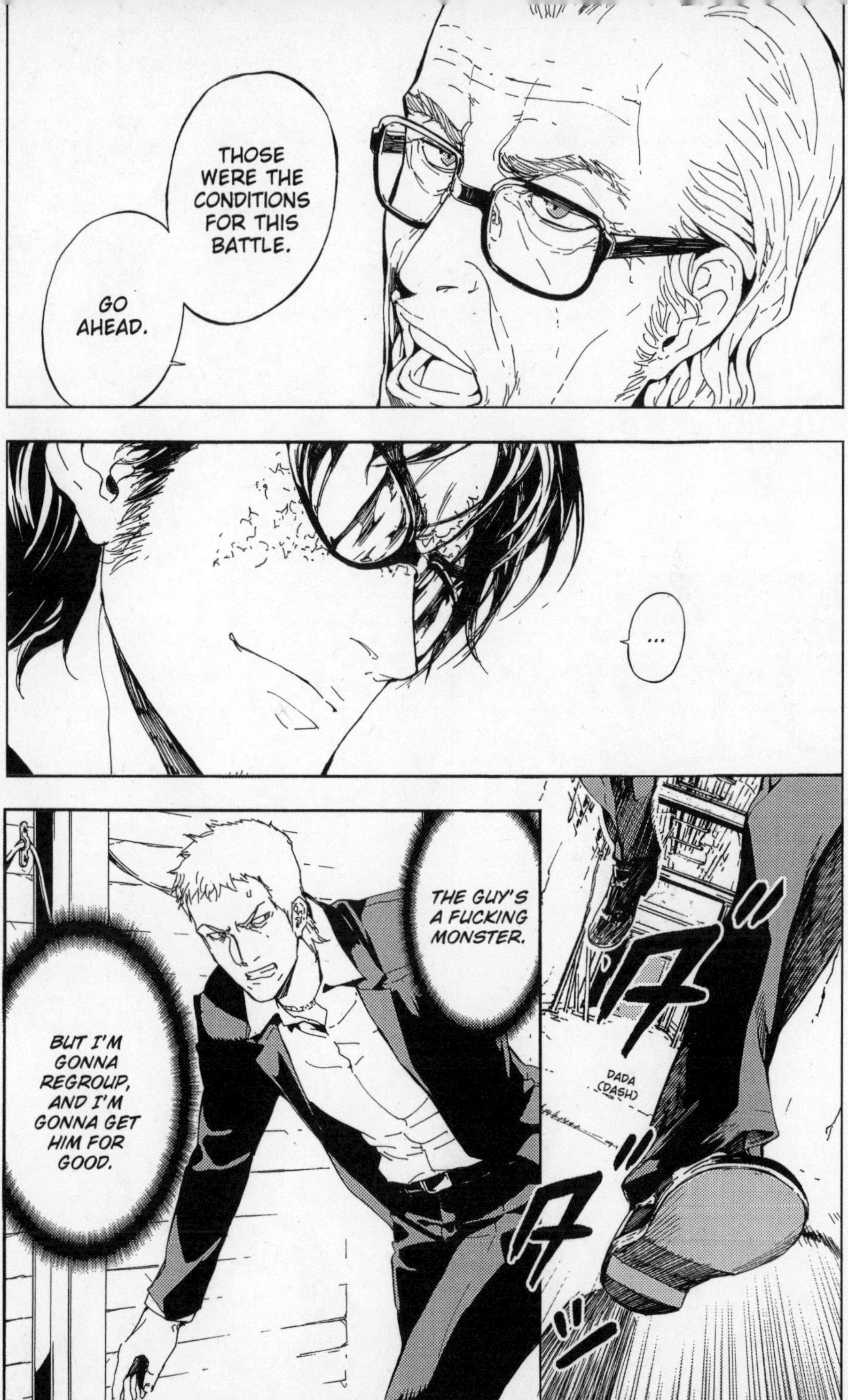
THOSE WERE THE CONDITIONS FOR THIS BATTLE.
GO AHEAD.
...
DADA (DASH)
THE GUY'S A FUCKING MONSTER.
BUT I'M GONNA REGROUP, AND I'M GONNA GET HIM FOR GOOD.

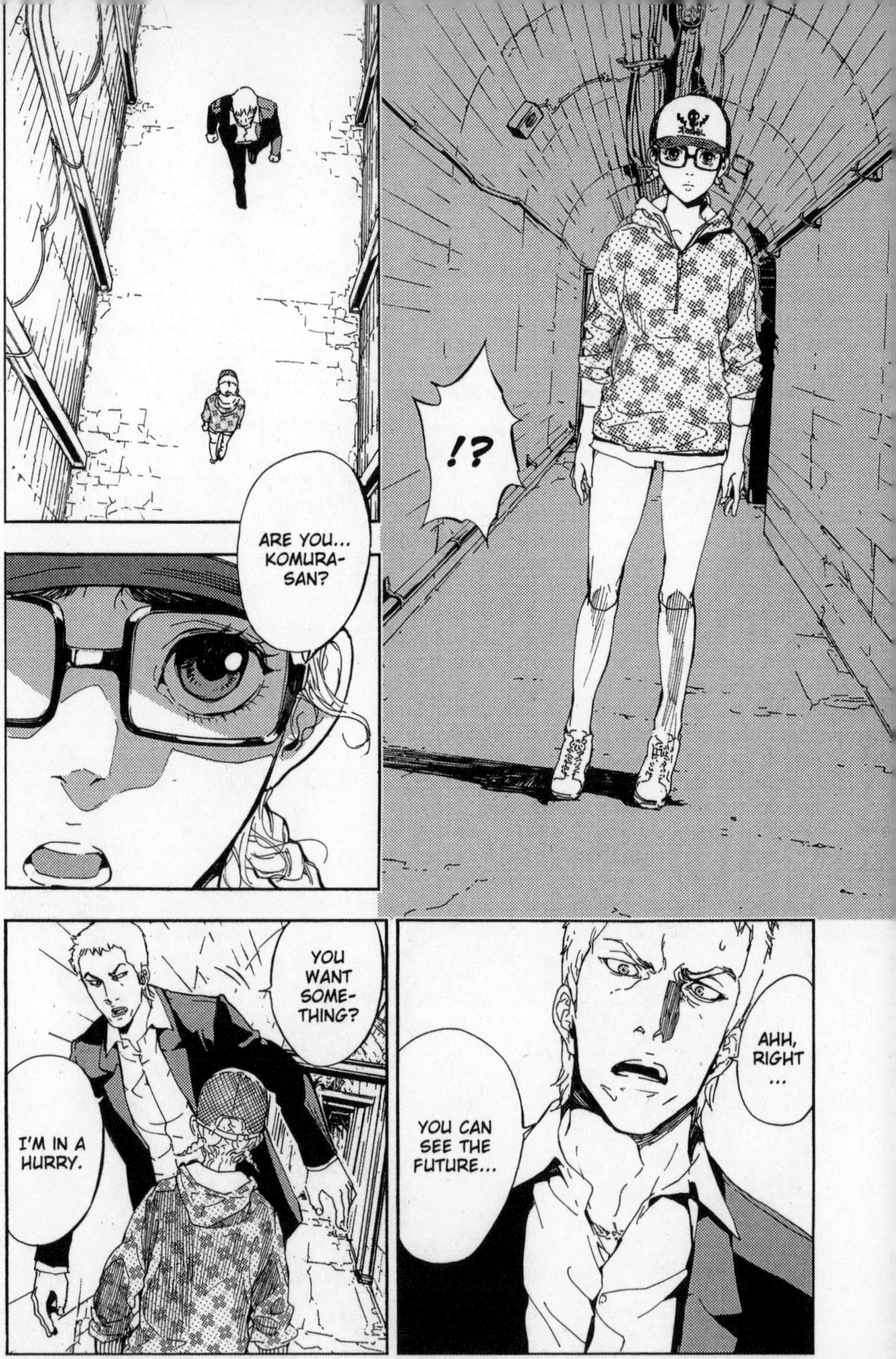
!?
ARE YOU... KOMURA-SAN?
AHH, RIGHT ...
YOU CAN SEE THE FUTURE...
YOU WANT SOME-THING?
I'M IN A HURRY.

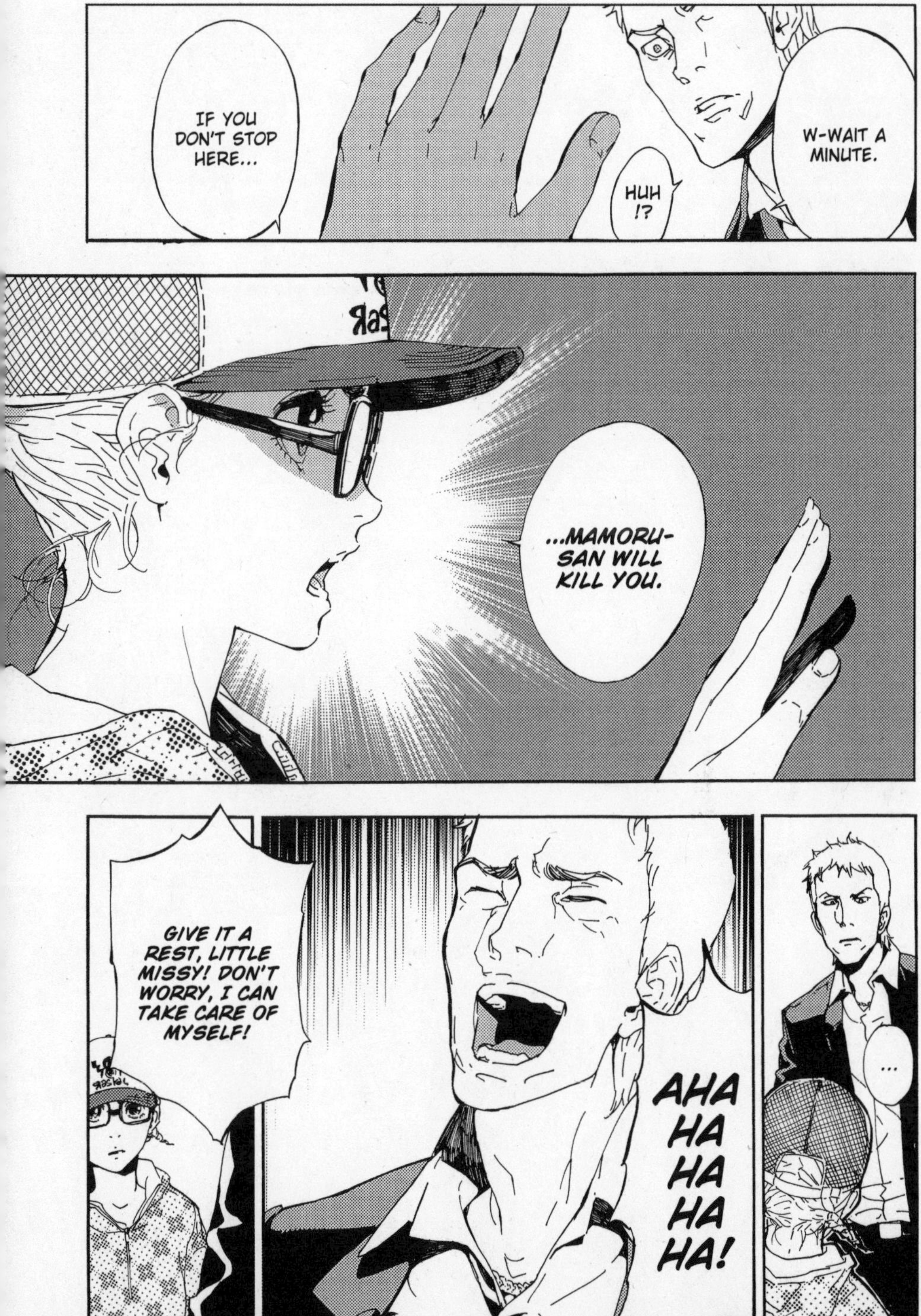
W-WAIT A MINUTE.
HUH !?
IF YOU DON'T STOP HERE...
...MAMORU-SAN WILL KILL YOU.
...
GIVE IT A REST, LITTLE MISSY! DON'T WORRY, I CAN TAKE CARE OF MYSELF!
AHA HA HA HA HA!

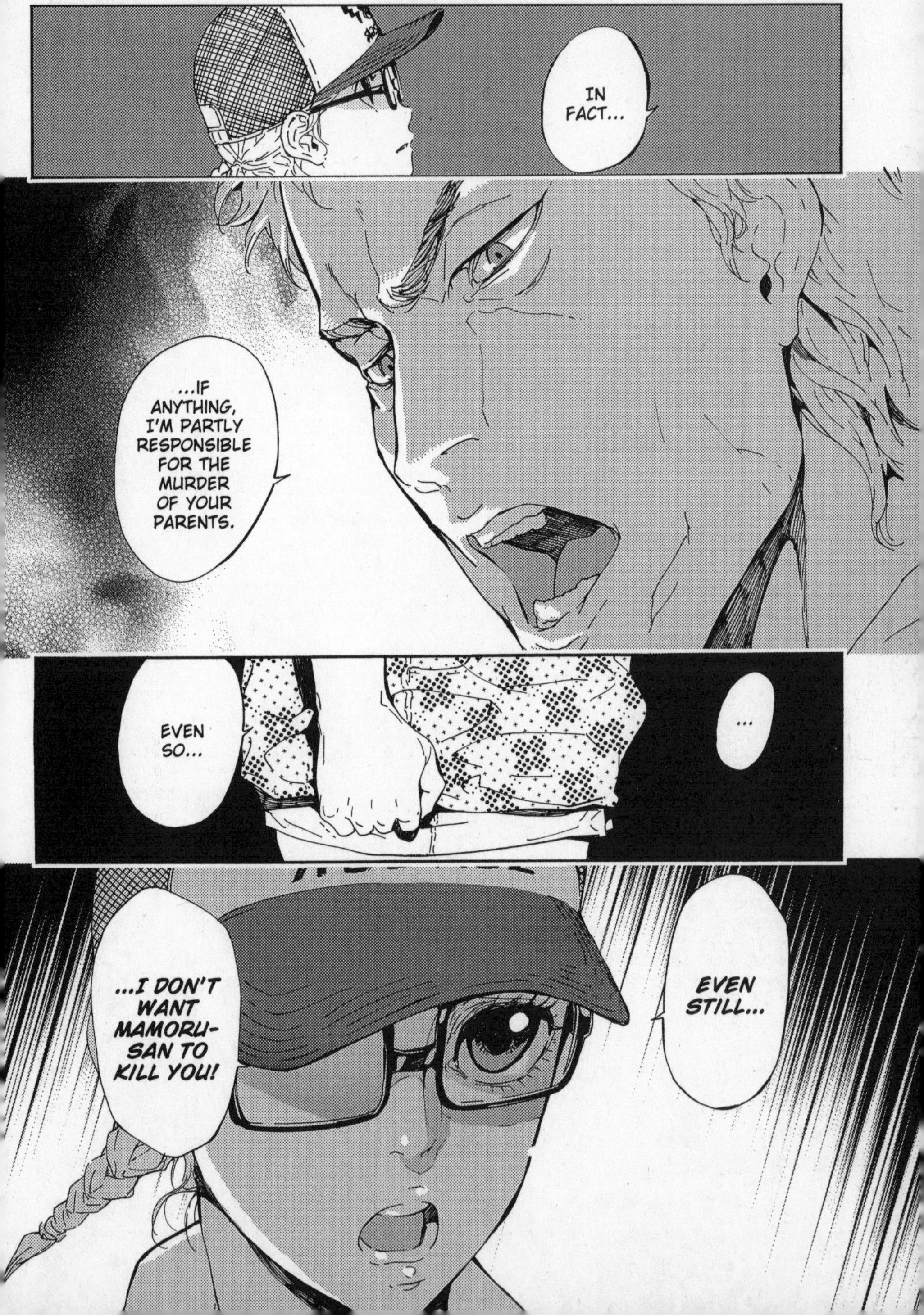
IN FACT...
...IF ANYTHING, I'M PARTLY RESPONSIBLE FOR THE MURDER OF YOUR PARENTS.
...
EVEN SO...
EVEN STILL...
...I DON'T WANT MAMORU-SAN TO KILL YOU!

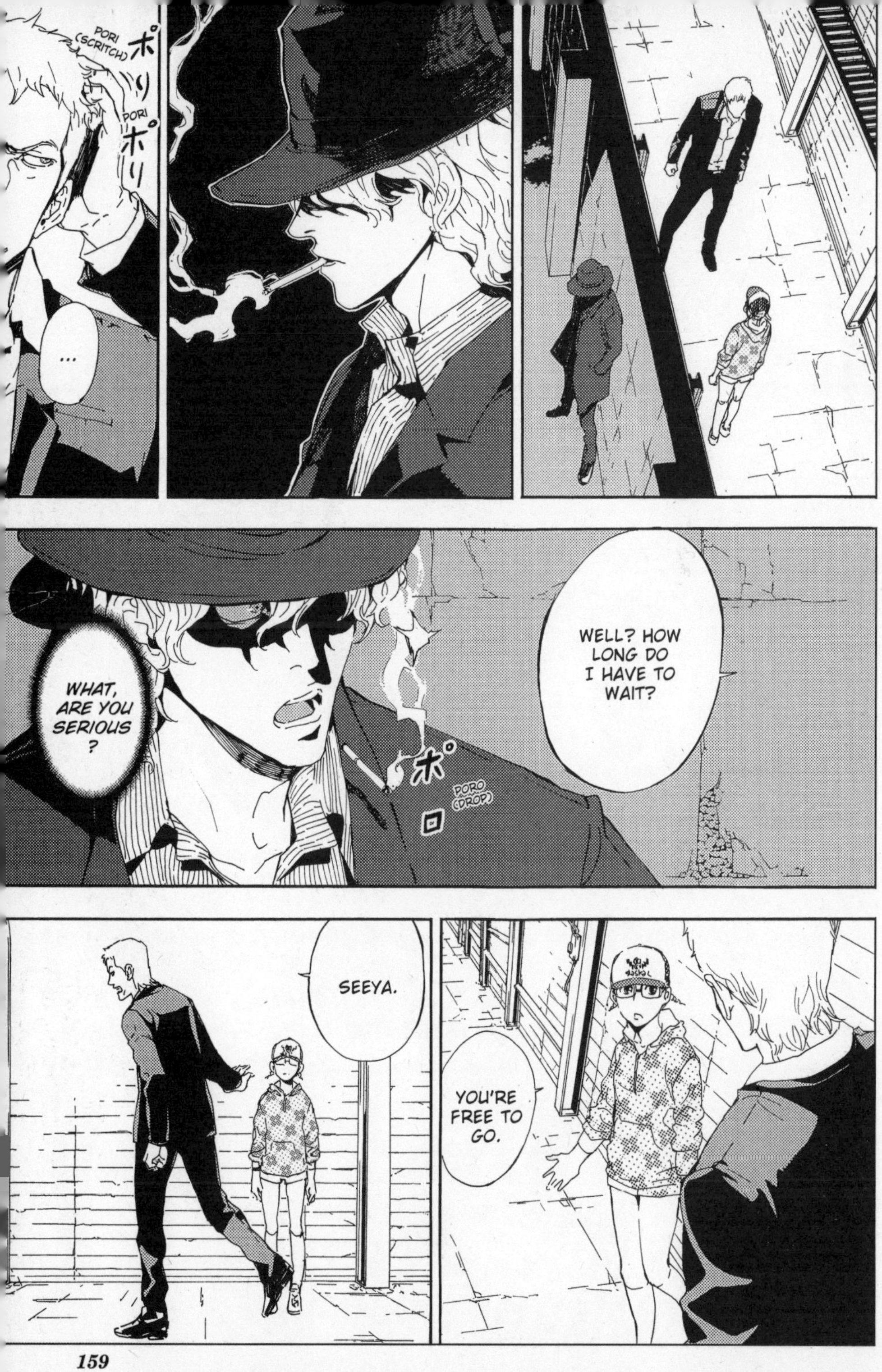

ポリ
PORI (SCRITCH)
ポリ
PORI
...
WELL? HOW LONG DO I HAVE TO WAIT?
ポロ
PORO (DROP)
WHAT, ARE YOU SERIOUS?
YOU'RE FREE TO GO.
SEEYA.

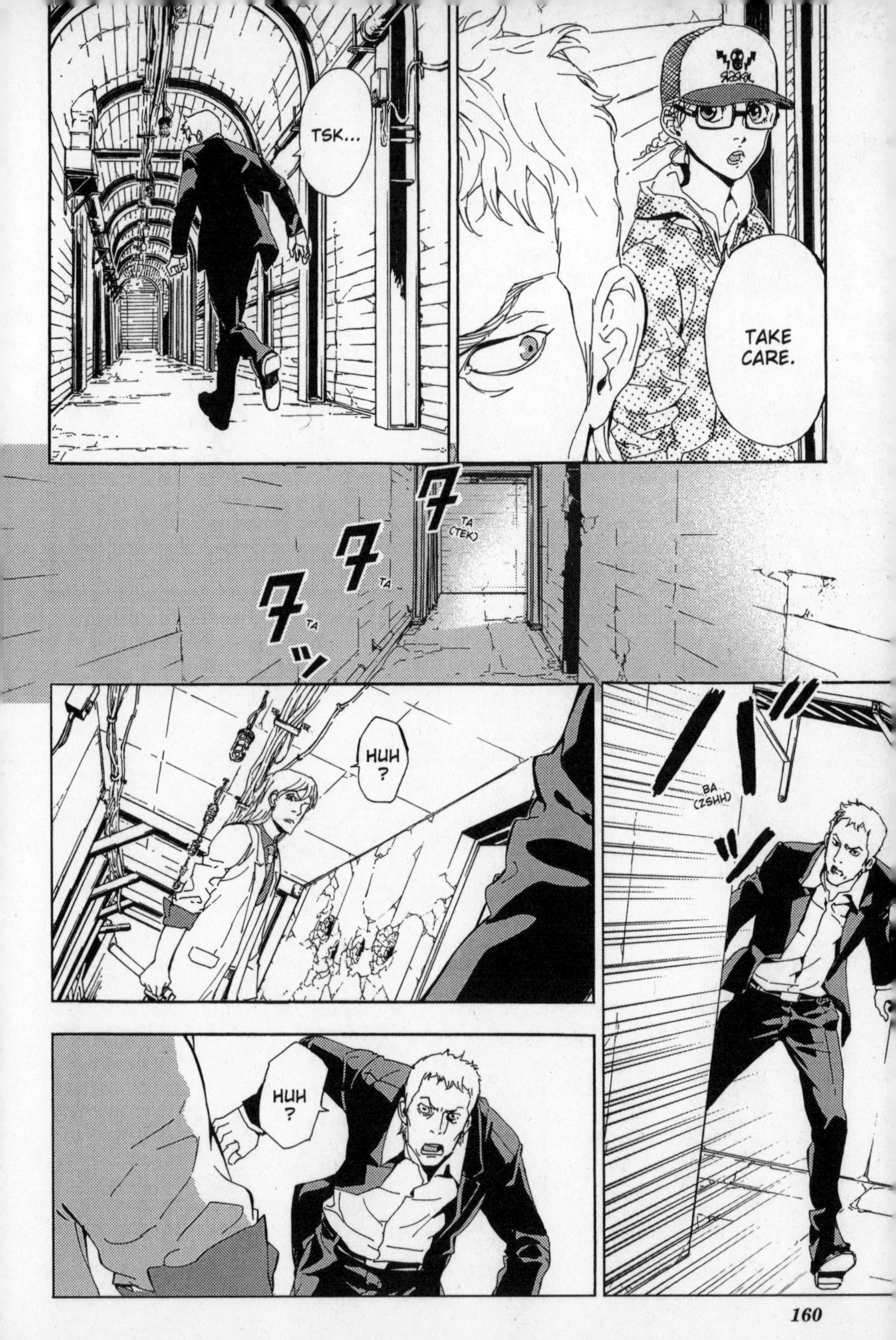
TAKE CARE.
TSK...
TA (TEK)
TA
TA
BA (ZSHH)
HUH ?
HUH ?

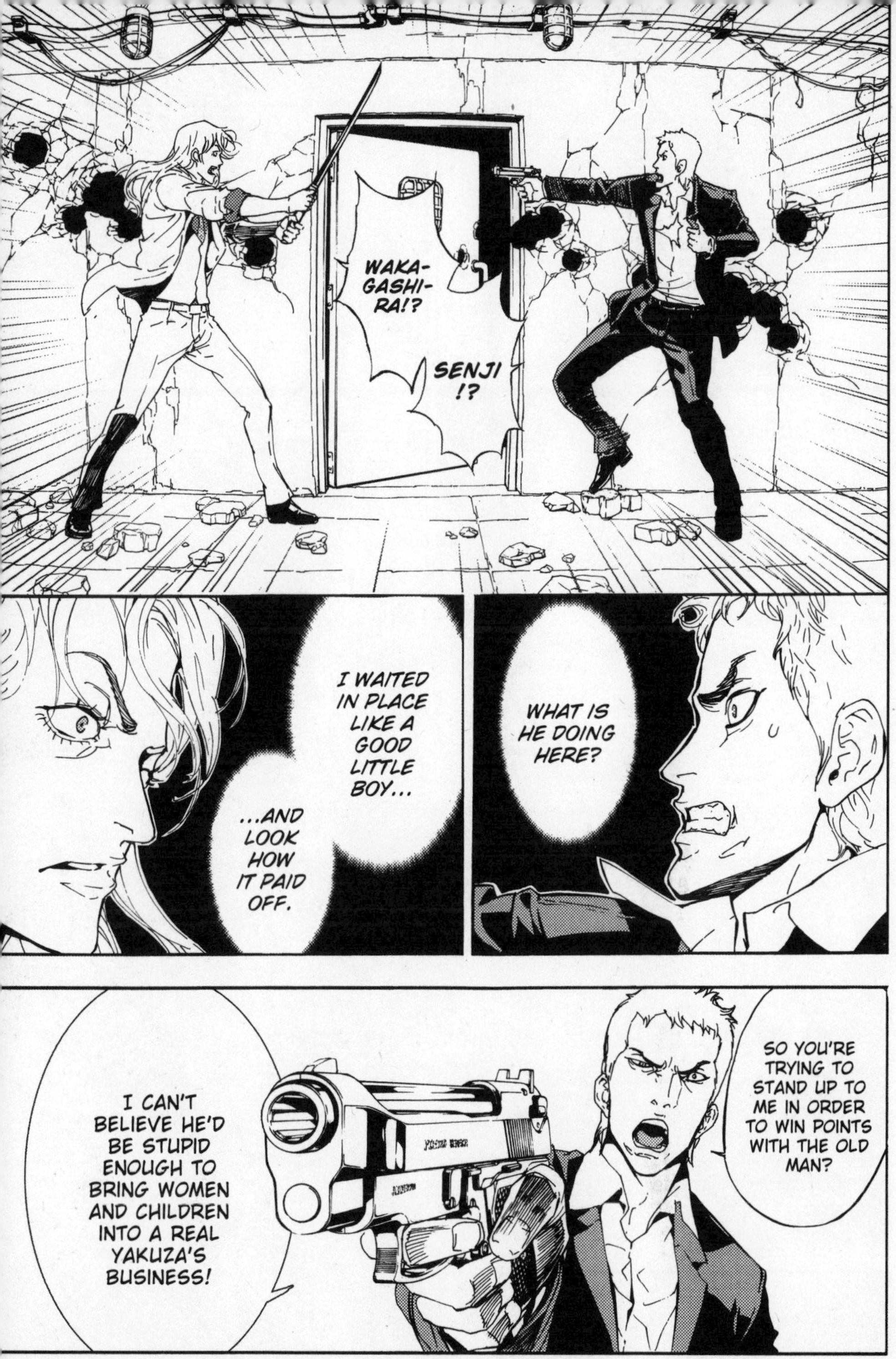
WAKA-GASHI-RA!?
SENJI!?
WHAT IS HE DOING HERE?
I WAITED IN PLACE LIKE A GOOD LITTLE BOY...
...AND LOOK HOW IT PAID OFF.
SO YOU'RE TRYING TO STAND UP TO ME IN ORDER TO WIN POINTS WITH THE OLD MAN?
I CAN'T BELIEVE HE'D BE STUPID ENOUGH TO BRING WOMEN AND CHILDREN INTO A REAL YAKUZA'S BUSINESS!

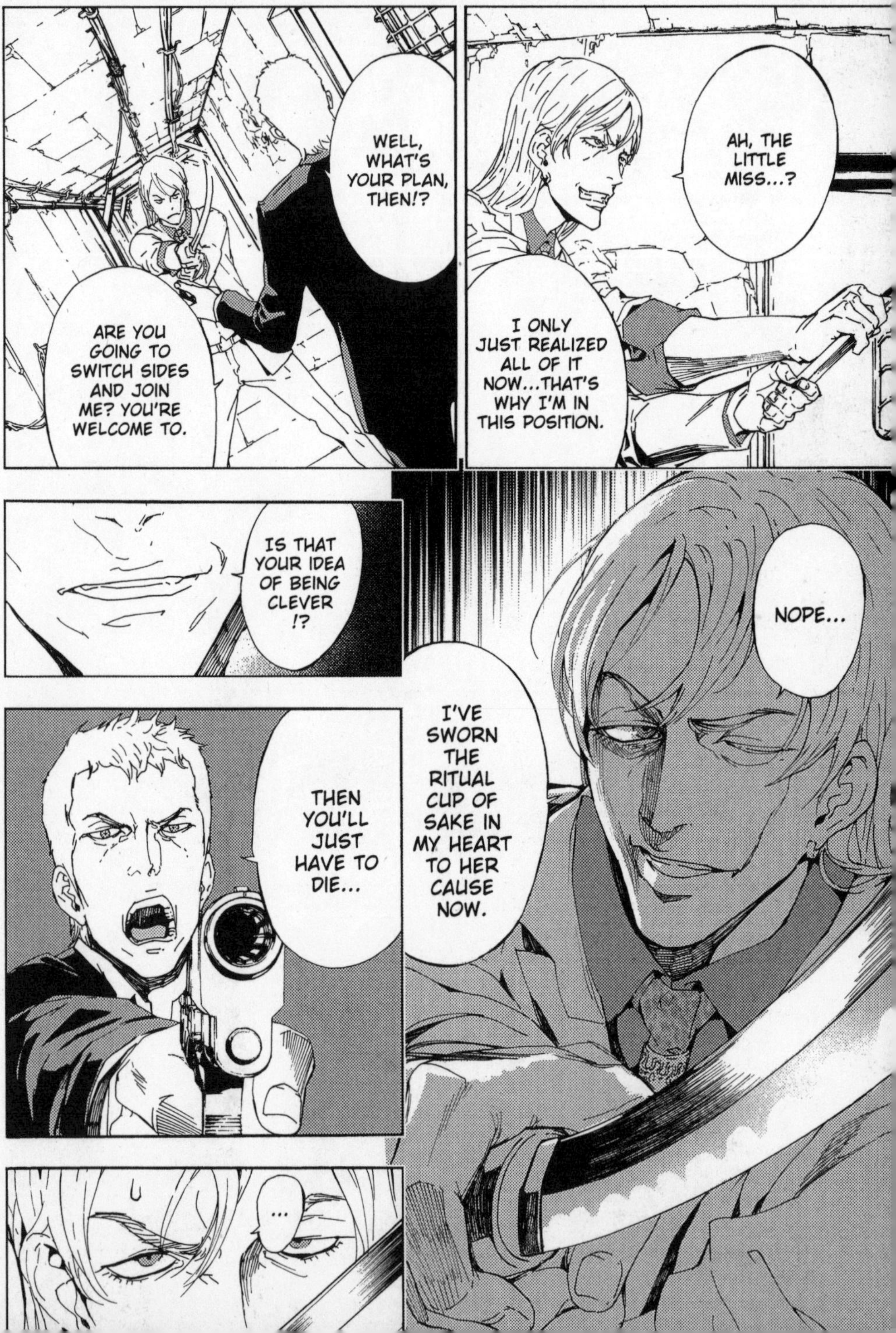
AH, THE LITTLE MISS...?
I ONLY JUST REALIZED ALL OF IT NOW...THAT'S WHY I'M IN THIS POSITION.
WELL, WHAT'S YOUR PLAN, THEN!?
ARE YOU GOING TO SWITCH SIDES AND JOIN ME? YOU'RE WELCOME TO.
NOPE...
I'VE SWORN THE RITUAL CUP OF SAKE IN MY HEART TO HER CAUSE NOW.
IS THAT YOUR IDEA OF BEING CLEVER !?
THEN YOU'LL JUST HAVE TO DIE...
...

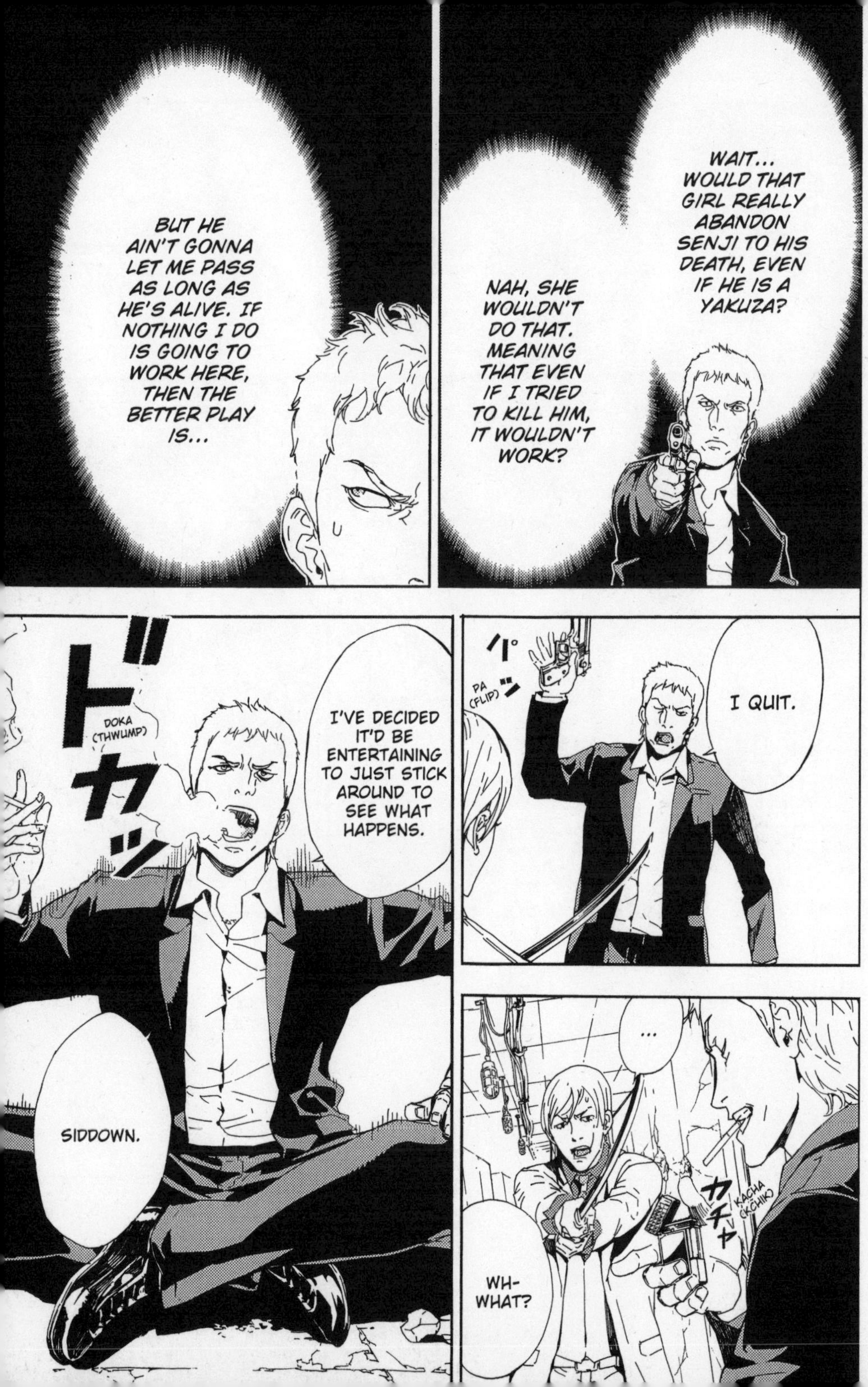
WAIT... WOULD THAT GIRL REALLY ABANDON SENJI TO HIS DEATH, EVEN IF HE IS A YAKUZA?
NAH, SHE WOULDN'T DO THAT. MEANING THAT EVEN IF I TRIED TO KILL HIM, IT WOULDN'T WORK?
BUT HE AIN'T GONNA LET ME PASS AS LONG AS HE'S ALIVE. IF NOTHING I DO IS GOING TO WORK HERE, THEN THE BETTER PLAY IS...
パッ
PA (FLIP)
I QUIT.
...
カチャ
KACHA (KCHIK)
WH- WHAT?
I'VE DECIDED IT'D BE ENTERTAINING TO JUST STICK AROUND TO SEE WHAT HAPPENS.
ドカッ
DOKA (THWUMP)
SIDDOWN.

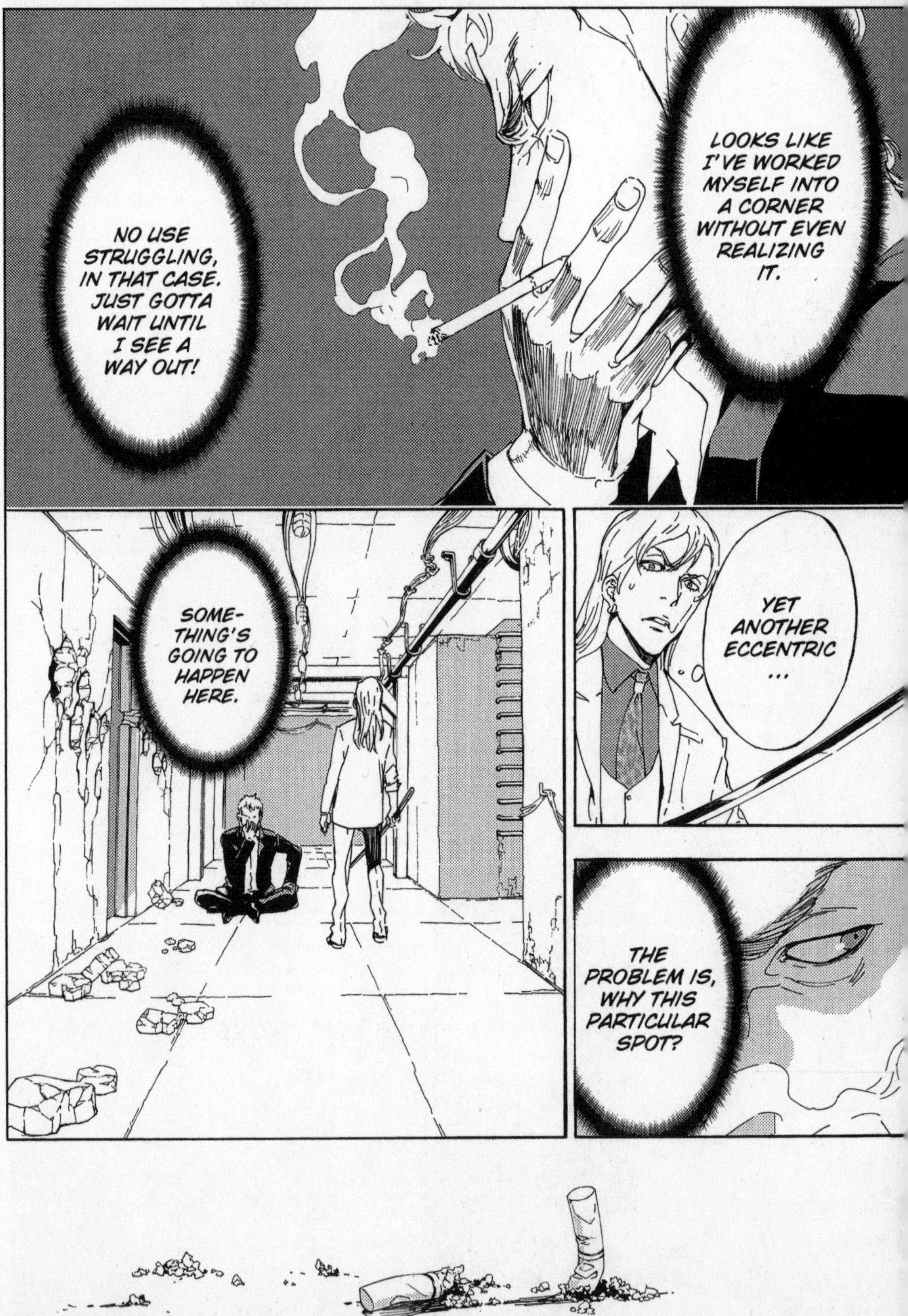
LOOKS LIKE I'VE WORKED MYSELF INTO A CORNER WITHOUT EVEN REALIZING IT.
NO USE STRUGGLING, IN THAT CASE. JUST GOTTA WAIT UNTIL I SEE A WAY OUT!
YET ANOTHER ECCENTRIC ...
THE PROBLEM IS, WHY THIS PARTICULAR SPOT?
SOME-THING'S GOING TO HAPPEN HERE.

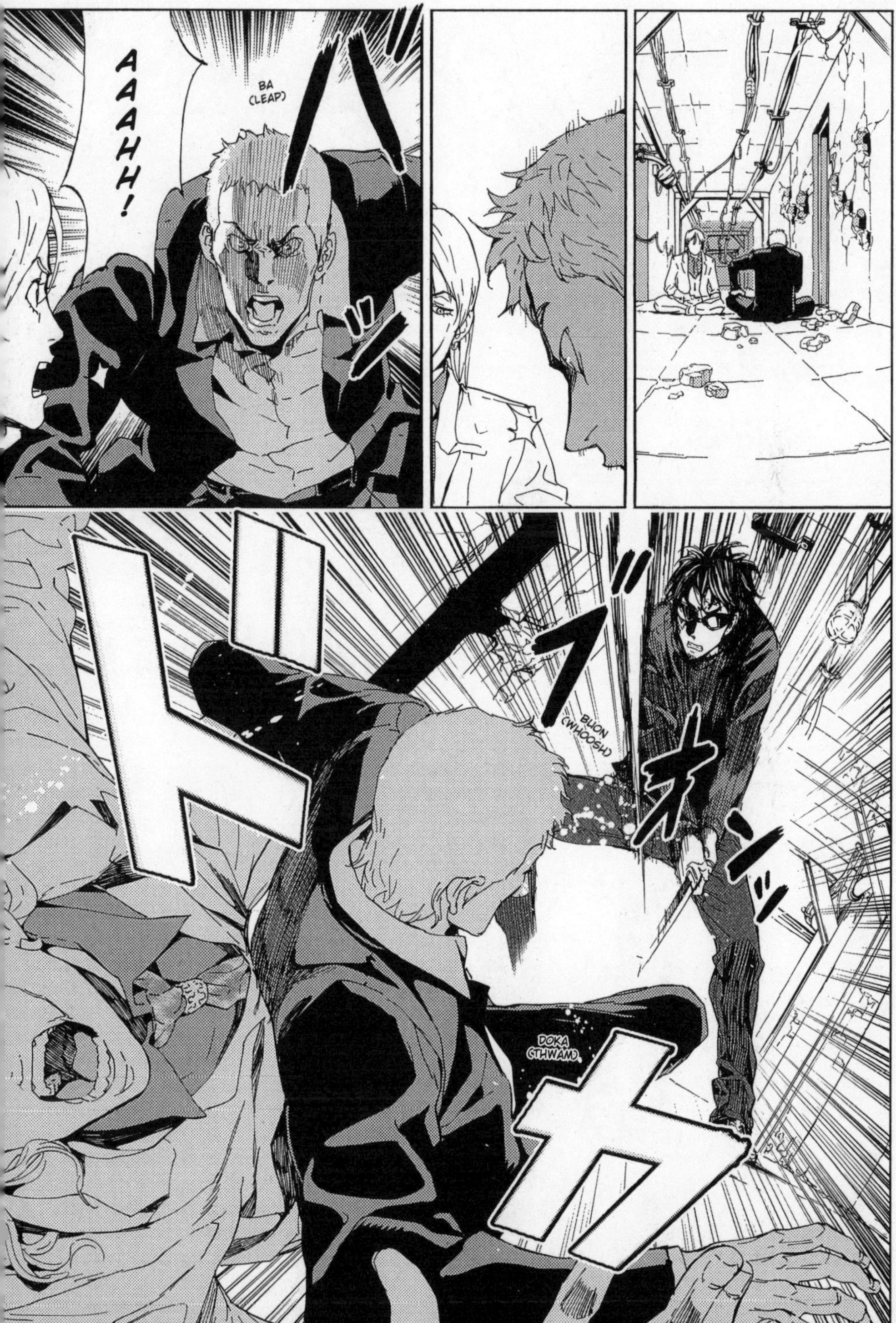
AAAAHH!
BA (LEAP)
BUON (WHOOSH)
DOKA (THWAM)

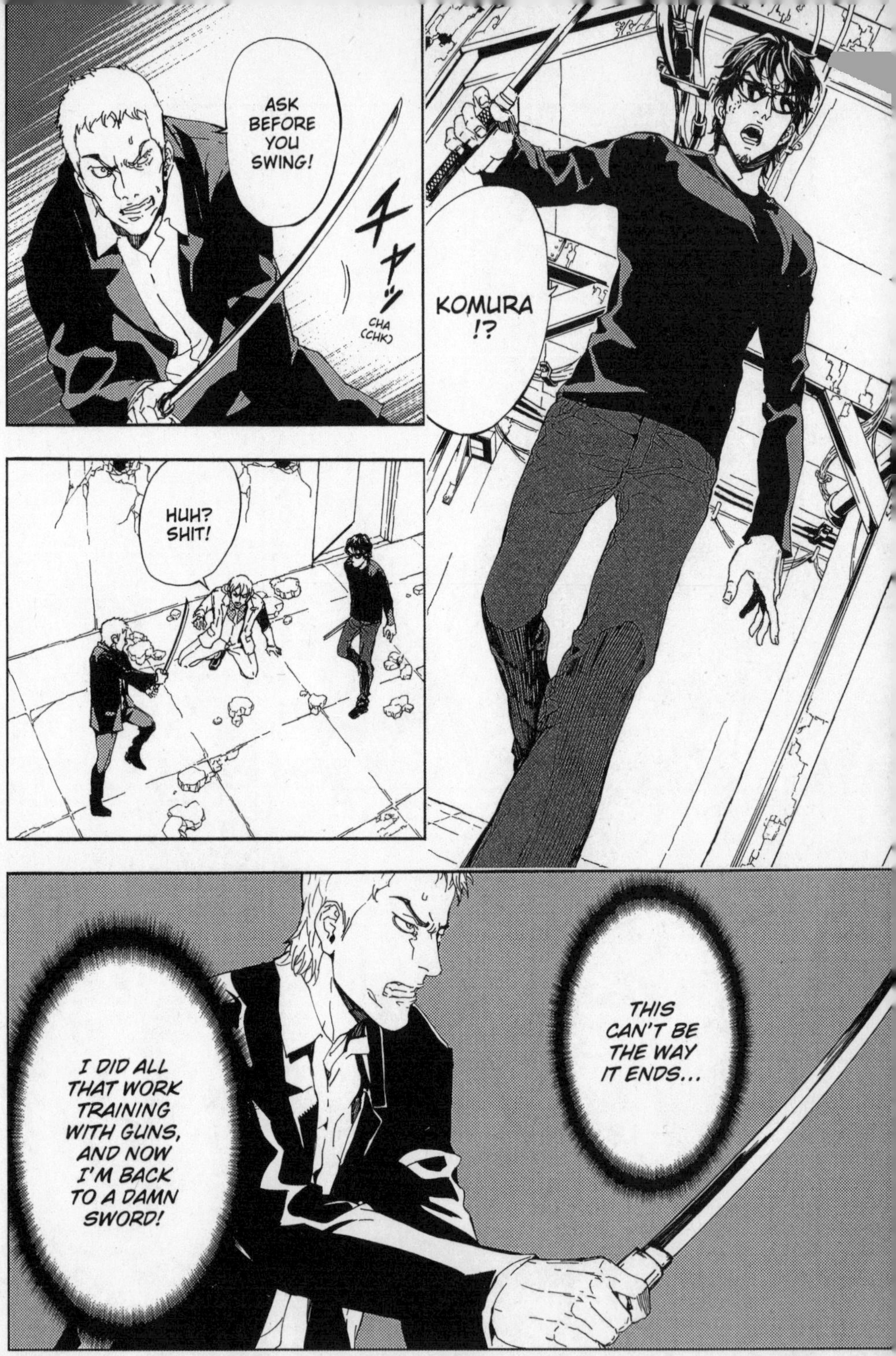
KOMURA!?
ASK BEFORE YOU SWING!
チャッ
CHA (CHK)
HUH? SHIT!
THIS CAN'T BE THE WAY IT ENDS...
I DID ALL THAT WORK TRAINING WITH GUNS, AND NOW I'M BACK TO A DAMN SWORD!

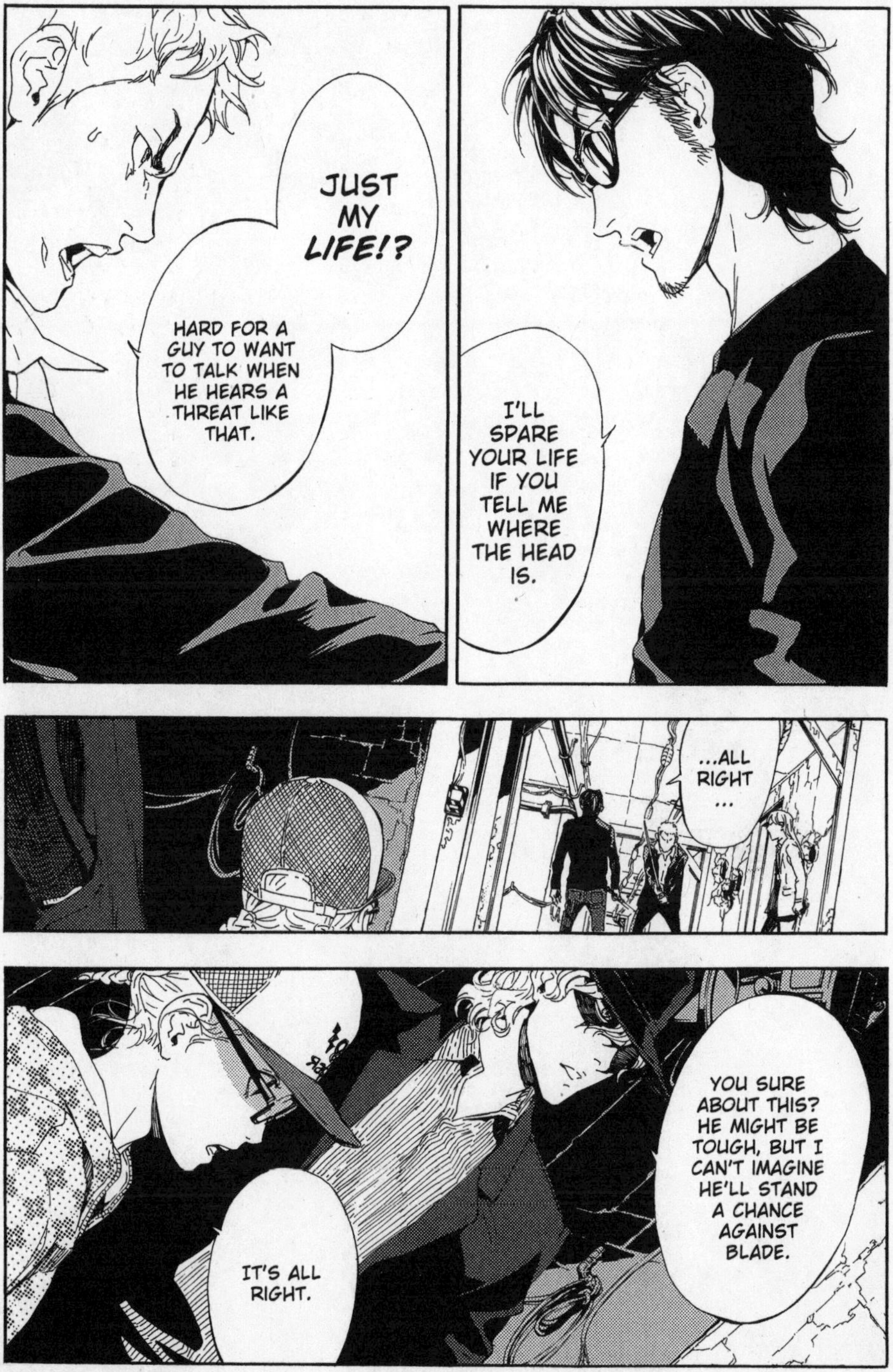
I'LL SPARE YOUR LIFE IF YOU TELL ME WHERE THE HEAD IS.
JUST MY *LIFE!?*
HARD FOR A GUY TO WANT TO TALK WHEN HE HEARS A THREAT LIKE THAT.
...ALL RIGHT ...
YOU SURE ABOUT THIS? HE MIGHT BE TOUGH, BUT I CAN'T IMAGINE HE'LL STAND A CHANCE AGAINST BLADE.
IT'S ALL RIGHT.

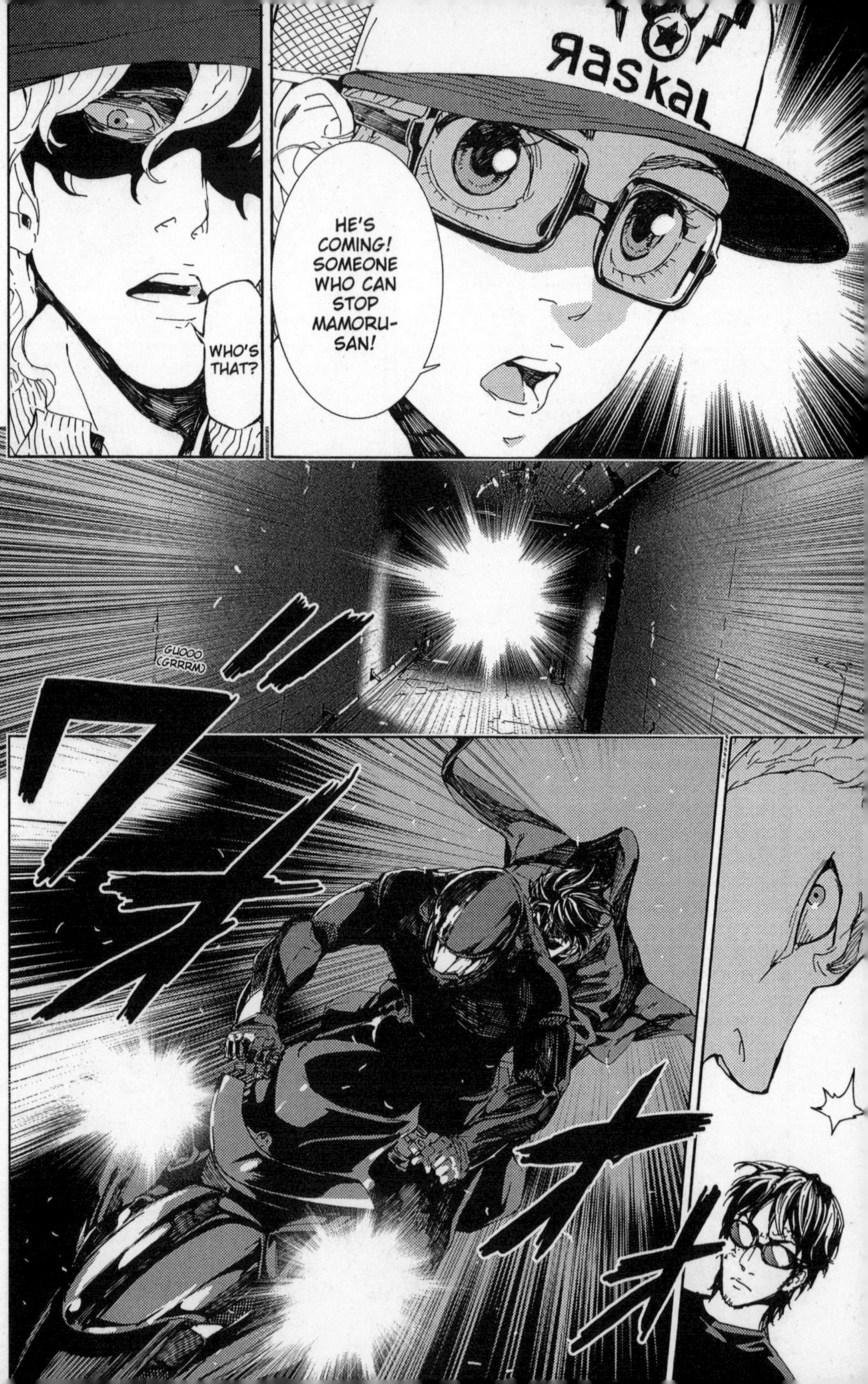
RASKAL
HE'S COMING! SOMEONE WHO CAN STOP MAMORU-SAN!
WHO'S THAT?
GUOOO (GRRRM)

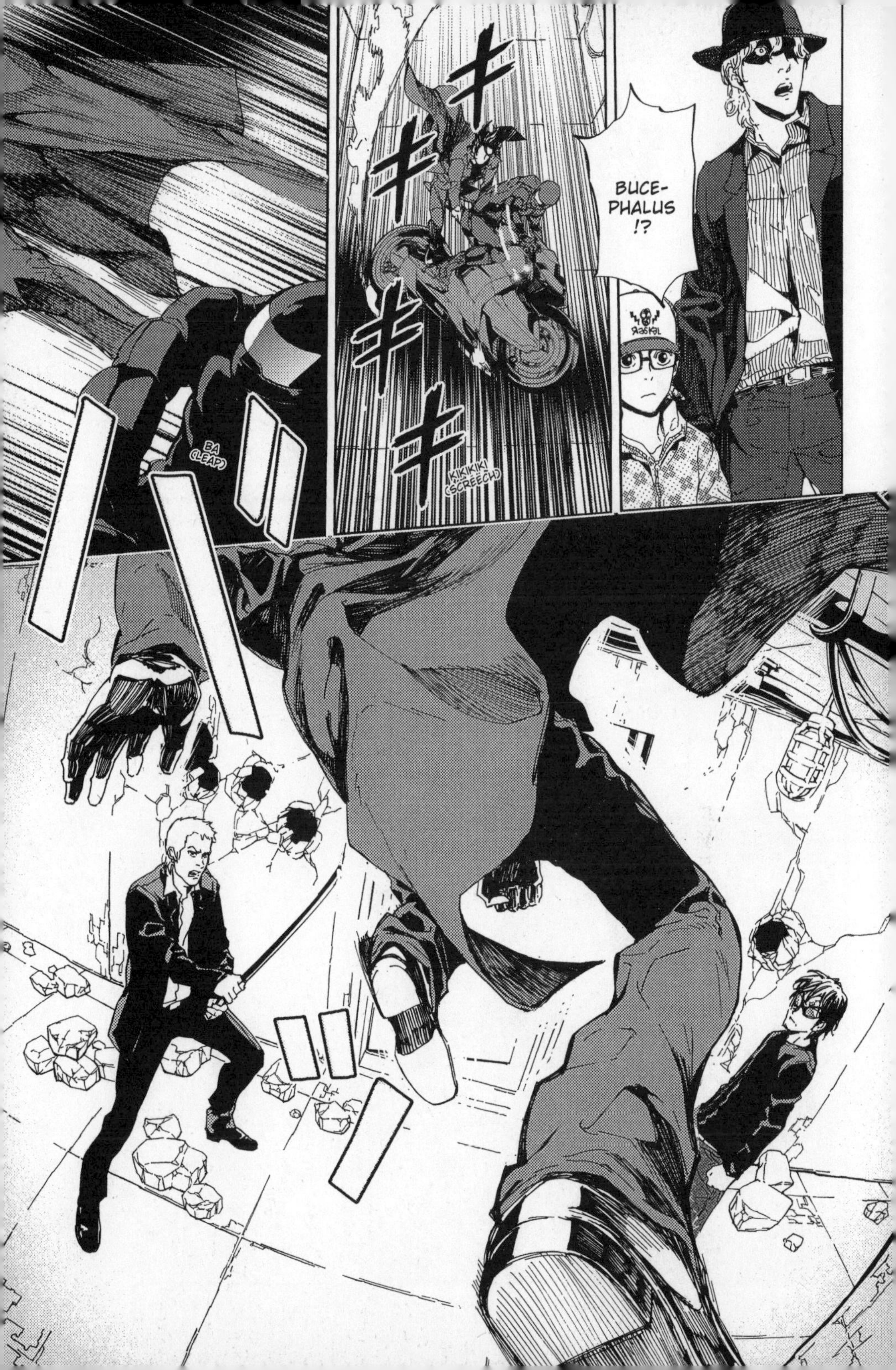
BUCE-PHALUS !?
KIKIKIKI (SCREECH)
BA (LEAP)

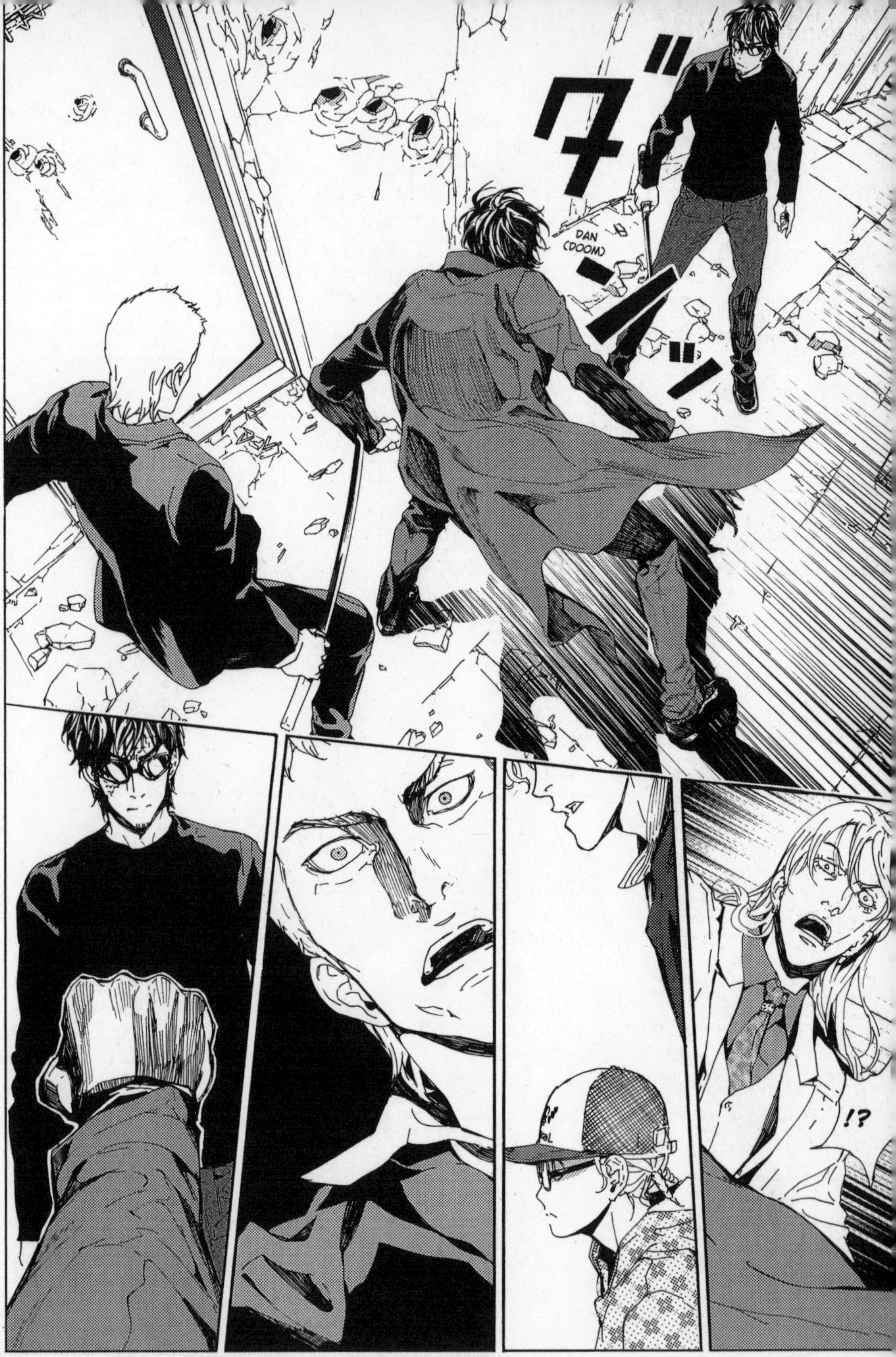
DAN (DOOM)
!?

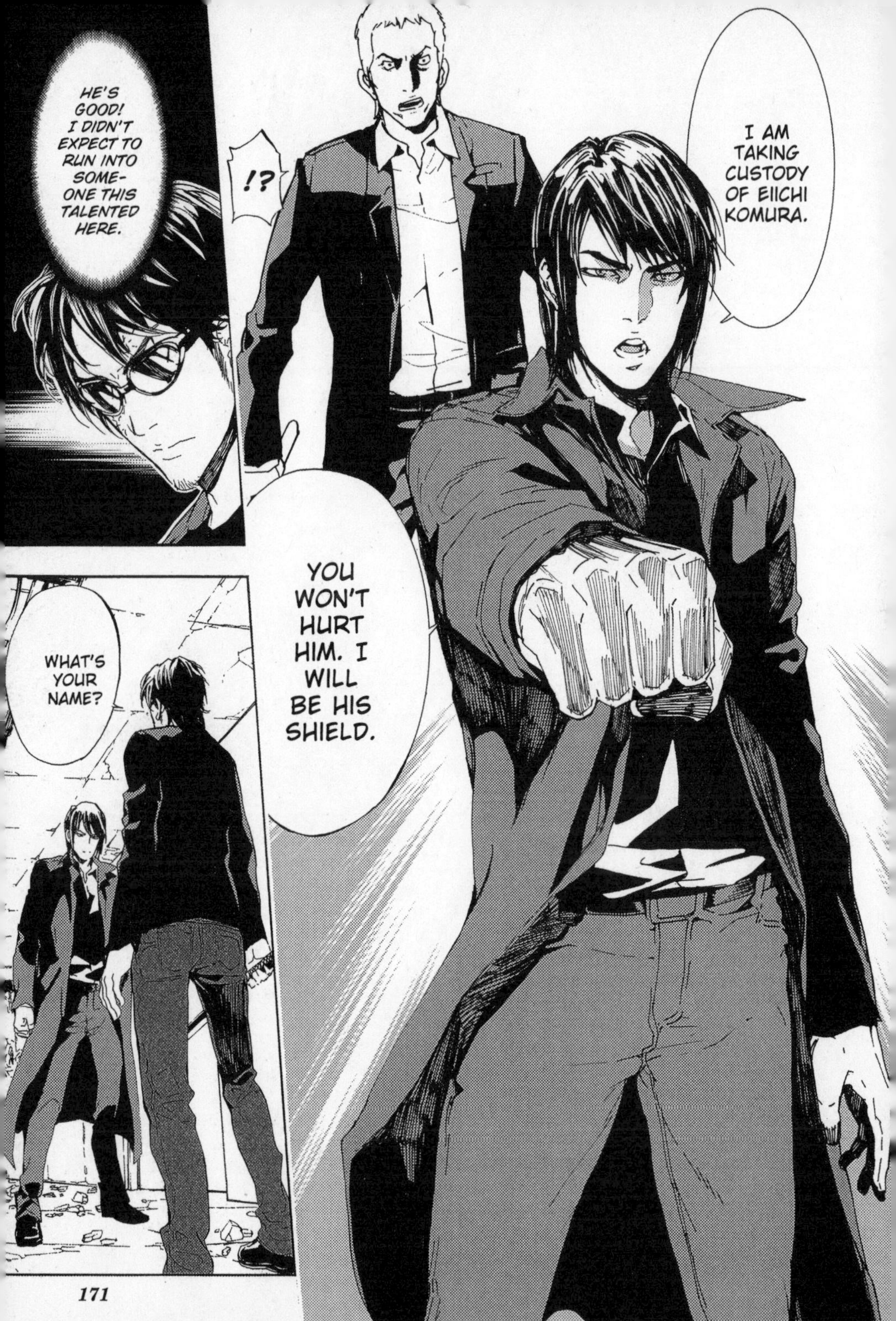
I AM TAKING CUSTODY OF EIICHI KOMURA.
!?
YOU WON'T HURT HIM. I WILL BE HIS SHIELD.
HE'S GOOD! I DIDN'T EXPECT TO RUN INTO SOME-ONE THIS TALENTED HERE.
WHAT'S YOUR NAME?

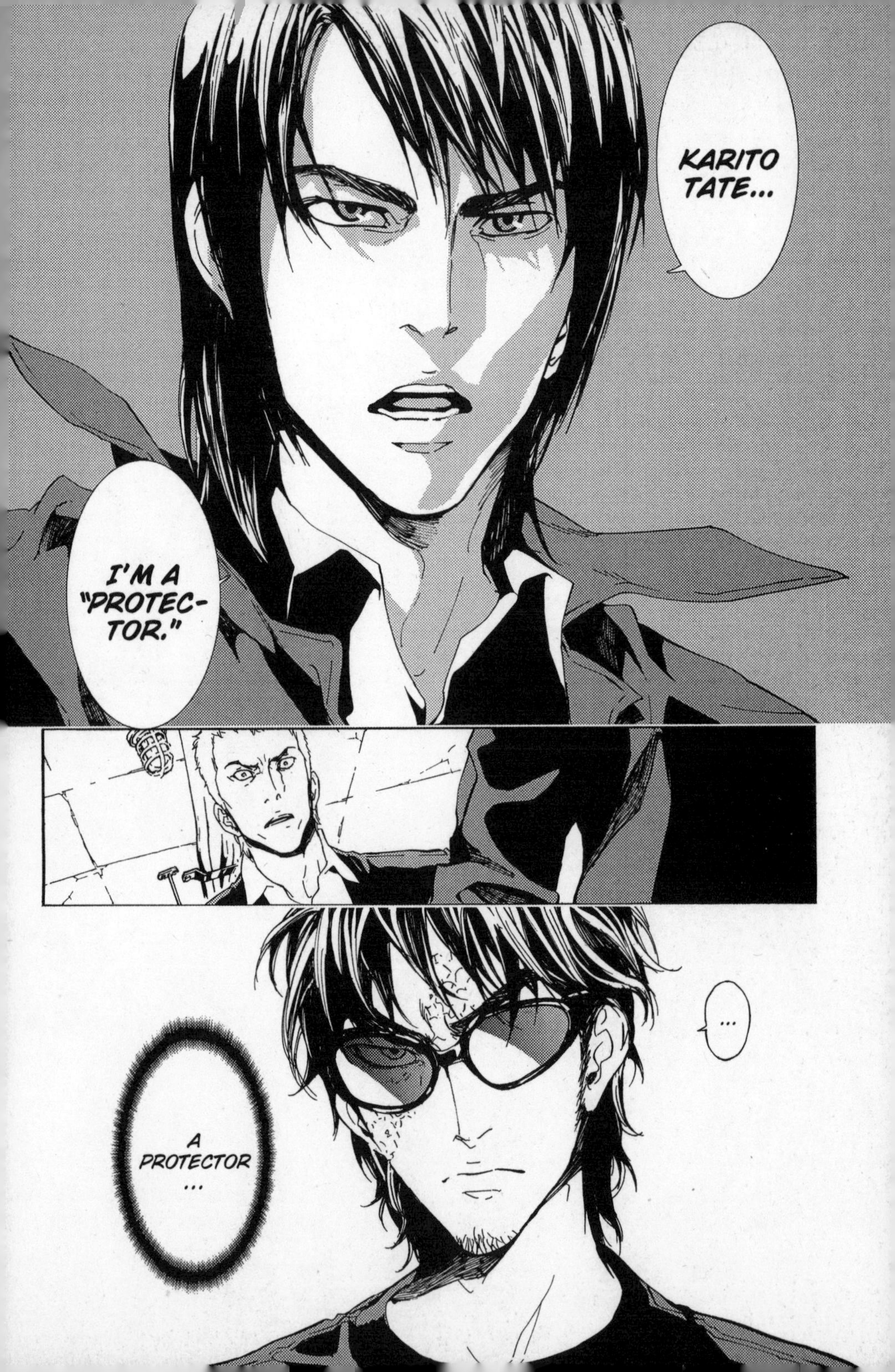
KARITO TATE...
I'M A "PROTEC-TOR."
...
A PROTECTOR ...

Until Death do us Part

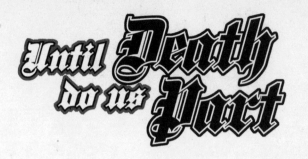

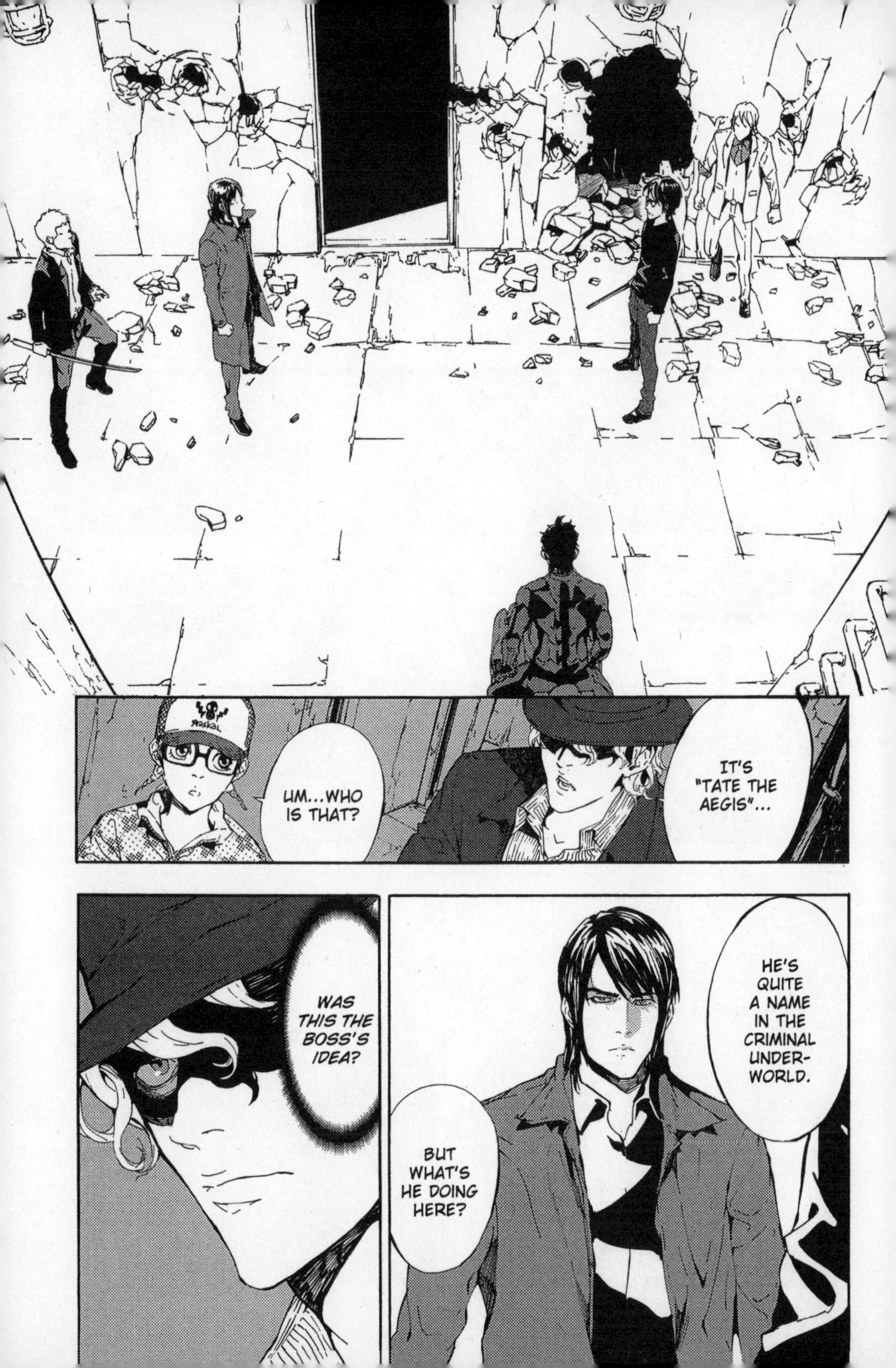
IT'S "TATE THE AEGIS"...
UM...WHO IS THAT?
HE'S QUITE A NAME IN THE CRIMINAL UNDER-WORLD.
BUT WHAT'S HE DOING HERE?
WAS THIS THE BOSS'S IDEA?

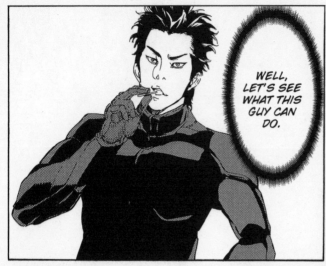

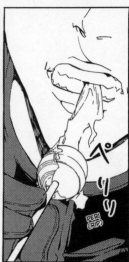

PERI (RIP)
WELL, LET'S SEE WHAT THIS GUY CAN DO.
WHAT THE HELL IS GOING ON!? IS THIS THE REAL AEGIS!?
WHO KNOWS WHAT MIGHT HAPPEN TO ME NOW?
HOLD UP!
FIRST OFF, I NEED TO KNOW IF YOU'RE REALLY THE FAMOUS TATE THE AEGIS...

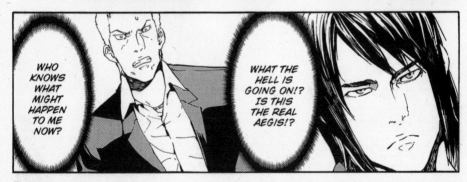

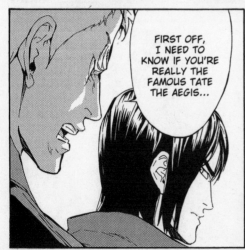

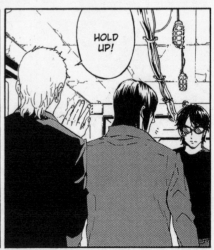

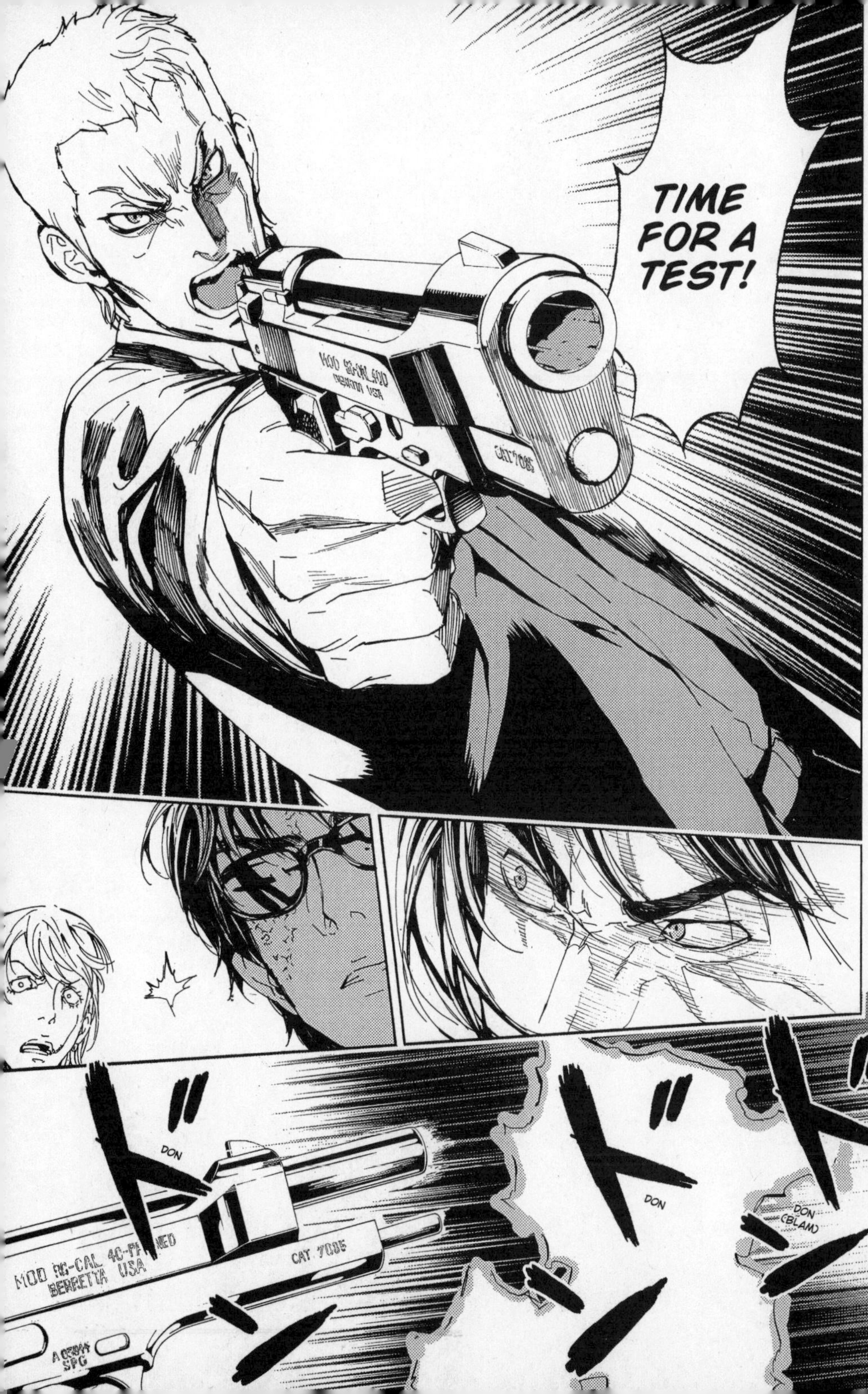
TIME FOR A TEST!
DON (BLAM)
DON
DON

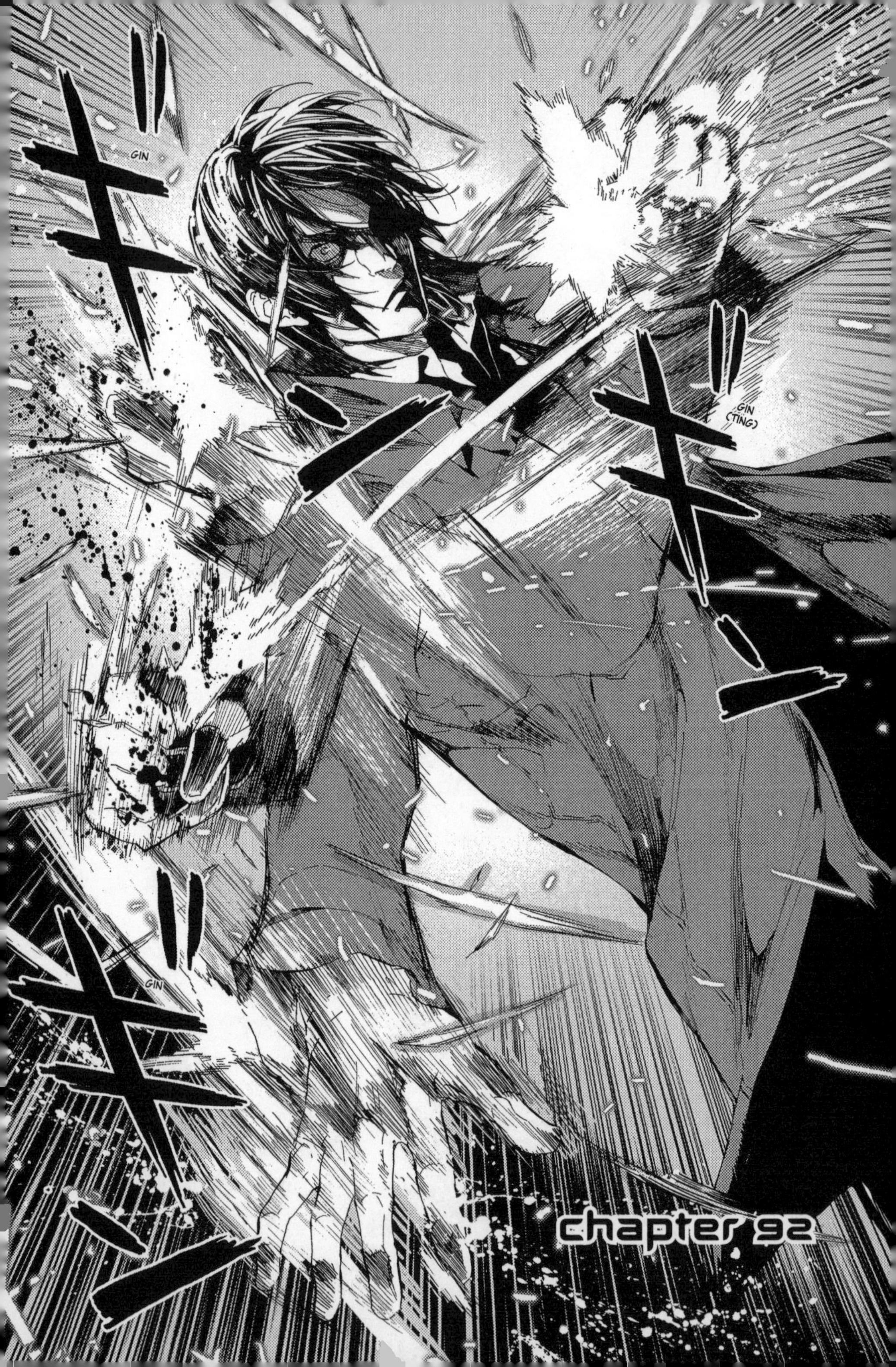
GIN
GIN
(TING)
GIN

chapter 92

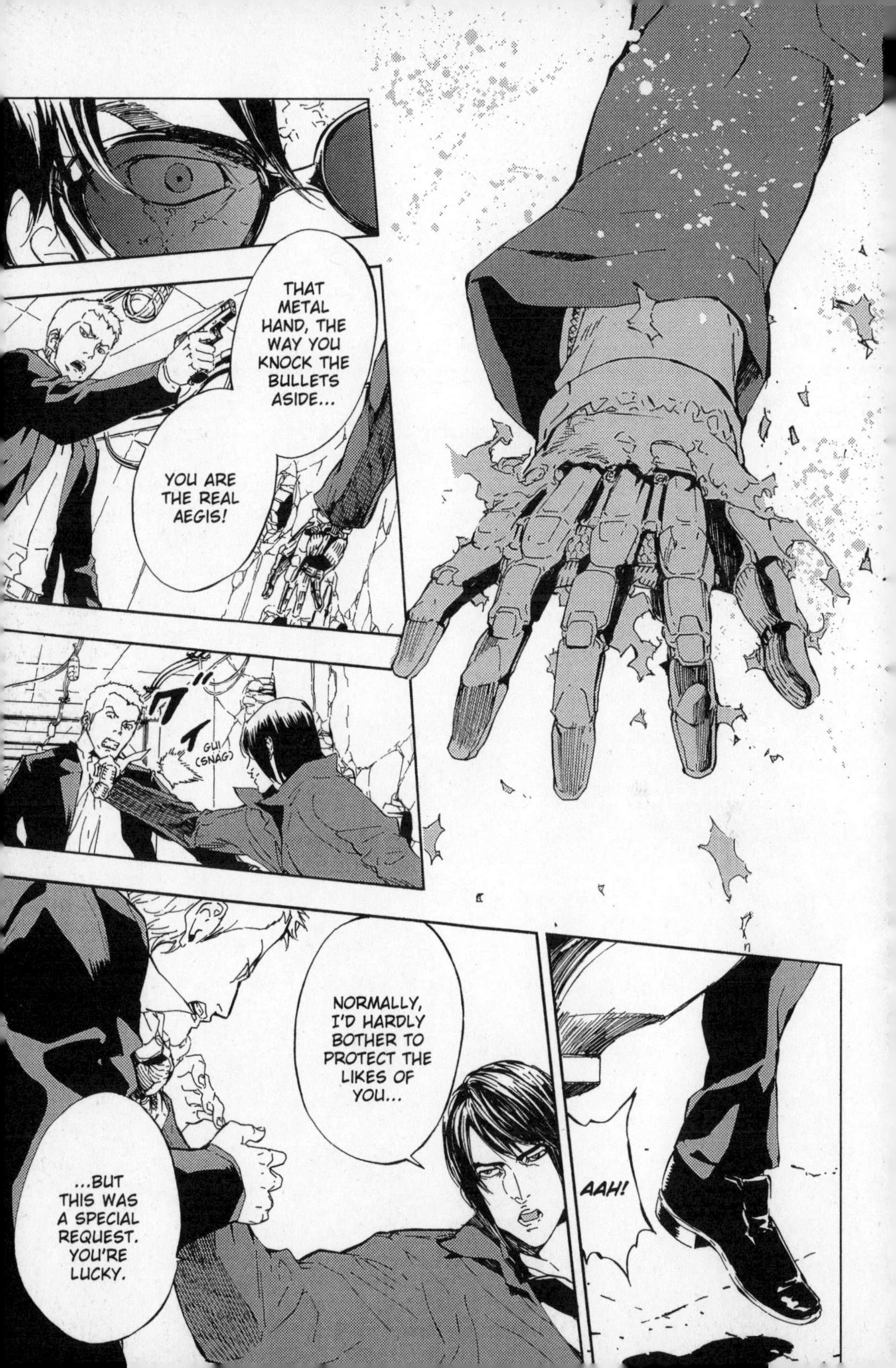
THAT METAL HAND, THE WAY YOU KNOCK THE BULLETS ASIDE...
YOU ARE THE REAL AEGIS!
GUI (SNAG)
AAH!
NORMALLY, I'D HARDLY BOTHER TO PROTECT THE LIKES OF YOU...
...BUT THIS WAS A SPECIAL REQUEST. YOU'RE LUCKY.

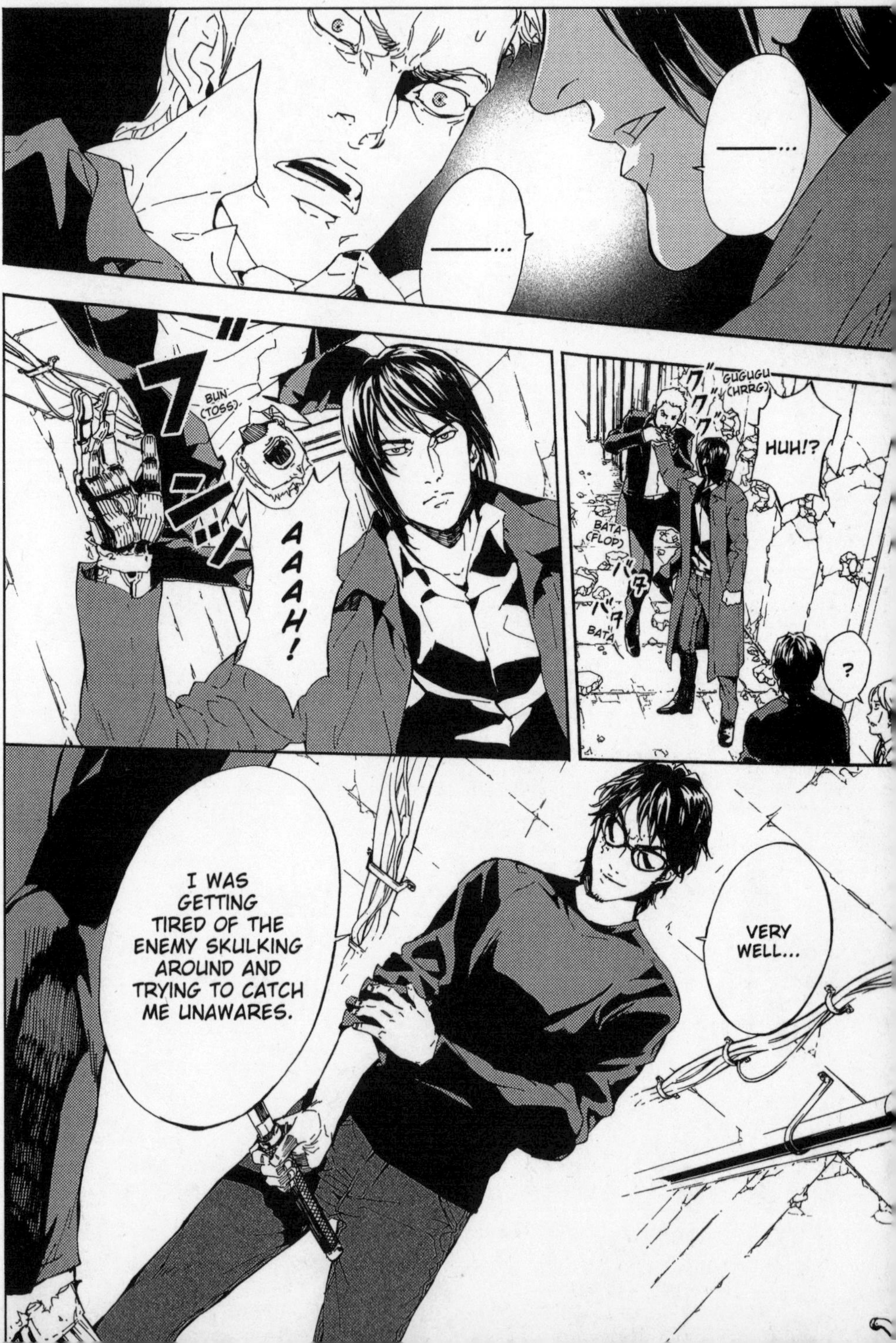
———...
———...
GUGUGU (HRRG)
HUH!?
BATA (FLOP)
BATA
?
BUN (TOSS)
AAAAH!
VERY WELL...
I WAS GETTING TIRED OF THE ENEMY SKULKING AROUND AND TRYING TO CATCH ME UNAWARES.

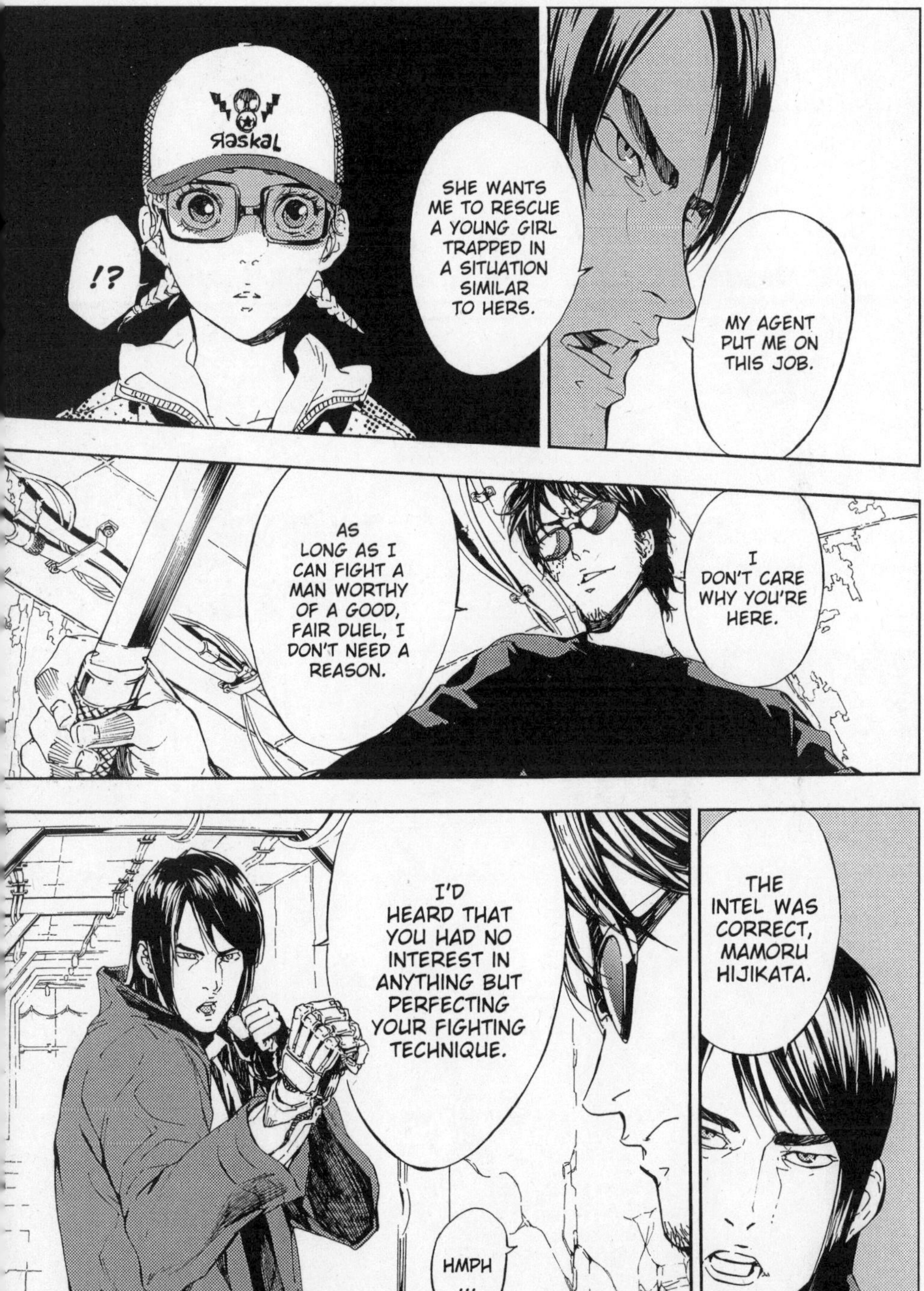
MY AGENT PUT ME ON THIS JOB.
SHE WANTS ME TO RESCUE A YOUNG GIRL TRAPPED IN A SITUATION SIMILAR TO HERS.
RASKAL
!?
I DON'T CARE WHY YOU'RE HERE.
AS LONG AS I CAN FIGHT A MAN WORTHY OF A GOOD, FAIR DUEL, I DON'T NEED A REASON.
THE INTEL WAS CORRECT, MAMORU HIJIKATA.
HMPH...
I'D HEARD THAT YOU HAD NO INTEREST IN ANYTHING BUT PERFECTING YOUR FIGHTING TECHNIQUE.

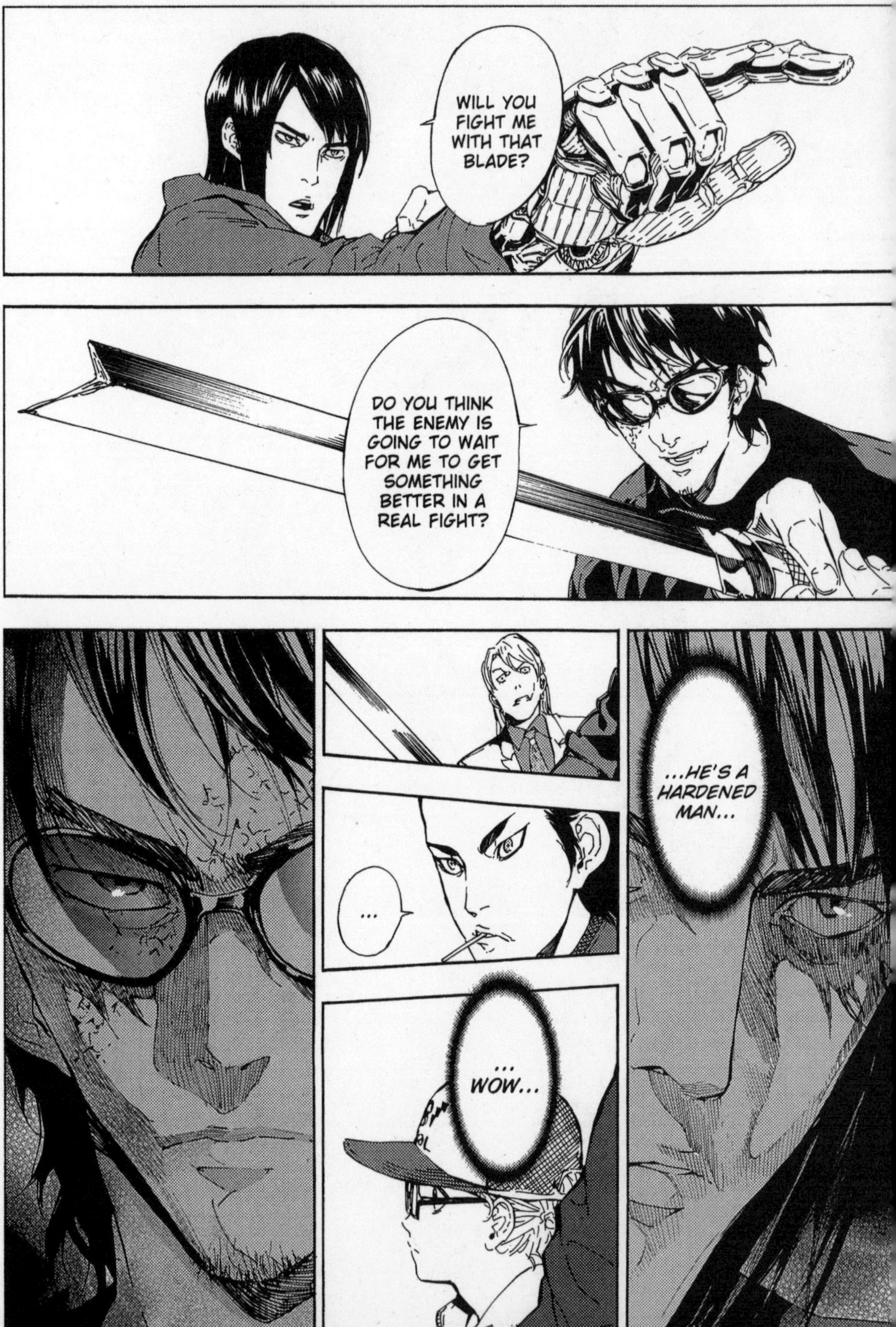
WILL YOU FIGHT ME WITH THAT BLADE?
DO YOU THINK THE ENEMY IS GOING TO WAIT FOR ME TO GET SOMETHING BETTER IN A REAL FIGHT?
...HE'S A HARDENED MAN...
...
... WOW...

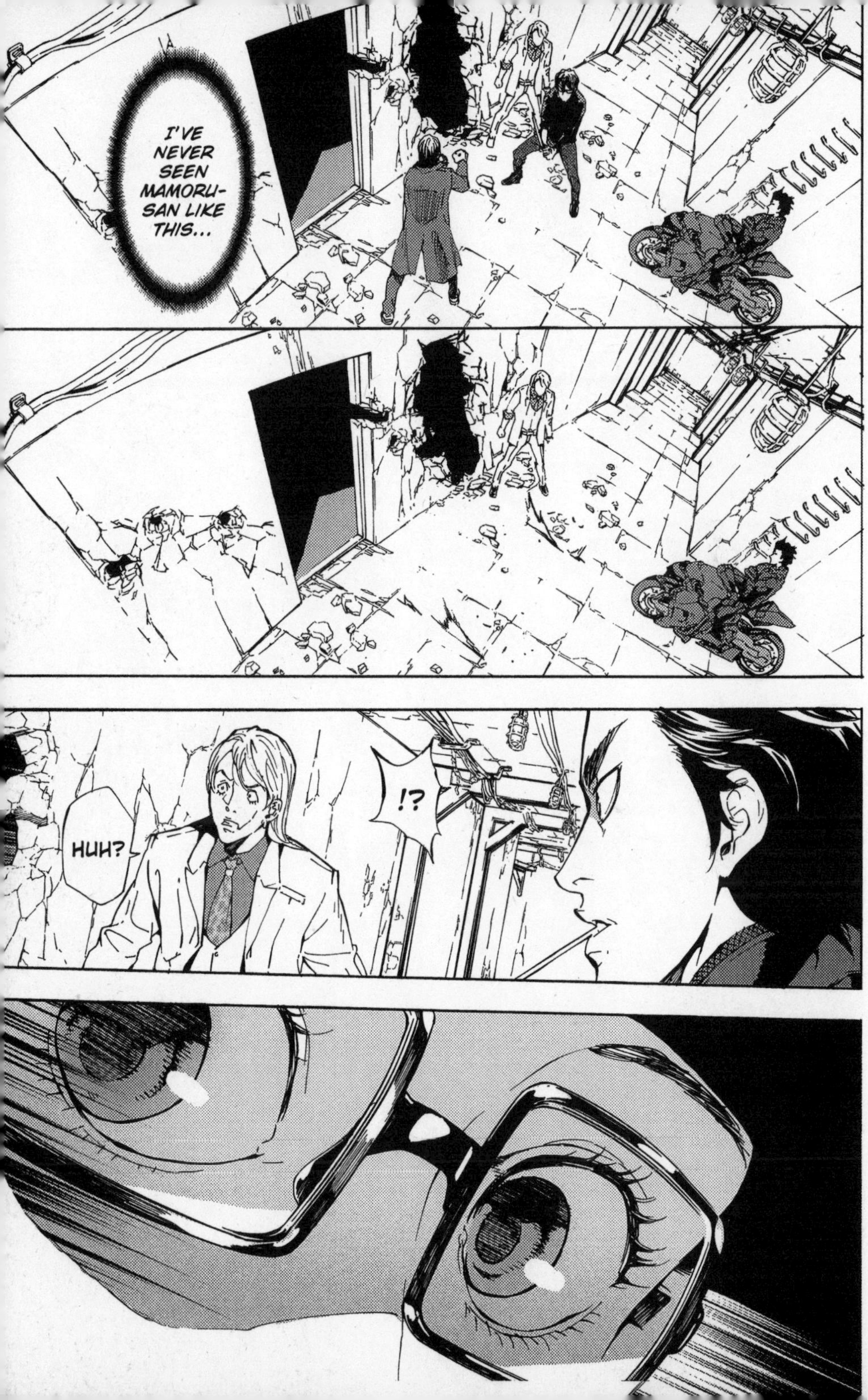
I'VE NEVER SEEN MAMORU-SAN LIKE THIS...
!?
HUH?

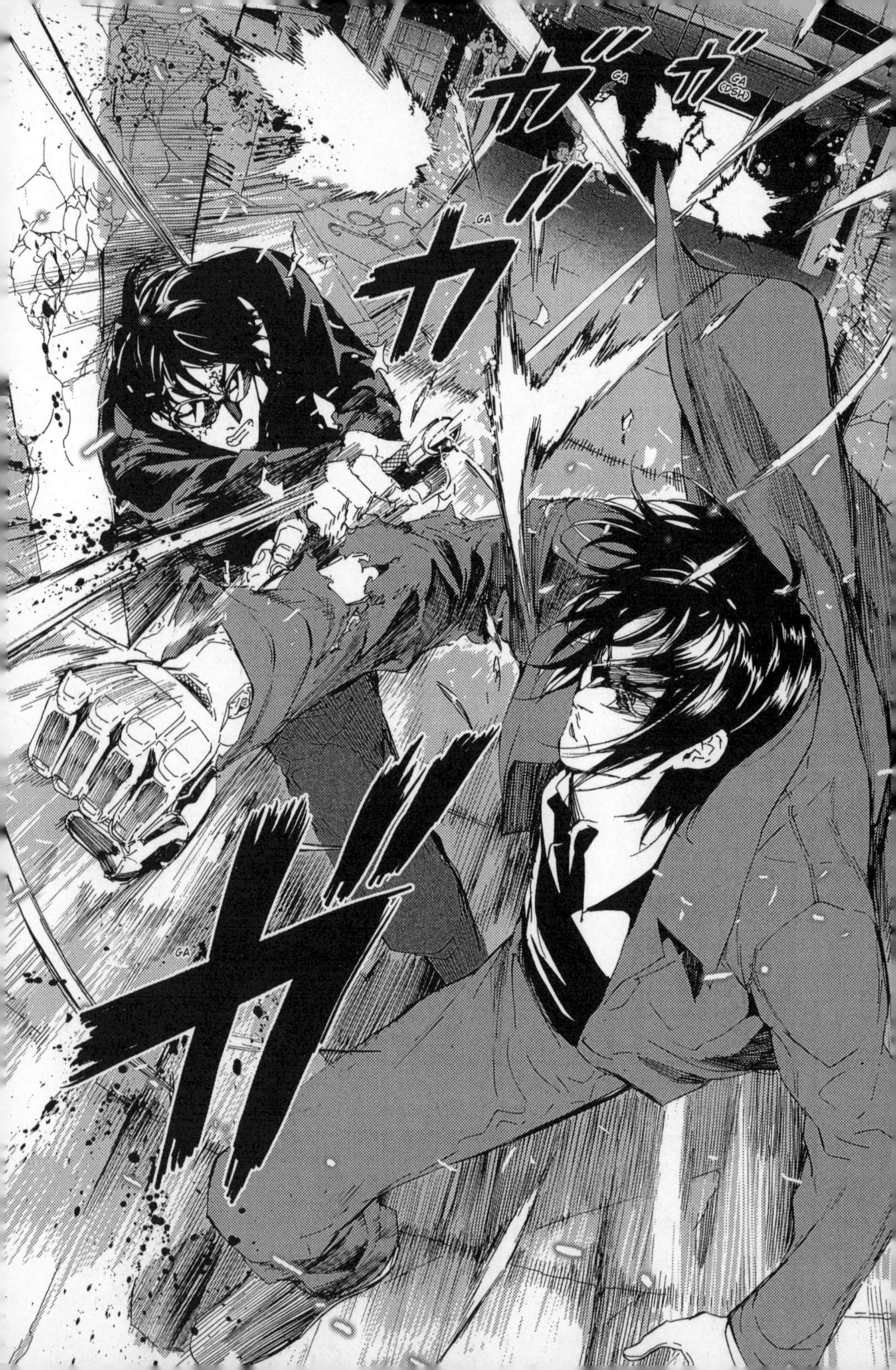
ガ
GA
(DSH)
ガ
GA
ガ
GA
ガ
GA

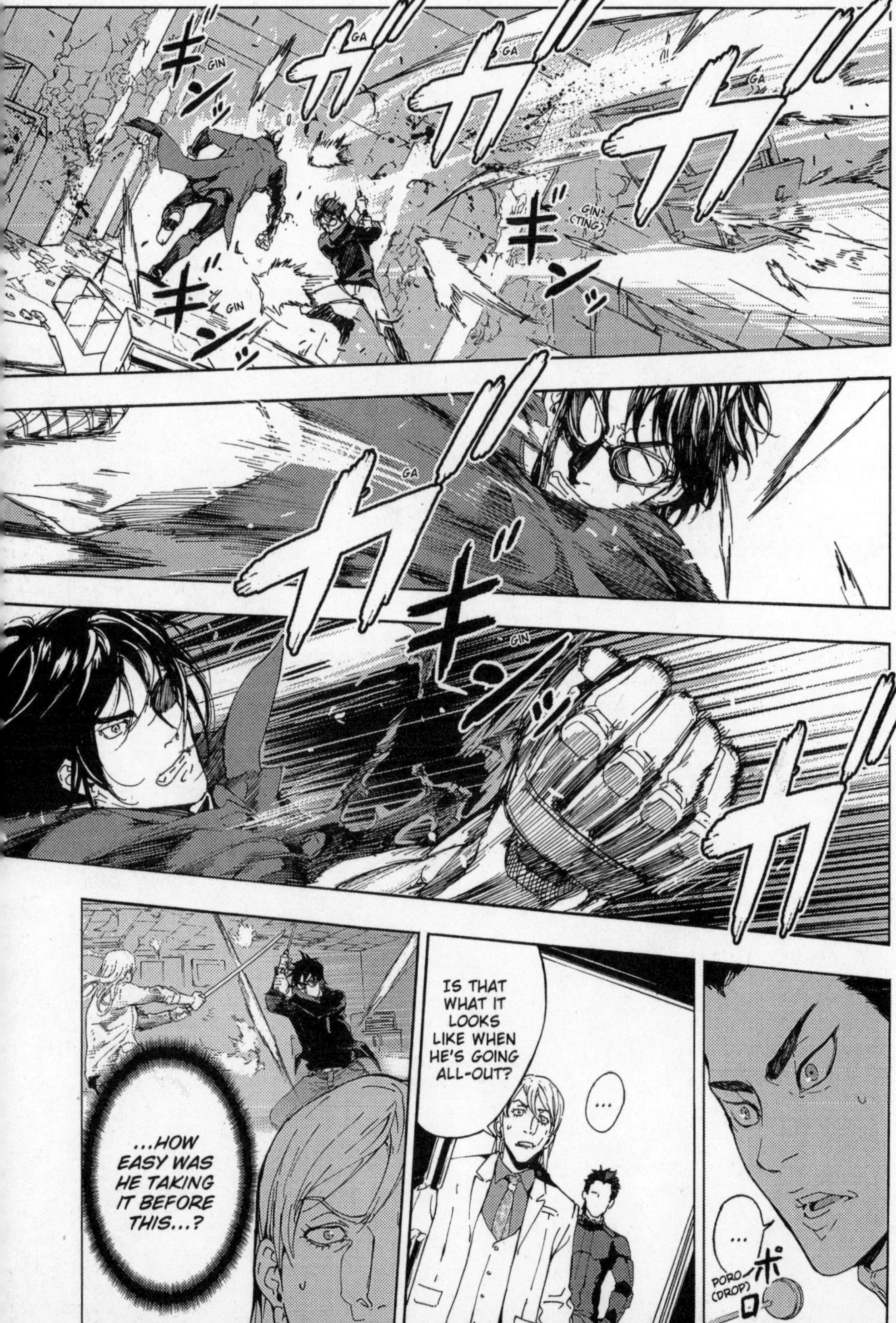
GA
GA
GA
GIN (TING)
GIN
GIN
GA
GIN
...
PORO (DROP)
IS THAT WHAT IT LOOKS LIKE WHEN HE'S GOING ALL-OUT?
...
...HOW EASY WAS HE TAKING IT BEFORE THIS...?

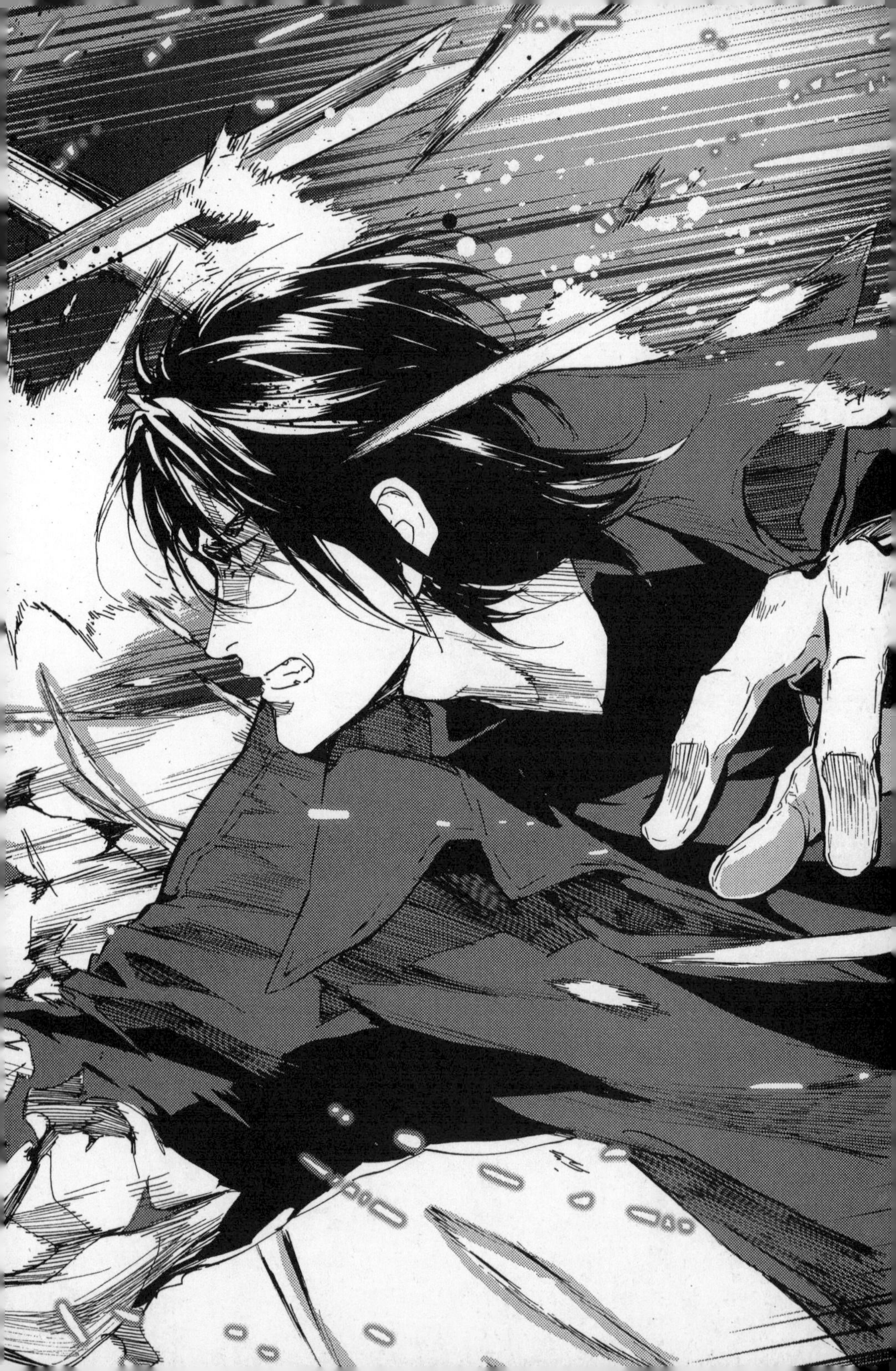

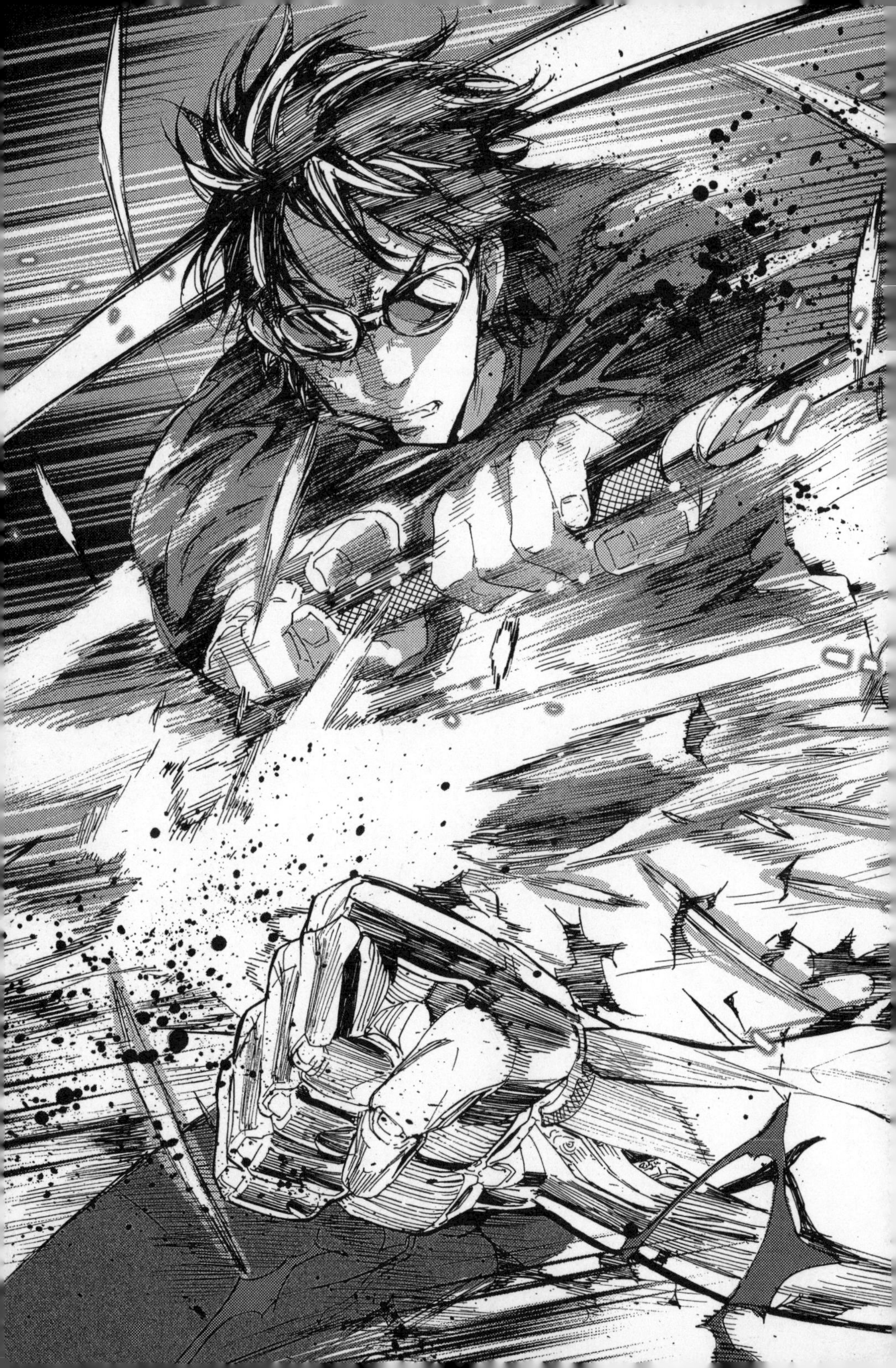

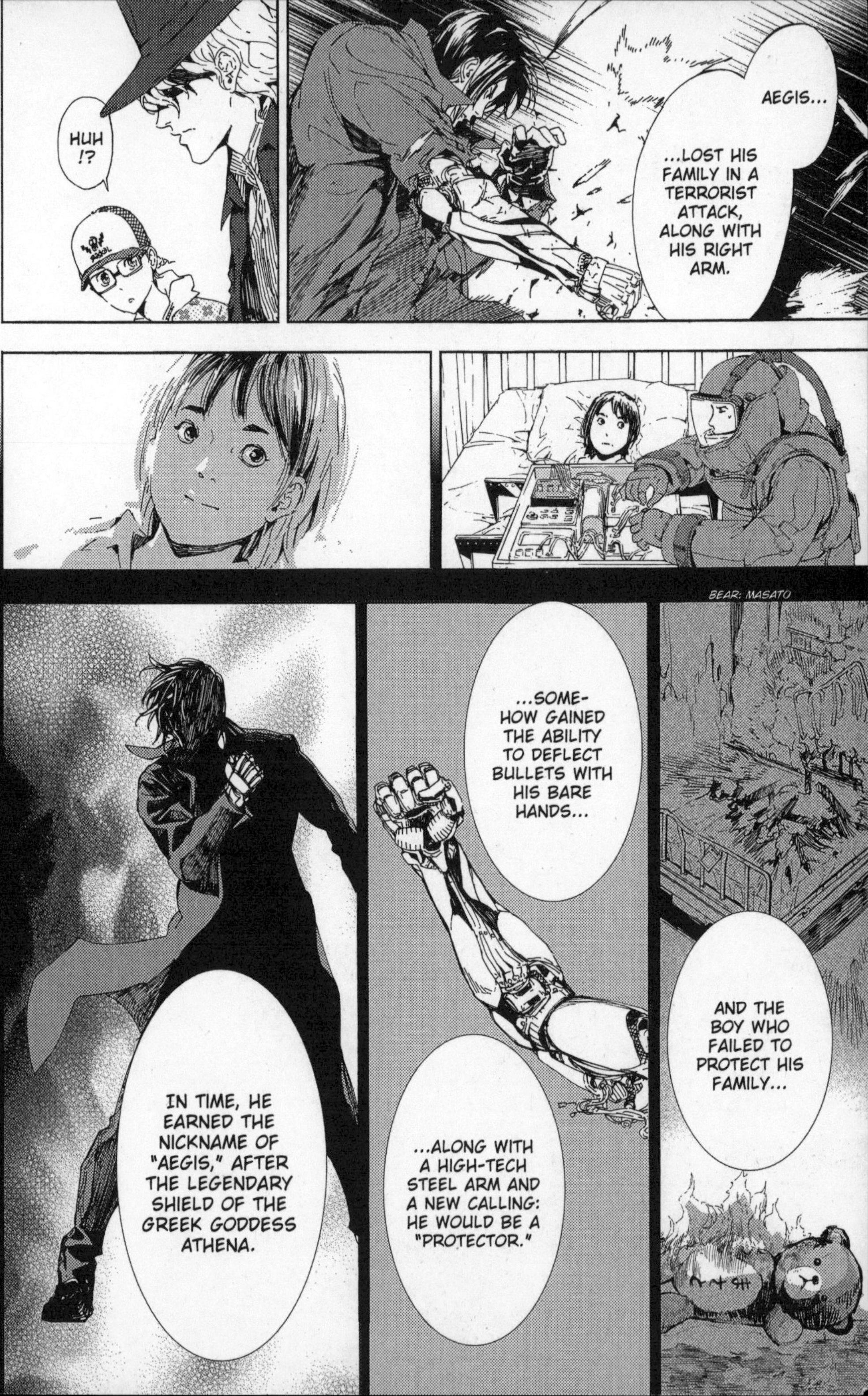

AEGIS...
...LOST HIS FAMILY IN A TERRORIST ATTACK, ALONG WITH HIS RIGHT ARM.
HUH !?
BEAR: MASATO
AND THE BOY WHO FAILED TO PROTECT HIS FAMILY...
...SOME-HOW GAINED THE ABILITY TO DEFLECT BULLETS WITH HIS BARE HANDS...
...ALONG WITH A HIGH-TECH STEEL ARM AND A NEW CALLING: HE WOULD BE A "PROTECTOR."
IN TIME, HE EARNED THE NICKNAME OF "AEGIS," AFTER THE LEGENDARY SHIELD OF THE GREEK GODDESS ATHENA.

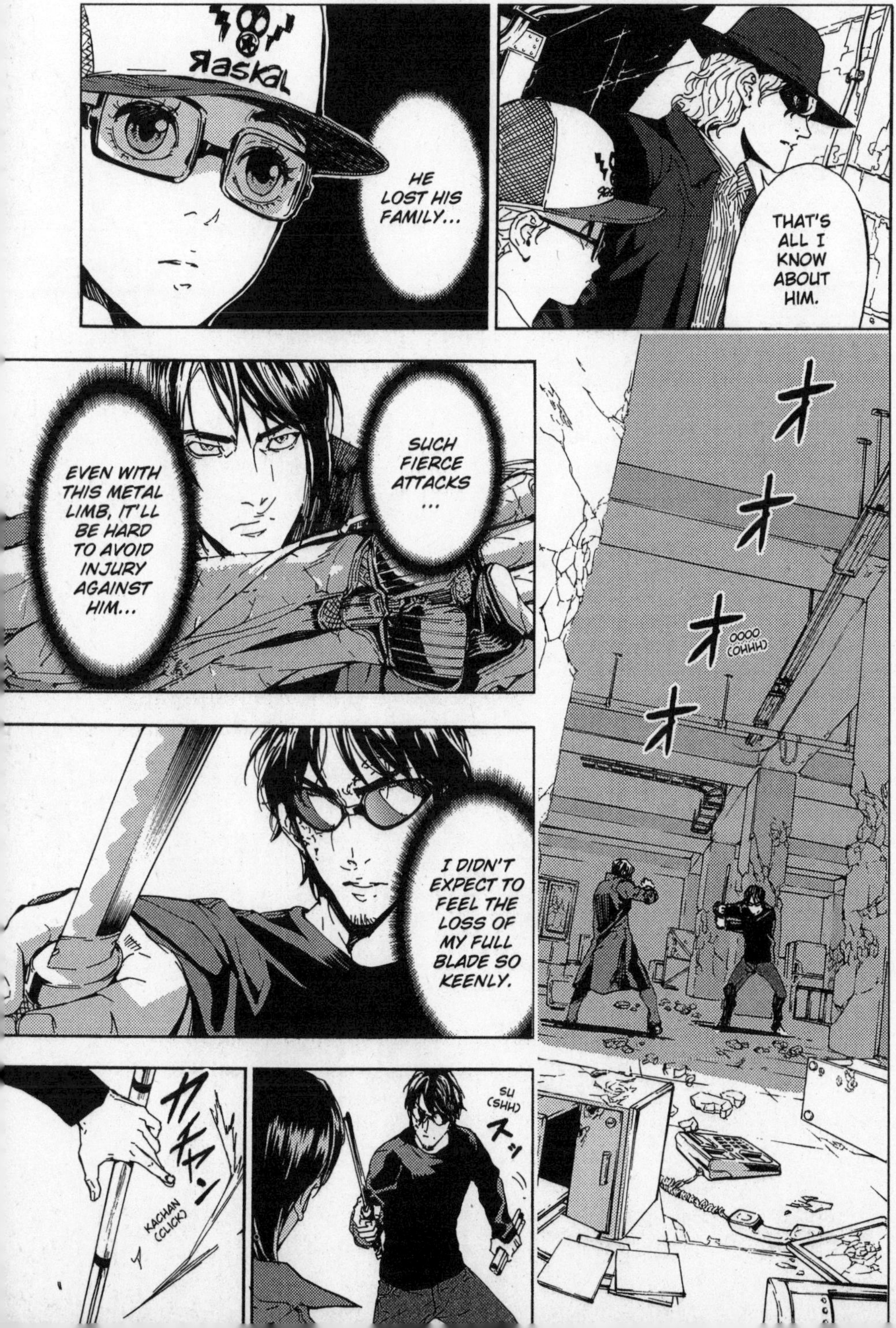
THAT'S ALL I KNOW ABOUT HIM.
HE LOST HIS FAMILY...
オオオオ
OOOO (OHHH)
SUCH FIERCE ATTACKS...
EVEN WITH THIS METAL LIMB, IT'LL BE HARD TO AVOID INJURY AGAINST HIM...
I DIDN'T EXPECT TO FEEL THE LOSS OF MY FULL BLADE SO KEENLY.
スッ
SU (SHH)
カチャン
KACHAN (CLICK)

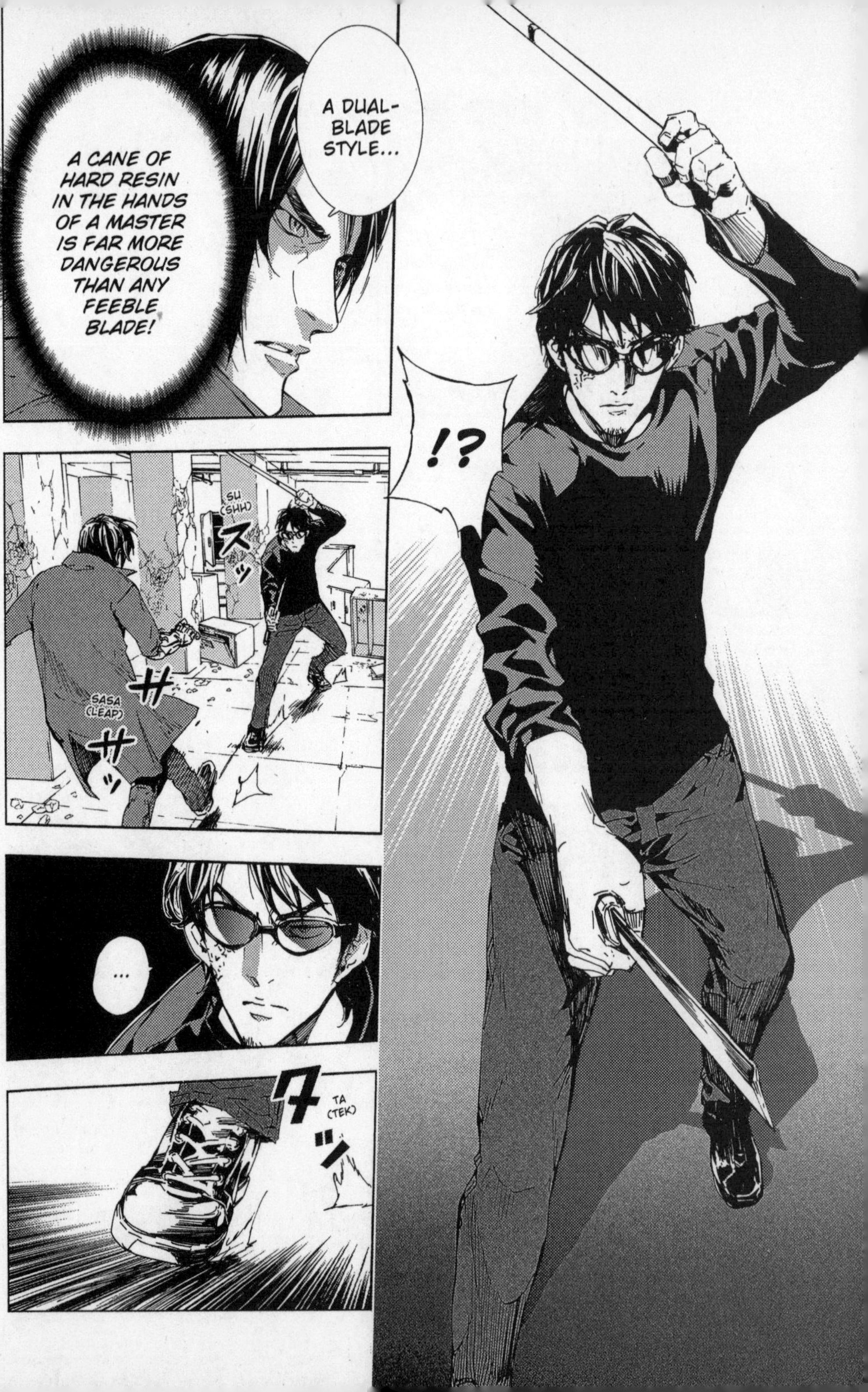
!?
A DUAL-BLADE STYLE...
A CANE OF HARD RESIN IN THE HANDS OF A MASTER IS FAR MORE DANGEROUS THAN ANY FEEBLE BLADE!
SU (SHH)
スッ
SASA (LEAP)
ササッ
...
タッ
TA (TEK)

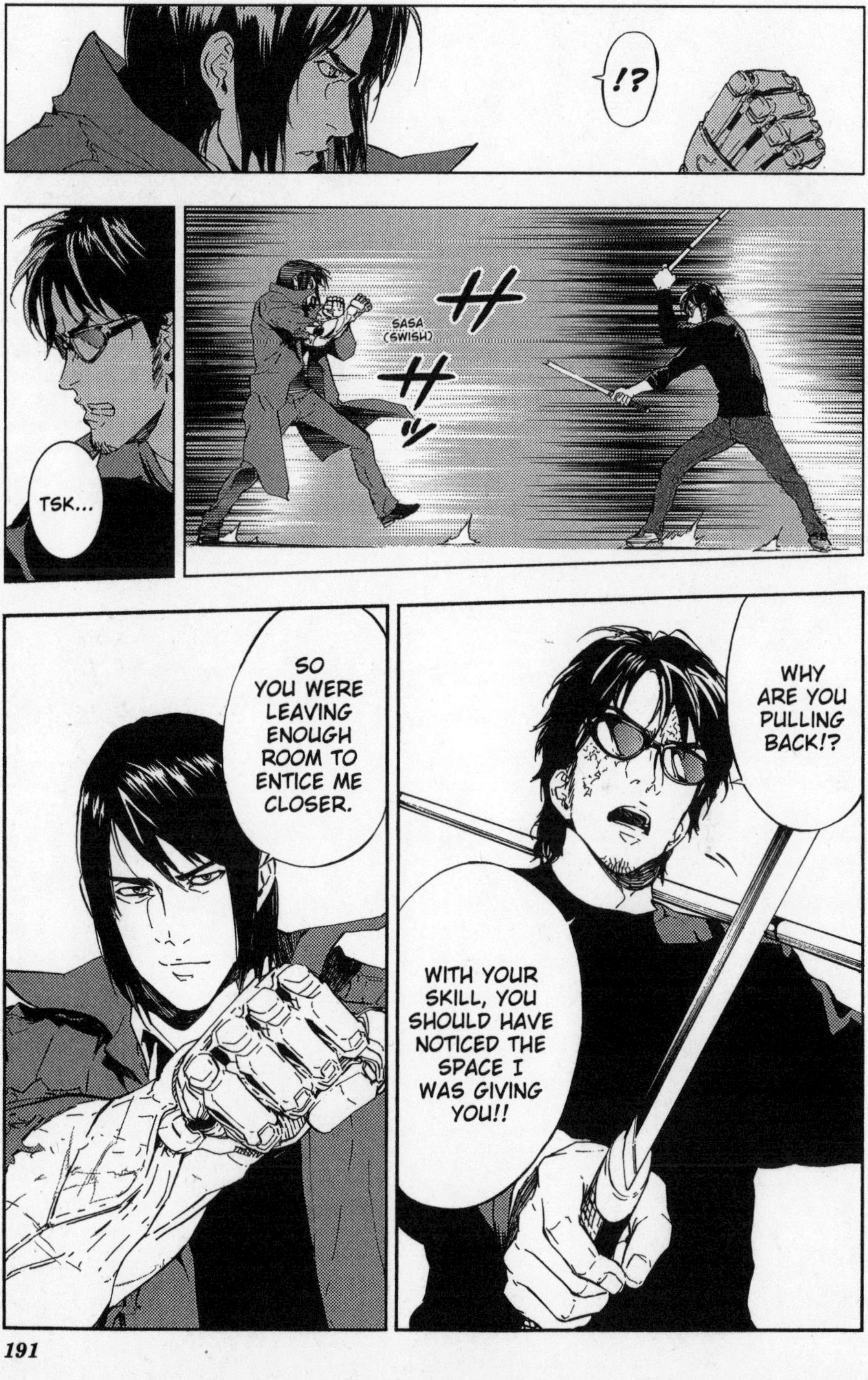
!?
SASA (SWISH)
TSK...
WHY ARE YOU PULLING BACK!?
WITH YOUR SKILL, YOU SHOULD HAVE NOTICED THE SPACE I WAS GIVING YOU!!
SO YOU WERE LEAVING ENOUGH ROOM TO ENTICE ME CLOSER.

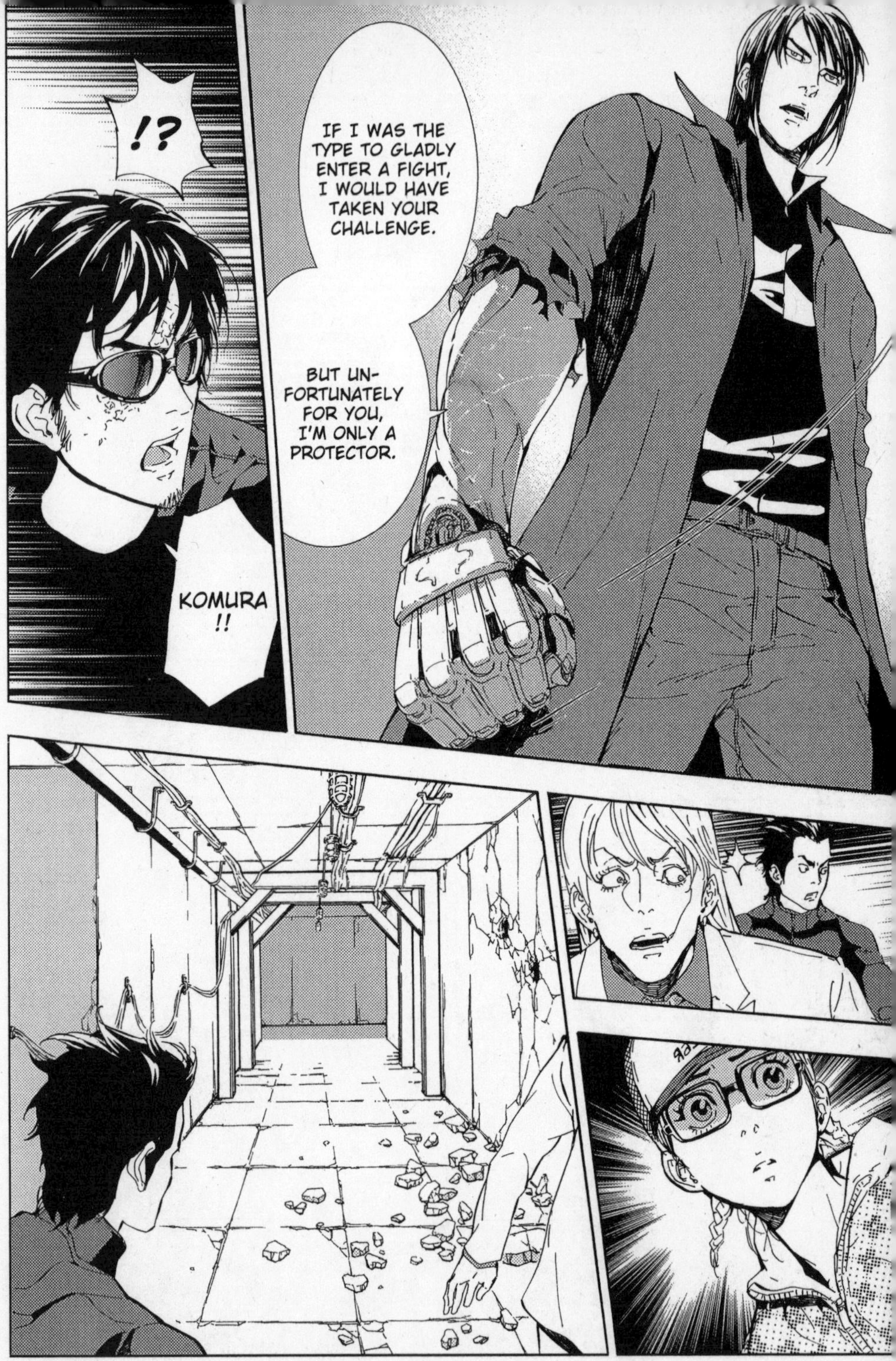
IF I WAS THE TYPE TO GLADLY ENTER A FIGHT, I WOULD HAVE TAKEN YOUR CHALLENGE.
BUT UN-FORTUNATELY FOR YOU, I'M ONLY A PROTECTOR.
!?
KOMURA !!

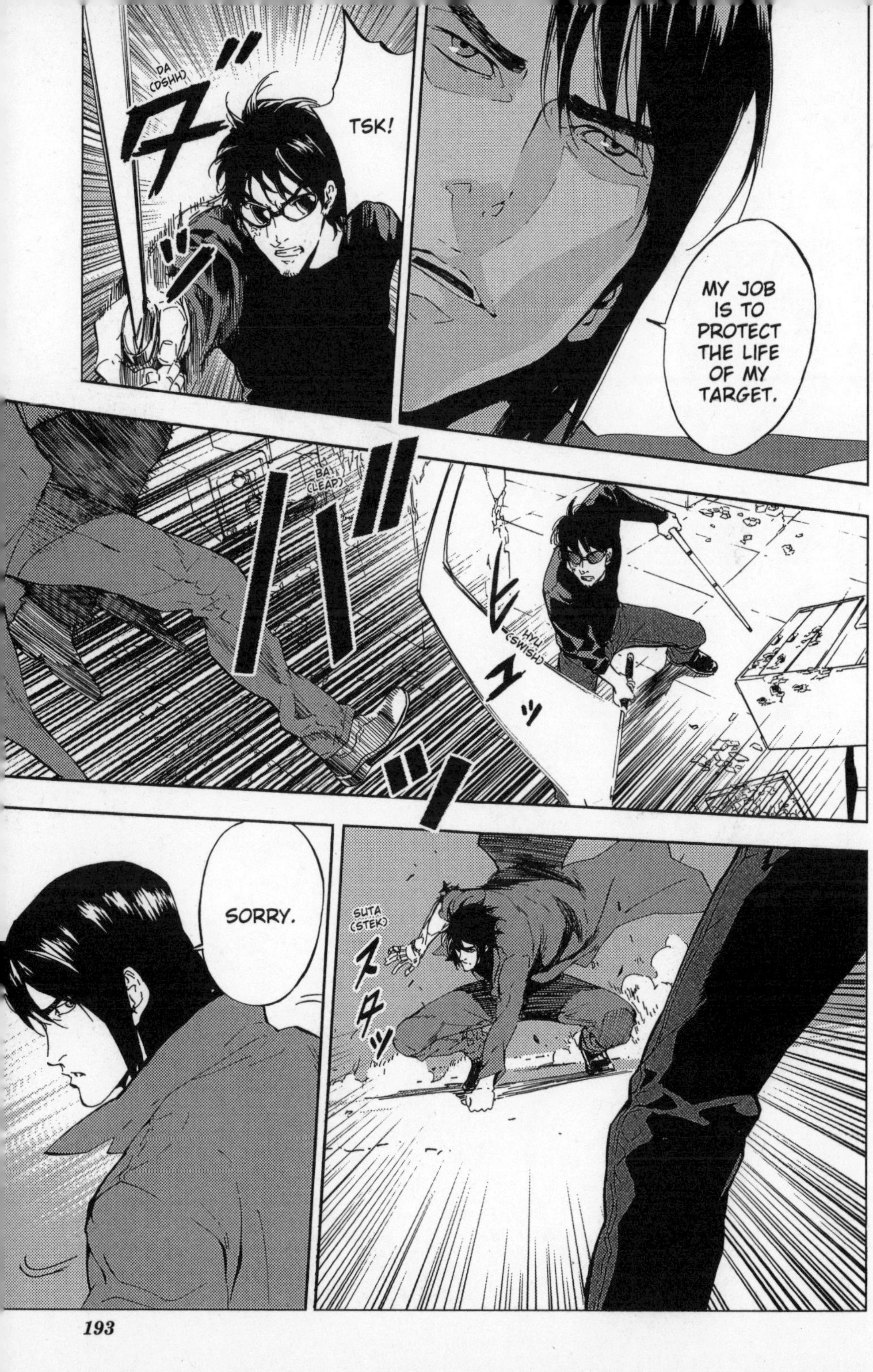
MY JOB IS TO PROTECT THE LIFE OF MY TARGET.
DA (DSHH)
TSK!
HYU (SWISH)
BA (LEAP)
SUTA (STEK)
SORRY.

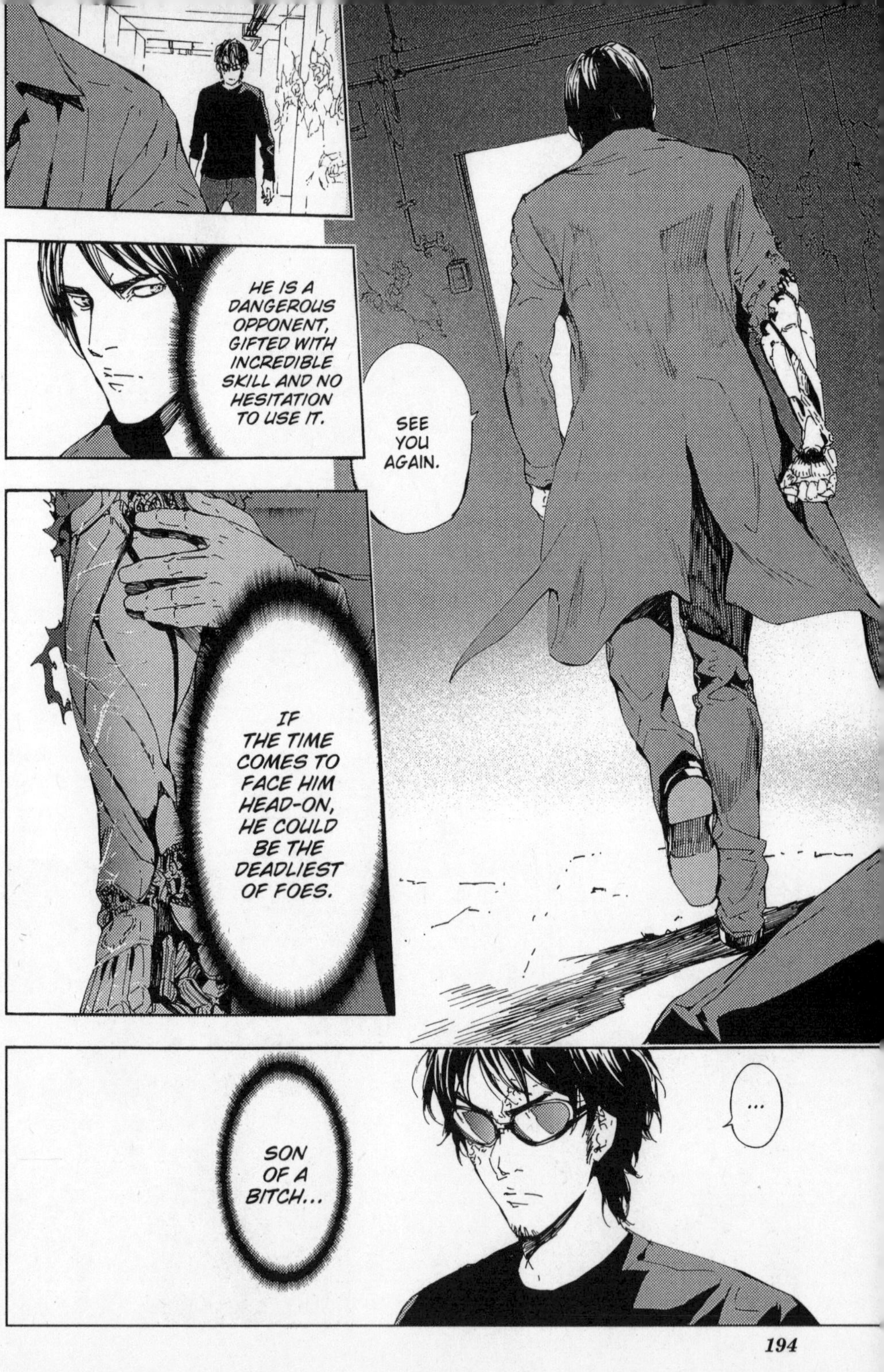
SEE YOU AGAIN.
HE IS A DANGEROUS OPPONENT, GIFTED WITH INCREDIBLE SKILL AND NO HESITATION TO USE IT.
IF THE TIME COMES TO FACE HIM HEAD-ON, HE COULD BE THE DEADLIEST OF FOES.
...
SON OF A BITCH...

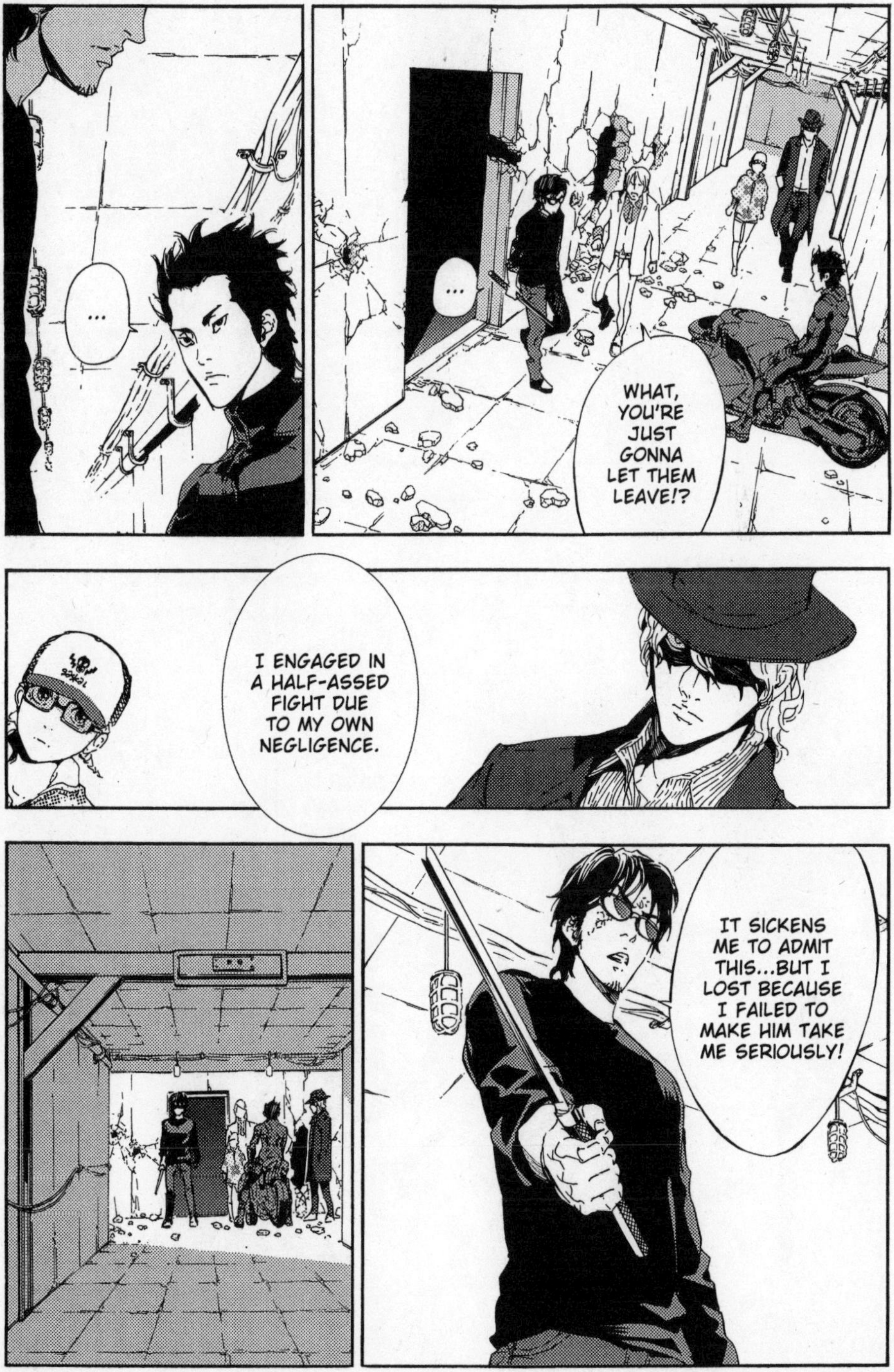

WHAT, YOU'RE JUST GONNA LET THEM LEAVE!?
...
...
I ENGAGED IN A HALF-ASSED FIGHT DUE TO MY OWN NEGLIGENCE.
IT SICKENS ME TO ADMIT THIS...BUT I LOST BECAUSE I FAILED TO MAKE HIM TAKE ME SERIOUSLY!

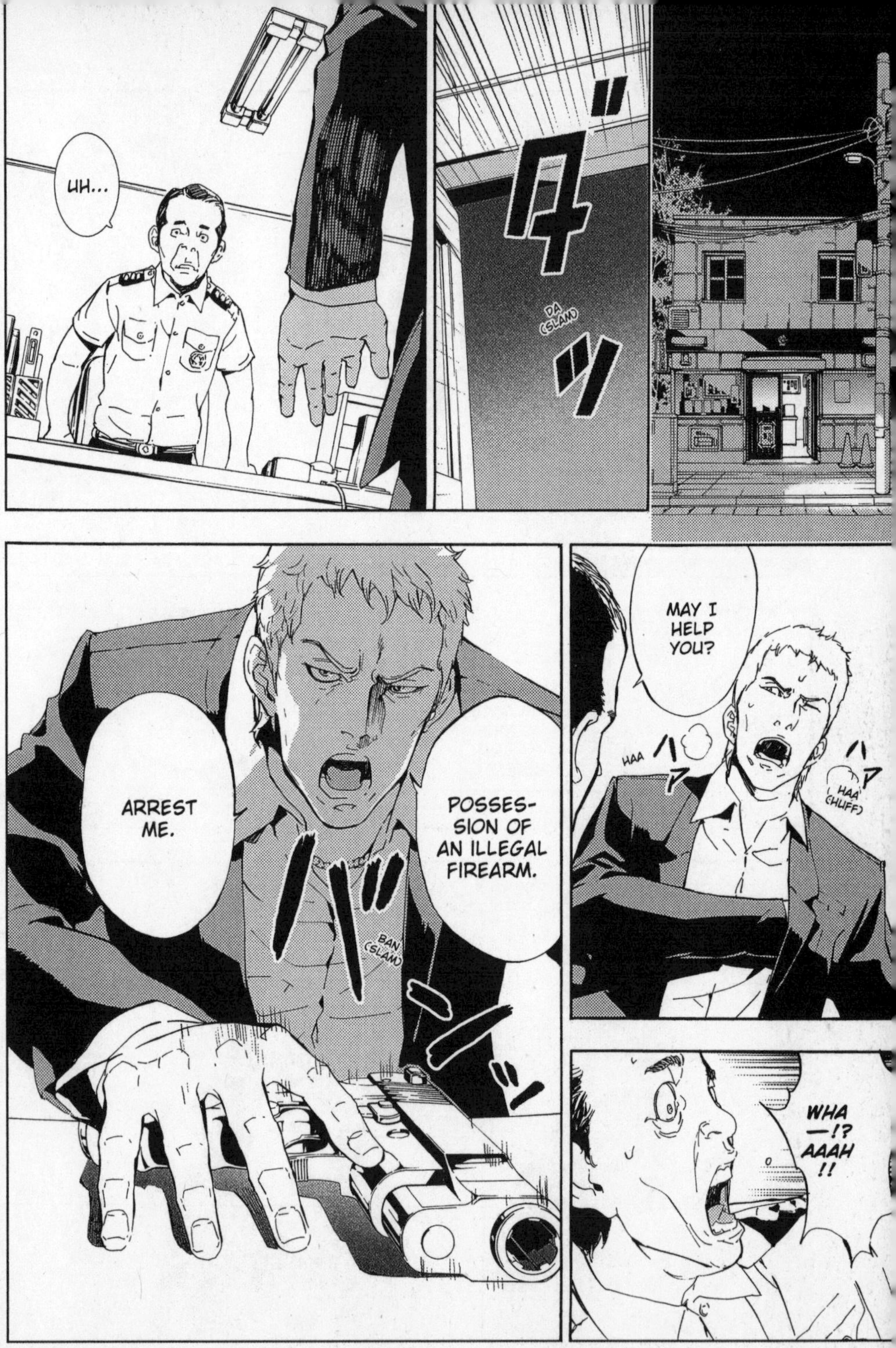
DA (SLAM)
UH...
MAY I HELP YOU?
HAA
HAA (HUFF)
WHA—!? AAAH!!
POSSES-SION OF AN ILLEGAL FIREARM.
ARREST ME.
BAN (SLAM)

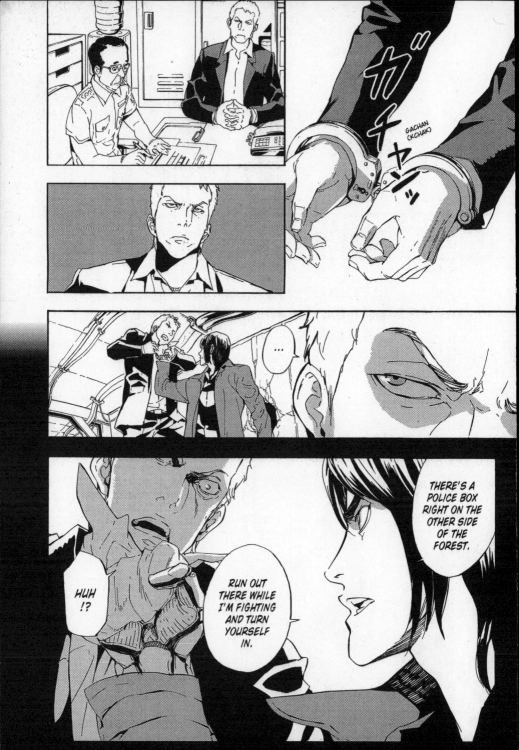

GACHAN
(KCHAK)

...

THERE'S A
POLICE BOX
RIGHT ON THE
OTHER SIDE
OF THE
FOREST.

RUN OUT
THERE WHILE
I'M FIGHTING
AND TURN
YOURSELF
IN.

HUH
!?

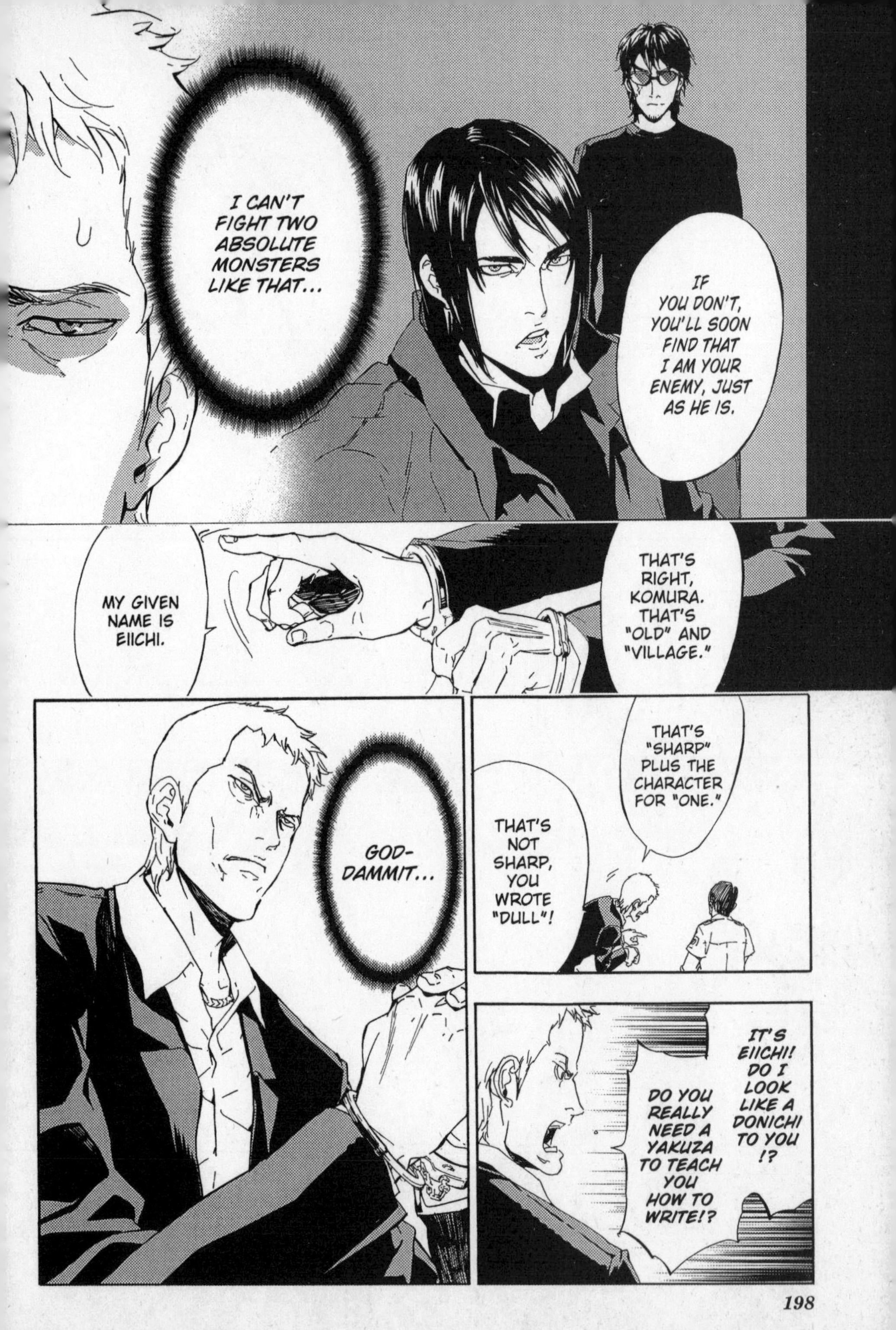
IF YOU DON'T, YOU'LL SOON FIND THAT I AM YOUR ENEMY, JUST AS HE IS.
I CAN'T FIGHT TWO ABSOLUTE MONSTERS LIKE THAT...
THAT'S RIGHT, KOMURA. THAT'S "OLD" AND "VILLAGE."
MY GIVEN NAME IS EIICHI.
THAT'S "SHARP" PLUS THE CHARACTER FOR "ONE."
THAT'S NOT SHARP, YOU WROTE "DULL"!
IT'S EIICHI! DO I LOOK LIKE A DONICHI TO YOU!?
DO YOU REALLY NEED A YAKUZA TO TEACH YOU HOW TO WRITE!?
GOD-DAMMIT...

Until Death do us Part

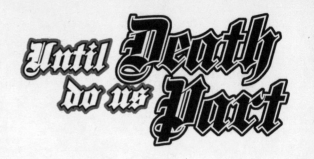

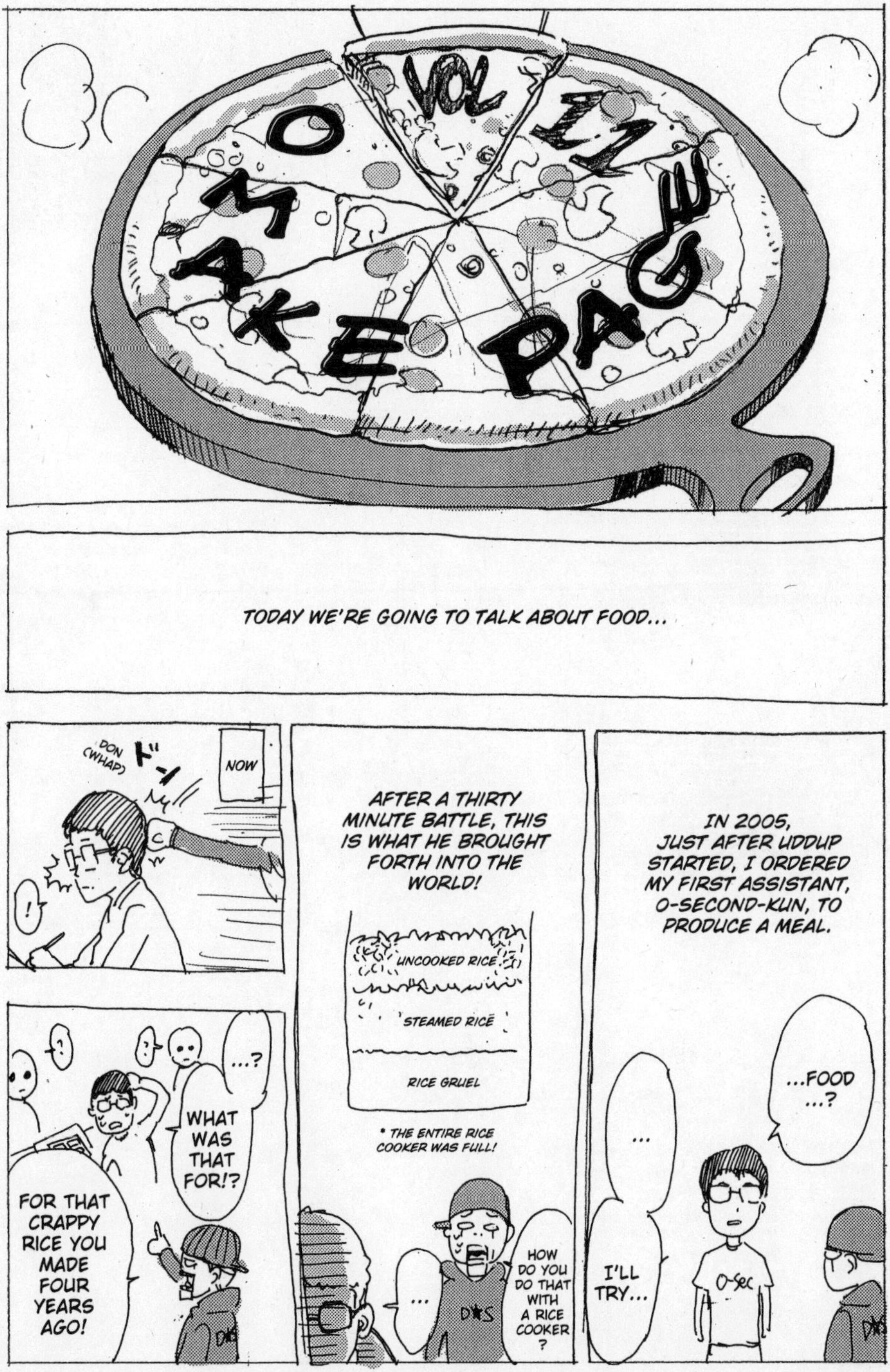
VOL 11
OMAKE PAGE
TODAY WE'RE GOING TO TALK ABOUT FOOD...
IN 2005, JUST AFTER UDDUP STARTED, I ORDERED MY FIRST ASSISTANT, O-SECOND-KUN, TO PRODUCE A MEAL.
...FOOD ...?
...
I'LL TRY...
O-Sec
AFTER A THIRTY MINUTE BATTLE, THIS IS WHAT HE BROUGHT FORTH INTO THE WORLD!
UNCOOKED RICE
STEAMED RICE
RICE GRUEL
* THE ENTIRE RICE COOKER WAS FULL!
HOW DO YOU DO THAT WITH A RICE COOKER?
...
NOW
DON (WHAP)
ドン
!
...?
WHAT WAS THAT FOR!?
FOR THAT CRAPPY RICE YOU MADE FOUR YEARS AGO!

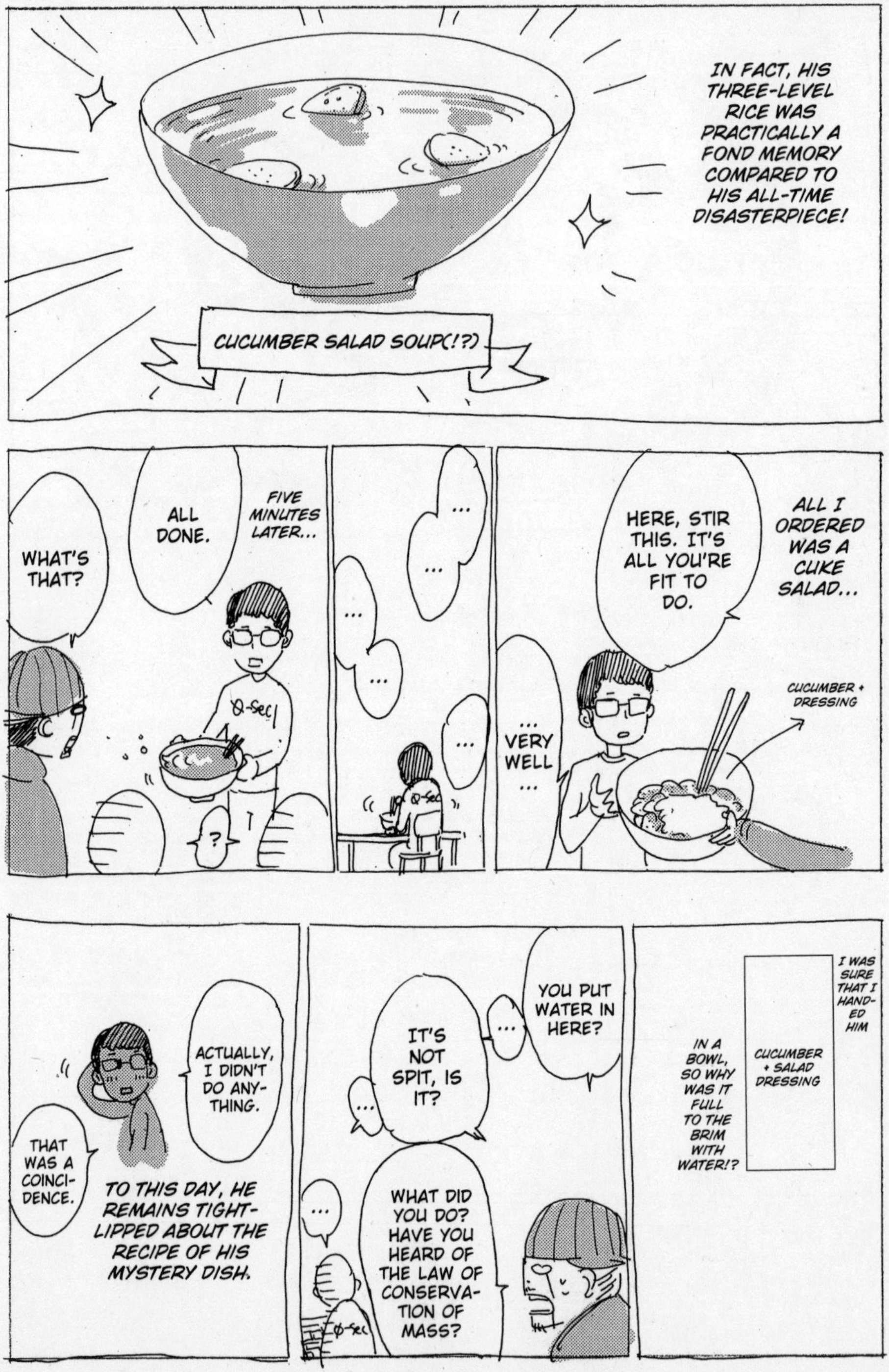
IN FACT, HIS THREE-LEVEL RICE WAS PRACTICALLY A FOND MEMORY COMPARED TO HIS ALL-TIME DISASTERPIECE!
CUCUMBER SALAD SOUP(!?)
ALL I ORDERED WAS A CUKE SALAD...
HERE, STIR THIS. IT'S ALL YOU'RE FIT TO DO.
CUCUMBER + DRESSING
...VERY WELL...
...
...
...
...
...
FIVE MINUTES LATER...
ALL DONE.
WHAT'S THAT?
?
I WAS SURE THAT I HANDED HIM
CUCUMBER + SALAD DRESSING
IN A BOWL, SO WHY WAS IT FULL TO THE BRIM WITH WATER!?
YOU PUT WATER IN HERE?
...
IT'S NOT SPIT, IS IT?
...
WHAT DID YOU DO? HAVE YOU HEARD OF THE LAW OF CONSERVATION OF MASS?
...
ACTUALLY, I DIDN'T DO ANYTHING.
THAT WAS A COINCIDENCE.
TO THIS DAY, HE REMAINS TIGHT-LIPPED ABOUT THE RECIPE OF HIS MYSTERY DISH.

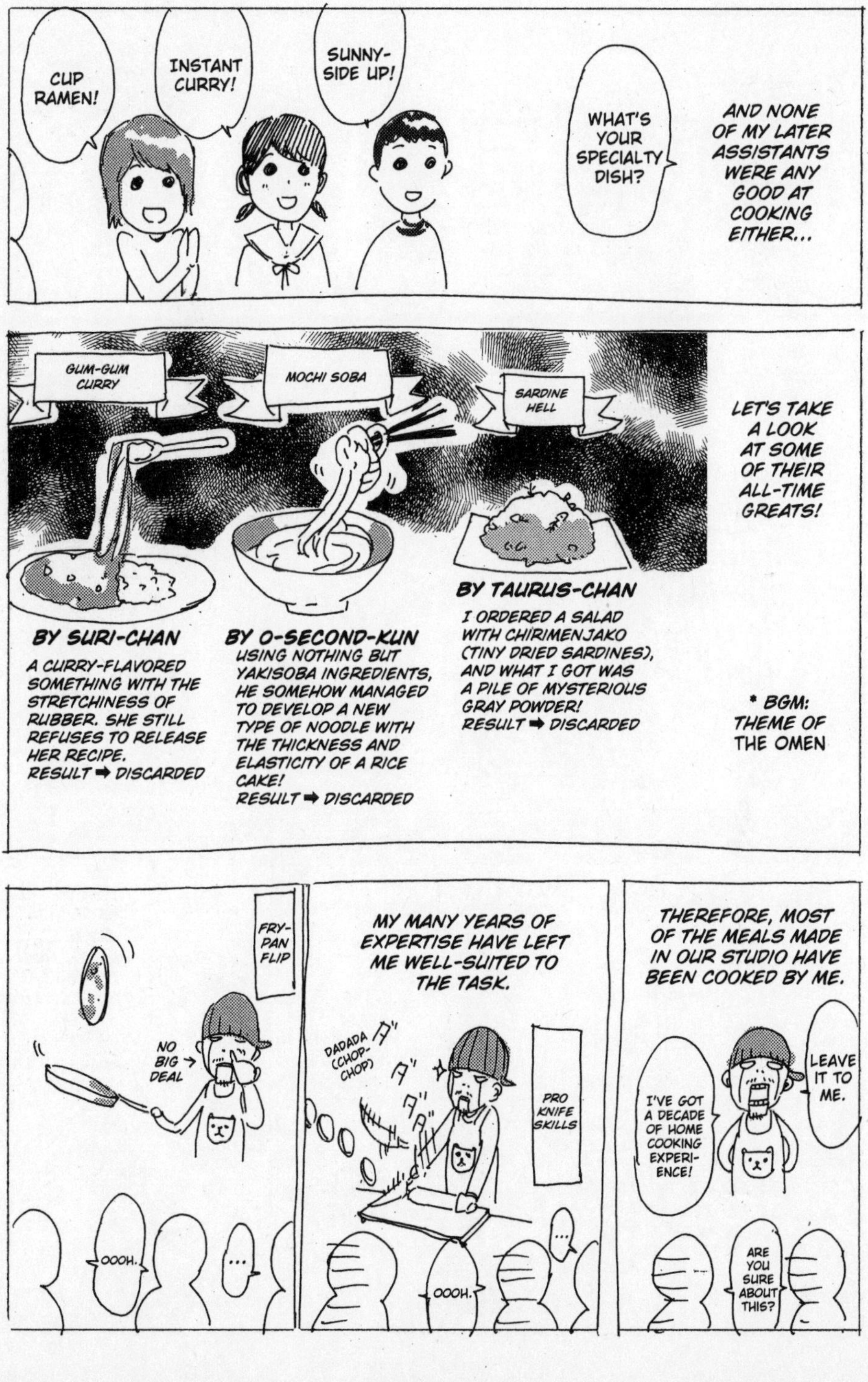
AND NONE OF MY LATER ASSISTANTS WERE ANY GOOD AT COOKING EITHER...
WHAT'S YOUR SPECIALTY DISH?
SUNNY-SIDE UP!
INSTANT CURRY!
CUP RAMEN!
LET'S TAKE A LOOK AT SOME OF THEIR ALL-TIME GREATS!
* BGM: THEME OF THE OMEN
SARDINE HELL
BY TAURUS-CHAN
I ORDERED A SALAD WITH CHIRIMENJAKO (TINY DRIED SARDINES), AND WHAT I GOT WAS A PILE OF MYSTERIOUS GRAY POWDER! RESULT ➡ DISCARDED
MOCHI SOBA
BY O-SECOND-KUN
USING NOTHING BUT YAKISOBA INGREDIENTS, HE SOMEHOW MANAGED TO DEVELOP A NEW TYPE OF NOODLE WITH THE THICKNESS AND ELASTICITY OF A RICE CAKE! RESULT ➡ DISCARDED
GUM-GUM CURRY
BY SURI-CHAN
A CURRY-FLAVORED SOMETHING WITH THE STRETCHINESS OF RUBBER. SHE STILL REFUSES TO RELEASE HER RECIPE. RESULT ➡ DISCARDED
THEREFORE, MOST OF THE MEALS MADE IN OUR STUDIO HAVE BEEN COOKED BY ME.
LEAVE IT TO ME.
I'VE GOT A DECADE OF HOME COOKING EXPERIENCE!
ARE YOU SURE ABOUT THIS?
MY MANY YEARS OF EXPERTISE HAVE LEFT ME WELL-SUITED TO THE TASK.
PRO KNIFE SKILLS
DADADA (CHOP-CHOP)
...
OOOH.
FRY-PAN FLIP
NO BIG DEAL
...
OOOH.

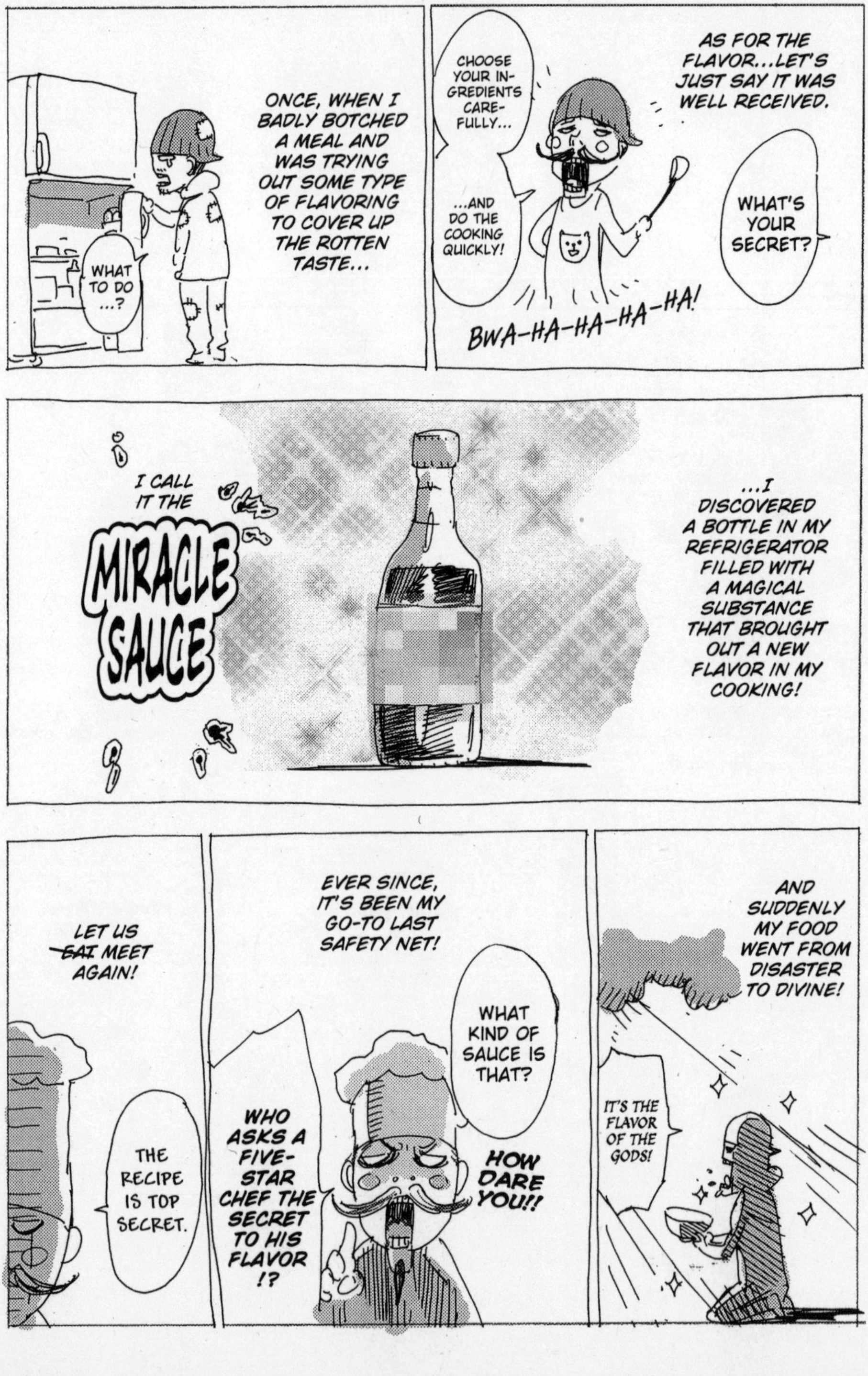
AS FOR THE FLAVOR...LET'S JUST SAY IT WAS WELL RECEIVED.
WHAT'S YOUR SECRET?
CHOOSE YOUR INGREDIENTS CAREFULLY...
...AND DO THE COOKING QUICKLY!
BWA-HA-HA-HA-HA!
ONCE, WHEN I BADLY BOTCHED A MEAL AND WAS TRYING OUT SOME TYPE OF FLAVORING TO COVER UP THE ROTTEN TASTE...
WHAT TO DO ...?
...I DISCOVERED A BOTTLE IN MY REFRIGERATOR FILLED WITH A MAGICAL SUBSTANCE THAT BROUGHT OUT A NEW FLAVOR IN MY COOKING!
I CALL IT THE
MIRACLE SAUCE
AND SUDDENLY MY FOOD WENT FROM DISASTER TO DIVINE!
IT'S THE FLAVOR OF THE GODS!
EVER SINCE, IT'S BEEN MY GO-TO LAST SAFETY NET!
WHAT KIND OF SAUCE IS THAT?
HOW DARE YOU!!
WHO ASKS A FIVE-STAR CHEF THE SECRET TO HIS FLAVOR!?
LET US ~~EAT~~ MEET AGAIN!
THE RECIPE IS TOP SECRET.

Art Staff
Suri ♀: Chief Assistant
0-Second ♂: Background Art
Taurus ♀: Background Art

Military Advisor
Lee Hyun Seok (warmania)

SPECIAL THANKS
Shingo Takano

Crossover Planning
JESUS—Sajin Kouro, Yami no Aegis, Akatsuki no Aegis
Written by Kyouichi Nanatsuki,
Art by Yoshihide Fujiwara
(Shogakukan)

Until Death do us Part

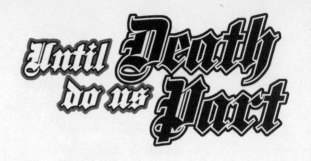

chapter 93

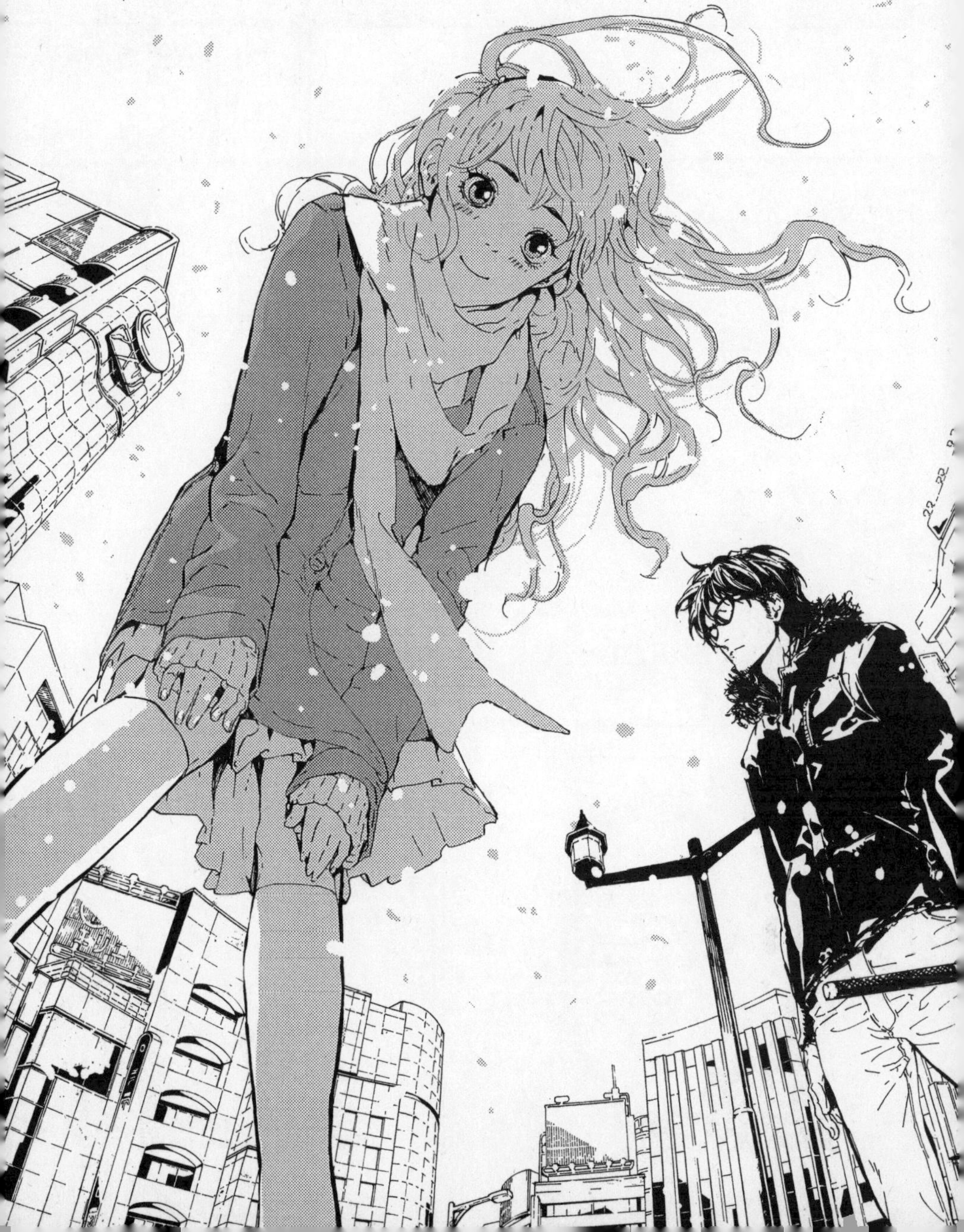

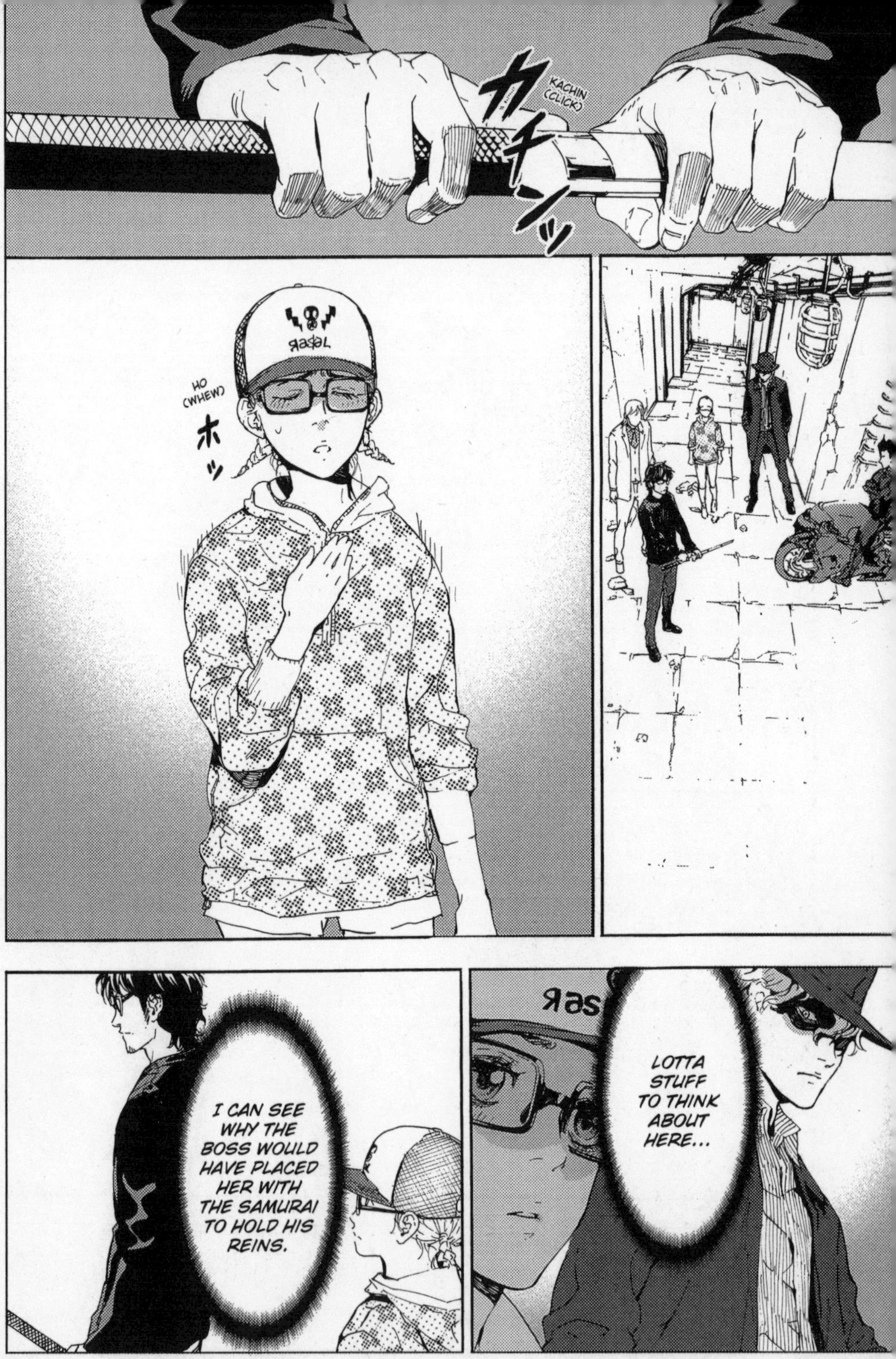

カチンッ
KACHIN (CLICK)
ホッ
HO (WHEW)
LOTTA STUFF TO THINK ABOUT HERE...
I CAN SEE WHY THE BOSS WOULD HAVE PLACED HER WITH THE SAMURAI TO HOLD HIS REINS.

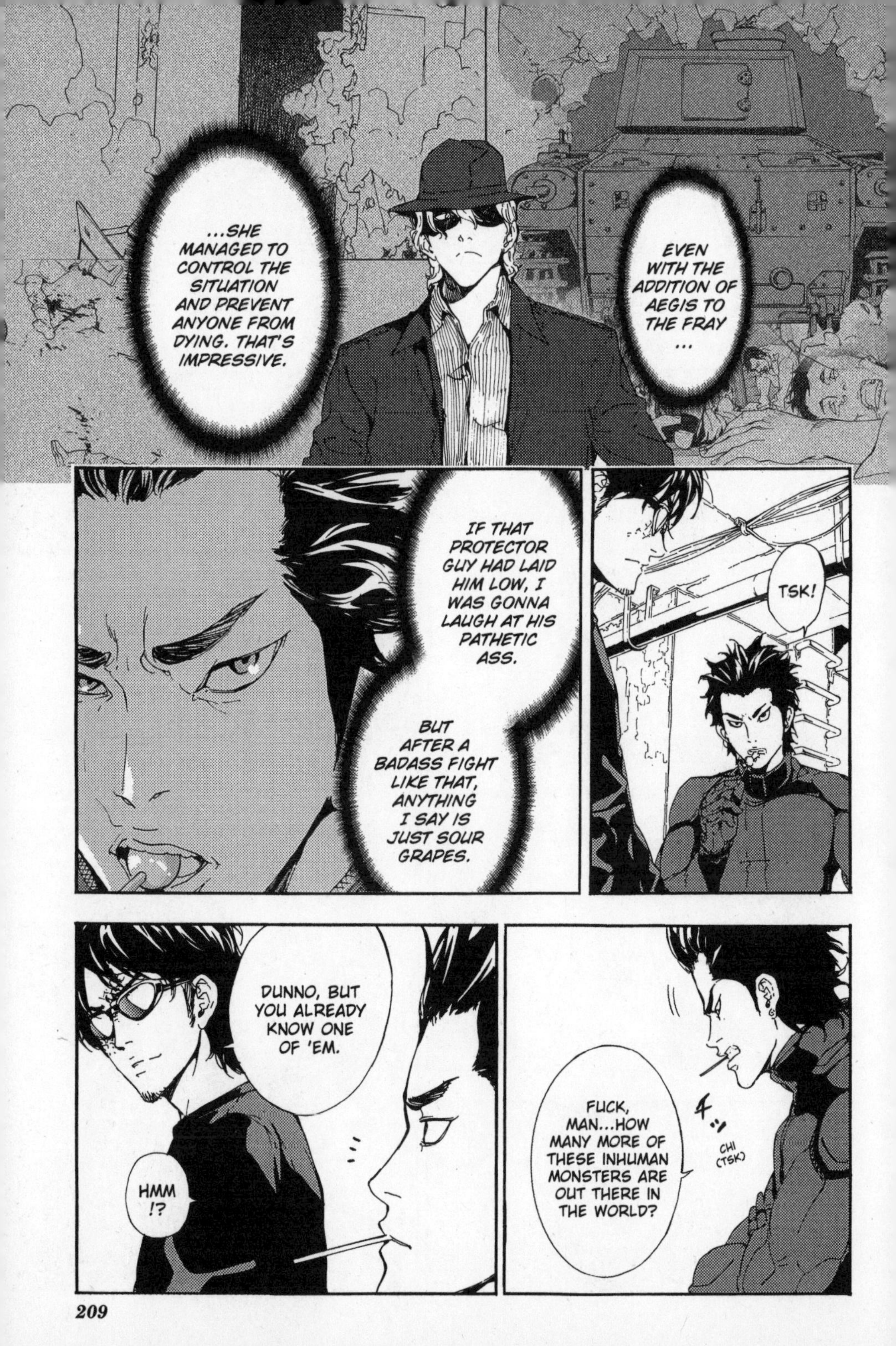
EVEN WITH THE ADDITION OF AEGIS TO THE FRAY...
...SHE MANAGED TO CONTROL THE SITUATION AND PREVENT ANYONE FROM DYING. THAT'S IMPRESSIVE.
TSK!
IF THAT PROTECTOR GUY HAD LAID HIM LOW, I WAS GONNA LAUGH AT HIS PATHETIC ASS.
BUT AFTER A BADASS FIGHT LIKE THAT, ANYTHING I SAY IS JUST SOUR GRAPES.
CHI (TSK)
FUCK, MAN...HOW MANY MORE OF THESE INHUMAN MONSTERS ARE OUT THERE IN THE WORLD?
DUNNO, BUT YOU ALREADY KNOW ONE OF 'EM.
HMM!?

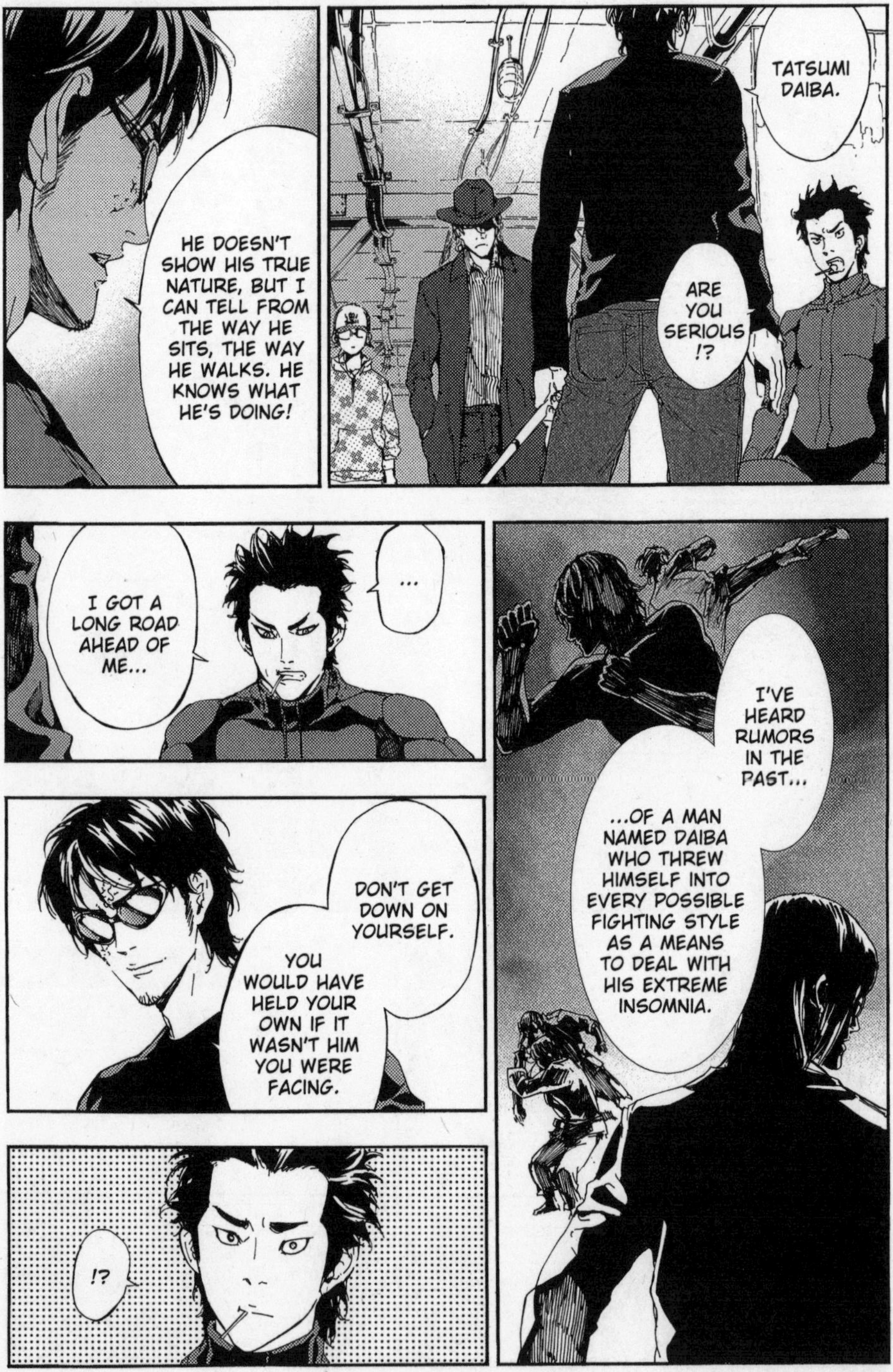
TATSUMI DAIBA.
ARE YOU SERIOUS!?
HE DOESN'T SHOW HIS TRUE NATURE, BUT I CAN TELL FROM THE WAY HE SITS, THE WAY HE WALKS. HE KNOWS WHAT HE'S DOING!
I'VE HEARD RUMORS IN THE PAST...
...OF A MAN NAMED DAIBA WHO THREW HIMSELF INTO EVERY POSSIBLE FIGHTING STYLE AS A MEANS TO DEAL WITH HIS EXTREME INSOMNIA.
...
I GOT A LONG ROAD AHEAD OF ME...
DON'T GET DOWN ON YOURSELF.
YOU WOULD HAVE HELD YOUR OWN IF IT WASN'T HIM YOU WERE FACING.
!?

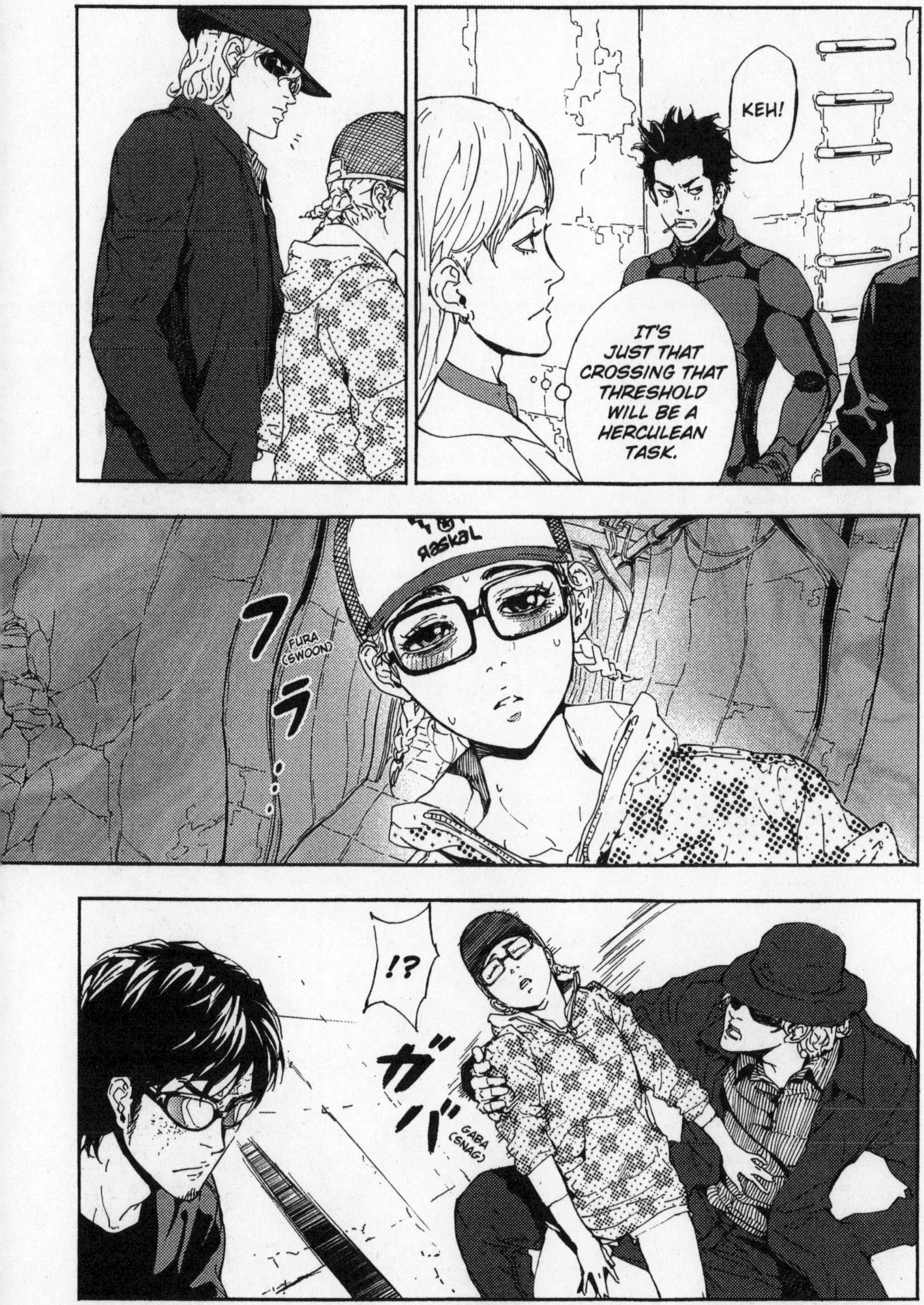
KEH!
IT'S JUST THAT CROSSING THAT THRESHOLD WILL BE A HERCULEAN TASK.
フラ…
FURA (SWOON)
!?
ガバ
GABA (SNAG)

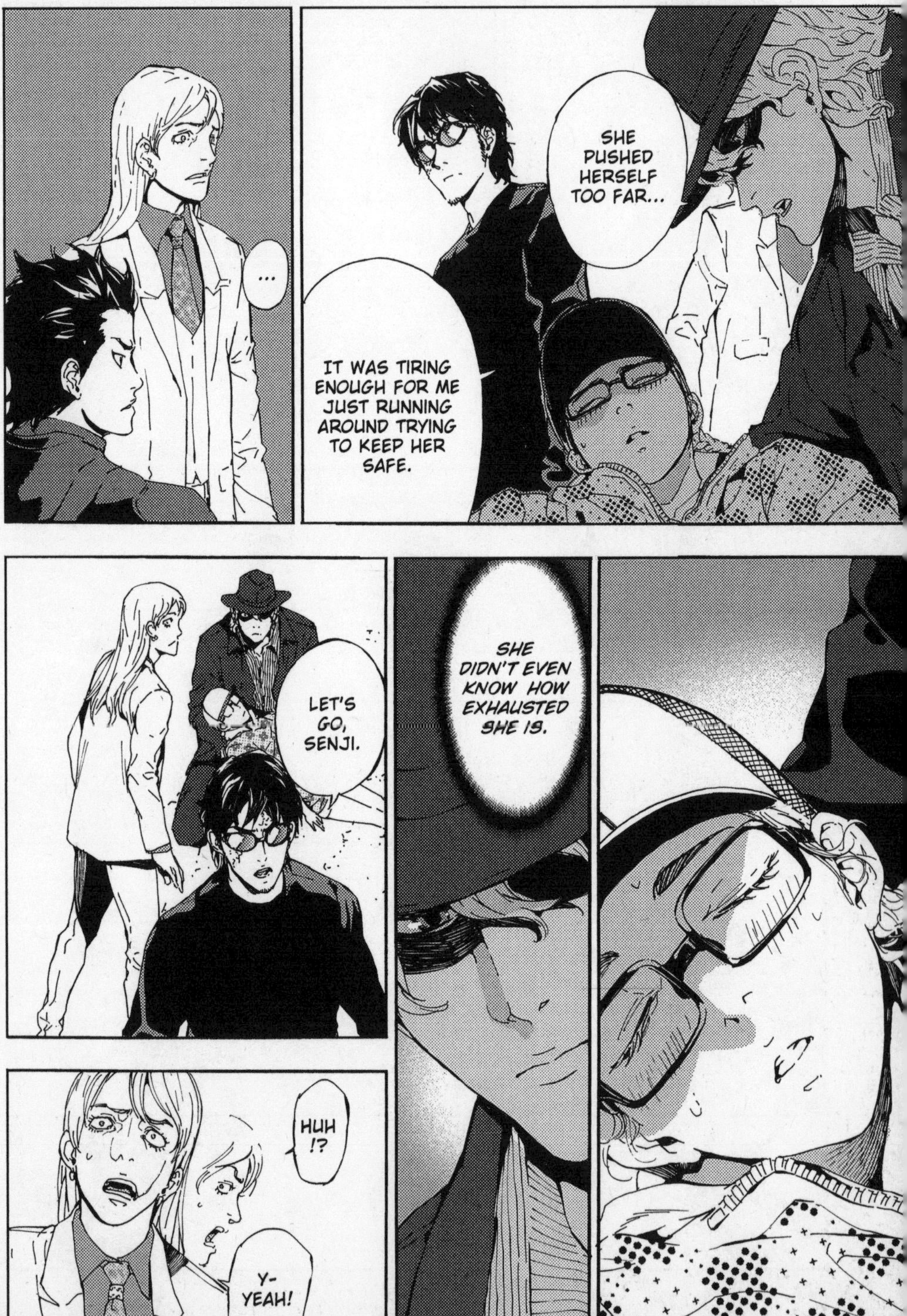
SHE PUSHED HERSELF TOO FAR...
IT WAS TIRING ENOUGH FOR ME JUST RUNNING AROUND TRYING TO KEEP HER SAFE.
...
SHE DIDN'T EVEN KNOW HOW EXHAUSTED SHE IS.
LET'S GO, SENJI.
HUH!?
Y-YEAH!

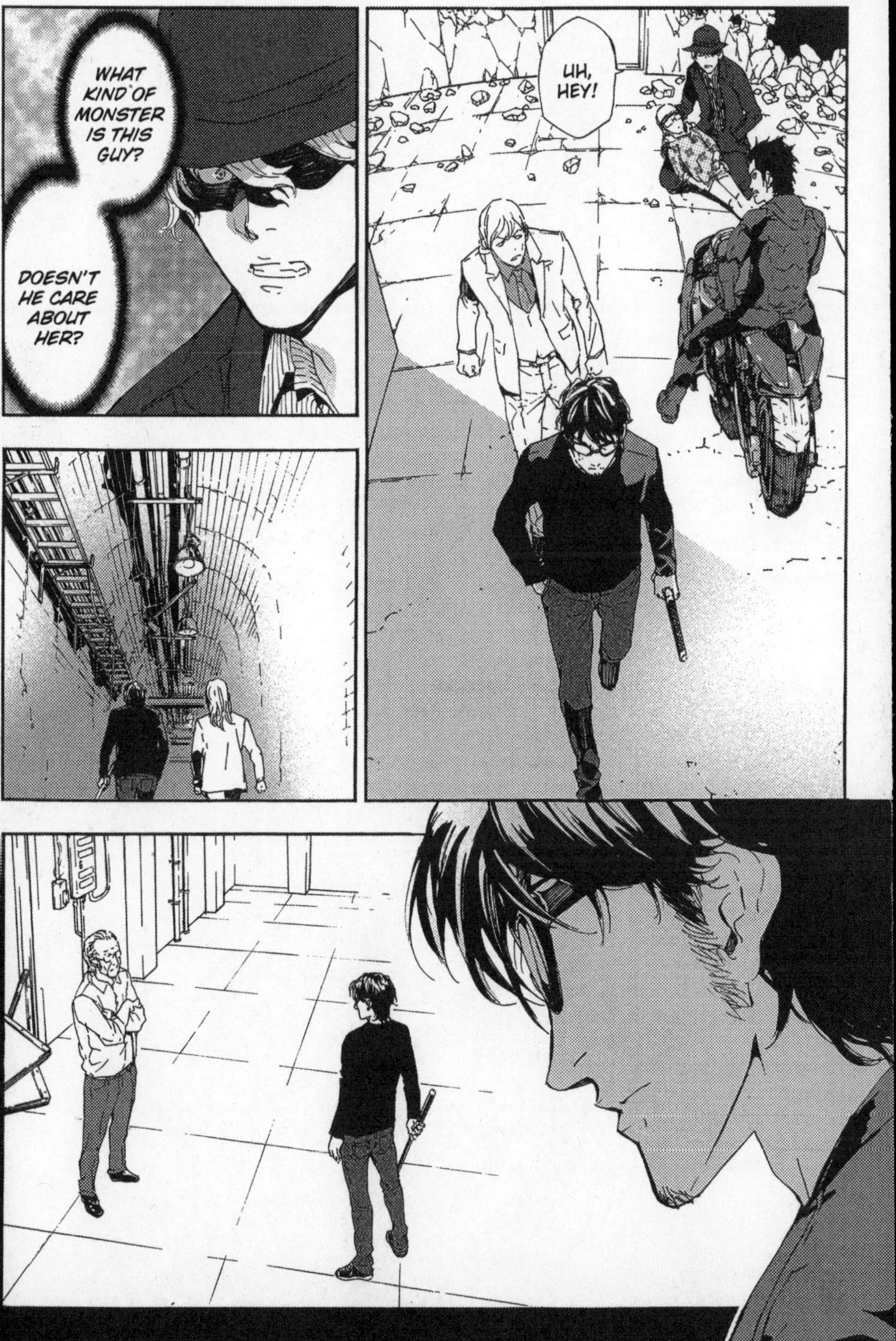
UH, HEY!
WHAT KIND OF MONSTER IS THIS GUY?
DOESN'T HE CARE ABOUT HER?

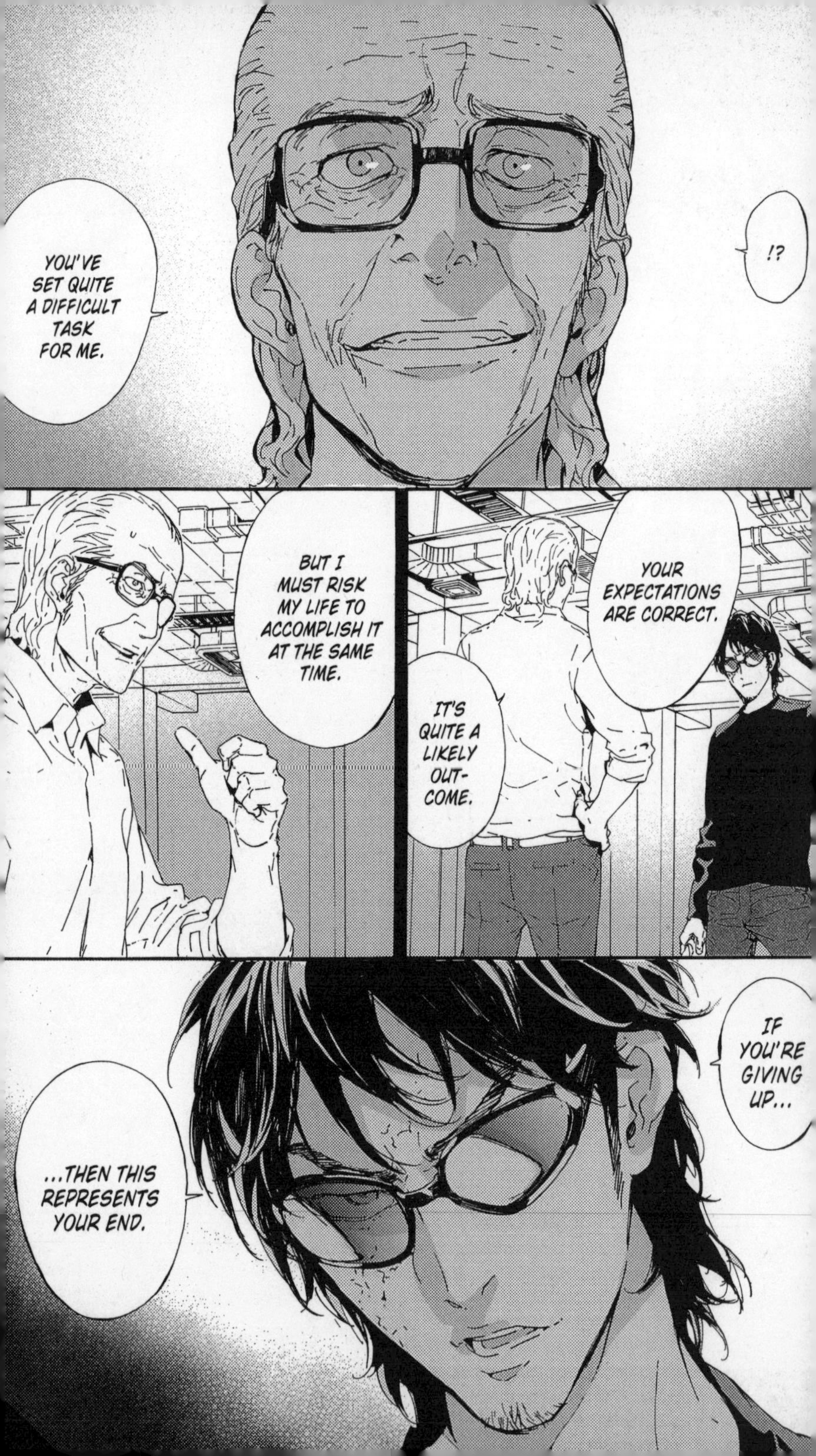
!?
YOU'VE SET QUITE A DIFFICULT TASK FOR ME.
YOUR EXPECTATIONS ARE CORRECT.
IT'S QUITE A LIKELY OUT-COME.
BUT I MUST RISK MY LIFE TO ACCOMPLISH IT AT THE SAME TIME.
IF YOU'RE GIVING UP...
...THEN THIS REPRESENTS YOUR END.

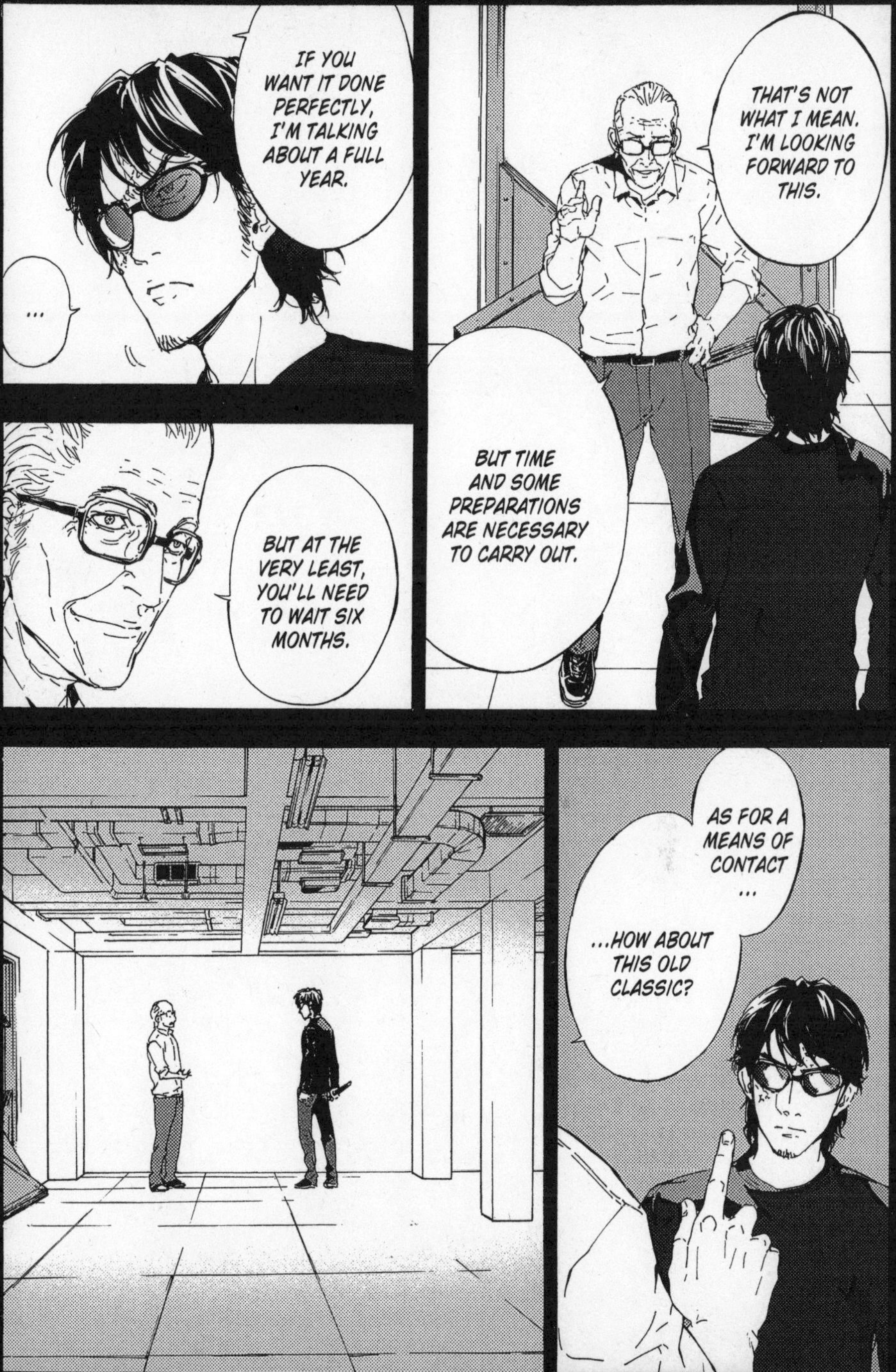
THAT'S NOT WHAT I MEAN. I'M LOOKING FORWARD TO THIS.
BUT TIME AND SOME PREPARATIONS ARE NECESSARY TO CARRY OUT.
IF YOU WANT IT DONE PERFECTLY, I'M TALKING ABOUT A FULL YEAR.
...
BUT AT THE VERY LEAST, YOU'LL NEED TO WAIT SIX MONTHS.
AS FOR A MEANS OF CONTACT ...
...HOW ABOUT THIS OLD CLASSIC?

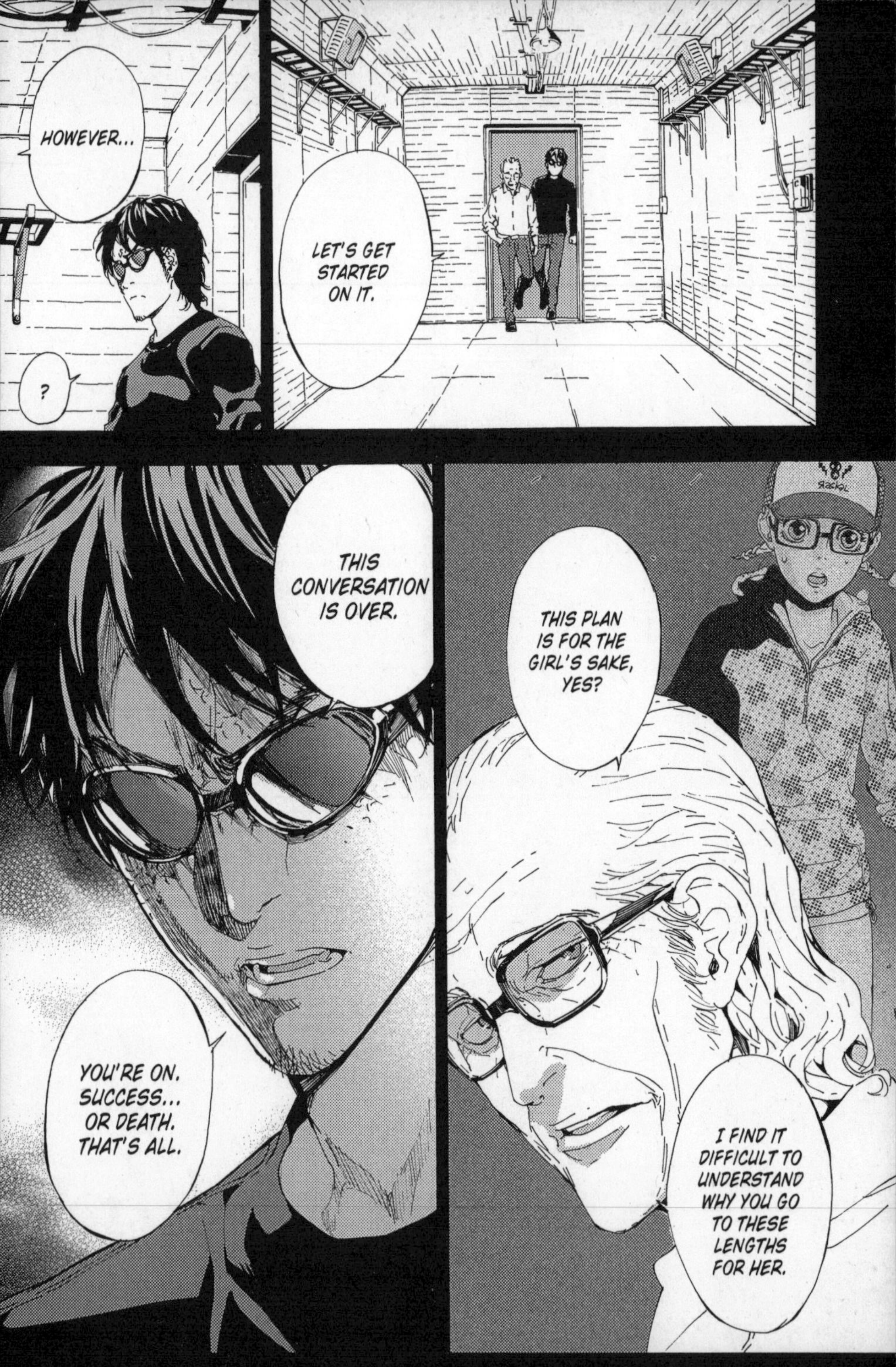
LET'S GET STARTED ON IT.
HOWEVER...
?
THIS PLAN IS FOR THE GIRL'S SAKE, YES?
I FIND IT DIFFICULT TO UNDERSTAND WHY YOU GO TO THESE LENGTHS FOR HER.
THIS CONVERSATION IS OVER.
YOU'RE ON. SUCCESS... OR DEATH. THAT'S ALL.

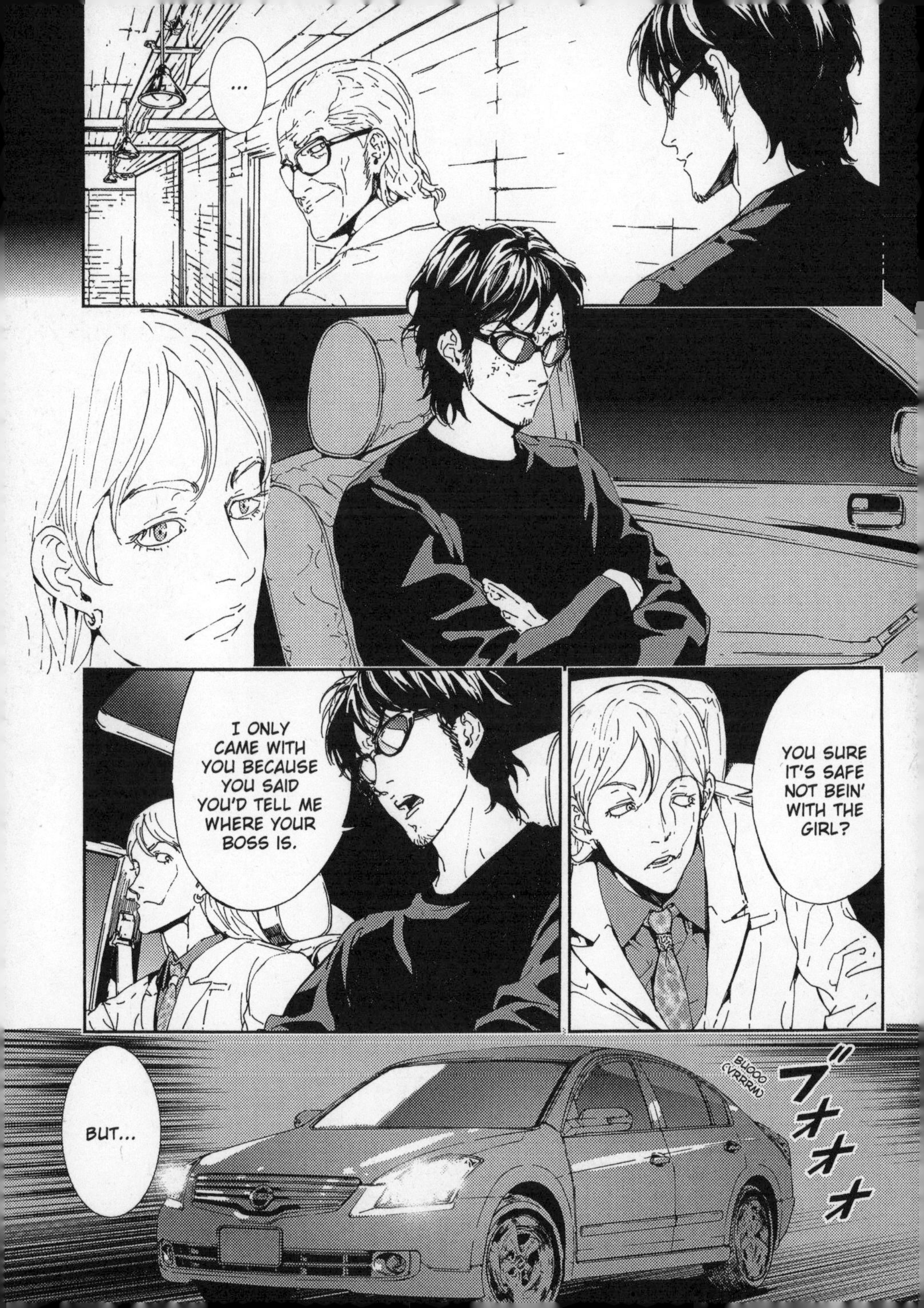
...
YOU SURE IT'S SAFE NOT BEIN' WITH THE GIRL?
I ONLY CAME WITH YOU BECAUSE YOU SAID YOU'D TELL ME WHERE YOUR BOSS IS.
ブオオオ
BUOOO (VRRRM)
BUT...

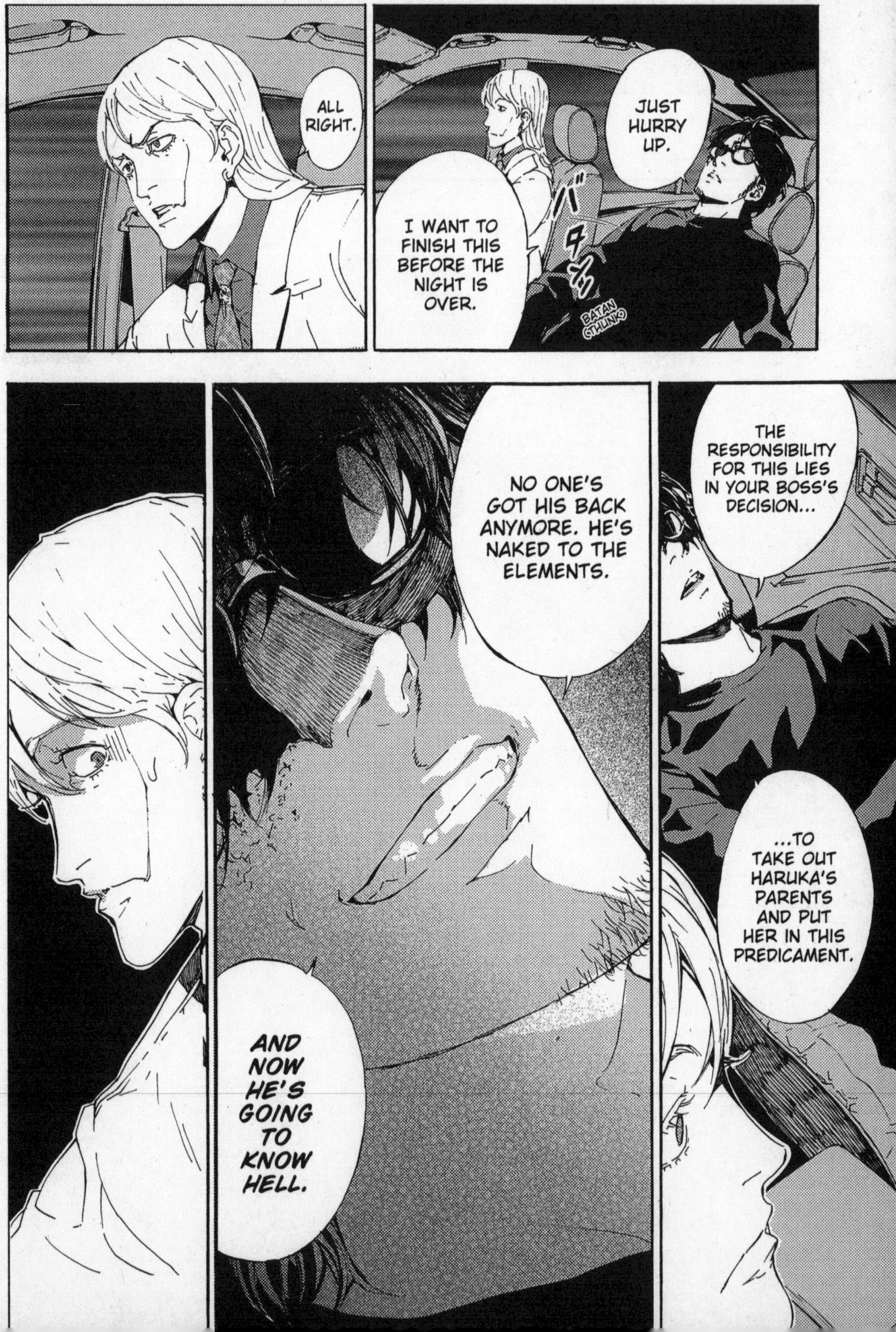
JUST HURRY UP.
I WANT TO FINISH THIS BEFORE THE NIGHT IS OVER.
BATAN (THUNK)
ALL RIGHT.
THE RESPONSIBILITY FOR THIS LIES IN YOUR BOSS'S DECISION...
...TO TAKE OUT HARUKA'S PARENTS AND PUT HER IN THIS PREDICAMENT.
NO ONE'S GOT HIS BACK ANYMORE. HE'S NAKED TO THE ELEMENTS.
AND NOW HE'S GOING TO KNOW HELL.

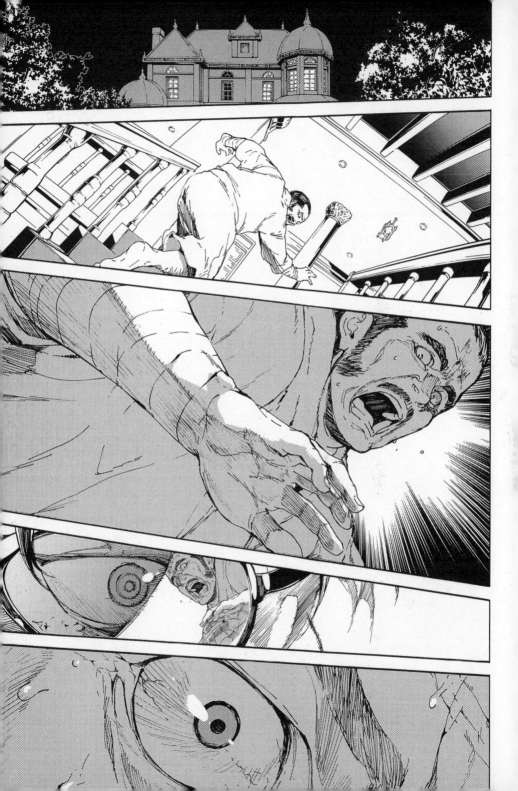

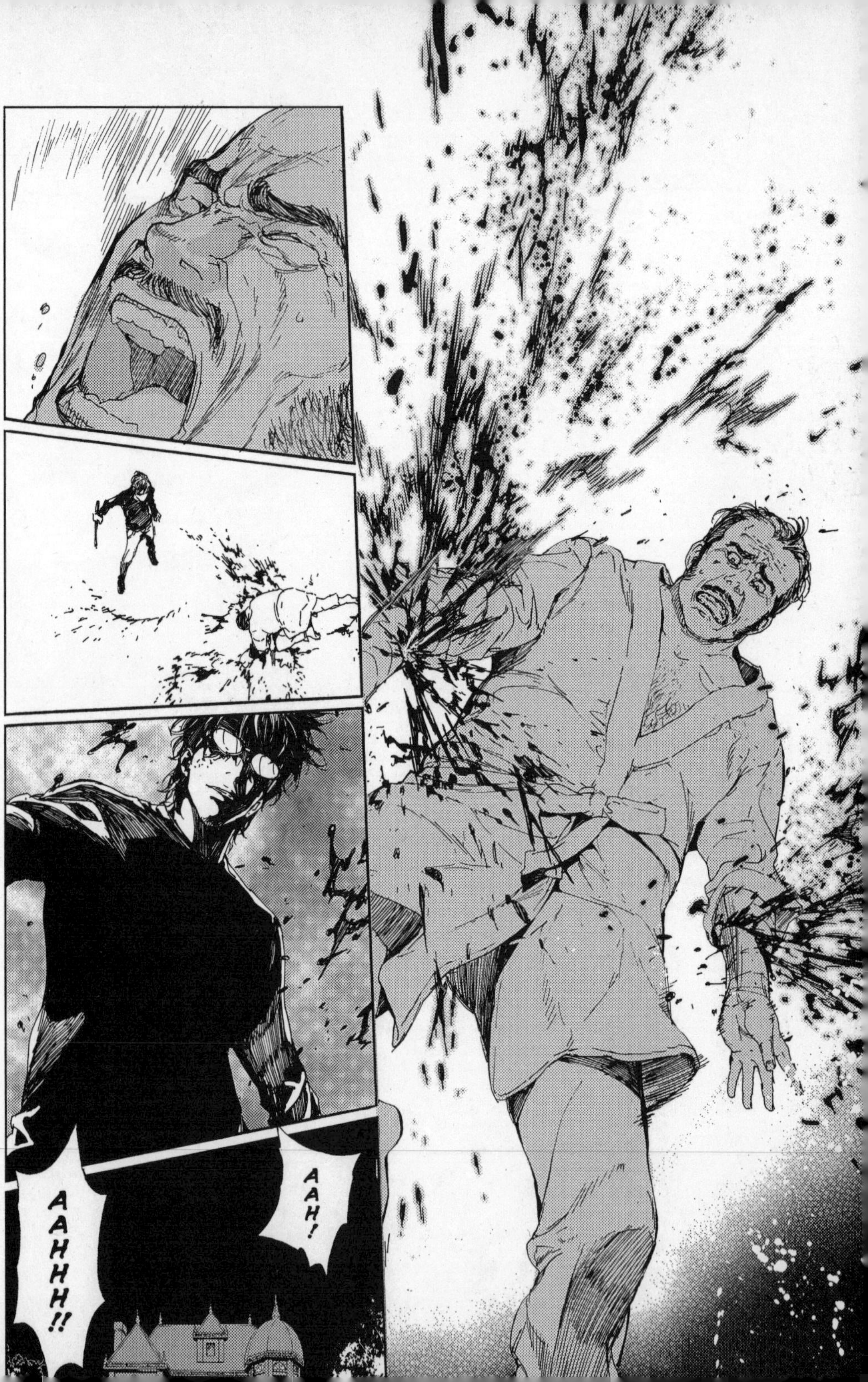
AAH!
AAHHH!!

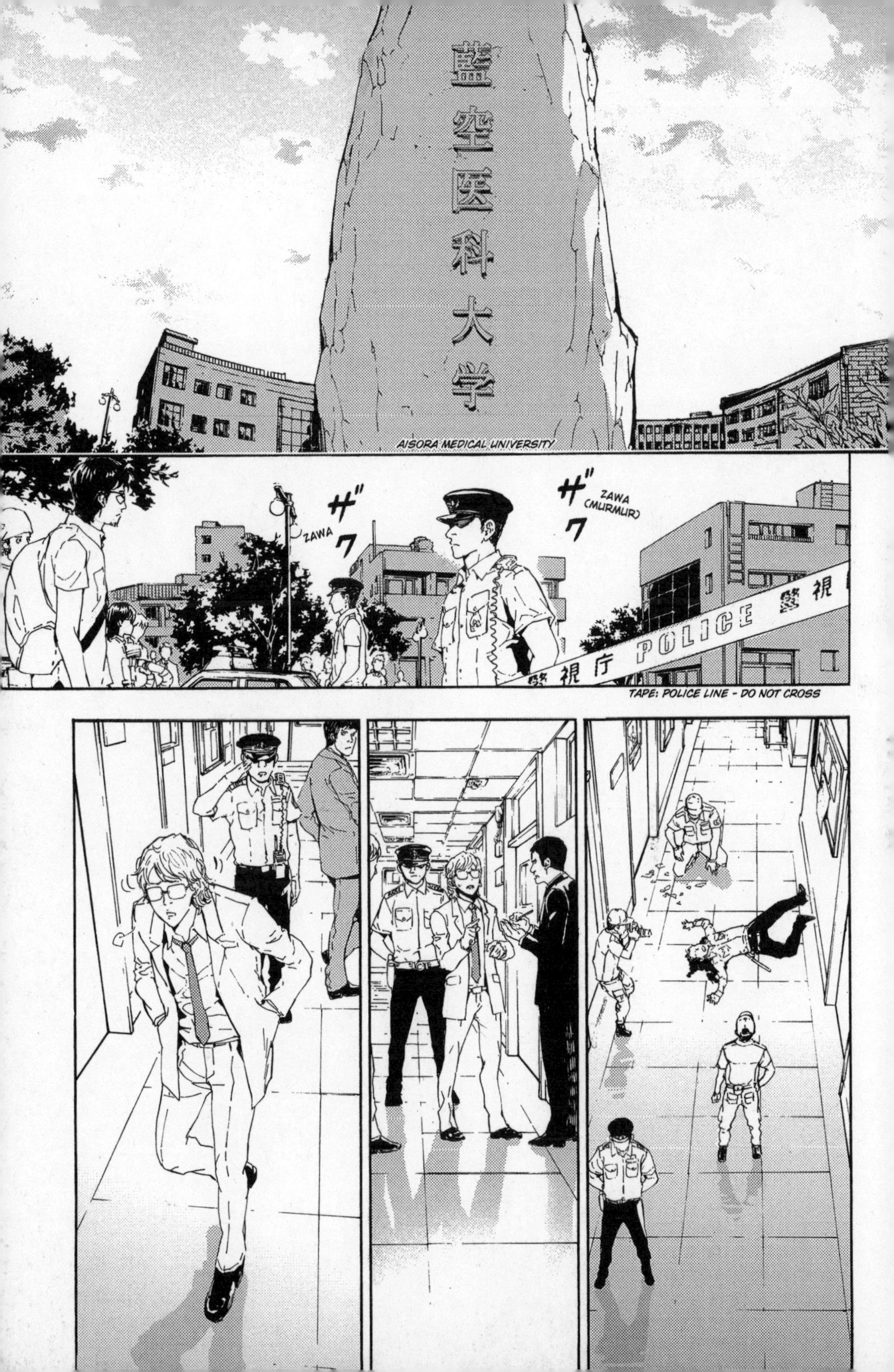
藍空医科大学
AISORA MEDICAL UNIVERSITY
ZAWA (MURMUR)
ZAWA
警視庁 POLICE
TAPE: POLICE LINE - DO NOT CROSS

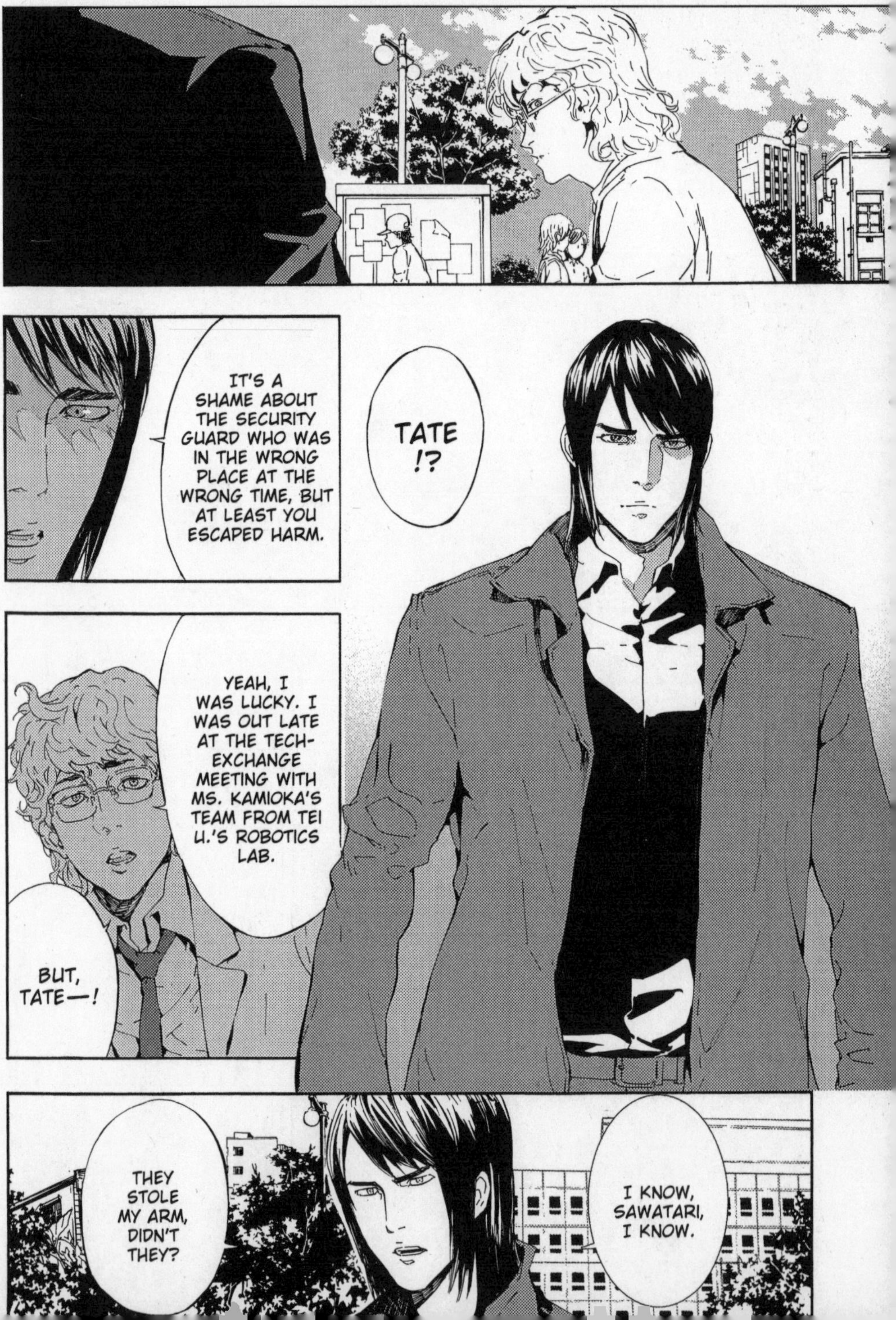
TATE !?
IT'S A SHAME ABOUT THE SECURITY GUARD WHO WAS IN THE WRONG PLACE AT THE WRONG TIME, BUT AT LEAST YOU ESCAPED HARM.
YEAH, I WAS LUCKY. I WAS OUT LATE AT THE TECH-EXCHANGE MEETING WITH MS. KAMIOKA'S TEAM FROM TEI U.'S ROBOTICS LAB.
BUT, TATE—!
I KNOW, SAWATARI, I KNOW.
THEY STOLE MY ARM, DIDN'T THEY?

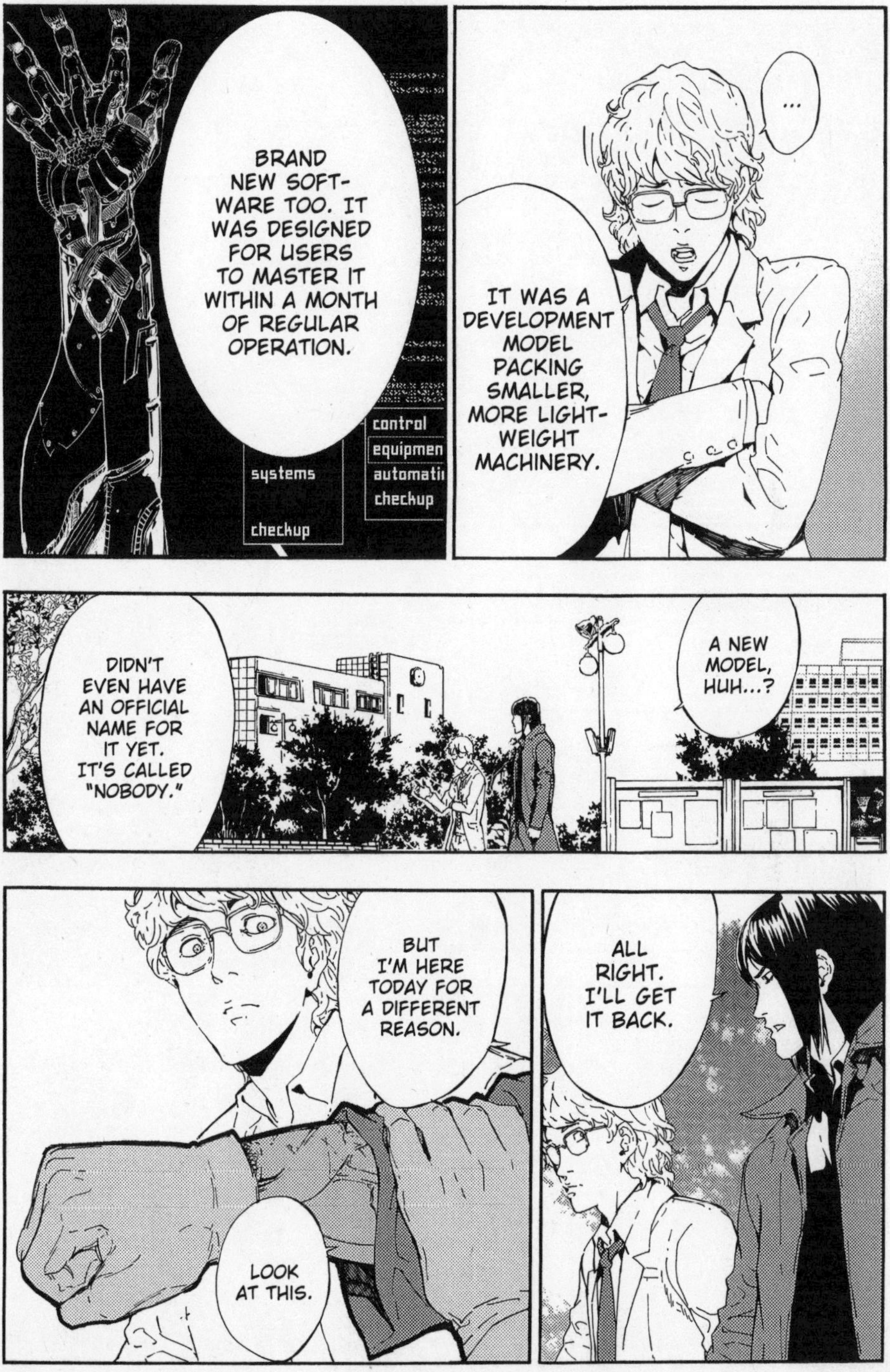
...
IT WAS A DEVELOPMENT MODEL PACKING SMALLER, MORE LIGHT-WEIGHT MACHINERY.
BRAND NEW SOFT-WARE TOO. IT WAS DESIGNED FOR USERS TO MASTER IT WITHIN A MONTH OF REGULAR OPERATION.
control
equipmen
automati
checkup
systems
checkup
A NEW MODEL, HUH...?
DIDN'T EVEN HAVE AN OFFICIAL NAME FOR IT YET. IT'S CALLED "NOBODY."
ALL RIGHT. I'LL GET IT BACK.
BUT I'M HERE TODAY FOR A DIFFERENT REASON.
LOOK AT THIS.

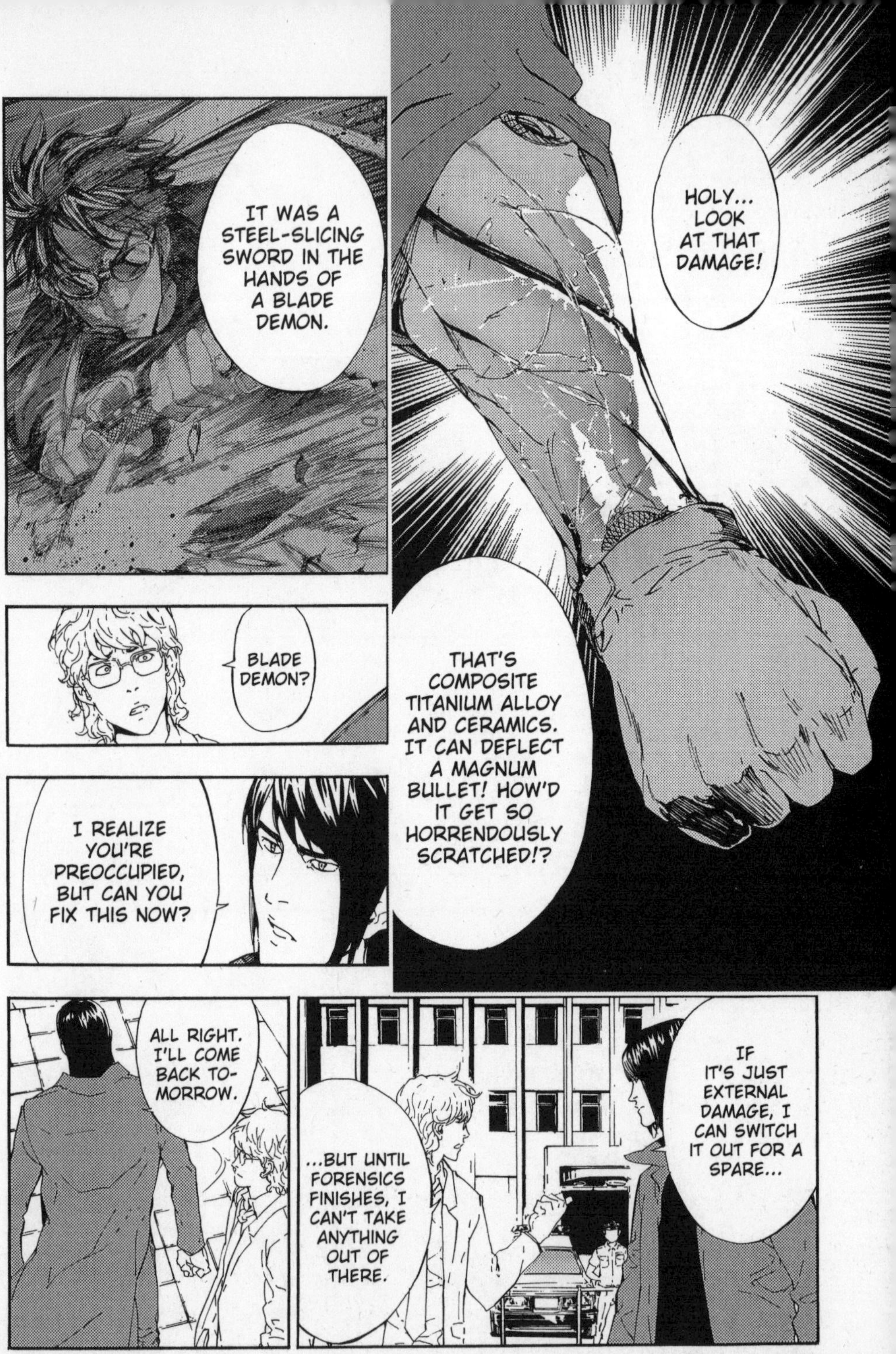
HOLY... LOOK AT THAT DAMAGE!
THAT'S COMPOSITE TITANIUM ALLOY AND CERAMICS. IT CAN DEFLECT A MAGNUM BULLET! HOW'D IT GET SO HORRENDOUSLY SCRATCHED!?
IT WAS A STEEL-SLICING SWORD IN THE HANDS OF A BLADE DEMON.
BLADE DEMON?
I REALIZE YOU'RE PREOCCUPIED, BUT CAN YOU FIX THIS NOW?
IF IT'S JUST EXTERNAL DAMAGE, I CAN SWITCH IT OUT FOR A SPARE...
...BUT UNTIL FORENSICS FINISHES, I CAN'T TAKE ANYTHING OUT OF THERE.
ALL RIGHT. I'LL COME BACK TO-MORROW.

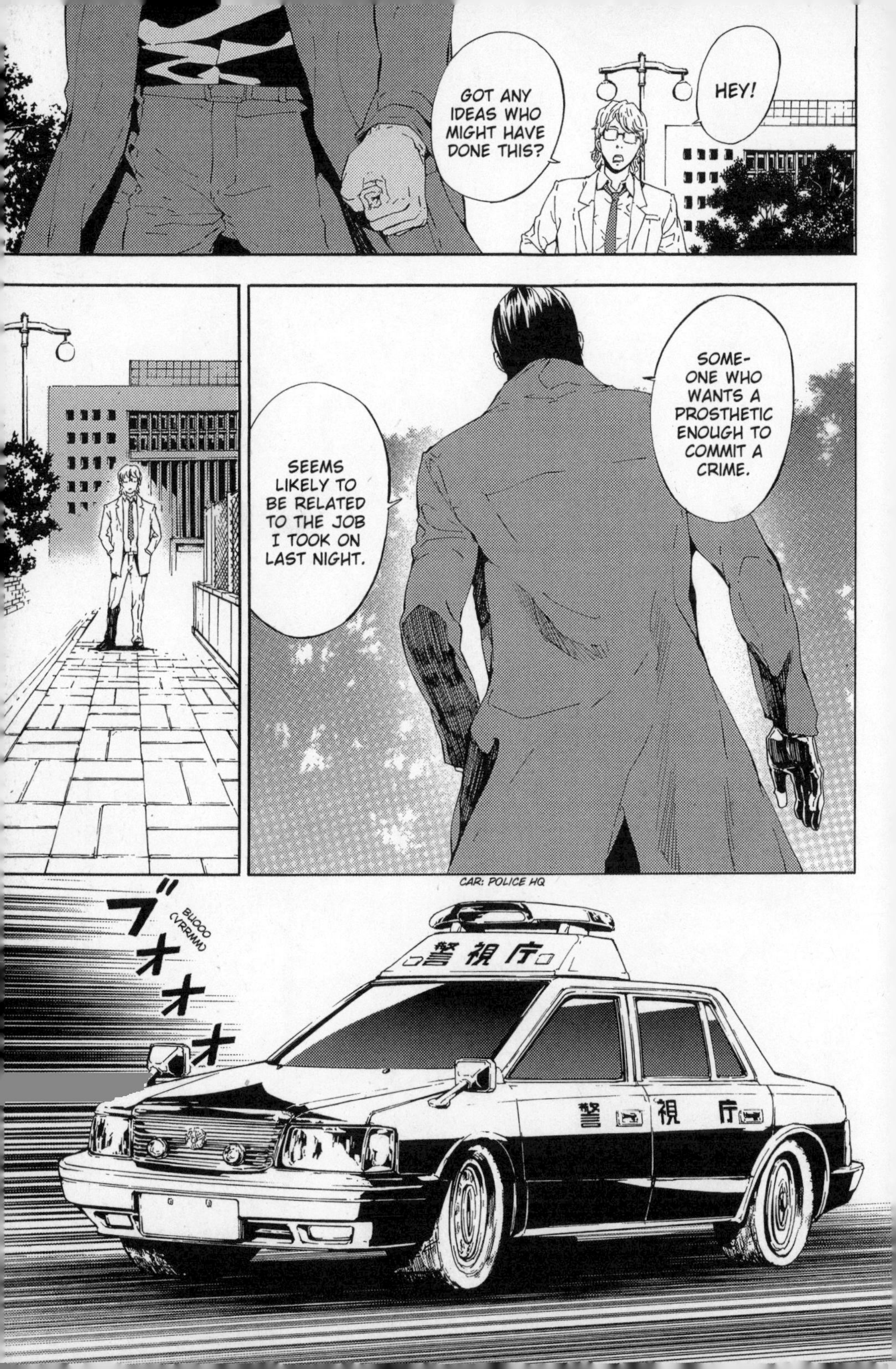
HEY!
GOT ANY IDEAS WHO MIGHT HAVE DONE THIS?
SOME-ONE WHO WANTS A PROSTHETIC ENOUGH TO COMMIT A CRIME.
SEEMS LIKELY TO BE RELATED TO THE JOB I TOOK ON LAST NIGHT.
CAR: POLICE HQ
ブオオオ
BUOOO (VRRMM)
警視庁
警視庁

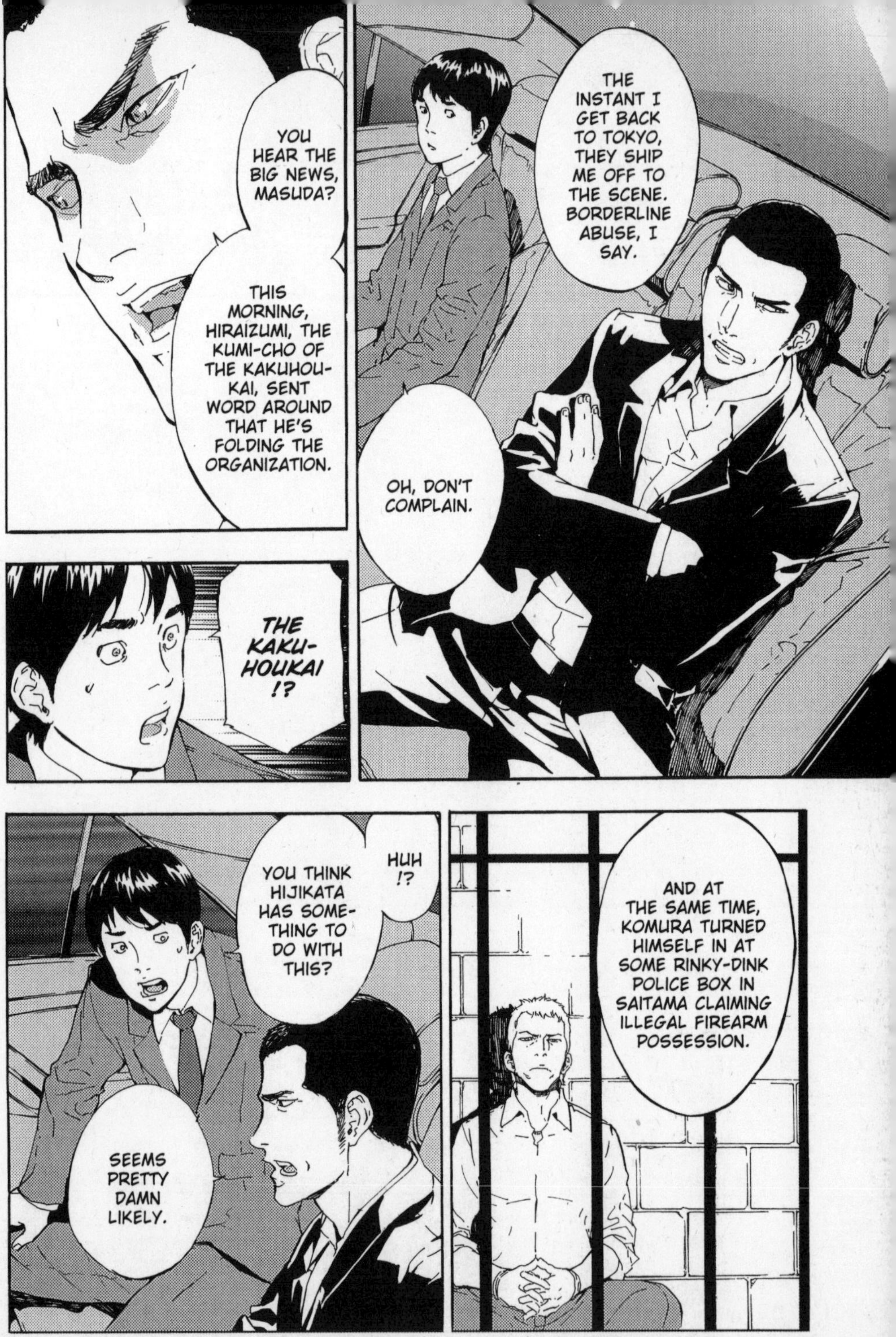
THE INSTANT I GET BACK TO TOKYO, THEY SHIP ME OFF TO THE SCENE. BORDERLINE ABUSE, I SAY.
OH, DON'T COMPLAIN.
YOU HEAR THE BIG NEWS, MASUDA?
THIS MORNING, HIRAIZUMI, THE KUMI-CHO OF THE KAKUHOU-KAI, SENT WORD AROUND THAT HE'S FOLDING THE ORGANIZATION.
THE KAKU-HOUKAI!?
AND AT THE SAME TIME, KOMURA TURNED HIMSELF IN AT SOME RINKY-DINK POLICE BOX IN SAITAMA CLAIMING ILLEGAL FIREARM POSSESSION.
HUH!?
YOU THINK HIJIKATA HAS SOME-THING TO DO WITH THIS?
SEEMS PRETTY DAMN LIKELY.

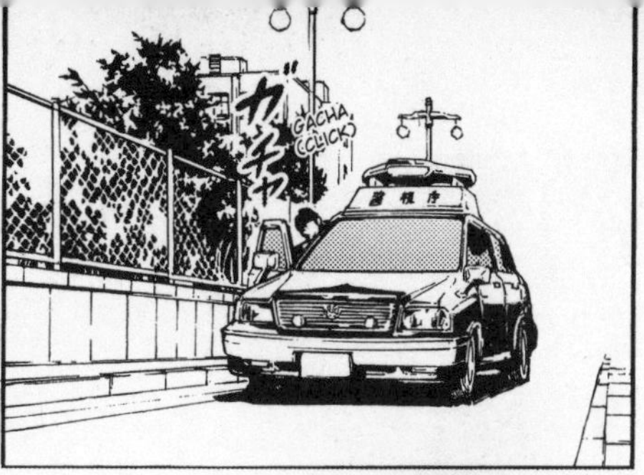
ガチャ
GACHA (CLICK)
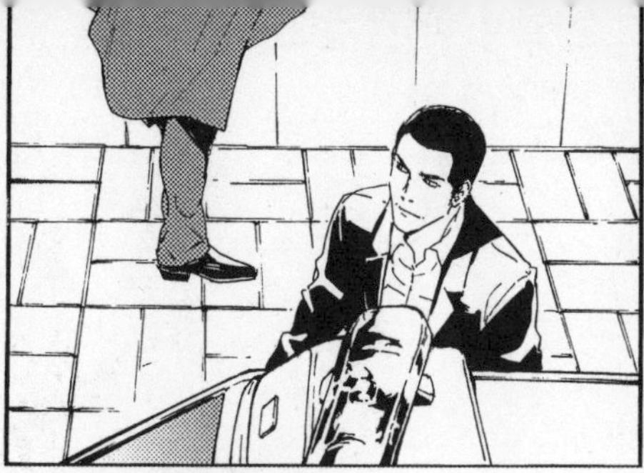
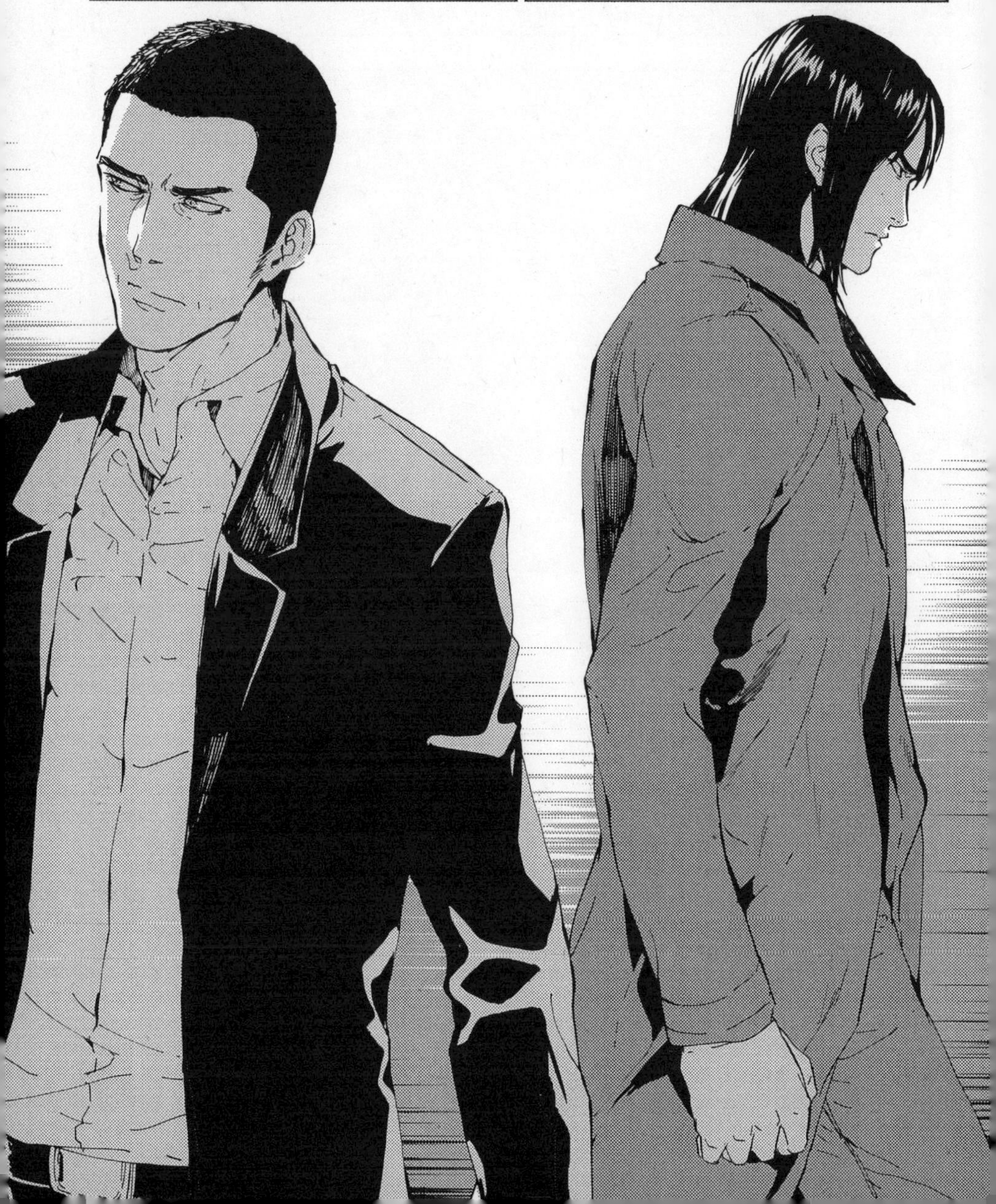

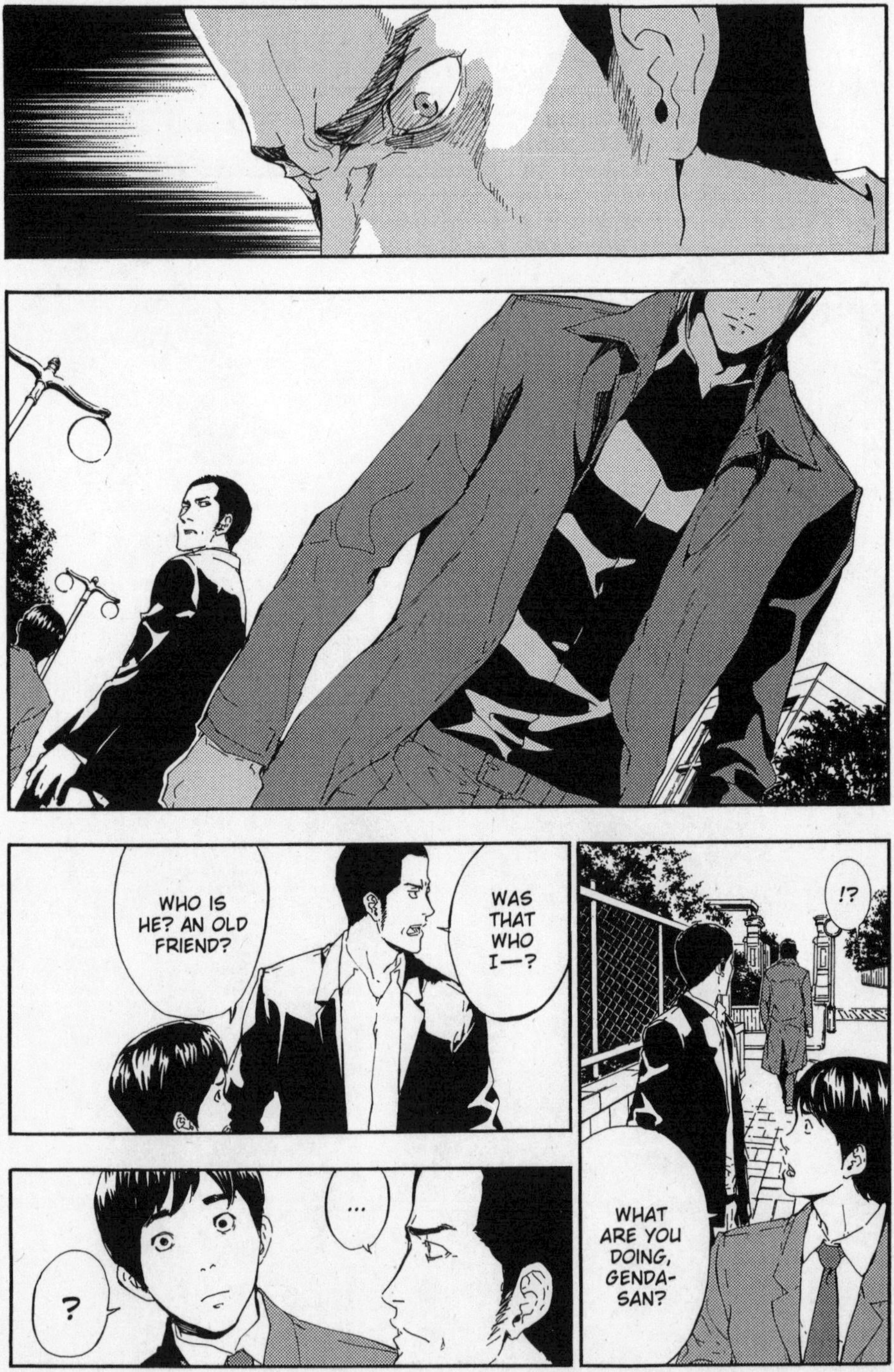
!?
WHAT ARE YOU DOING, GENDA-SAN?
WAS THAT WHO I—?
WHO IS HE? AN OLD FRIEND?
...
?

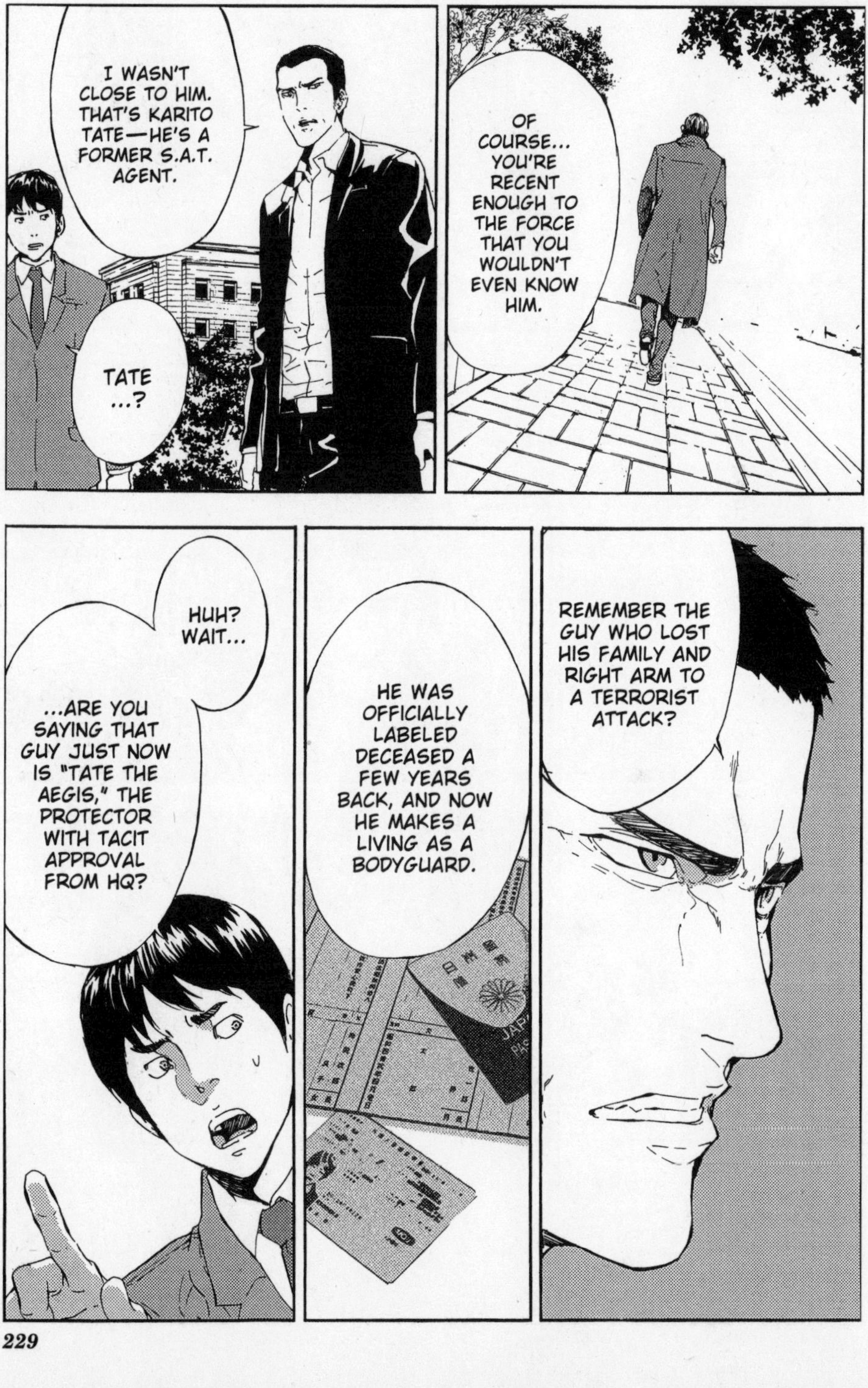
OF COURSE... YOU'RE RECENT ENOUGH TO THE FORCE THAT YOU WOULDN'T EVEN KNOW HIM.
I WASN'T CLOSE TO HIM. THAT'S KARITO TATE—HE'S A FORMER S.A.T. AGENT.
TATE ...?
REMEMBER THE GUY WHO LOST HIS FAMILY AND RIGHT ARM TO A TERRORIST ATTACK?
HE WAS OFFICIALLY LABELED DECEASED A FEW YEARS BACK, AND NOW HE MAKES A LIVING AS A BODYGUARD.
HUH? WAIT...
...ARE YOU SAYING THAT GUY JUST NOW IS "TATE THE AEGIS," THE PROTECTOR WITH TACIT APPROVAL FROM HQ?

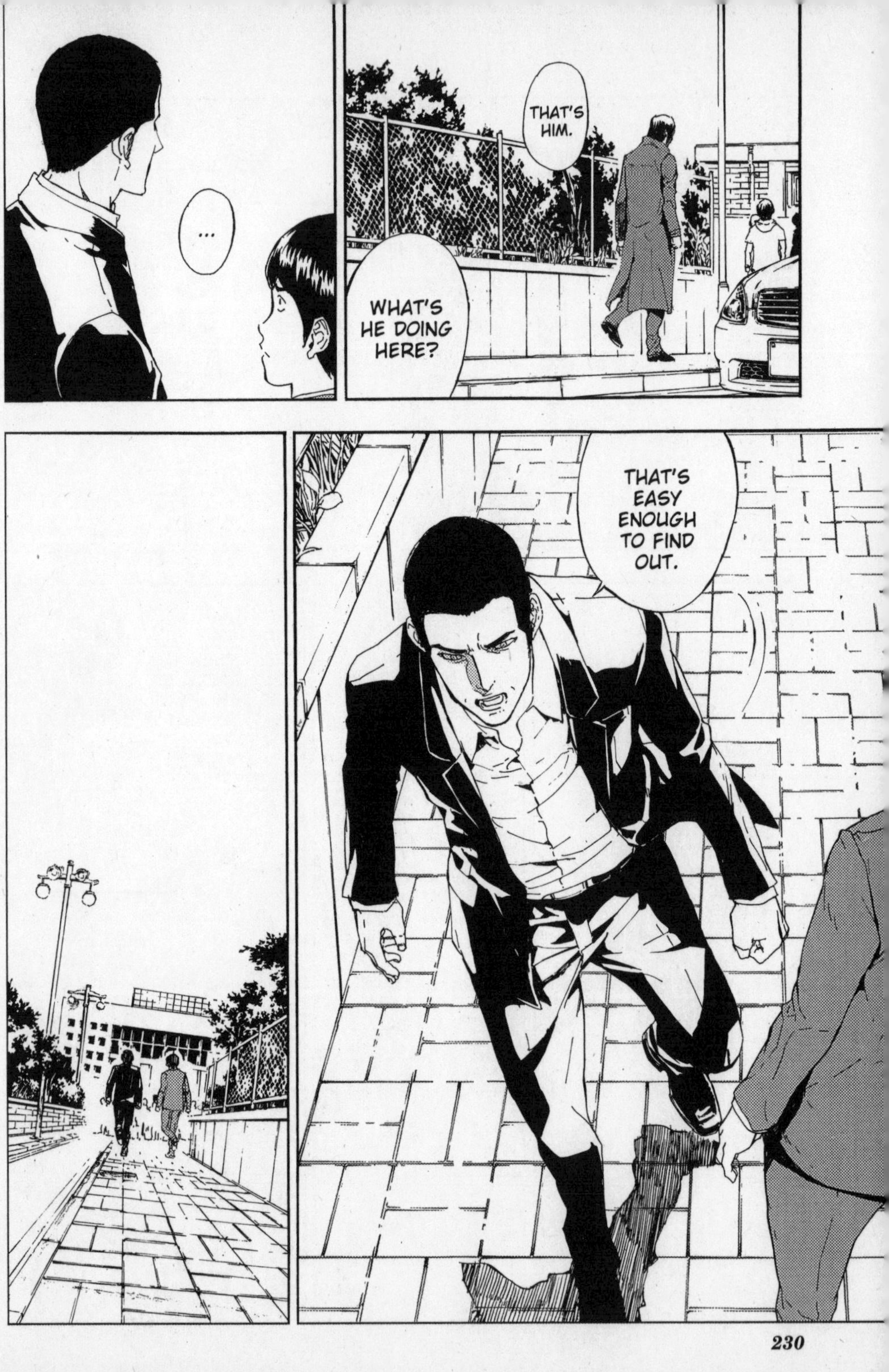
THAT'S HIM.
WHAT'S HE DOING HERE?
...
THAT'S EASY ENOUGH TO FIND OUT.

Until Death do us Part

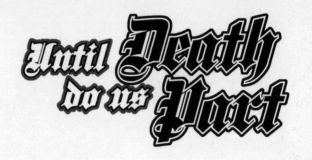

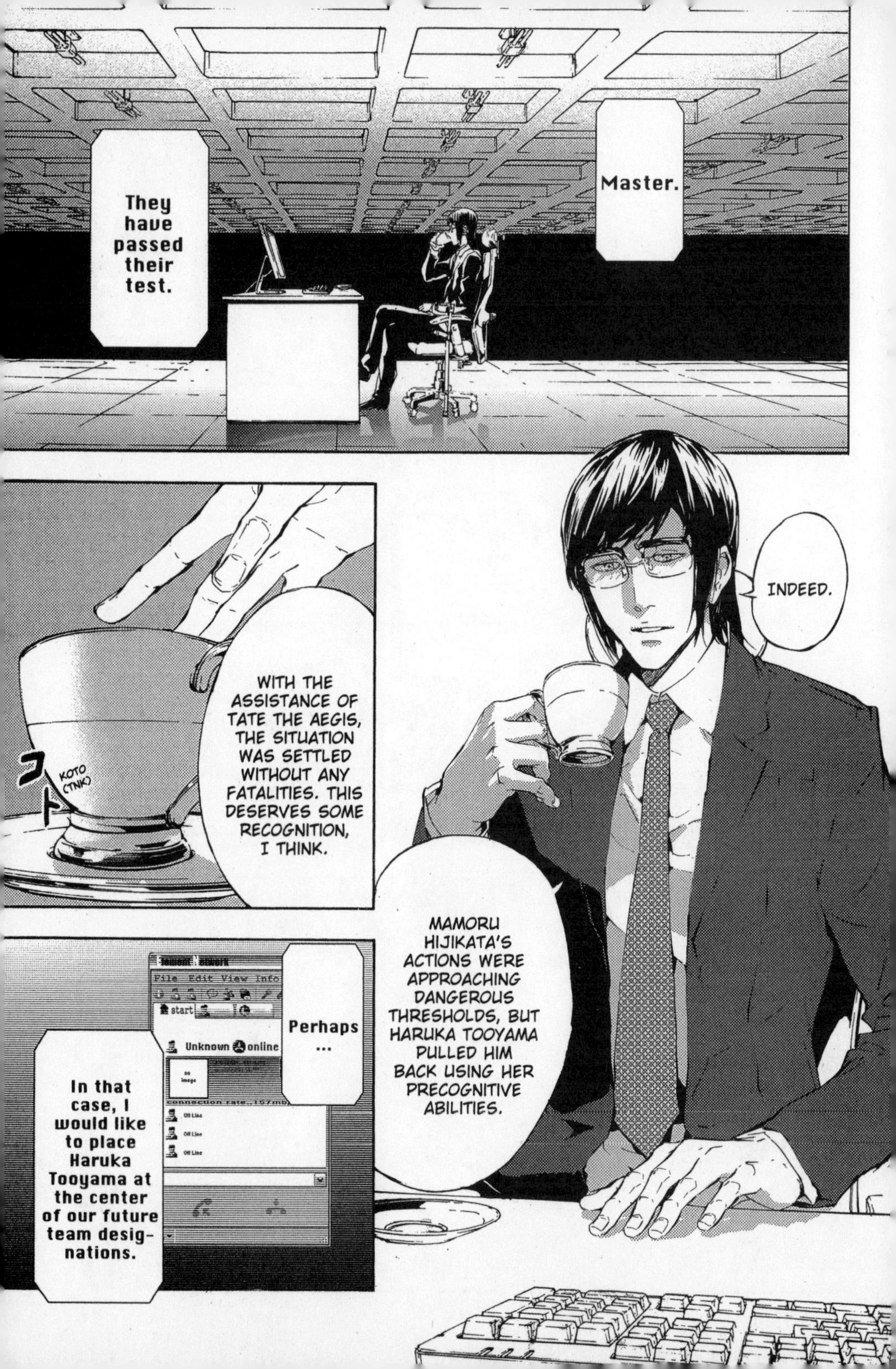
Master.
They have passed their test.
WITH THE ASSISTANCE OF TATE THE AEGIS, THE SITUATION WAS SETTLED WITHOUT ANY FATALITIES. THIS DESERVES SOME RECOGNITION, I THINK.
コト
KOTO (TNK)
INDEED.
MAMORU HIJIKATA'S ACTIONS WERE APPROACHING DANGEROUS THRESHOLDS, BUT HARUKA TOOYAMA PULLED HIM BACK USING HER PRECOGNITIVE ABILITIES.
Perhaps ...
In that case, I would like to place Haruka Tooyama at the center of our future team desig-nations.
File Edit View Info
start
Unknown online
Off Line
Off Line
Off Line

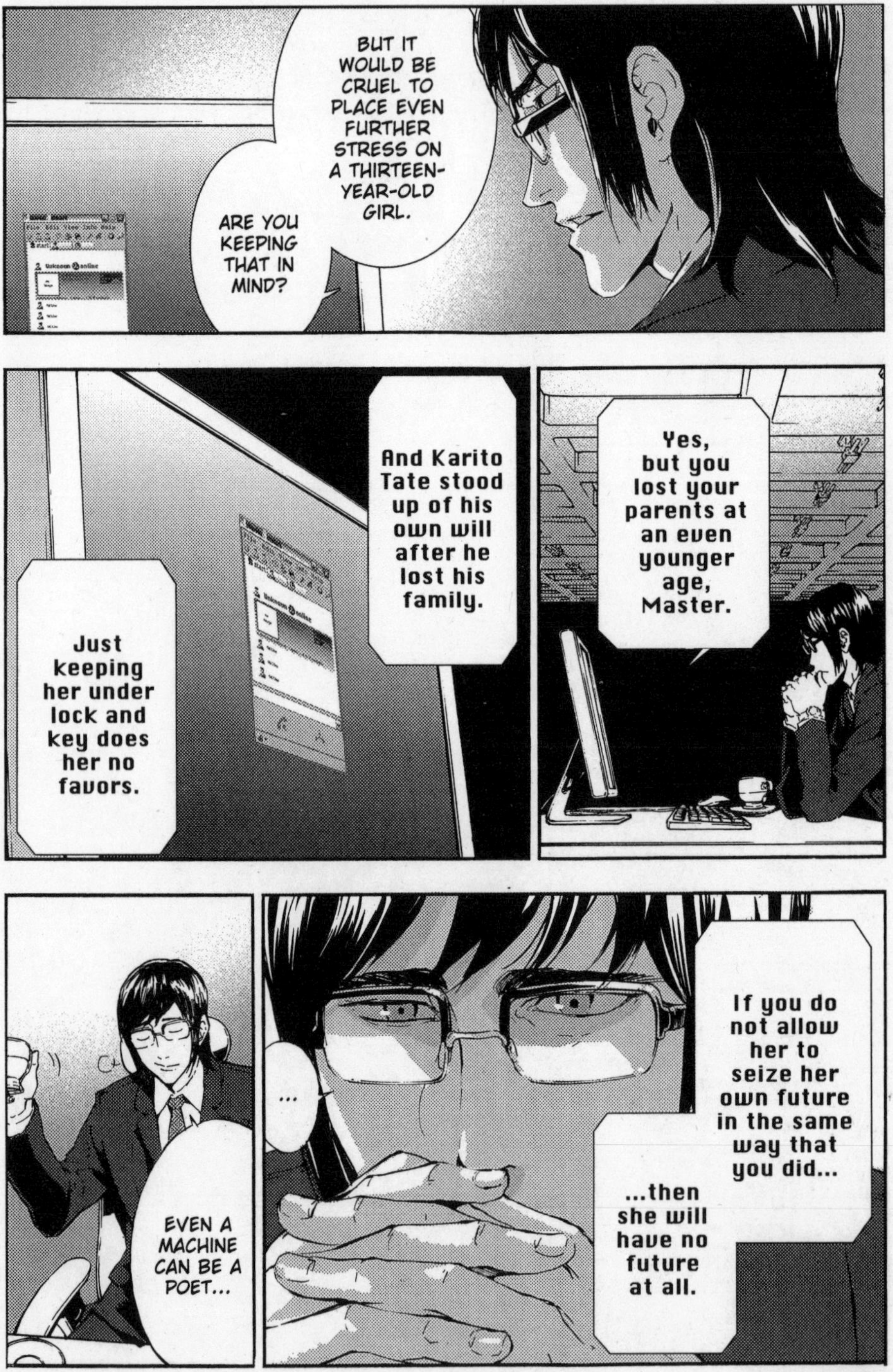
BUT IT WOULD BE CRUEL TO PLACE EVEN FURTHER STRESS ON A THIRTEEN-YEAR-OLD GIRL.
ARE YOU KEEPING THAT IN MIND?
Yes, but you lost your parents at an even younger age, Master.
And Karito Tate stood up of his own will after he lost his family.
Just keeping her under lock and key does her no favors.
If you do not allow her to seize her own future in the same way that you did...
...then she will have no future at all.
...
EVEN A MACHINE CAN BE A POET...

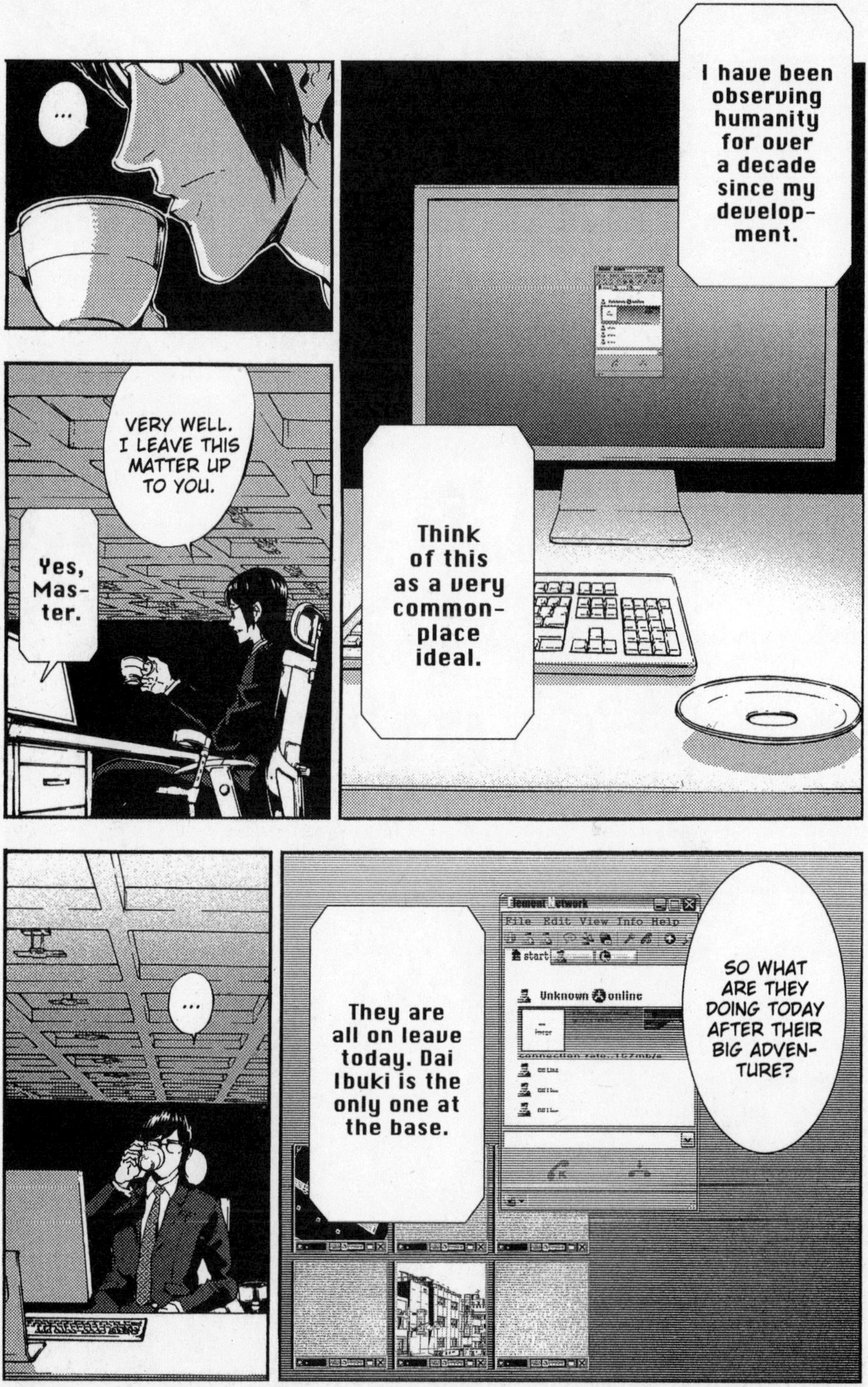
I have been observing humanity for over a decade since my development.
Think of this as a very commonplace ideal.
...
VERY WELL. I LEAVE THIS MATTER UP TO YOU.
Yes, Master.
SO WHAT ARE THEY DOING TODAY AFTER THEIR BIG ADVENTURE?
They are all on leave today. Dai Ibuki is the only one at the base.
...

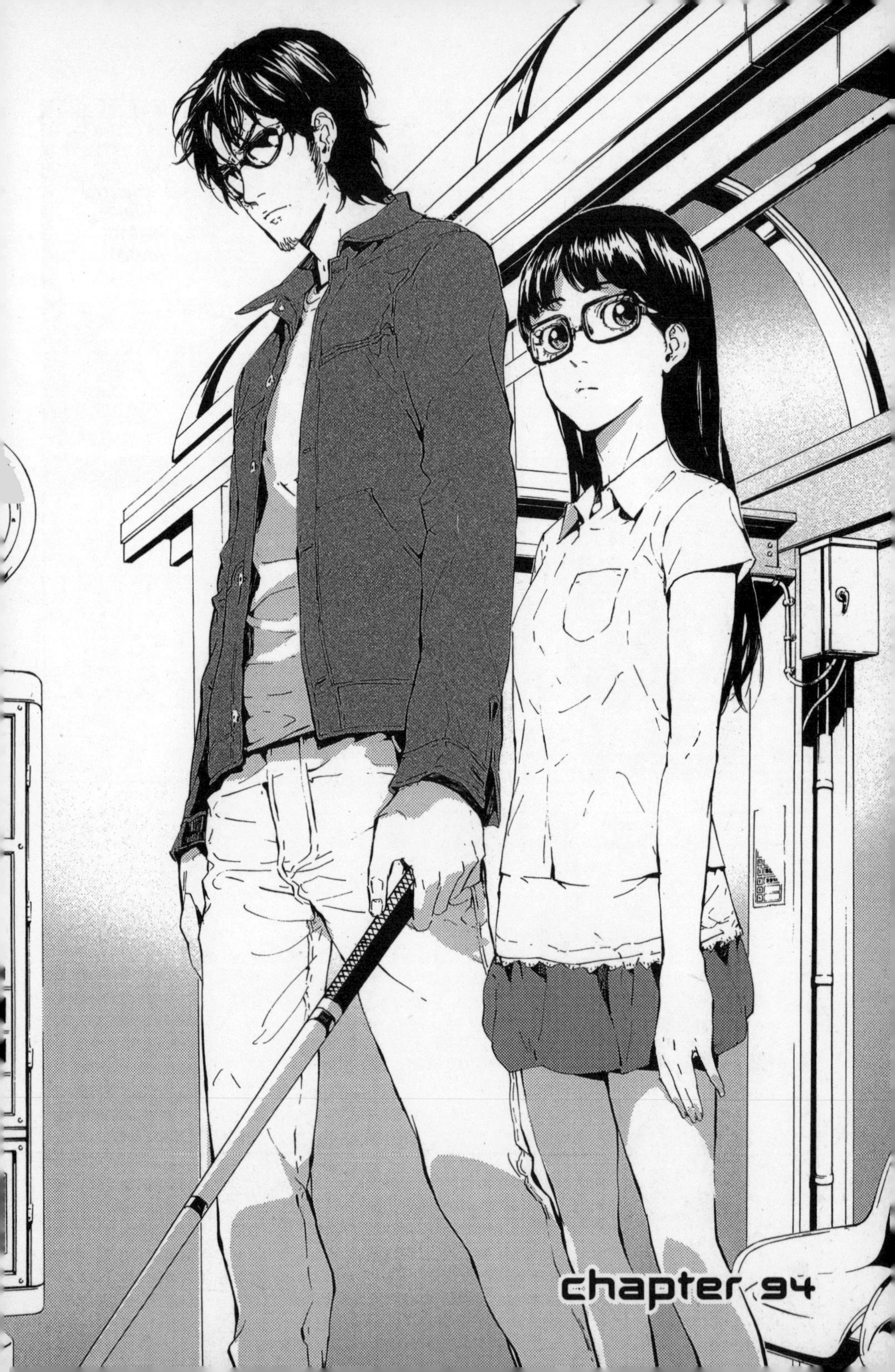
chapter 94

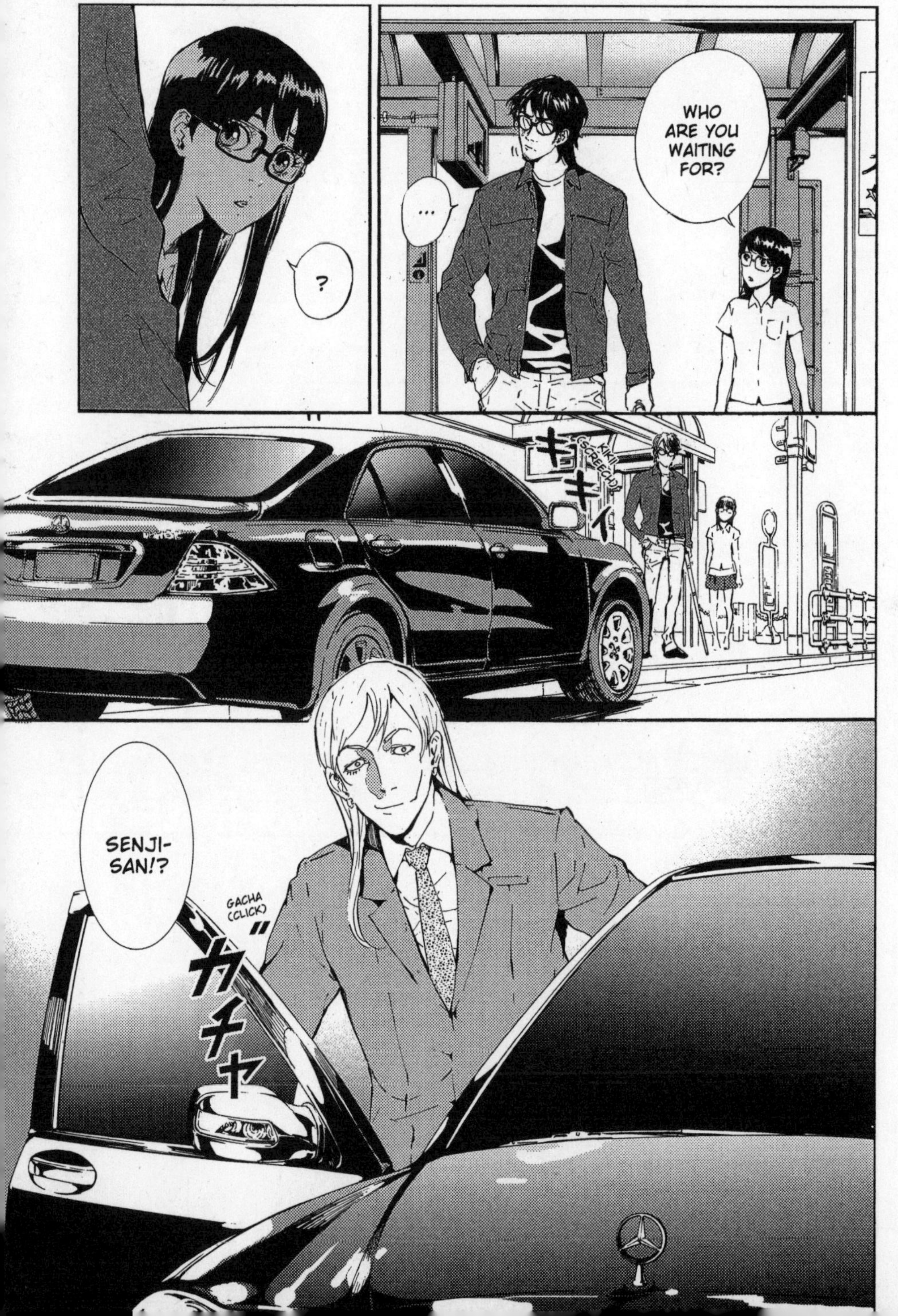
WHO ARE YOU WAITING FOR?
...
?
キキイ
KIKII (SCREECH)
SENJI-SAN!?
ガチャ
GACHA (CLICK)

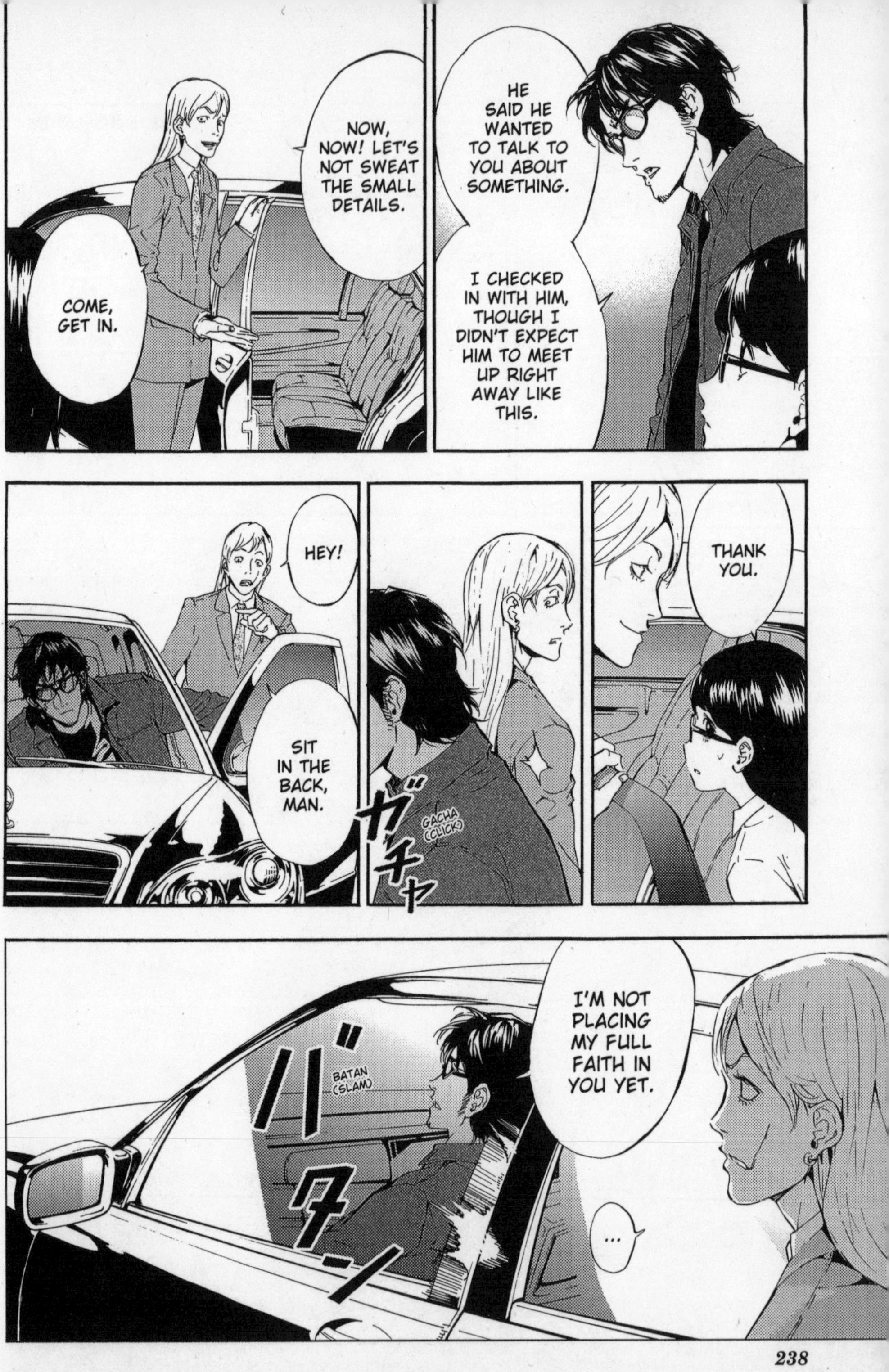
HE SAID HE WANTED TO TALK TO YOU ABOUT SOMETHING.
I CHECKED IN WITH HIM, THOUGH I DIDN'T EXPECT HIM TO MEET UP RIGHT AWAY LIKE THIS.
NOW, NOW! LET'S NOT SWEAT THE SMALL DETAILS.
COME, GET IN.
THANK YOU.
ガチャ
GACHA (CLICK)
HEY!
SIT IN THE BACK, MAN.
I'M NOT PLACING MY FULL FAITH IN YOU YET.
BATAN (SLAM)
...

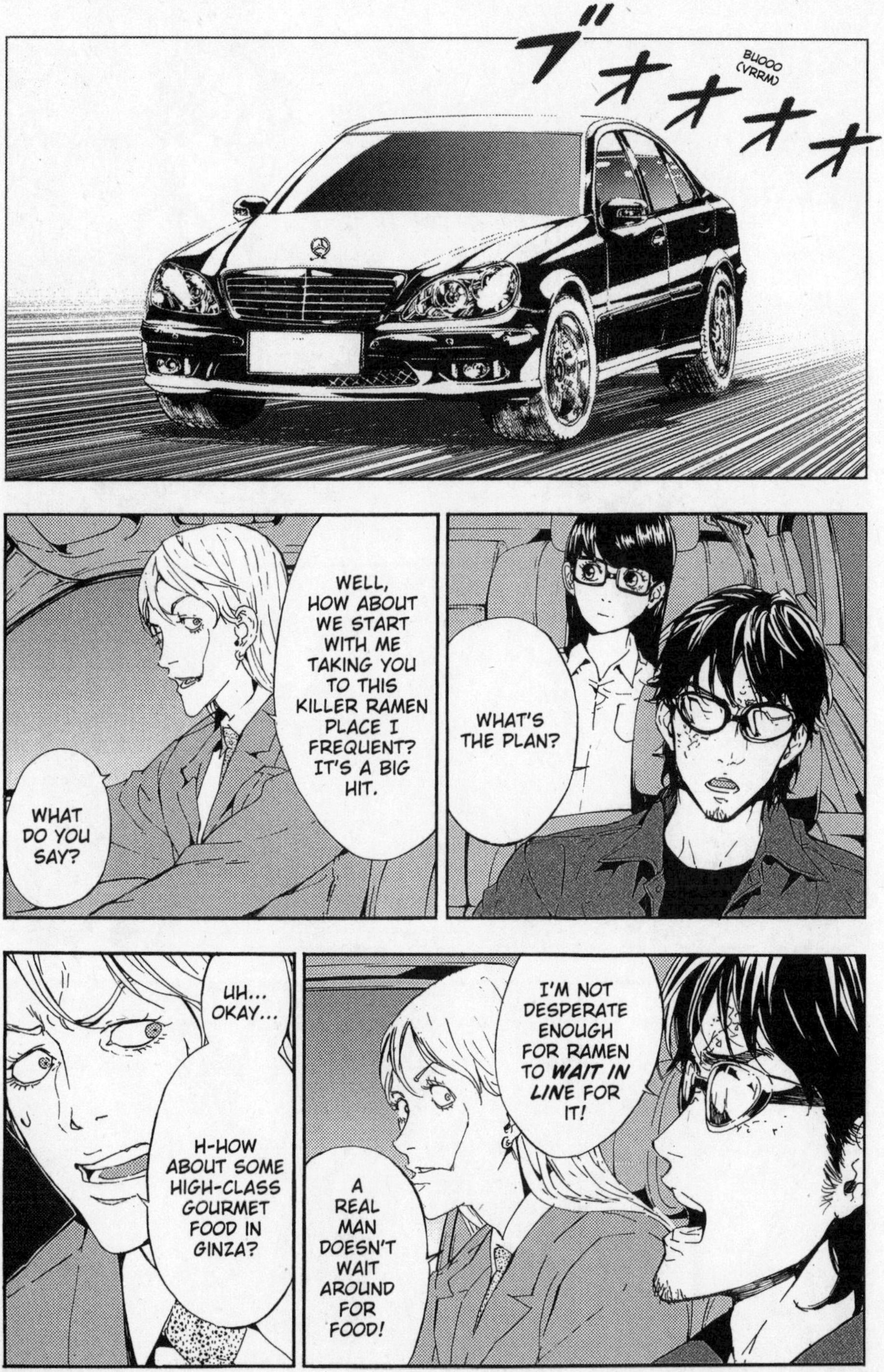
ブオオオオ
BUOOO (VRRM)
WHAT'S THE PLAN?
WELL, HOW ABOUT WE START WITH ME TAKING YOU TO THIS KILLER RAMEN PLACE I FREQUENT? IT'S A BIG HIT.
WHAT DO YOU SAY?
I'M NOT DESPERATE ENOUGH FOR RAMEN TO ***WAIT IN LINE*** FOR IT!
A REAL MAN DOESN'T WAIT AROUND FOR FOOD!
UH... OKAY...
H-HOW ABOUT SOME HIGH-CLASS GOURMET FOOD IN GINZA?

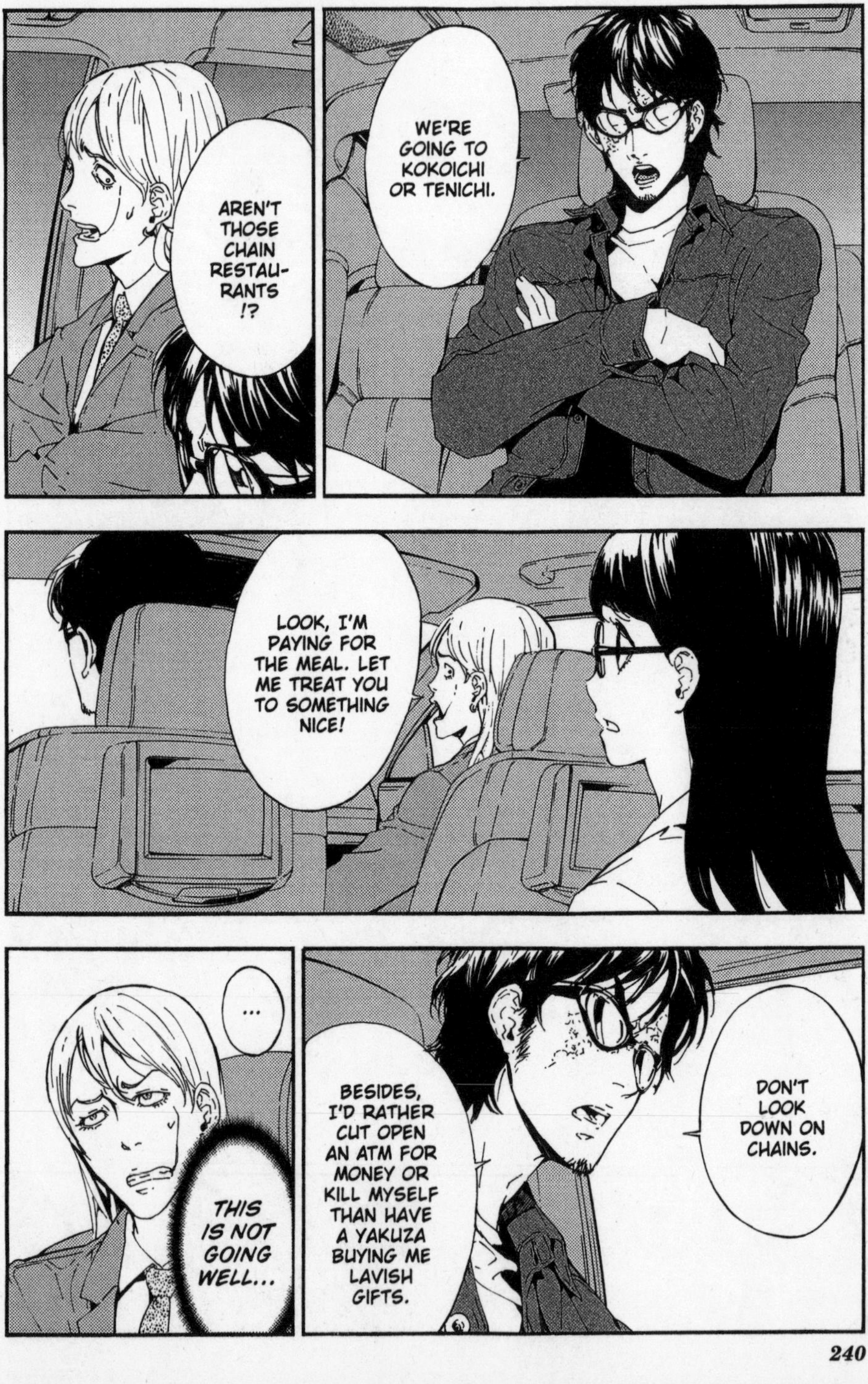
WE'RE GOING TO KOKOICHI OR TENICHI.
AREN'T THOSE CHAIN RESTAURANTS!?
LOOK, I'M PAYING FOR THE MEAL. LET ME TREAT YOU TO SOMETHING NICE!
DON'T LOOK DOWN ON CHAINS.
BESIDES, I'D RATHER CUT OPEN AN ATM FOR MONEY OR KILL MYSELF THAN HAVE A YAKUZA BUYING ME LAVISH GIFTS.
...
THIS IS NOT GOING WELL...

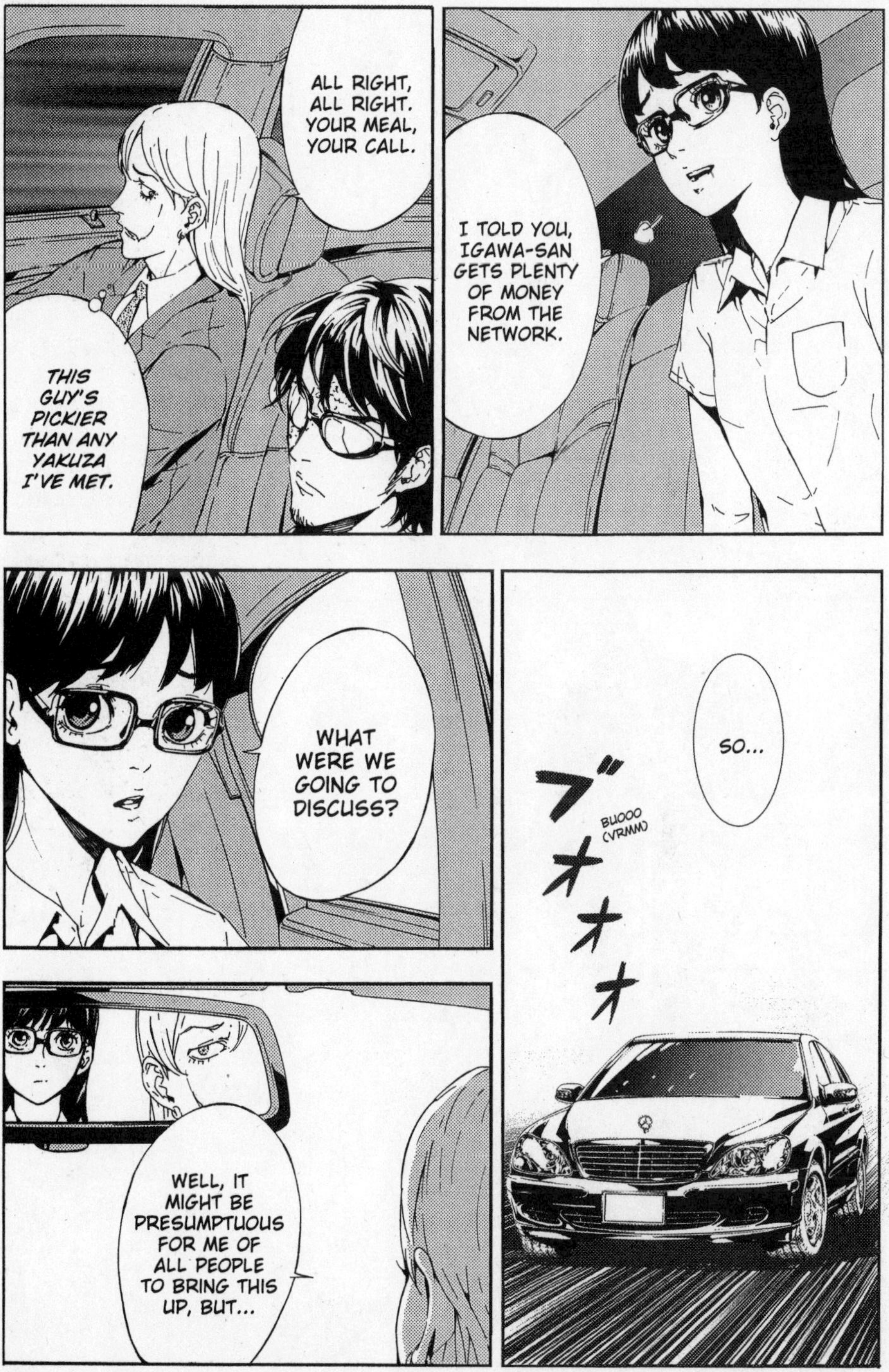
I TOLD YOU, IGAWA-SAN GETS PLENTY OF MONEY FROM THE NETWORK.
ALL RIGHT, ALL RIGHT. YOUR MEAL, YOUR CALL.
THIS GUY'S PICKIER THAN ANY YAKUZA I'VE MET.
SO...
BUOOO (VRMM)
WHAT WERE WE GOING TO DISCUSS?
WELL, IT MIGHT BE PRESUMPTUOUS FOR ME OF ALL PEOPLE TO BRING THIS UP, BUT...

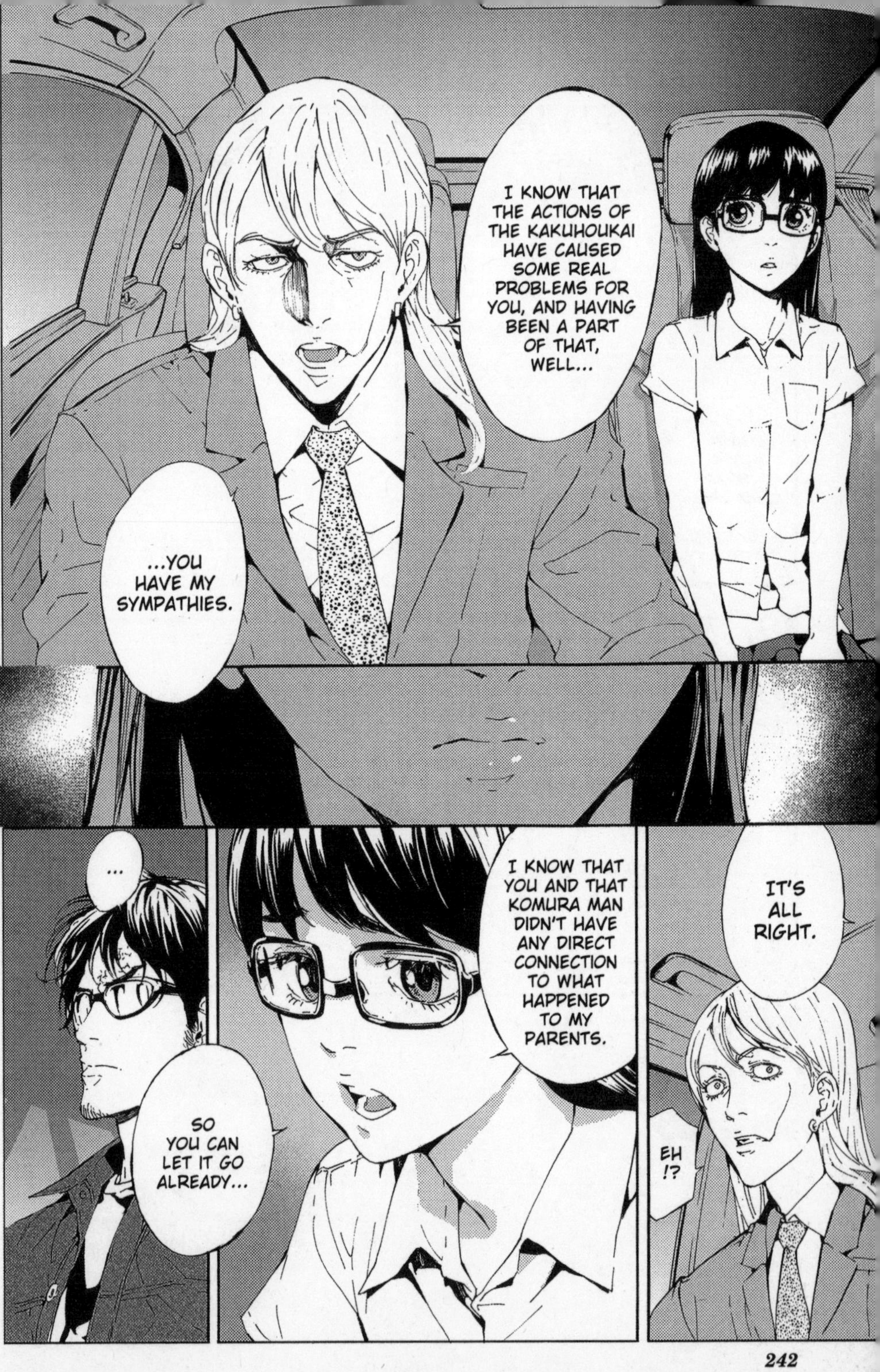
I KNOW THAT THE ACTIONS OF THE KAKUHOUKAI HAVE CAUSED SOME REAL PROBLEMS FOR YOU, AND HAVING BEEN A PART OF THAT, WELL...
...YOU HAVE MY SYMPATHIES.
IT'S ALL RIGHT.
EH !?
I KNOW THAT YOU AND THAT KOMURA MAN DIDN'T HAVE ANY DIRECT CONNECTION TO WHAT HAPPENED TO MY PARENTS.
...
SO YOU CAN LET IT GO ALREADY...

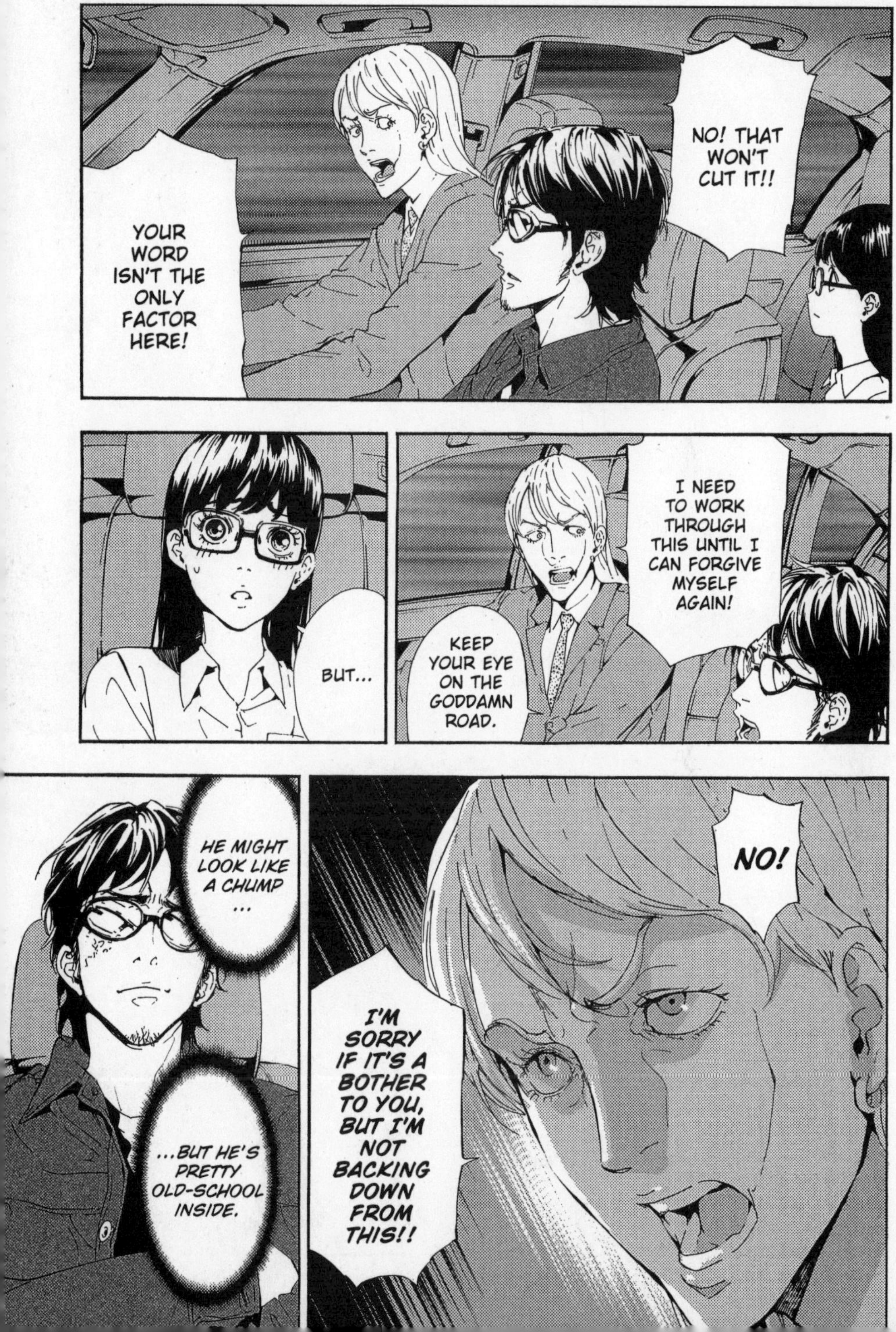
NO! THAT WON'T CUT IT!!
YOUR WORD ISN'T THE ONLY FACTOR HERE!
I NEED TO WORK THROUGH THIS UNTIL I CAN FORGIVE MYSELF AGAIN!
KEEP YOUR EYE ON THE GODDAMN ROAD.
BUT...
NO!
I'M SORRY IF IT'S A BOTHER TO YOU, BUT I'M NOT BACKING DOWN FROM THIS!!
HE MIGHT LOOK LIKE A CHUMP ...
...BUT HE'S PRETTY OLD-SCHOOL INSIDE.

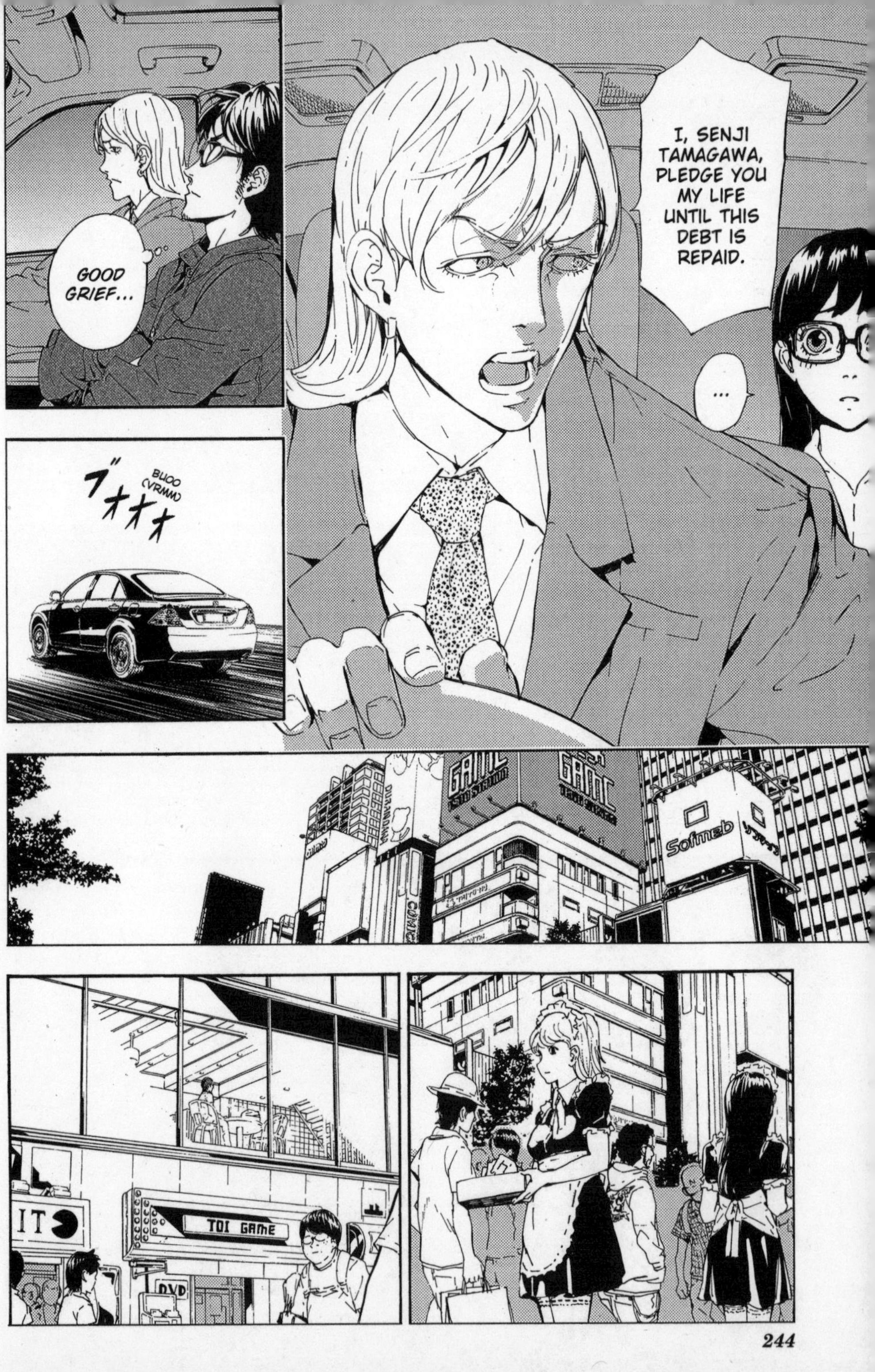
I, SENJI TAMAGAWA, PLEDGE YOU MY LIFE UNTIL THIS DEBT IS REPAID.
...
GOOD GRIEF...
ブオオオ
BUOO (VRMM)
Sofmeb
TOI GAME
DVD

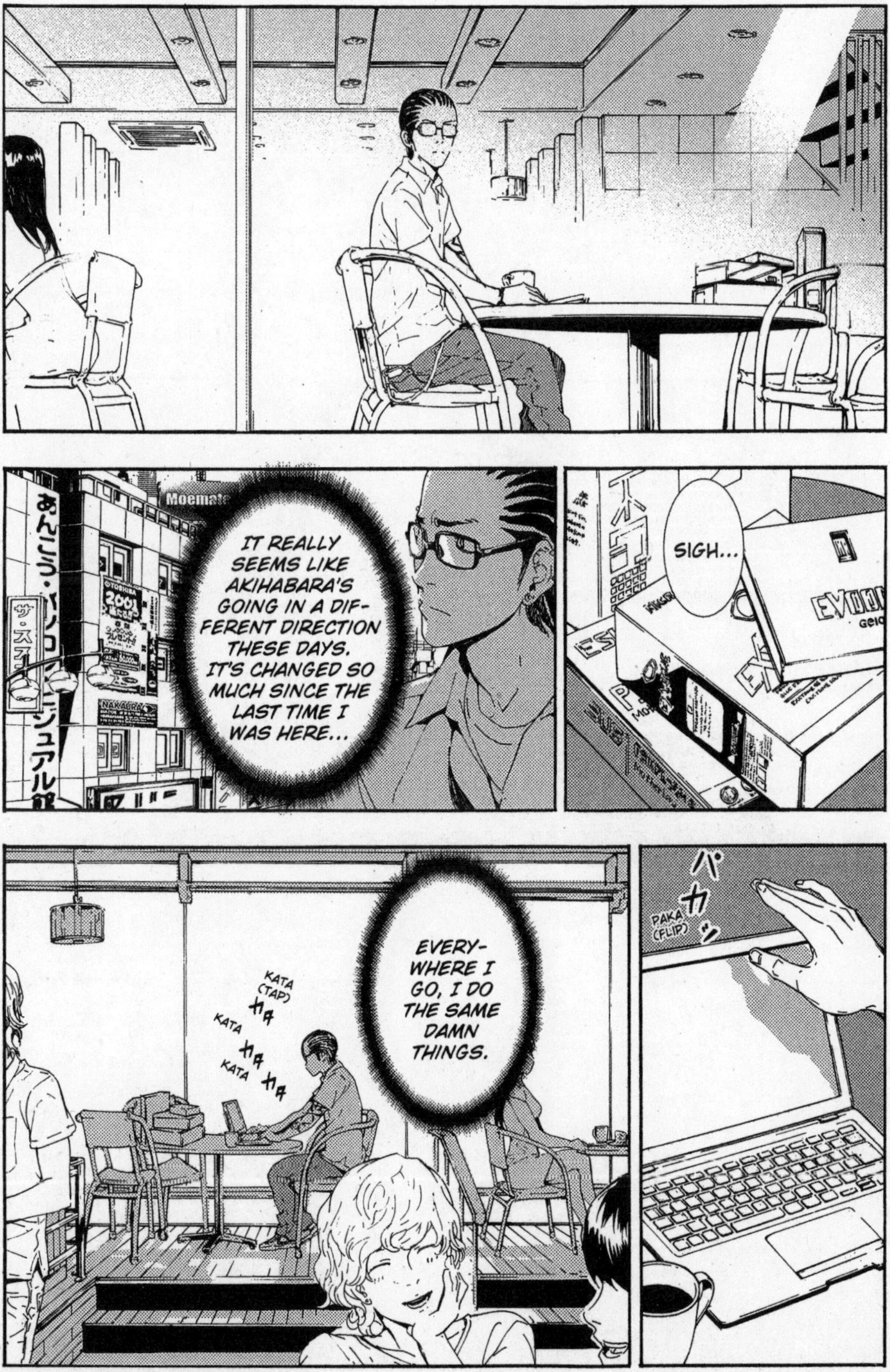
SIGH...
IT REALLY SEEMS LIKE AKIHABARA'S GOING IN A DIFFERENT DIRECTION THESE DAYS. IT'S CHANGED SO MUCH SINCE THE LAST TIME I WAS HERE...
パカッ
PAKA (FLIP)
KATA (TAP) カタ
KATA カタ
KATA カタ
EVERYWHERE I GO, I DO THE SAME DAMN THINGS.

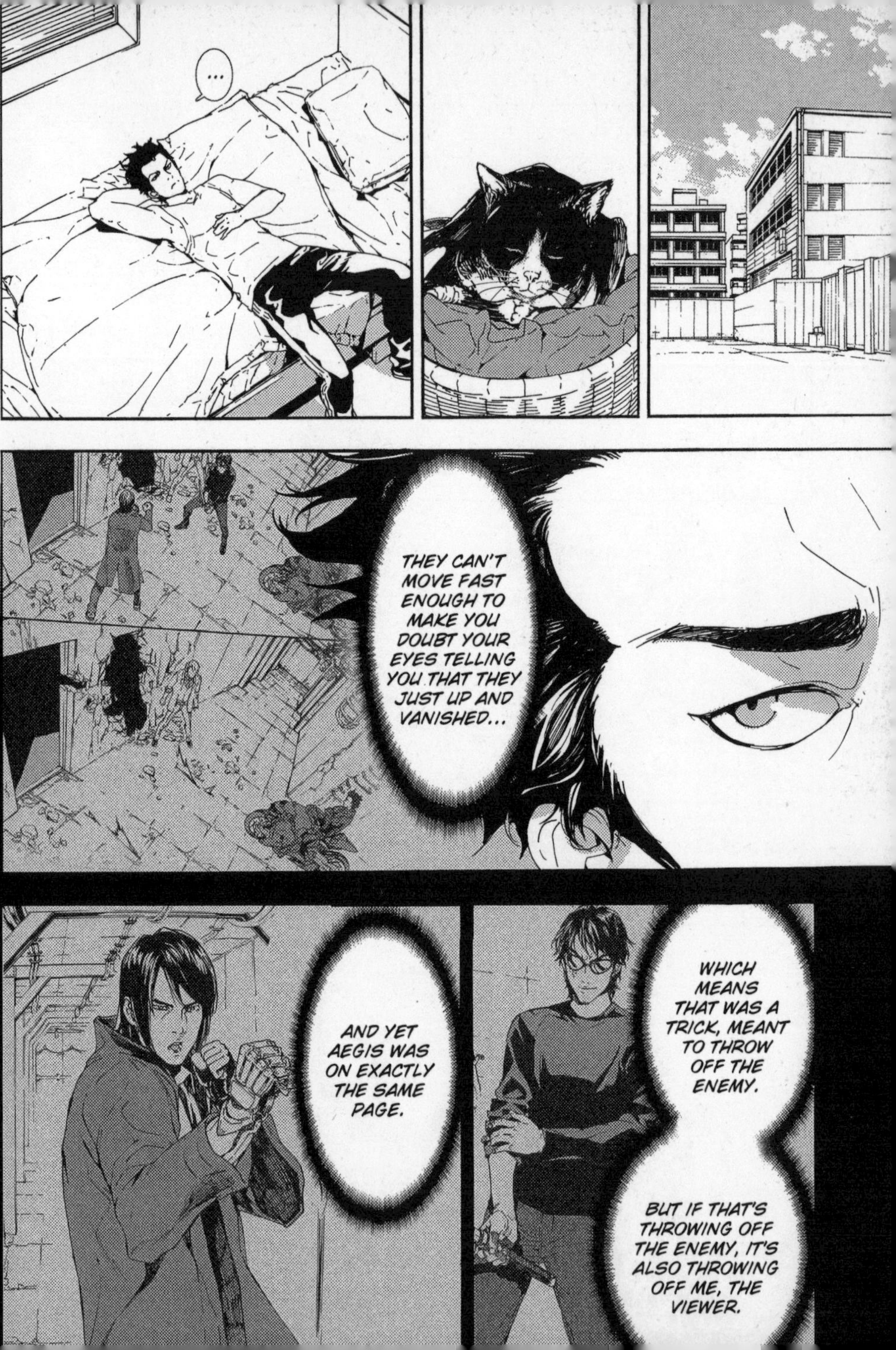
...
THEY CAN'T MOVE FAST ENOUGH TO MAKE YOU DOUBT YOUR EYES TELLING YOU THAT THEY JUST UP AND VANISHED...
WHICH MEANS THAT WAS A TRICK, MEANT TO THROW OFF THE ENEMY.
BUT IF THAT'S THROWING OFF THE ENEMY, IT'S ALSO THROWING OFF ME, THE VIEWER.
AND YET AEGIS WAS ON EXACTLY THE SAME PAGE.

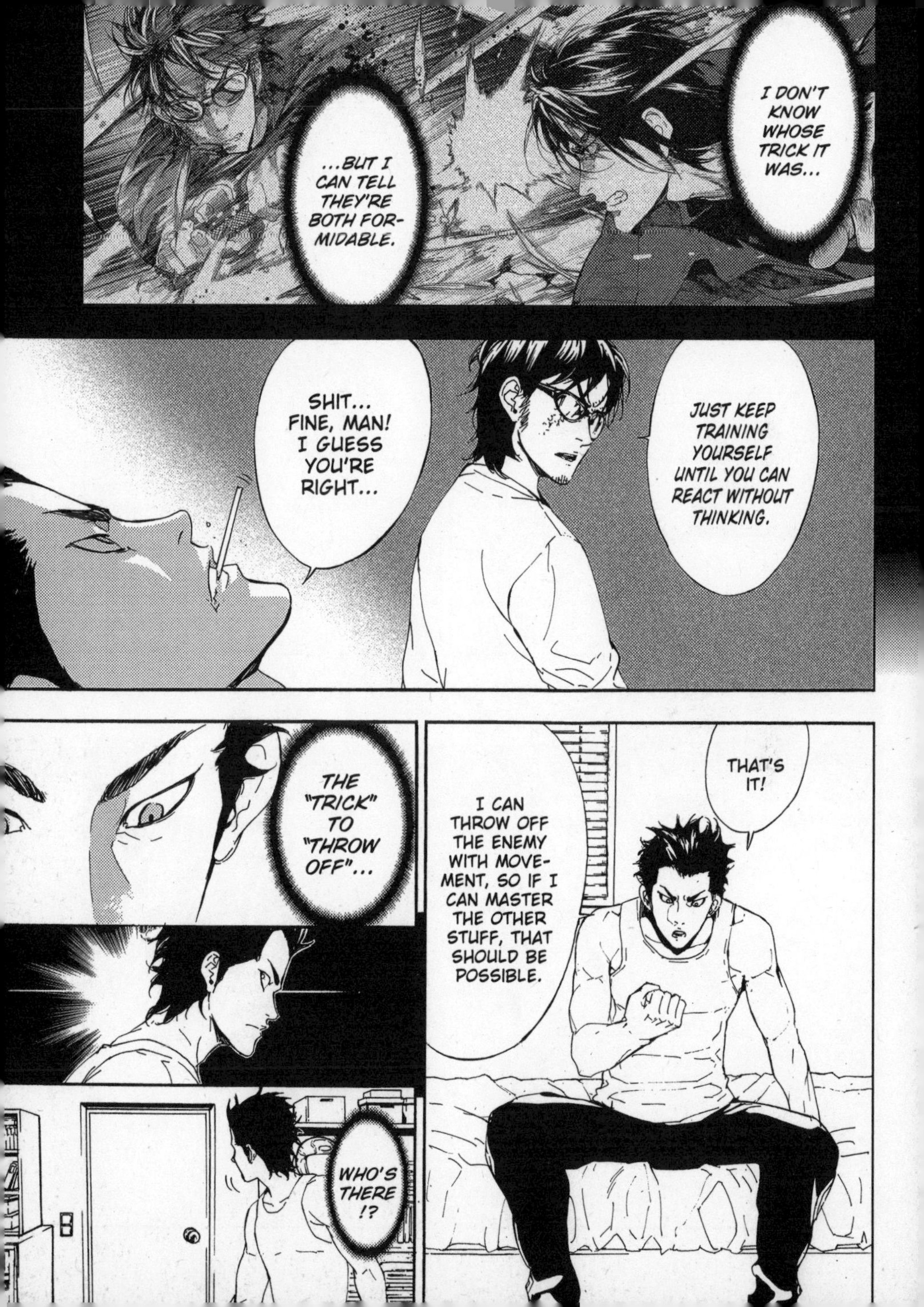
I DON'T KNOW WHOSE TRICK IT WAS...
...BUT I CAN TELL THEY'RE BOTH FOR-MIDABLE.
JUST KEEP TRAINING YOURSELF UNTIL YOU CAN REACT WITHOUT THINKING.
SHIT... FINE, MAN! I GUESS YOU'RE RIGHT...
THAT'S IT!
I CAN THROW OFF THE ENEMY WITH MOVE-MENT, SO IF I CAN MASTER THE OTHER STUFF, THAT SHOULD BE POSSIBLE.
THE "TRICK" TO "THROW OFF"...
WHO'S THERE !?

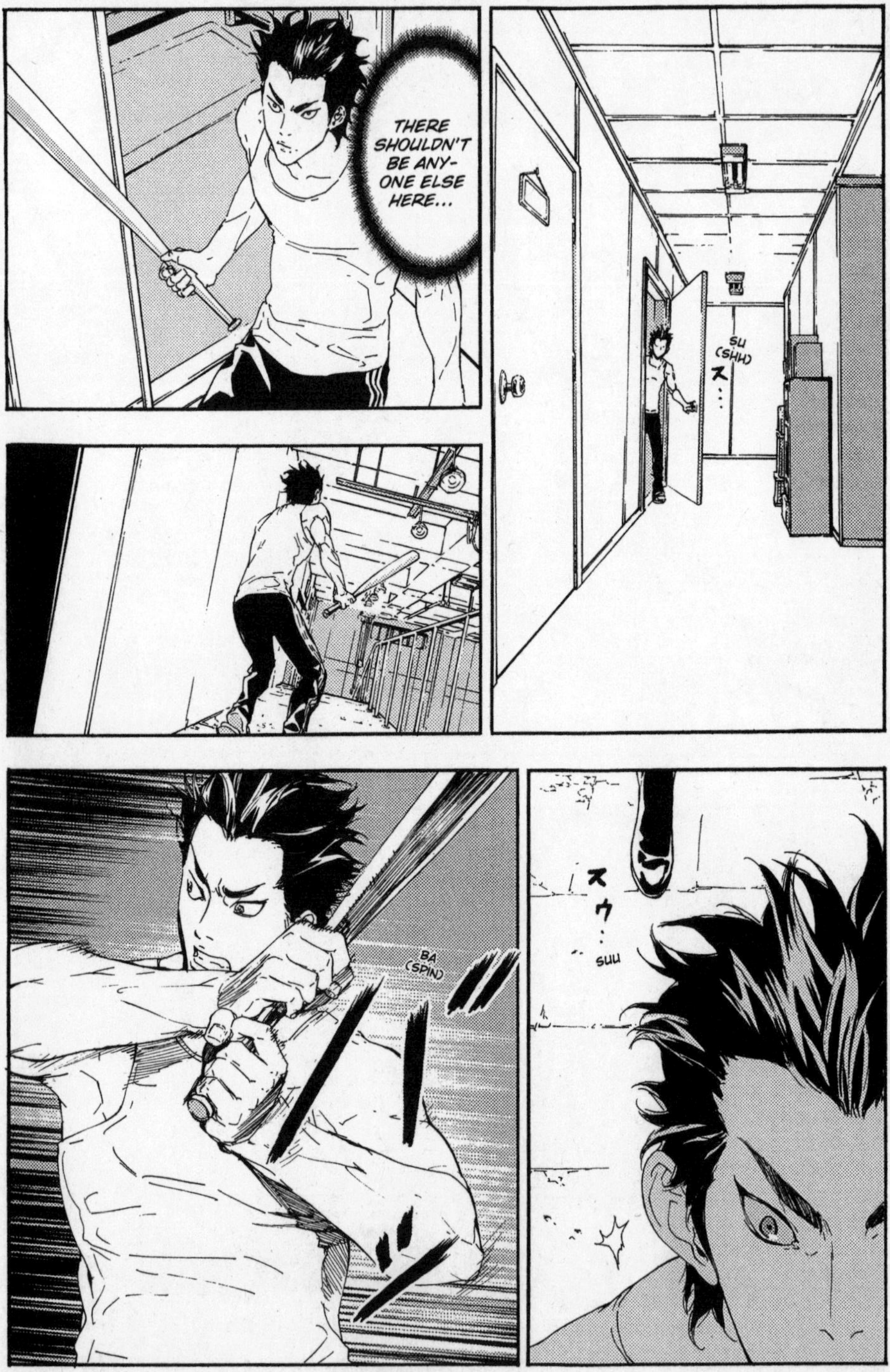
SU (SHH)
ス…
THERE SHOULDN'T BE ANY-ONE ELSE HERE...
スウ…
SUU
BA (SPIN)

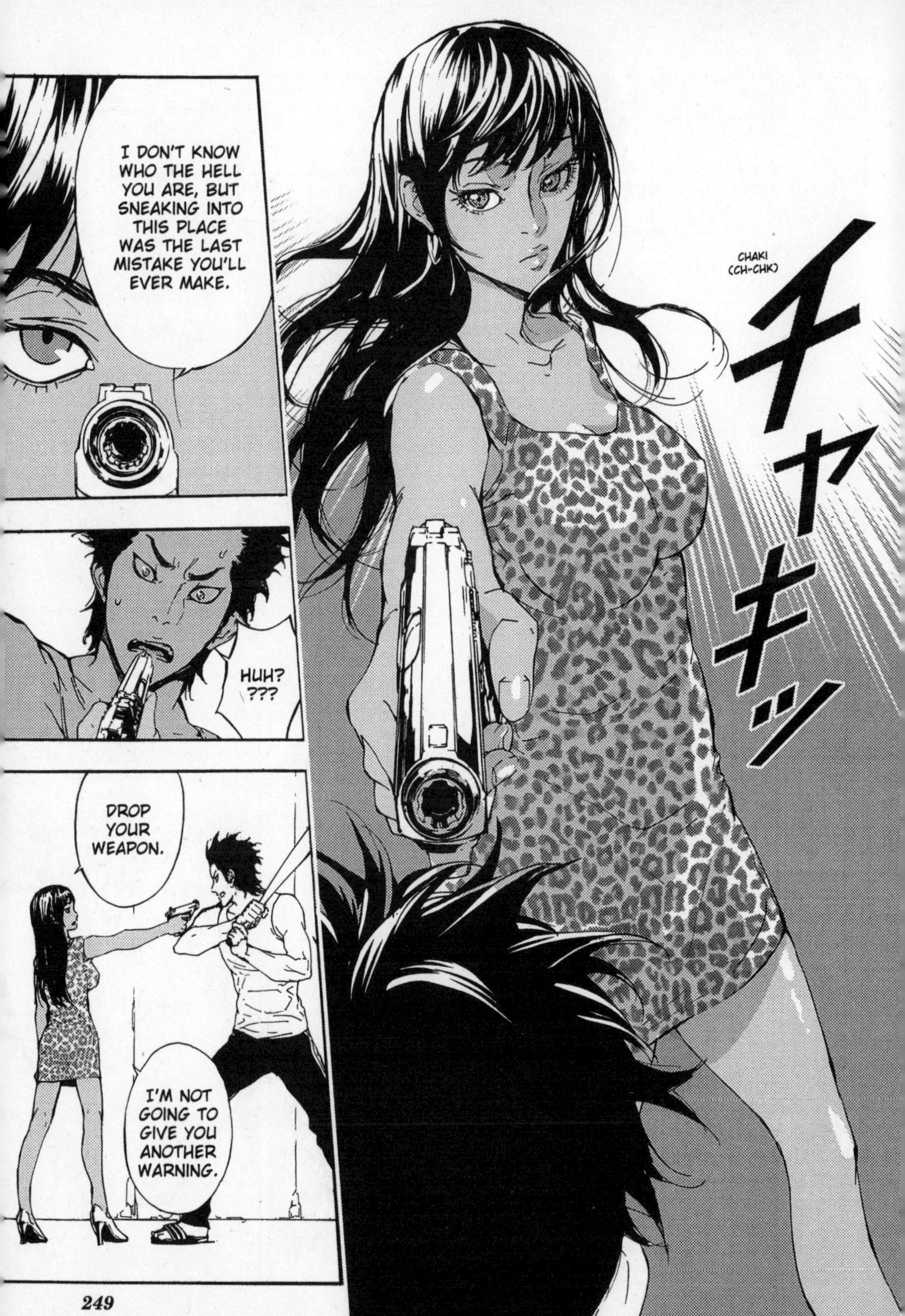
チャキッ
CHAKI (CH-CHK)
I DON'T KNOW WHO THE HELL YOU ARE, BUT SNEAKING INTO THIS PLACE WAS THE LAST MISTAKE YOU'LL EVER MAKE.
HUH? ???
DROP YOUR WEAPON.
I'M NOT GOING TO GIVE YOU ANOTHER WARNING.

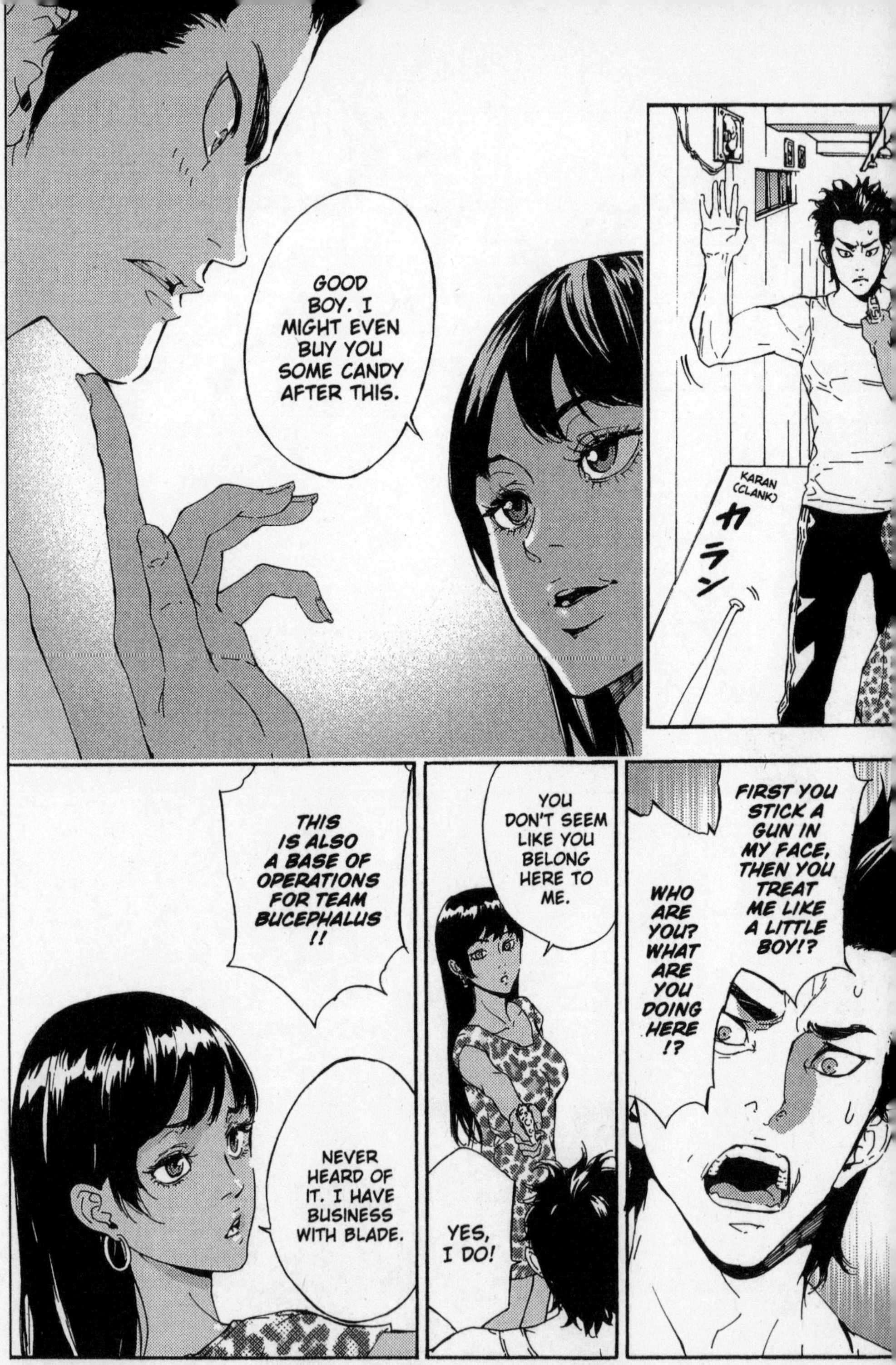
KARAN (CLANK)
カラン
GOOD BOY. I MIGHT EVEN BUY YOU SOME CANDY AFTER THIS.
FIRST YOU STICK A GUN IN MY FACE, THEN YOU TREAT ME LIKE A LITTLE BOY!?
WHO ARE YOU? WHAT ARE YOU DOING HERE!?
YOU DON'T SEEM LIKE YOU BELONG HERE TO ME.
YES, I DO!
THIS IS ALSO A BASE OF OPERATIONS FOR TEAM BUCEPHALUS!!
NEVER HEARD OF IT. I HAVE BUSINESS WITH BLADE.

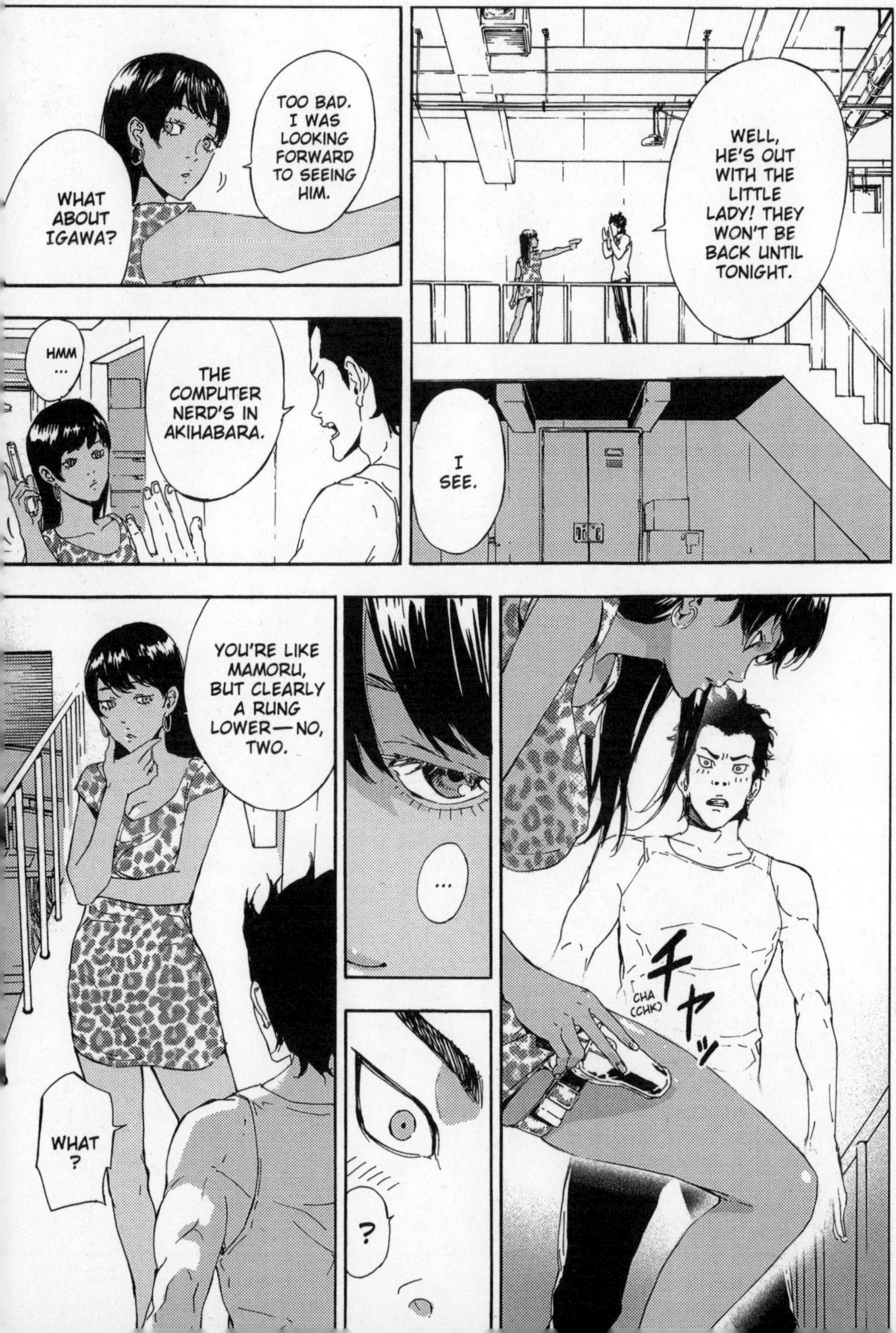
WELL, HE'S OUT WITH THE LITTLE LADY! THEY WON'T BE BACK UNTIL TONIGHT.
TOO BAD. I WAS LOOKING FORWARD TO SEEING HIM.
WHAT ABOUT IGAWA?
THE COMPUTER NERD'S IN AKIHABARA.
HMM ...
I SEE.
YOU'RE LIKE MAMORU, BUT CLEARLY A RUNG LOWER—NO, TWO.
WHAT ?
...
?
チャッ
CHA (CHK)

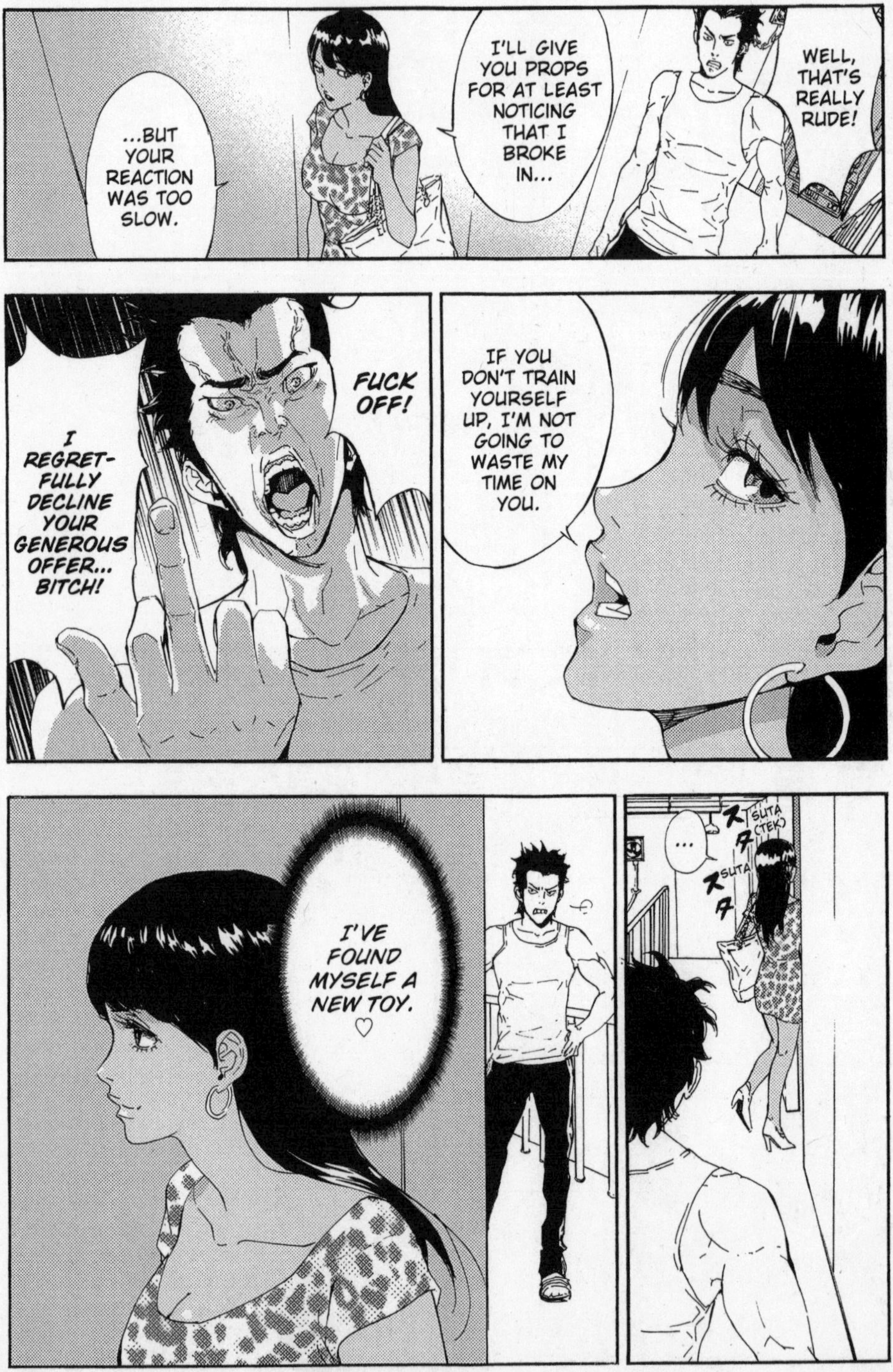
WELL, THAT'S REALLY RUDE!
I'LL GIVE YOU PROPS FOR AT LEAST NOTICING THAT I BROKE IN...
...BUT YOUR REACTION WAS TOO SLOW.
IF YOU DON'T TRAIN YOURSELF UP, I'M NOT GOING TO WASTE MY TIME ON YOU.
FUCK OFF!
I REGRETFULLY DECLINE YOUR GENEROUS OFFER... BITCH!
スタ (SUTA (TEK)
...
スタ SUTA
I'VE FOUND MYSELF A NEW TOY. ♡

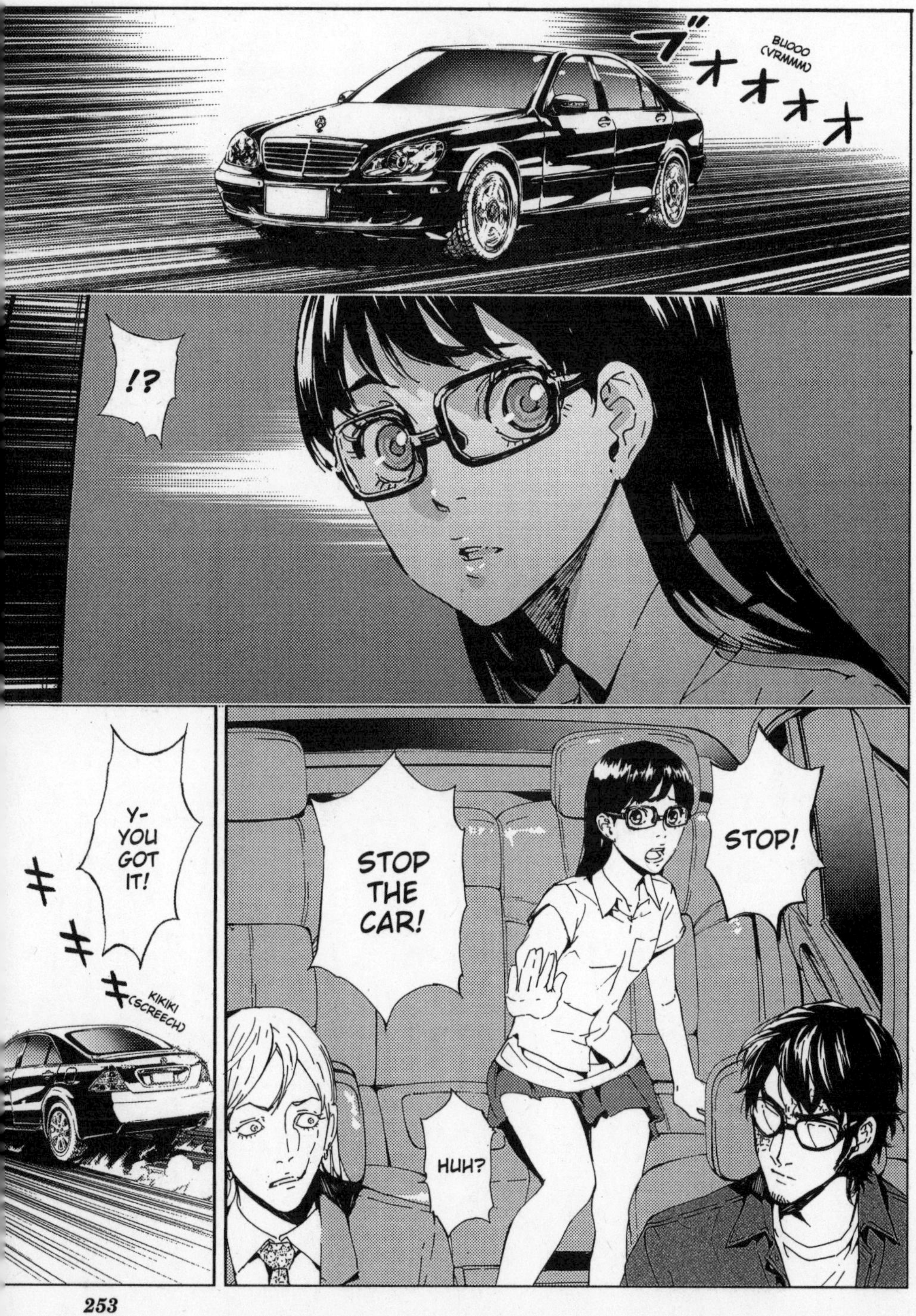

ブオオオオ
BUOOO (VRMMM)
!?
STOP!
STOP THE CAR!
HUH?
Y-YOU GOT IT!
キキキ
KIKIKI (SCREECH)

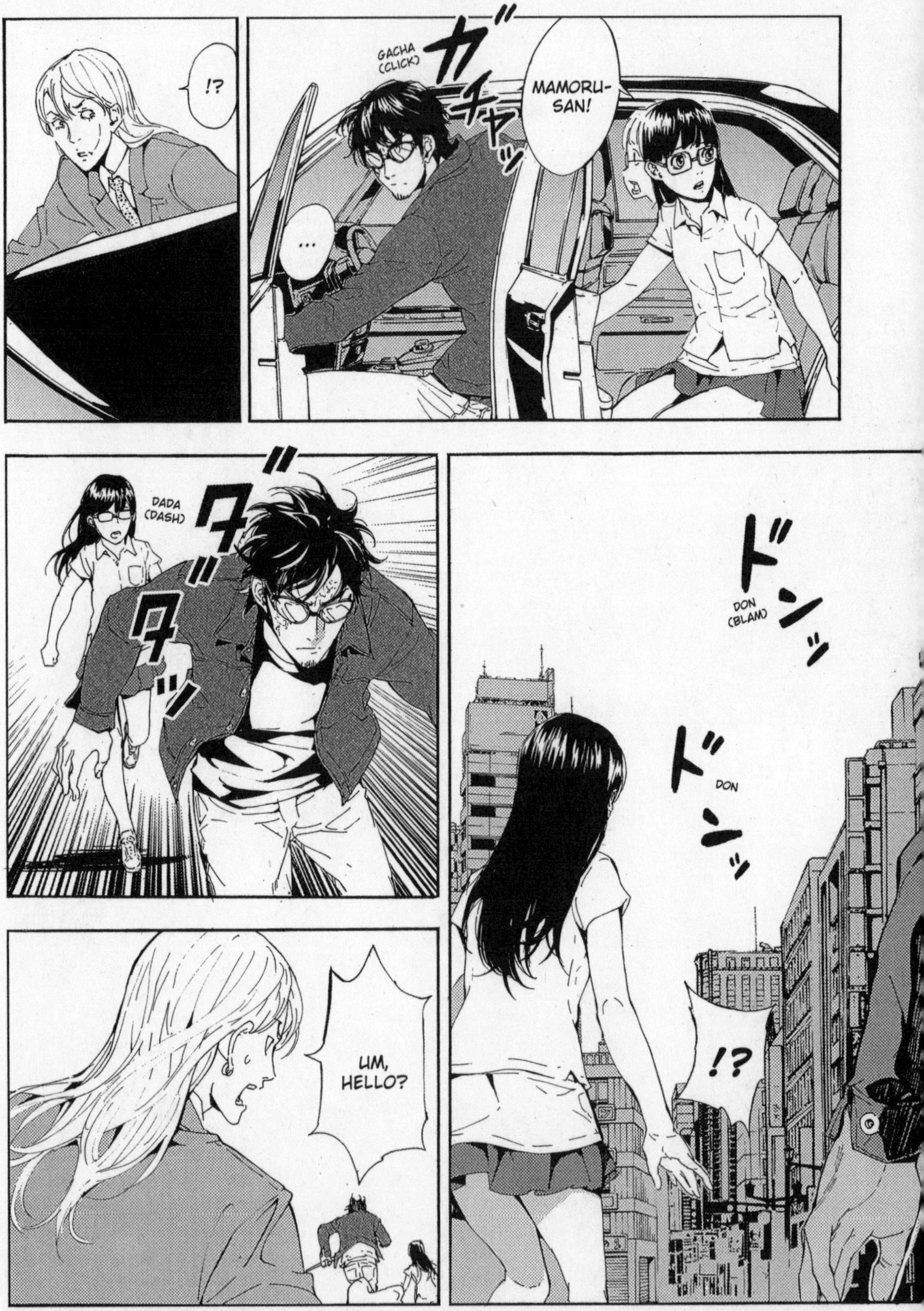
MAMORU-SAN!
ガチャッ
GACHA (CLICK)
...
!?
ドンッ
DON (BLAM)
ドンッ
DON
!?
ダダッ
DADA (DASH)
UM, HELLO?

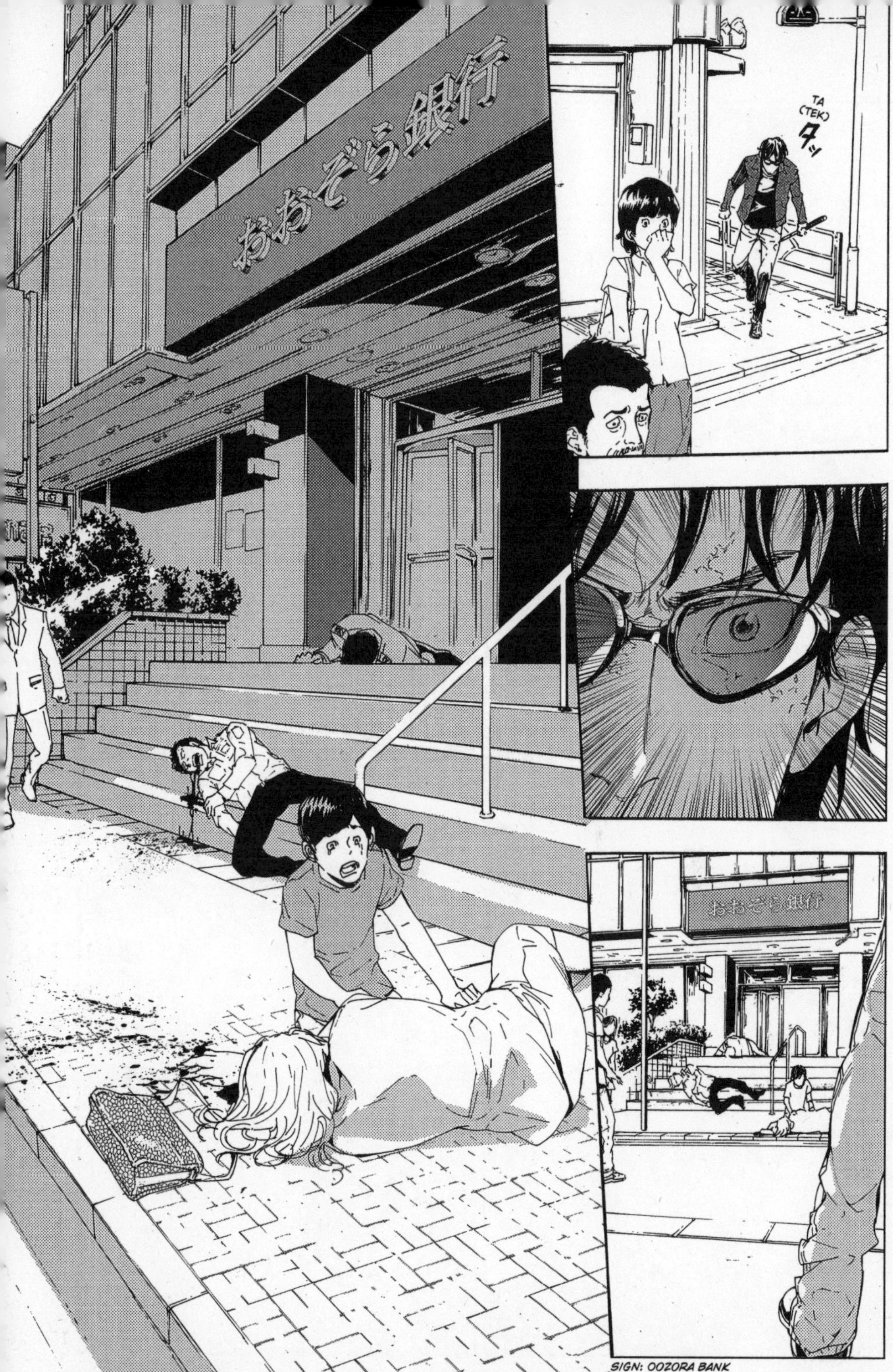
TA
(TEK)
タッ
おおぞら銀行
おおぞら銀行
SIGN: OOZORA BANK

MOMMY!

MOMMY!

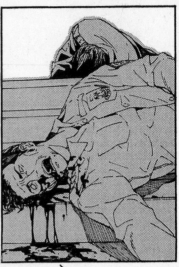

...

THIS WAS A BANK ROBBERY.

YOU SHOULDN'T SEE WHAT HAPPENED HERE.

STAY BACK !!

Until Death do us Part

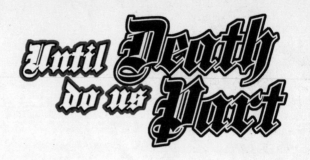

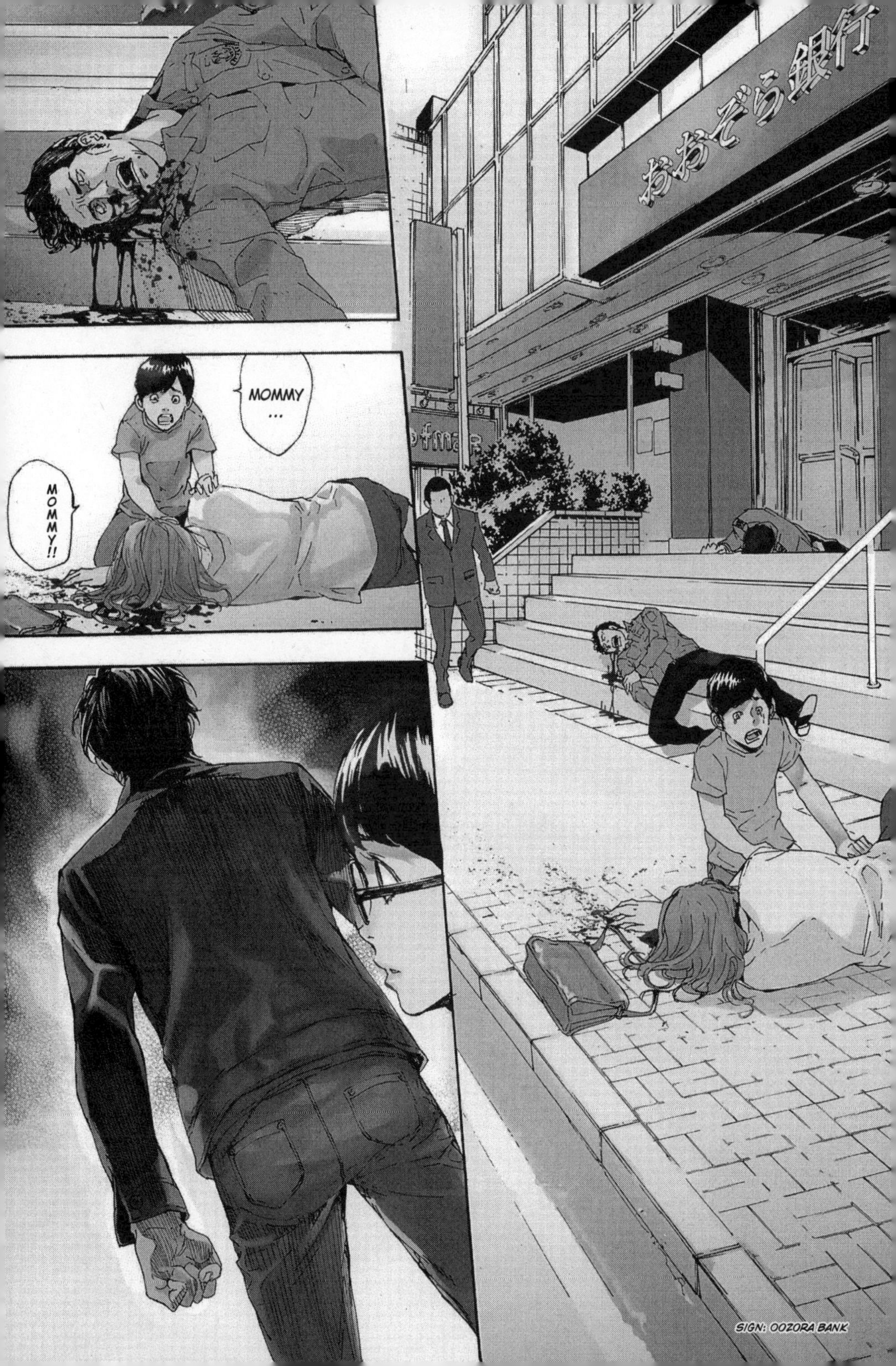
おおぞら銀行
SIGN: OOZORA BANK
MOMMY ...
MOMMY!!

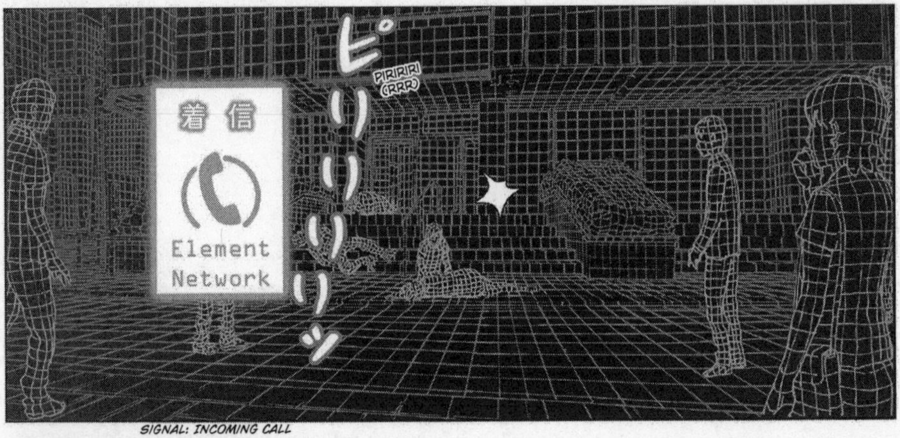
ピリリリリリッ
PIRIRIRI (RRR)
着信
Element Network

SIGNAL: INCOMING CALL

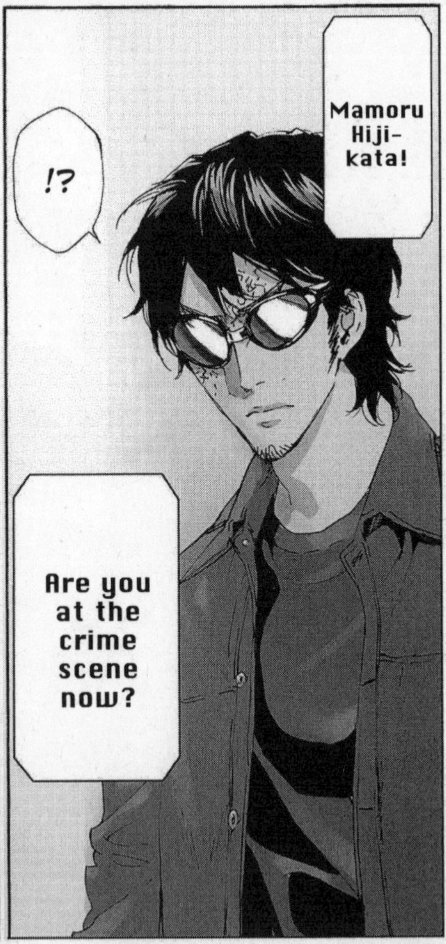
Mamoru Hiji-kata!
!?
Are you at the crime scene now?

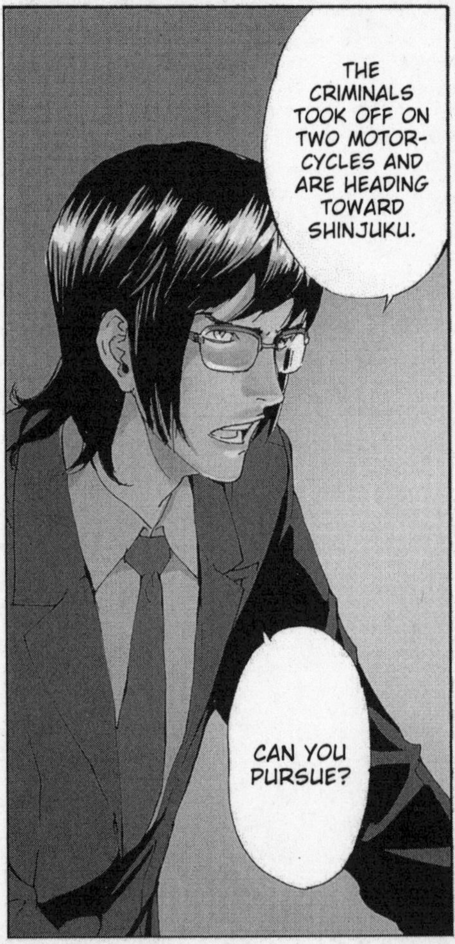
THE CRIMINALS TOOK OFF ON TWO MOTOR-CYCLES AND ARE HEADING TOWARD SHINJUKU.
CAN YOU PURSUE?

chapter 95

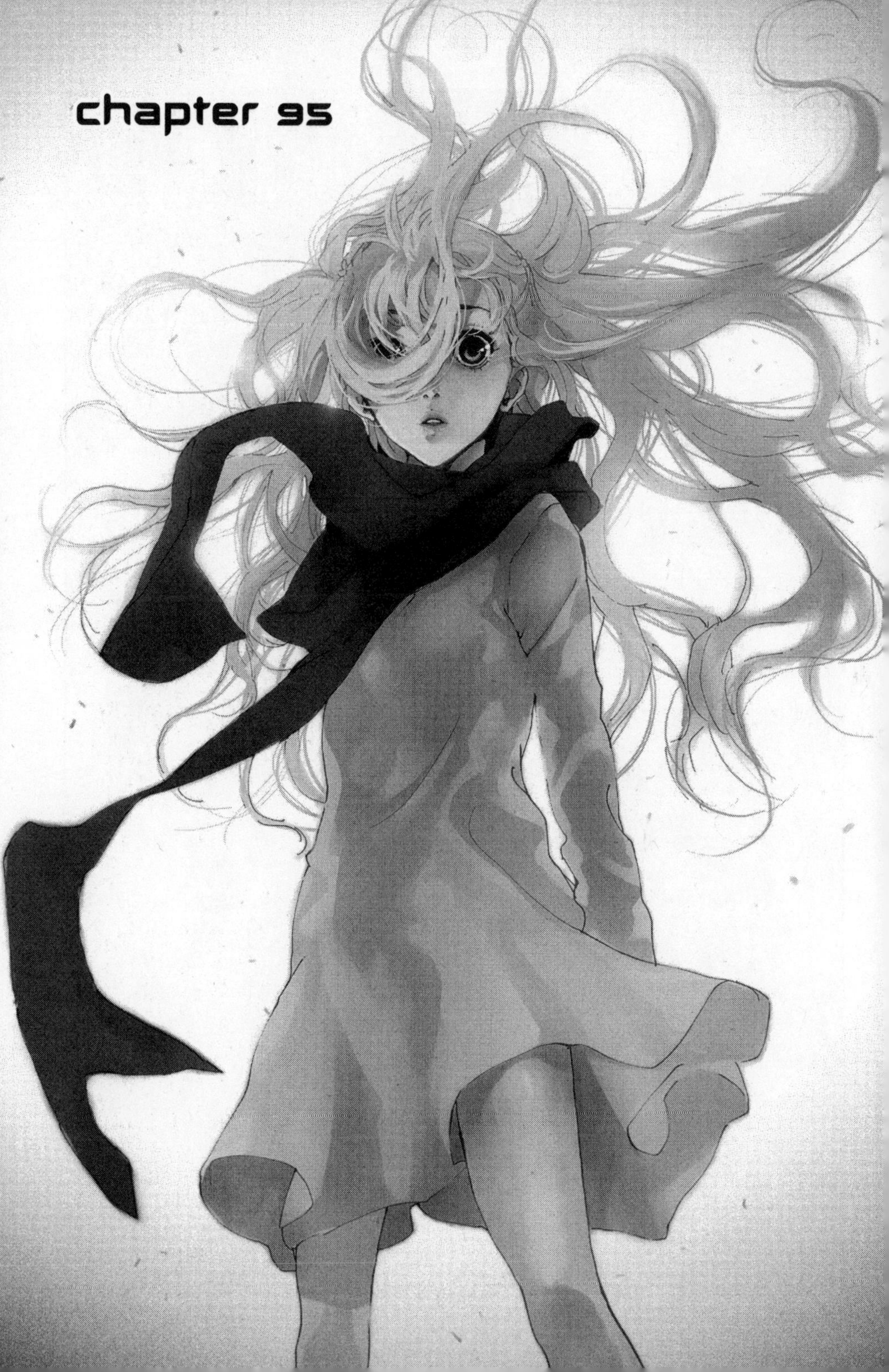

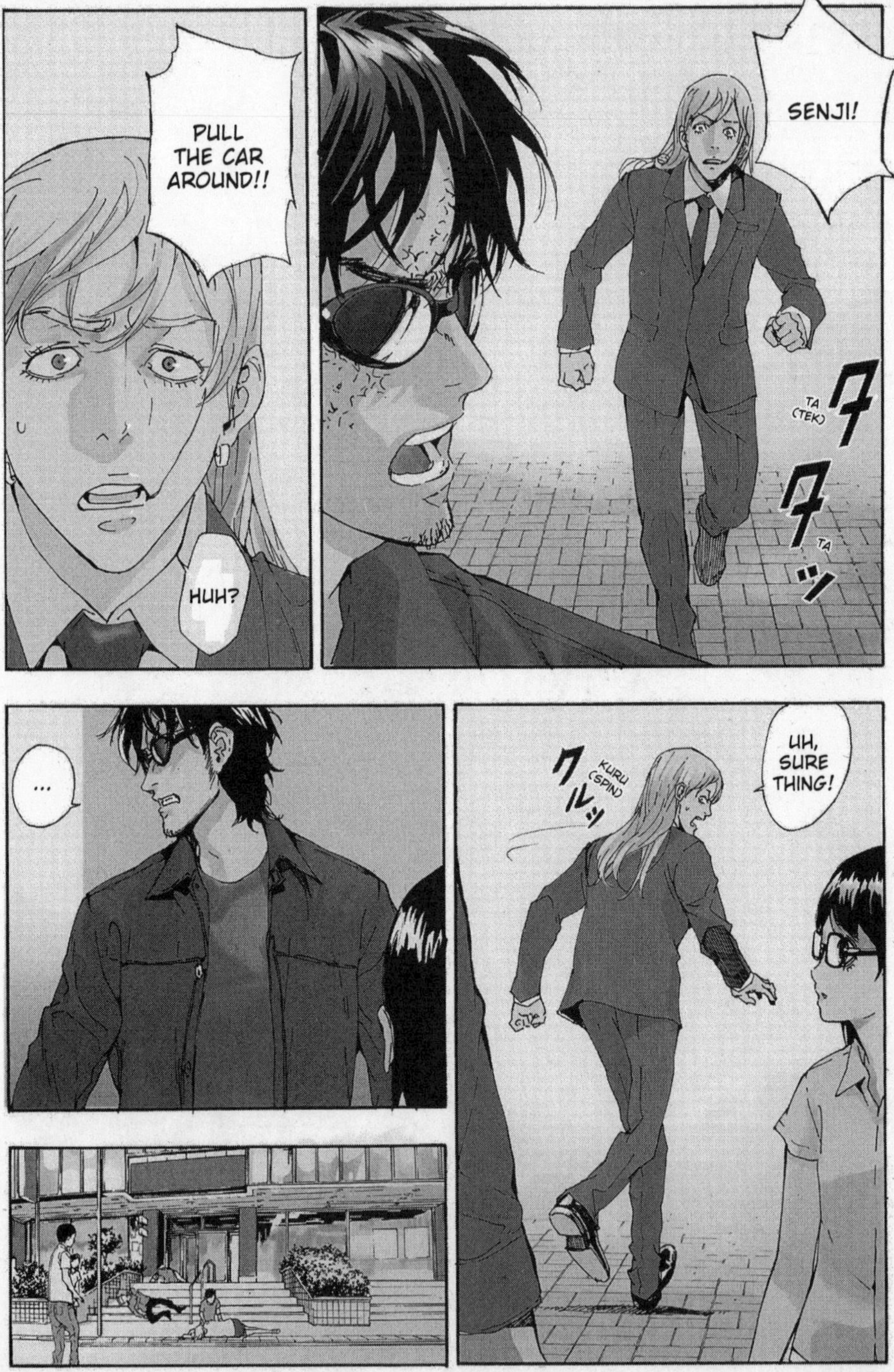
SENJI!
TA (TEK)
TA
PULL THE CAR AROUND!!
HUH?
UH, SURE THING!
KURU (SPIN)
...

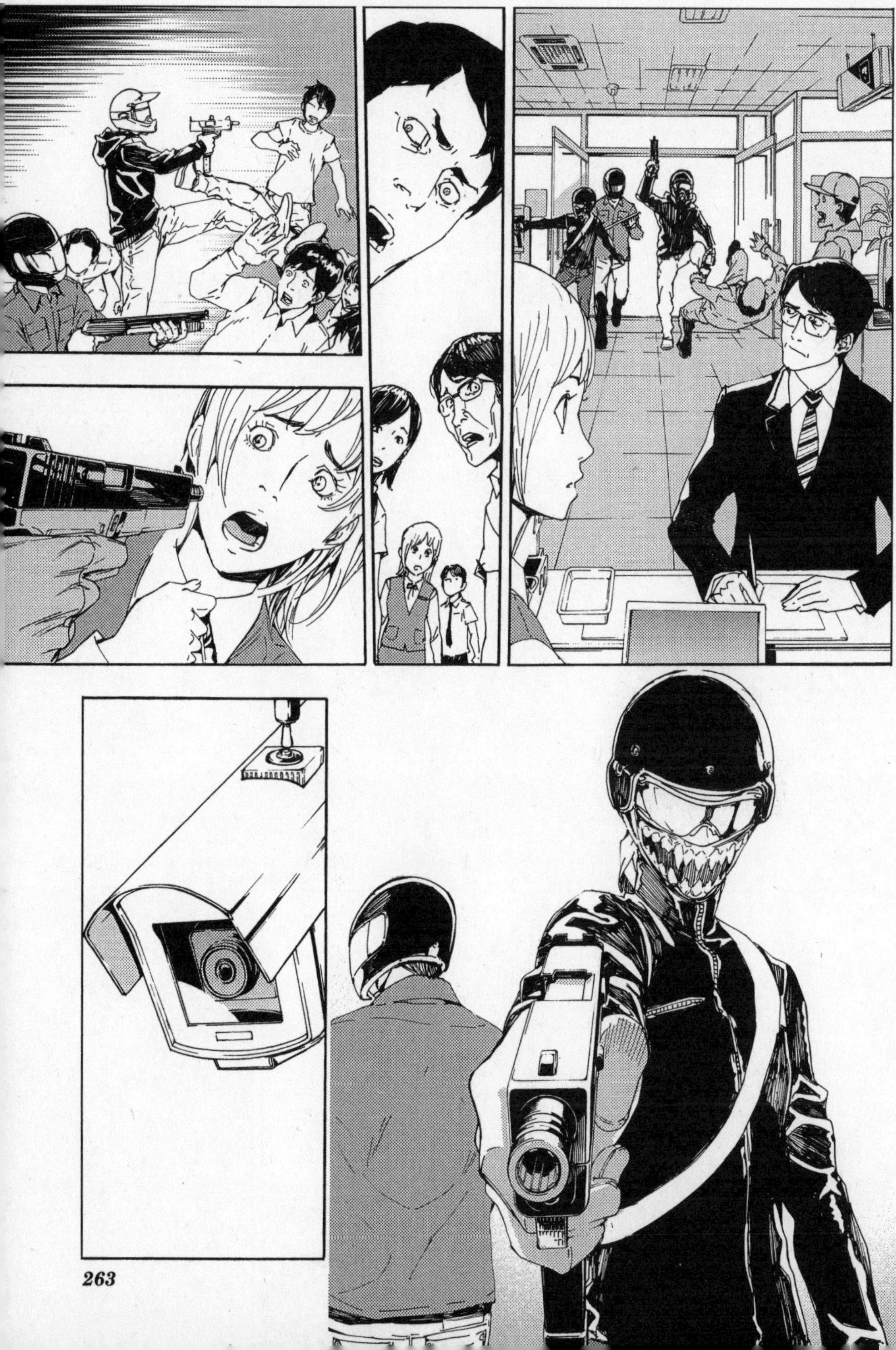

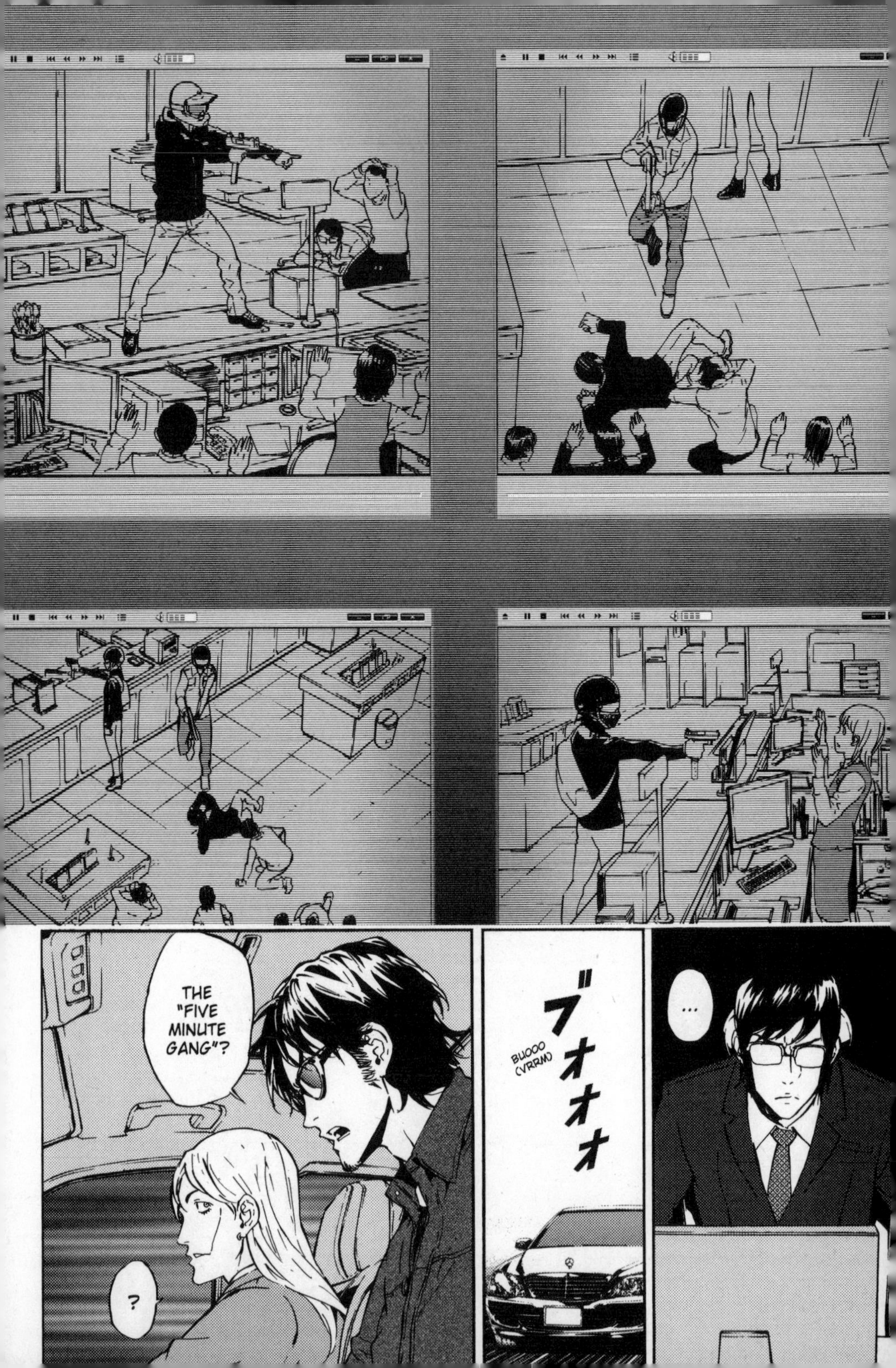
...
ブオオオ
BUOOO (VRRM)
THE "FIVE MINUTE GANG"?
?

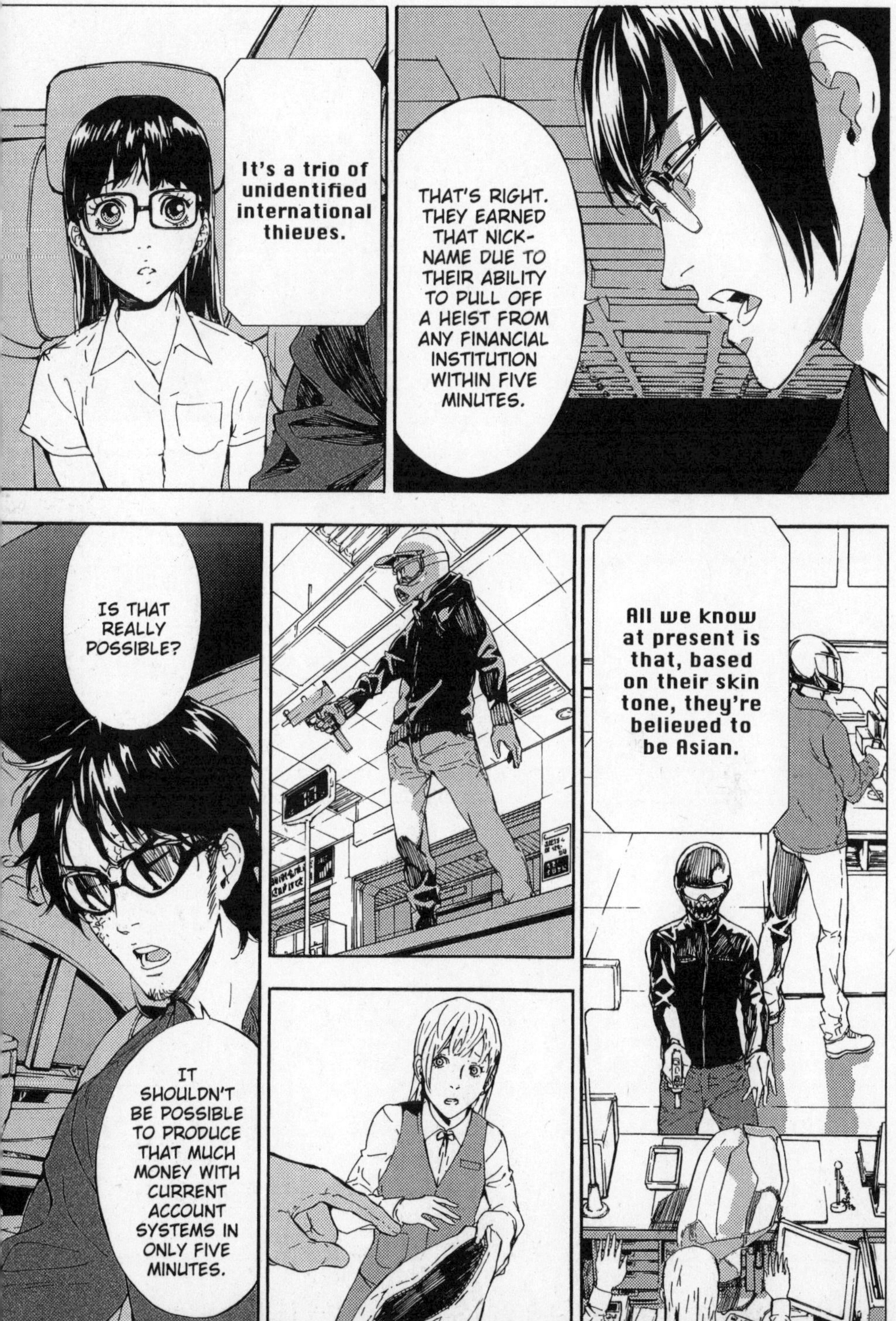
THAT'S RIGHT. THEY EARNED THAT NICKNAME DUE TO THEIR ABILITY TO PULL OFF A HEIST FROM ANY FINANCIAL INSTITUTION WITHIN FIVE MINUTES.
It's a trio of unidentified international thieves.
All we know at present is that, based on their skin tone, they're believed to be Asian.
IS THAT REALLY POSSIBLE?
IT SHOULDN'T BE POSSIBLE TO PRODUCE THAT MUCH MONEY WITH CURRENT ACCOUNT SYSTEMS IN ONLY FIVE MINUTES.

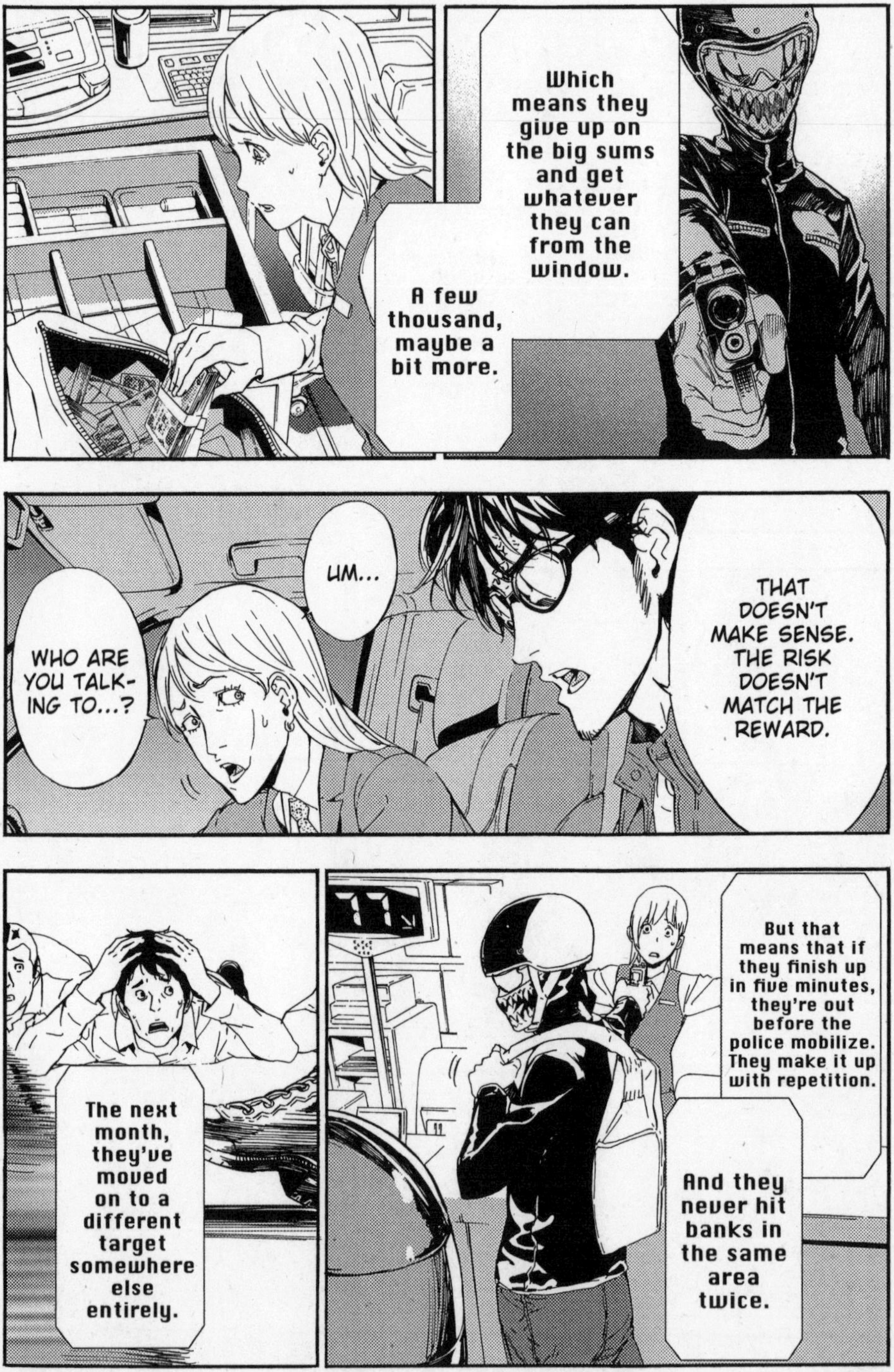

Which means they give up on the big sums and get whatever they can from the window.
A few thousand, maybe a bit more.
THAT DOESN'T MAKE SENSE. THE RISK DOESN'T MATCH THE REWARD.
UM...
WHO ARE YOU TALKING TO...?
But that means that if they finish up in five minutes, they're out before the police mobilize. They make it up with repetition.
And they never hit banks in the same area twice.
The next month, they've moved on to a different target somewhere else entirely.

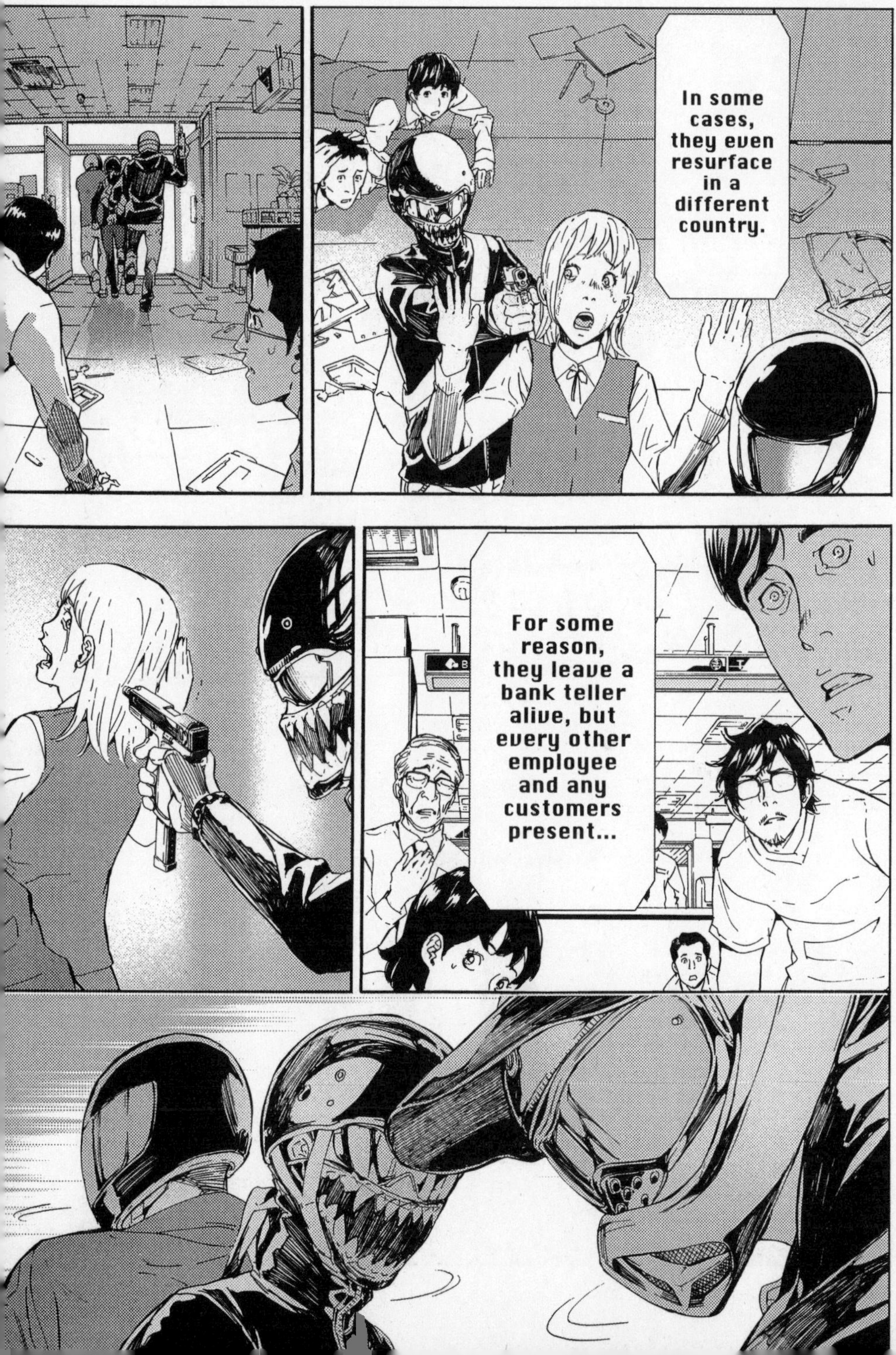
In some cases, they even resurface in a different country.
For some reason, they leave a bank teller alive, but every other employee and any customers present...

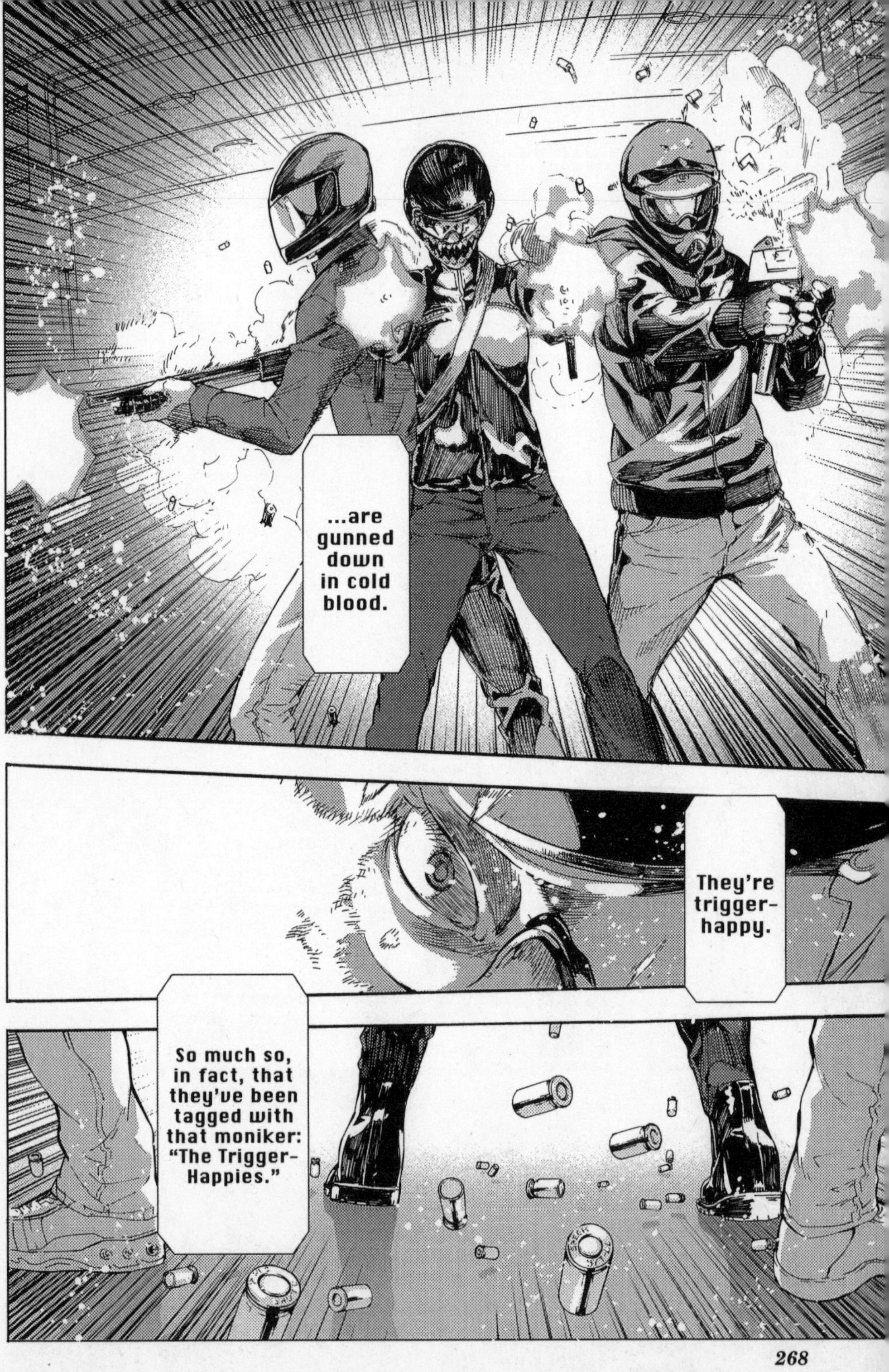
...are gunned down in cold blood.
They're trigger-happy.
So much so, in fact, that they've been tagged with that moniker: "The Trigger-Happies."

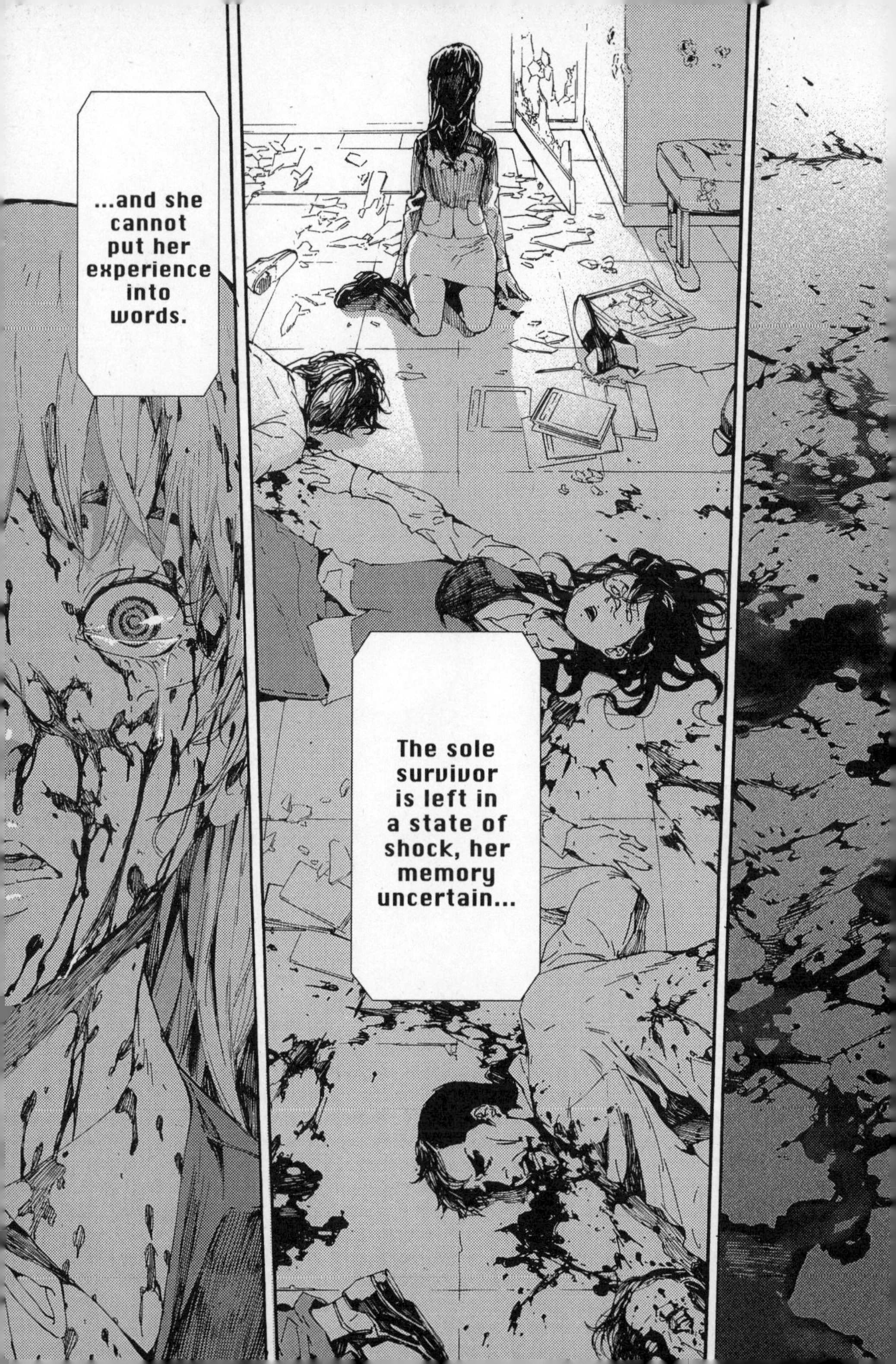
The sole survivor is left in a state of shock, her memory uncertain...
...and she cannot put her experience into words.

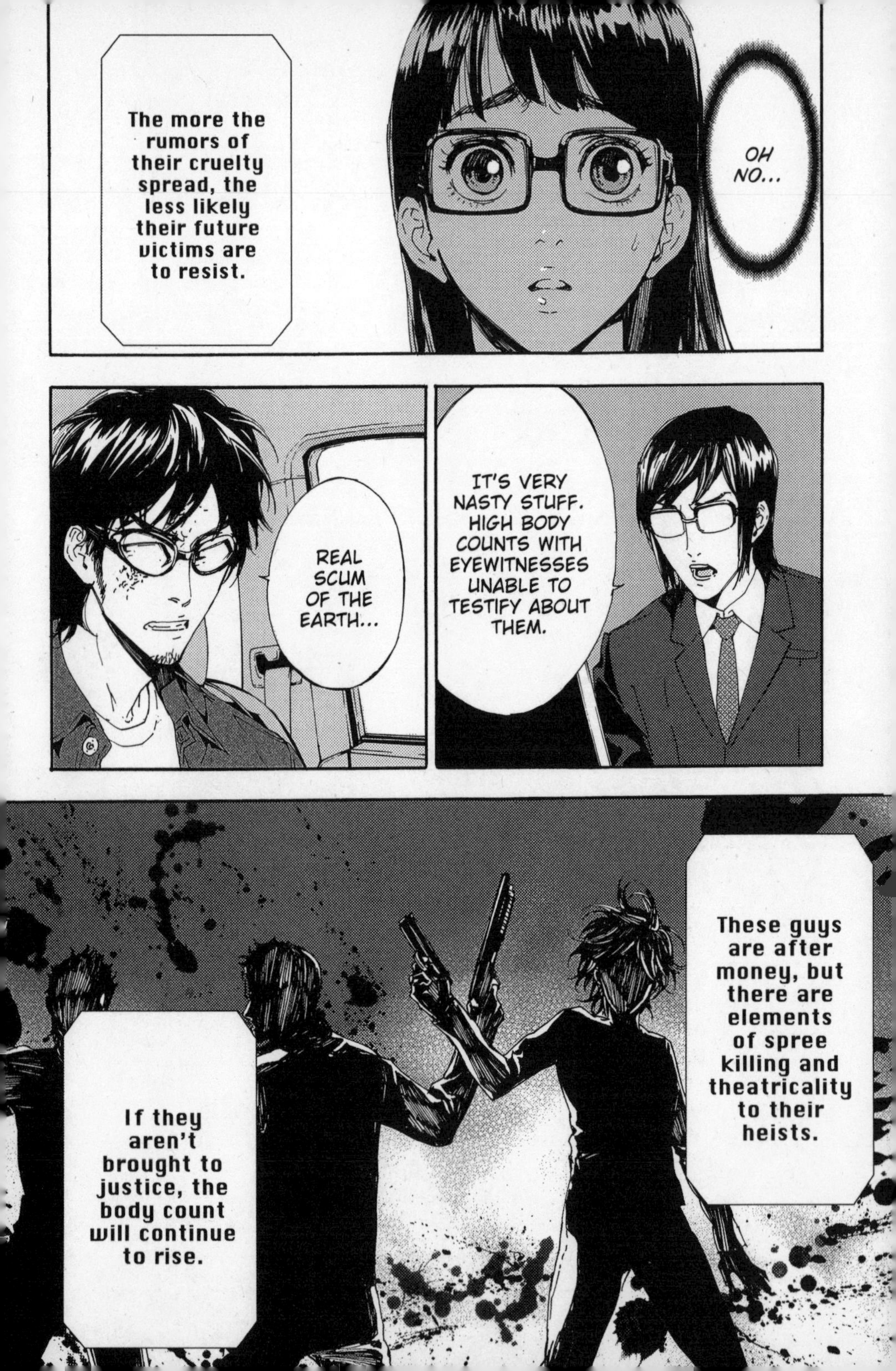
OH NO...
The more the rumors of their cruelty spread, the less likely their future victims are to resist.
IT'S VERY NASTY STUFF. HIGH BODY COUNTS WITH EYEWITNESSES UNABLE TO TESTIFY ABOUT THEM.
REAL SCUM OF THE EARTH...
These guys are after money, but there are elements of spree killing and theatricality to their heists.
If they aren't brought to justice, the body count will continue to rise.

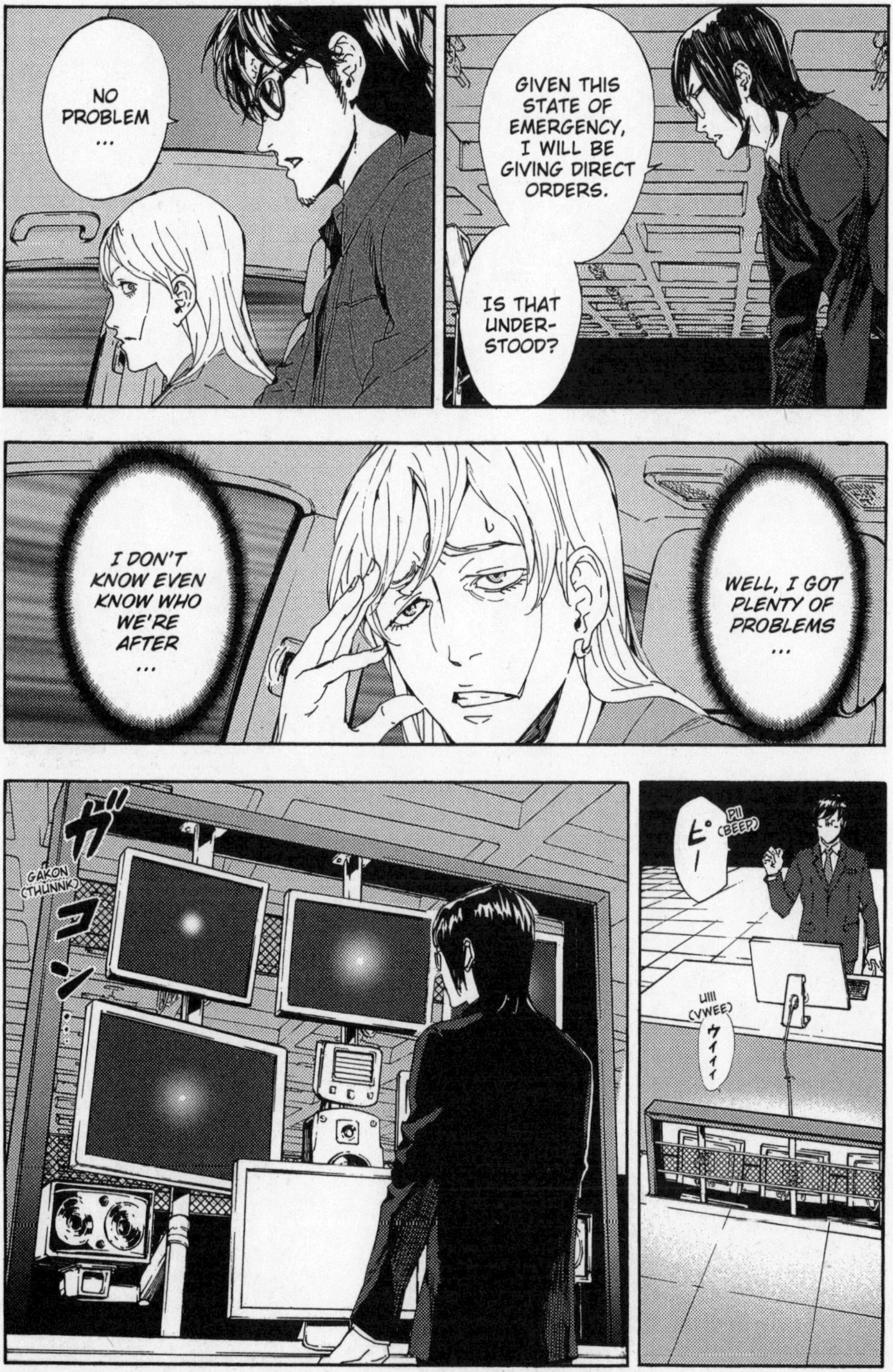
GIVEN THIS STATE OF EMERGENCY, I WILL BE GIVING DIRECT ORDERS.
IS THAT UNDER-STOOD?
NO PROBLEM ...
WELL, I GOT PLENTY OF PROBLEMS ...
I DON'T KNOW EVEN KNOW WHO WE'RE AFTER ...
ピー
PII (BEEP)
ウイイイ
UIII (VWEE)
ガコン
GAKON (THUNNK)

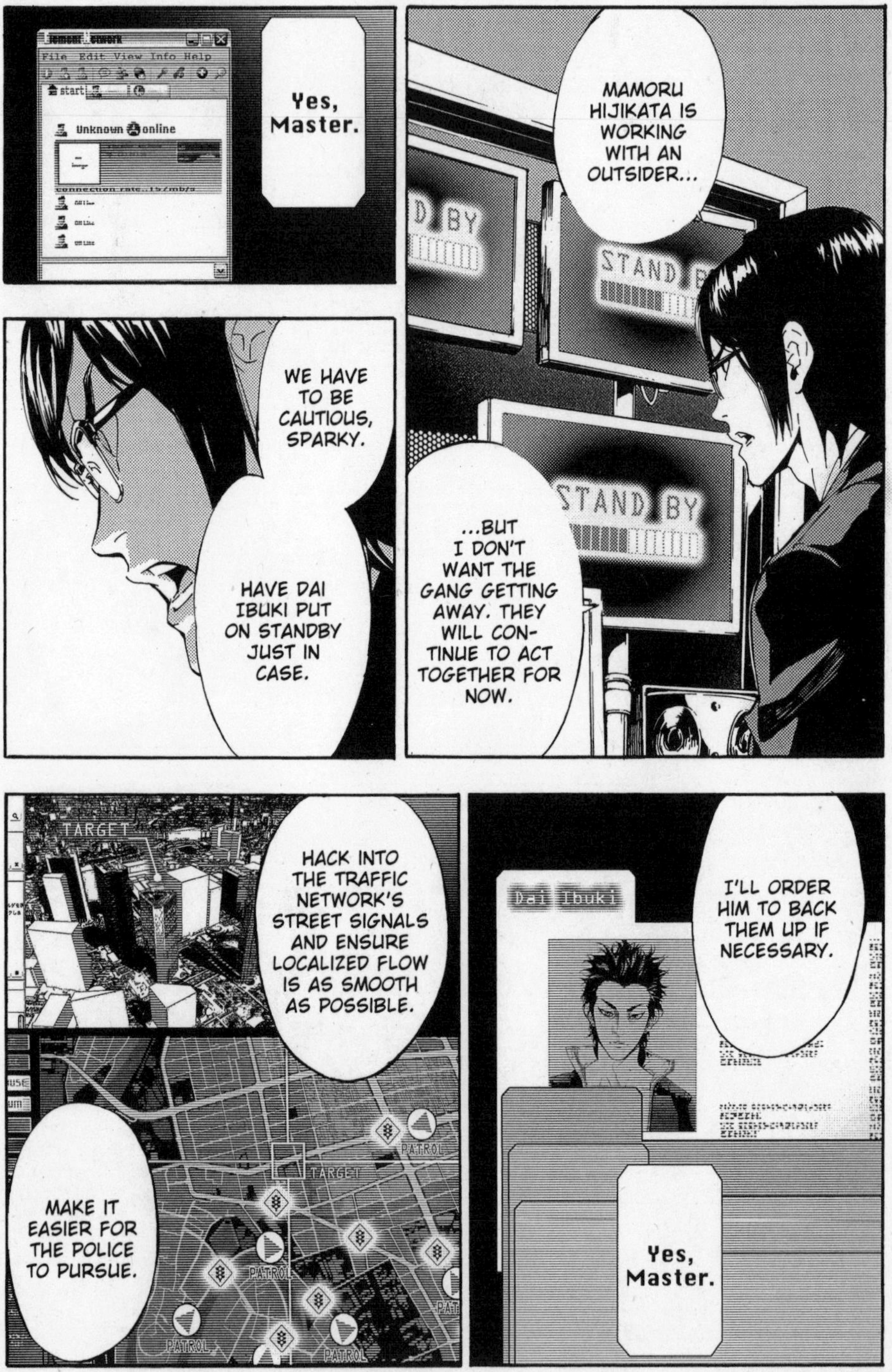
STAND BY
MAMORU HIJIKATA IS WORKING WITH AN OUTSIDER...
...BUT I DON'T WANT THE GANG GETTING AWAY. THEY WILL CONTINUE TO ACT TOGETHER FOR NOW.
File Edit View Info Help
start
Unknown online
Yes, Master.
WE HAVE TO BE CAUTIOUS, SPARKY.
HAVE DAI IBUKI PUT ON STANDBY JUST IN CASE.
Dai Ibuki
I'LL ORDER HIM TO BACK THEM UP IF NECESSARY.
Yes, Master.
TARGET
HACK INTO THE TRAFFIC NETWORK'S STREET SIGNALS AND ENSURE LOCALIZED FLOW IS AS SMOOTH AS POSSIBLE.
PATROL
TARGET
MAKE IT EASIER FOR THE POLICE TO PURSUE.

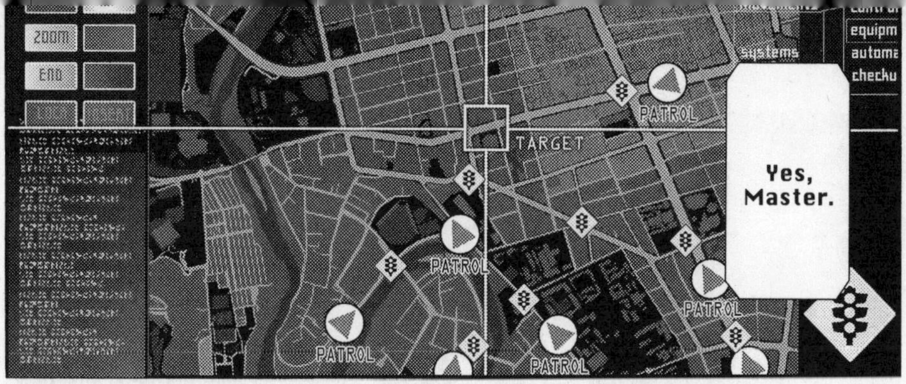
ZOOM
END
systems
equipm
automa
checku
TARGET
PATROL
PATROL
PATROL
PATROL
PATROL
Yes, Master.

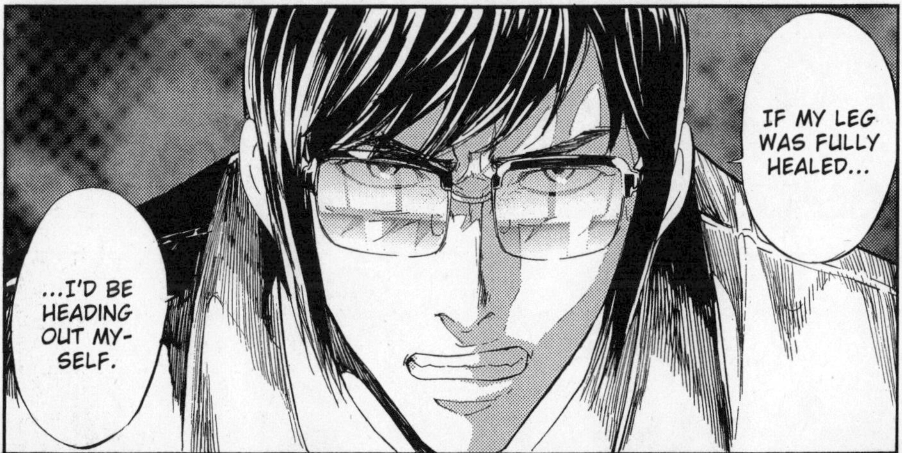
IF MY LEG WAS FULLY HEALED...
...I'D BE HEADING OUT MY-SELF.

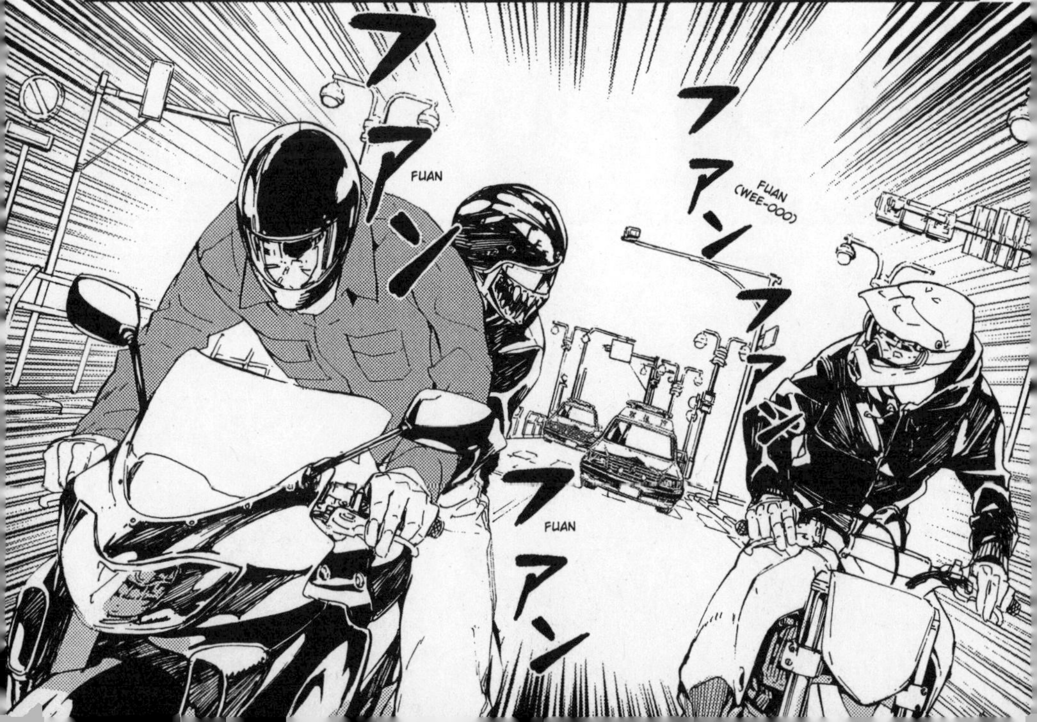
FUAN (WEE-OOO)
FUAN
FUAN

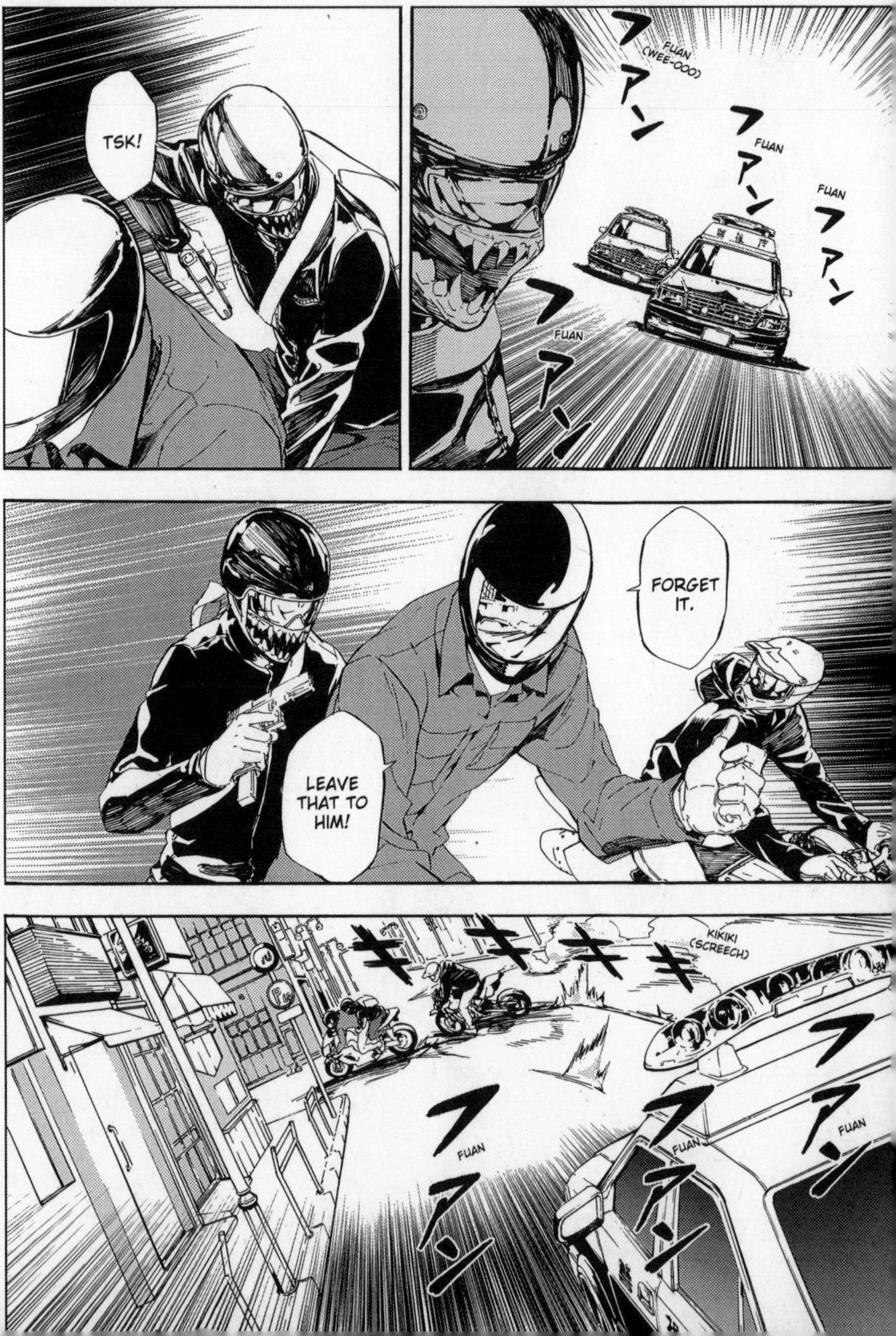
ファン
FUAN (WEE-OOO)
ファン
FUAN
ファン
FUAN
ファン
FUAN
TSK!
FORGET IT.
LEAVE THAT TO HIM!
キキキキ
KIKIKI (SCREECH)
ファン
FUAN
ファン
FUAN
ファン
FUAN

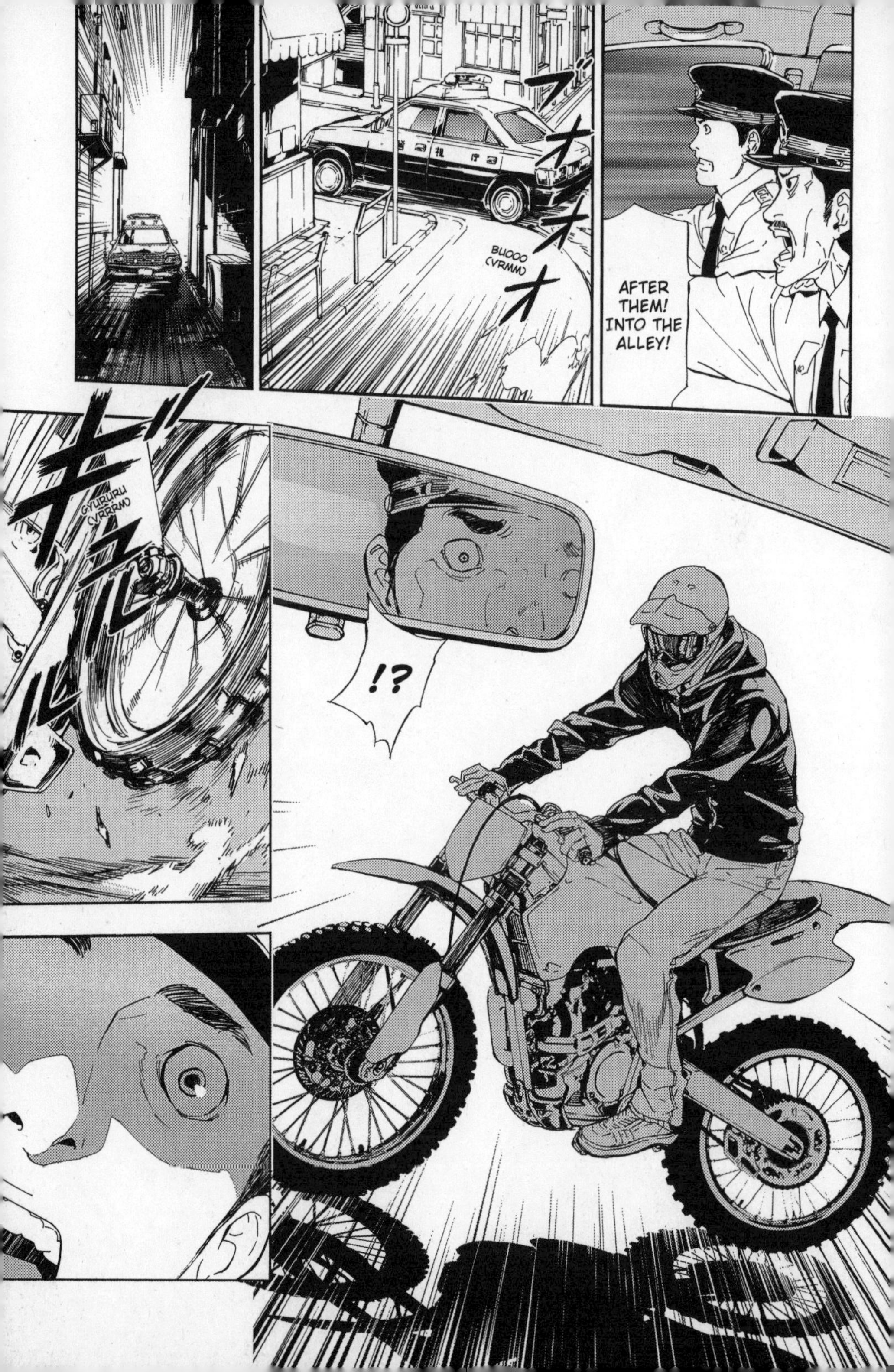
AFTER THEM! INTO THE ALLEY!
BUOOO (VRMM)
!?
GYURURU (VRRRM)

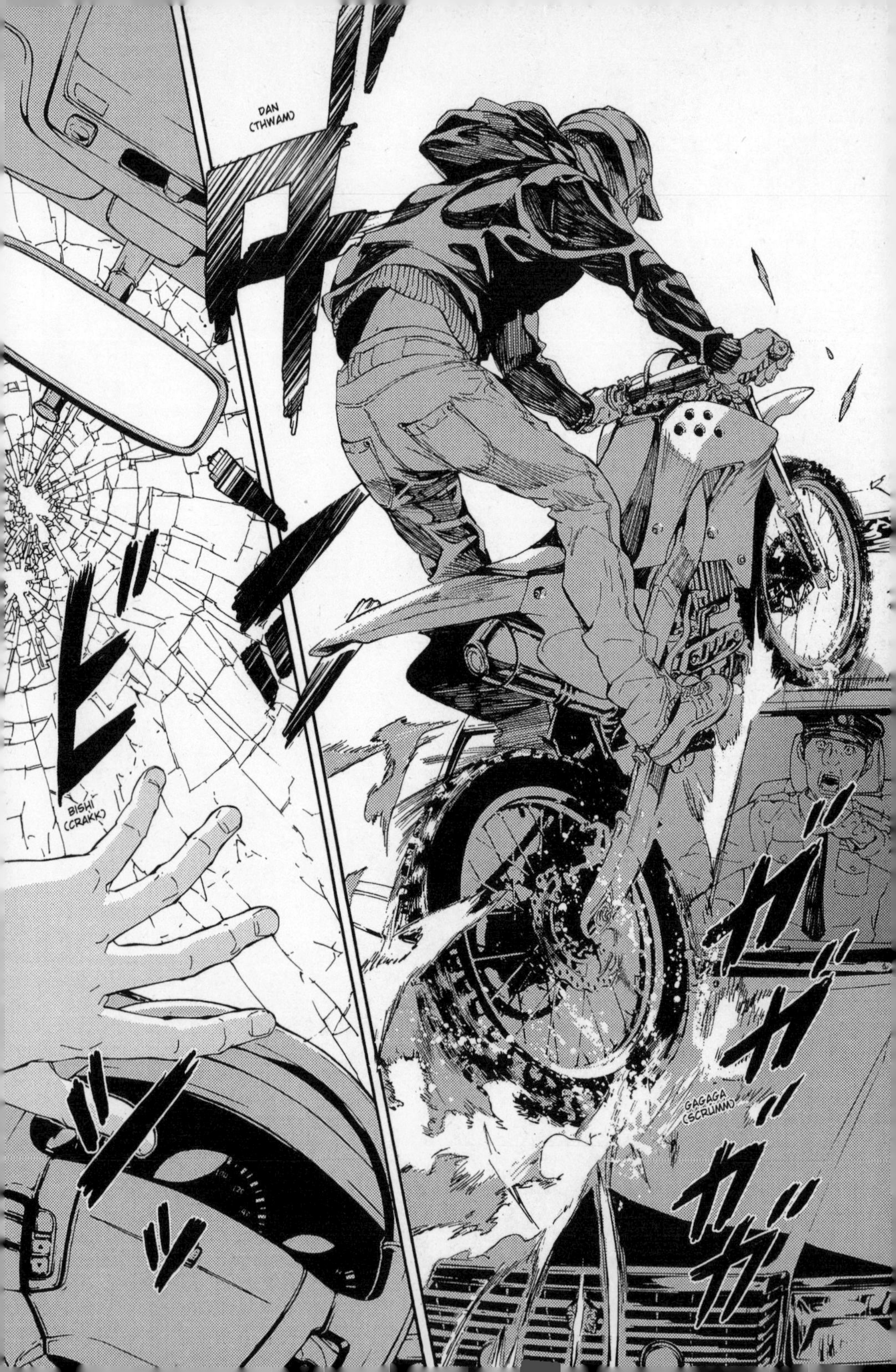
DAN (THWAM)
GAGAGA (SCRUMM)
BISHI (CRAKK)

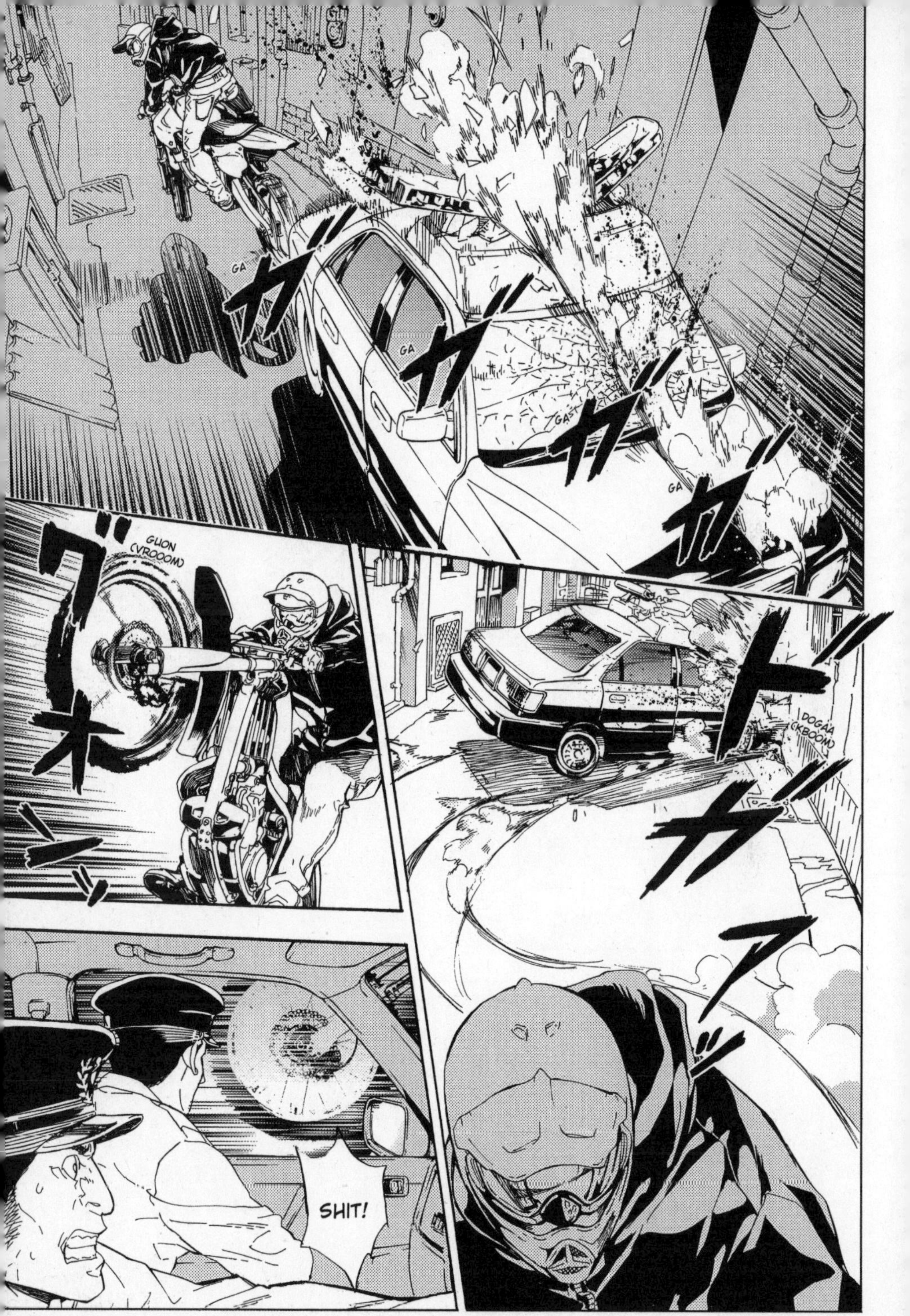
GA
GA
GAST
GA
DOGAA (KBOOM)
GUON (VROOOM)
SHIT!

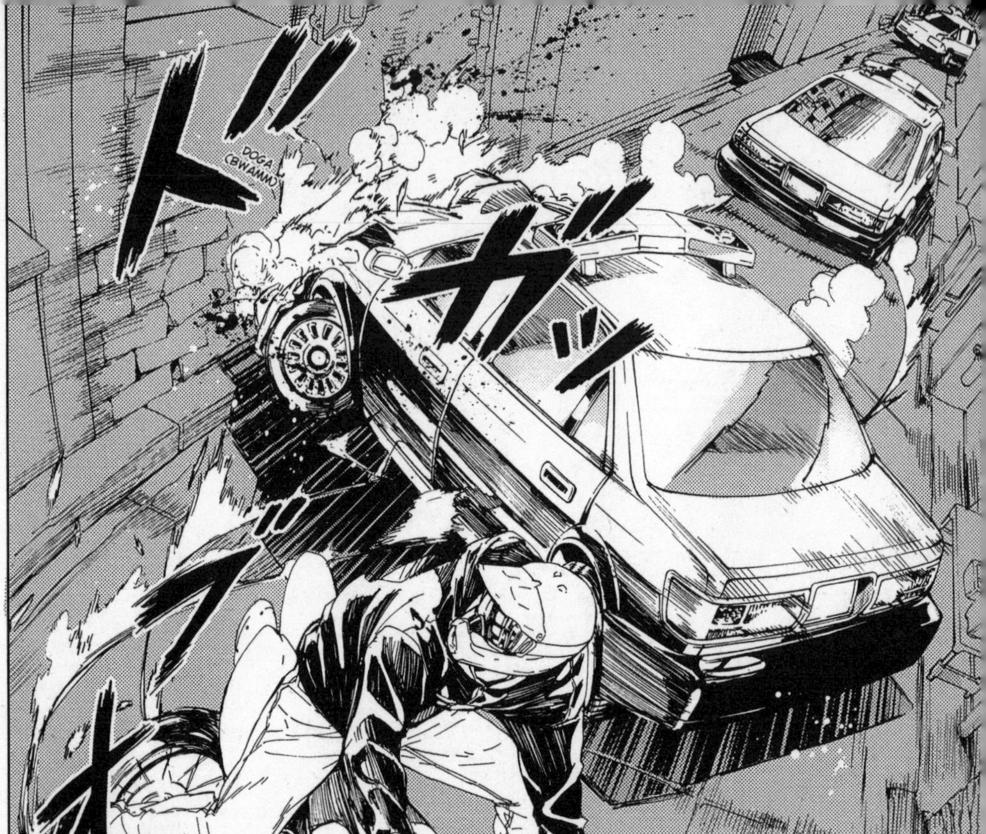
DOGA
(BWAMM)
BUON
(VWOOM)

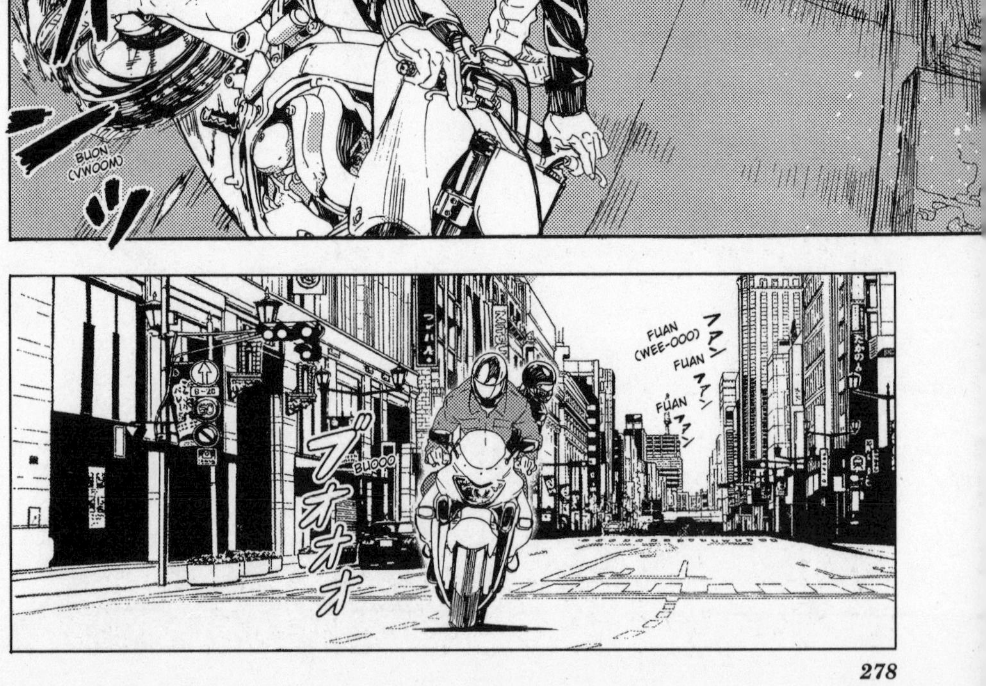
FUAN
(WEE-OOO)
FUAN
FUAN
BUOOO

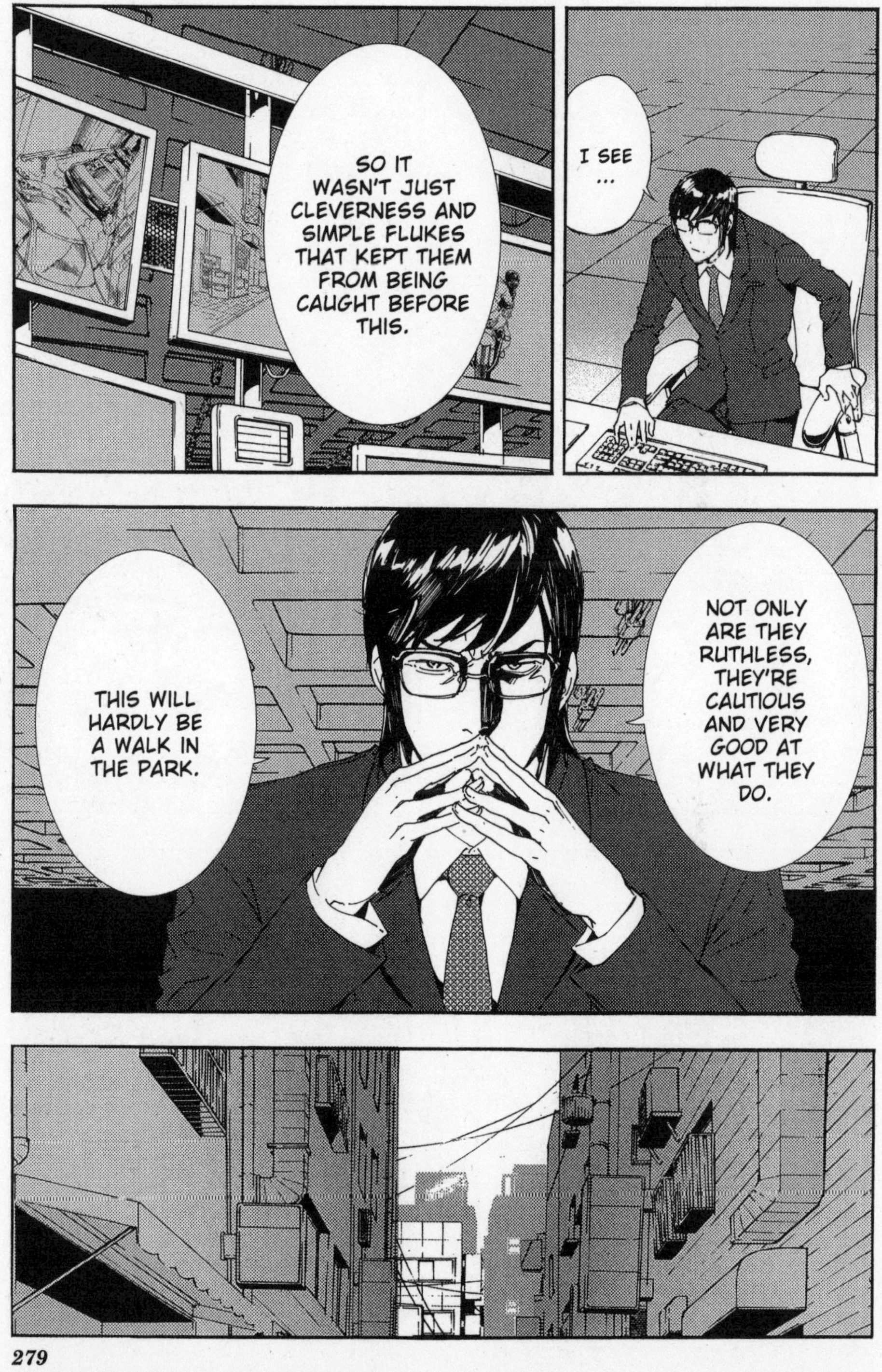
I SEE ...
SO IT WASN'T JUST CLEVERNESS AND SIMPLE FLUKES THAT KEPT THEM FROM BEING CAUGHT BEFORE THIS.
NOT ONLY ARE THEY RUTHLESS, THEY'RE CAUTIOUS AND VERY GOOD AT WHAT THEY DO.
THIS WILL HARDLY BE A WALK IN THE PARK.

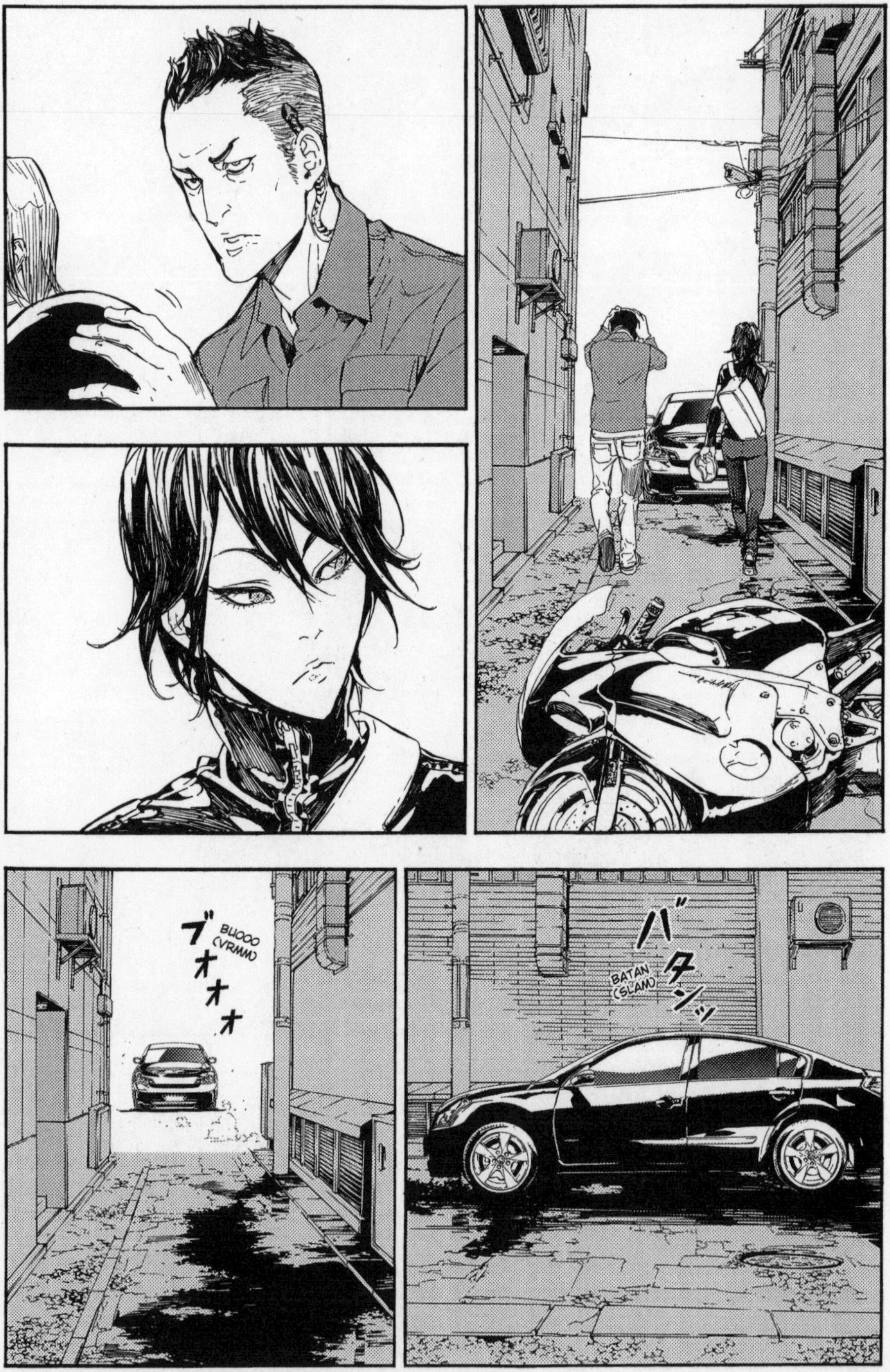
バタンッ
BATAN (SLAM)
ブオオオ
BUOOO (VRMM)

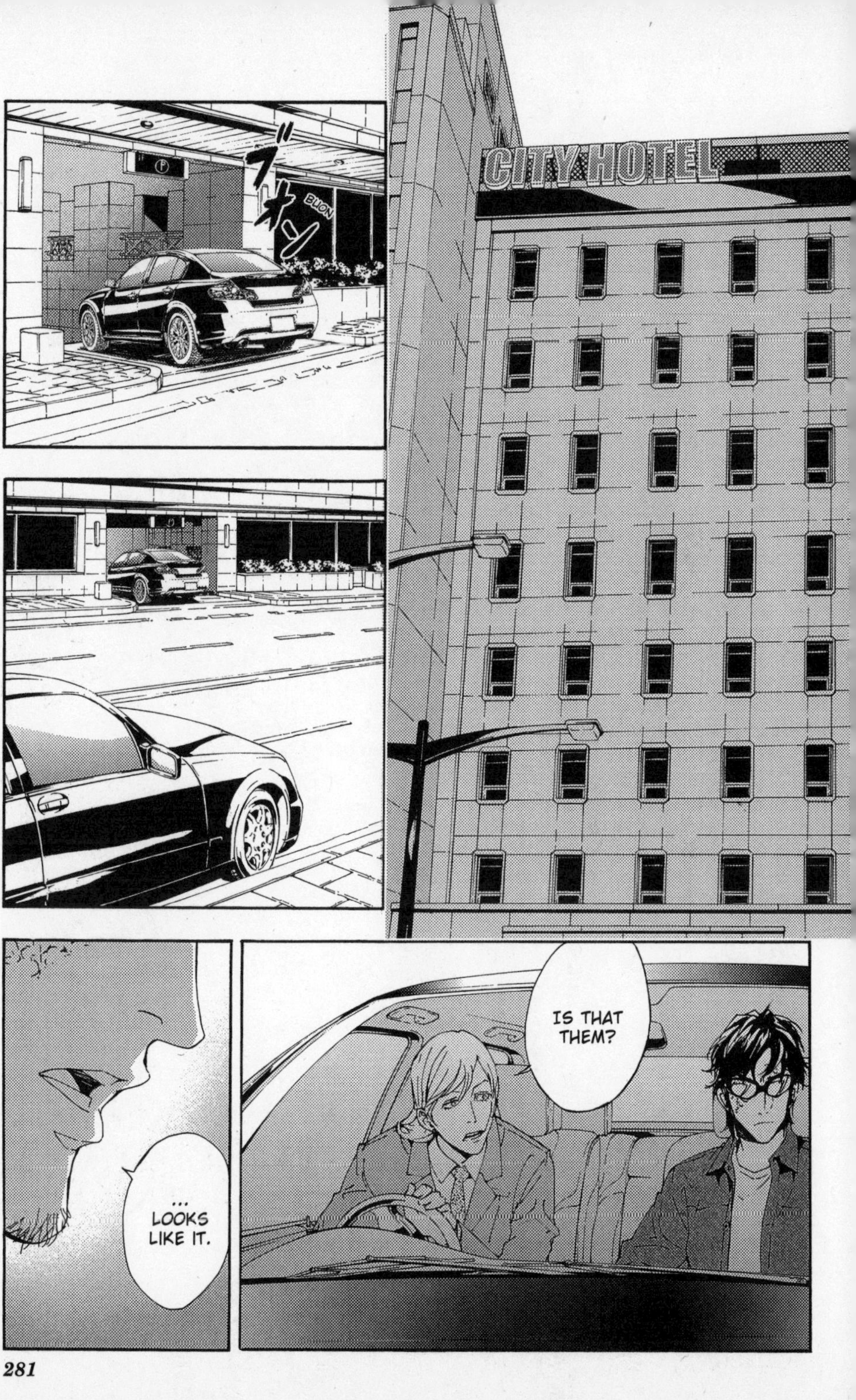
CITY HOTEL
ブオン
BUON
IS THAT THEM?
... LOOKS LIKE IT.

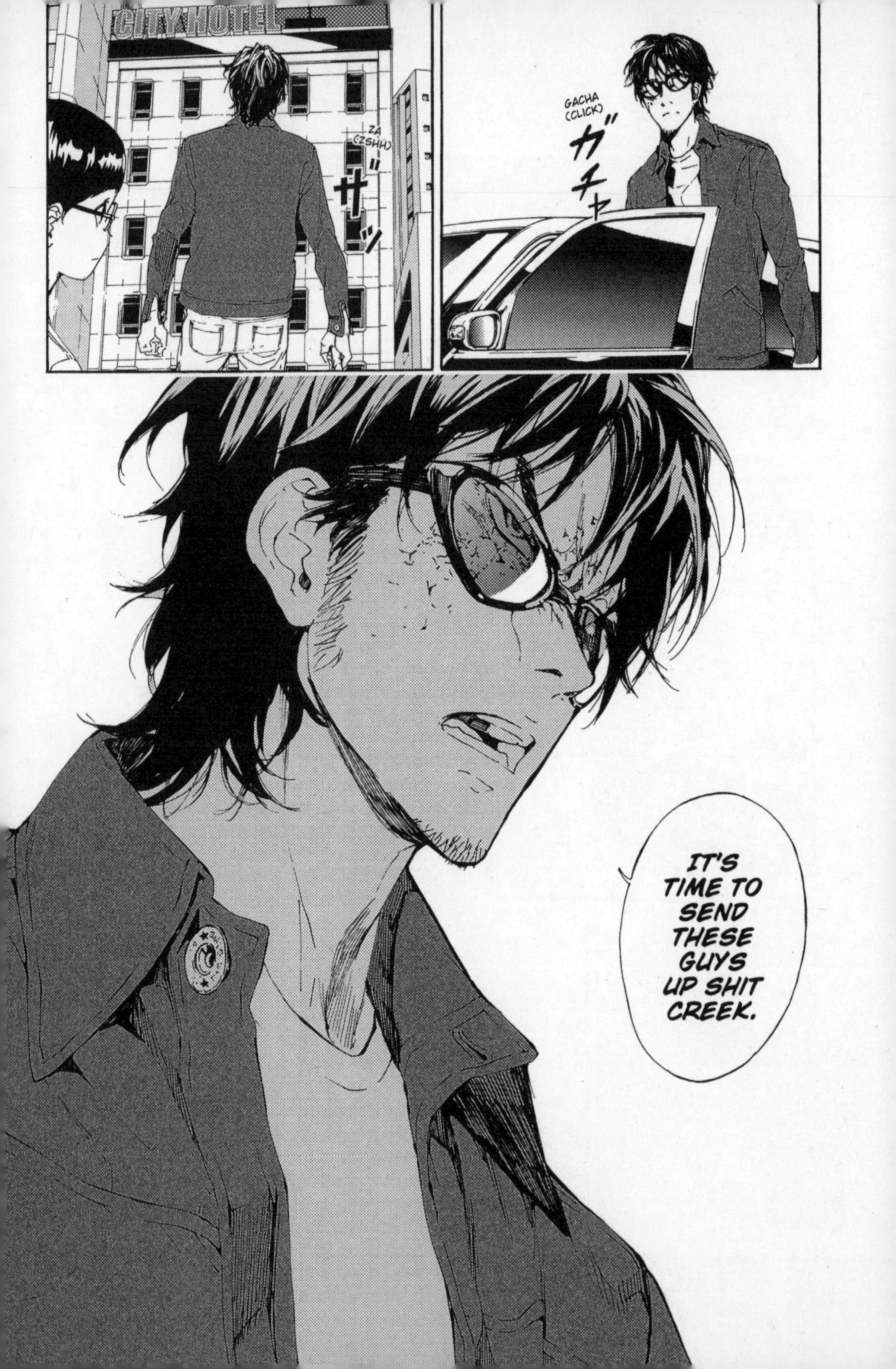
GACHA (CLICK)
ガチャ
CITY HOTEL
ZA (ZSHH)
ザッ
IT'S TIME TO SEND THESE GUYS UP SHIT CREEK.

Until Death do us Part

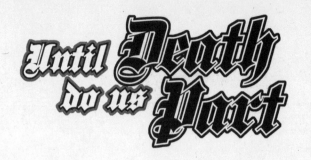

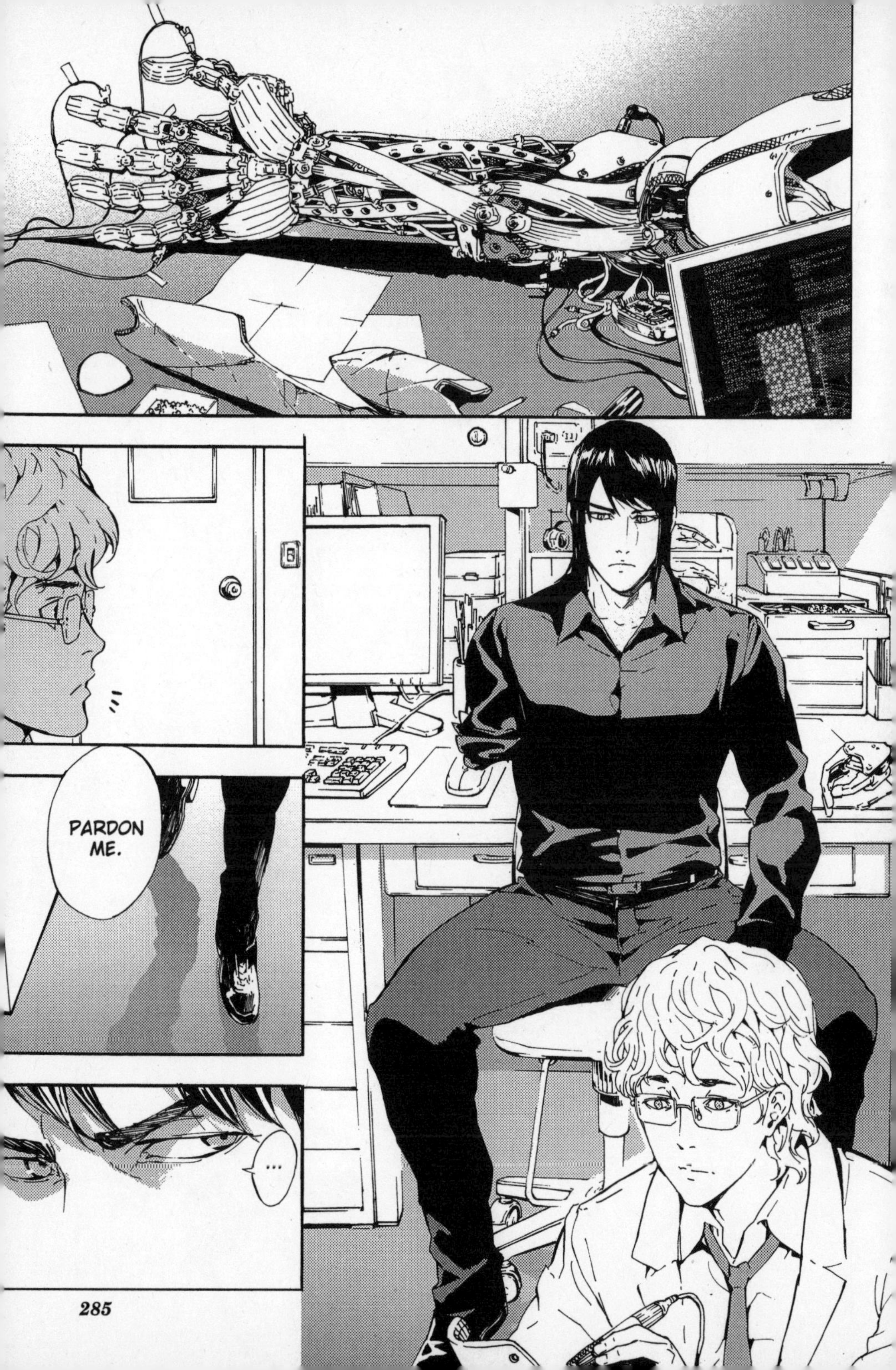
PARDON ME.
...

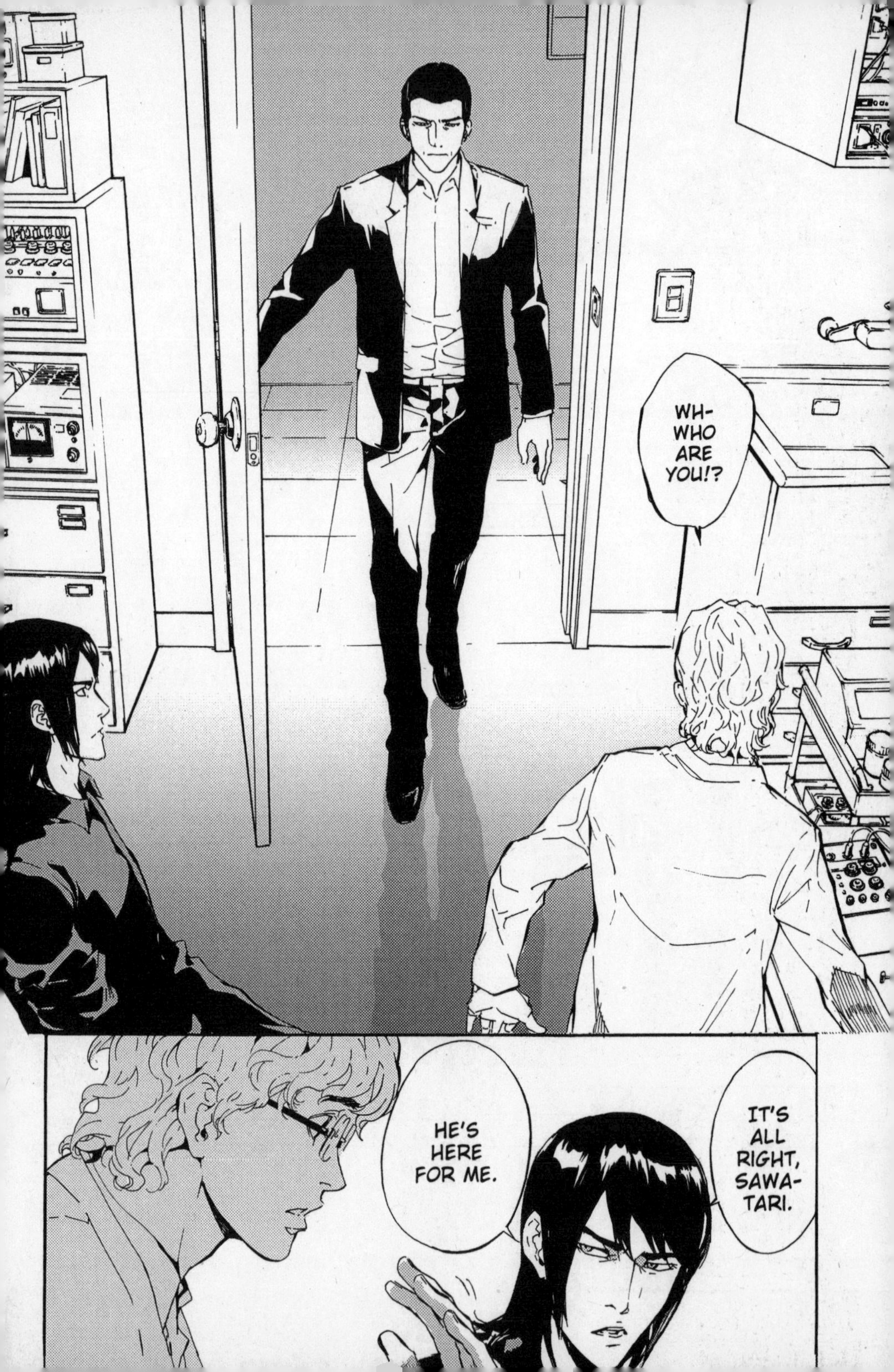
WH- WHO ARE YOU!?
IT'S ALL RIGHT, SAWA-TARI.
HE'S HERE FOR ME.

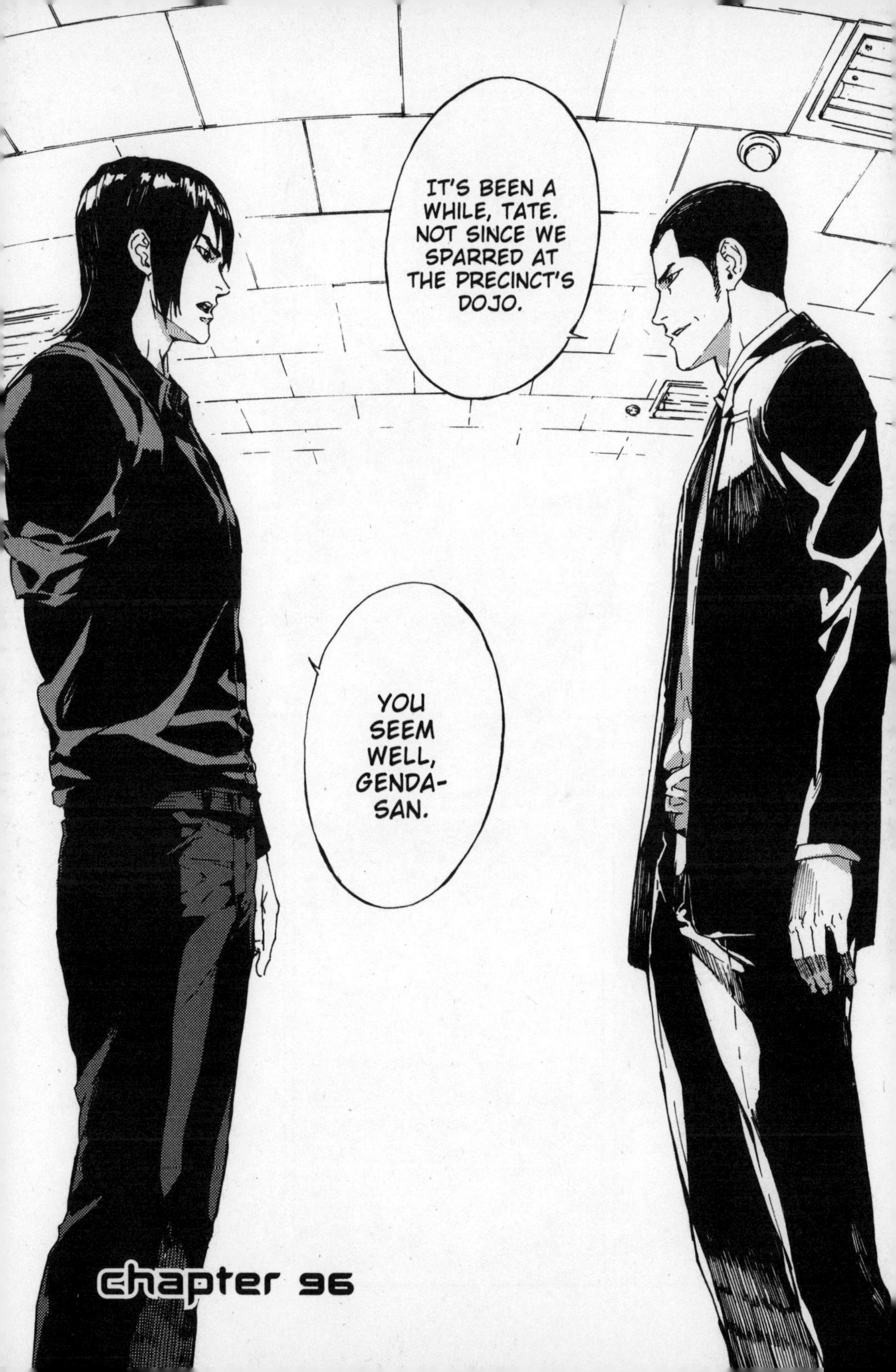
IT'S BEEN A WHILE, TATE. NOT SINCE WE SPARRED AT THE PRECINCT'S DOJO.
YOU SEEM WELL, GENDA-SAN.
chapter 96

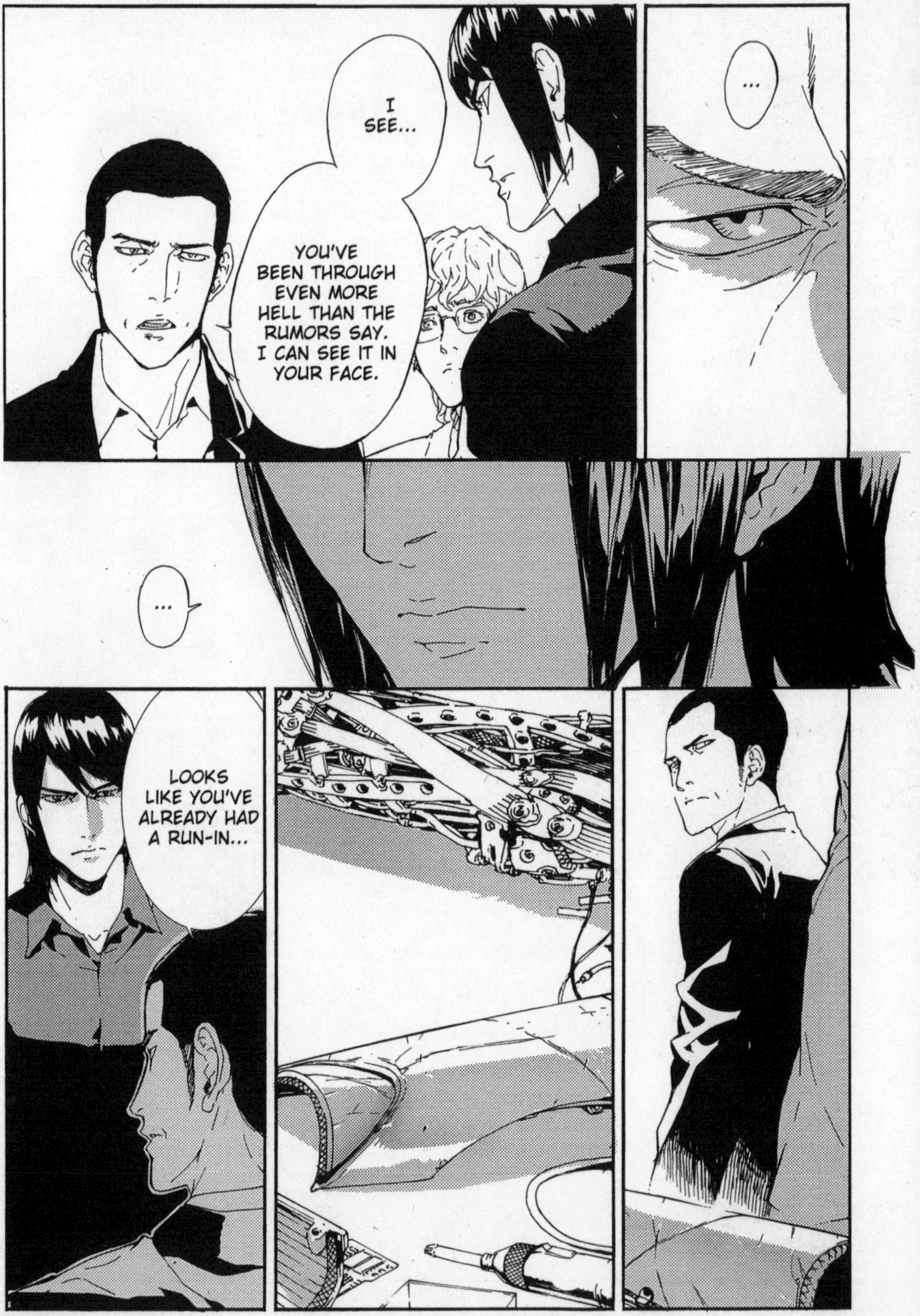
...
I SEE...
YOU'VE BEEN THROUGH EVEN MORE HELL THAN THE RUMORS SAY. I CAN SEE IT IN YOUR FACE.
...
LOOKS LIKE YOU'VE ALREADY HAD A RUN-IN...

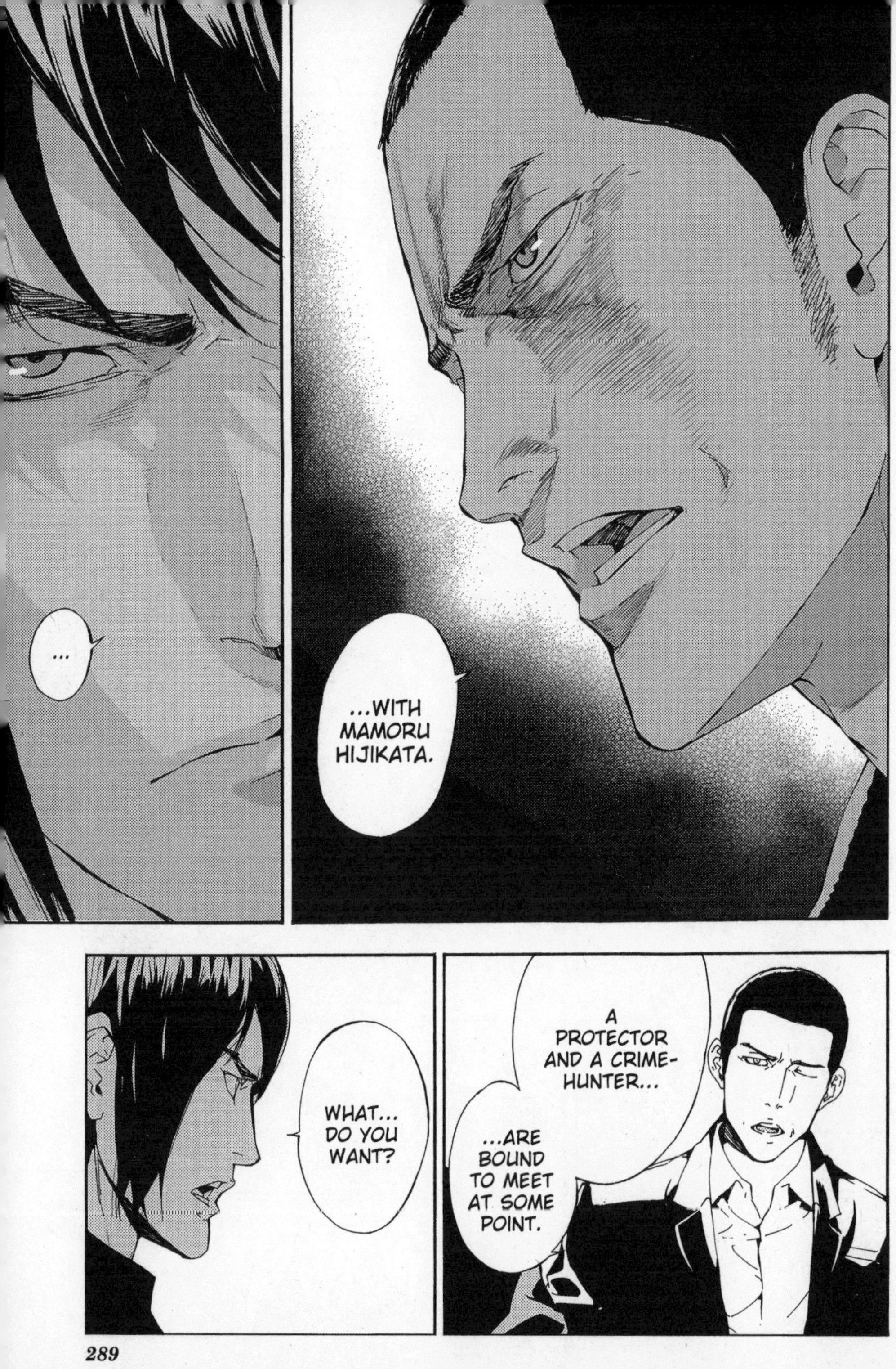
...WITH MAMORU HIJIKATA.
...
A PROTECTOR AND A CRIME-HUNTER...
...ARE BOUND TO MEET AT SOME POINT.
WHAT... DO YOU WANT?

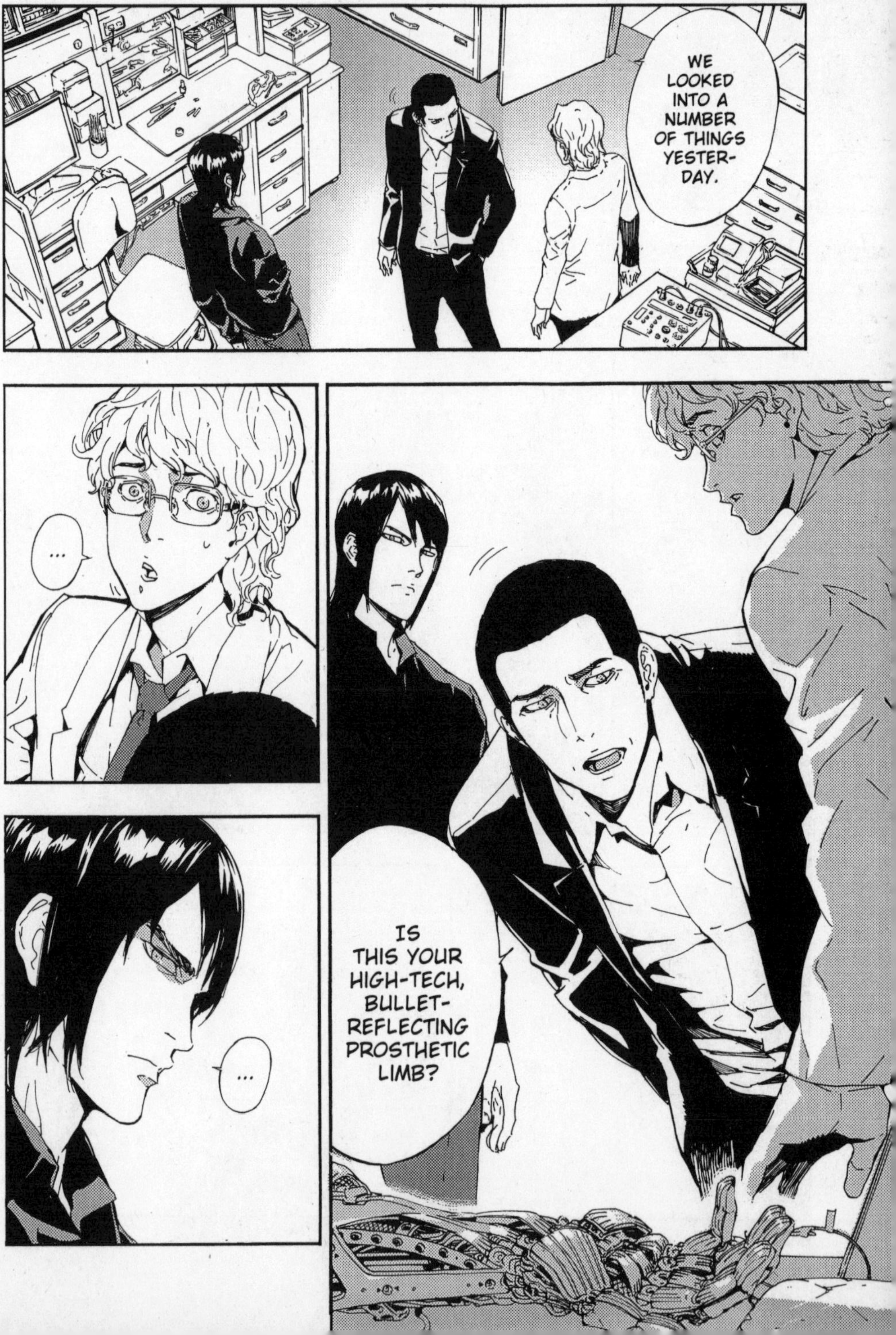
WE LOOKED INTO A NUMBER OF THINGS YESTER-DAY.
IS THIS YOUR HIGH-TECH, BULLET-REFLECTING PROSTHETIC LIMB?
...
...

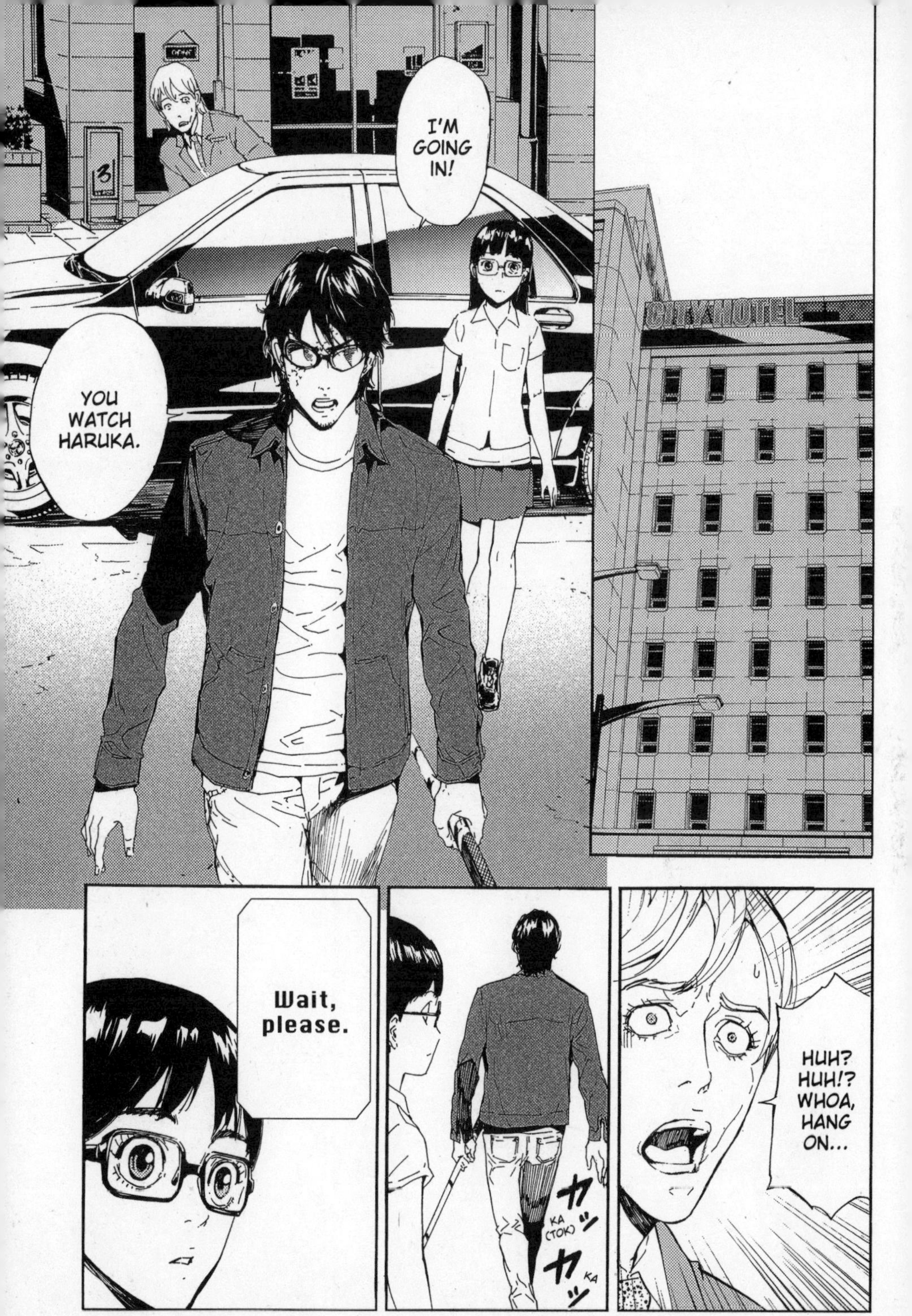
I'M GOING IN!
YOU WATCH HARUKA.
HUH? HUH!? WHOA, HANG ON...
カッ KA (TOK)
カッ KA
Wait, please.

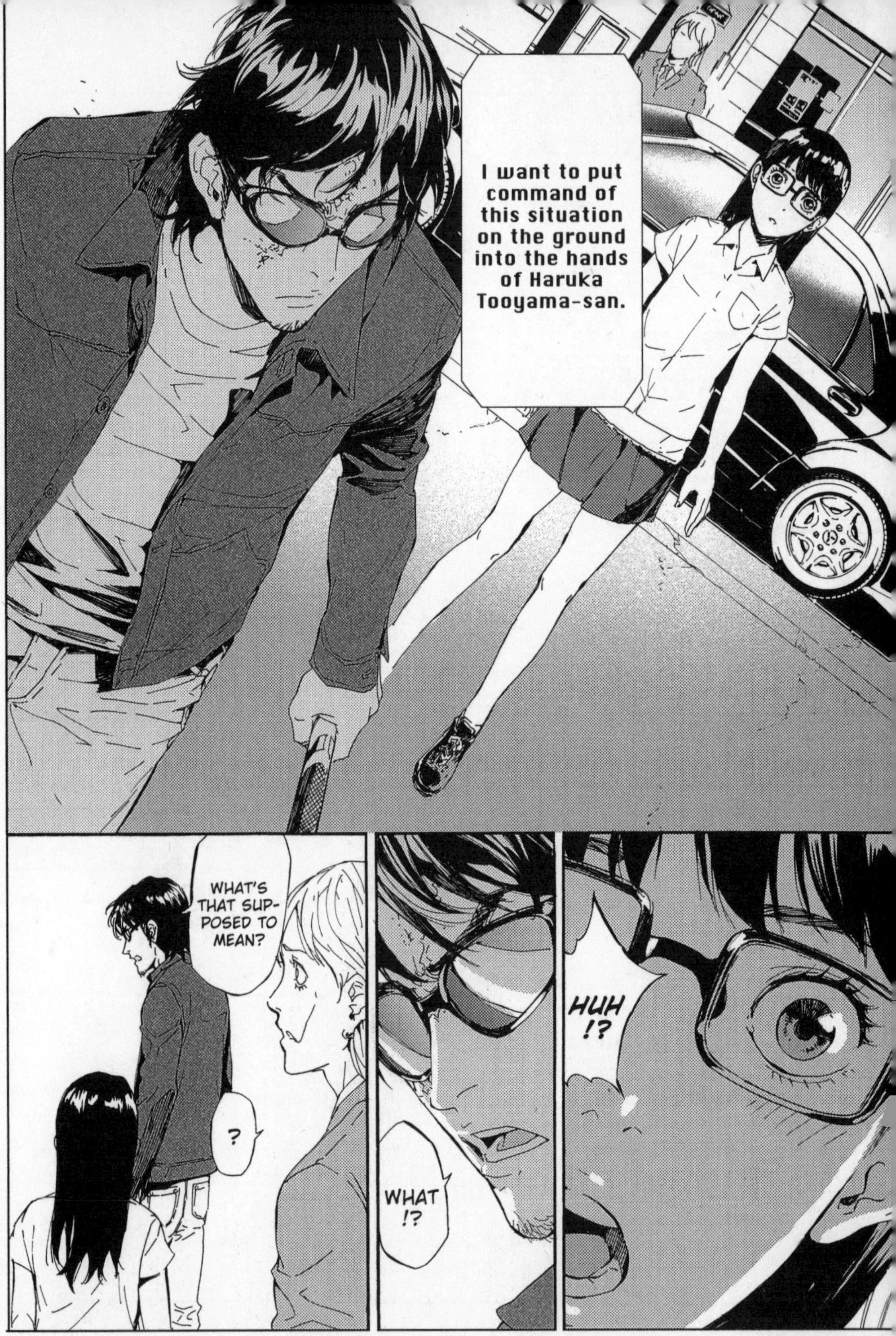
I want to put command of this situation on the ground into the hands of Haruka Tooyama-san.
HUH !?
WHAT !?
WHAT'S THAT SUP-POSED TO MEAN?
?

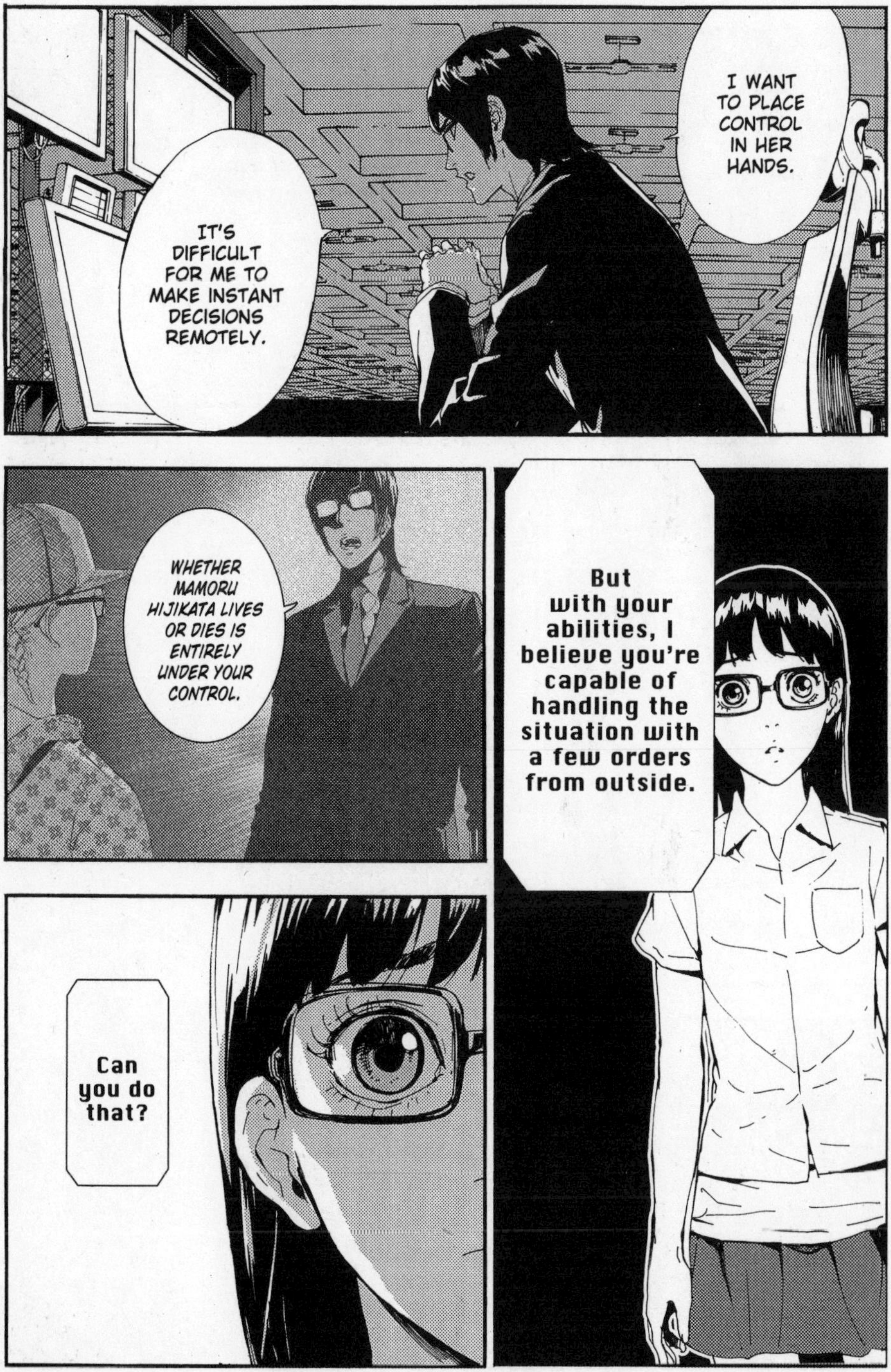
I WANT TO PLACE CONTROL IN HER HANDS.
IT'S DIFFICULT FOR ME TO MAKE INSTANT DECISIONS REMOTELY.
But with your abilities, I believe you're capable of handling the situation with a few orders from outside.
WHETHER MAMORU HIJIKATA LIVES OR DIES IS ENTIRELY UNDER YOUR CONTROL.
Can you do that?

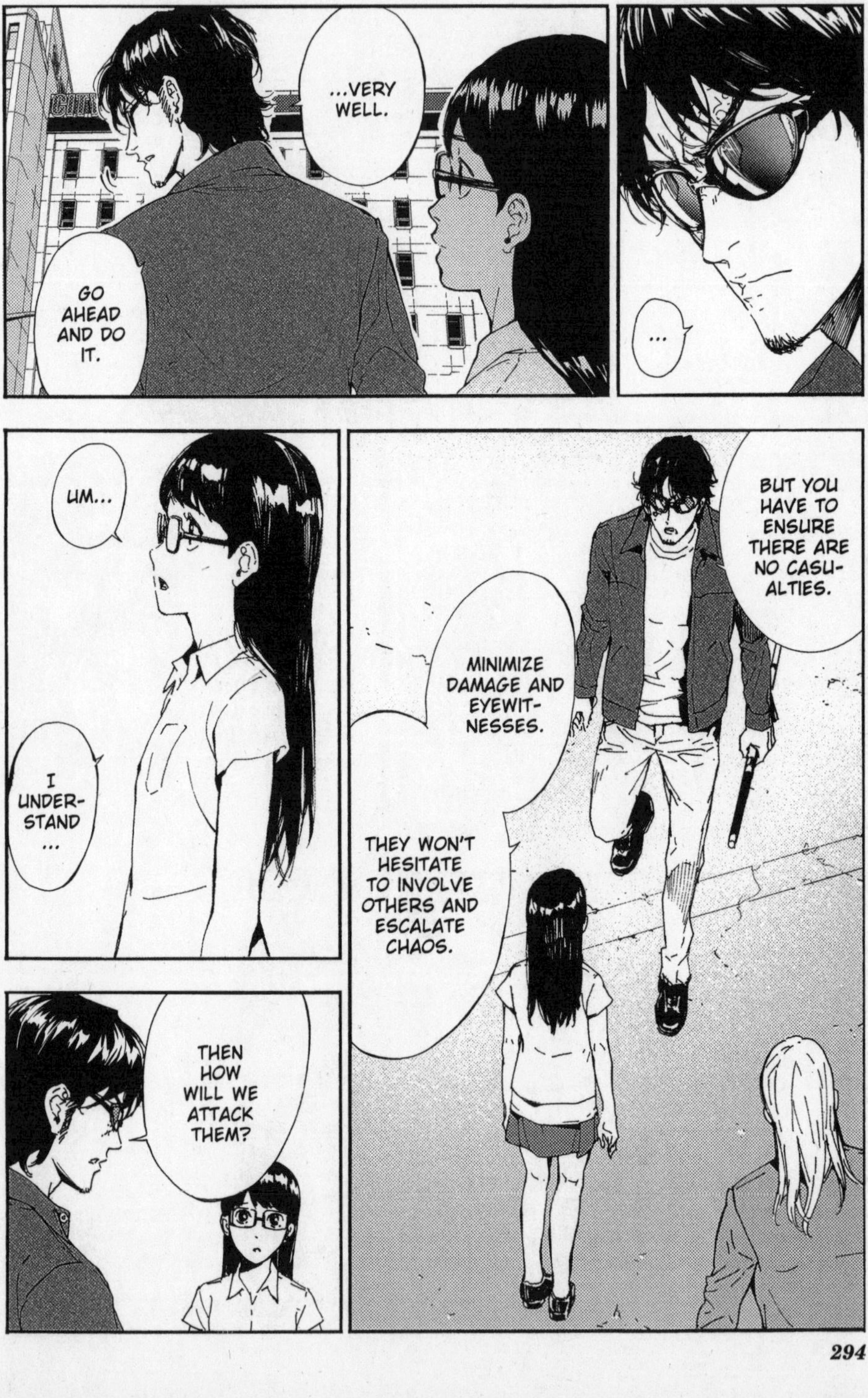
...
...VERY WELL.
GO AHEAD AND DO IT.
BUT YOU HAVE TO ENSURE THERE ARE NO CASUALTIES.
MINIMIZE DAMAGE AND EYEWITNESSES.
THEY WON'T HESITATE TO INVOLVE OTHERS AND ESCALATE CHAOS.
UM...
I UNDERSTAND...
THEN HOW WILL WE ATTACK THEM?

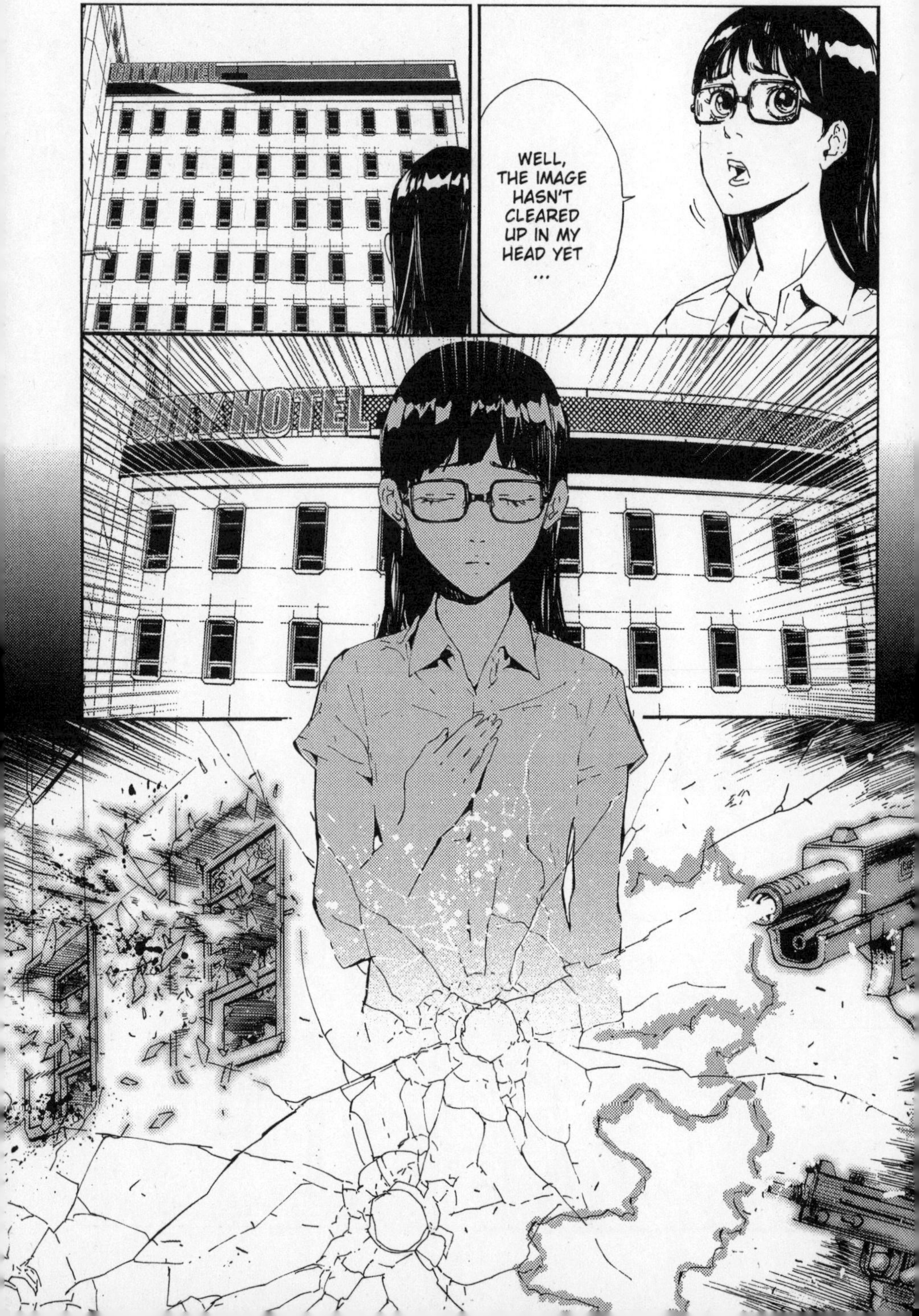
WELL, THE IMAGE HASN'T CLEARED UP IN MY HEAD YET ...
CITY HOTEL

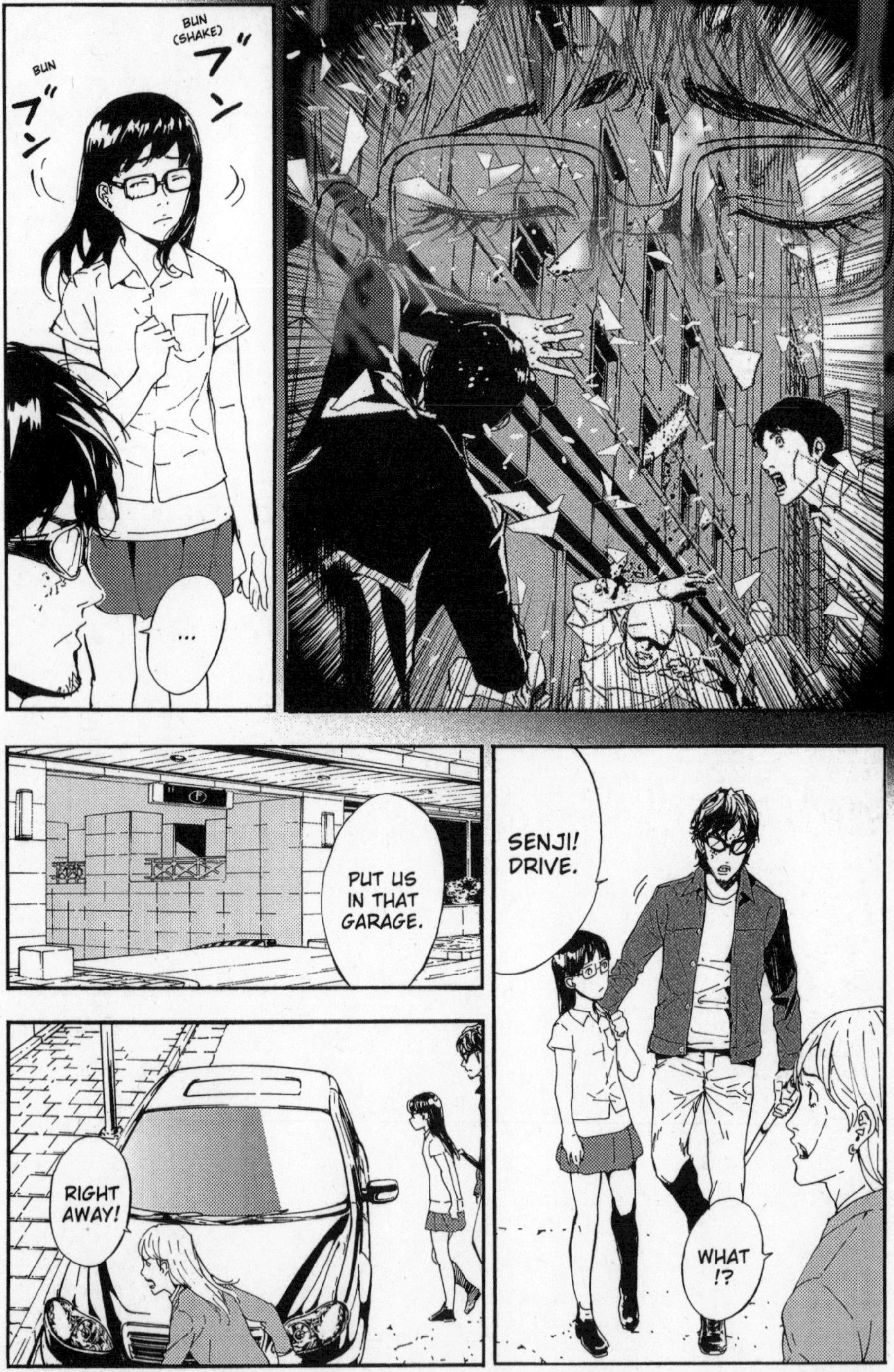
BUN (SHAKE)
ブン
BUN
ブン
...
SENJI! DRIVE.
WHAT !?
PUT US IN THAT GARAGE.
RIGHT AWAY!

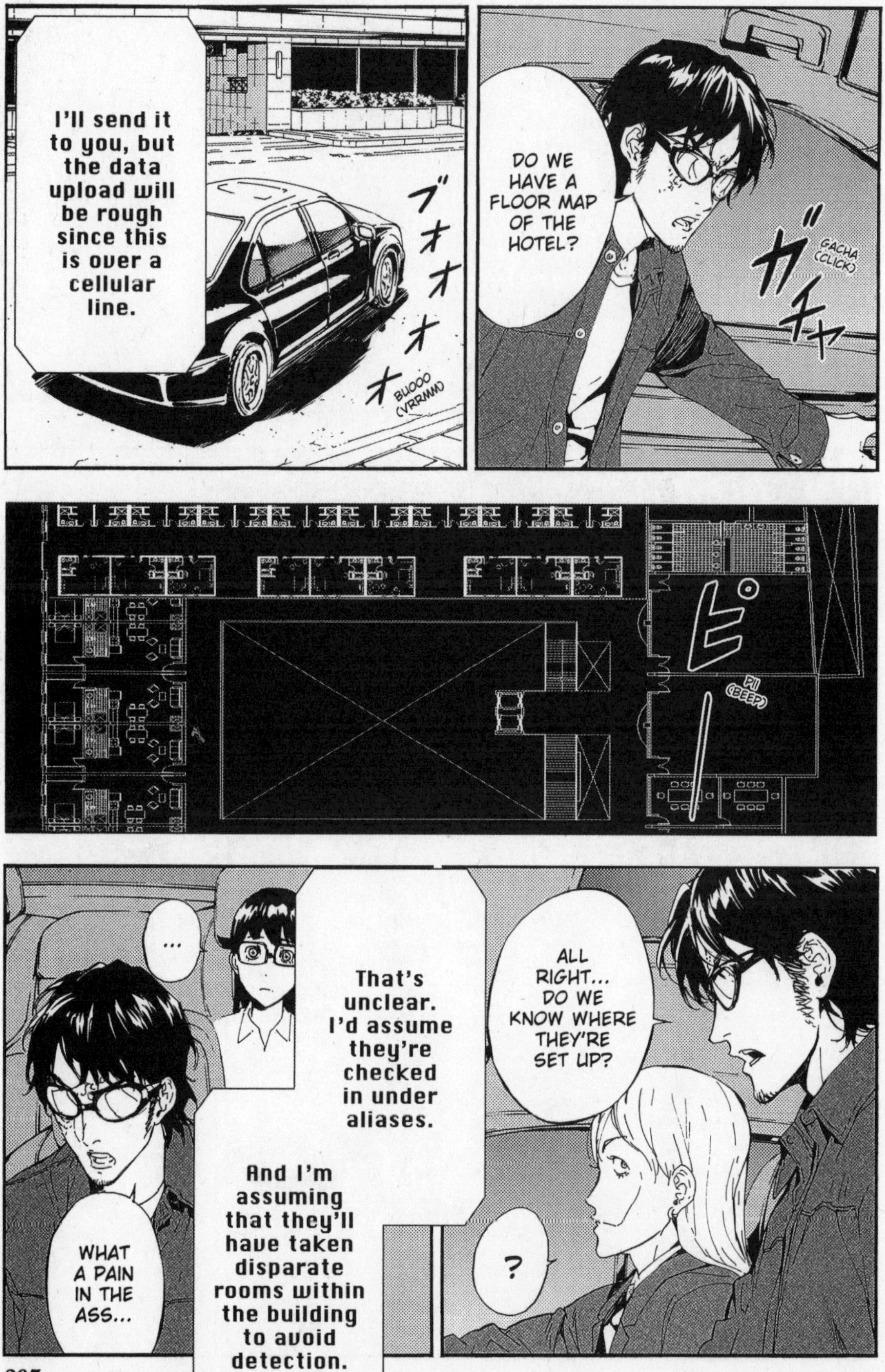
DO WE HAVE A FLOOR MAP OF THE HOTEL?
ガチャ
GACHA (CLICK)
I'll send it to you, but the data upload will be rough since this is over a cellular line.
ブォォォォ
BUOOO (VRRMM)
ピー
PII (BEEP)
ALL RIGHT... DO WE KNOW WHERE THEY'RE SET UP?
That's unclear. I'd assume they're checked in under aliases.
And I'm assuming that they'll have taken disparate rooms within the building to avoid detection.
?
...
WHAT A PAIN IN THE ASS...

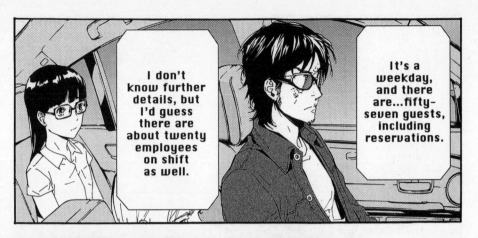

It's a weekday, and there are...fifty-seven guests, including reservations.
I don't know further details, but I'd guess there are about twenty employees on shift as well.
THIS ISN'T THE TIME OF DAY THAT HOTEL GUESTS WILL BE HANGING AROUND THEIR ROOMS.
ONLY A SMALL PERCENTAGE WILL BE PRESENT.
YES.
...
WHATEVER, I'M ONLY ALONG FOR THE RIDE.
WHATEVER'S GOING ON, I HAVE NO CHOICE BUT TO STICK WITH THEM.

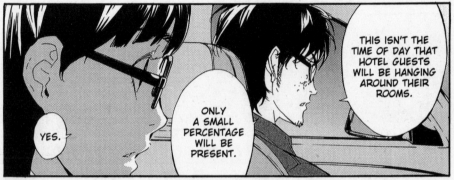

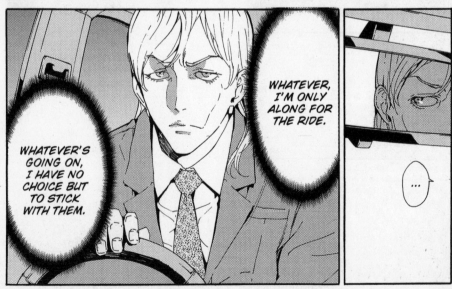

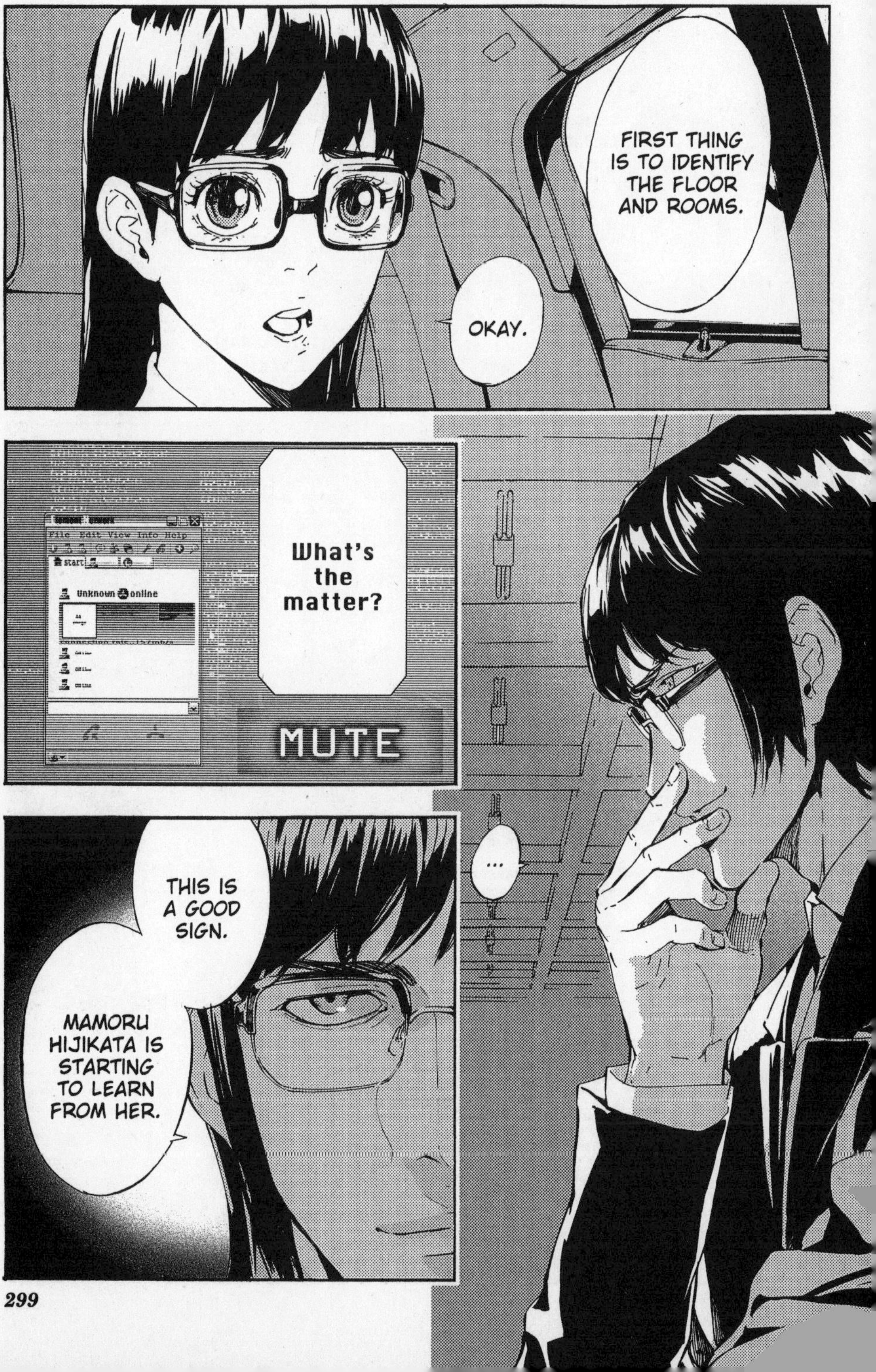
FIRST THING IS TO IDENTIFY THE FLOOR AND ROOMS.
OKAY.
...
File Edit View Info Help
start
Unknown online
What's the matter?
MUTE
THIS IS A GOOD SIGN.
MAMORU HIJIKATA IS STARTING TO LEARN FROM HER.

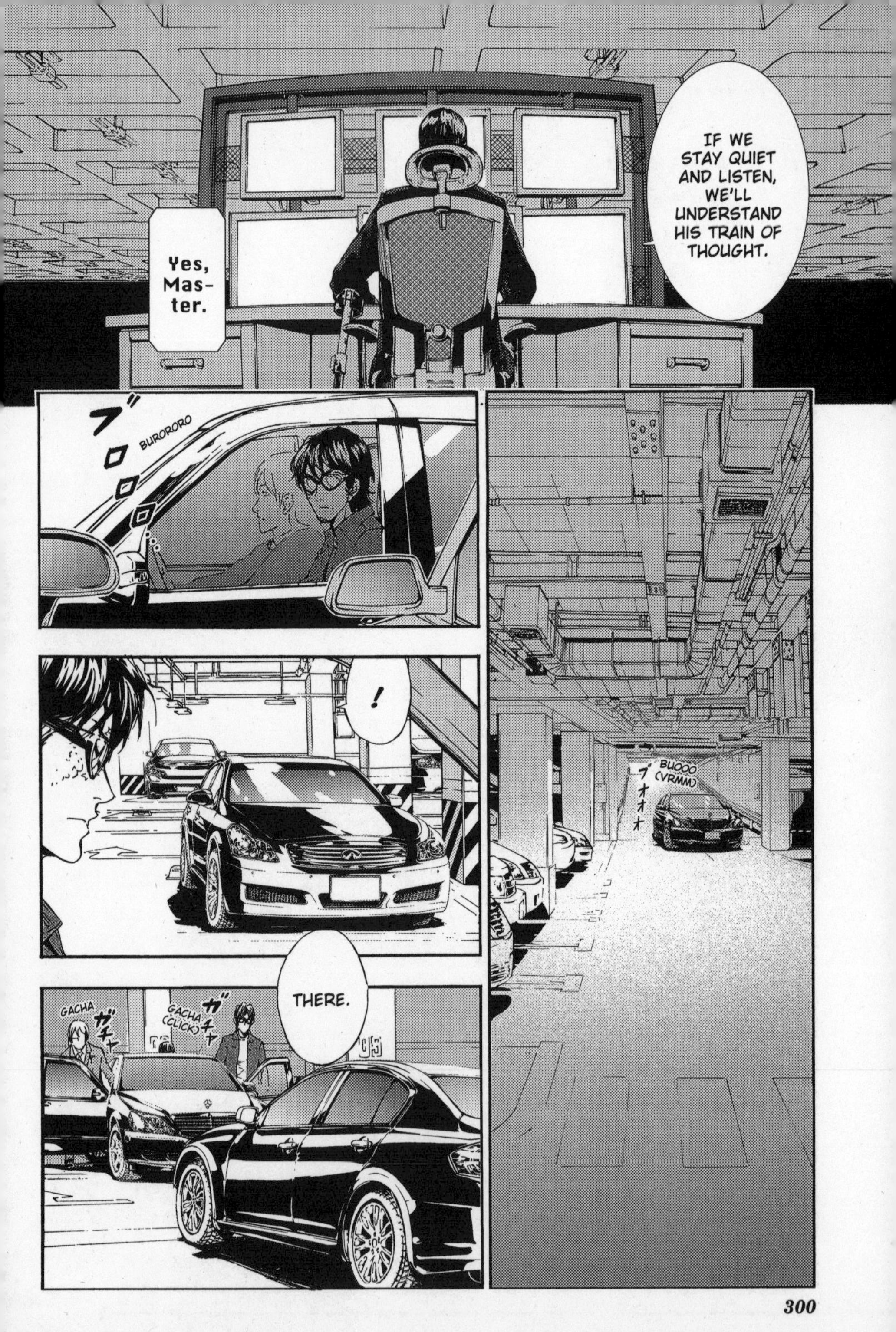
IF WE STAY QUIET AND LISTEN, WE'LL UNDERSTAND HIS TRAIN OF THOUGHT.
Yes, Master.
BUOOO (VRMM)
BURORORO
!
THERE.
GACHA (CLICK)
GACHA

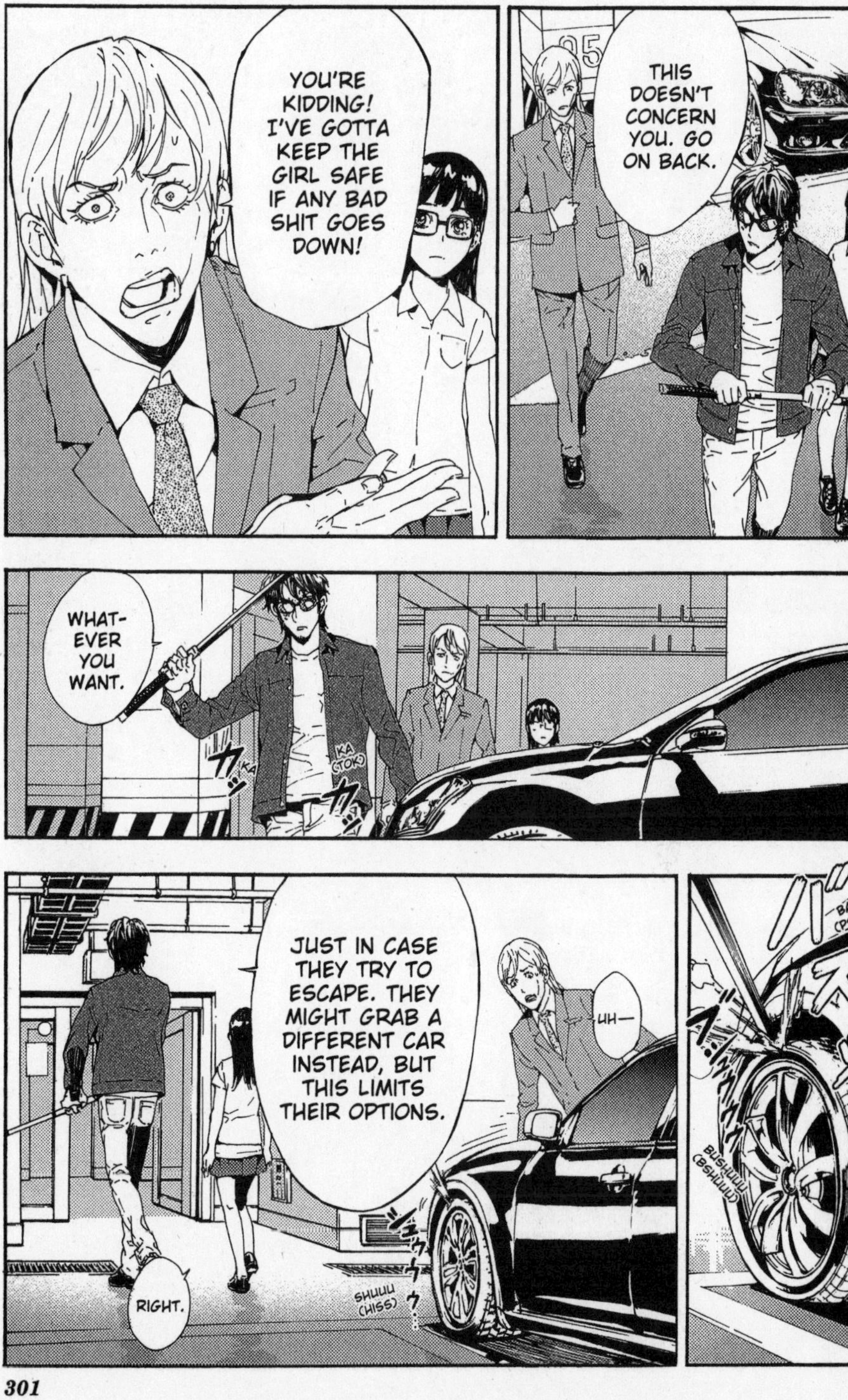
THIS DOESN'T CONCERN YOU. GO ON BACK.
YOU'RE KIDDING! I'VE GOTTA KEEP THE GIRL SAFE IF ANY BAD SHIT GOES DOWN!
WHATEVER YOU WANT.
KA (TOK)
KA
BASU (P.SHUT)
BUSHUUU (BSHUUU)
UH—
JUST IN CASE THEY TRY TO ESCAPE. THEY MIGHT GRAB A DIFFERENT CAR INSTEAD, BUT THIS LIMITS THEIR OPTIONS.
SHUUU (HISS)
RIGHT.

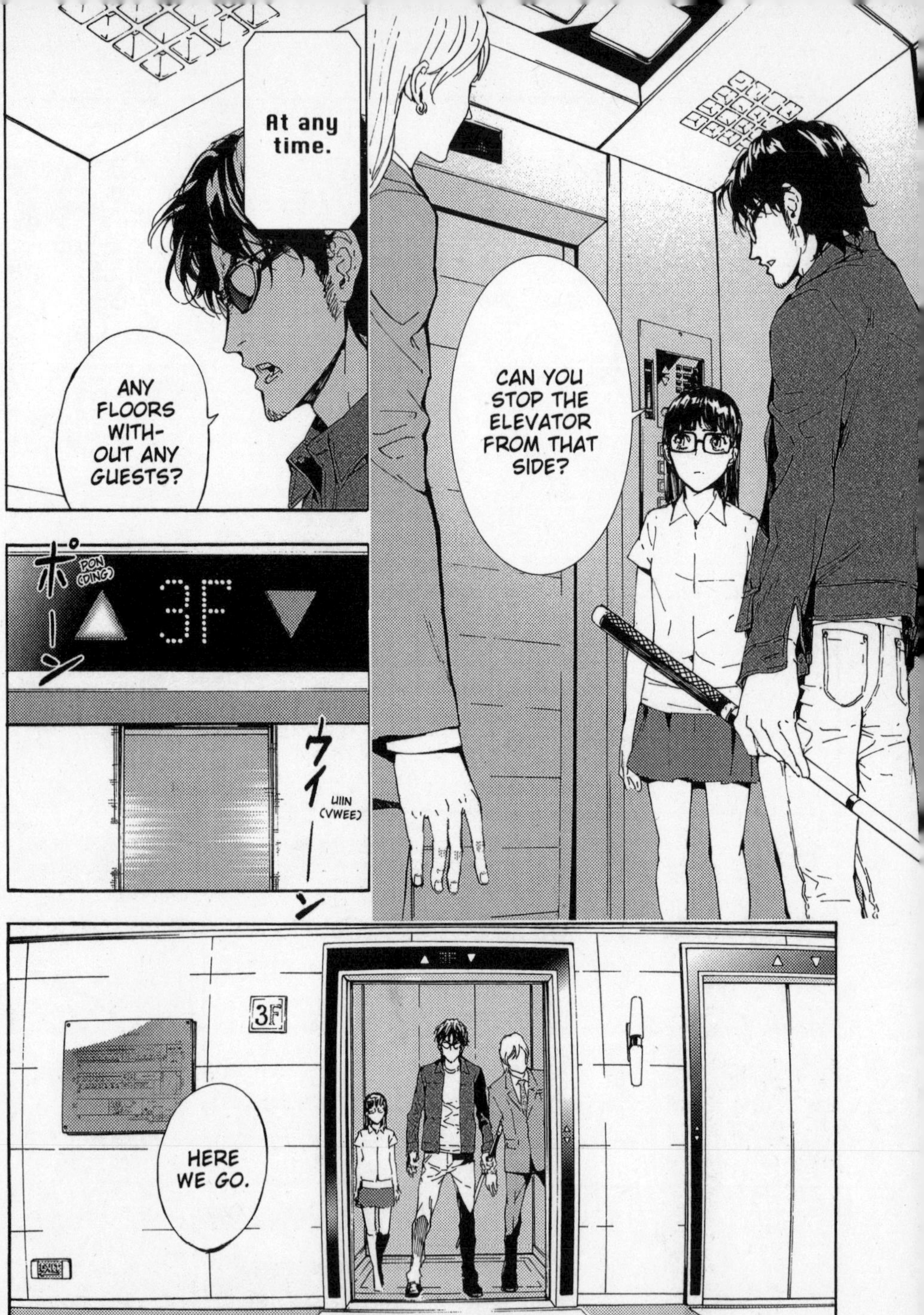
CAN YOU STOP THE ELEVATOR FROM THAT SIDE?
At any time.
ANY FLOORS WITH-OUT ANY GUESTS?
ポーン
PON (DING)
3F
ウィーン
UIIN (VWEE)
HERE WE GO.

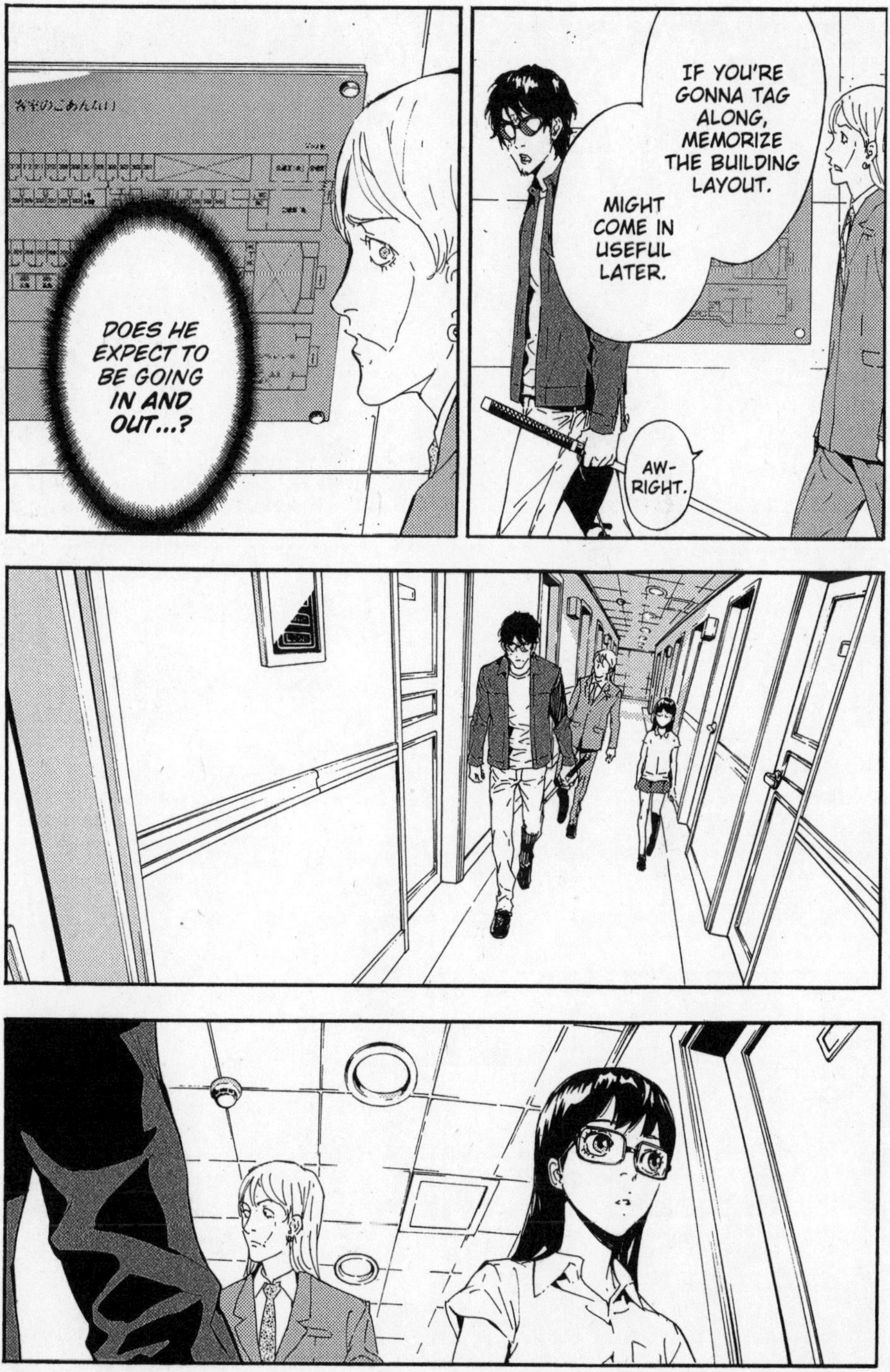
IF YOU'RE GONNA TAG ALONG, MEMORIZE THE BUILDING LAYOUT.
MIGHT COME IN USEFUL LATER.
AW-RIGHT.
DOES HE EXPECT TO BE GOING IN AND OUT...?

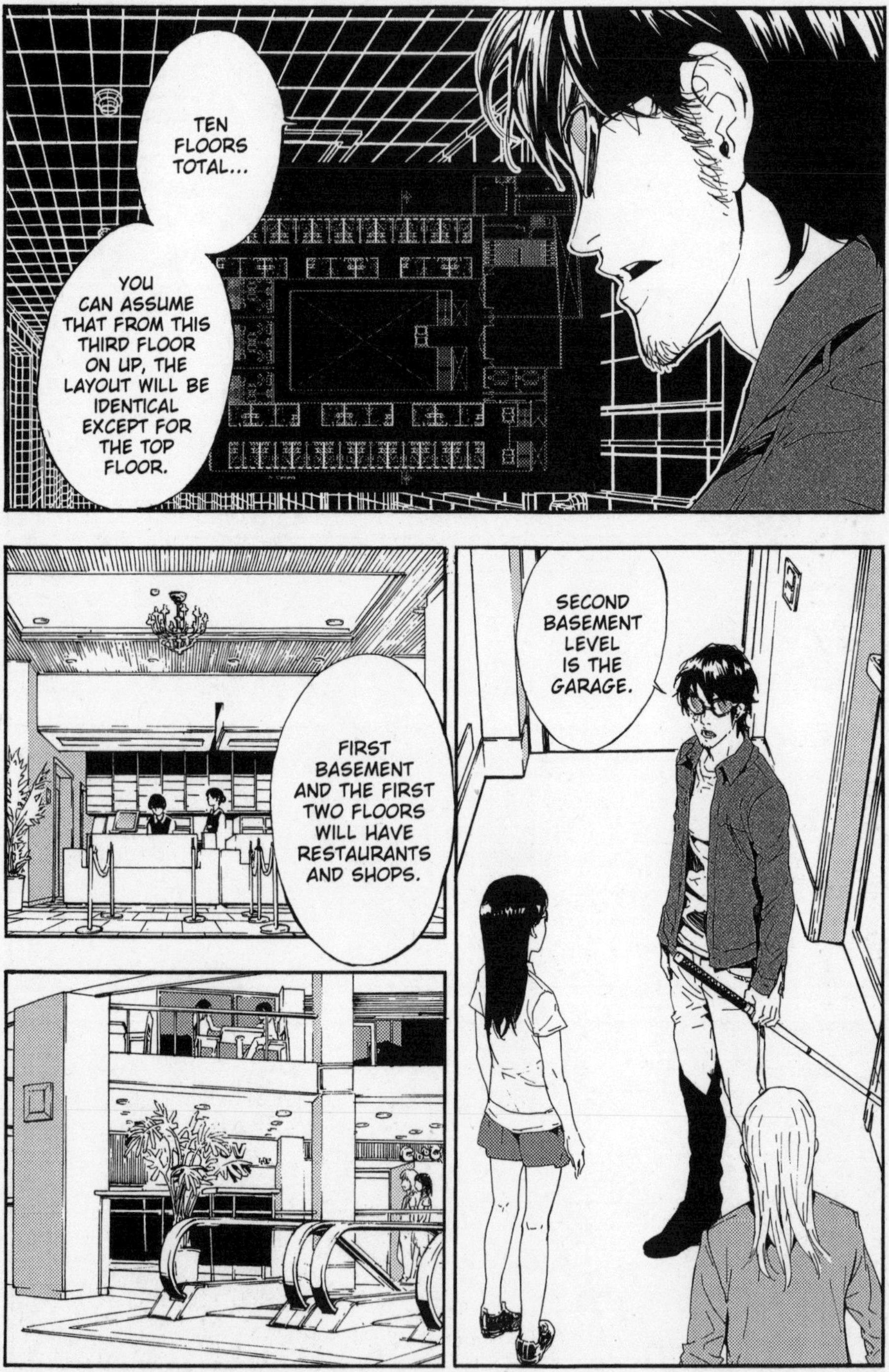
TEN FLOORS TOTAL...
YOU CAN ASSUME THAT FROM THIS THIRD FLOOR ON UP, THE LAYOUT WILL BE IDENTICAL EXCEPT FOR THE TOP FLOOR.
SECOND BASEMENT LEVEL IS THE GARAGE.
FIRST BASEMENT AND THE FIRST TWO FLOORS WILL HAVE RESTAURANTS AND SHOPS.

O-OKAY.

Third one's coming back, Master.

NOT BAD, AS FAR AS TIMING GOES.

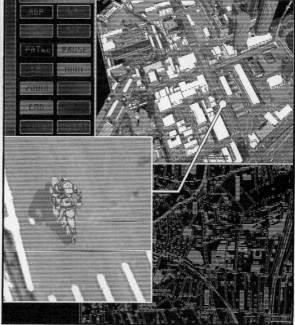

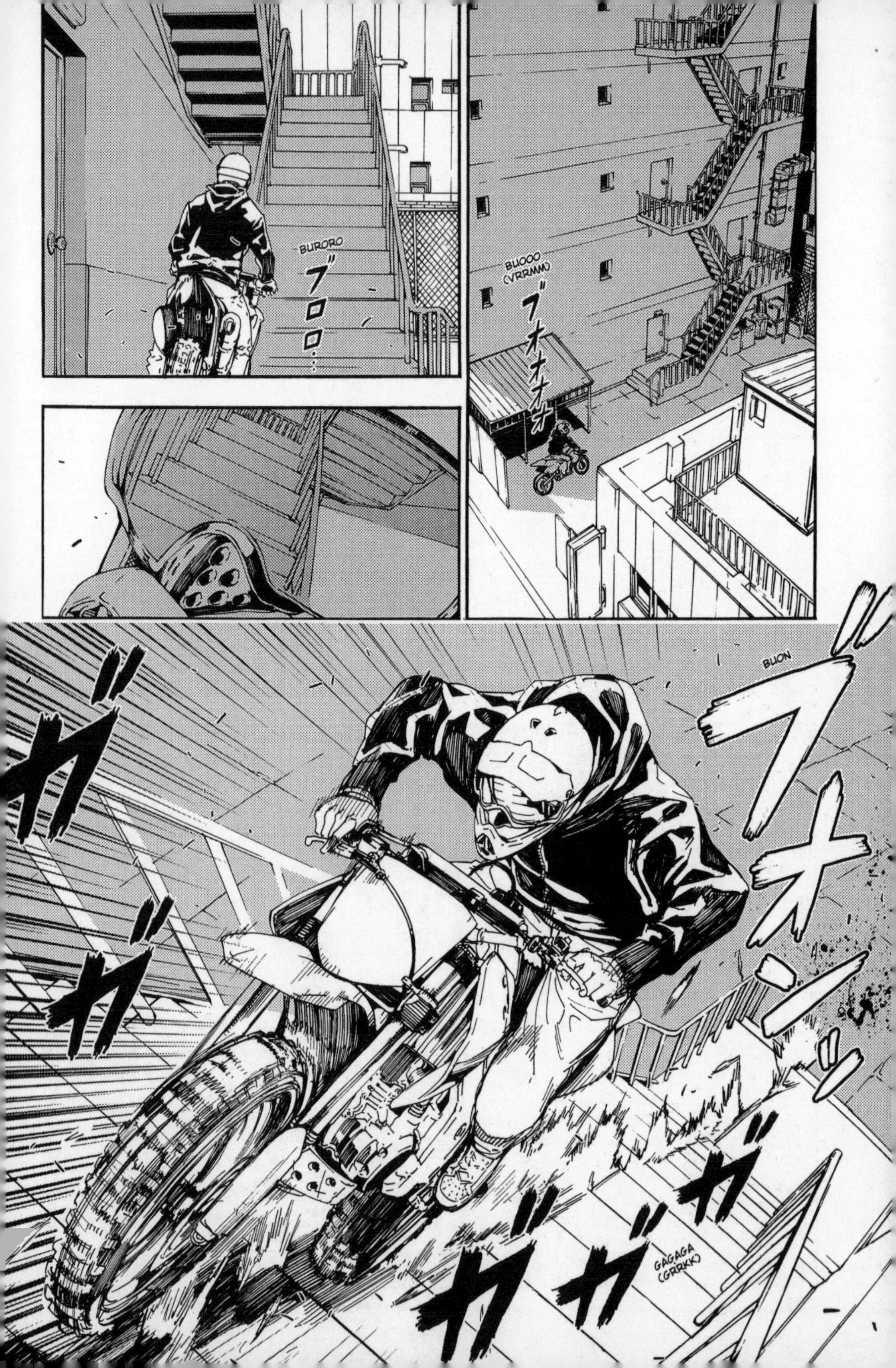

BUOOO (VRRMM)
ブオオオオ
BURORO
ブロロ…
BUON
ブオン
GAGAGA (GRRKK)
ガガガ
ガガガ

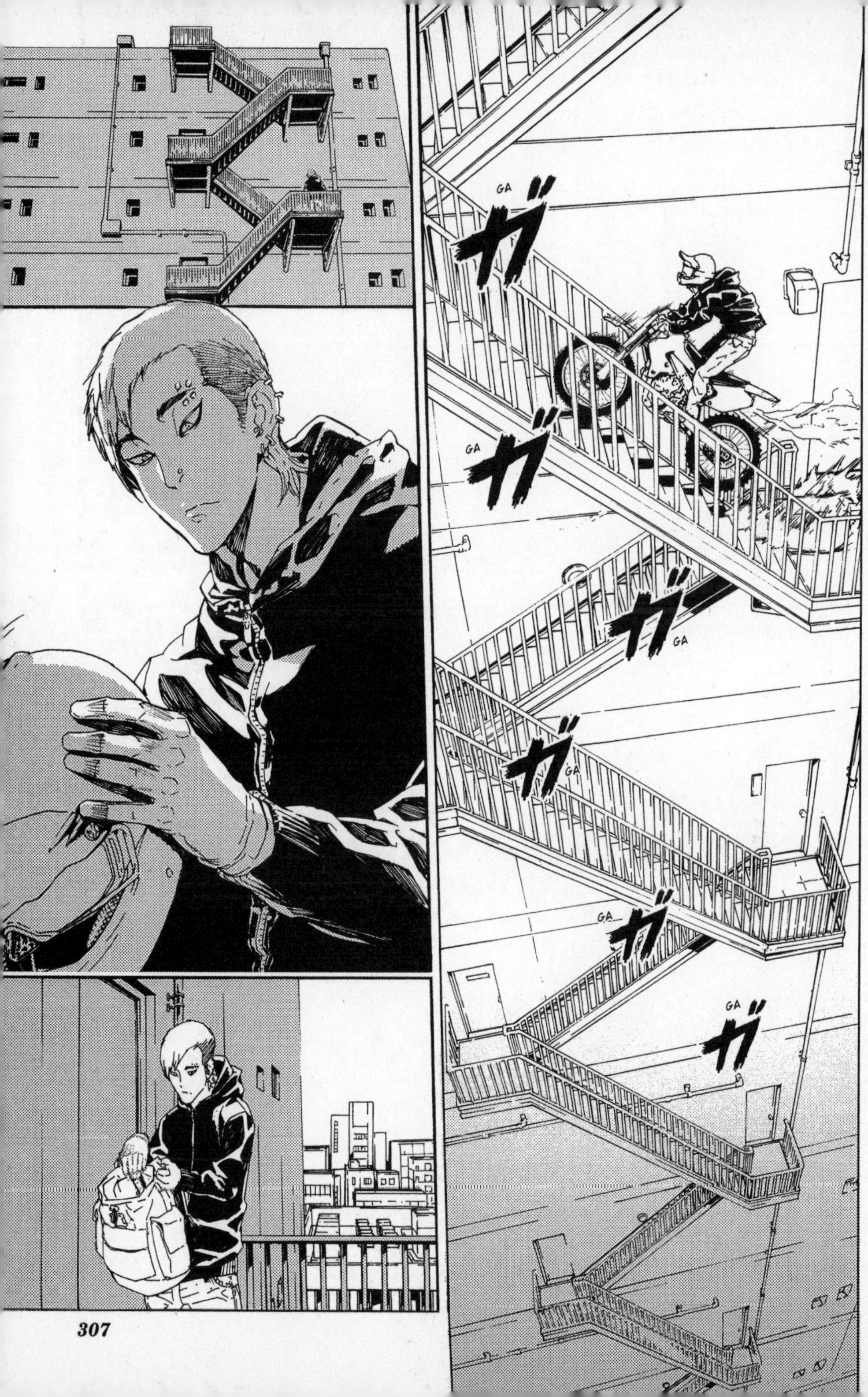

GA ガ
GA ガ
ガ GA
ガ GA
GA ガ
GA ガ

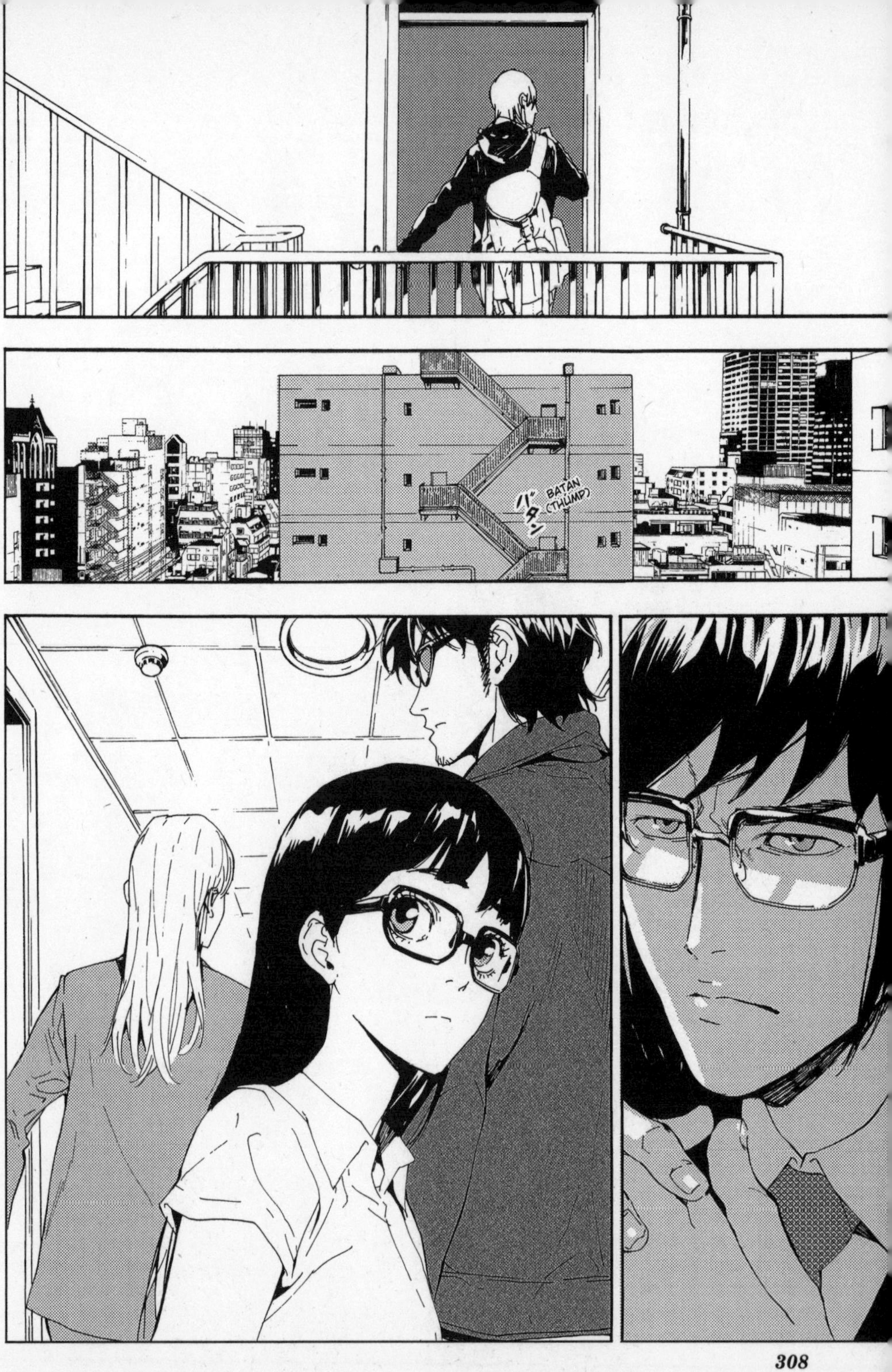
バタン
BATAN (THUMP)

chapter 97

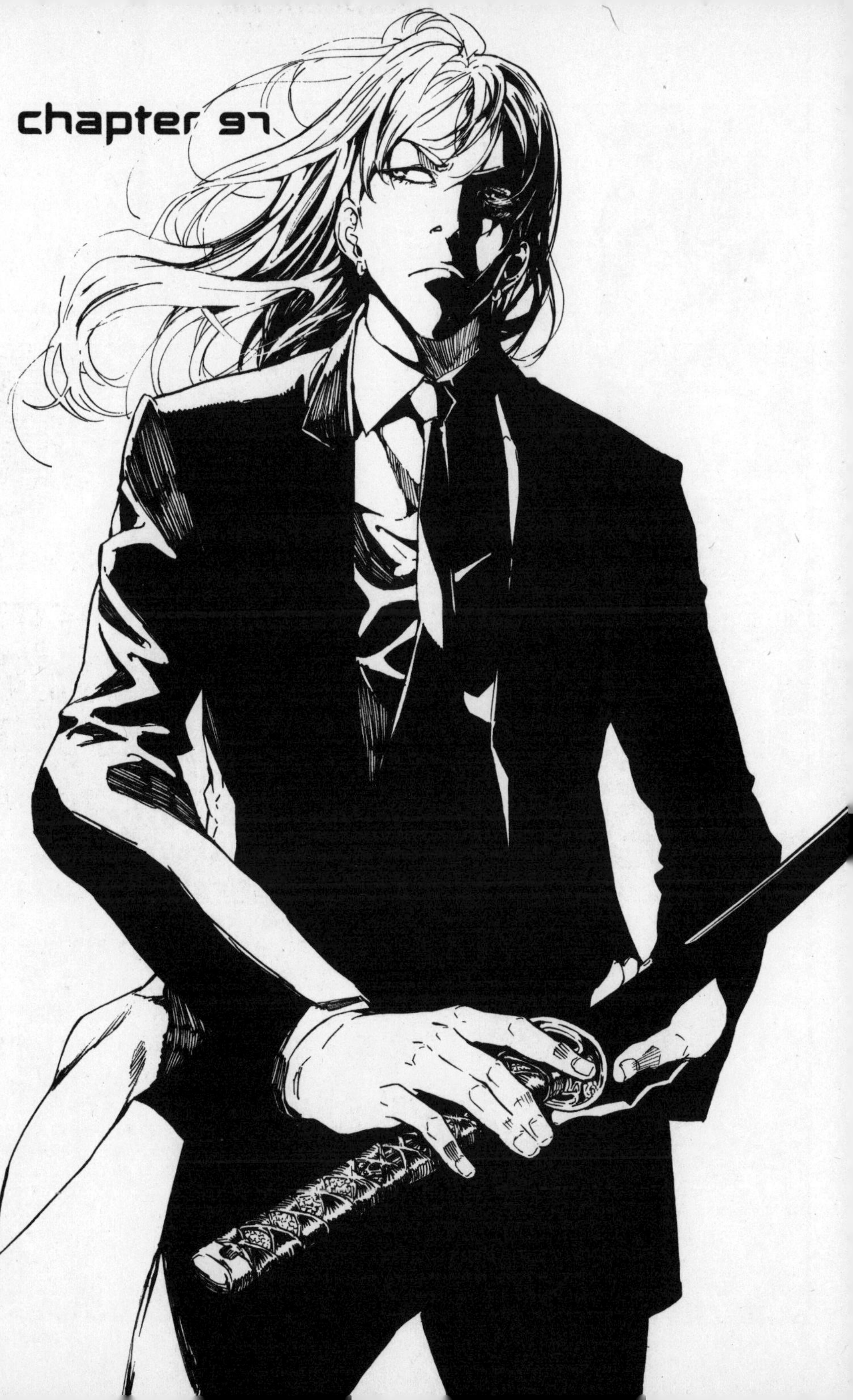

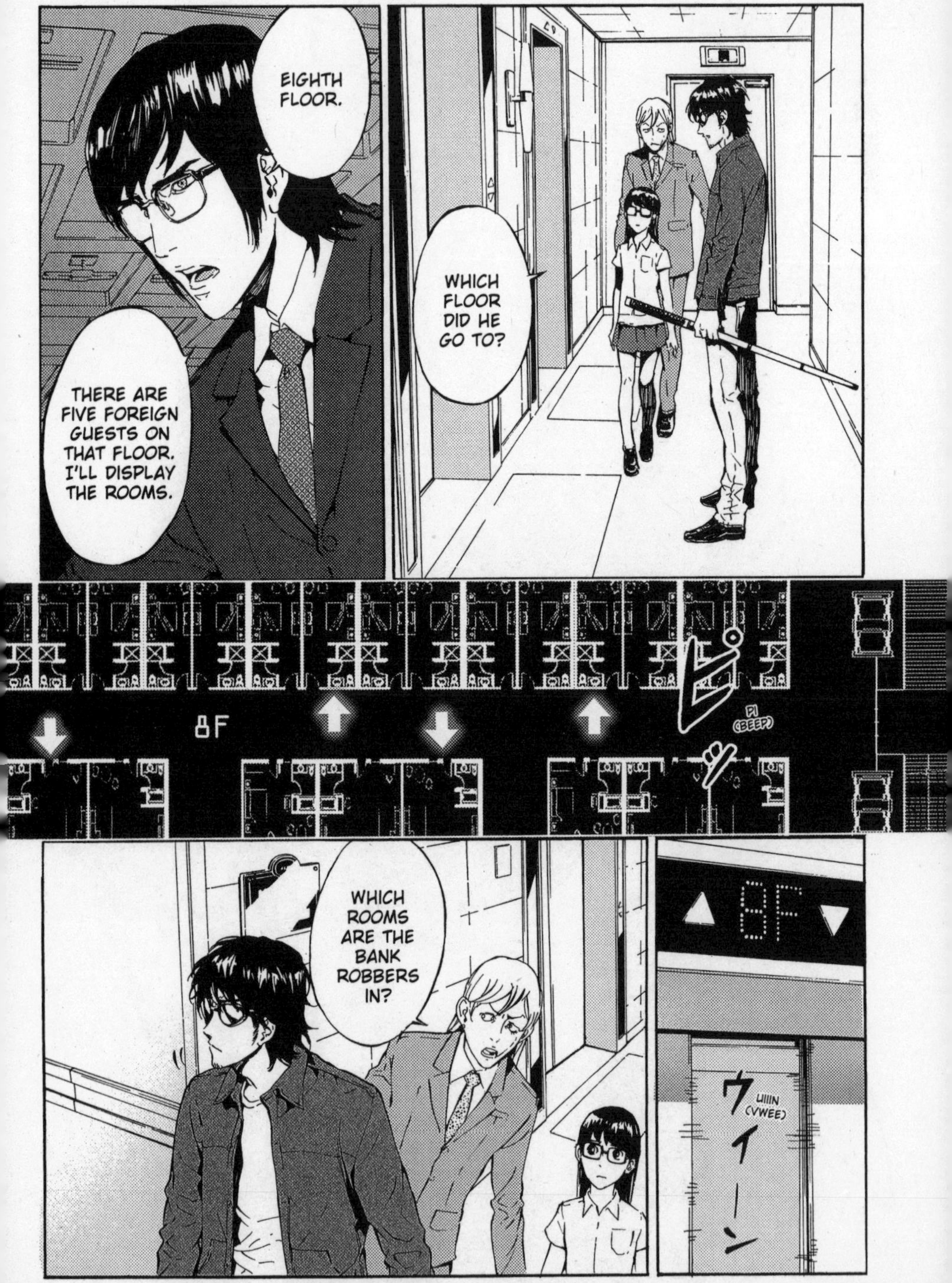
WHICH FLOOR DID HE GO TO?
EIGHTH FLOOR.
THERE ARE FIVE FOREIGN GUESTS ON THAT FLOOR. I'LL DISPLAY THE ROOMS.
ピッ
PI (BEEP)
8F
8F
ウィーン
UIIIN (VWEE)
WHICH ROOMS ARE THE BANK ROBBERS IN?

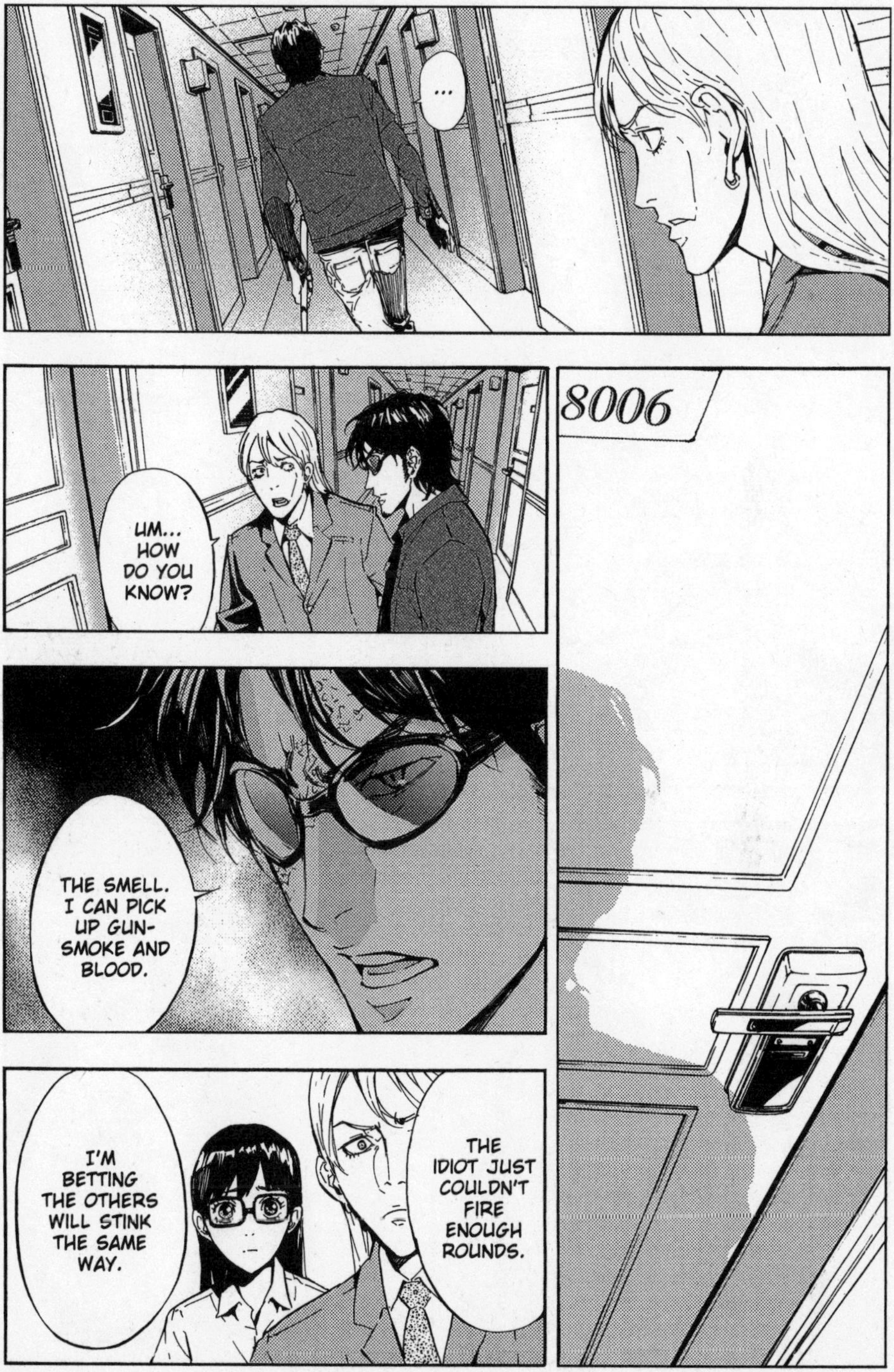
...
8006
UM... HOW DO YOU KNOW?
THE SMELL. I CAN PICK UP GUN-SMOKE AND BLOOD.
THE IDIOT JUST COULDN'T FIRE ENOUGH ROUNDS.
I'M BETTING THE OTHERS WILL STINK THE SAME WAY.

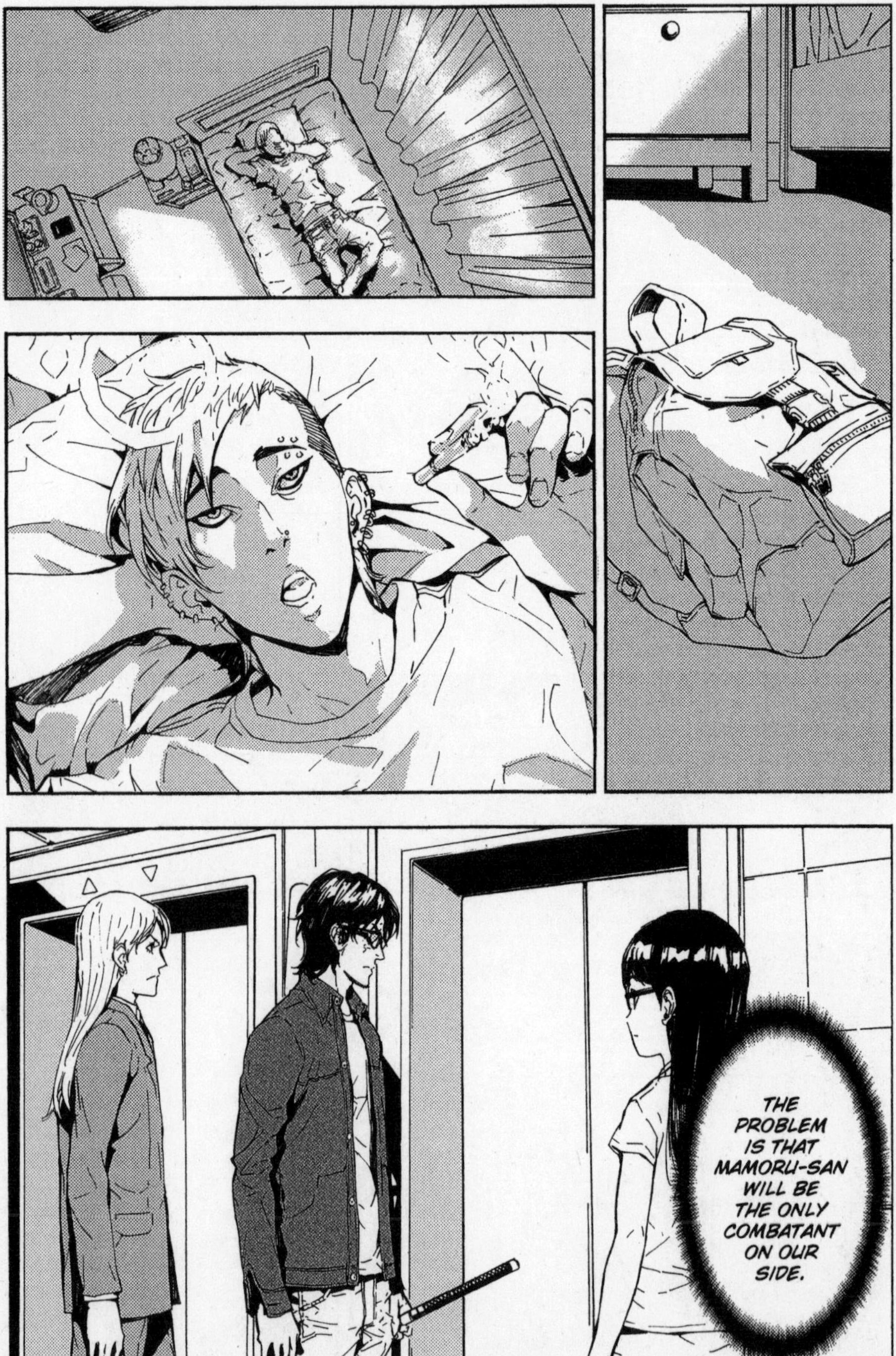
THE PROBLEM IS THAT MAMORU-SAN WILL BE THE ONLY COMBATANT ON OUR SIDE.

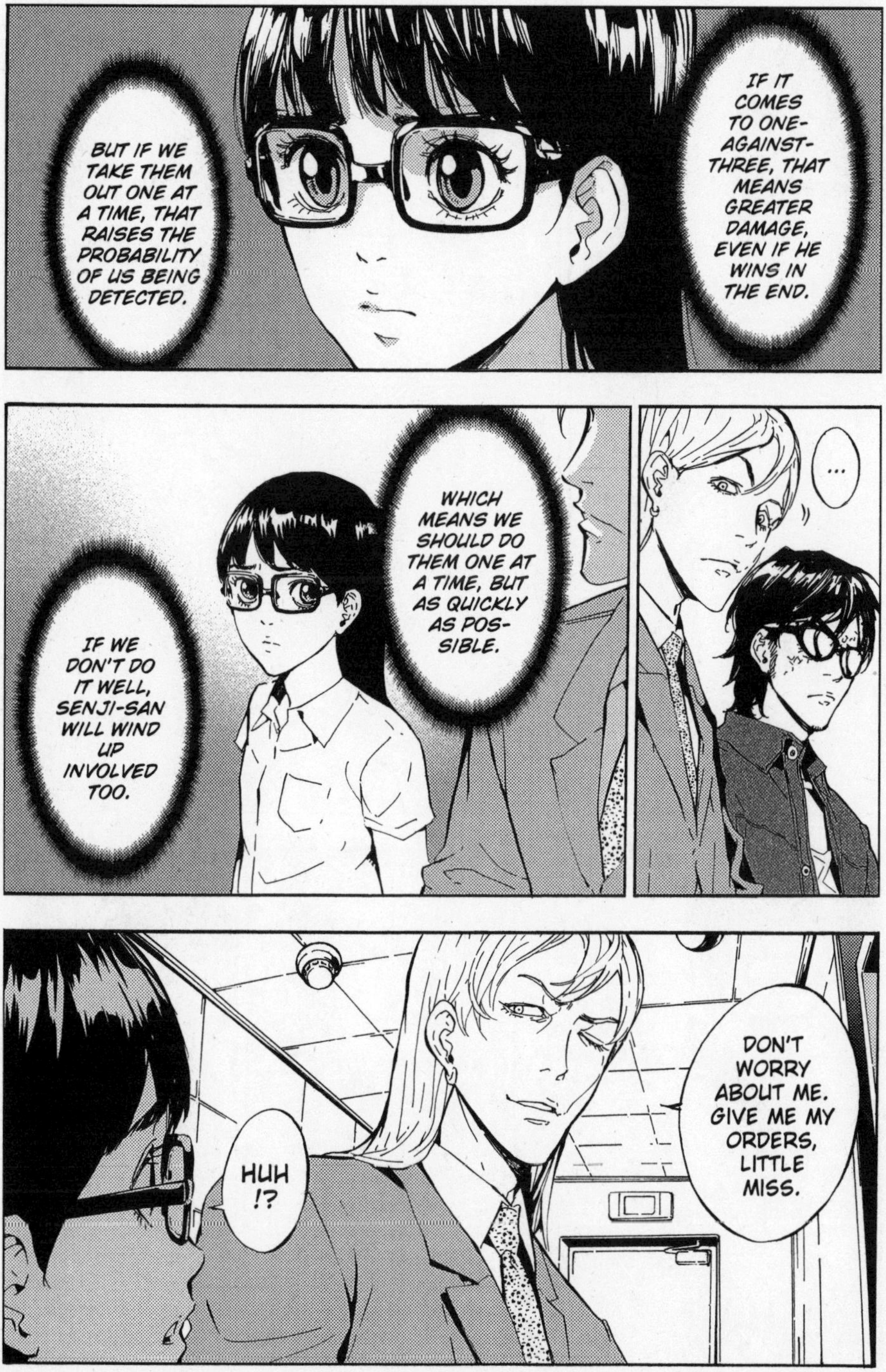
IF IT COMES TO ONE-AGAINST-THREE, THAT MEANS GREATER DAMAGE, EVEN IF HE WINS IN THE END.
BUT IF WE TAKE THEM OUT ONE AT A TIME, THAT RAISES THE PROBABILITY OF US BEING DETECTED.
...
WHICH MEANS WE SHOULD DO THEM ONE AT A TIME, BUT AS QUICKLY AS POS-SIBLE.
IF WE DON'T DO IT WELL, SENJI-SAN WILL WIND UP INVOLVED TOO.
DON'T WORRY ABOUT ME. GIVE ME MY ORDERS, LITTLE MISS.
HUH !?

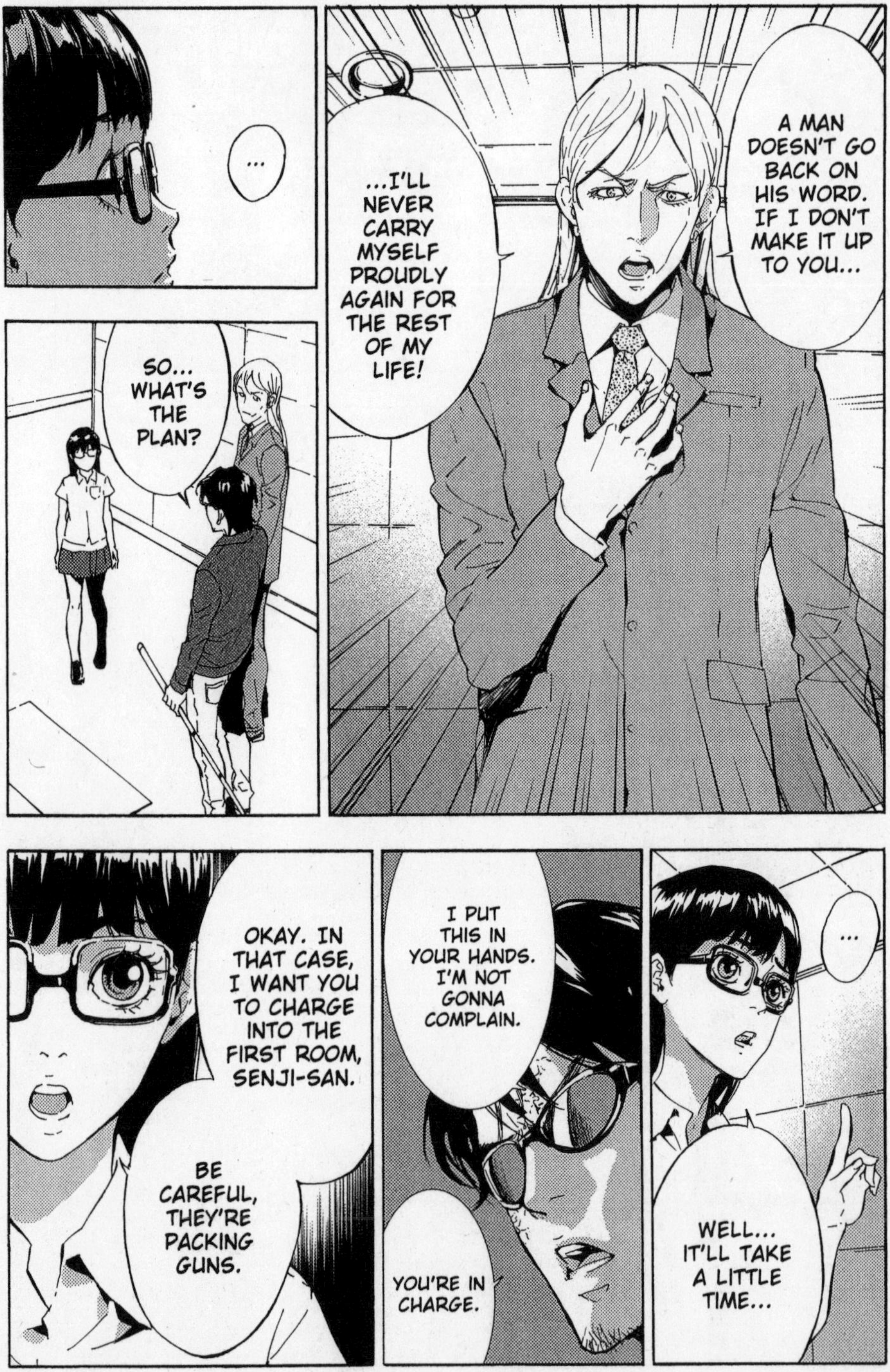
A MAN DOESN'T GO BACK ON HIS WORD. IF I DON'T MAKE IT UP TO YOU...
...I'LL NEVER CARRY MYSELF PROUDLY AGAIN FOR THE REST OF MY LIFE!
...
SO... WHAT'S THE PLAN?
...
WELL... IT'LL TAKE A LITTLE TIME...
I PUT THIS IN YOUR HANDS. I'M NOT GONNA COMPLAIN.
YOU'RE IN CHARGE.
OKAY. IN THAT CASE, I WANT YOU TO CHARGE INTO THE FIRST ROOM, SENJI-SAN.
BE CAREFUL, THEY'RE PACKING GUNS.

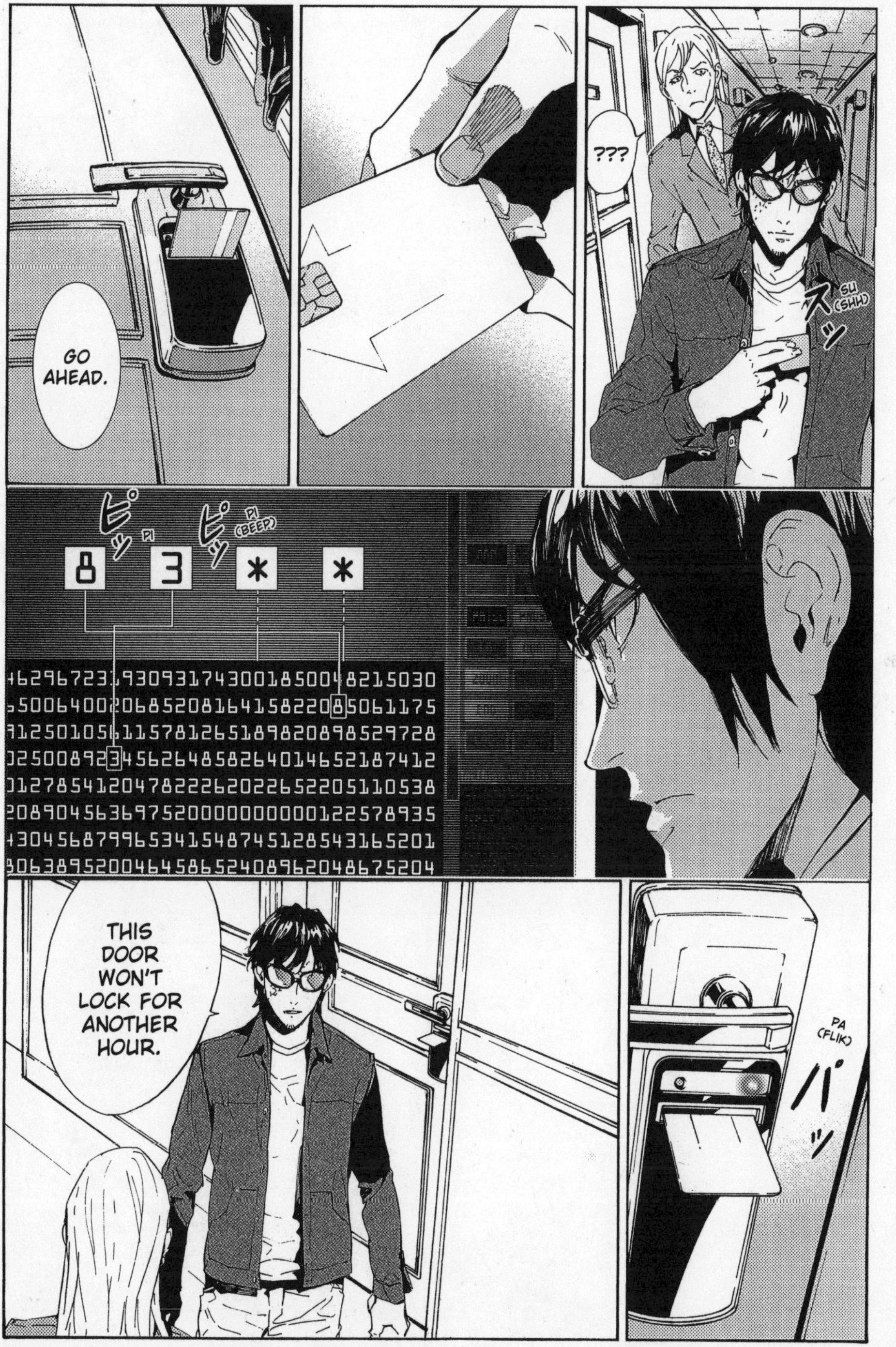
???
SU (SHH)
スッ
GO AHEAD.
ピッ
PI
ピッ
PI (BEEP)
8 3 * *
PA (FLIK)
パッ
THIS DOOR WON'T LOCK FOR ANOTHER HOUR.

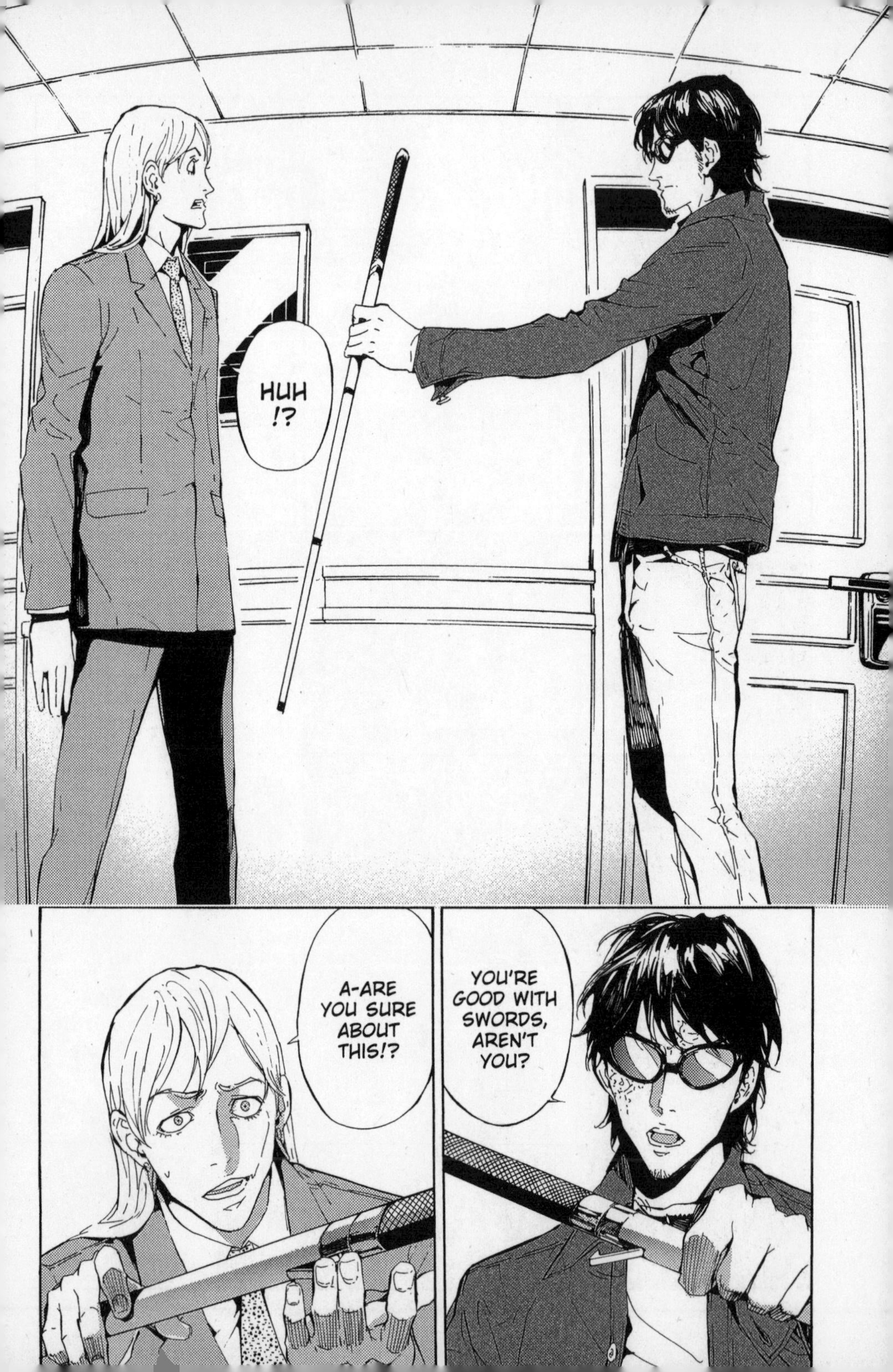
HUH !?
YOU'RE GOOD WITH SWORDS, AREN'T YOU?
A-ARE YOU SURE ABOUT THIS!?

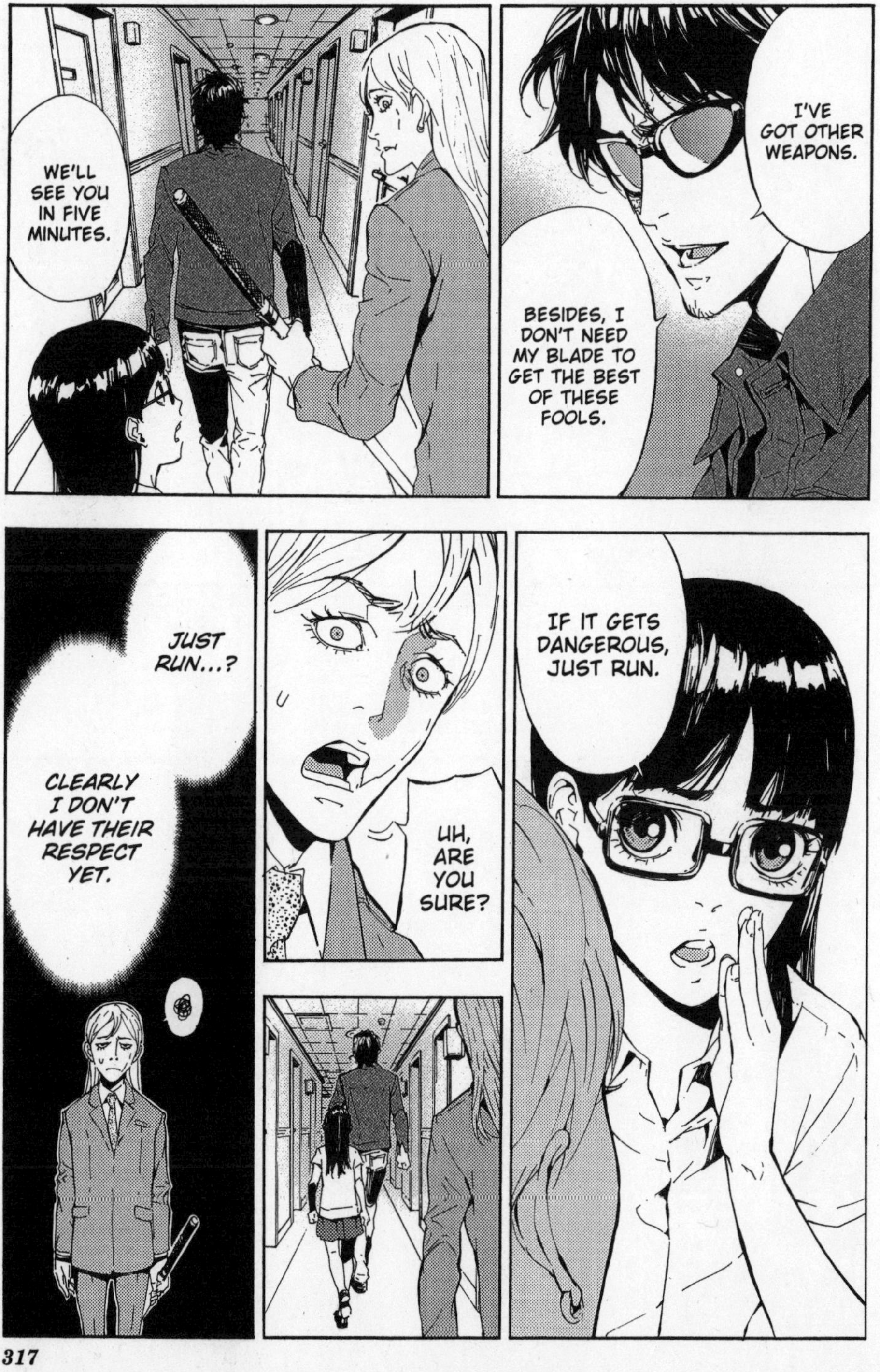
I'VE GOT OTHER WEAPONS.
BESIDES, I DON'T NEED MY BLADE TO GET THE BEST OF THESE FOOLS.
WE'LL SEE YOU IN FIVE MINUTES.
IF IT GETS DANGEROUS, JUST RUN.
UH, ARE YOU SURE?
JUST RUN...?
CLEARLY I DON'T HAVE THEIR RESPECT YET.

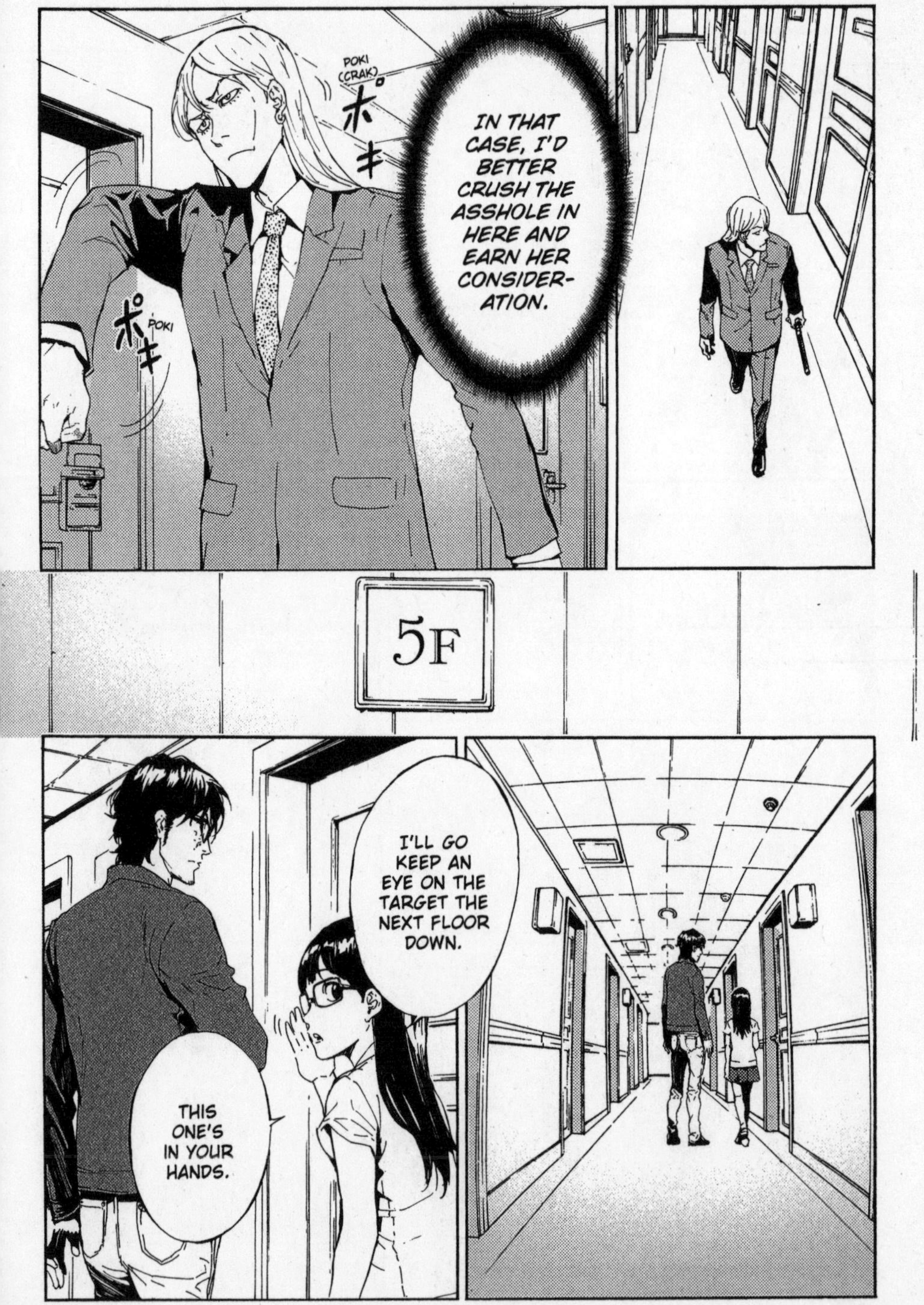
IN THAT CASE, I'D BETTER CRUSH THE ASSHOLE IN HERE AND EARN HER CONSIDER-ATION.
ポキ POKI (CRAK)
ポキ POKI
5F
I'LL GO KEEP AN EYE ON THE TARGET THE NEXT FLOOR DOWN.
THIS ONE'S IN YOUR HANDS.

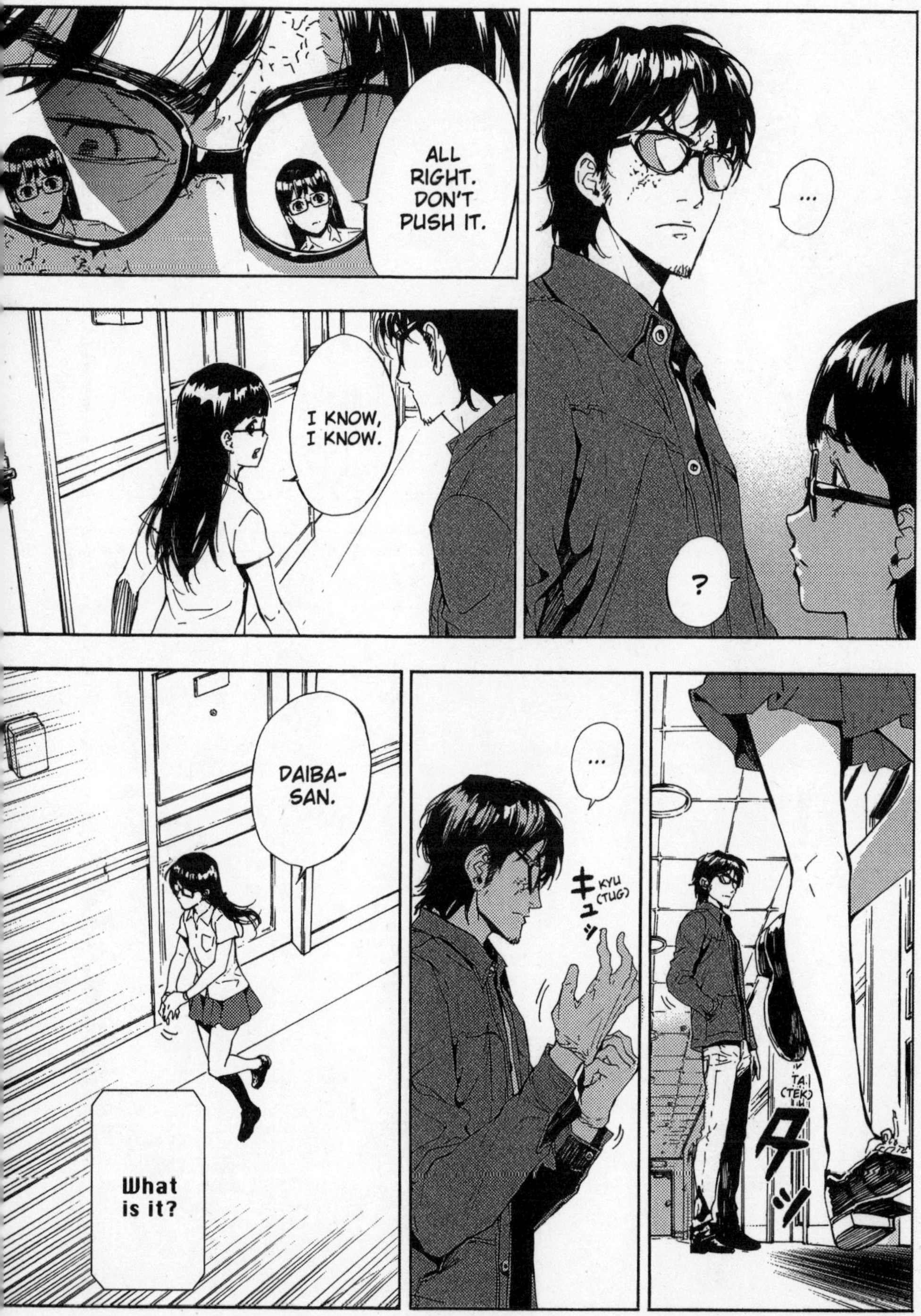
...
?
ALL RIGHT. DON'T PUSH IT.
I KNOW, I KNOW.
タッ
TA (TEK)
...
キュッ
KYU (TUG)
DAIBA-SAN.
What is it?

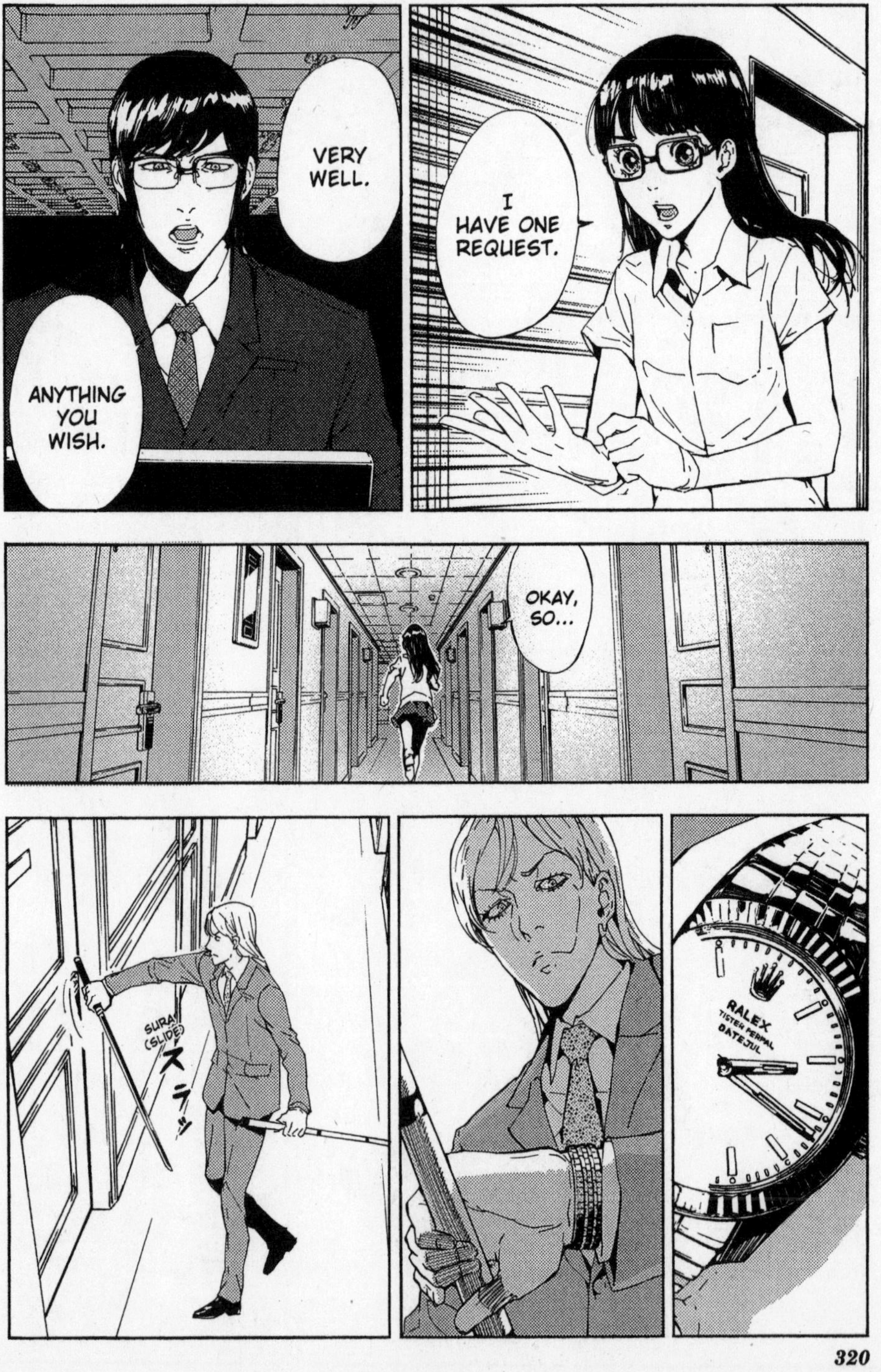
I HAVE ONE REQUEST.
VERY WELL.
ANYTHING YOU WISH.
OKAY, SO...
RALEX
TISTER PERPAL
DATEJUL
SURA! (SLIDE)
スラッ

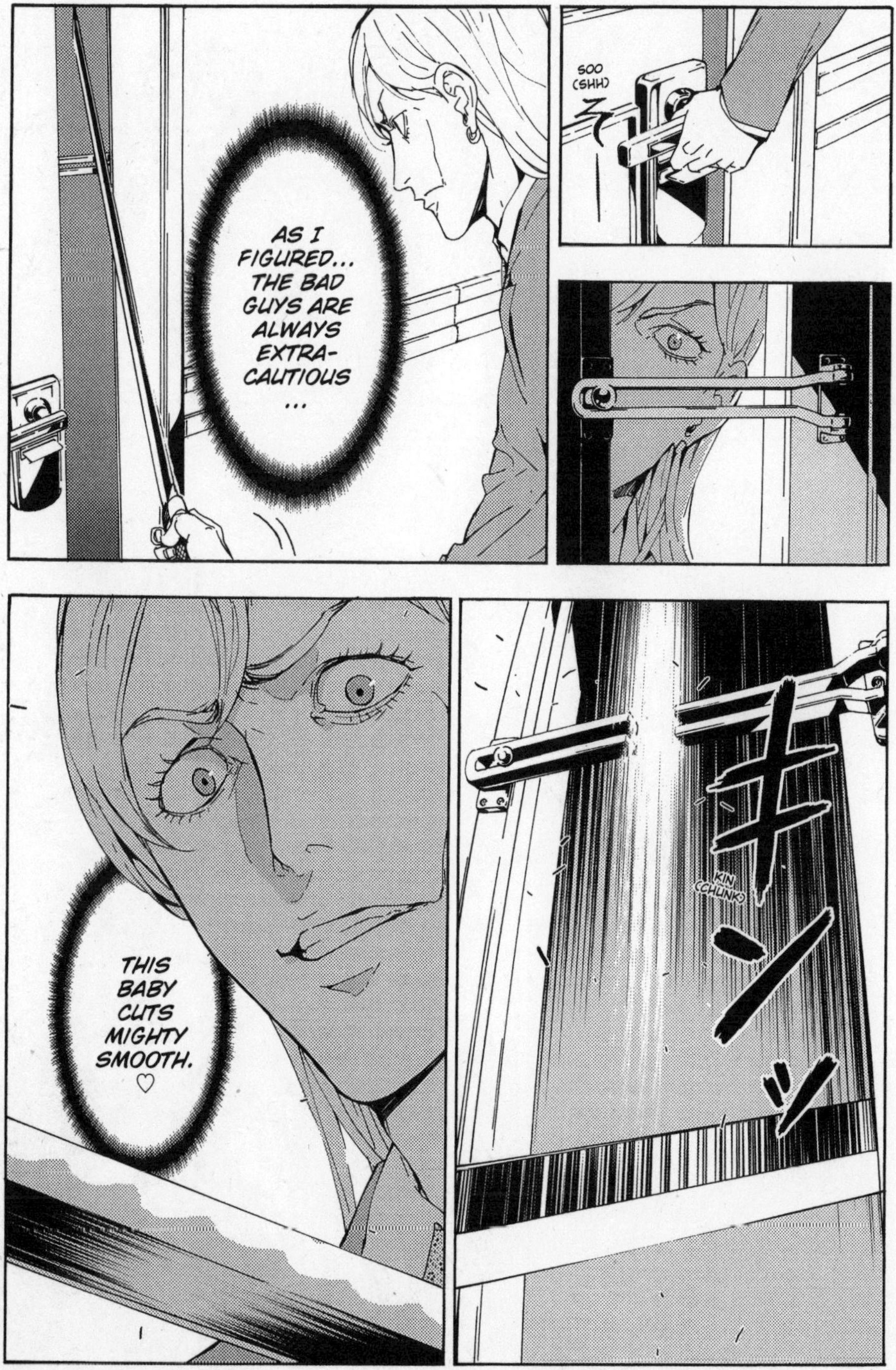
SOO (SHH)
AS I FIGURED... THE BAD GUYS ARE ALWAYS EXTRA-CAUTIOUS...
KIN (CHUNK)
THIS BABY CUTS MIGHTY SMOOTH. ♡

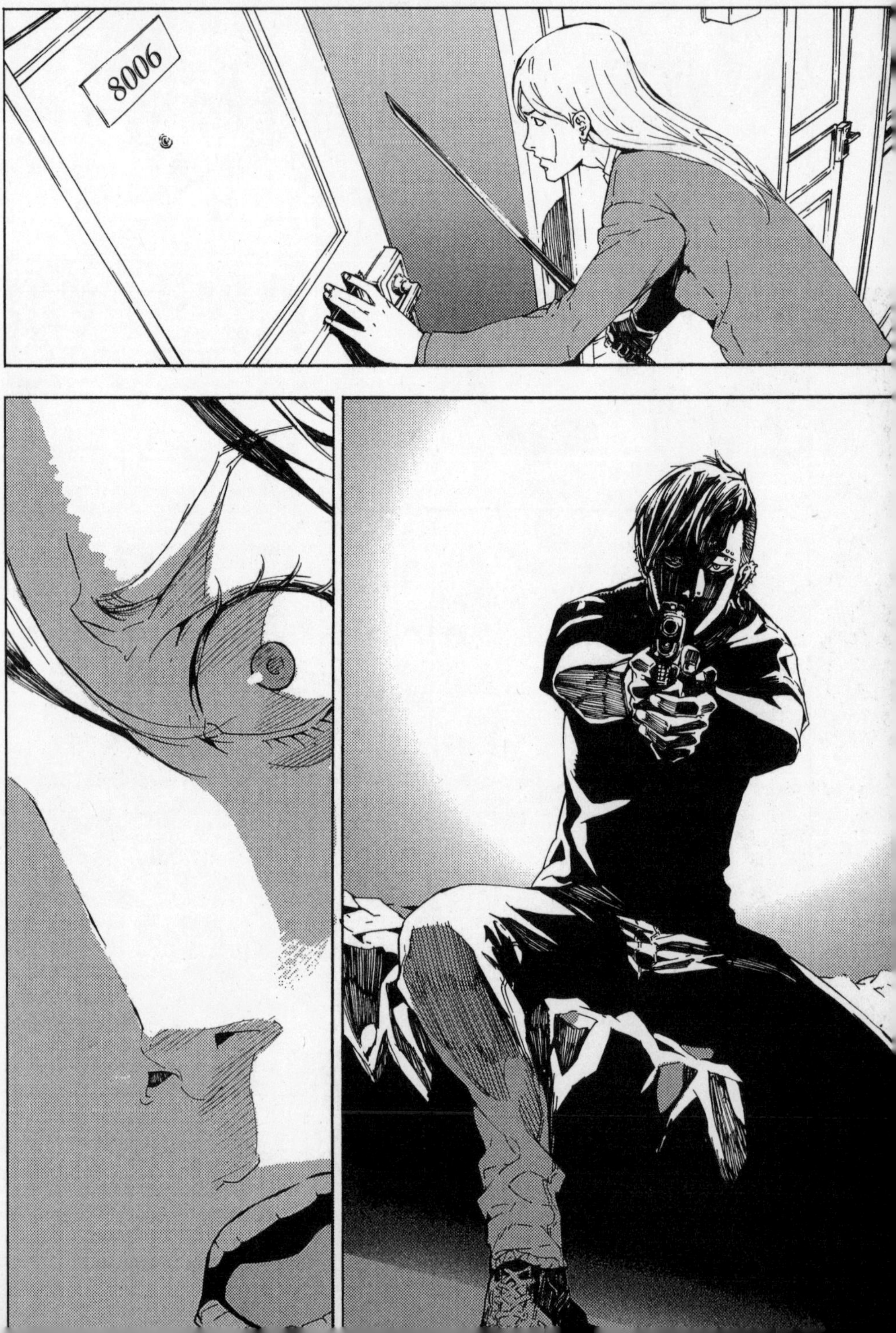
8006

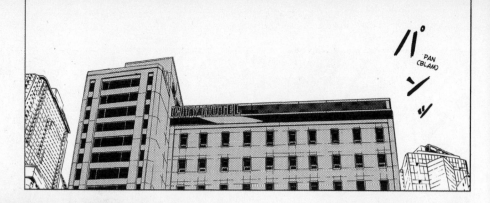

パン
PAN
(BLAM)
ン
ツ

...I
FUCKED
UP...

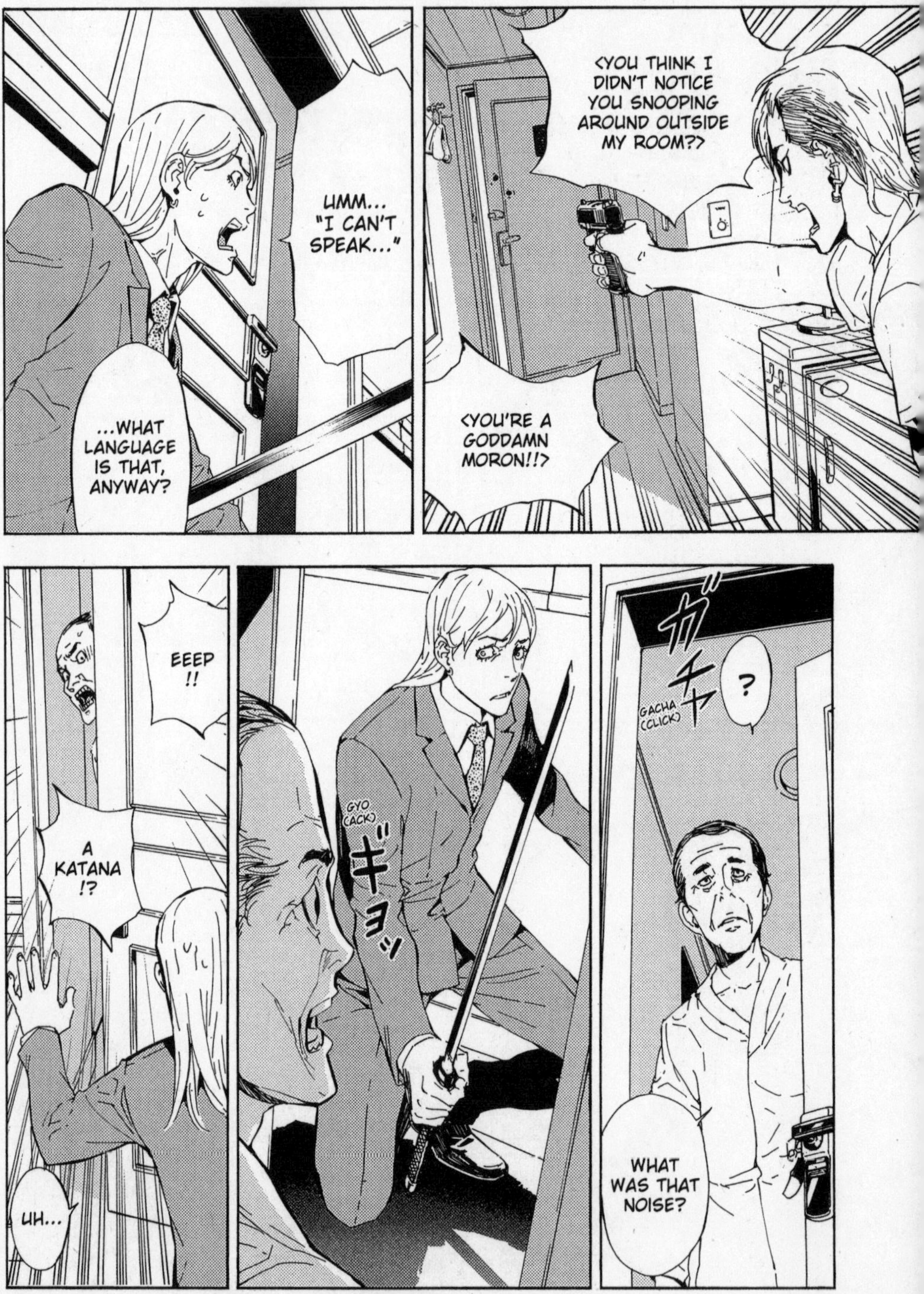
<YOU THINK I DIDN'T NOTICE YOU SNOOPING AROUND OUTSIDE MY ROOM?>
<YOU'RE A GODDAMN MORON!!>
UMM... "I CAN'T SPEAK..."
...WHAT LANGUAGE IS THAT, ANYWAY?
ガチャ
GACHA (CLICK)
?
WHAT WAS THAT NOISE?
ギョッ
GYO (ACK)
EEEP !!
A KATANA !?
UH...

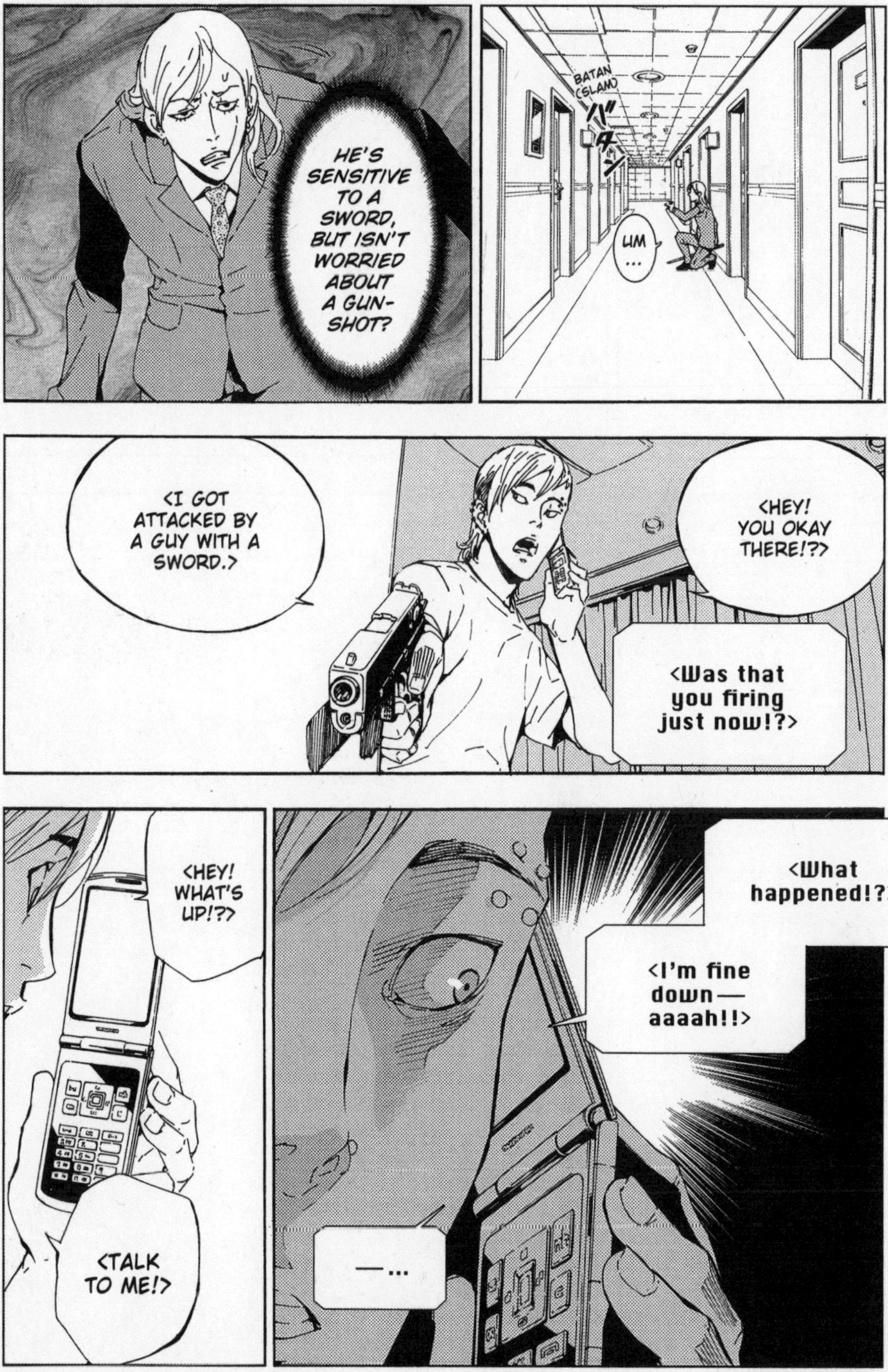
BATAN (SLAM)
バタン
UM ...
HE'S SENSITIVE TO A SWORD, BUT ISN'T WORRIED ABOUT A GUN-SHOT?
<HEY! YOU OKAY THERE!?>
<I GOT ATTACKED BY A GUY WITH A SWORD.>
<Was that you firing just now!?>
<What happened!?>
<I'm fine down— aaaah!!>
—...
<HEY! WHAT'S UP!?>
<TALK TO ME!>

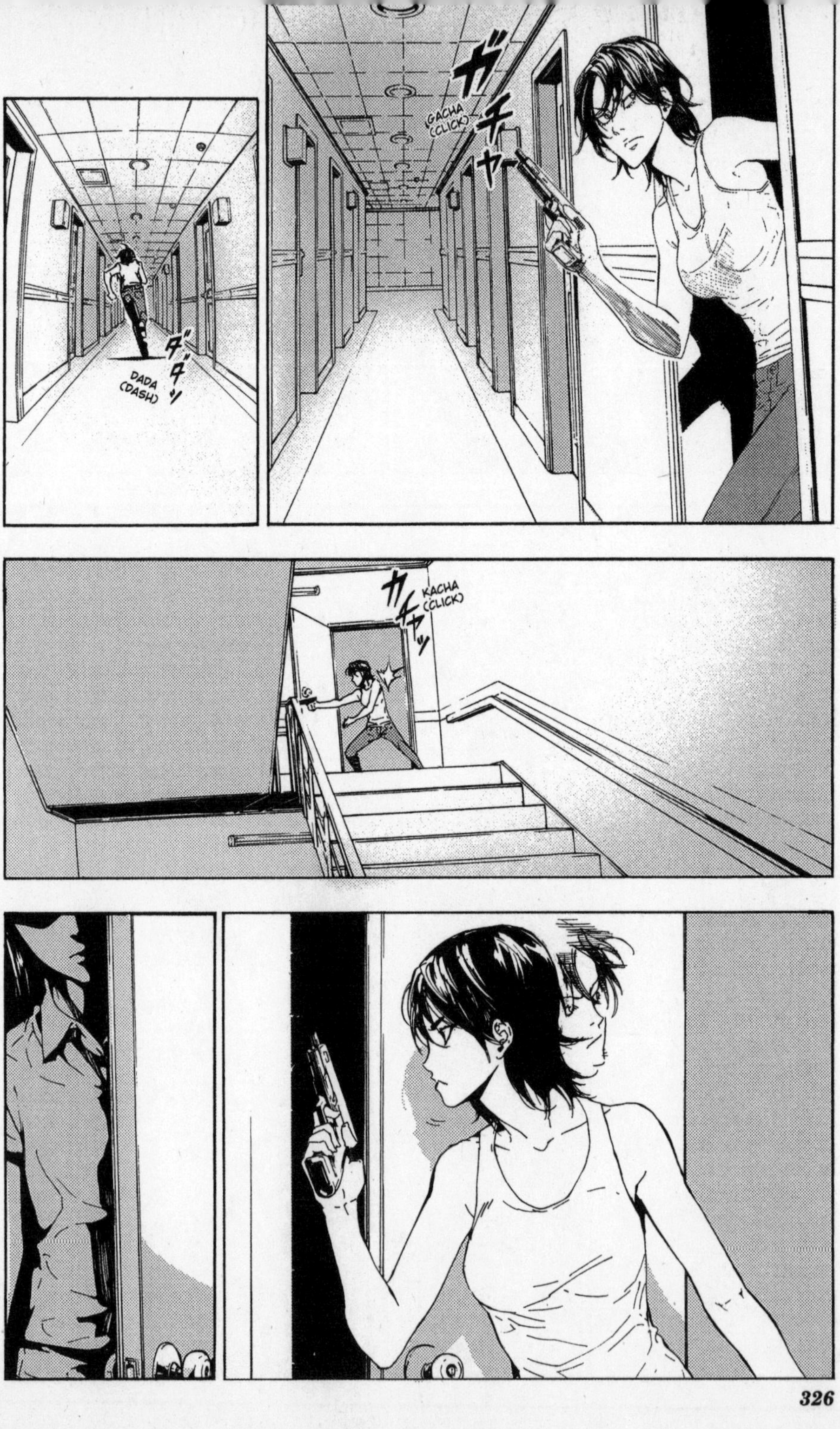
ガチャ
GACHA (CLICK)
ダダッ
DADA (DASH)
カチャッ
KACHA (CLICK)

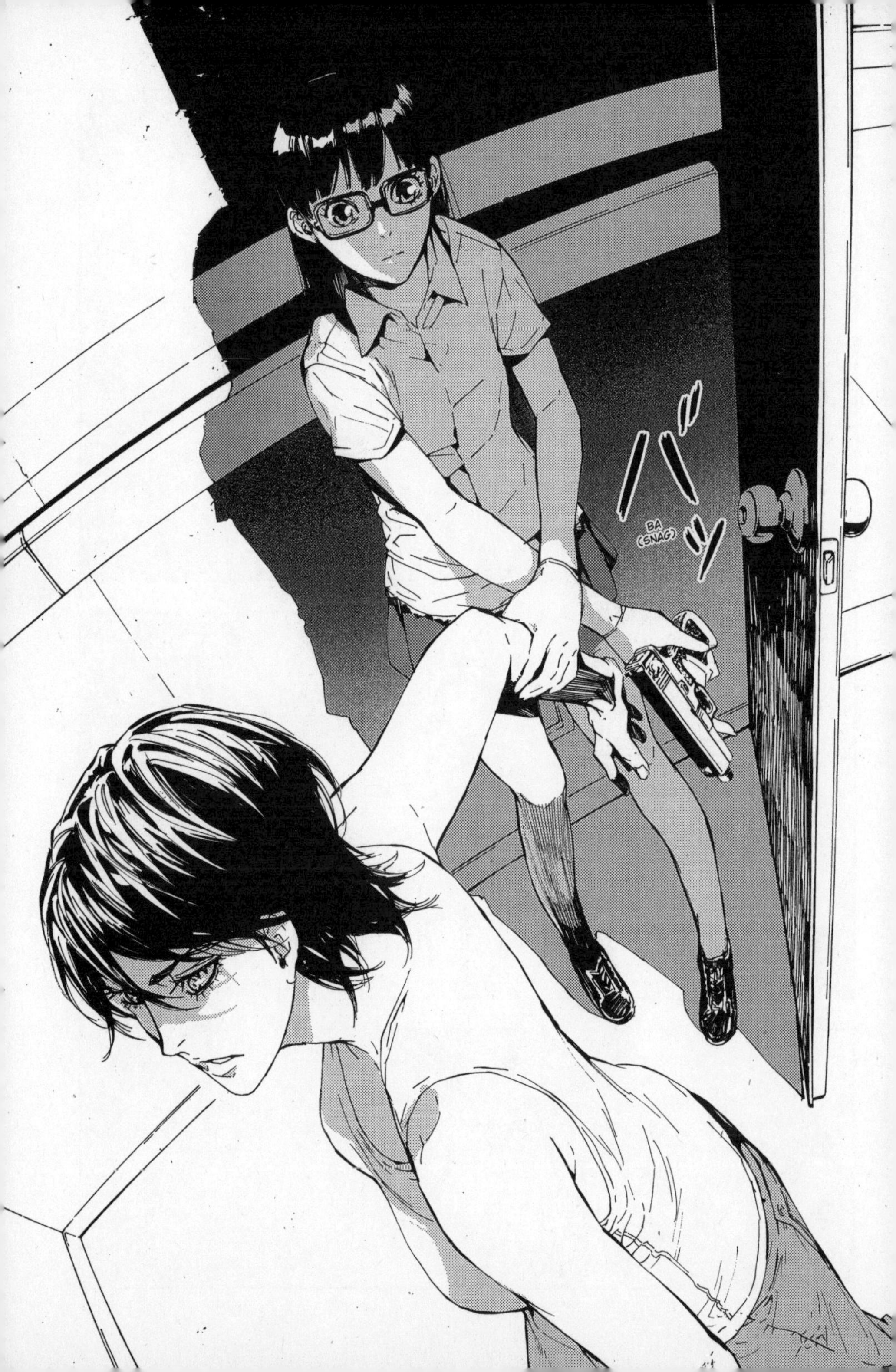
バッ
BA
(SNAG)

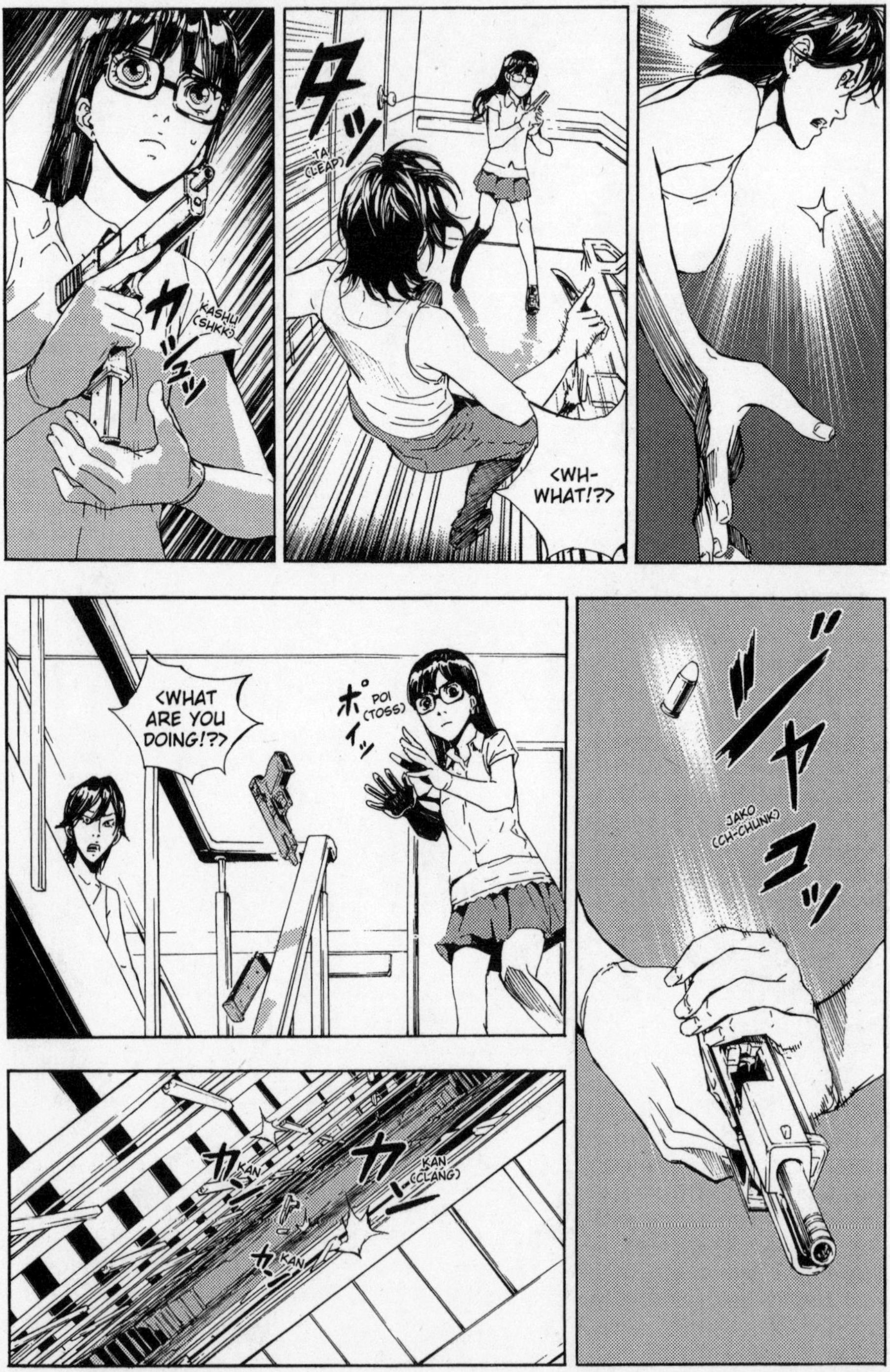

タッ
TA (LEAP)
<WH-WHAT!?>
カシュッ
KASHU (SHKK)
ジャコッ
JAKO (CH-CHUNK)
ポイッ
POI (TOSS)
<WHAT ARE YOU DOING!?>
カーン
KAN (CLANG)
KAN
KAN

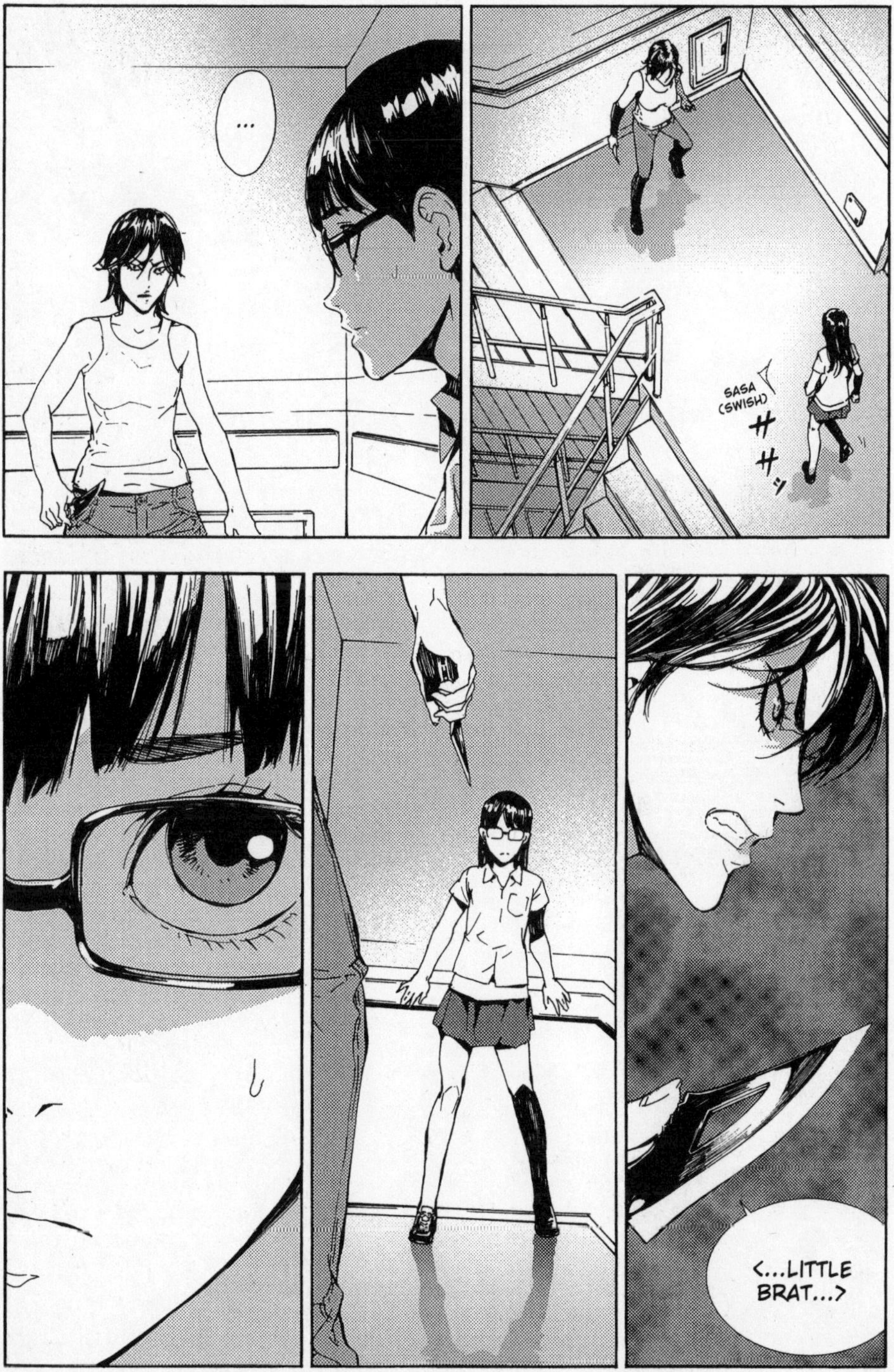
SASA (SWISH)
ササッ
...
<...LITTLE BRAT...>

Until Death do us Part

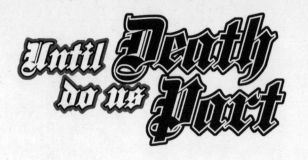

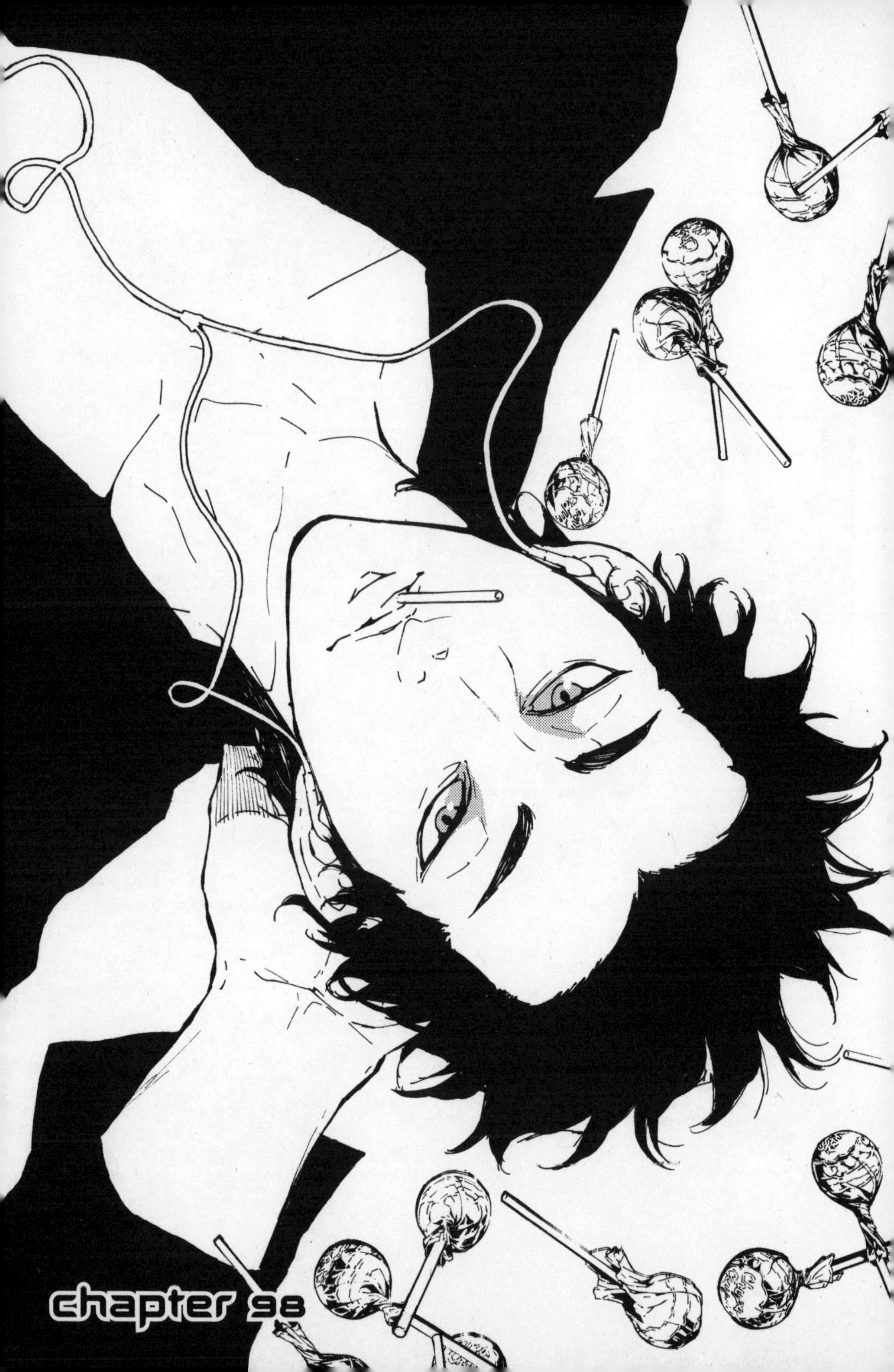
chapter 98

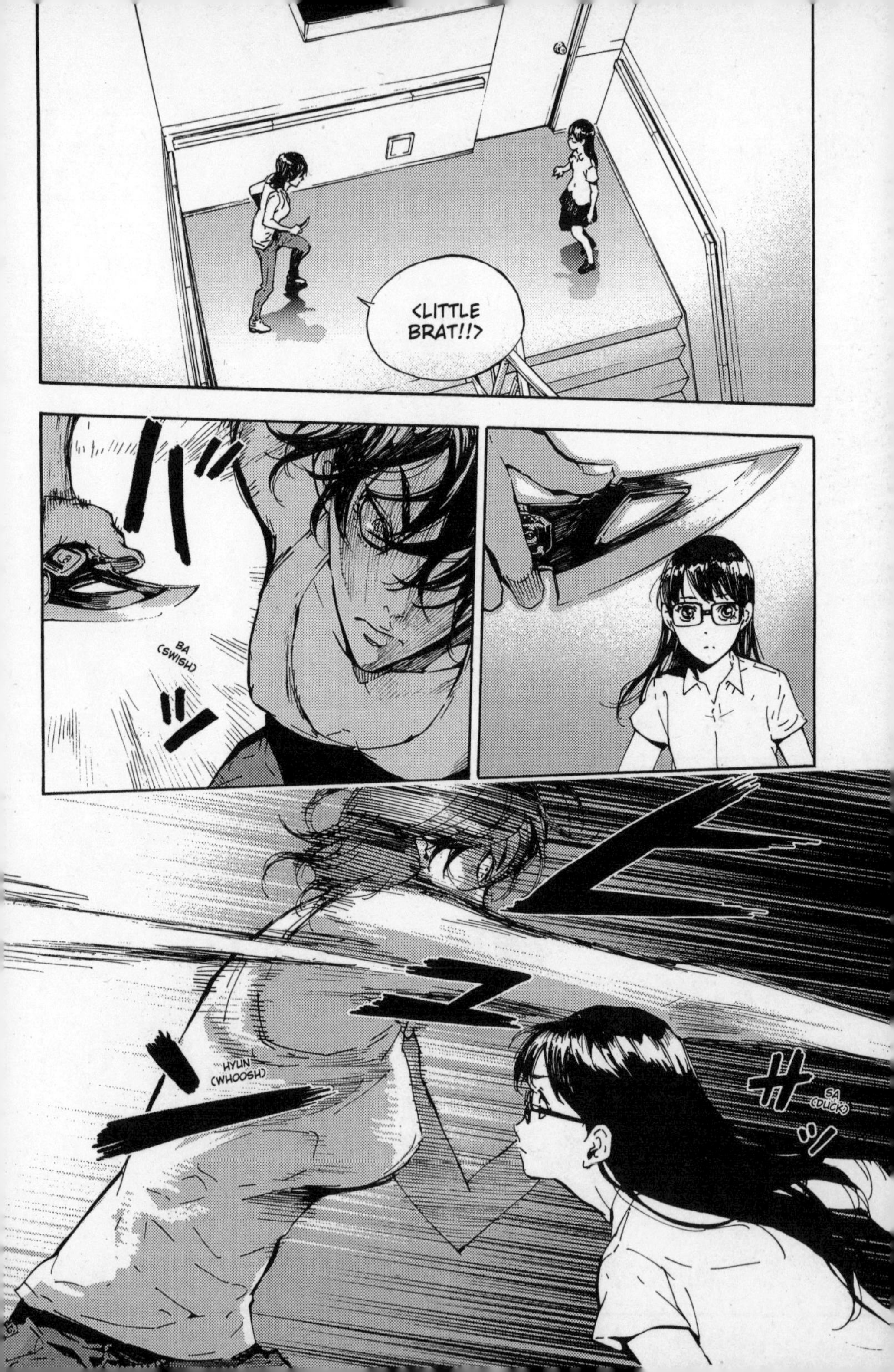
<LITTLE BRAT!!>
BA (SWISH)
SA (DUCK)
HYUN (WHOOSH)

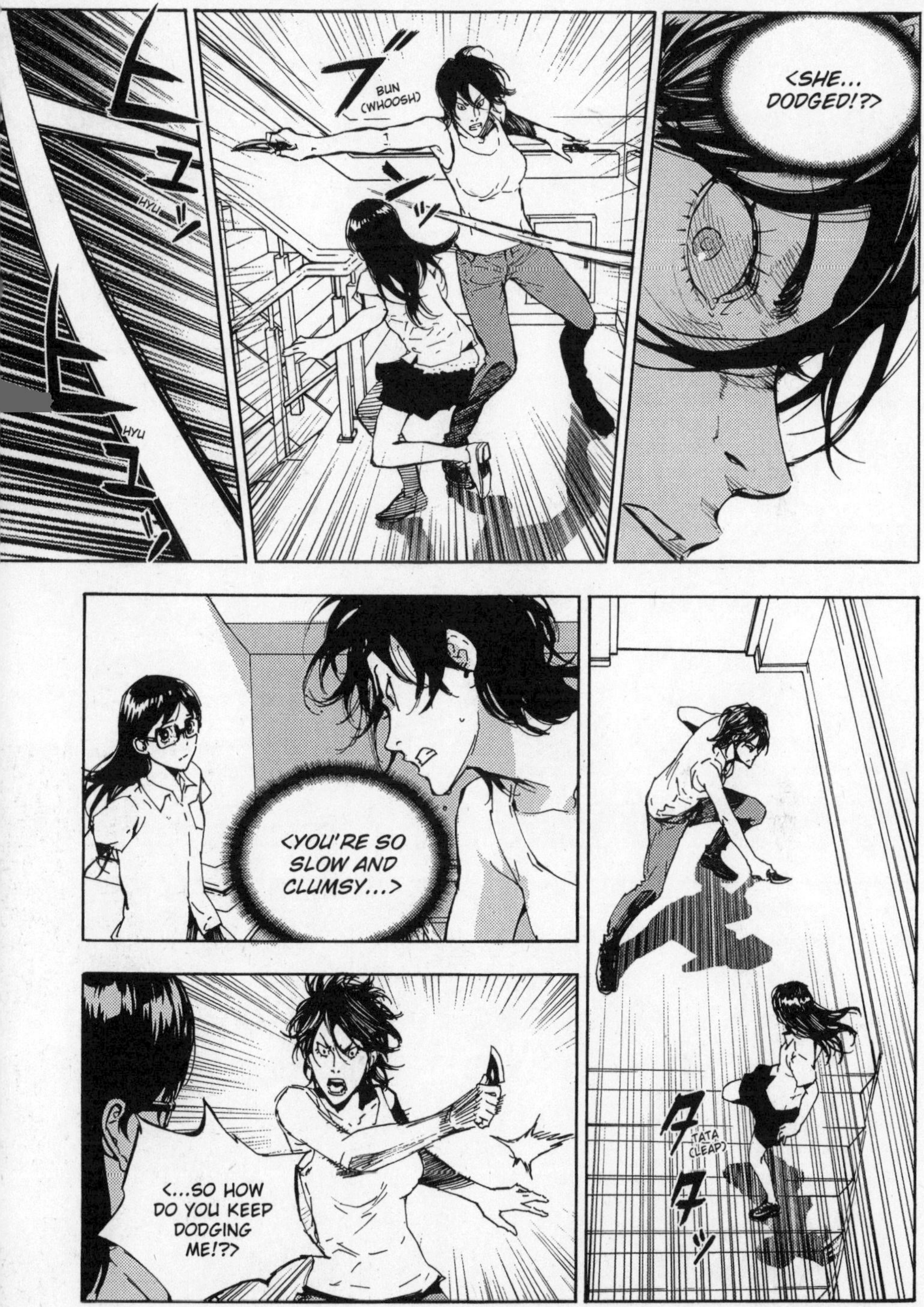

<SHE... DODGED!?>
BUN (WHOOSH)
HYU
HYU
TATA (LEAP)
<YOU'RE SO SLOW AND CLUMSY...>
<...SO HOW DO YOU KEEP DODGING ME!?>

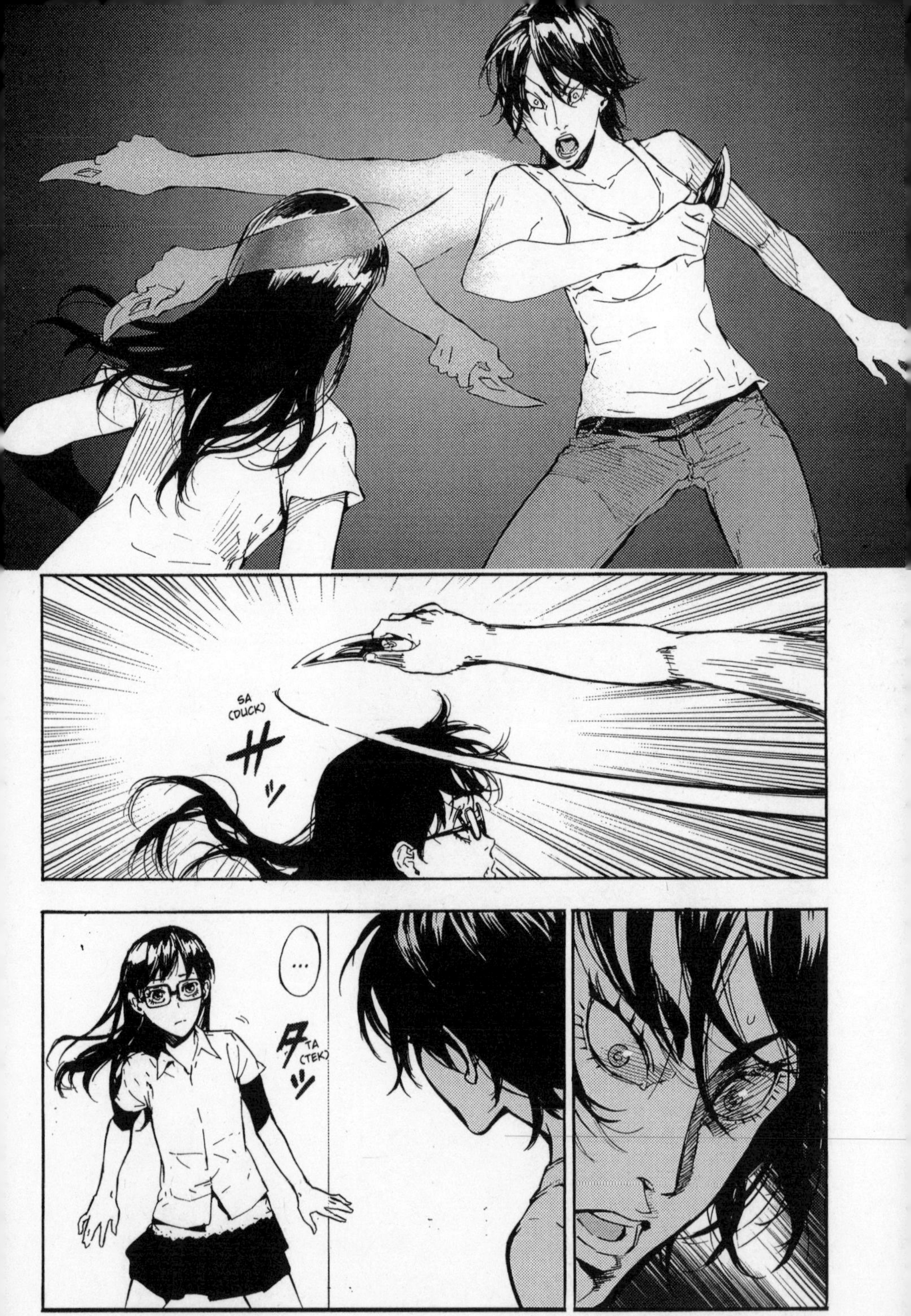
SA
(DUCK)
サッ
...
タッ
TA
(TEK)

I NEED TO KEEP HER OCCUPIED LONGER...

<LITTLE... BITCH!>

8F

(CHA (CHK))

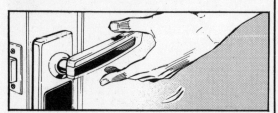

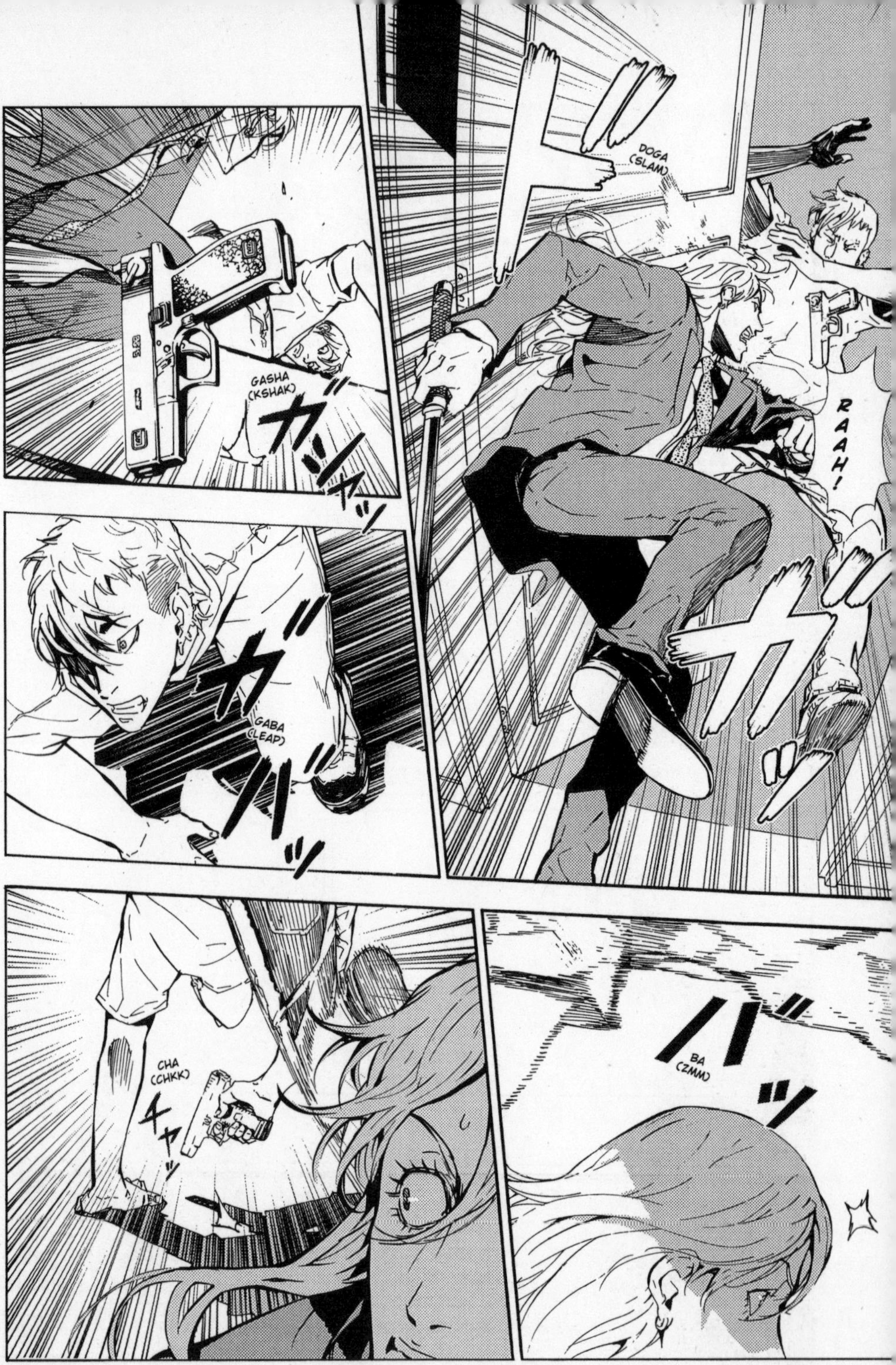
DOGA (SLAM)
RAAAH!
GASHA (KSHAK)
GABA (LEAP)
BA (ZMM)
CHA (CHKK)

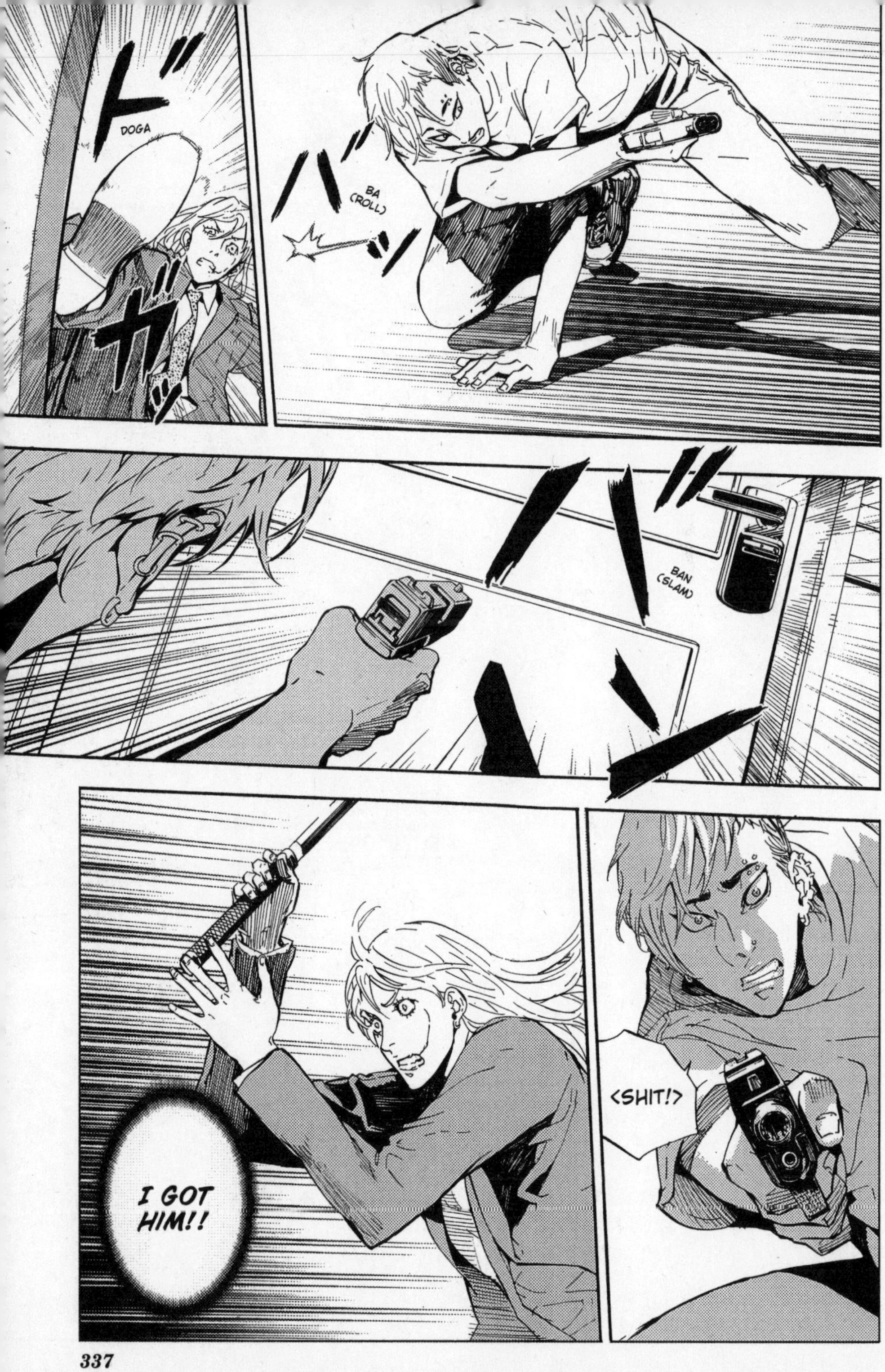
BA (ROLL)
DOGA
BAN (SLAM)
<SHIT!>
I GOT HIM!!

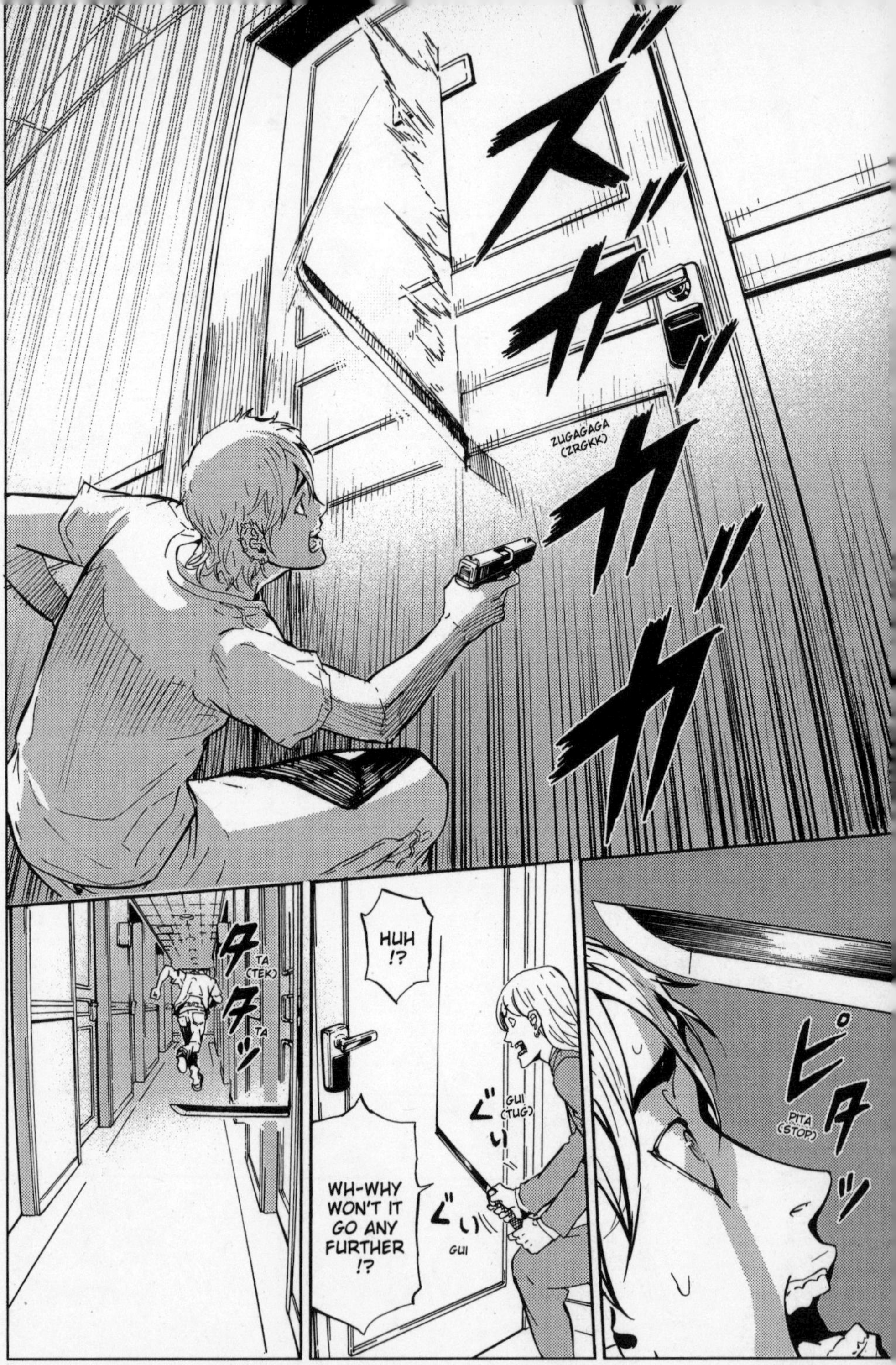
ズガガガ
ZUGAGAGA (ZRGKK)
ピタッ
PITA (STOP)
HUH !?
ぐい
GUI (TUG)
ぐい
GUI
WH-WHY WON'T IT GO ANY FURTHER !?
タタッ
TA (TEK)
TA

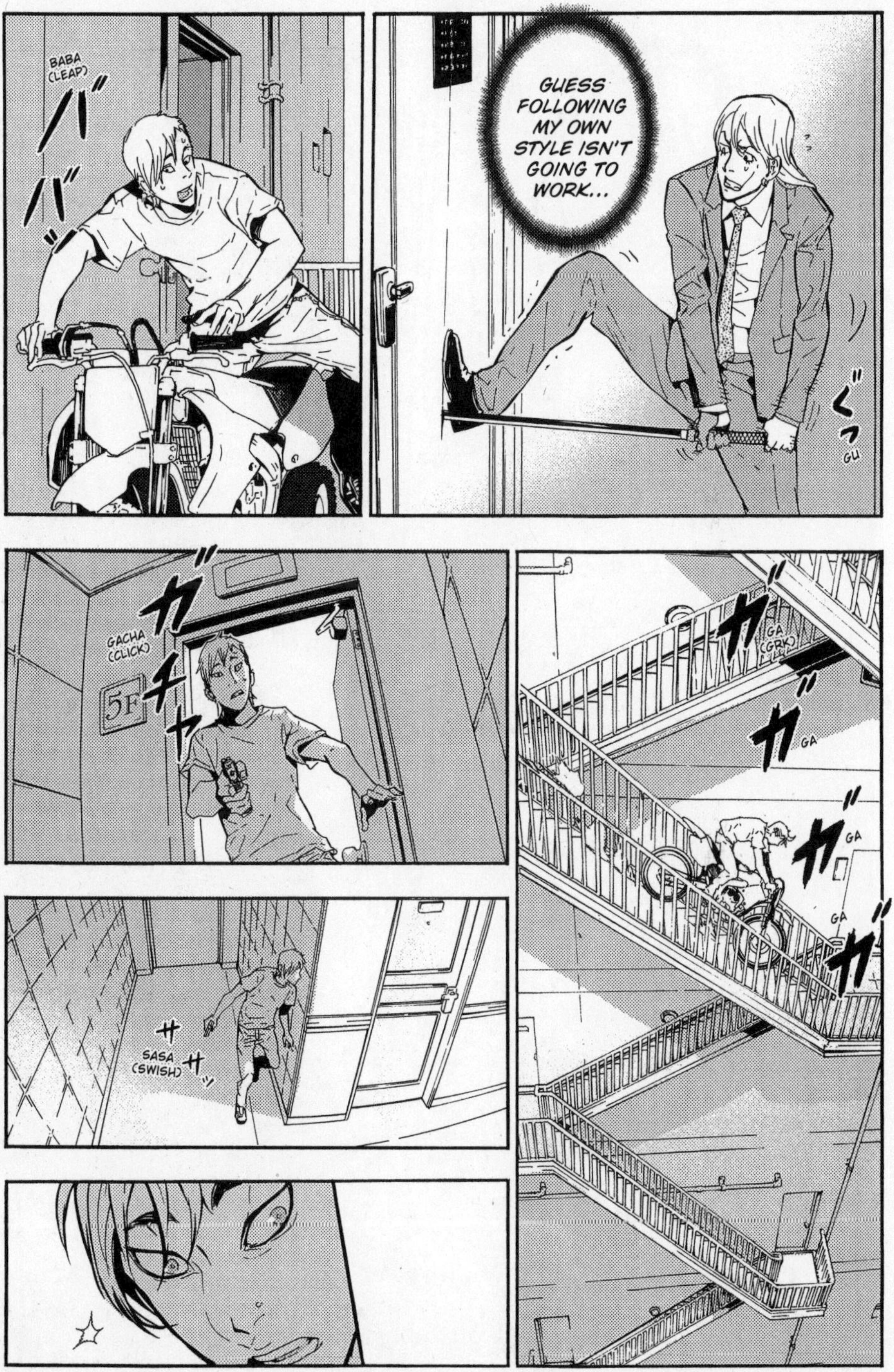
GUESS FOLLOWING MY OWN STYLE ISN'T GOING TO WORK...
ぐっ
GU
バババ
BABA (LEAP)
ガガガガ
GA (GRK)
GA
GA
GA
ガチャ
GACHA (CLICK)
ササッ
SASA (SWISH)
5F

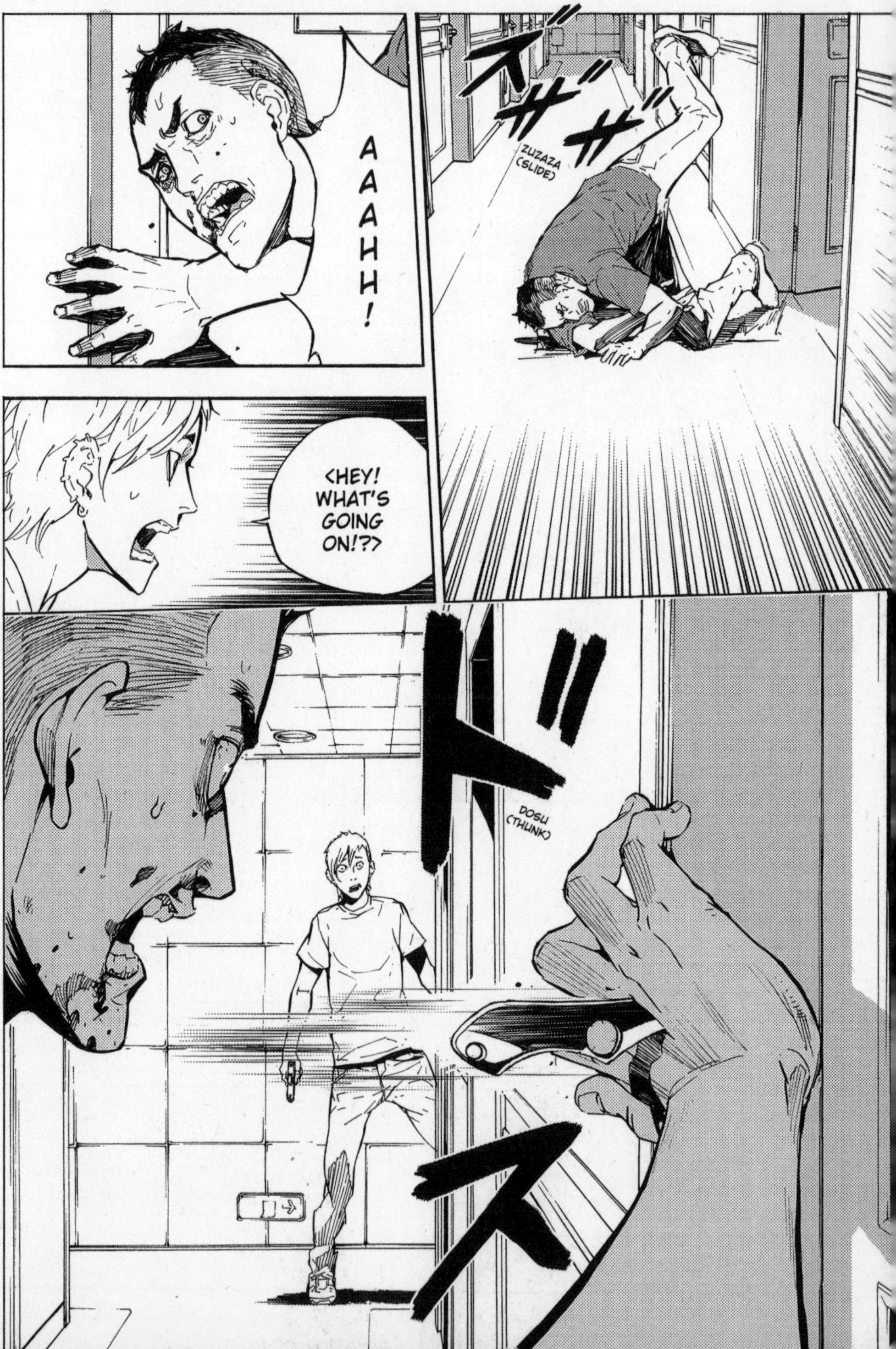
ZUZAZA (SLIDE)
AAAAHH!
<HEY! WHAT'S GOING ON!?>
DOSU (THUNK)

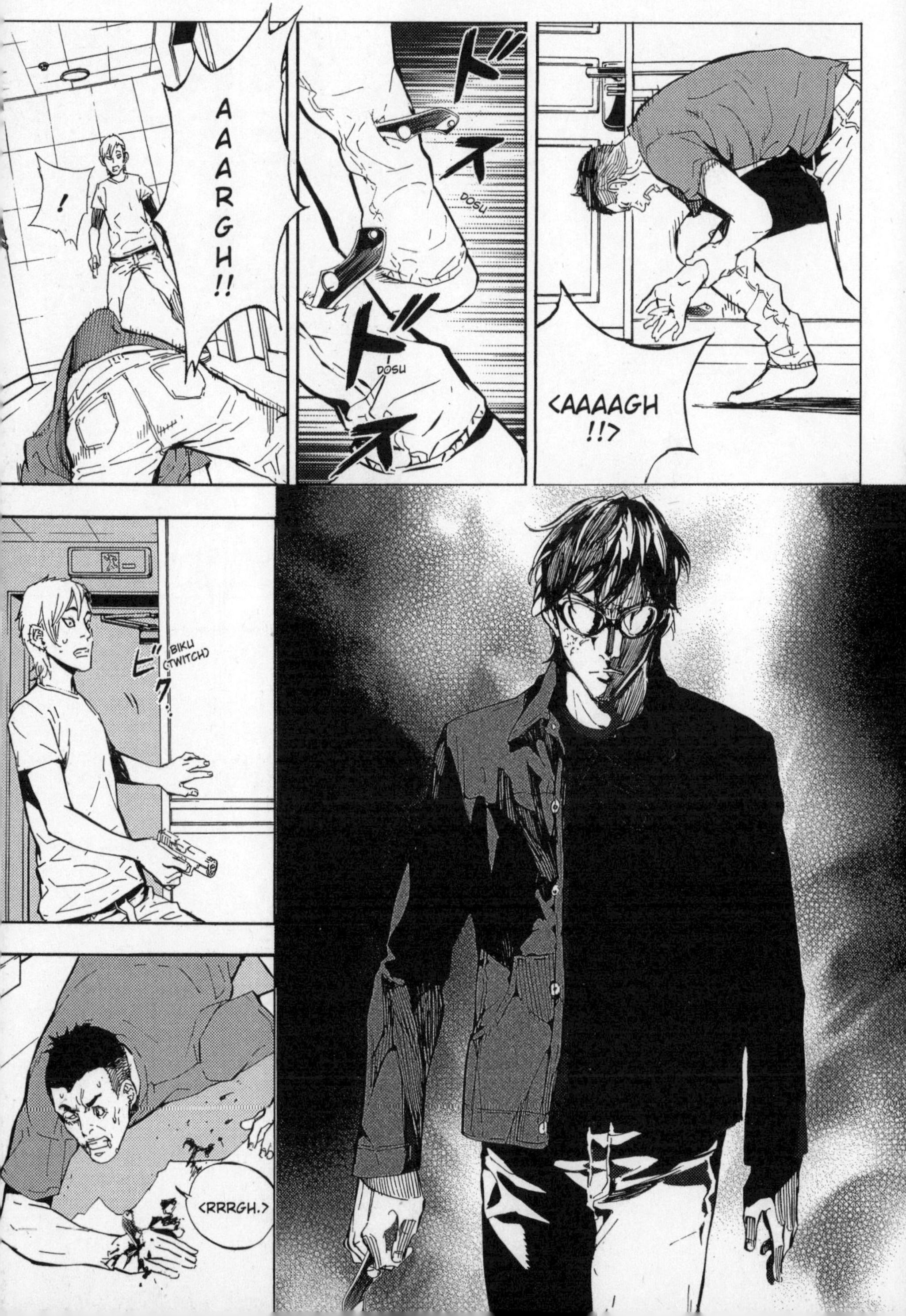

<AAAAGH !!>
ドス
DOSU
ドス
DOSU
!
AAAARGH!!
ビク
BIKU (TWITCH)
<RRRGH.>

AAAH! AAGHH!!

グッ

ジグッ

GUSHA (CRUNCH)

THE PEOPLE YOU SHOT SUFFERED FAR WORSE.

YOU'RE NEXT...

...

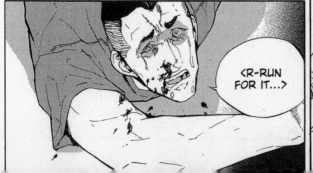

<R-RUN FOR IT...>

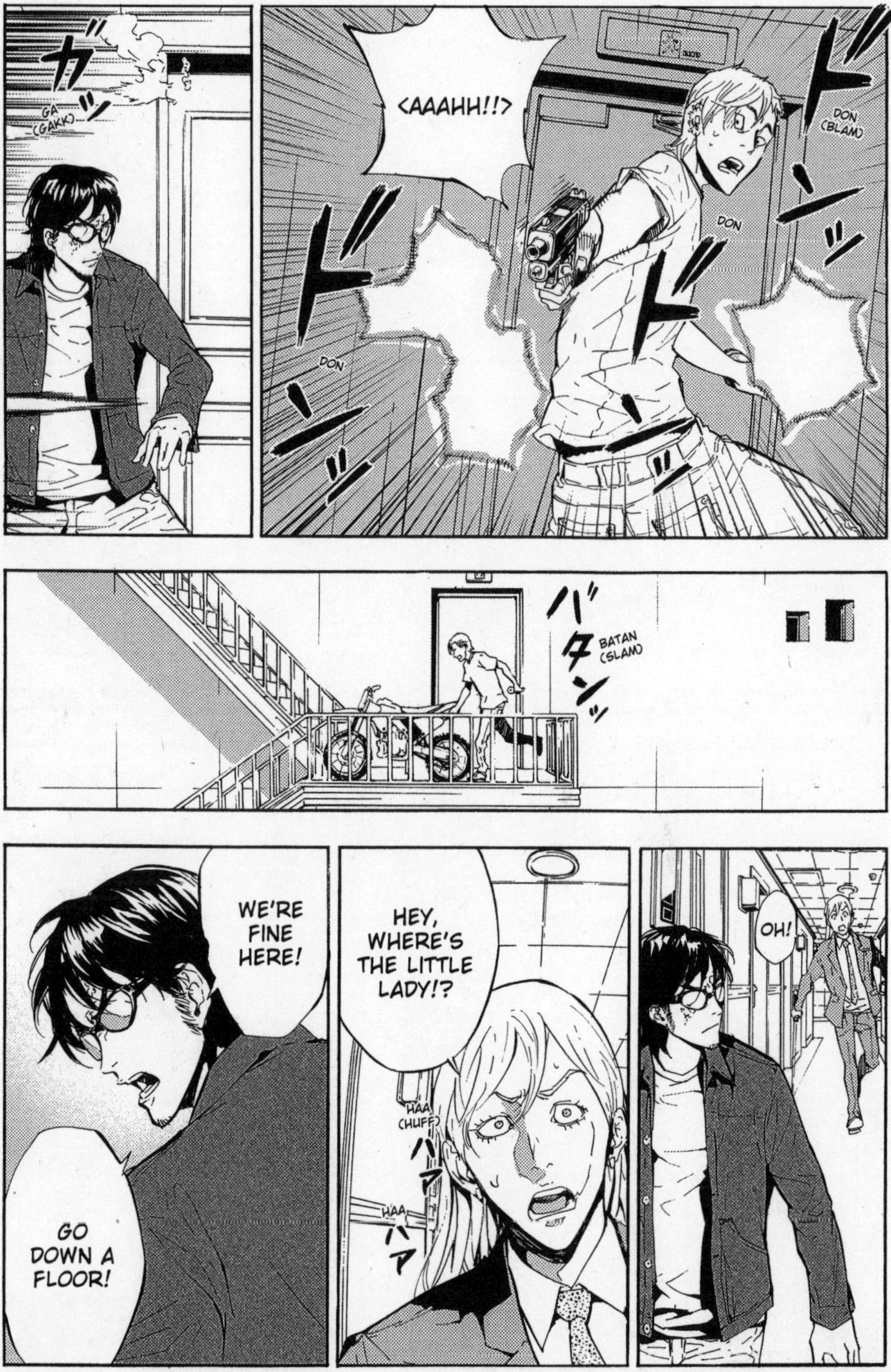
DON (BLAM)
<AAAHH!!>
DON
DON
GA (GAKK)
BATAN (SLAM)
OH!
HEY, WHERE'S THE LITTLE LADY!?
HAA (HUFF)
HAA
WE'RE FINE HERE!
GO DOWN A FLOOR!

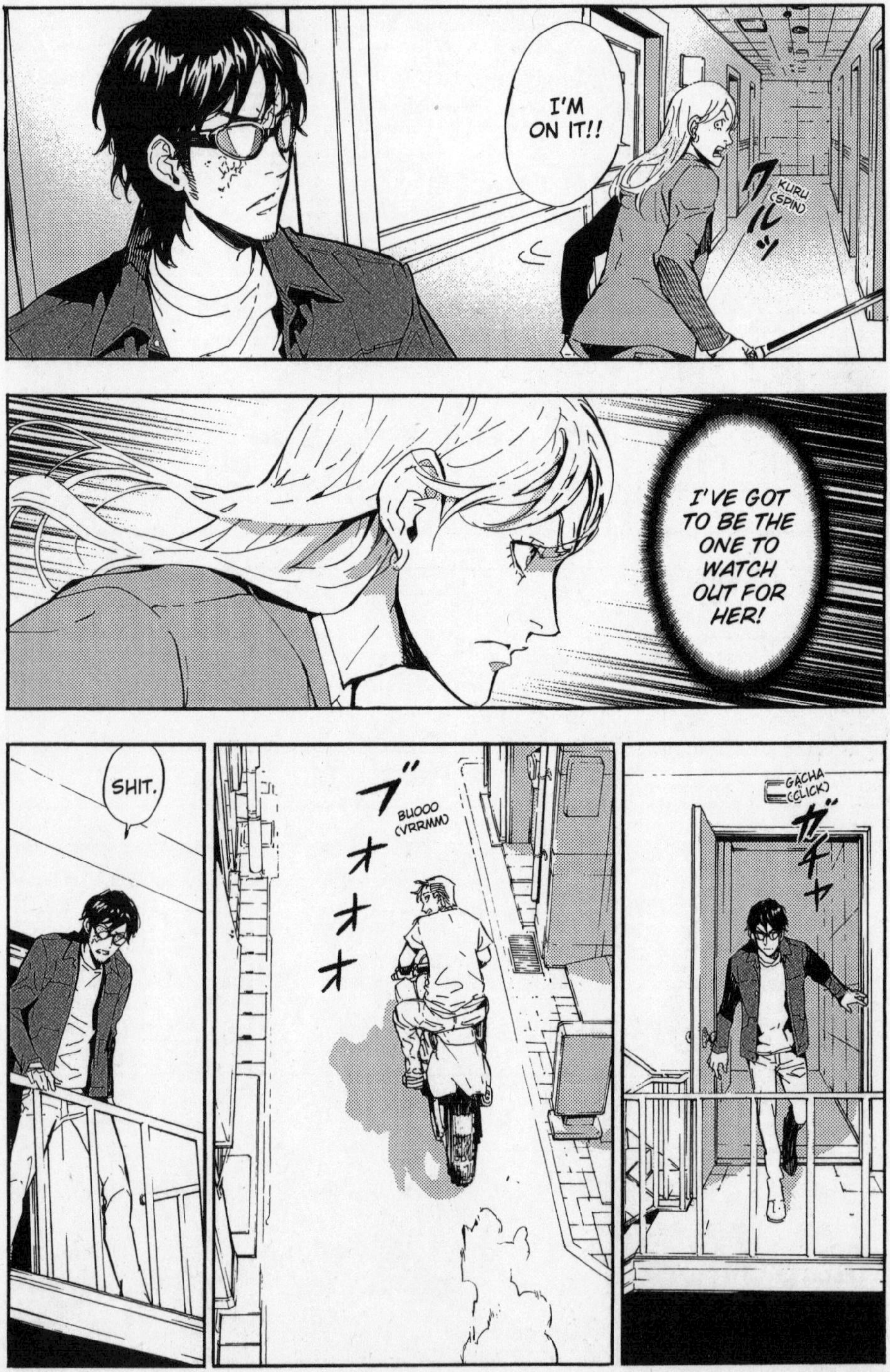
I'M ON IT!!
KURU (SPIN)
クルッ
I'VE GOT TO BE THE ONE TO WATCH OUT FOR HER!
GACHA (CLICK)
ガチャ
BUOOO (VRRMM)
ブォオオ
SHIT.

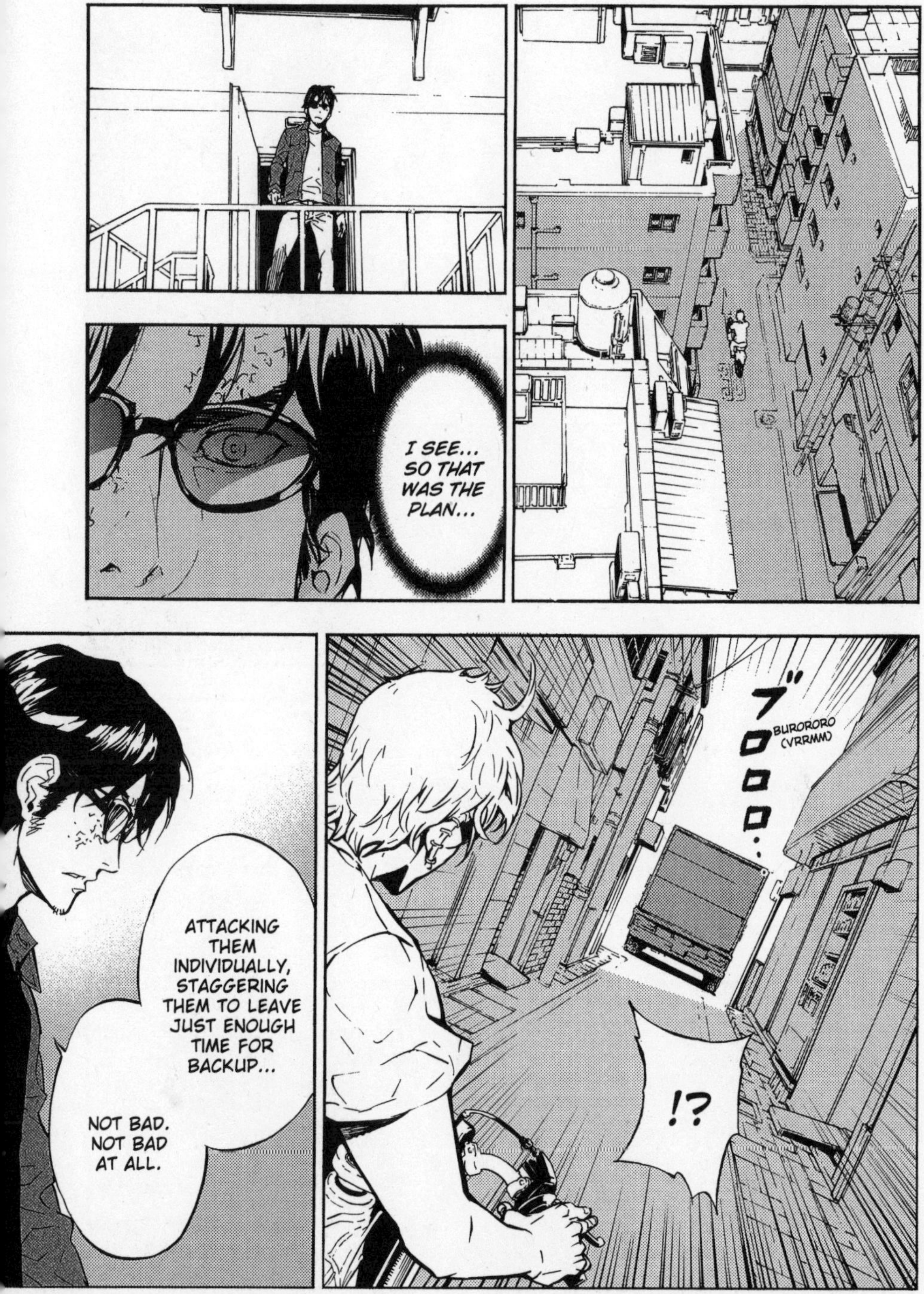
I SEE... SO THAT WAS THE PLAN...
ブロロロ..
BURORORO (VRRMM)
!?
ATTACKING THEM INDIVIDUALLY, STAGGERING THEM TO LEAVE JUST ENOUGH TIME FOR BACKUP...
NOT BAD. NOT BAD AT ALL.

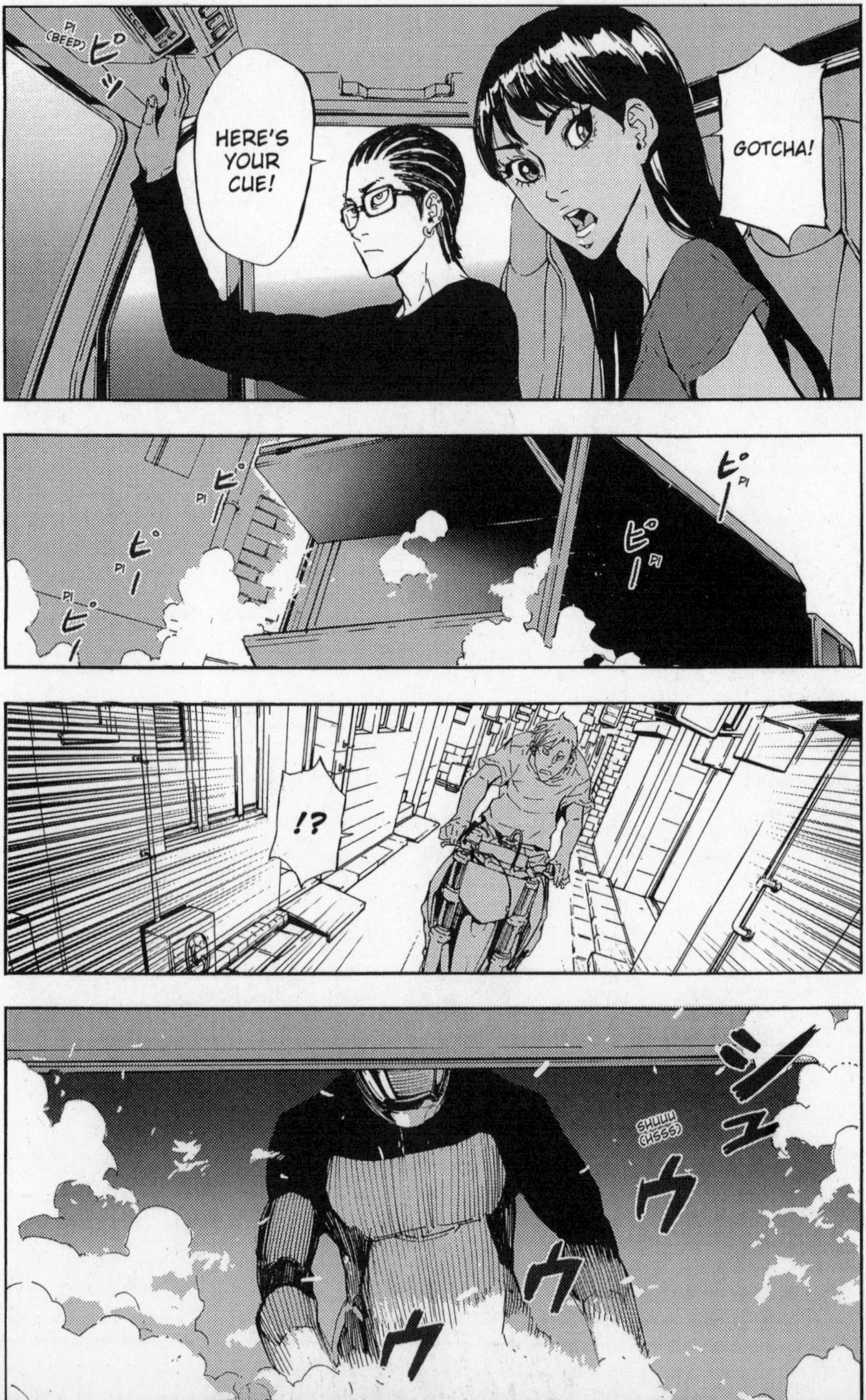
GOTCHA!
HERE'S YOUR CUE!
ピッ
PI (BEEP)
ピー
PI
ピー
PI
ピー
PI
ピー
PI
!?
シュウウウ
SHUUU (HSSS)

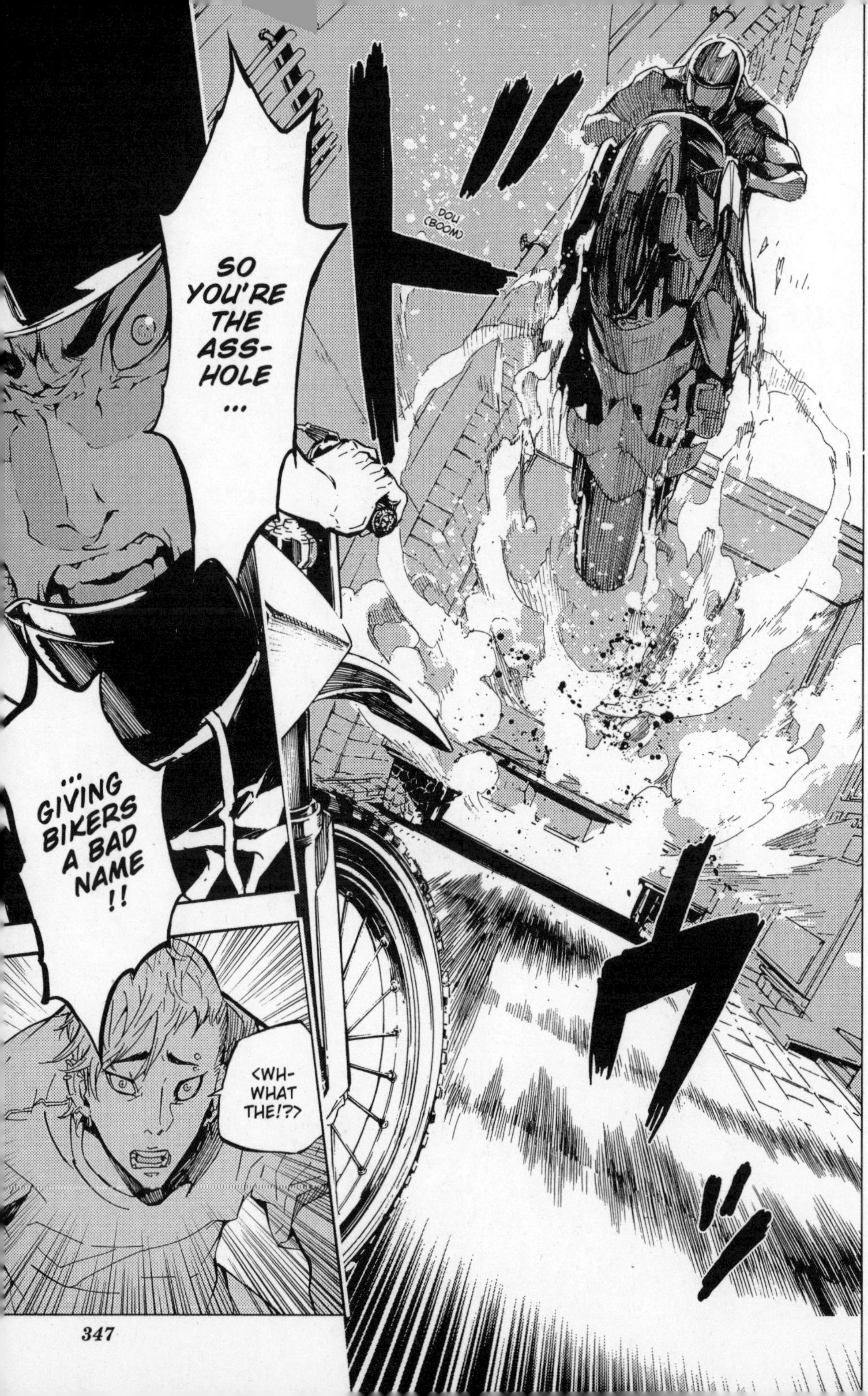
DOU (BOOM)
SO YOU'RE THE ASS-HOLE ...
... GIVING BIKERS A BAD NAME !!
<WH-WHAT THE!?>

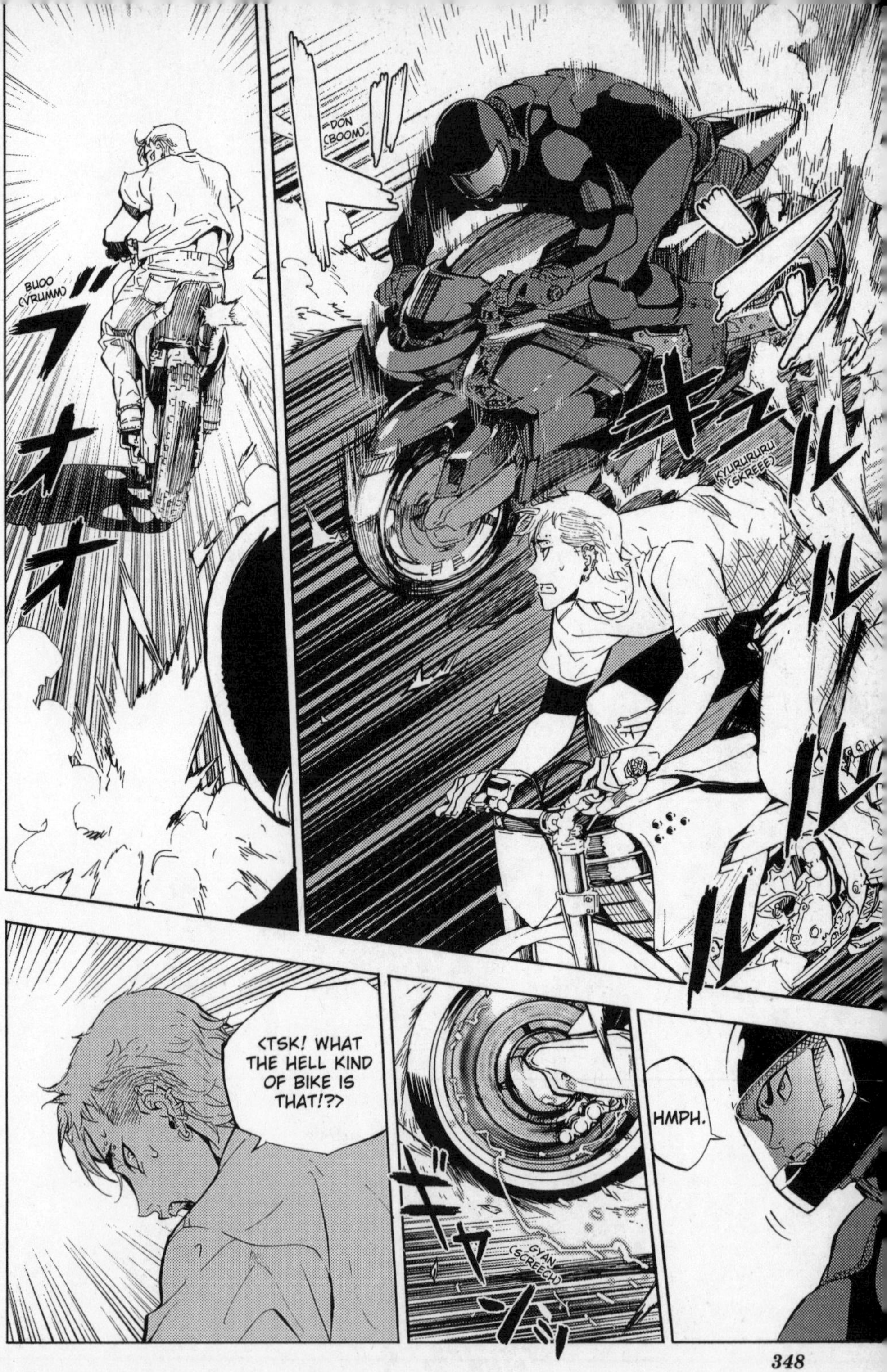
DON (BOOM)
KYURURURU (SKREEE)
BUOO (VRUMM)
HMPH.
GYAN (SCREECH)
<TSK! WHAT THE HELL KIND OF BIKE IS THAT!?>

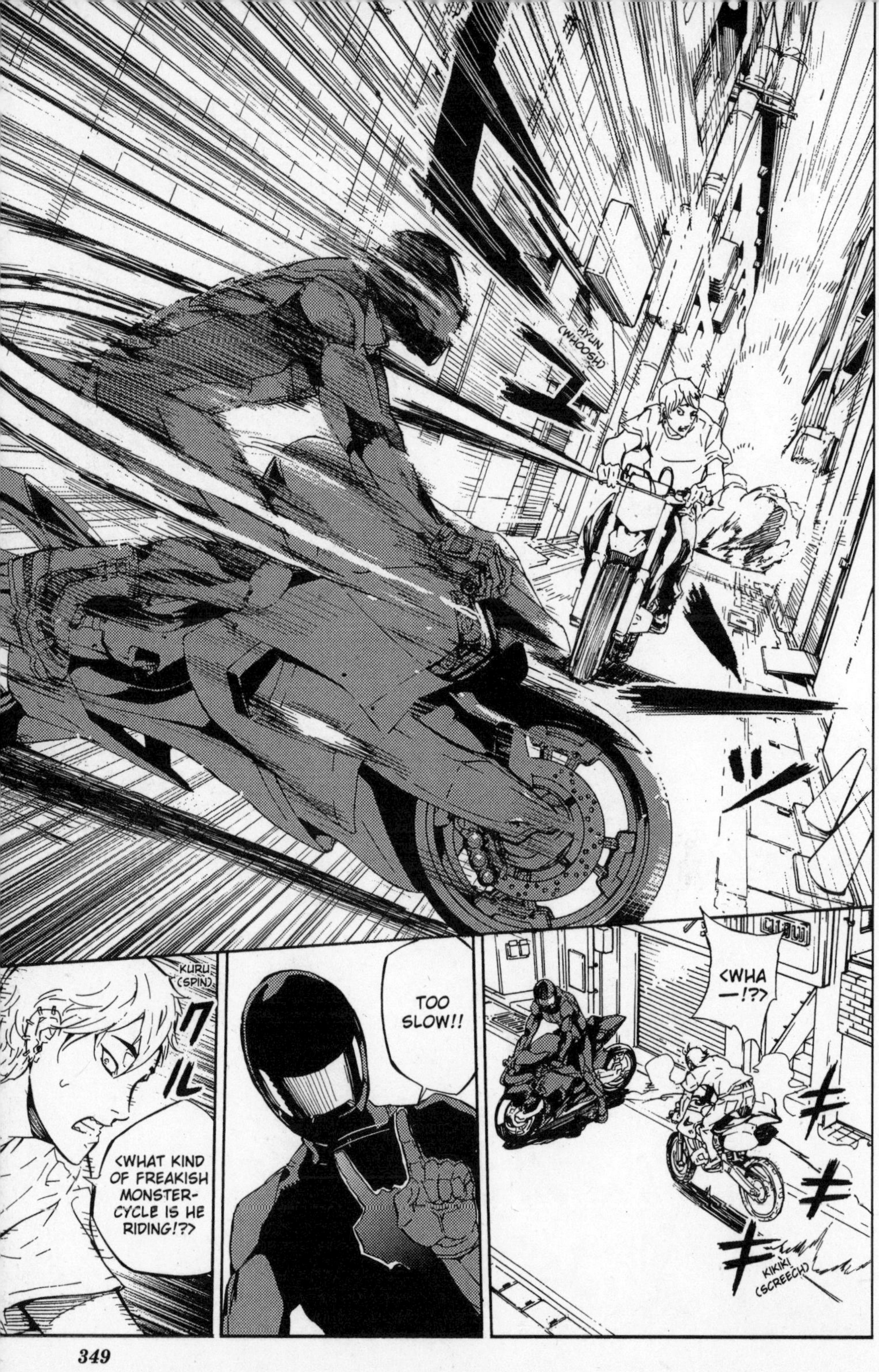
HYUN (WHOOSH)
<WHA—!?>
KIKIKI (SCREECH)
TOO SLOW!!
KURU (SPIN)
<WHAT KIND OF FREAKISH MONSTER-CYCLE IS HE RIDING!?>

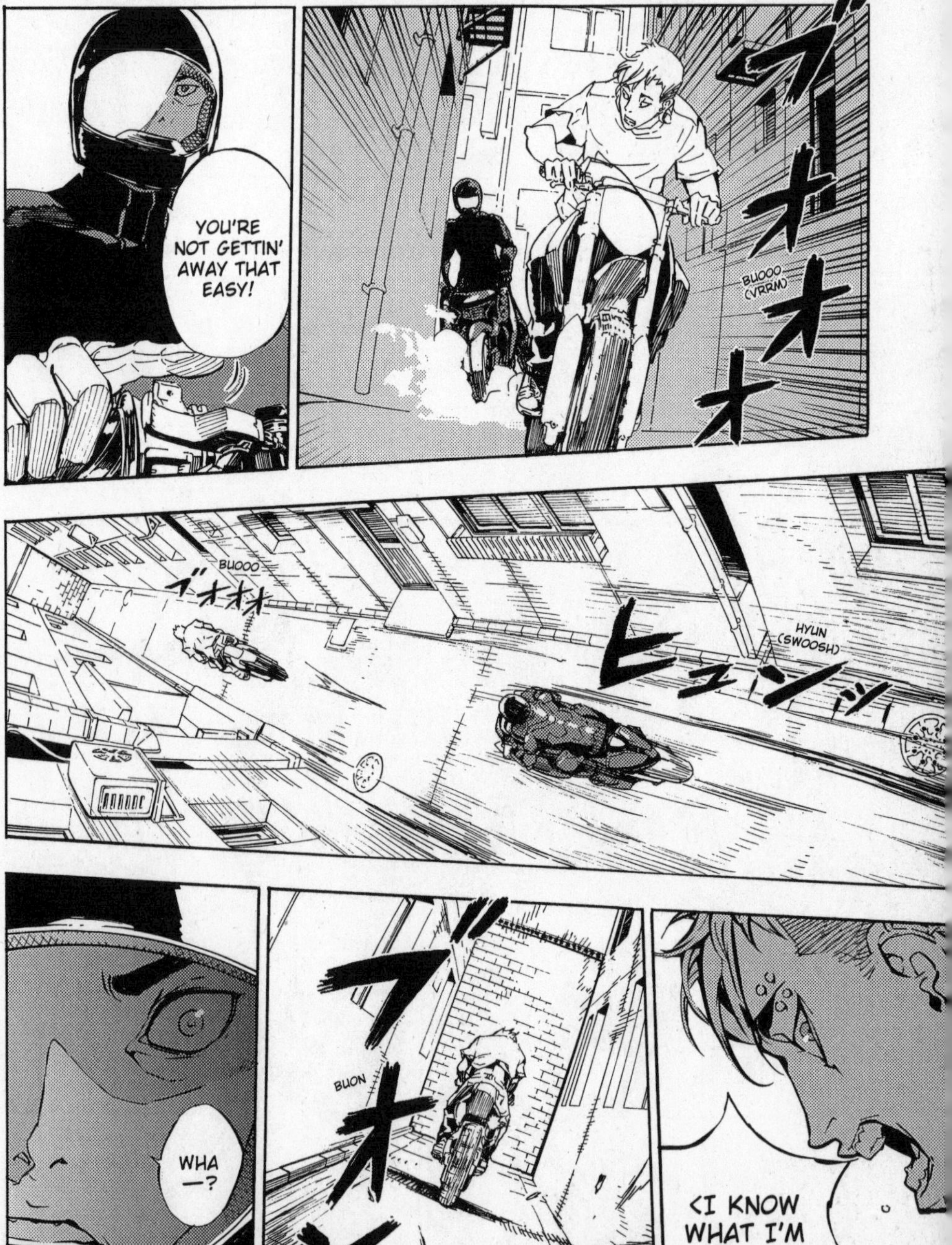
ブオオオ
BUOOO (VRRM)
YOU'RE NOT GETTIN' AWAY THAT EASY!
ヒュンッ
HYUN (SWOOSH)
ブオオオ
BUOOO
<I KNOW WHAT I'M DOING TOO!>
ブオン
BUON
WHA—?

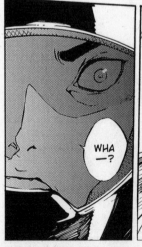

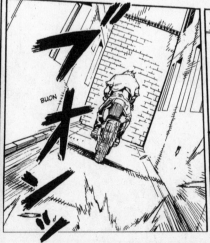

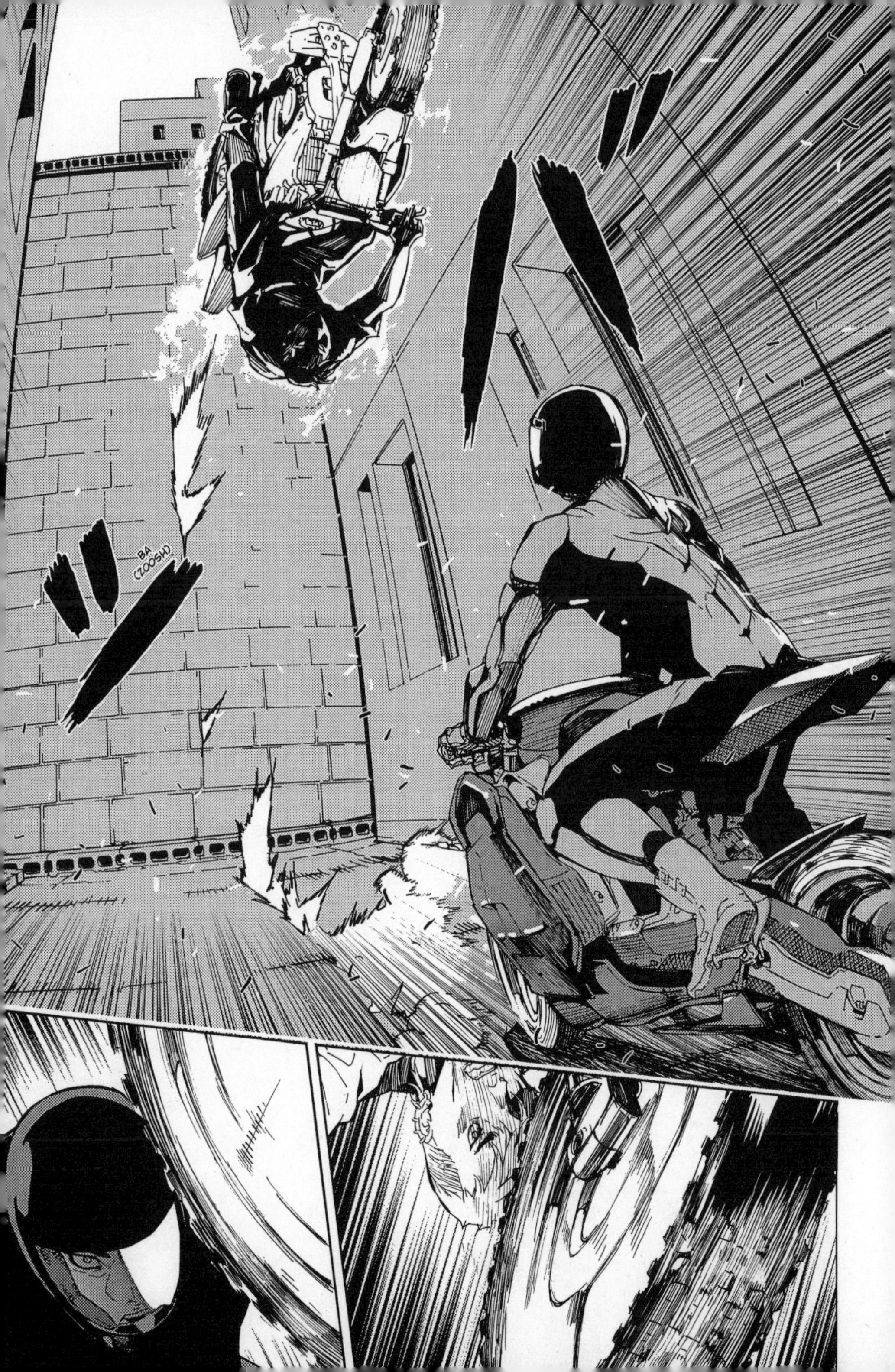
BA
(ZOOSH)

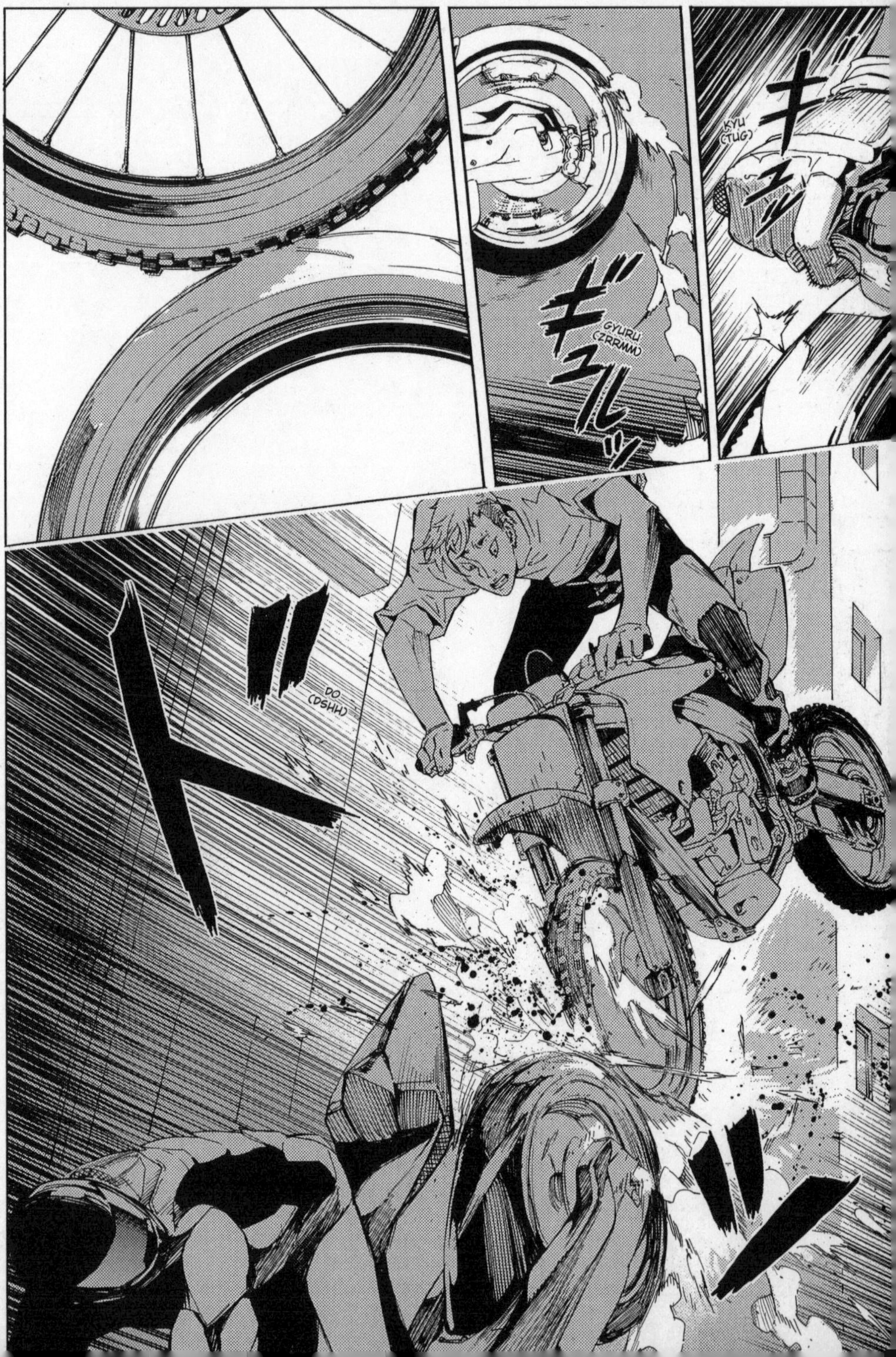
KYU (TUG)
GYURU (ZRRMM)
DO (DSHH)

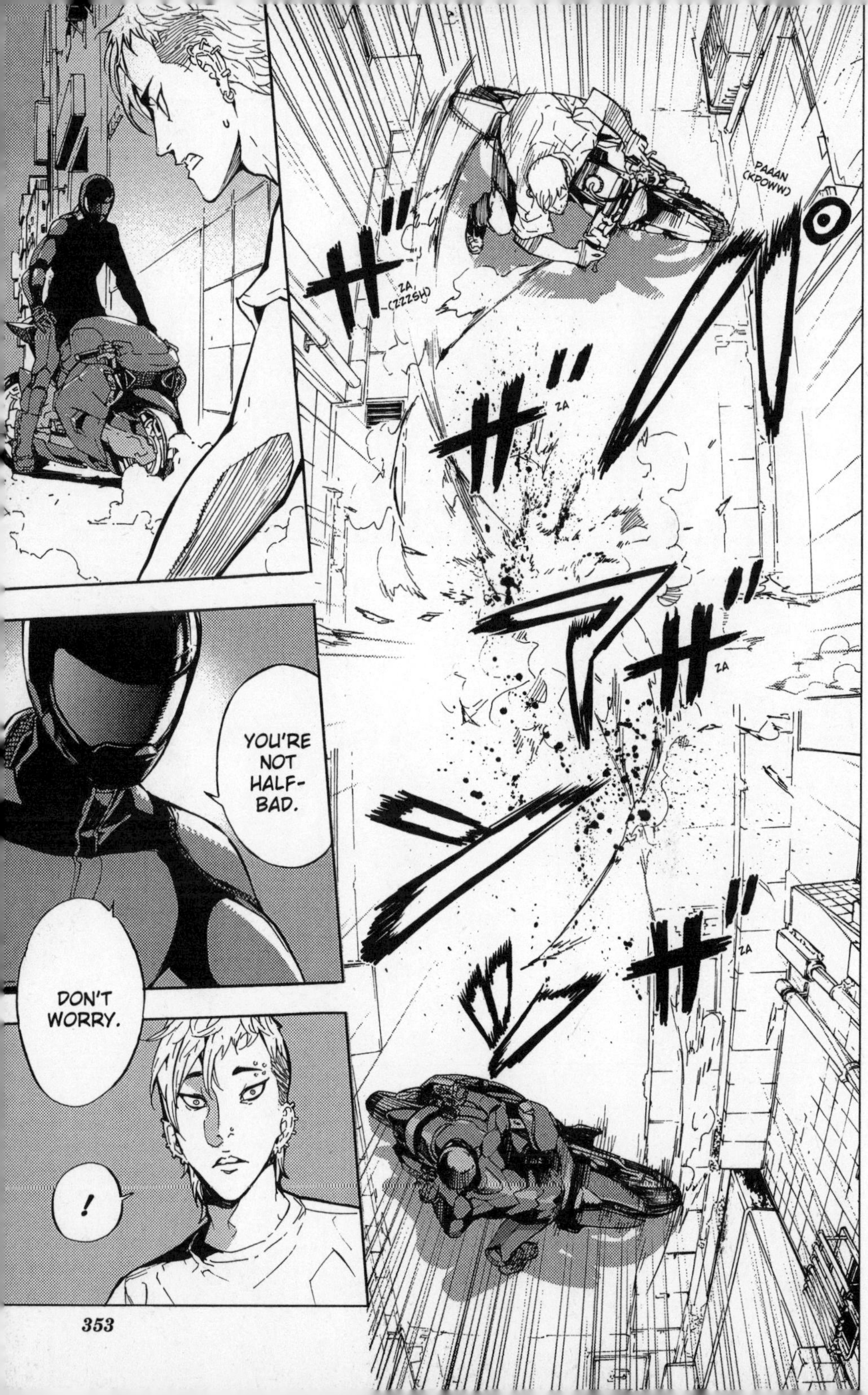
PAAAN (KPOWW)
ZA (ZZZSH)
ZA
ZA
ZA
YOU'RE NOT HALF-BAD.
DON'T WORRY.
!

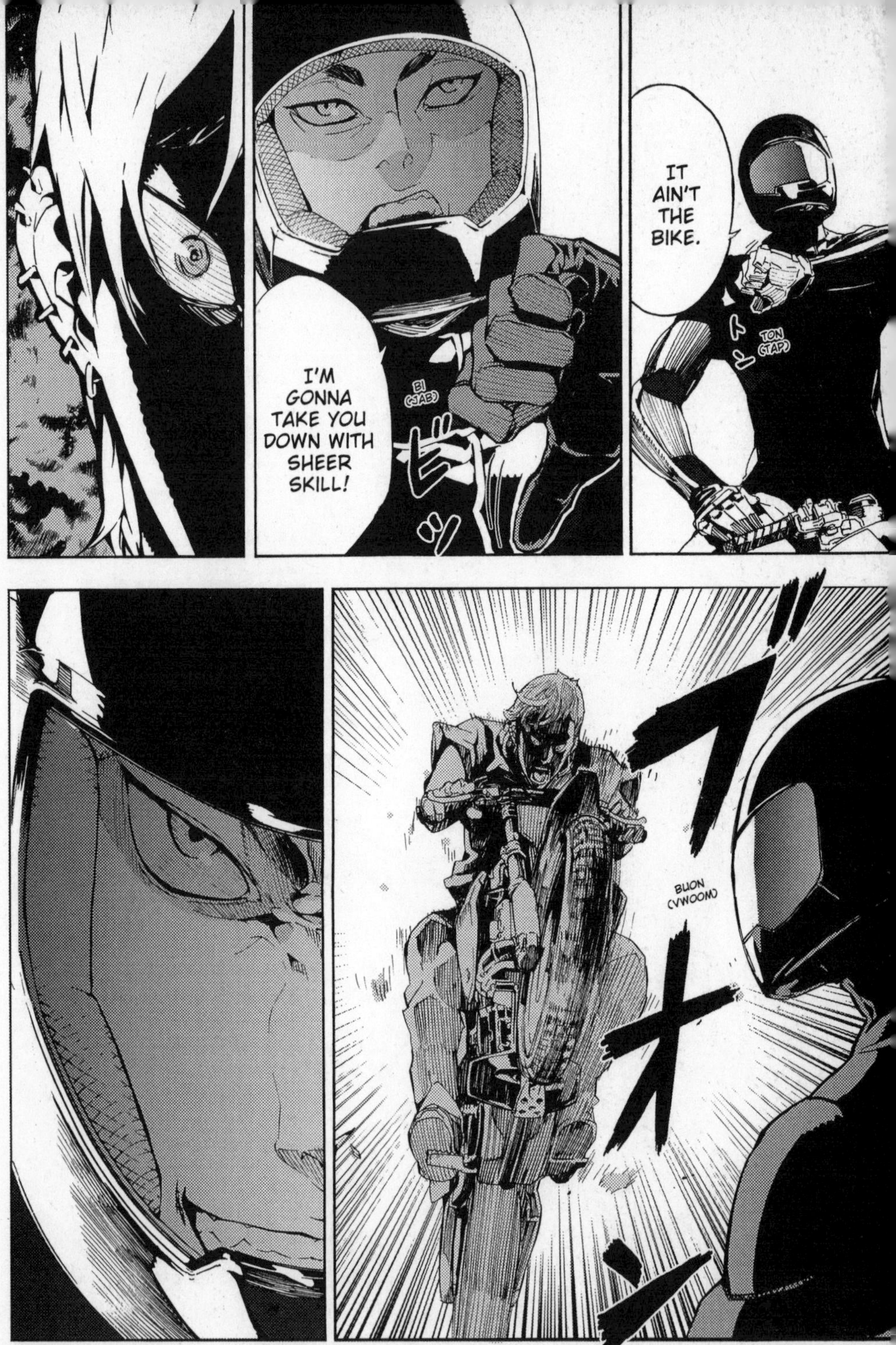

IT AIN'T THE BIKE.
TON (TAP)
I'M GONNA TAKE YOU DOWN WITH SHEER SKILL!
BI (JAB)
BUON (VWOOM)

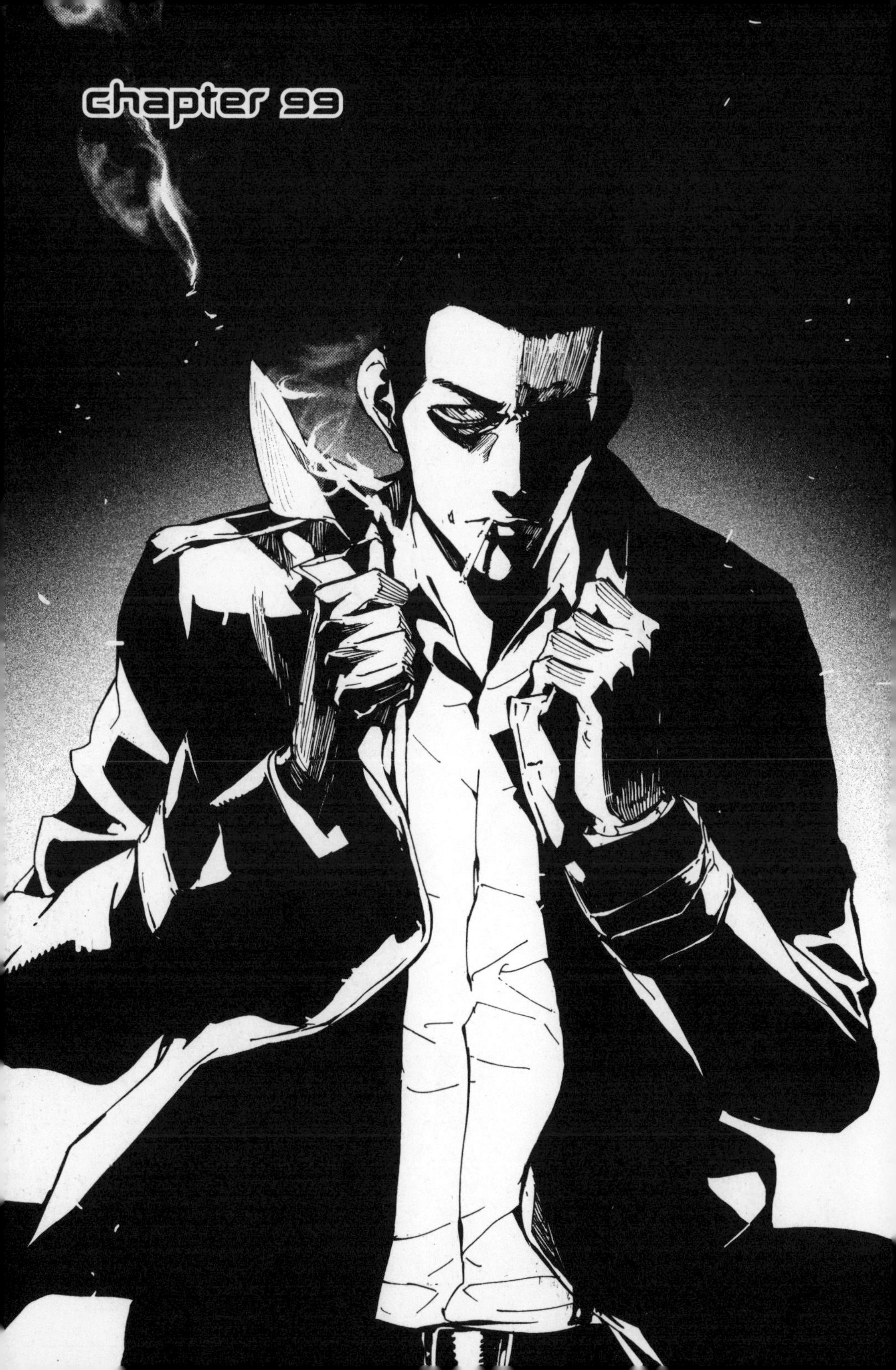
chapter 99

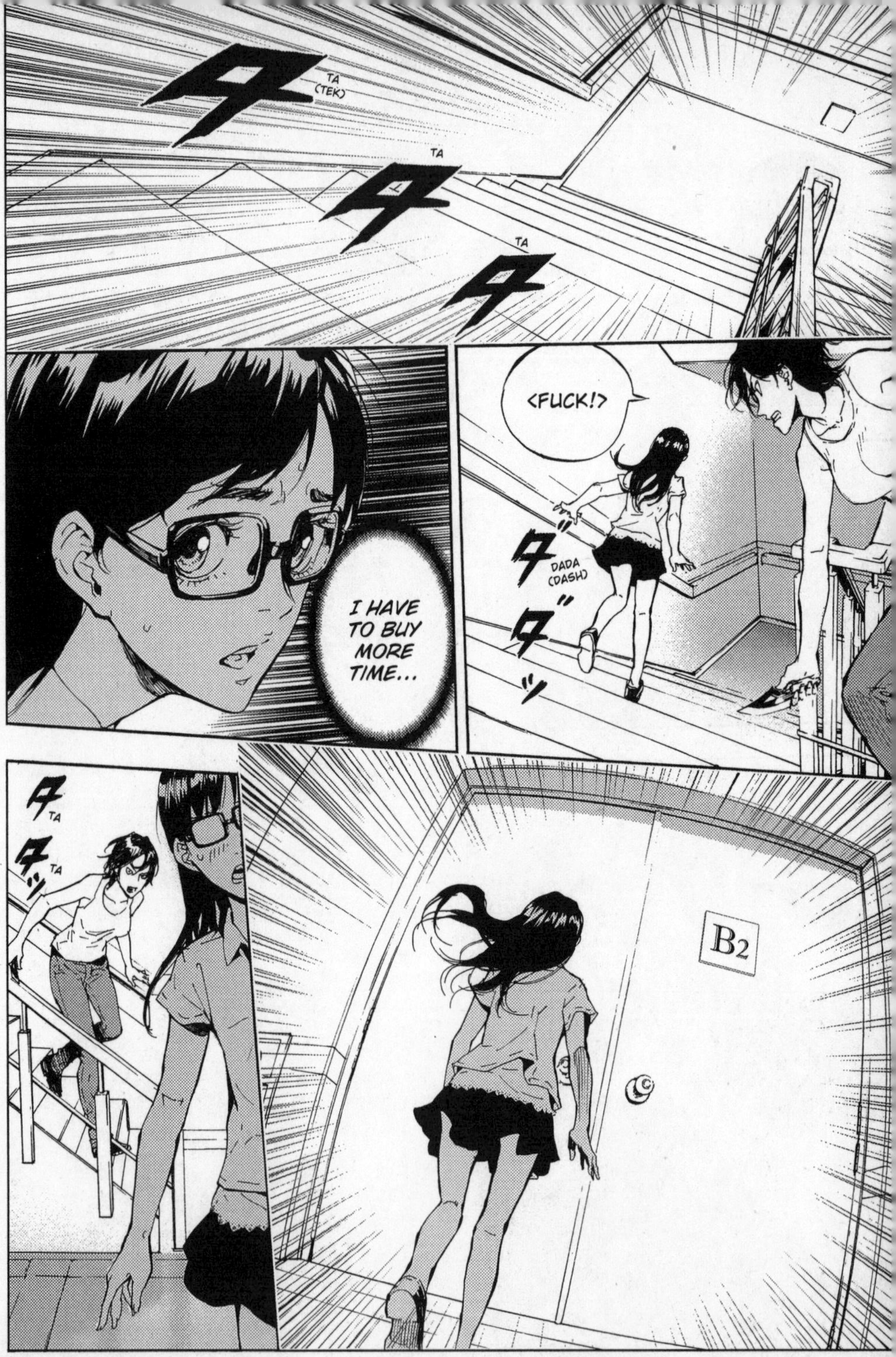
TA (TEK)
TA
TA
<FUCK!>
DADA (DASH)
I HAVE TO BUY MORE TIME...
B2
TA
TA

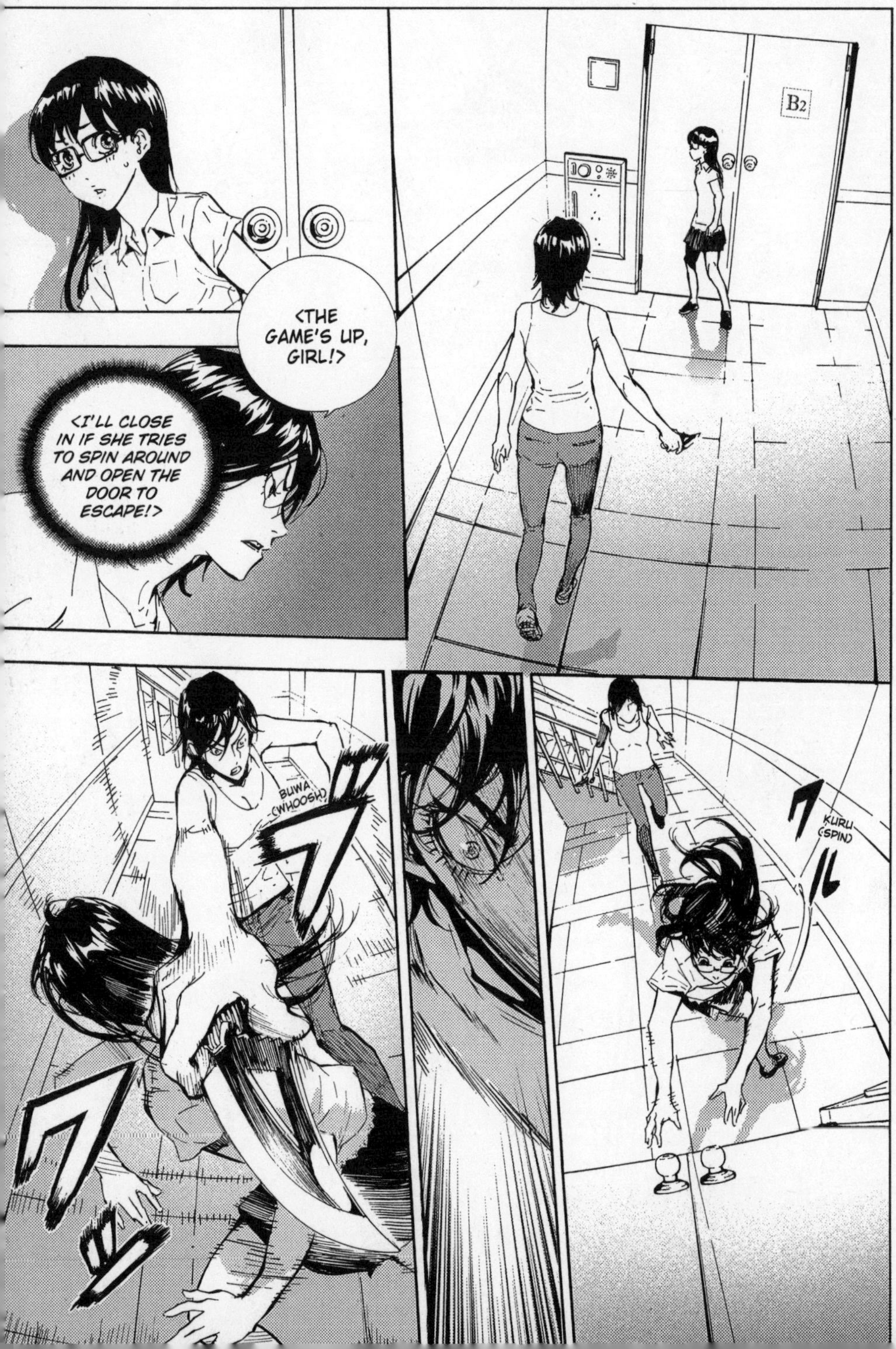
<THE GAME'S UP, GIRL!>
<I'LL CLOSE IN IF SHE TRIES TO SPIN AROUND AND OPEN THE DOOR TO ESCAPE!>
B2
KURU (SPIN)
BUWA (WHOOSH)

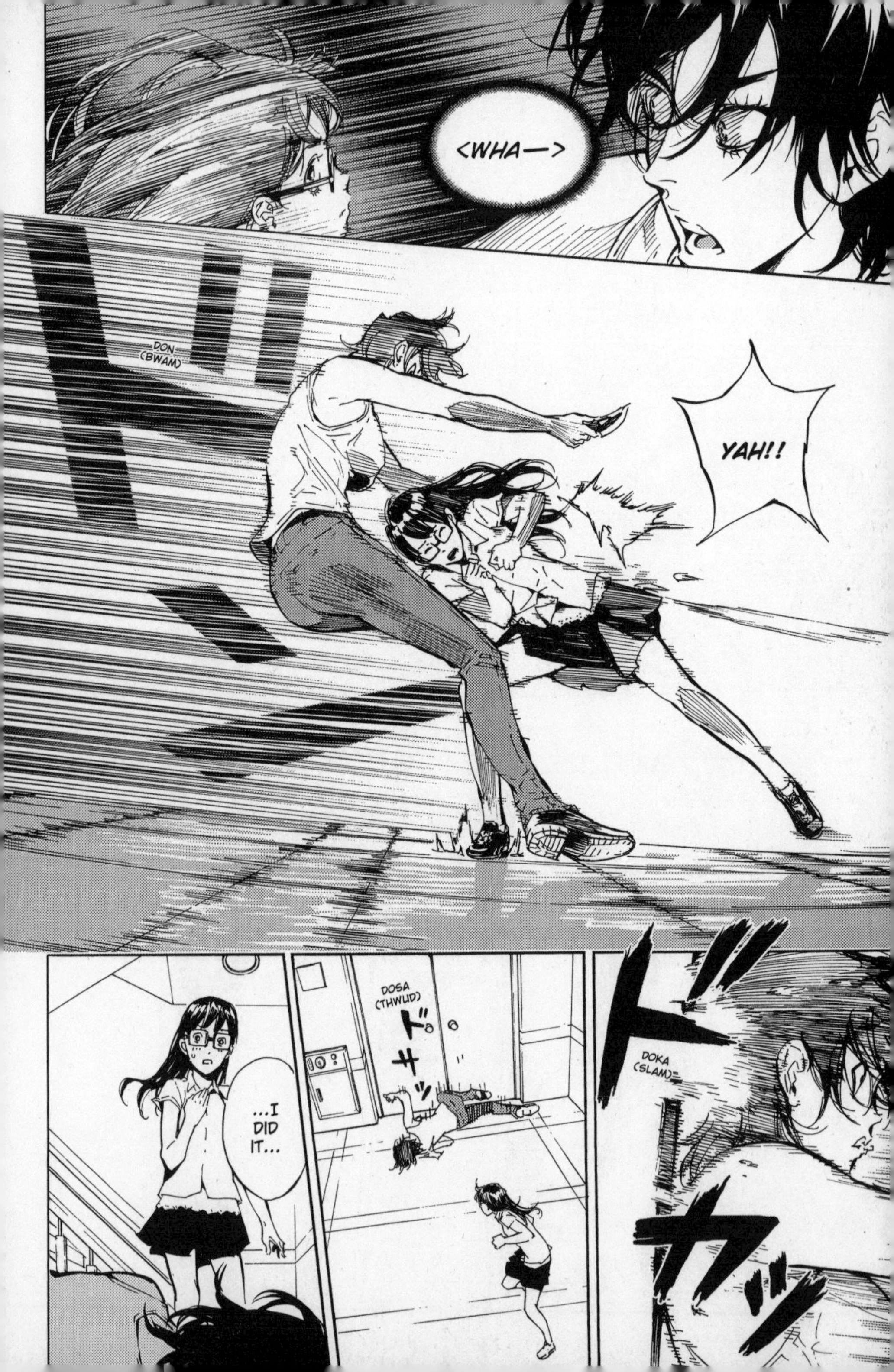
<WHA—>
YAH!!
DON (BWAM)
DOKA (SLAM)
DOSA (THWUD)
...I DID IT...

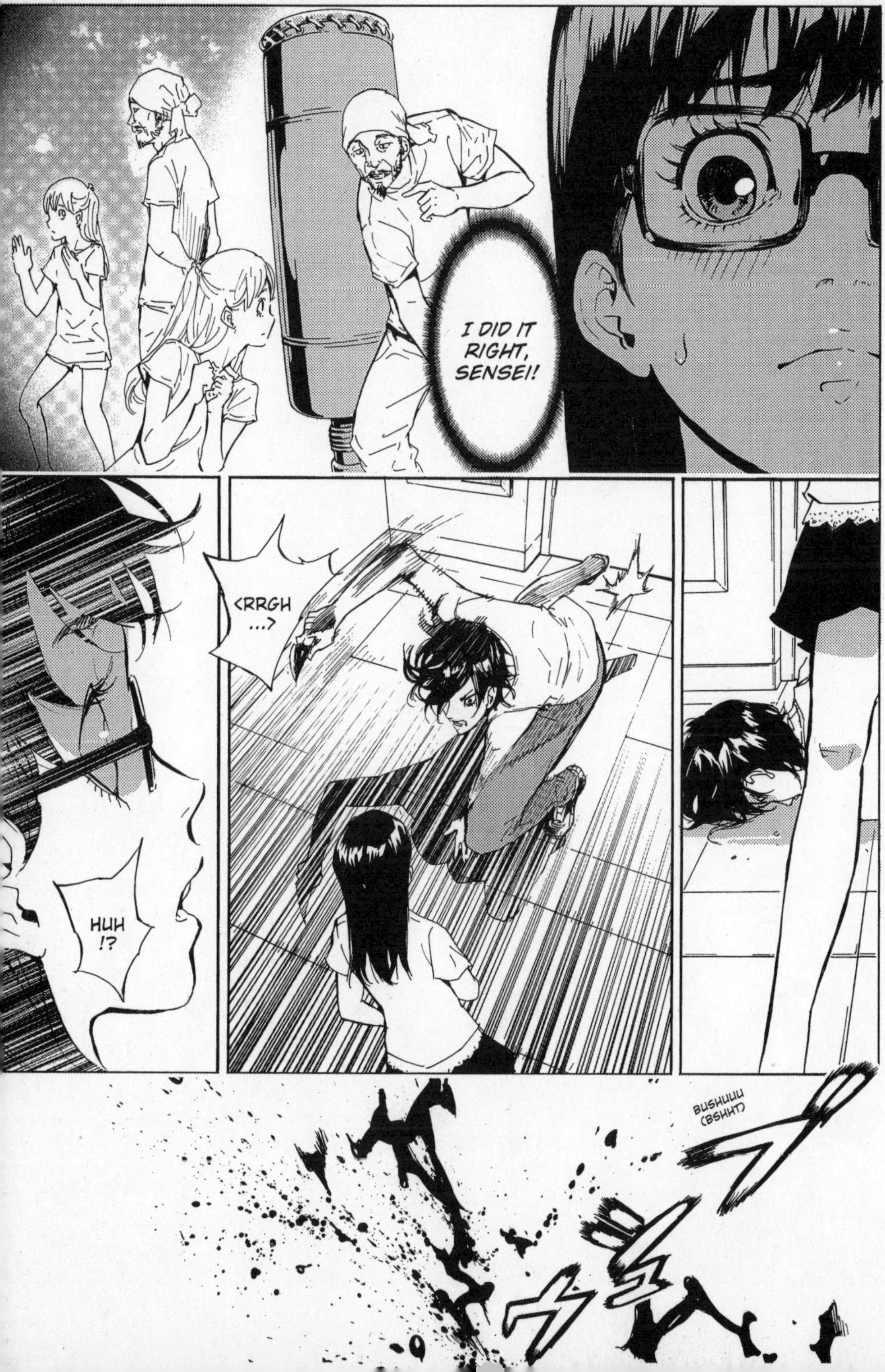
I DID IT RIGHT, SENSEI!
<RRGH ...>
HUH !?
BUSHUUU (BSHHT)

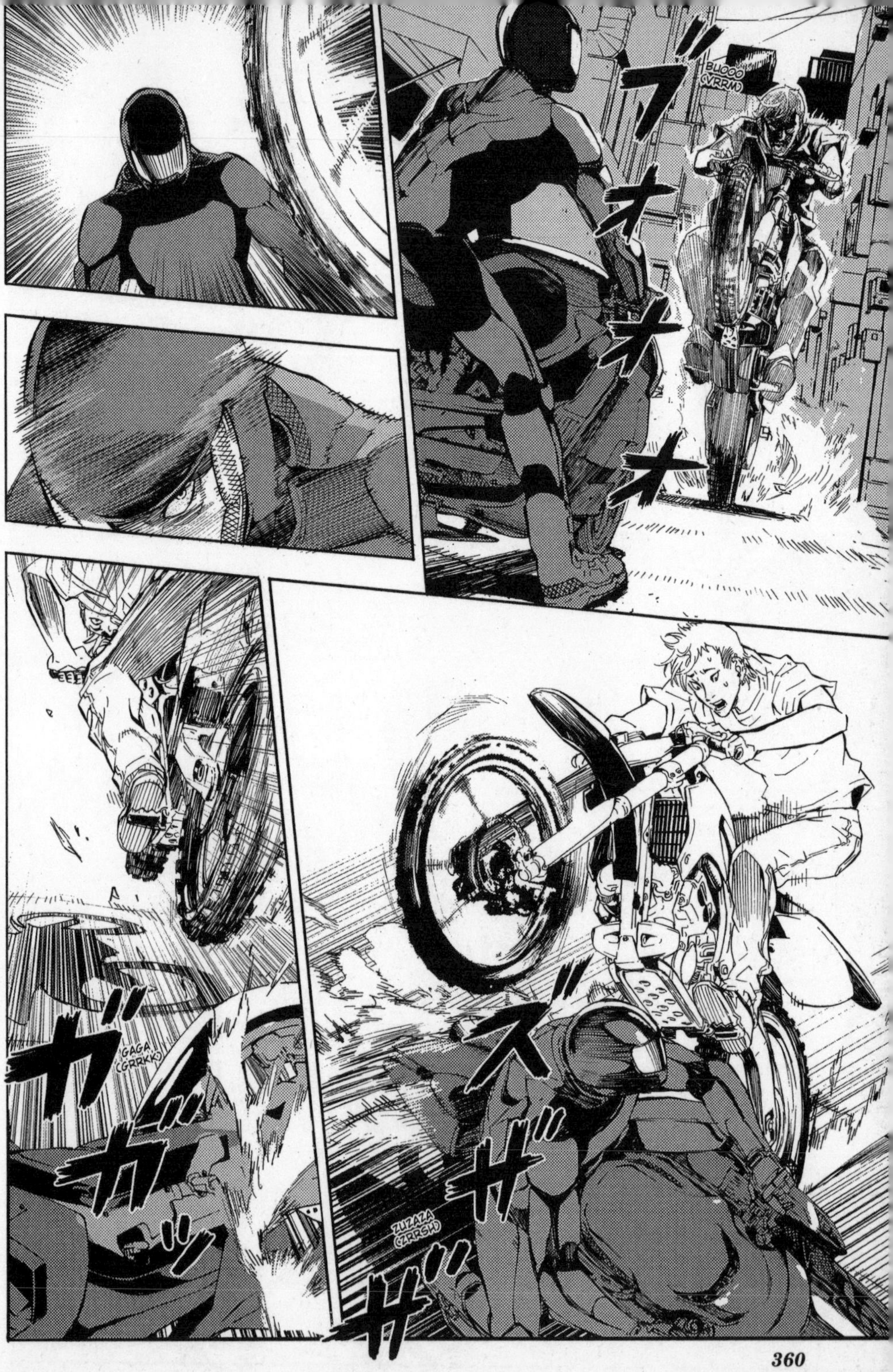
BUOOO (VRRM)
ZUZAZA (ZRRSH)
GAGA (GRRKK)

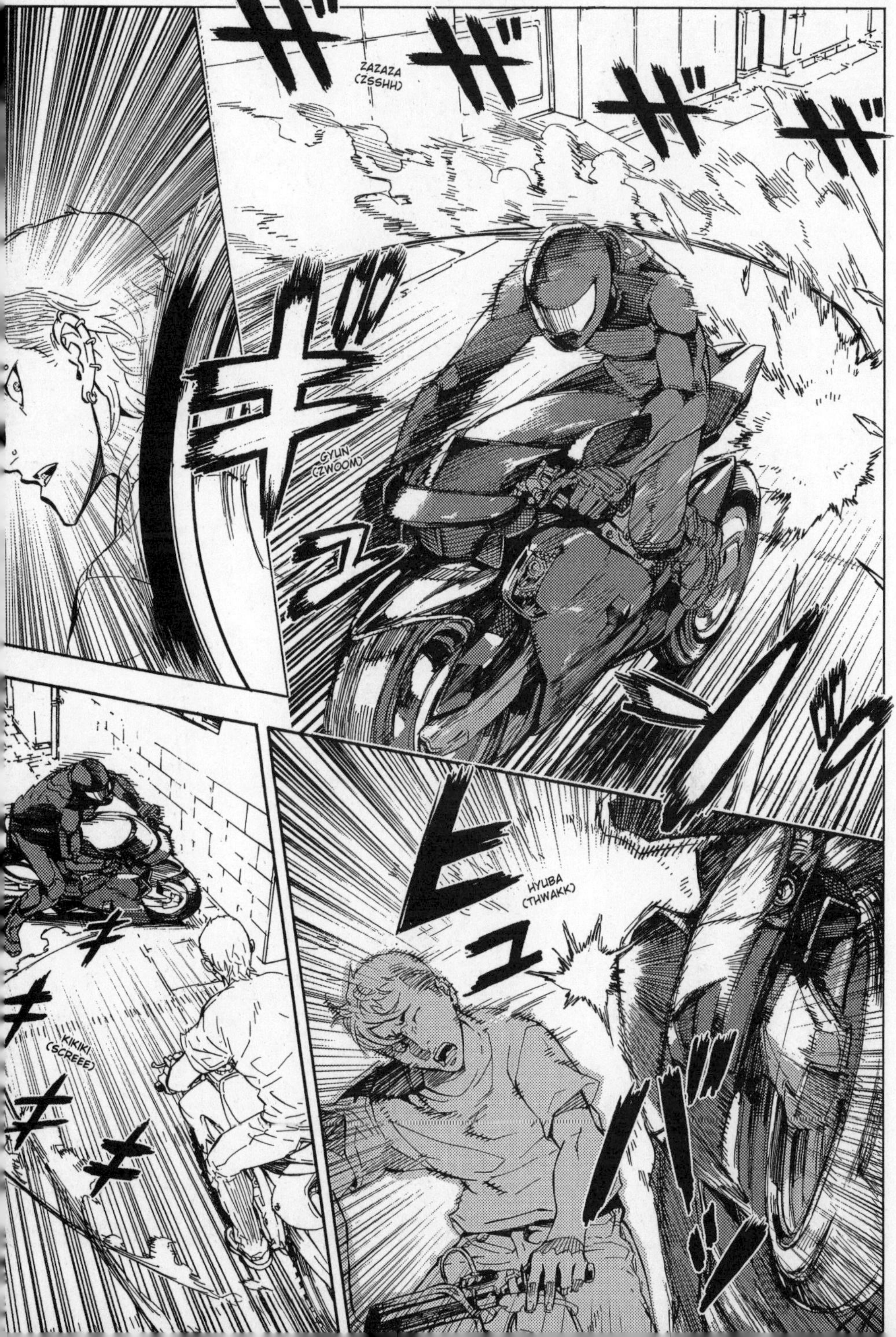
ZAZAZA
(ZSSHH)
GYUN
(ZWOOM)
HYUBA
(THWAKK)
KIKIKI
(SCREEE)

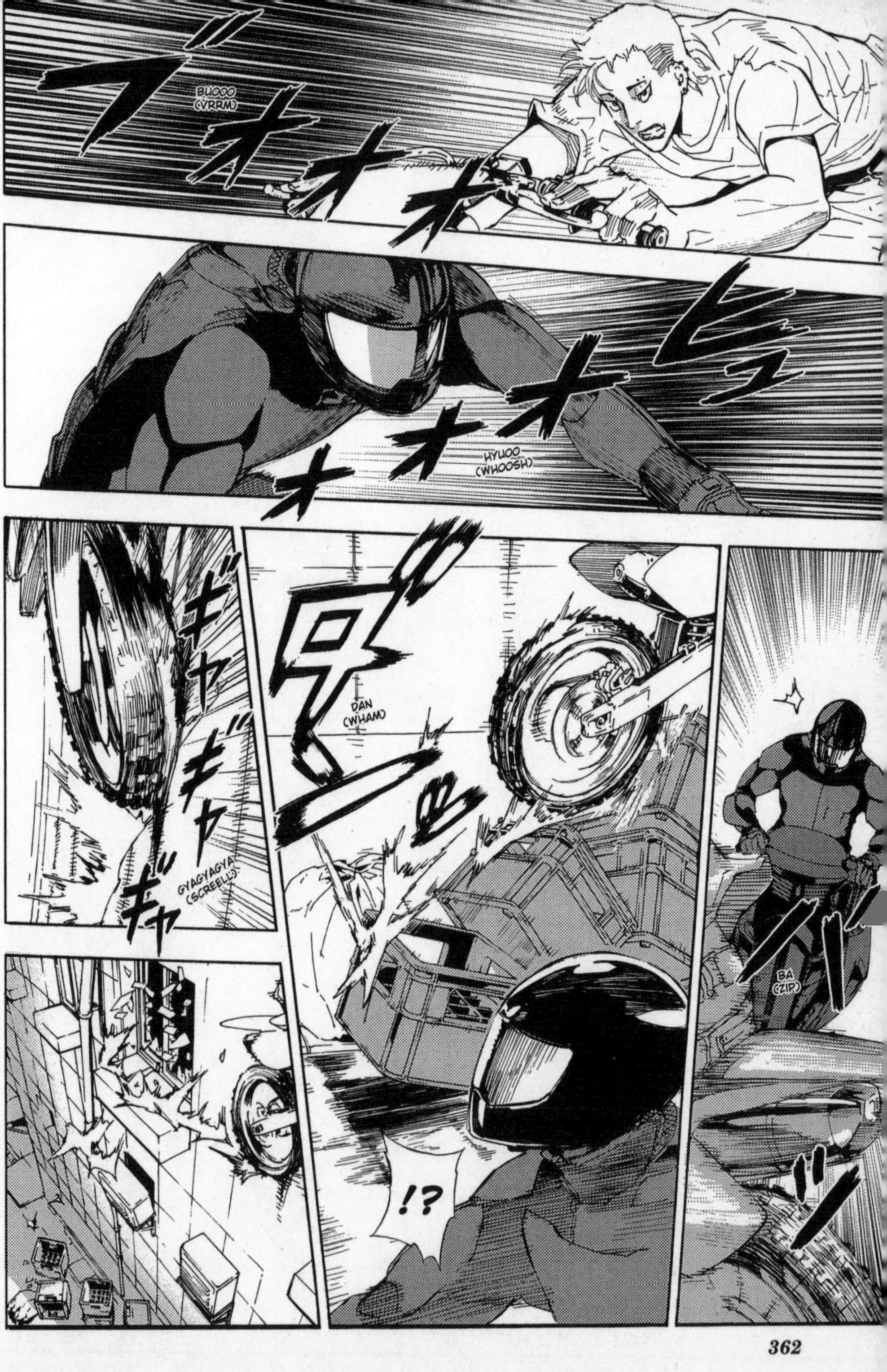

BUOOO (VRRM)
HYUOO (WHOOSH)
BA (ZIP)
DAN (WHAM)
!?
GYAGYAGYA (SCREEE)

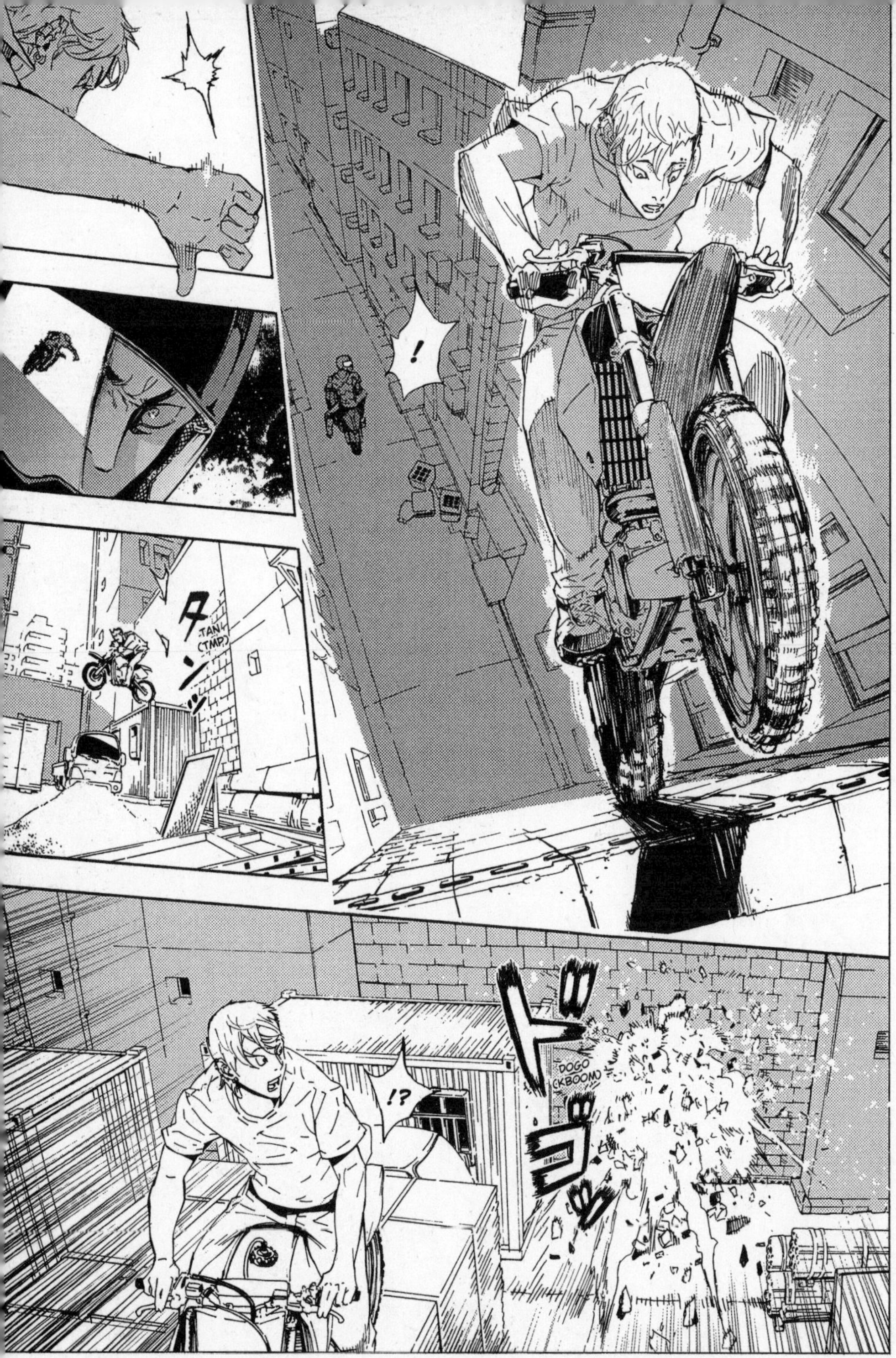
!
タン
TAN
(TMP)
ドゴゴ
DOGO
(KBOOM)
!?

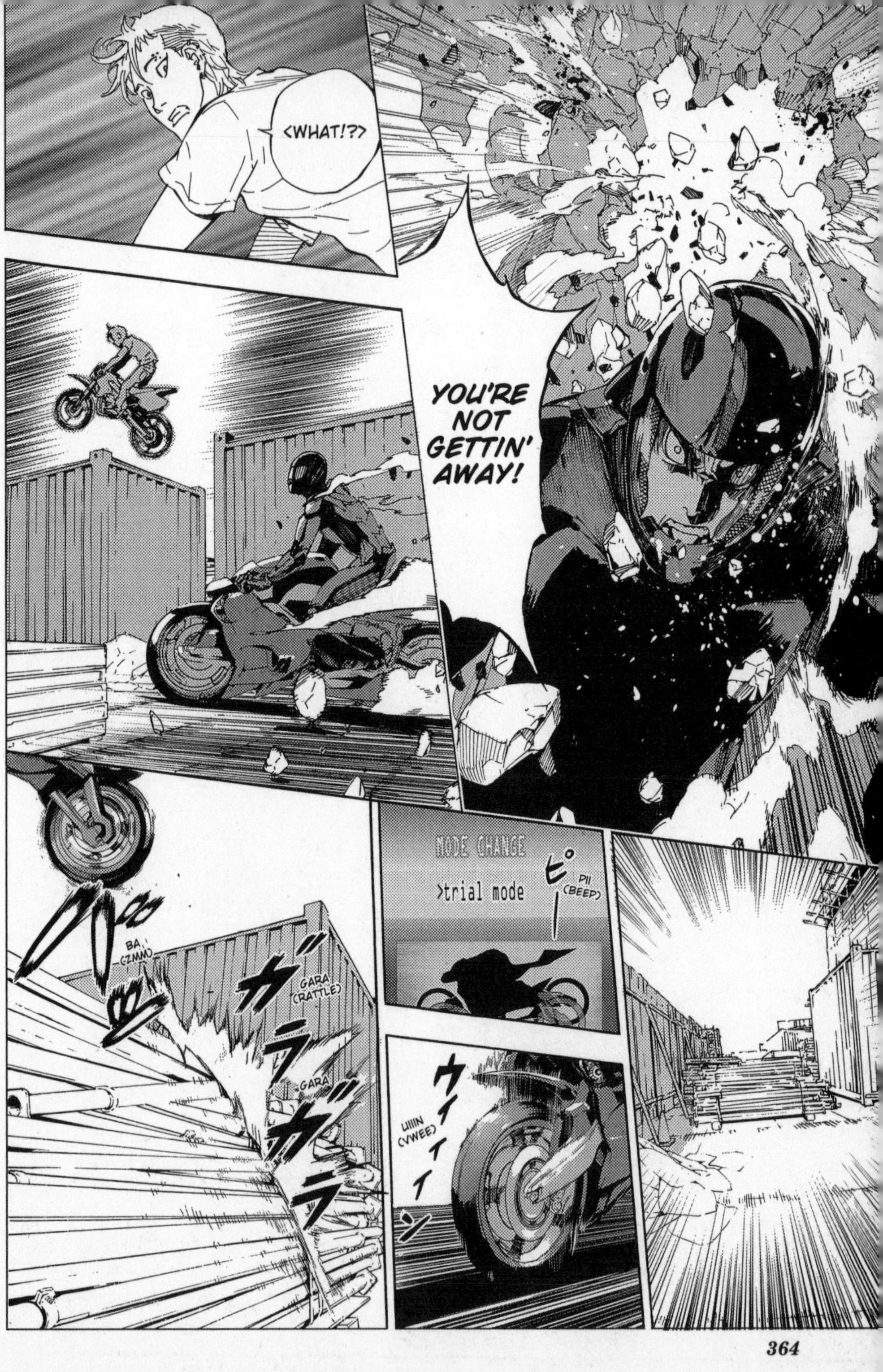
YOU'RE NOT GETTIN' AWAY!
<WHAT!?>
MODE CHANGE
>trial mode
PII (BEEP)
UIIIN (VWEE)
BA (ZMM)
GARA (RATTLE)
GARA

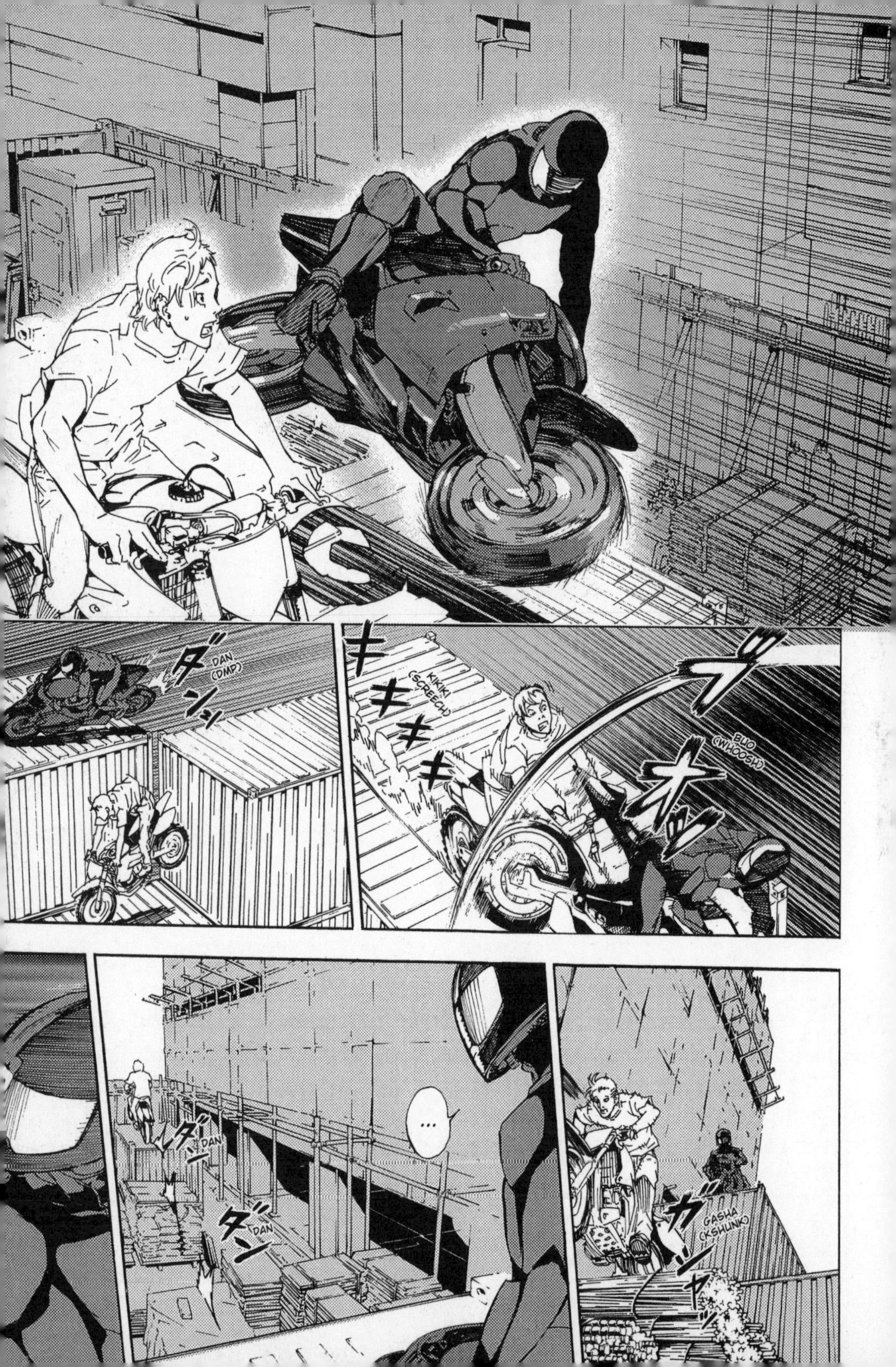
BUO (WHOOSH)
KIKIKI (SCREECH)
DAN (DMP)
GASHA (KSHUNK)
...
DAN
DAN

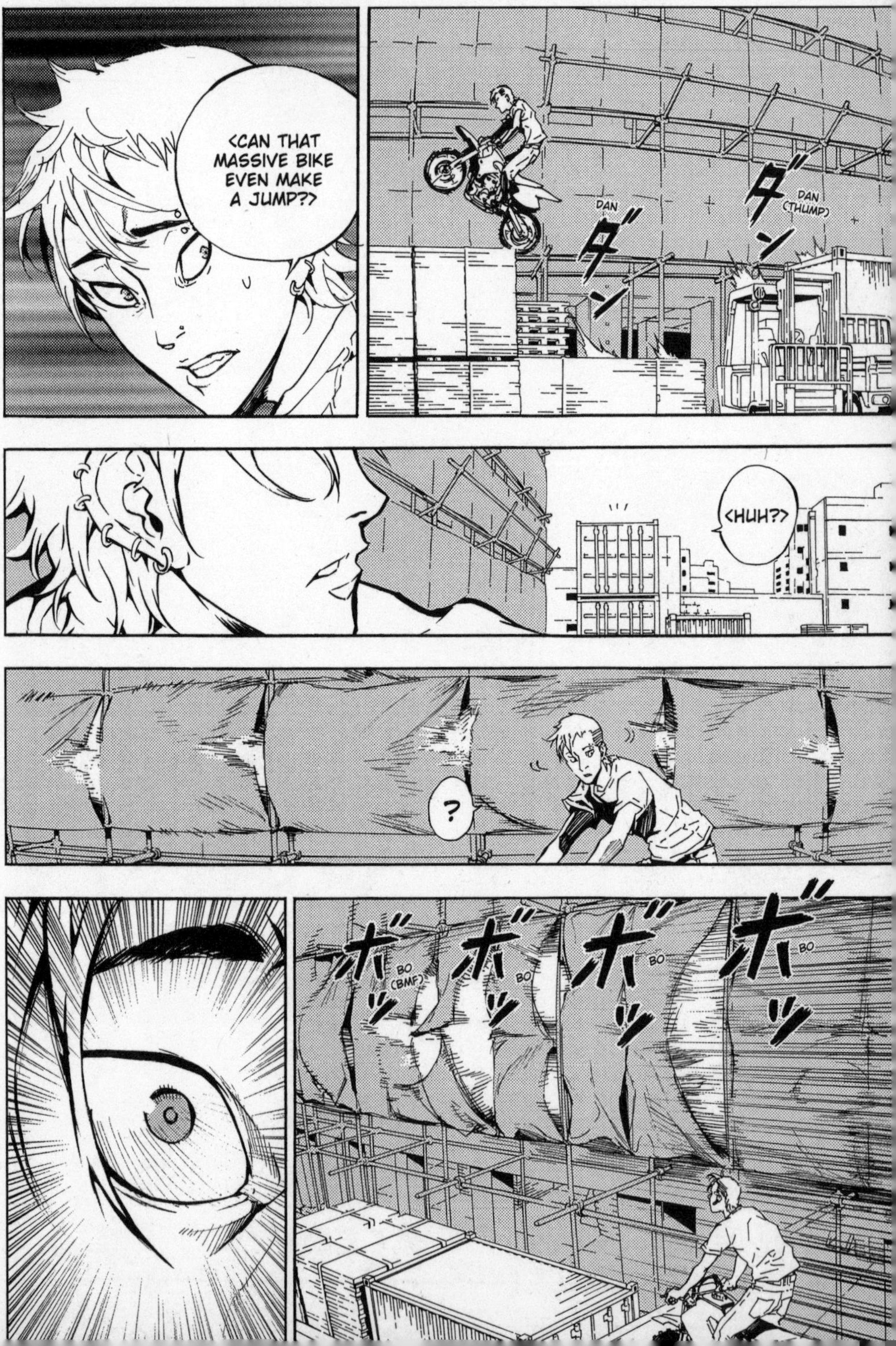
ダン
DAN (THUMP)
ダン
DAN
<CAN THAT MASSIVE BIKE EVEN MAKE A JUMP??>
<HUH?>
?
ボッ
BO
ボッ
BO
ボッ
BO
ボッ
BO (BMF)

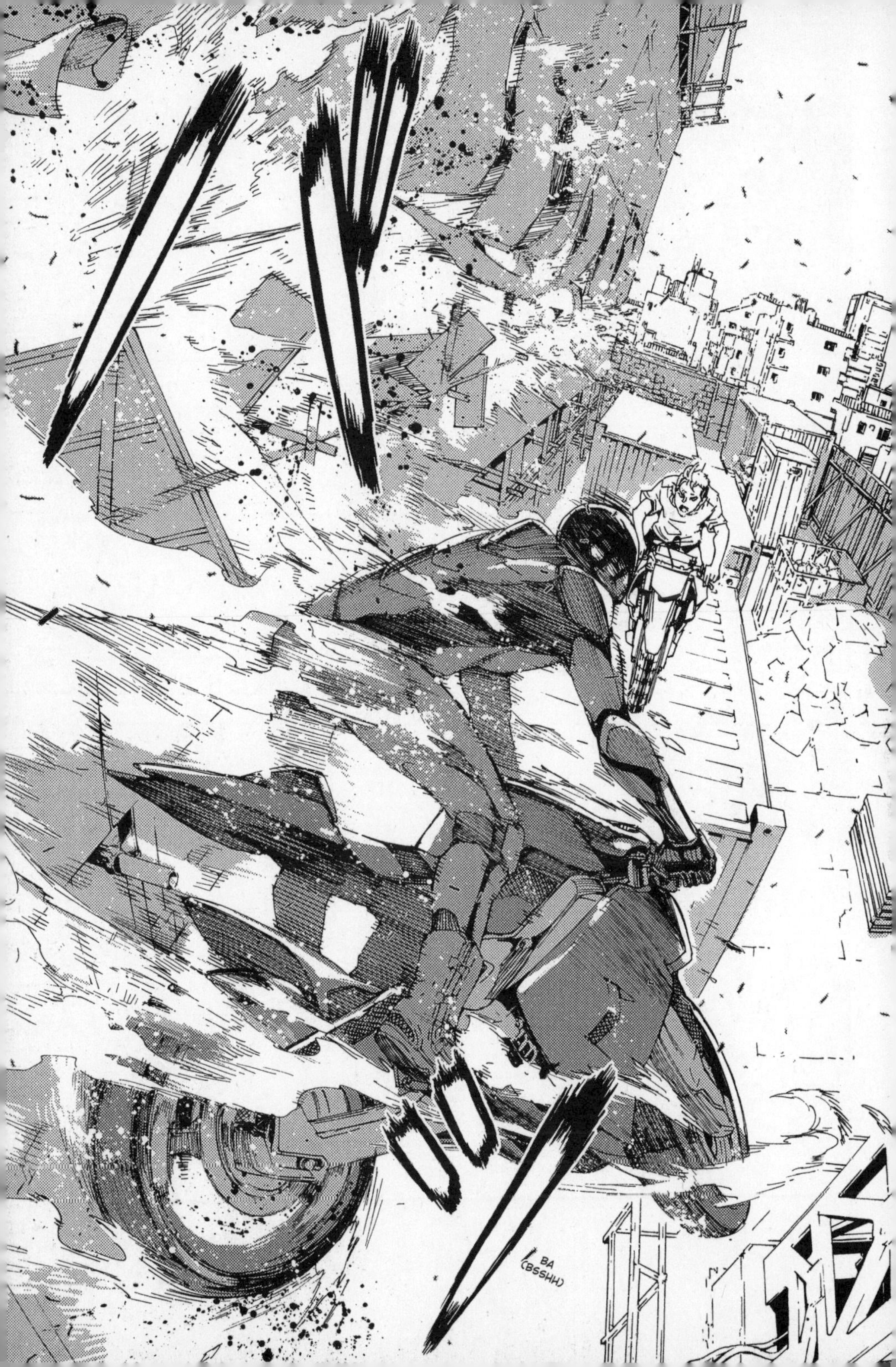
BA
(BSSHH)

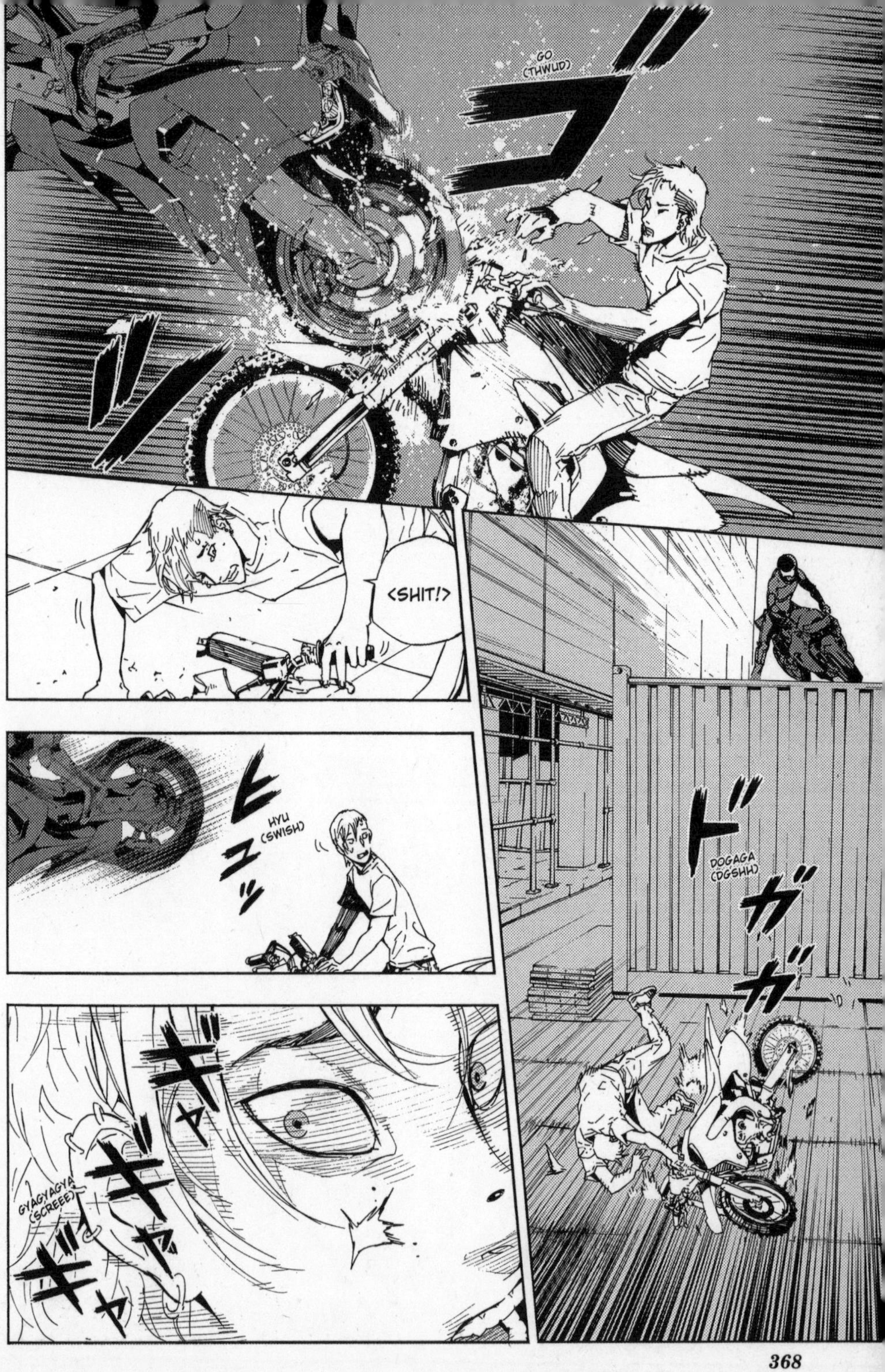
GO
(THWUD)
DOGAGA
(DGSHH)
<SHIT!>
HYU
(SWISH)
GYAGYAGYA
(SCREEE)

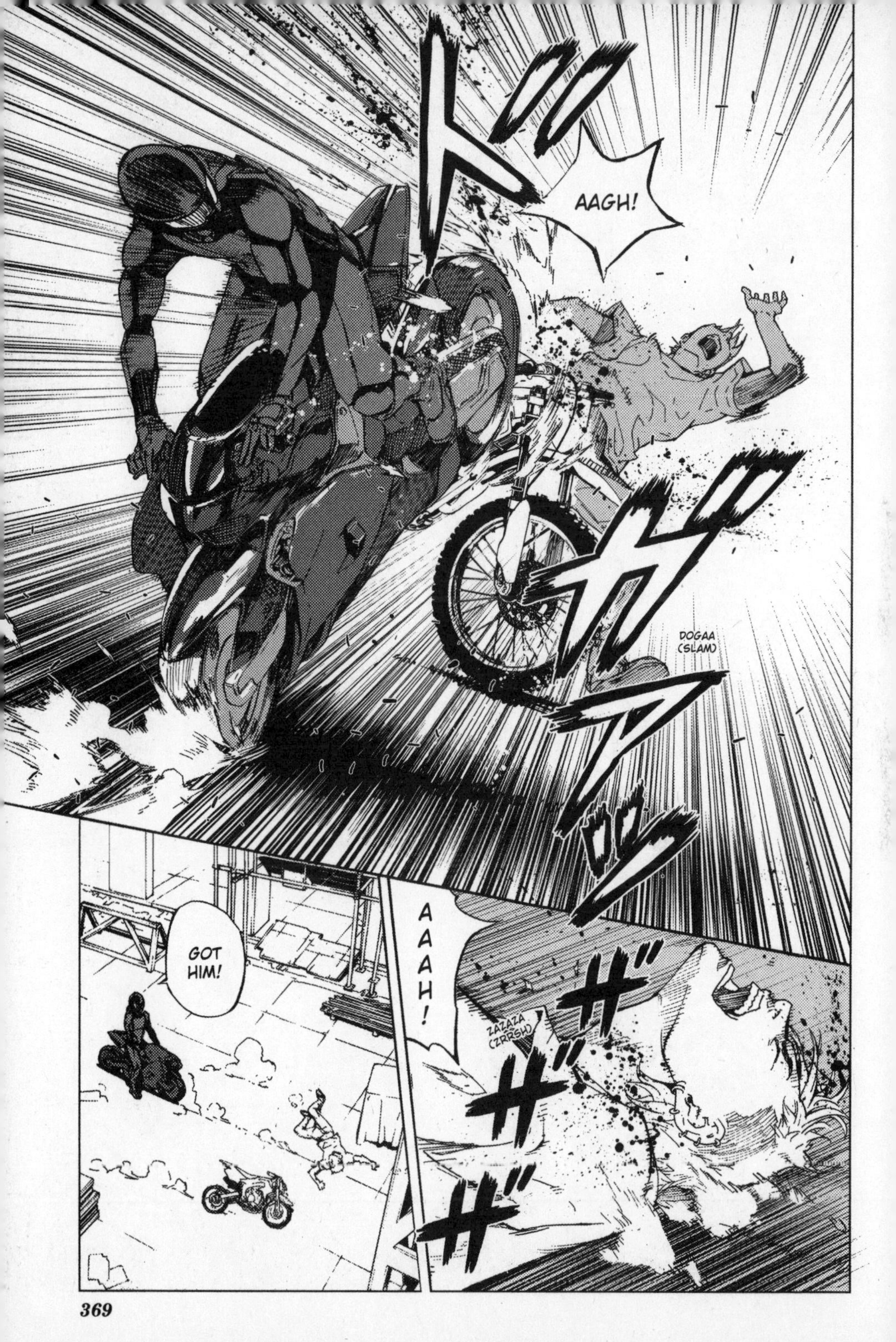
AAGH!
DOGAA (SLAM)
AAAAH!
ZAZAZA (ZRRSH)
GOT HIM!

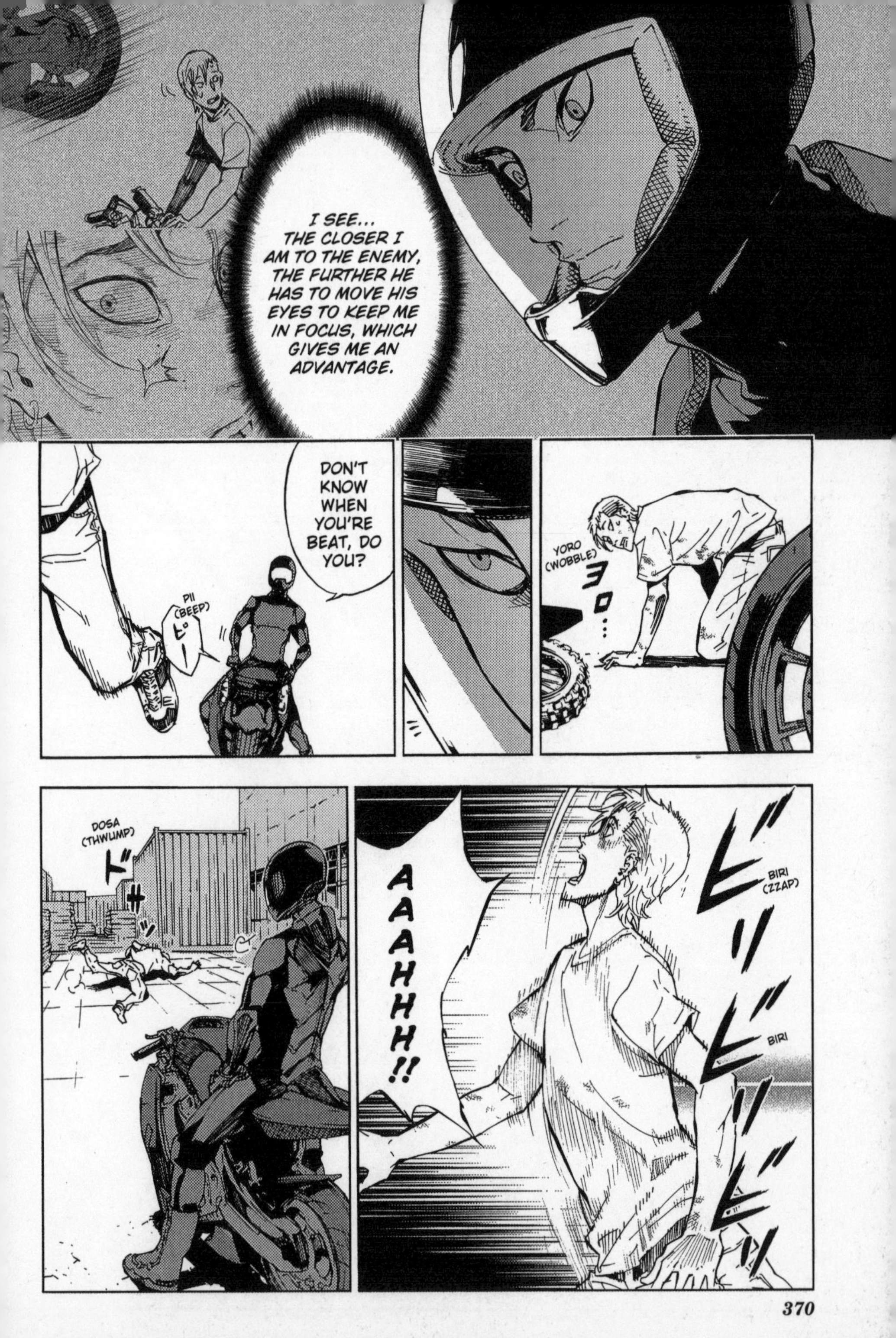
I SEE... THE CLOSER I AM TO THE ENEMY, THE FURTHER HE HAS TO MOVE HIS EYES TO KEEP ME IN FOCUS, WHICH GIVES ME AN ADVANTAGE.
YORO (WOBBLE)
ヨロ…
DON'T KNOW WHEN YOU'RE BEAT, DO YOU?
PII (BEEP)
ピー
AAAAHHH!!
BIRI (ZZAP)
BIRI
DOSA (THWUMP)
ドサッ

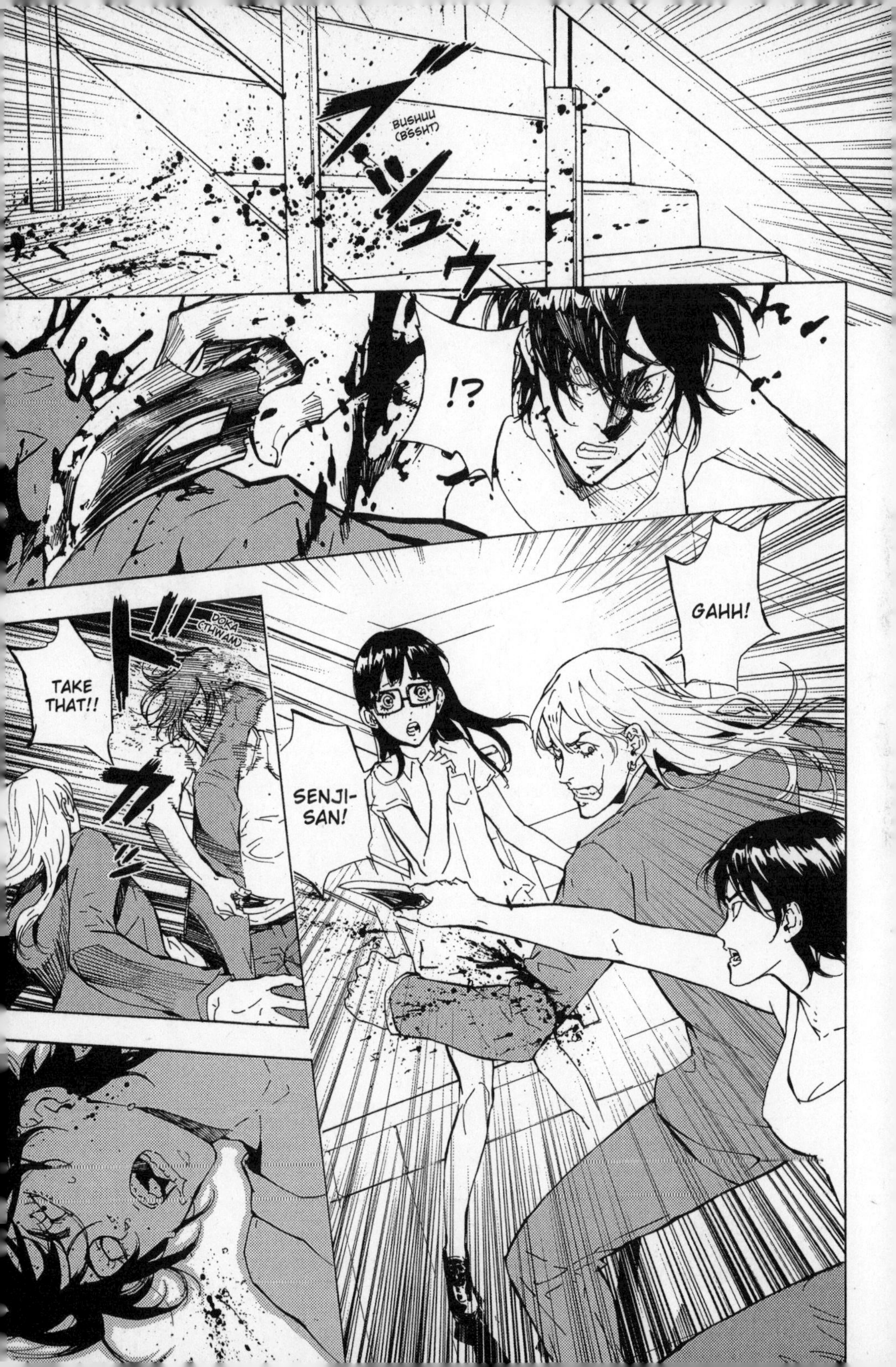
BUSHUU (B'SSHT)
!?
GAHH!
SENJI-SAN!
DOKA (THWAM)
TAKE THAT!!

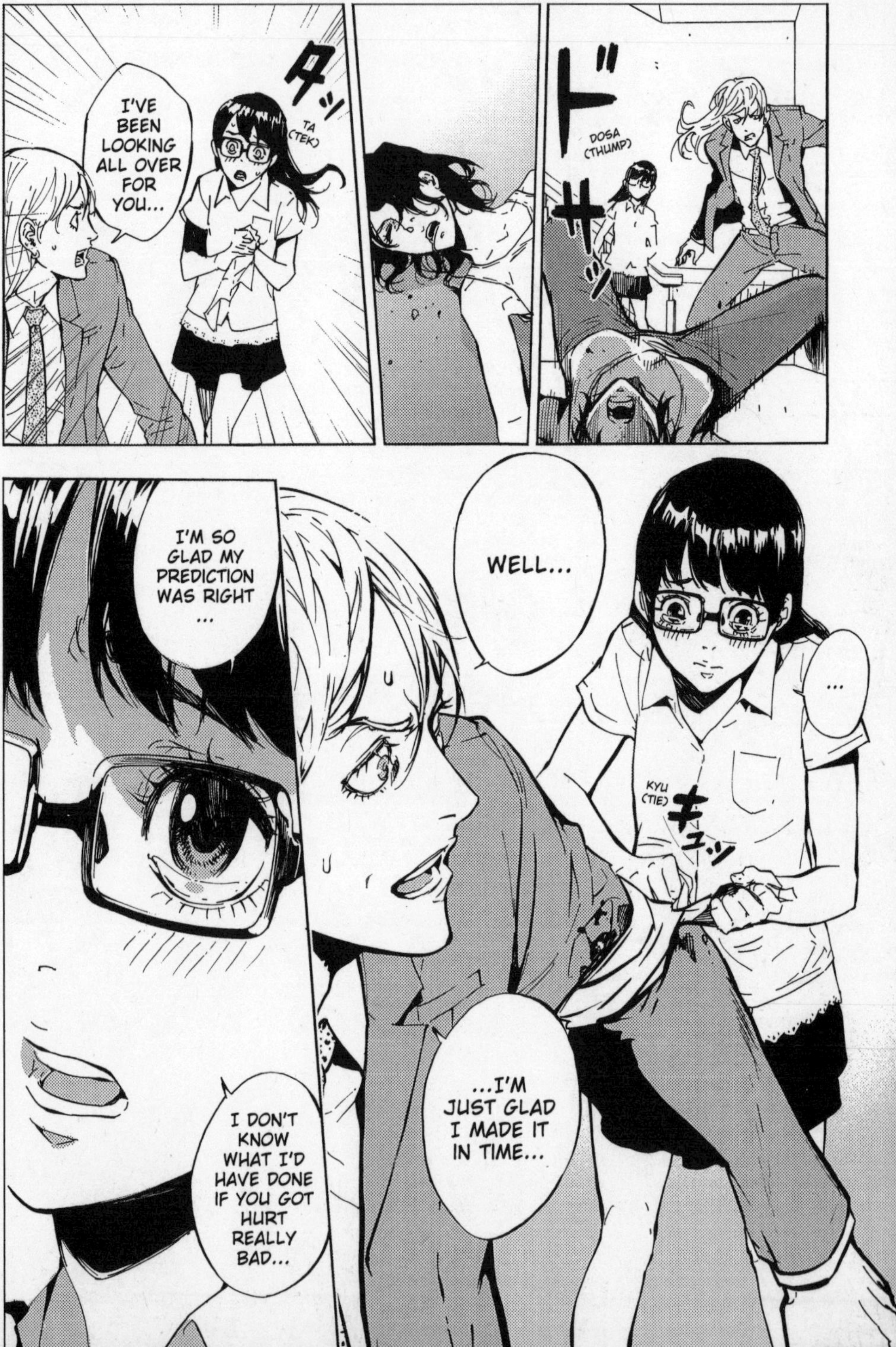
ドザッ
DOSA (THUMP)
タッ
TA (TEK)
I'VE BEEN LOOKING ALL OVER FOR YOU...
WELL...
...
キュッ
KYU (TIE)
...I'M JUST GLAD I MADE IT IN TIME...
I'M SO GLAD MY PREDICTION WAS RIGHT ...
I DON'T KNOW WHAT I'D HAVE DONE IF YOU GOT HURT REALLY BAD...

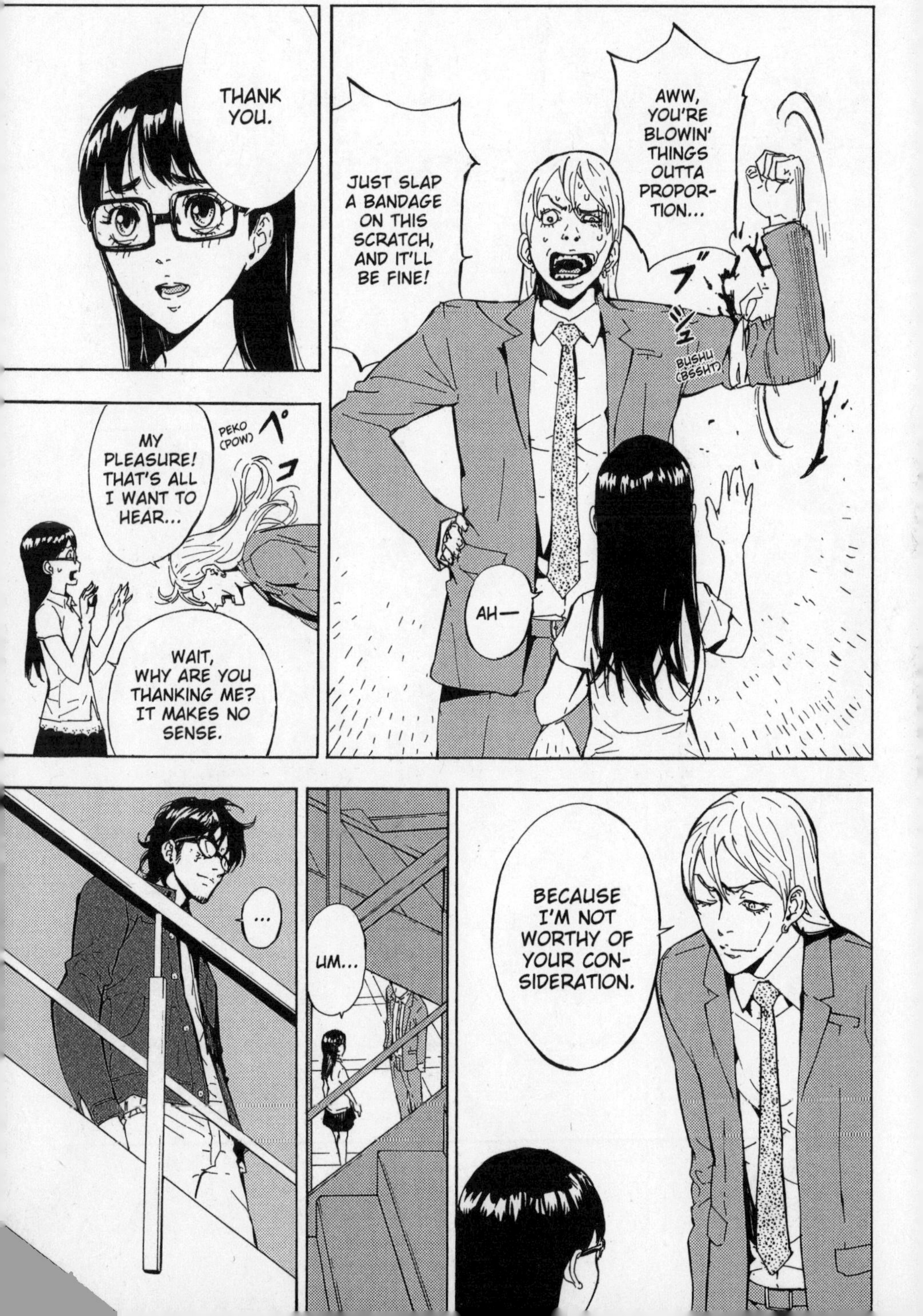
AWW, YOU'RE BLOWIN' THINGS OUTTA PROPOR-TION...
JUST SLAP A BANDAGE ON THIS SCRATCH, AND IT'LL BE FINE!
BUSHU (BSSHT)
AH—
THANK YOU.
PEKO (POW)
MY PLEASURE! THAT'S ALL I WANT TO HEAR...
WAIT, WHY ARE YOU THANKING ME? IT MAKES NO SENSE.
BECAUSE I'M NOT WORTHY OF YOUR CON-SIDERATION.
UM...
...

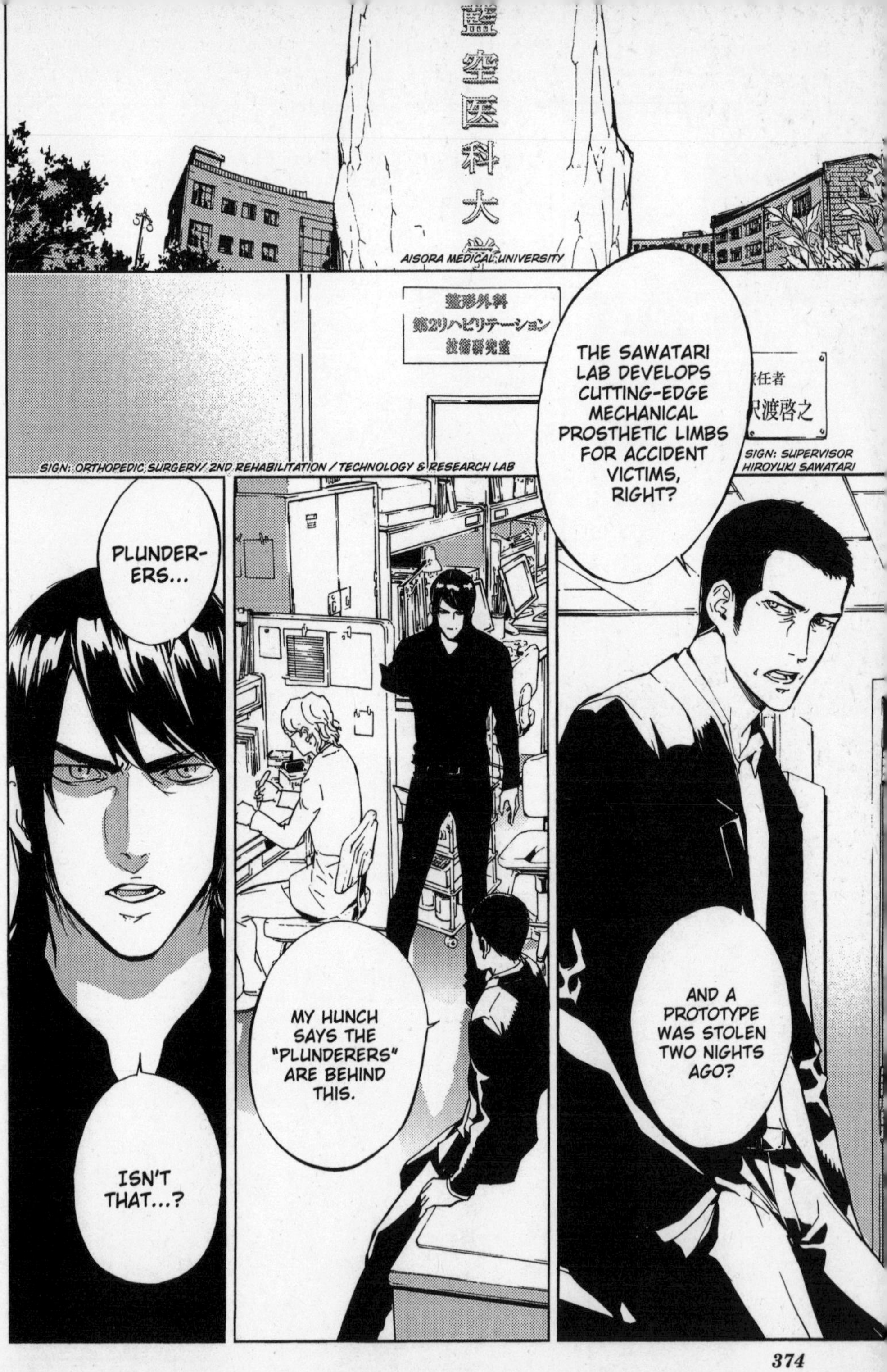

AISORA MEDICAL UNIVERSITY
整形外科
第2リハビリテーション
技術研究室
SIGN: SUPERVISOR HIROYUKI SAWATARI
SIGN: ORTHOPEDIC SURGERY/ 2ND REHABILITATION / TECHNOLOGY & RESEARCH LAB
THE SAWATARI LAB DEVELOPS CUTTING-EDGE MECHANICAL PROSTHETIC LIMBS FOR ACCIDENT VICTIMS, RIGHT?
AND A PROTOTYPE WAS STOLEN TWO NIGHTS AGO?
MY HUNCH SAYS THE "PLUNDERERS" ARE BEHIND THIS.
PLUNDERERS...
ISN'T THAT...?

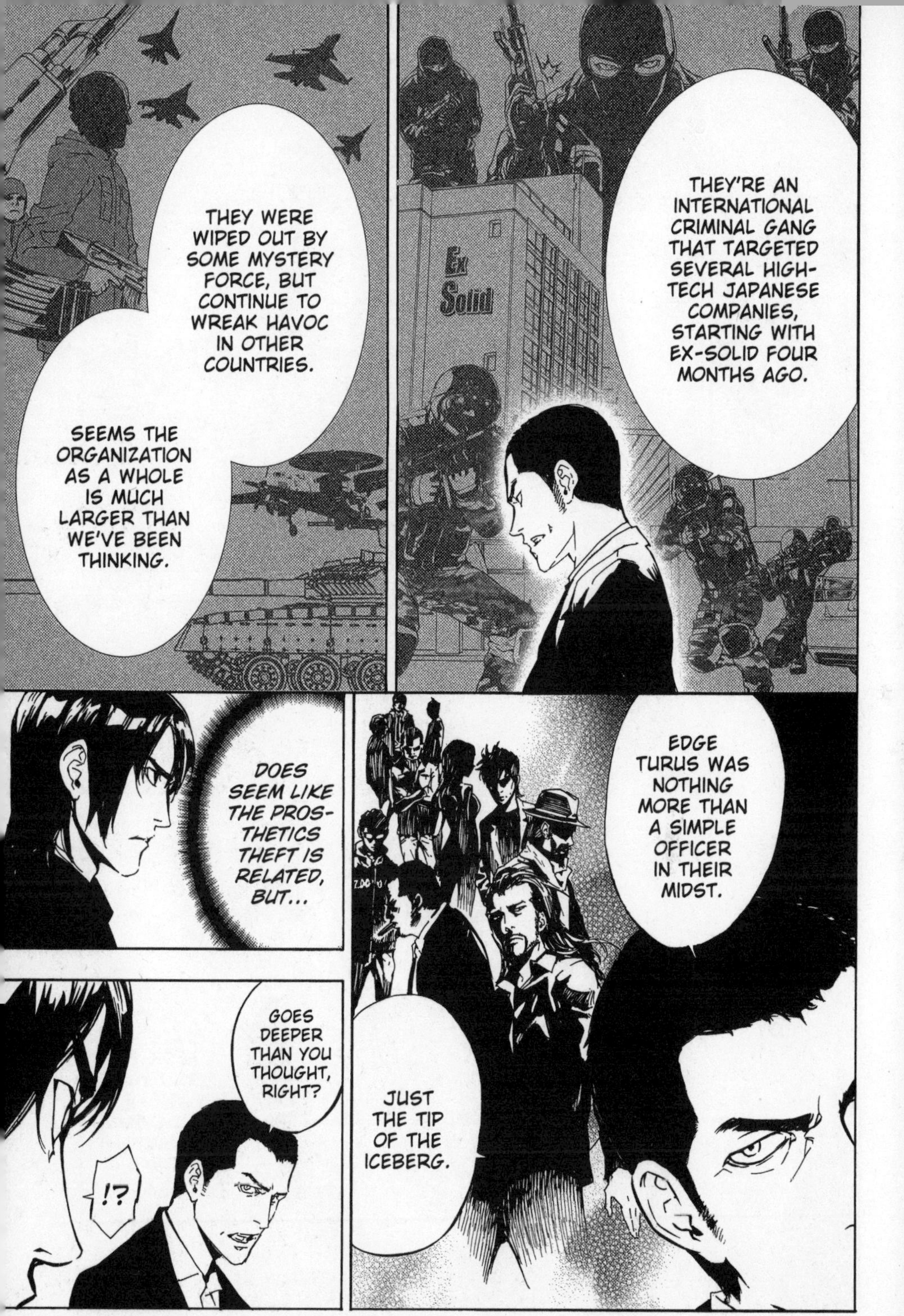
THEY'RE AN INTERNATIONAL CRIMINAL GANG THAT TARGETED SEVERAL HIGH-TECH JAPANESE COMPANIES, STARTING WITH EX-SOLID FOUR MONTHS AGO.
Ex Solid
THEY WERE WIPED OUT BY SOME MYSTERY FORCE, BUT CONTINUE TO WREAK HAVOC IN OTHER COUNTRIES.
SEEMS THE ORGANIZATION AS A WHOLE IS MUCH LARGER THAN WE'VE BEEN THINKING.
EDGE TURUS WAS NOTHING MORE THAN A SIMPLE OFFICER IN THEIR MIDST.
JUST THE TIP OF THE ICEBERG.
DOES SEEM LIKE THE PROSTHETICS THEFT IS RELATED, BUT...
GOES DEEPER THAN YOU THOUGHT, RIGHT?
!?

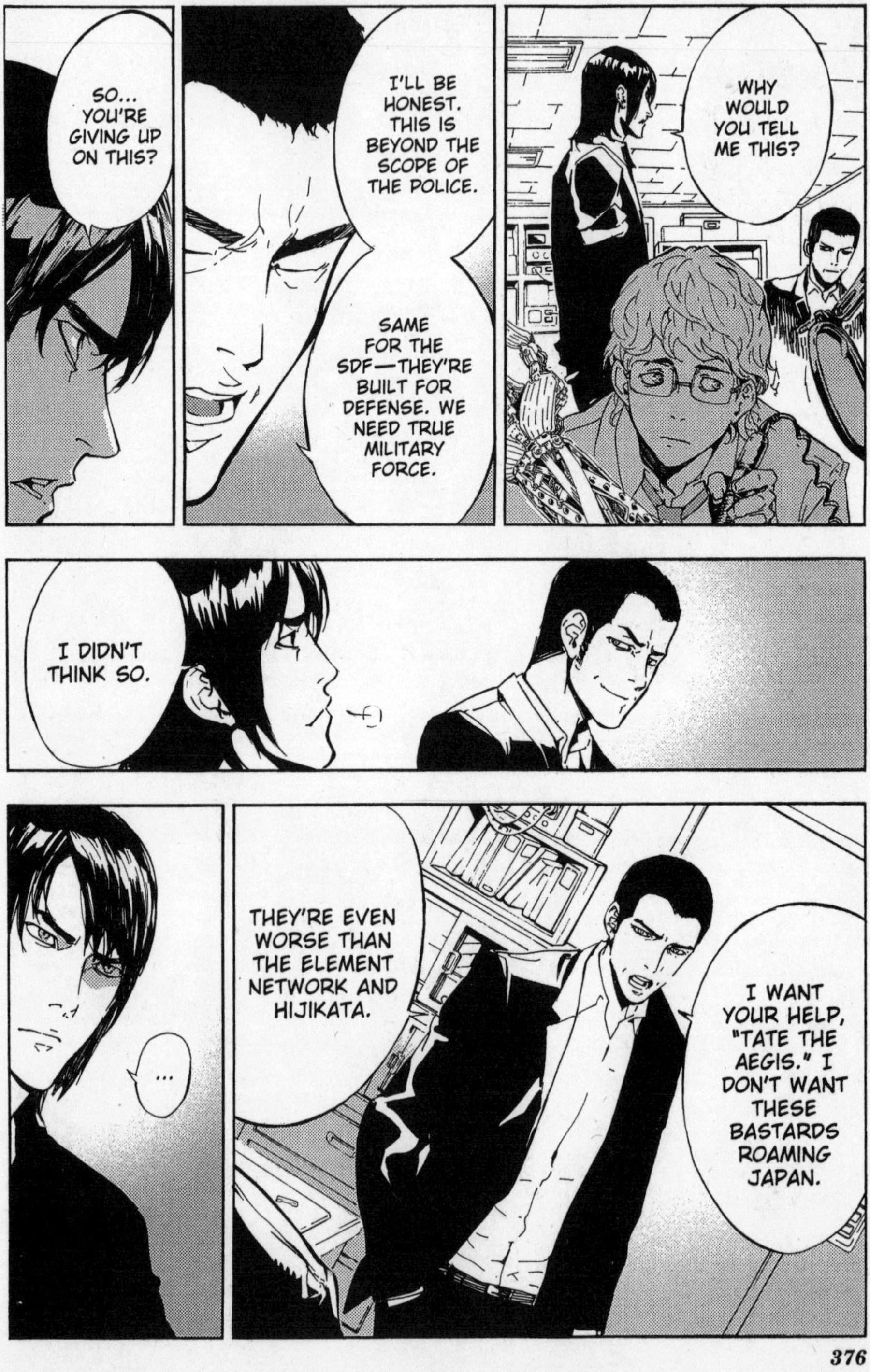
WHY WOULD YOU TELL ME THIS?
I'LL BE HONEST. THIS IS BEYOND THE SCOPE OF THE POLICE.
SAME FOR THE SDF—THEY'RE BUILT FOR DEFENSE. WE NEED TRUE MILITARY FORCE.
SO... YOU'RE GIVING UP ON THIS?
I DIDN'T THINK SO.
I WANT YOUR HELP, "TATE THE AEGIS." I DON'T WANT THESE BASTARDS ROAMING JAPAN.
THEY'RE EVEN WORSE THAN THE ELEMENT NETWORK AND HIJIKATA.
...

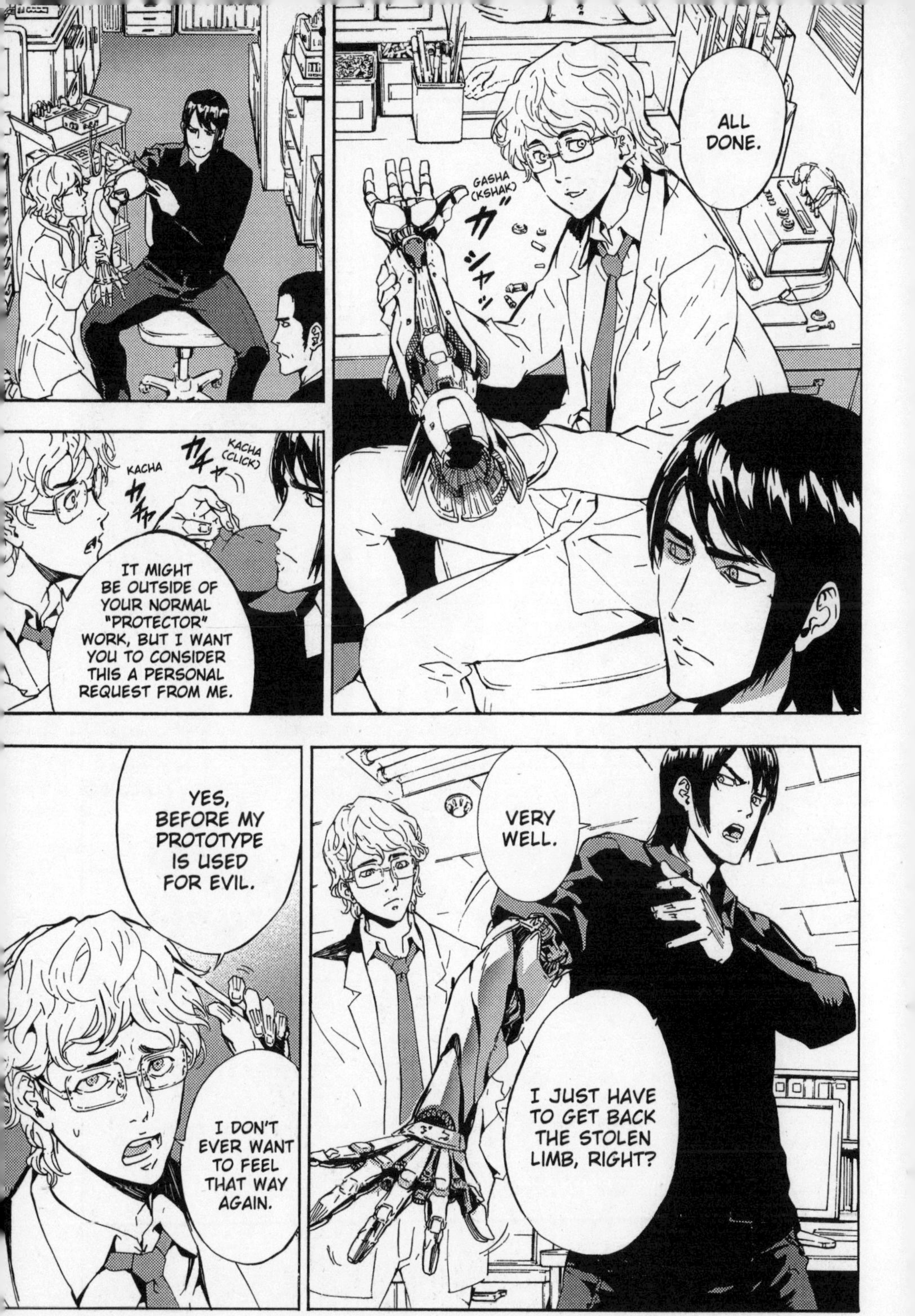
ALL DONE.
GASHA (KSHAK)
ガシャッ
KACHA (CLICK)
カチャ
KACHA
カチャ
IT MIGHT BE OUTSIDE OF YOUR NORMAL "PROTECTOR" WORK, BUT I WANT YOU TO CONSIDER THIS A PERSONAL REQUEST FROM ME.
VERY WELL.
I JUST HAVE TO GET BACK THE STOLEN LIMB, RIGHT?
YES, BEFORE MY PROTOTYPE IS USED FOR EVIL.
I DON'T EVER WANT TO FEEL THAT WAY AGAIN.

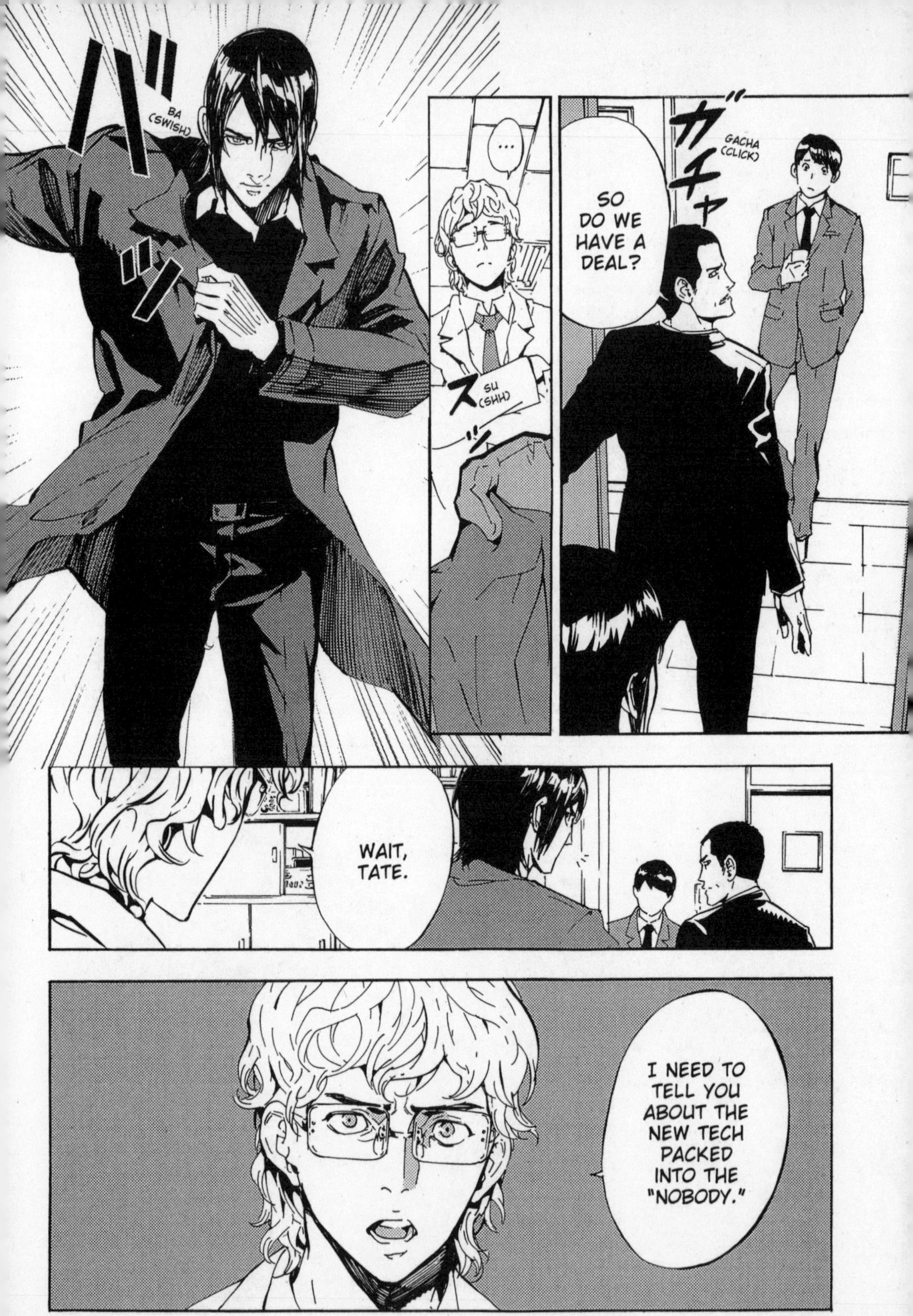
ガチャ
GACHA (CLICK)
SO DO WE HAVE A DEAL?
...
ス
SU (SHH)
バ
BA (SWISH)
WAIT, TATE.
I NEED TO TELL YOU ABOUT THE NEW TECH PACKED INTO THE "NOBODY."

Until Death do us Part

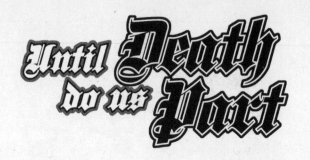

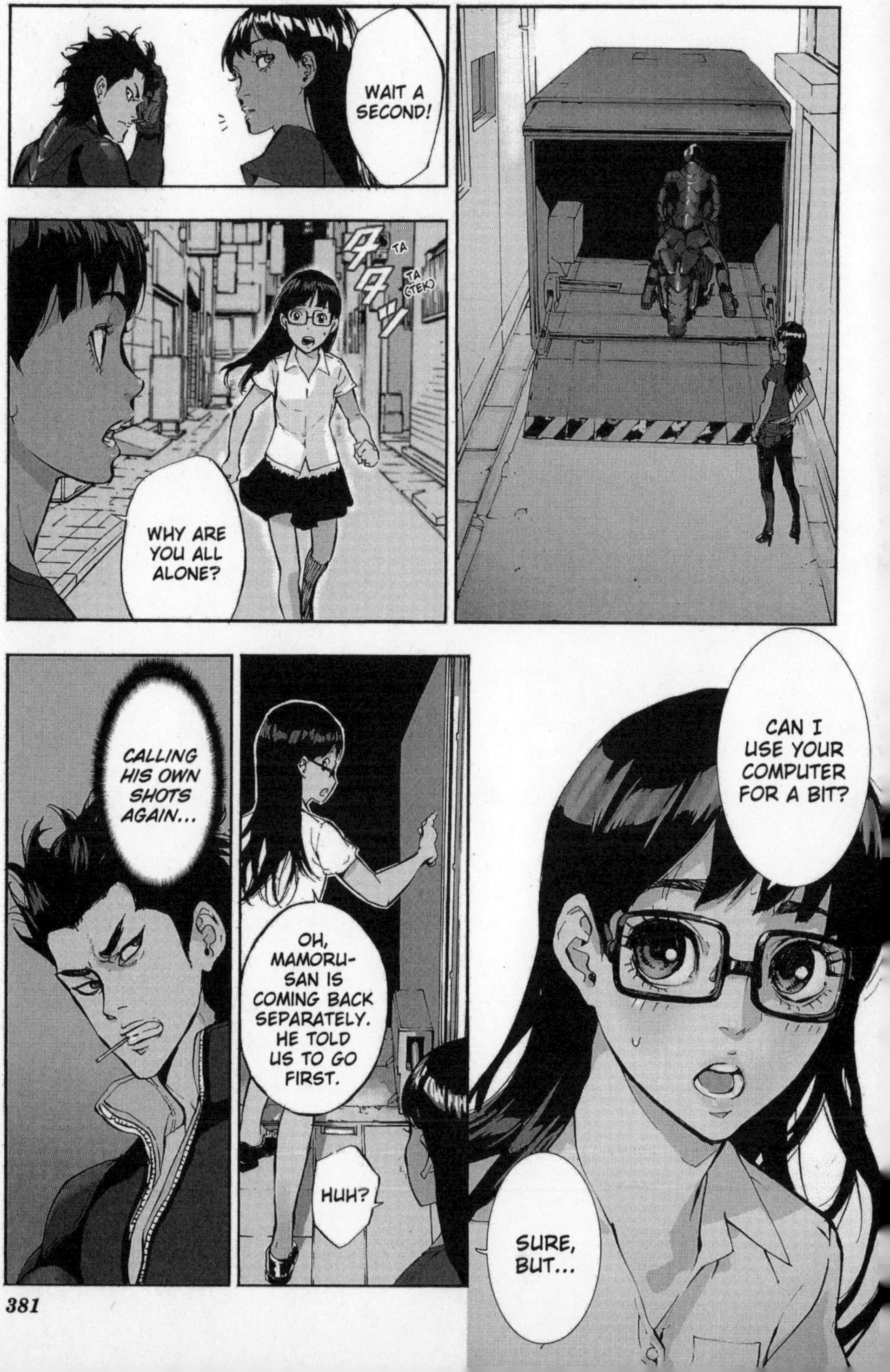
WAIT A SECOND!
タタッ
TA
TA (TEK)
WHY ARE YOU ALL ALONE?
CAN I USE YOUR COMPUTER FOR A BIT?
SURE, BUT...
OH, MAMORU-SAN IS COMING BACK SEPARATELY. HE TOLD US TO GO FIRST.
HUH?
CALLING HIS OWN SHOTS AGAIN...

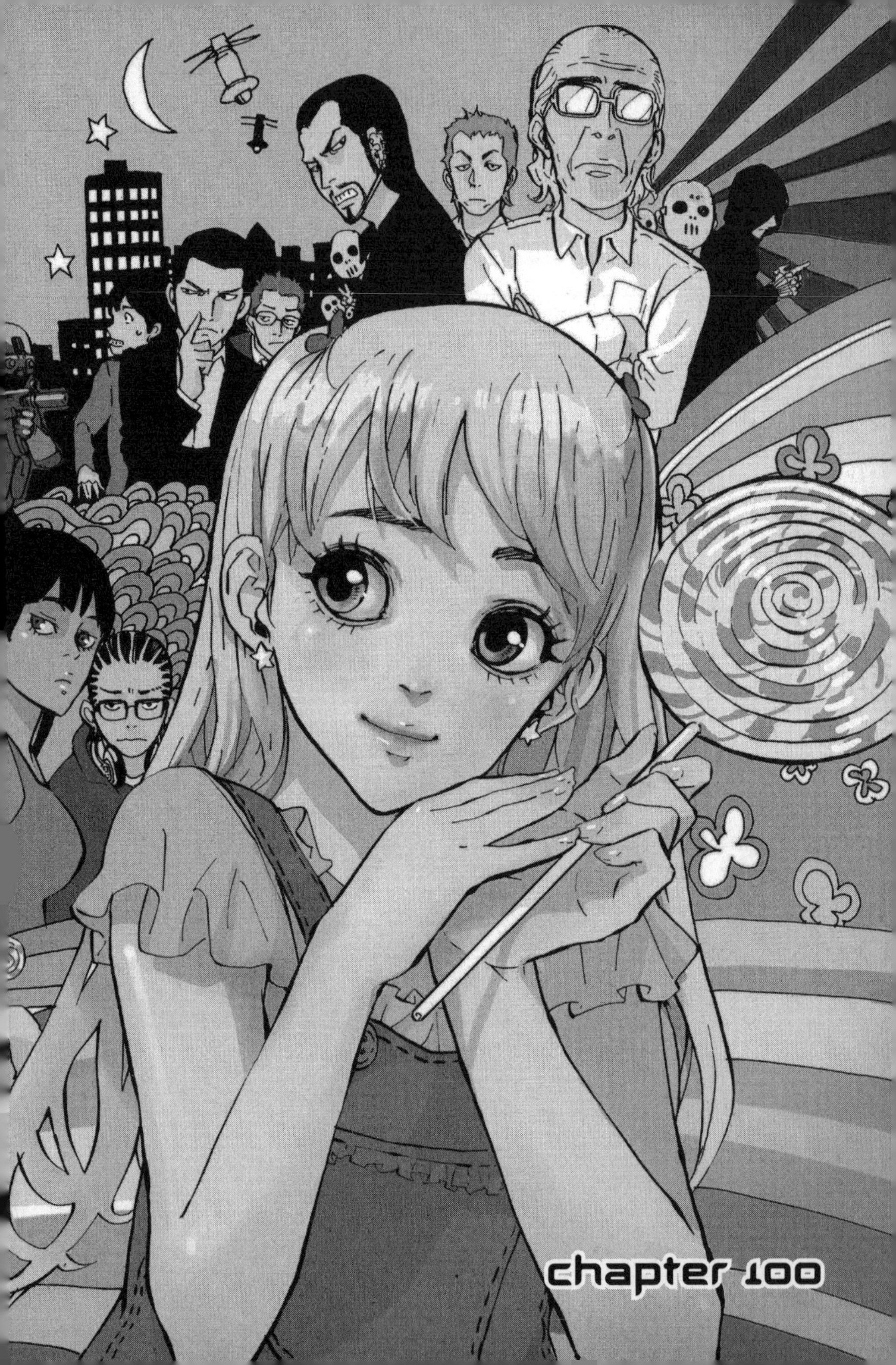
chapter 100

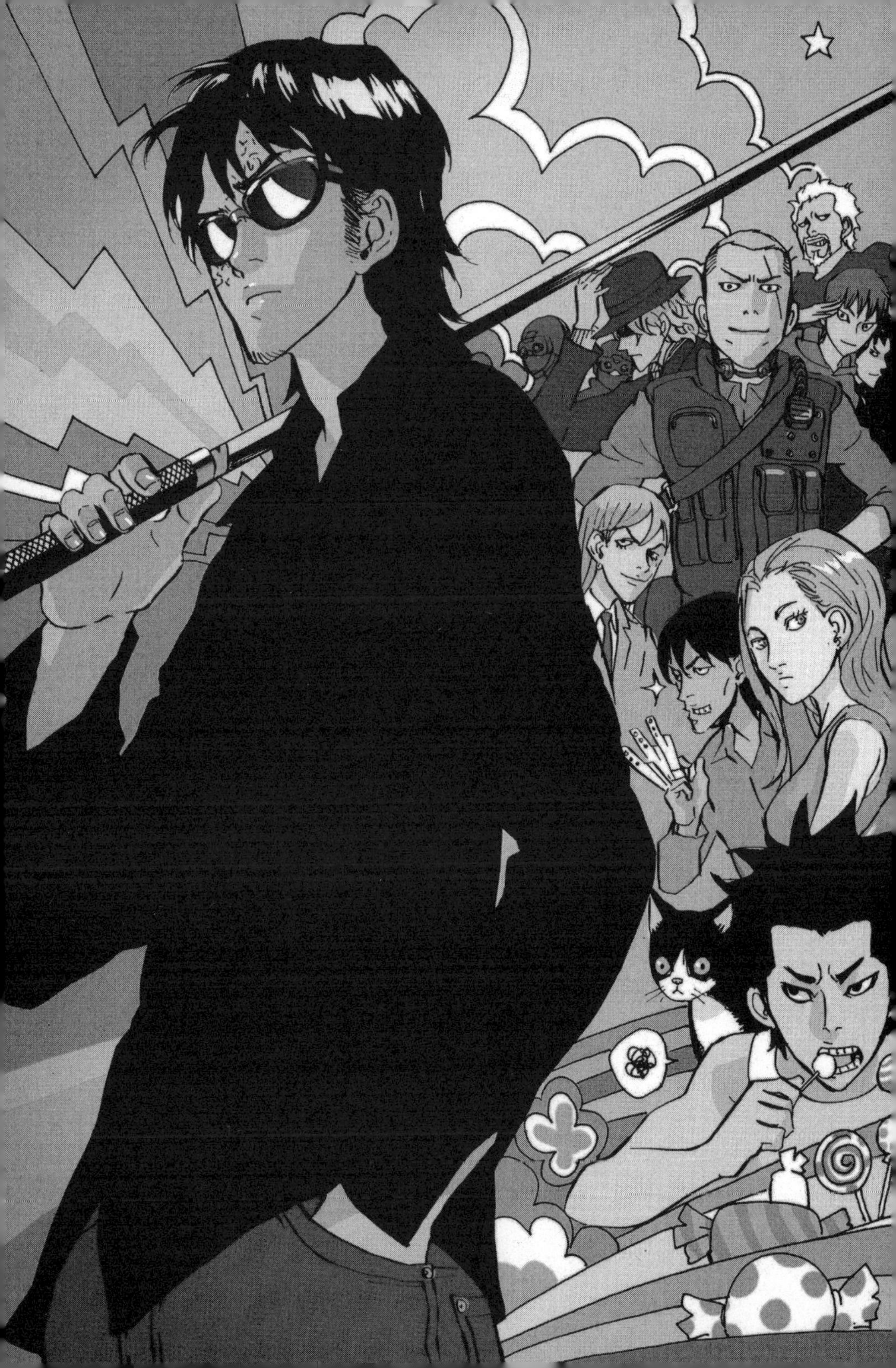

Until Death do us Part

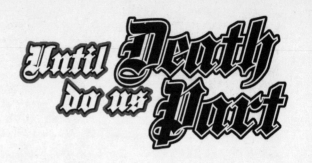

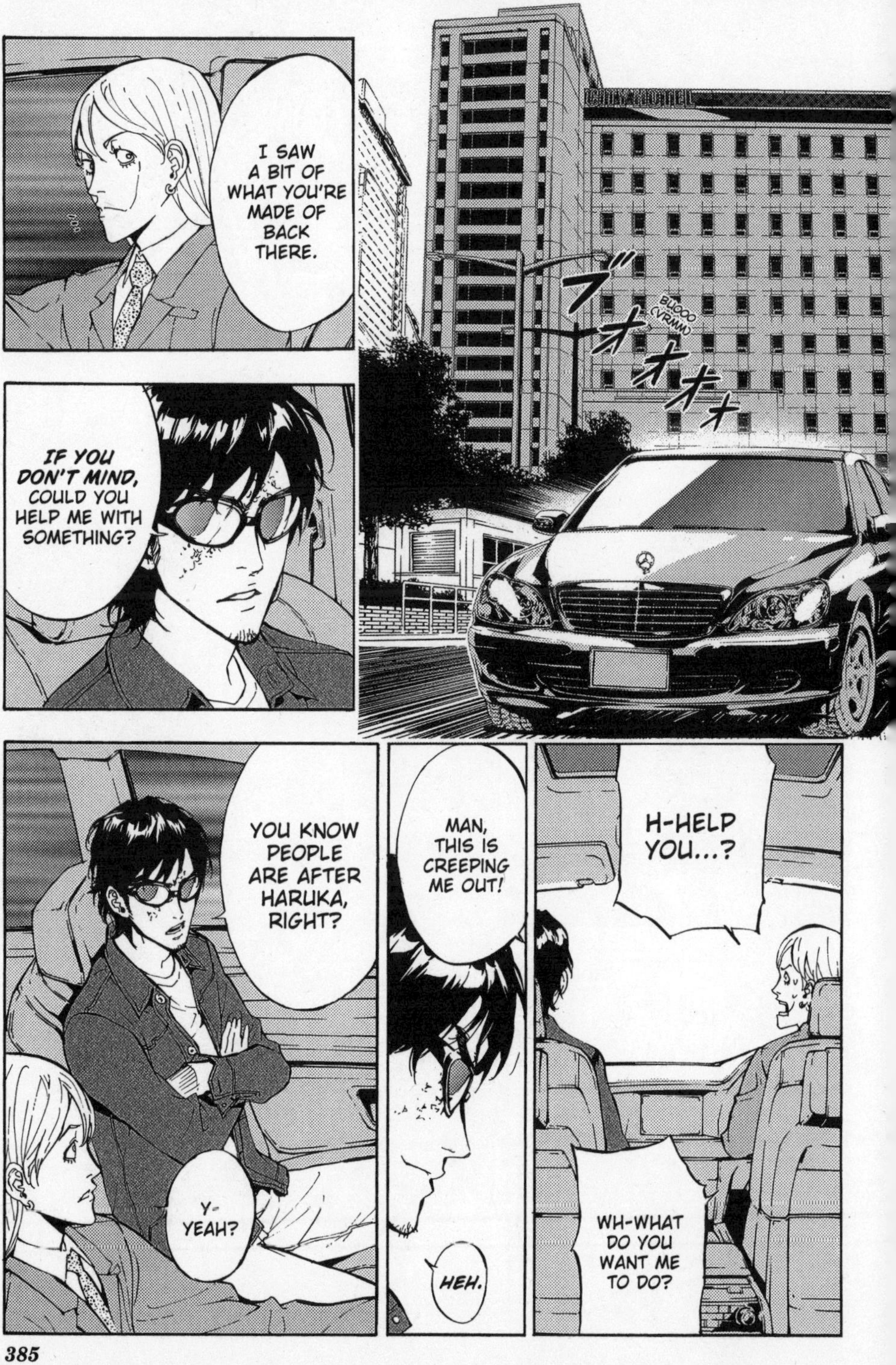
ブオオオオォ
BUOOO (VRMM)
I SAW A BIT OF WHAT YOU'RE MADE OF BACK THERE.
IF YOU DON'T MIND, COULD YOU HELP ME WITH SOMETHING?
H-HELP YOU...?
WH-WHAT DO YOU WANT ME TO DO?
MAN, THIS IS CREEPING ME OUT!
HEH.
YOU KNOW PEOPLE ARE AFTER HARUKA, RIGHT?
Y-YEAH?

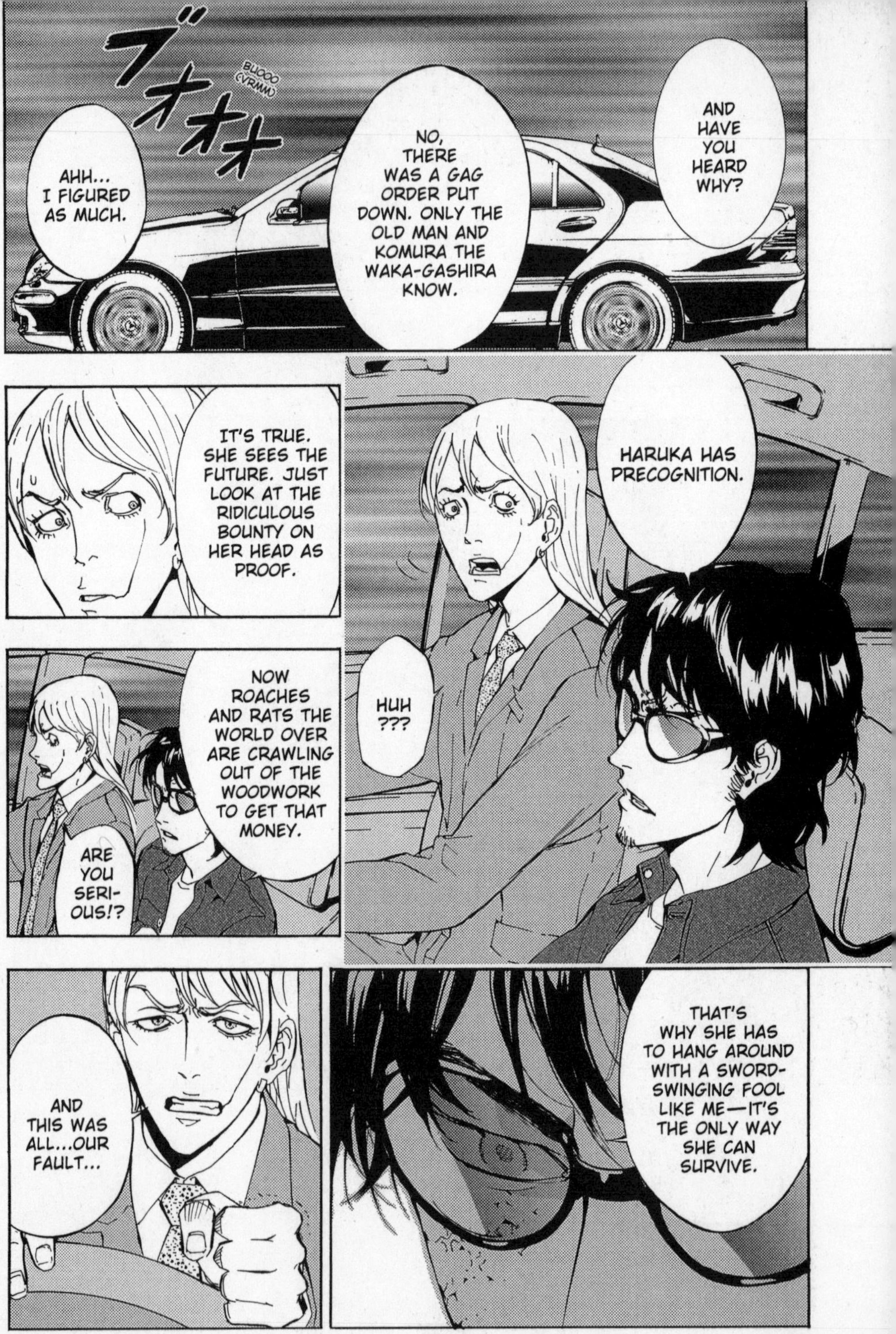
AND HAVE YOU HEARD WHY?
NO, THERE WAS A GAG ORDER PUT DOWN. ONLY THE OLD MAN AND KOMURA THE WAKA-GASHIRA KNOW.
ブオオオ
BUOOO (VRMM)
AHH... I FIGURED AS MUCH.
HARUKA HAS PRECOGNITION.
HUH ???
IT'S TRUE. SHE SEES THE FUTURE. JUST LOOK AT THE RIDICULOUS BOUNTY ON HER HEAD AS PROOF.
NOW ROACHES AND RATS THE WORLD OVER ARE CRAWLING OUT OF THE WOODWORK TO GET THAT MONEY.
ARE YOU SERI-OUS!?
THAT'S WHY SHE HAS TO HANG AROUND WITH A SWORD-SWINGING FOOL LIKE ME—IT'S THE ONLY WAY SHE CAN SURVIVE.
AND THIS WAS ALL...OUR FAULT...

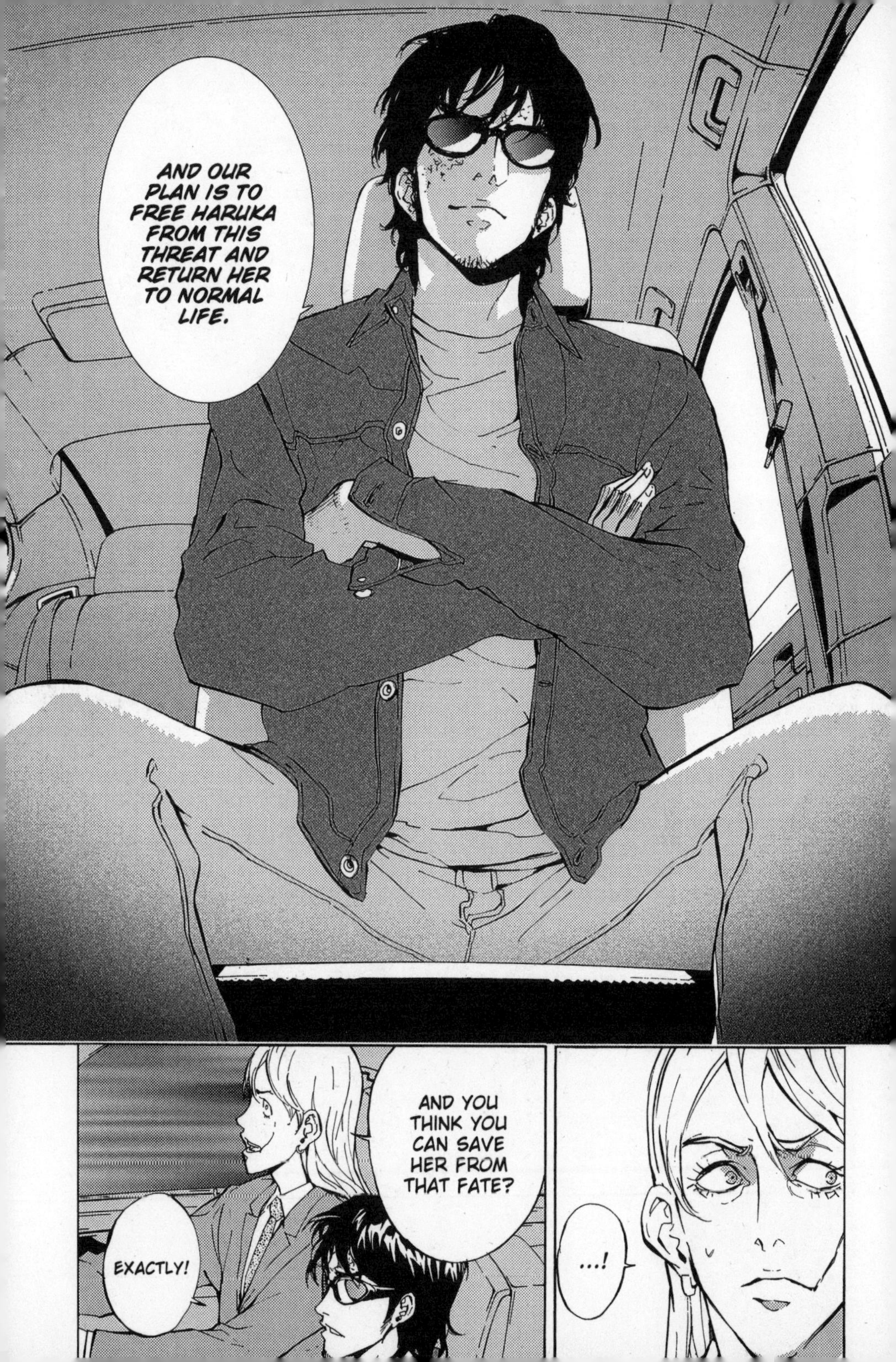
AND OUR PLAN IS TO FREE HARUKA FROM THIS THREAT AND RETURN HER TO NORMAL LIFE.
...!
AND YOU THINK YOU CAN SAVE HER FROM THAT FATE?
EXACTLY!

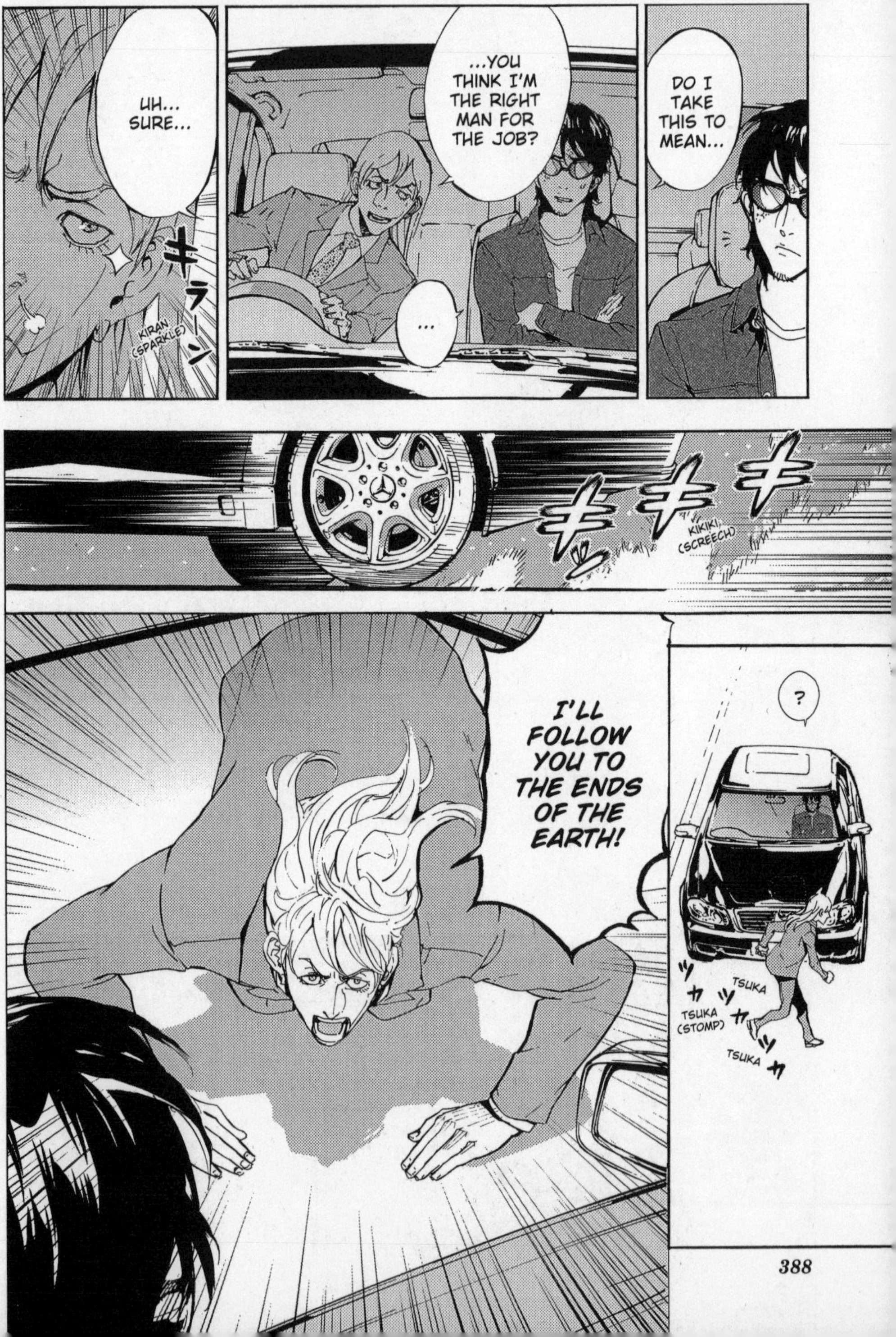
DO I TAKE THIS TO MEAN...
...YOU THINK I'M THE RIGHT MAN FOR THE JOB?
...
UH... SURE...
キラーン
KIRAN (SPARKLE)
キキキ
KIKIKI (SCREECH)
?
ツカツカツカ
TSUKA TSUKA (STOMP) TSUKA
I'LL FOLLOW YOU TO THE ENDS OF THE EARTH!

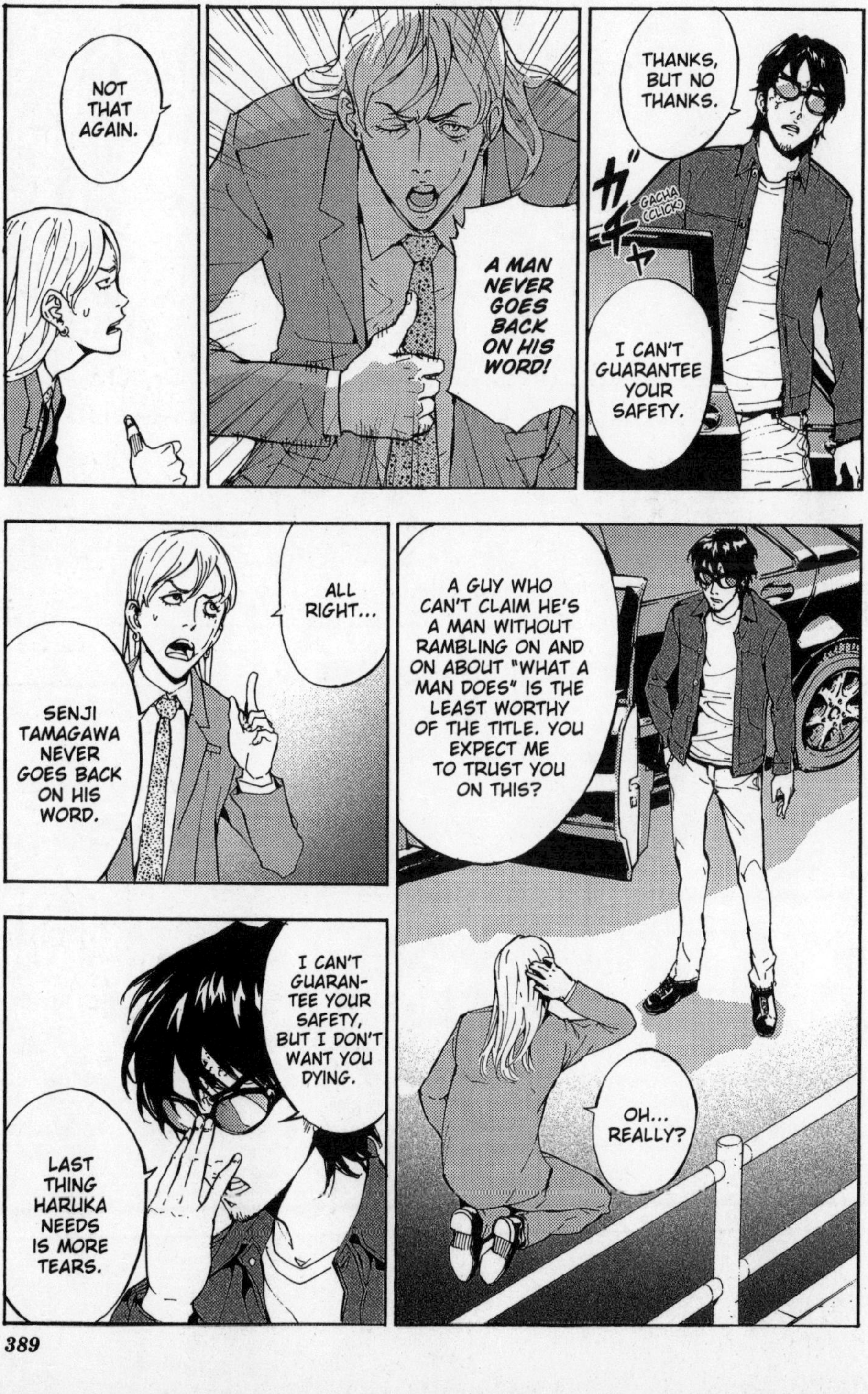
THANKS, BUT NO THANKS.
ガチャ
GACHA (CLICK)
I CAN'T GUARANTEE YOUR SAFETY.
A MAN NEVER GOES BACK ON HIS WORD!
NOT THAT AGAIN.
A GUY WHO CAN'T CLAIM HE'S A MAN WITHOUT RAMBLING ON AND ON ABOUT "WHAT A MAN DOES" IS THE LEAST WORTHY OF THE TITLE. YOU EXPECT ME TO TRUST YOU ON THIS?
OH... REALLY?
ALL RIGHT...
SENJI TAMAGAWA NEVER GOES BACK ON HIS WORD.
I CAN'T GUARAN-TEE YOUR SAFETY, BUT I DON'T WANT YOU DYING.
LAST THING HARUKA NEEDS IS MORE TEARS.

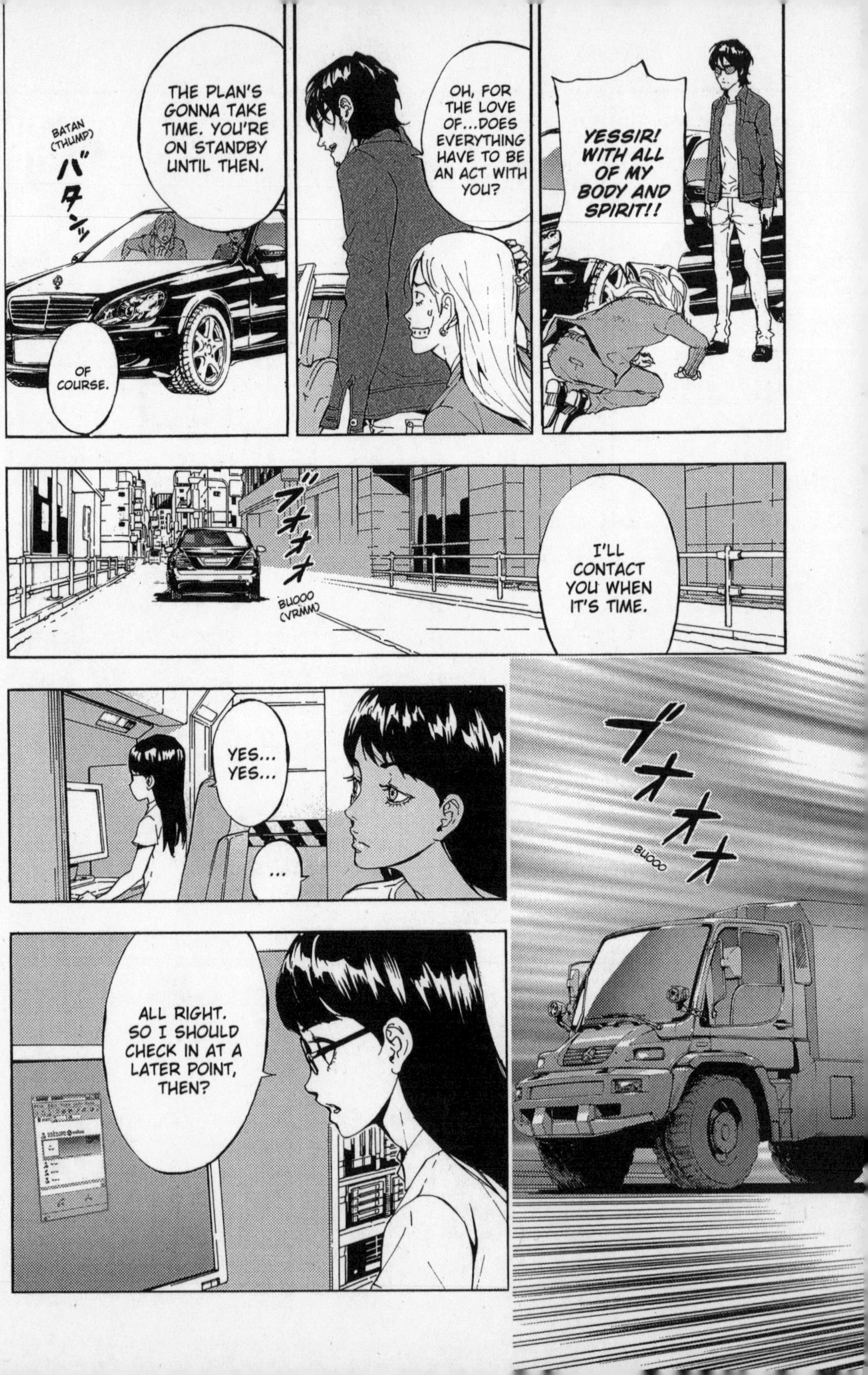
YESSIR! WITH ALL OF MY BODY AND SPIRIT!!
OH, FOR THE LOVE OF...DOES EVERYTHING HAVE TO BE AN ACT WITH YOU?
THE PLAN'S GONNA TAKE TIME. YOU'RE ON STANDBY UNTIL THEN.
バタンッ
BATAN (THUMP)
OF COURSE.
I'LL CONTACT YOU WHEN IT'S TIME.
ブオオオ
BUOOO (VRMM)
ブオオオ
BUOOO
YES... YES...
...
ALL RIGHT. SO I SHOULD CHECK IN AT A LATER POINT, THEN?

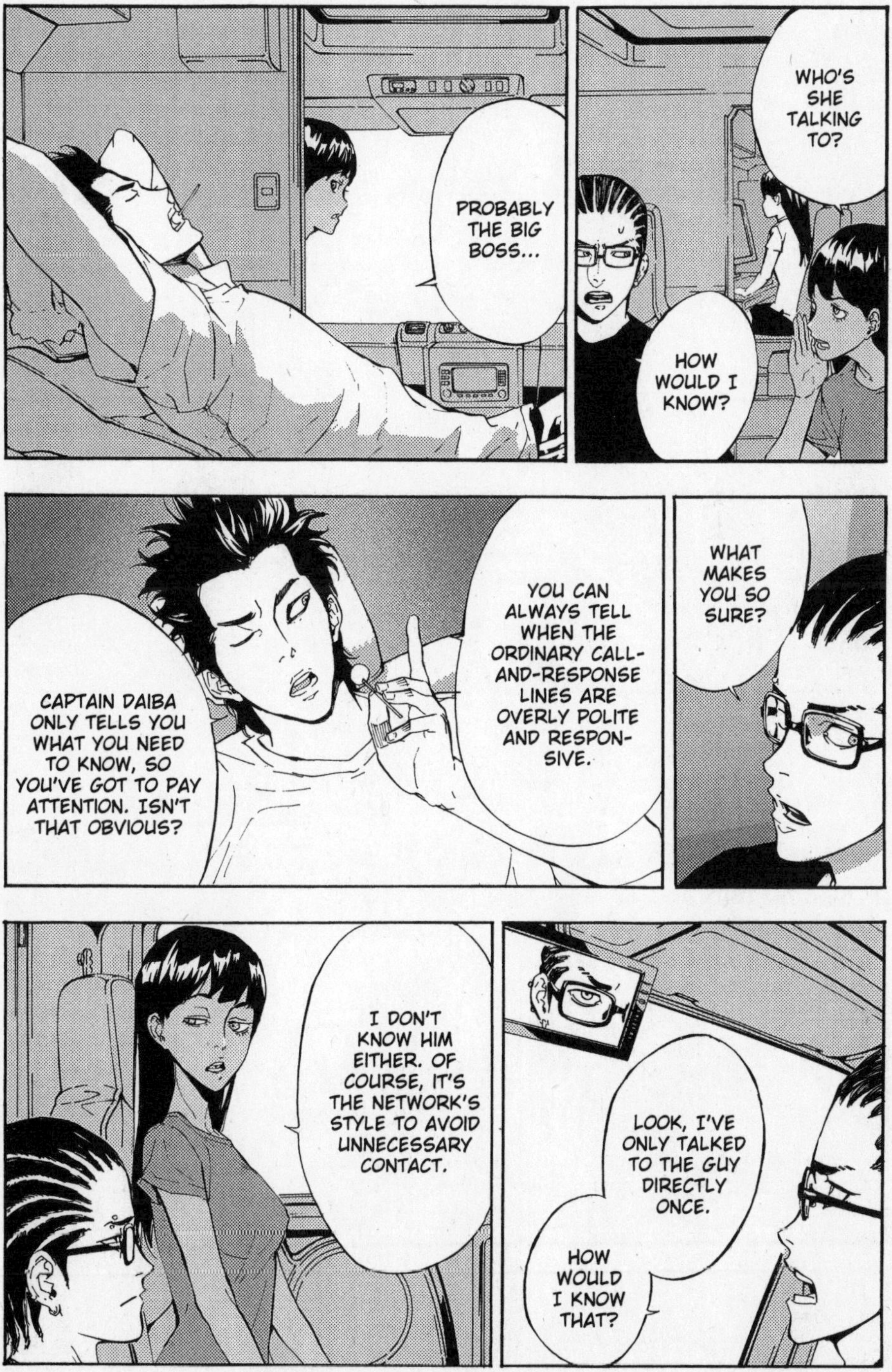
WHO'S SHE TALKING TO?
HOW WOULD I KNOW?
PROBABLY THE BIG BOSS...
WHAT MAKES YOU SO SURE?
YOU CAN ALWAYS TELL WHEN THE ORDINARY CALL-AND-RESPONSE LINES ARE OVERLY POLITE AND RESPONSIVE.
CAPTAIN DAIBA ONLY TELLS YOU WHAT YOU NEED TO KNOW, SO YOU'VE GOT TO PAY ATTENTION. ISN'T THAT OBVIOUS?
LOOK, I'VE ONLY TALKED TO THE GUY DIRECTLY ONCE.
HOW WOULD I KNOW THAT?
I DON'T KNOW HIM EITHER. OF COURSE, IT'S THE NETWORK'S STYLE TO AVOID UNNECESSARY CONTACT.

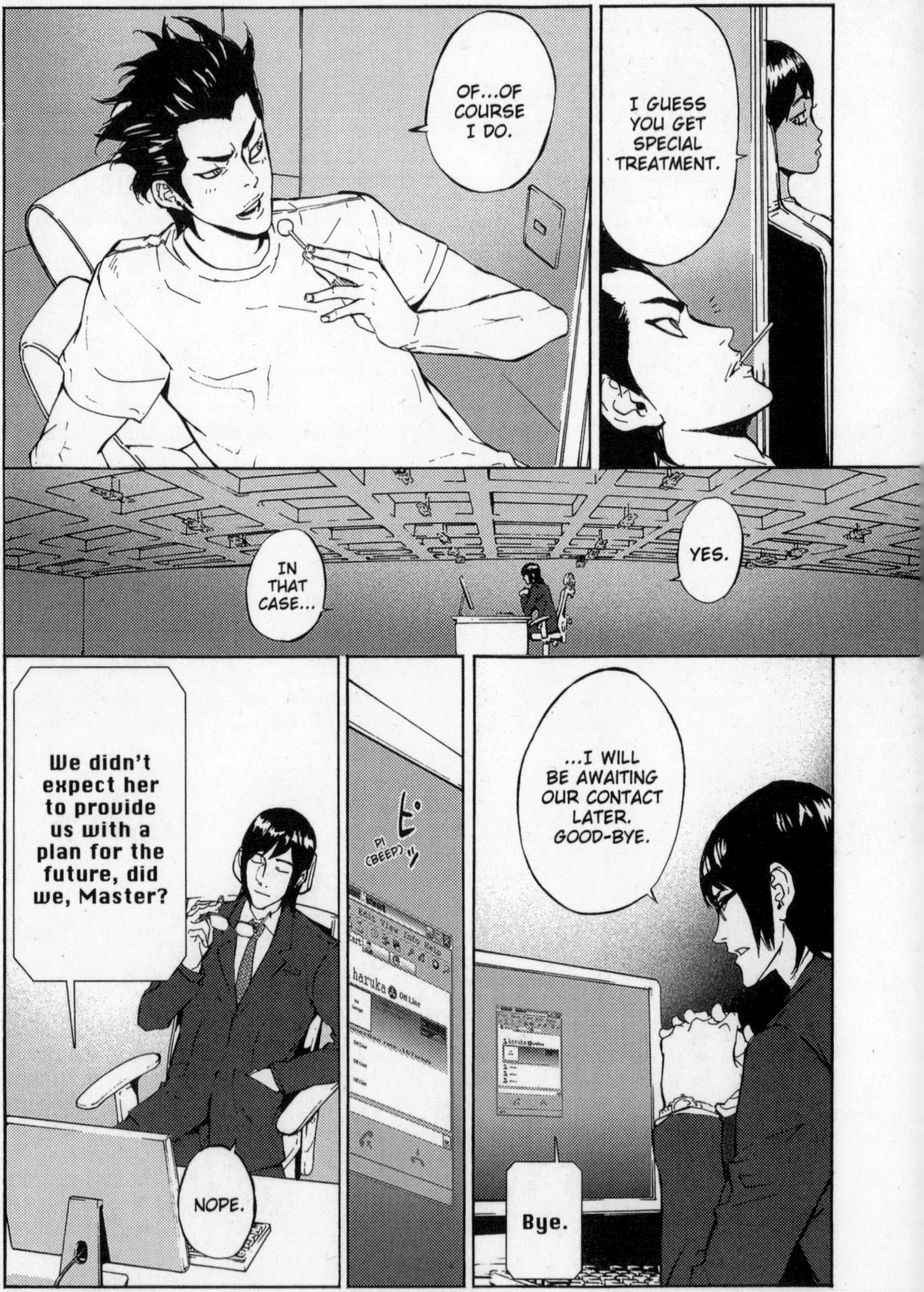
I GUESS YOU GET SPECIAL TREATMENT.
OF...OF COURSE I DO.
YES.
IN THAT CASE...
...I WILL BE AWAITING OUR CONTACT LATER. GOOD-BYE.
Bye.
ピ
PI (BEEP)
haruka Off Line
We didn't expect her to provide us with a plan for the future, did we, Master?
NOPE.

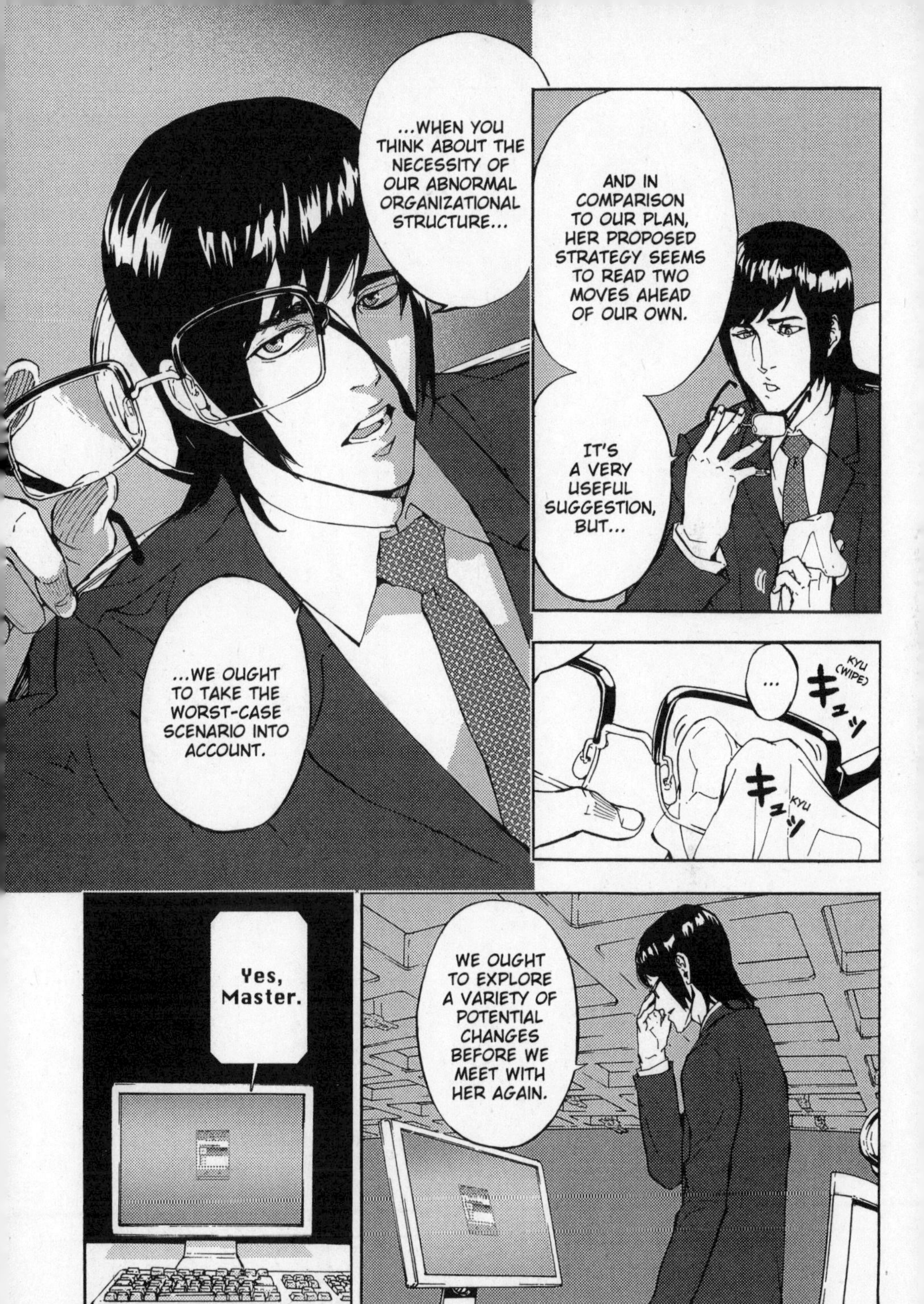
AND IN COMPARISON TO OUR PLAN, HER PROPOSED STRATEGY SEEMS TO READ TWO MOVES AHEAD OF OUR OWN.
IT'S A VERY USEFUL SUGGESTION, BUT...
...
キュッ
KYU (WIPE)
キュッ
KYU
...WHEN YOU THINK ABOUT THE NECESSITY OF OUR ABNORMAL ORGANIZATIONAL STRUCTURE...
...WE OUGHT TO TAKE THE WORST-CASE SCENARIO INTO ACCOUNT.
WE OUGHT TO EXPLORE A VARIETY OF POTENTIAL CHANGES BEFORE WE MEET WITH HER AGAIN.
Yes, Master.

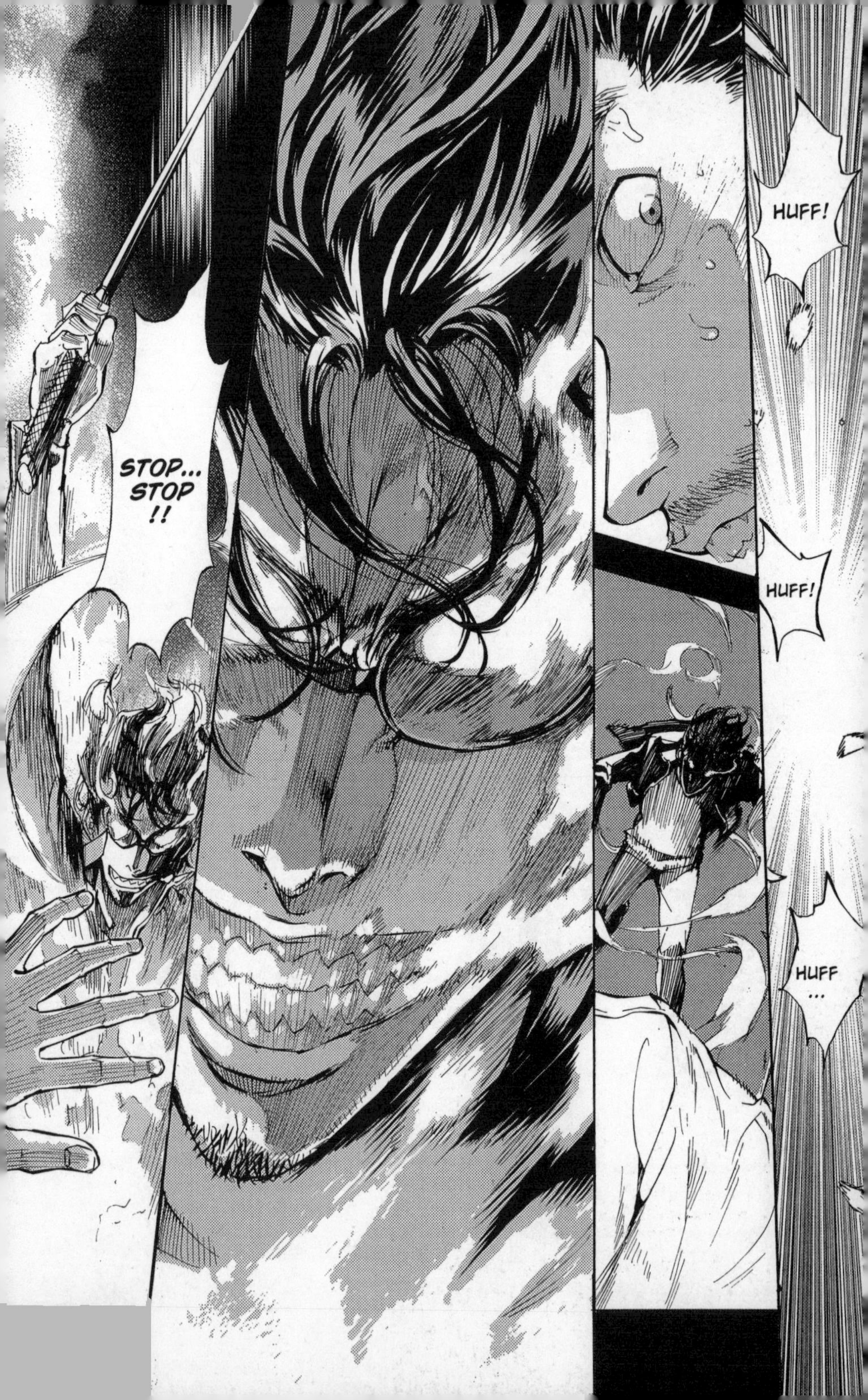
HUFF!
HUFF!
HUFF ...
STOP... STOP !!

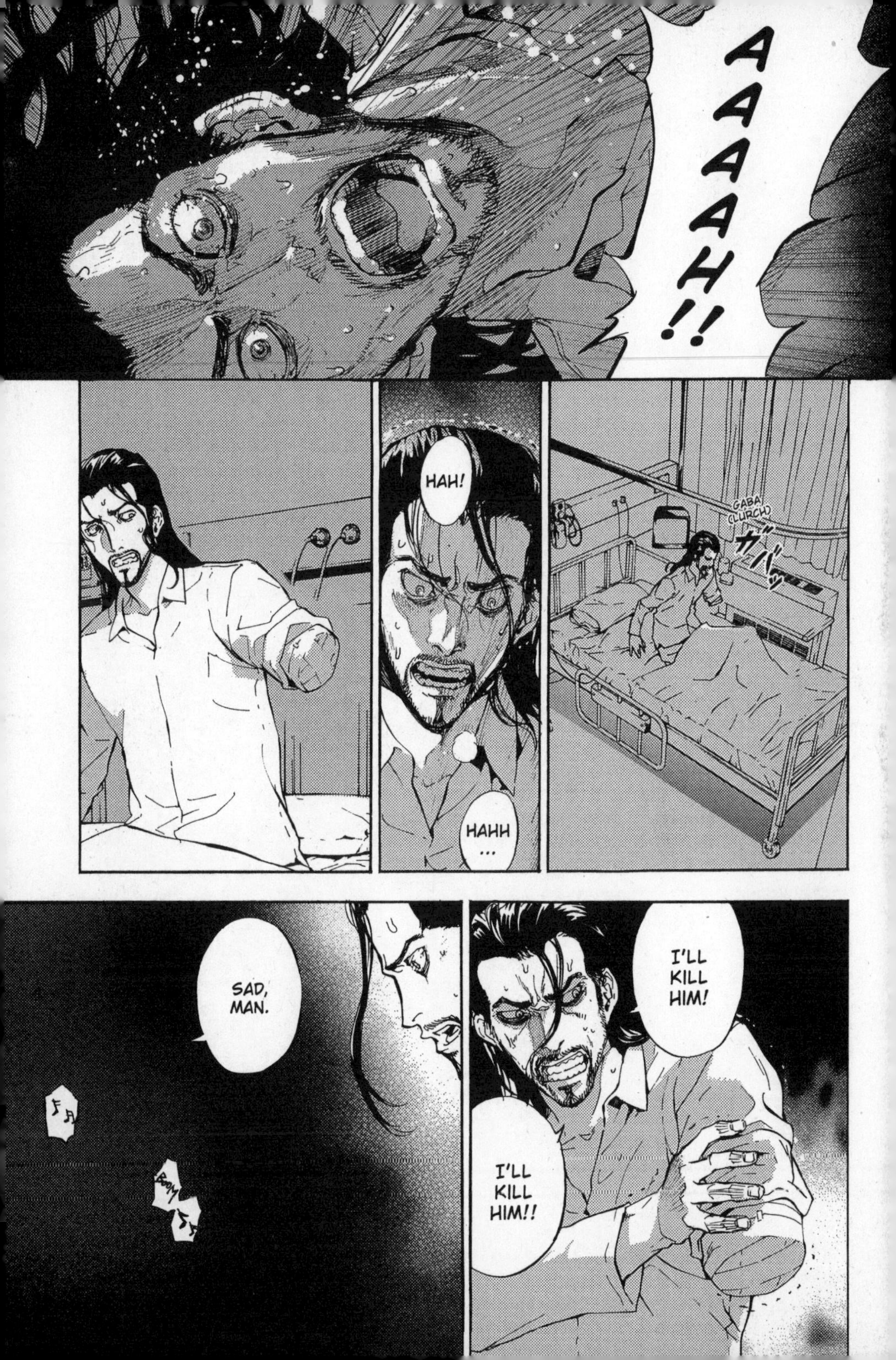
AAAAAH!!
GABA (LURCH)
ガバッ
HAH!
HAHH...
I'LL KILL HIM!
I'LL KILL HIM!!
SAD, MAN.
BOOM

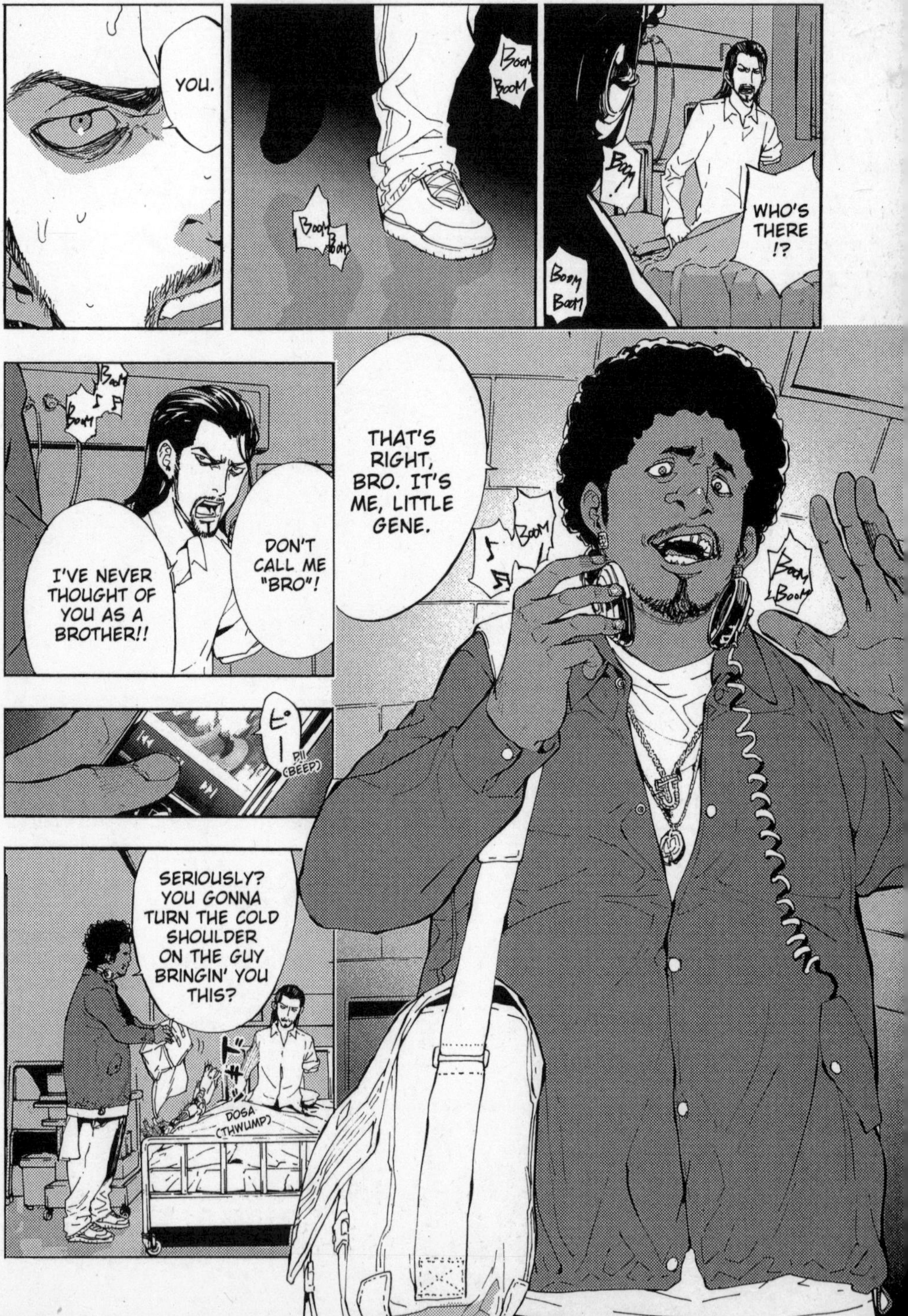
BOOM BOOM
BOOM
BOOM BOOM
WHO'S THERE !?
BOOM BOOM
YOU.
THAT'S RIGHT, BRO. IT'S ME, LITTLE GENE.
BOOM
BOOM BOOM
BOOM BOOM
DON'T CALL ME "BRO"!
I'VE NEVER THOUGHT OF YOU AS A BROTHER!!
ピー
PII (BEEP)
SERIOUSLY? YOU GONNA TURN THE COLD SHOULDER ON THE GUY BRINGIN' YOU THIS?
DOSA (THWUMP)

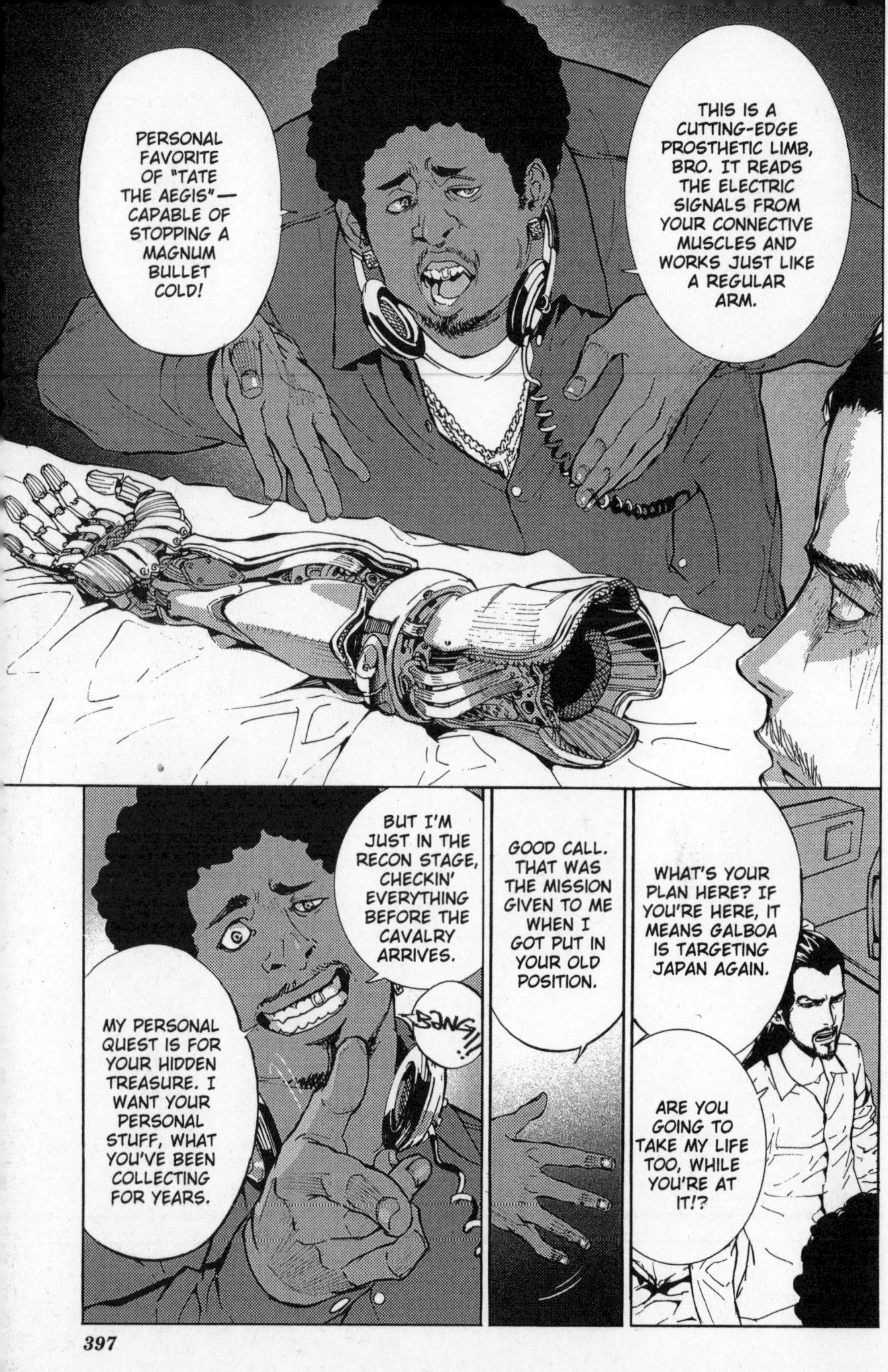
THIS IS A CUTTING-EDGE PROSTHETIC LIMB, BRO. IT READS THE ELECTRIC SIGNALS FROM YOUR CONNECTIVE MUSCLES AND WORKS JUST LIKE A REGULAR ARM.
PERSONAL FAVORITE OF "TATE THE AEGIS"—CAPABLE OF STOPPING A MAGNUM BULLET COLD!
WHAT'S YOUR PLAN HERE? IF YOU'RE HERE, IT MEANS GALBOA IS TARGETING JAPAN AGAIN.
ARE YOU GOING TO TAKE MY LIFE TOO, WHILE YOU'RE AT IT!?
GOOD CALL. THAT WAS THE MISSION GIVEN TO ME WHEN I GOT PUT IN YOUR OLD POSITION.
BUT I'M JUST IN THE RECON STAGE, CHECKIN' EVERYTHING BEFORE THE CAVALRY ARRIVES.
BANG!!
MY PERSONAL QUEST IS FOR YOUR HIDDEN TREASURE. I WANT YOUR PERSONAL STUFF, WHAT YOU'VE BEEN COLLECTING FOR YEARS.

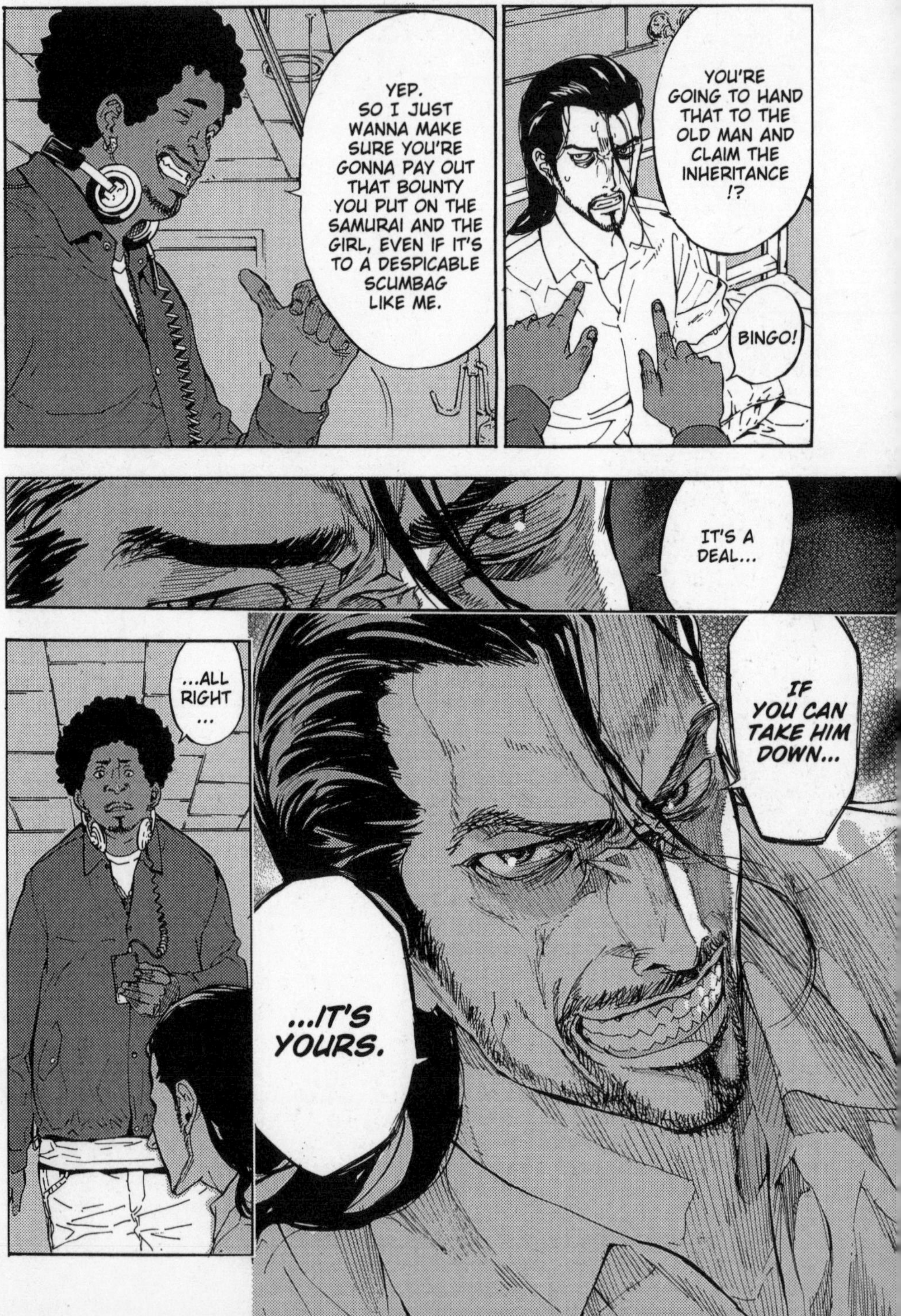
YOU'RE GOING TO HAND THAT TO THE OLD MAN AND CLAIM THE INHERITANCE !?
BINGO!
YEP. SO I JUST WANNA MAKE SURE YOU'RE GONNA PAY OUT THAT BOUNTY YOU PUT ON THE SAMURAI AND THE GIRL, EVEN IF IT'S TO A DESPICABLE SCUMBAG LIKE ME.
IT'S A DEAL...
IF YOU CAN TAKE HIM DOWN...
...IT'S YOURS.
...ALL RIGHT ...

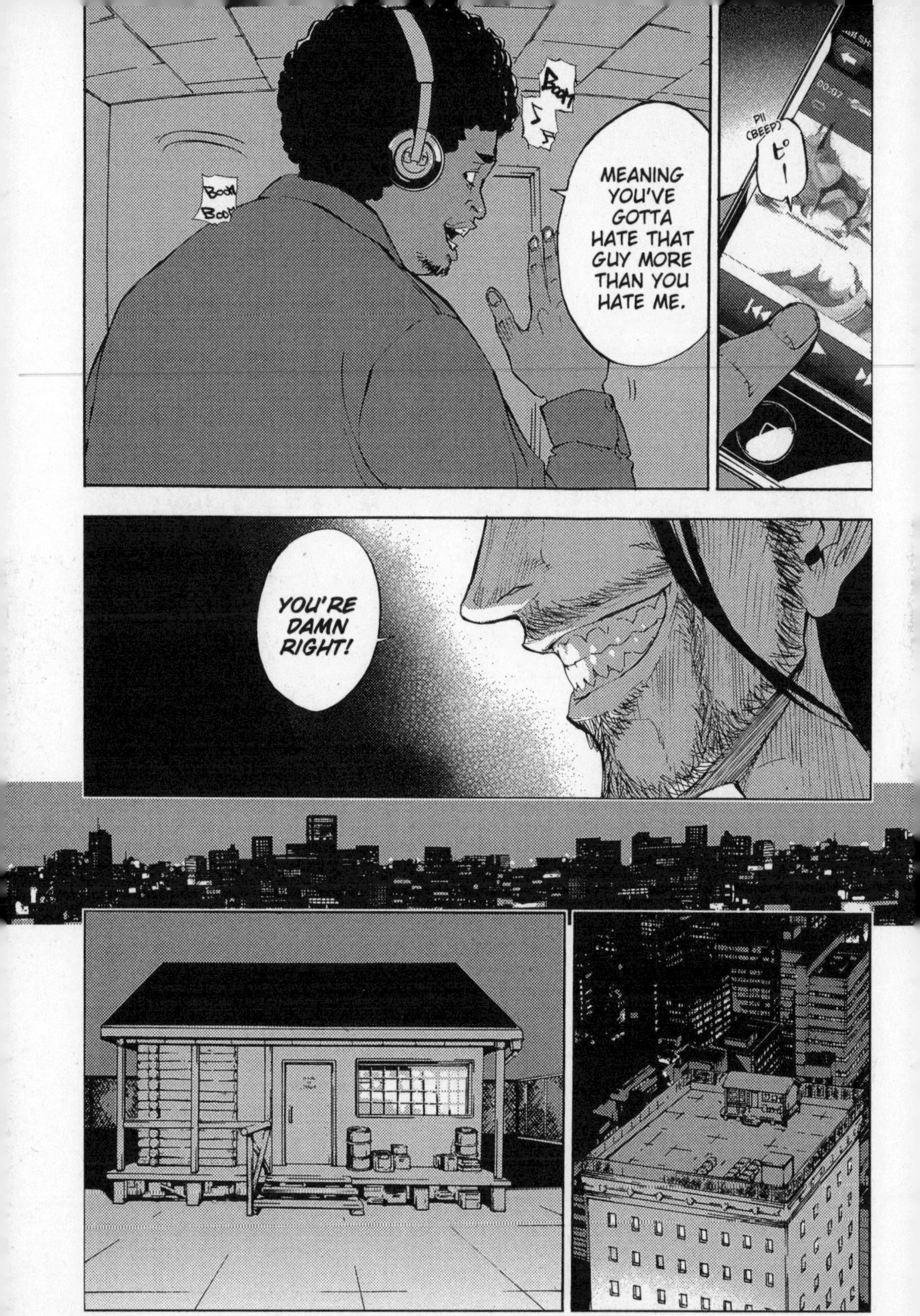
PII (BEEP)
BOOM
BOOM BOOM
MEANING YOU'VE GOTTA HATE THAT GUY MORE THAN YOU HATE ME.
YOU'RE DAMN RIGHT!

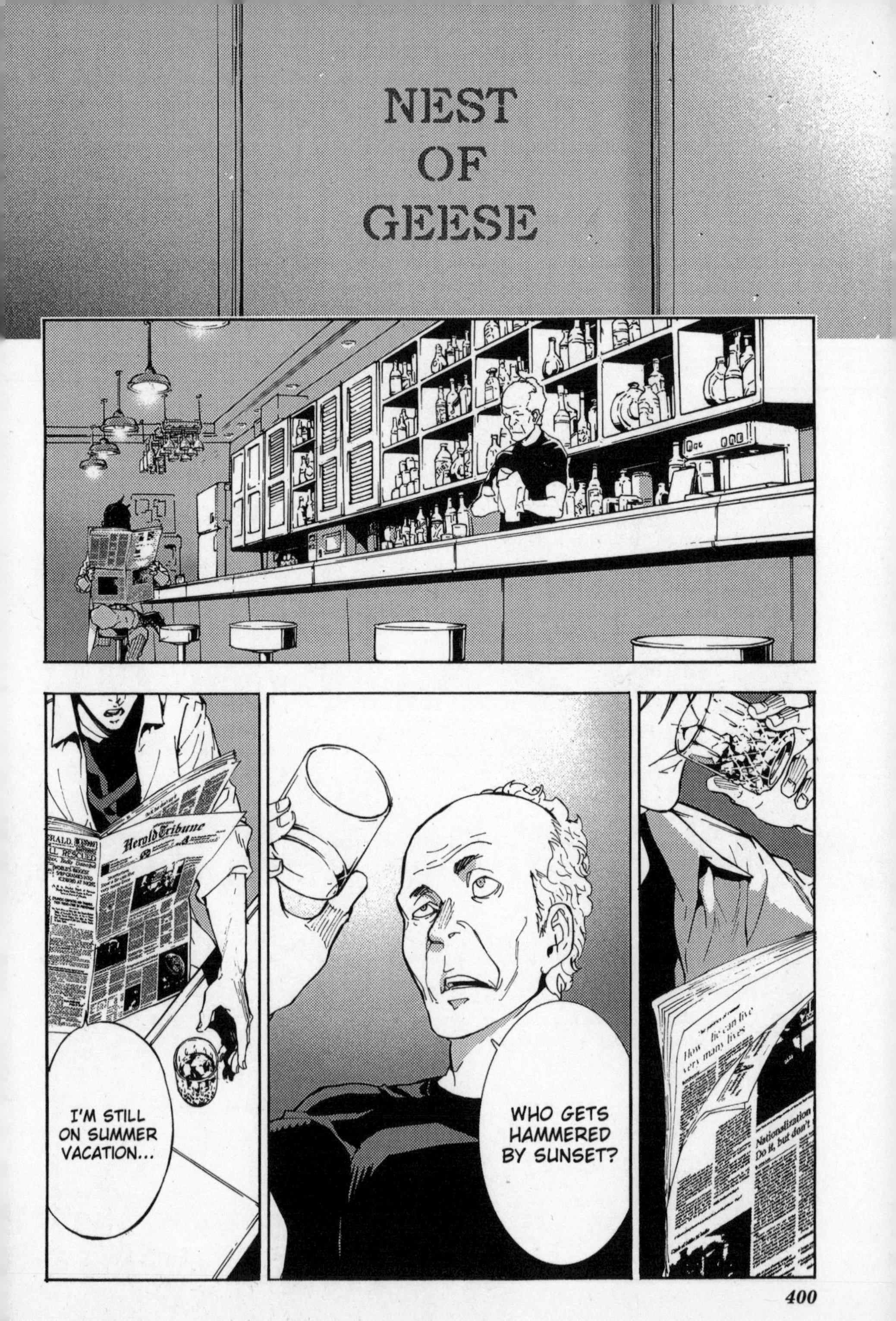
NEST OF GEESE
How he can live very many lives
Nationalization
Do it, but don't
WHO GETS HAMMERED BY SUNSET?
Herald Tribune
I'M STILL ON SUMMER VACATION...

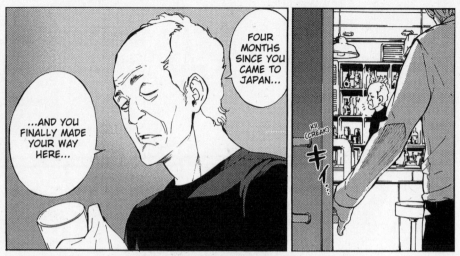

FOUR MONTHS SINCE YOU CAME TO JAPAN...

...AND YOU FINALLY MADE YOUR WAY HERE...

...

...THOMAS JEFFERSON.

IS THAT HOW LONG IT TOOK FOR YOU TO MAKE SOME TIME?

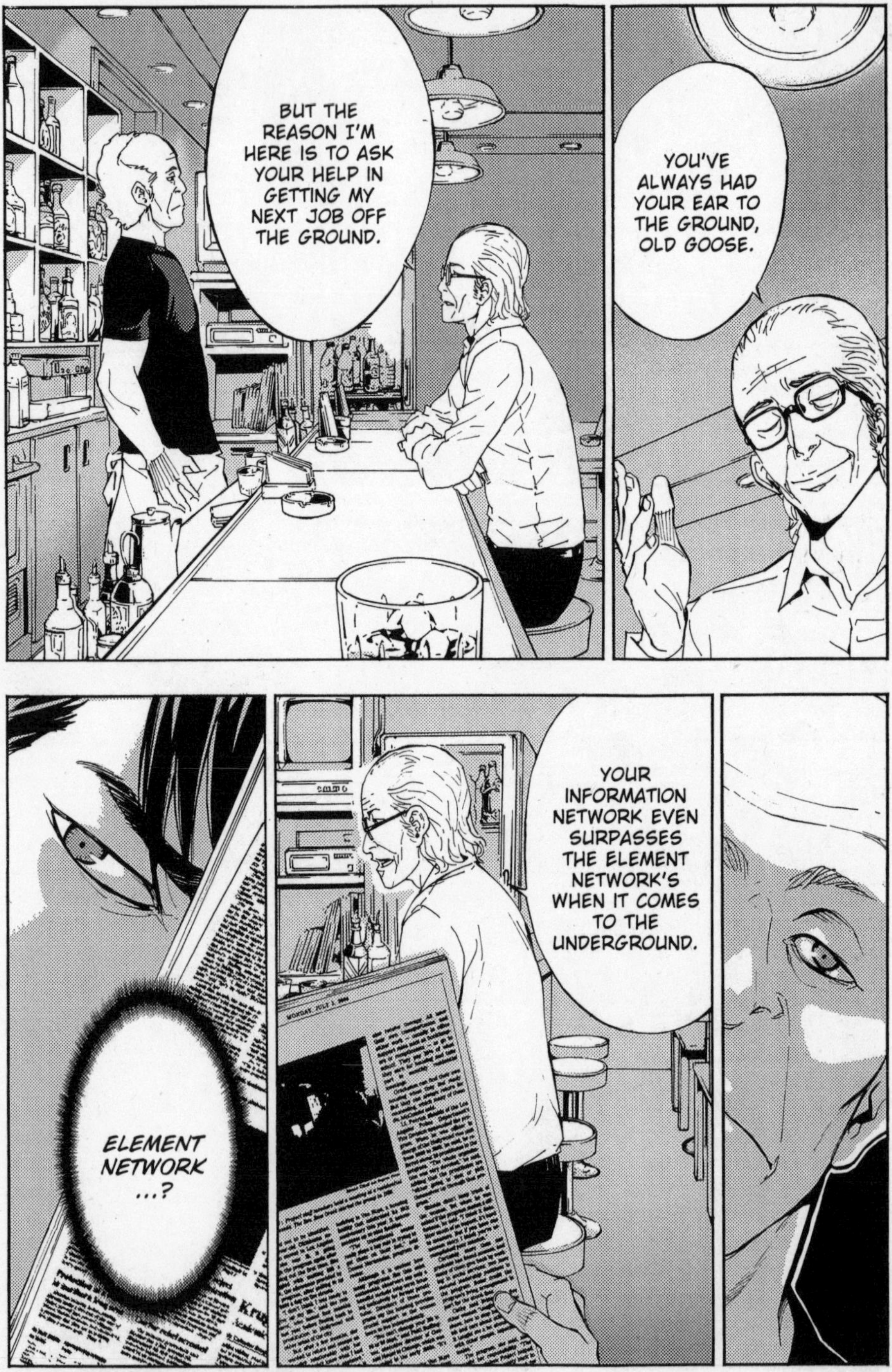
YOU'VE ALWAYS HAD YOUR EAR TO THE GROUND, OLD GOOSE.
BUT THE REASON I'M HERE IS TO ASK YOUR HELP IN GETTING MY NEXT JOB OFF THE GROUND.
YOUR INFORMATION NETWORK EVEN SURPASSES THE ELEMENT NETWORK'S WHEN IT COMES TO THE UNDERGROUND.
ELEMENT NETWORK ...?

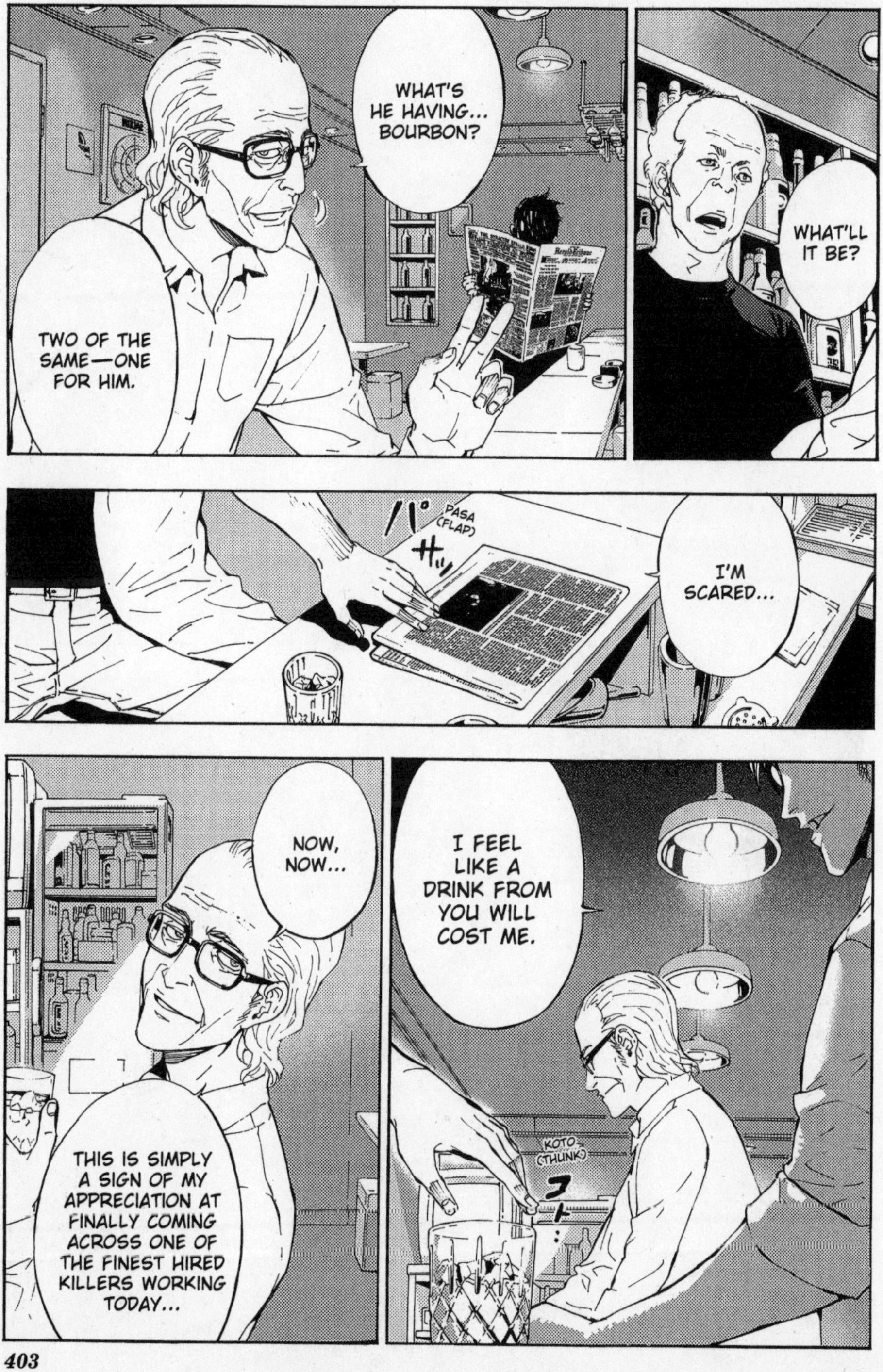
WHAT'LL IT BE?
WHAT'S HE HAVING... BOURBON?
TWO OF THE SAME—ONE FOR HIM.
PASA (FLAP)
I'M SCARED...
I FEEL LIKE A DRINK FROM YOU WILL COST ME.
KOTO (THUNK)
NOW, NOW...
THIS IS SIMPLY A SIGN OF MY APPRECIATION AT FINALLY COMING ACROSS ONE OF THE FINEST HIRED KILLERS WORKING TODAY...

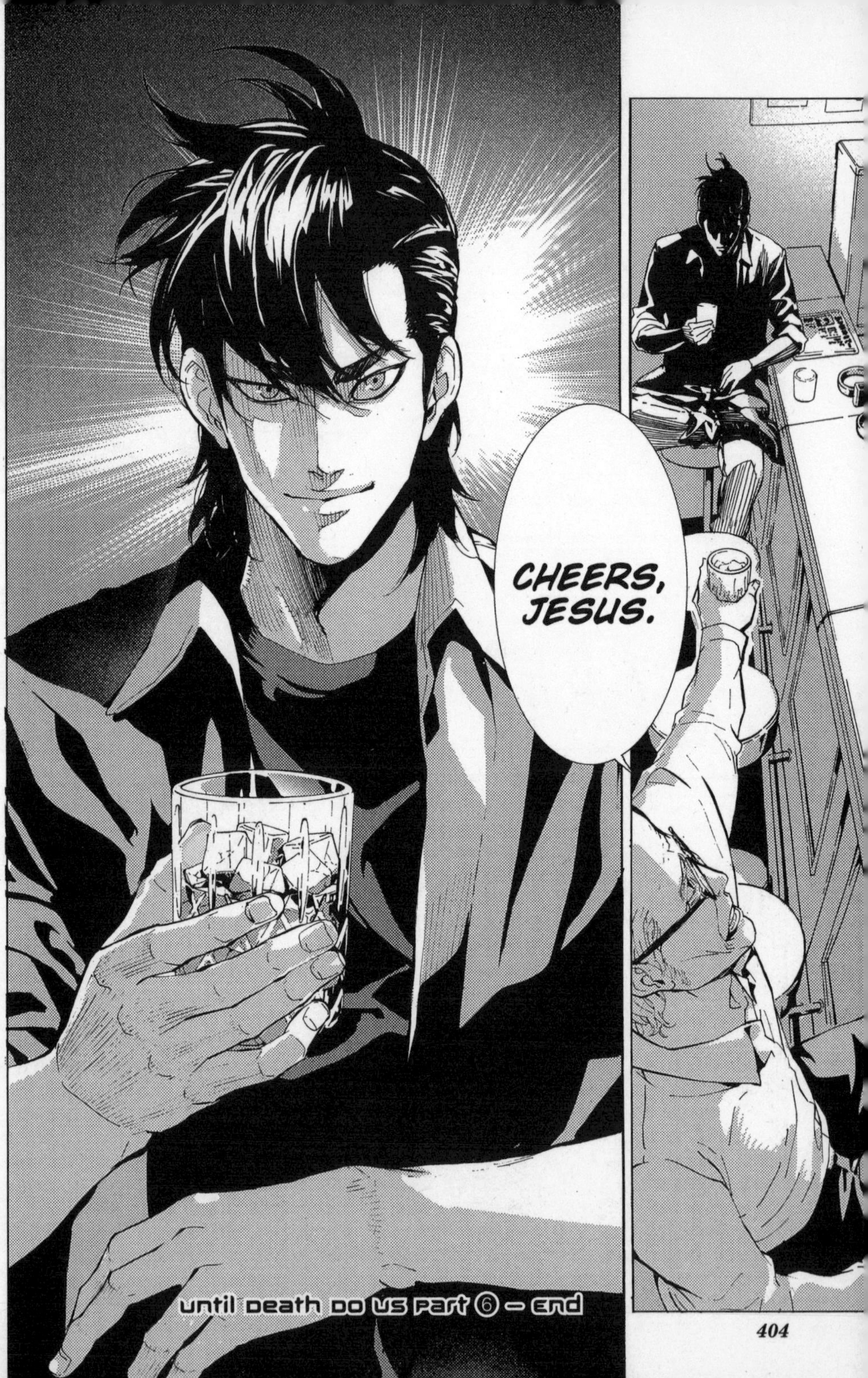
CHEERS, JESUS.
until death do us part ⑥ – end

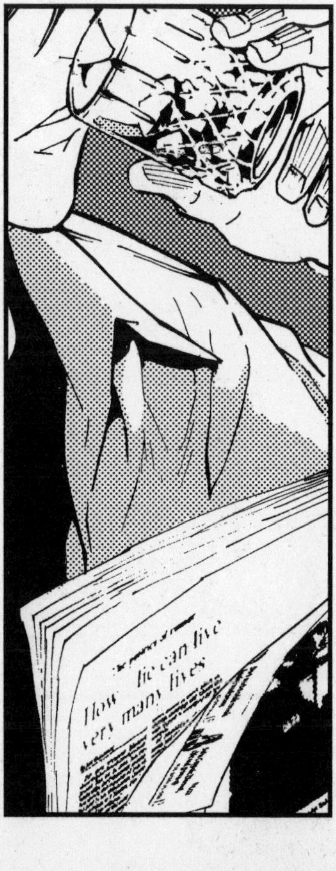
How lie can live
very many lives

Until Death do us Part

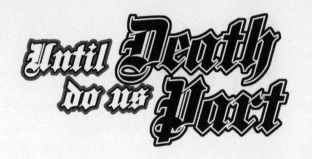

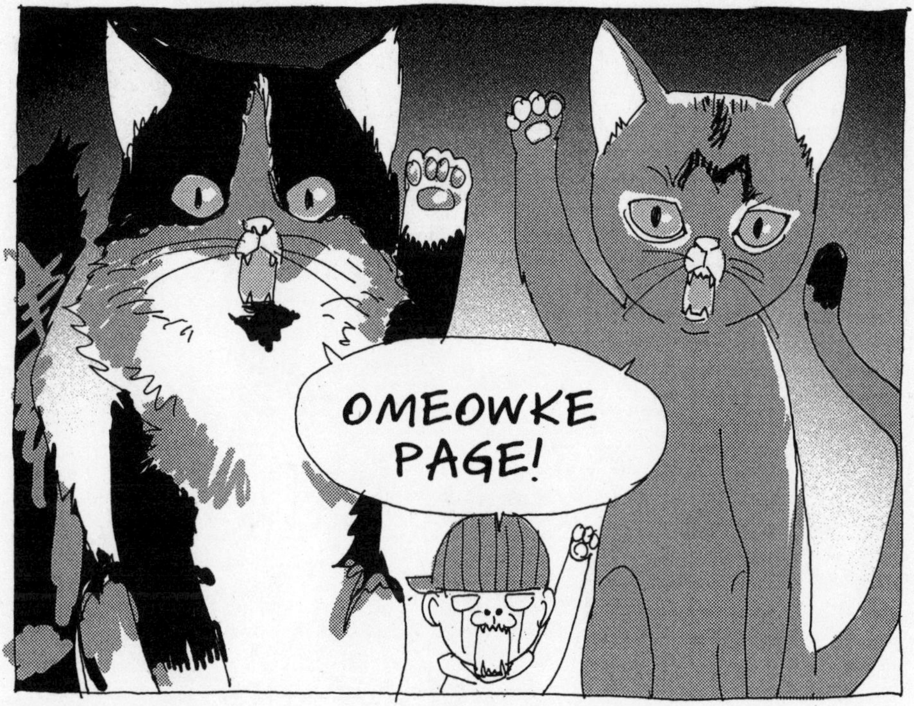
OMEOWKE PAGE!

AT ONE POINT, MY DOG FANG, BORN FROM A MALTESE MOTHER AND MUTT FATHER, WAS A TINY LITTLE PUPPY I COULD HOLD IN THE PALM OF MY HAND...

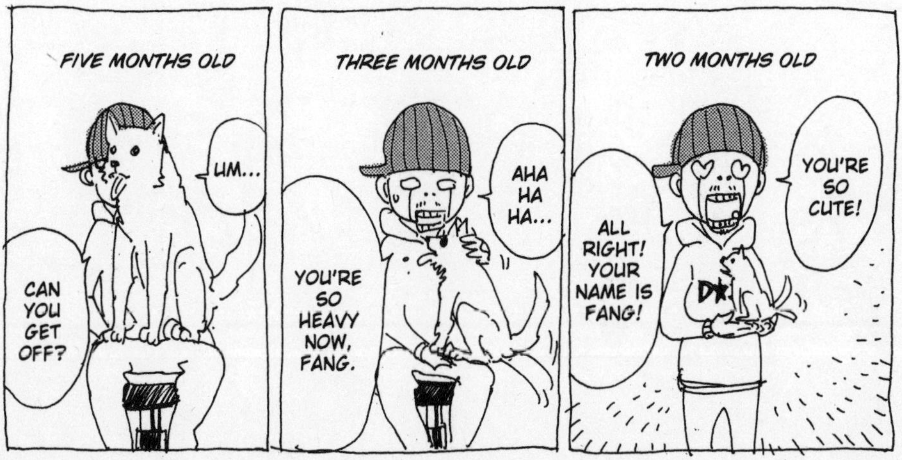
TWO MONTHS OLD
YOU'RE SO CUTE!
ALL RIGHT! YOUR NAME IS FANG!
THREE MONTHS OLD
AHA HA HA...
YOU'RE SO HEAVY NOW, FANG.
FIVE MONTHS OLD
UM...
CAN YOU GET OFF?

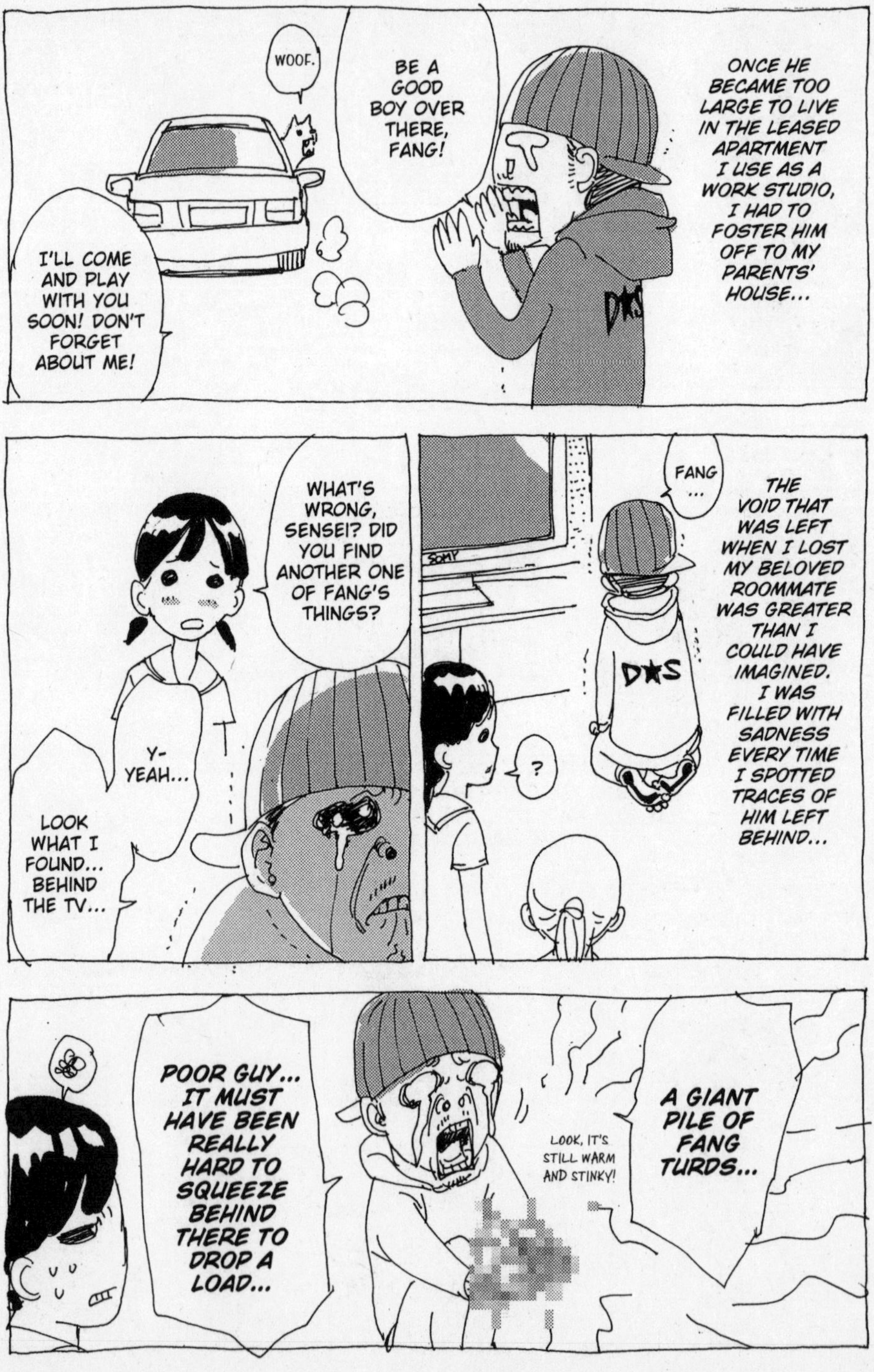
ONCE HE BECAME TOO LARGE TO LIVE IN THE LEASED APARTMENT I USE AS A WORK STUDIO, I HAD TO FOSTER HIM OFF TO MY PARENTS' HOUSE...
BE A GOOD BOY OVER THERE, FANG!
WOOF.
I'LL COME AND PLAY WITH YOU SOON! DON'T FORGET ABOUT ME!
THE VOID THAT WAS LEFT WHEN I LOST MY BELOVED ROOMMATE WAS GREATER THAN I COULD HAVE IMAGINED. I WAS FILLED WITH SADNESS EVERY TIME I SPOTTED TRACES OF HIM LEFT BEHIND...
FANG...
?
WHAT'S WRONG, SENSEI? DID YOU FIND ANOTHER ONE OF FANG'S THINGS?
Y-YEAH...
LOOK WHAT I FOUND... BEHIND THE TV...
A GIANT PILE OF FANG TURDS...
LOOK, IT'S STILL WARM AND STINKY!
POOR GUY... IT MUST HAVE BEEN REALLY HARD TO SQUEEZE BEHIND THERE TO DROP A LOAD...

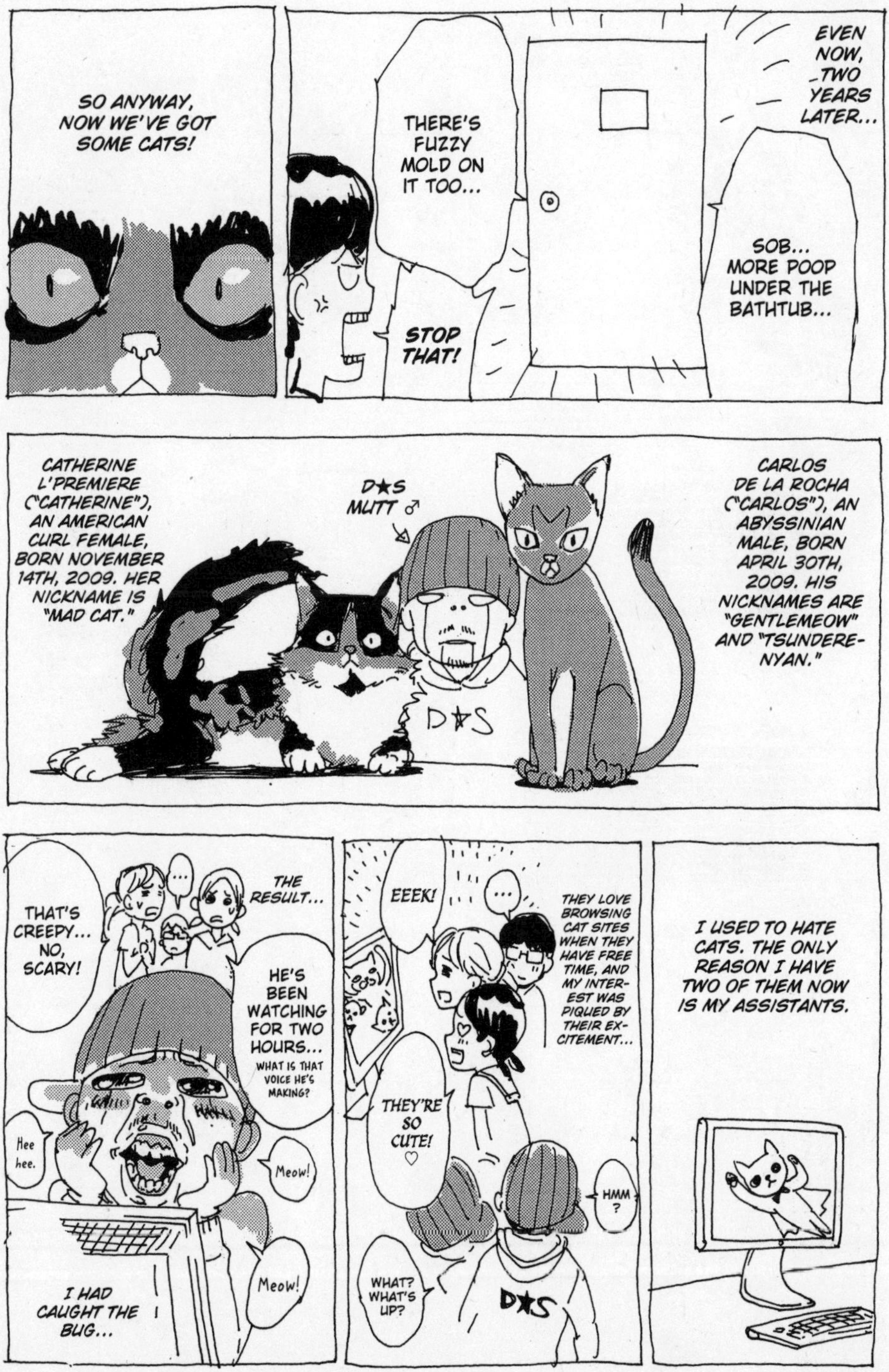
EVEN NOW, TWO YEARS LATER...
SOB... MORE POOP UNDER THE BATHTUB...
THERE'S FUZZY MOLD ON IT TOO...
STOP THAT!
SO ANYWAY, NOW WE'VE GOT SOME CATS!
CARLOS DE LA ROCHA ("CARLOS"), AN ABYSSINIAN MALE, BORN APRIL 30TH, 2009. HIS NICKNAMES ARE "GENTLEMEOW" AND "TSUNDERE-NYAN."
D★S MUTT ♂
D★S
CATHERINE L'PREMIERE ("CATHERINE"), AN AMERICAN CURL FEMALE, BORN NOVEMBER 14TH, 2009. HER NICKNAME IS "MAD CAT."
I USED TO HATE CATS. THE ONLY REASON I HAVE TWO OF THEM NOW IS MY ASSISTANTS.
THEY LOVE BROWSING CAT SITES WHEN THEY HAVE FREE TIME, AND MY INTEREST WAS PIQUED BY THEIR EXCITEMENT...
...
EEEK!
THEY'RE SO CUTE! ♡
HMM ?
WHAT? WHAT'S UP?
D★S
THE RESULT...
...
THAT'S CREEPY... NO, SCARY!
HE'S BEEN WATCHING FOR TWO HOURS...
WHAT IS THAT VOICE HE'S MAKING?
Meow!
Hee hee.
Meow!
I HAD CAUGHT THE BUG...

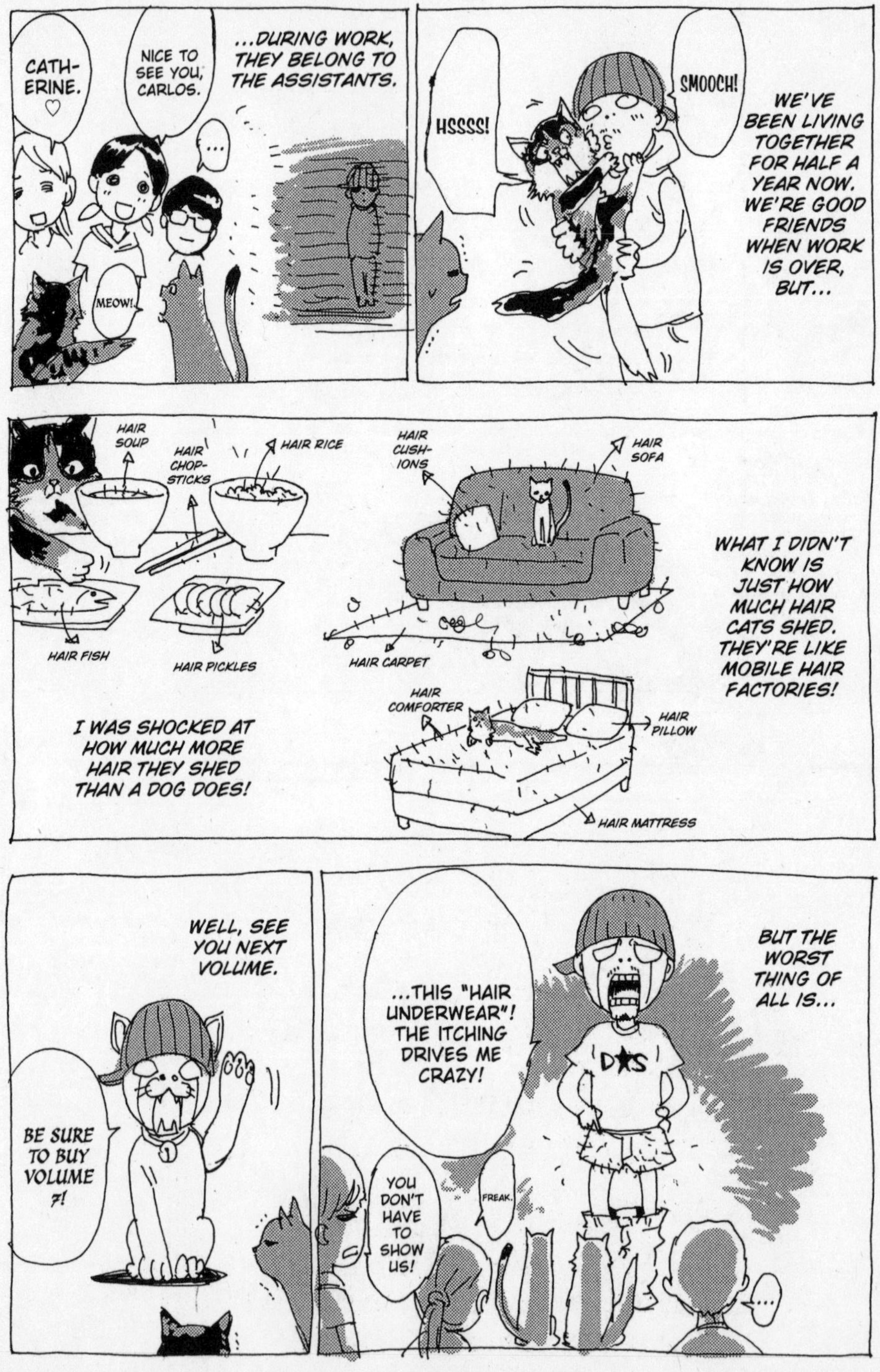
WE'VE BEEN LIVING TOGETHER FOR HALF A YEAR NOW. WE'RE GOOD FRIENDS WHEN WORK IS OVER, BUT...
SMOOCH!
HSSSS!
...DURING WORK, THEY BELONG TO THE ASSISTANTS.
NICE TO SEE YOU, CARLOS.
CATH-ERINE. ♡
...
MEOW!
WHAT I DIDN'T KNOW IS JUST HOW MUCH HAIR CATS SHED. THEY'RE LIKE MOBILE HAIR FACTORIES!
HAIR SOFA
HAIR CUSH-IONS
HAIR CARPET
HAIR PILLOW
HAIR COMFORTER
HAIR MATTRESS
HAIR RICE
HAIR CHOP-STICKS
HAIR SOUP
HAIR PICKLES
HAIR FISH
I WAS SHOCKED AT HOW MUCH MORE HAIR THEY SHED THAN A DOG DOES!
BUT THE WORST THING OF ALL IS...
...THIS "HAIR UNDERWEAR"! THE ITCHING DRIVES ME CRAZY!
D★S
...
FREAK.
YOU DON'T HAVE TO SHOW US!
WELL, SEE YOU NEXT VOLUME.
BE SURE TO BUY VOLUME 7!

Art Staff
Suri ♀: Chief Assistant
0-Second ♂: Background Art
Taurus ♀: Background Art

Military Advisor
Lee Hyun Seok (warmania)

SPECIAL THANKS
Shingo Takano

Crossover Planning
JESUS—Sajin Kouro, Yami no Aegis, Akatsuki no Aegis
Written by Kyouichi Nanatsuki,
Art by Yoshihide Fujiwara
(Shogakukan)

Translation Notes

Common Honorifics
no honorific: Indicates familiarity or closeness; if used without permission or reason, addressing someone in this manner would constitute an insult.
-san: The Japanese equivalent of Mr./Mrs./Miss. If a situation calls for politeness, this is the fail-safe honorific.
-sama: Conveys great respect; may also indicate that the social status of the speaker is lower than that of the addressee.
-kun: Used most often when referring to boys, this indicates affection or familiarity. Occasionally used by older men among their peers, but it may also be used by anyone referring to a person of lower standing.
-chan: An affectionate honorific indicating familiarity used mostly in reference to girls; also used in reference to cute persons or animals of either gender.
-senpai: A suffix used to address upperclassmen or more experienced coworkers.
-sensei: A respectful term for teachers, artists, or high-level professionals.

Yen conversion: While exchange rates fluctuate daily, a convenient conversion estimation is about ¥100 to 1 USD.

Page 68
Type-3 Chi-Nu: A medium-sized Imperial Japanese Army tank manufactured for use in World War II. The Chi-Nu was equipped with one of the largest guns the Japanese made during the war, though it was never actually used in combat, the units having been held back on the Japanese mainland in the event of an Allied invasion.

Page 161
Waka-gashira: The "young head" of a yakuza organization. Typically the waka-gashira (or waka) is the next in line to inherit the syndicate when the leader (*kumi-cho*) dies or steps down, and he is often responsible for organizing forces and carrying out raids. In this story, Komura is the waka-gashira of the Kakuhoukai yakuza.

Page 162
Ritual sake: Within the yakuza, which often places its members into "family" hierarchies such as father/sons or elder and younger brothers despite no actual blood relationship, the sharing of sake using special formal saucer-like cups called *sakazuki* is a special ritual that binds the drinkers. This practice is not limited to the yakuza, however, as the sakazuki cups are also utilized in religious ceremonies, traditional marriages, formal award ceremonies, and so on.

Page 172
Karito Tate: The titular protagonist of a manga series titled *Yami no Aegis* (Aegis in the Dark). His nickname comes from the legendary shield of the Greek goddess Athena. At this point in *Until Death Do Us Part*, the series becomes a crossover with the characters Karito Tate (whose surname means "shield") from *Yami no Aegis* and the hitman named Jesus from the 1990s hit action series *Jesus*, both written by Kyouichi Nanatsuki and drawn by Yoshihide Fujiwara. The Aegis series is serialized alongside UDDUP in the magazine *Young Gangan*.

Page 229
S.A.T.: Special Assault Team, the Japanese form of SWAT-style tactical law enforcement and counterterrorism squads.

Page 409
Tsundere: An archetype within anime and manga of a character who alternates between outward hostility (*tsun-tsun*) and sappy affection (*dere-dere*). Although this character model is typically a romantic interest, it sure does sound like the average housecat!